Financial Information Systems

Theory and Practice

James B. Bower

Professor, Graduate School of Business

University of Wisconsin

Madison, Wisconsin

Robert E. Schlosser

Director, Division of Professional Development

American Institute of Certified Public Accountants

New York City, New York

Charles T. Zlatkovich

Professor, College of Business Administration

University of Texas

Austin, Texas

FINANCIAL

INFORMATION SYSTEMS

THEORY AND PRACTICE

Allyn and Bacon, Inc.

Boston

Library of Congress Catalog Card Number: 69-11845
Printed in the United States of America

PREFACE

Financial Information Systems: Theory and Practice is the outgrowth of a need experienced by the authors for conceptual material to be used in teaching both an understanding of systems subject material and the approach of the systems analyst to the design of a system. Many methods of organizing and presenting systems material have been attempted, but little has been done to codify principles of systems design as part of the theoretical structure of systems or to explain the many difficulties encountered by the analyst. Further, many teachers have hesitated to instruct in the systems area as there were few strong or tangible questions, problems, or cases to use as a foundation for instruction. This book postulates not only a systems theory, but also a great number of questions, problems, and cases in which the systems theory presented can be applied to enable a depth of understanding and effectiveness in systems work.

The book is organized onto four Units and three Appendices. Unit 1, Chapters 1 to 9, presents and explains the basic systems theory. Chapter 1 provides an overview of the entire theory, with chapters 2 through 9 expanding and explaining the detail of the theory. Unit 2, Chapters 10 to 13, presents the work and tools of the systems analyst in the context of his basic service—the systems investigation. The approach of the analyst to a systems investigation through a study of the existing system, the design of a new or revised system, the installation and maintenance of the system, and proper documentation, is presented. Emphasis on the techniques of the analyst in accomplishing his engagement is evident. Unit 3, Chapters 14 to 17, is an extension of the systems theory to the small business and to card and computer systems. Concepts rather than operating details are emphasized.

Unit 4, Chapters 18 and 19, presents a series of typical procedures with a liberal amount of strong problem material relating to each procedure. Included are procedures for purchases, payables, sales, receivables, cash receipts, cash disbursements, payroll, inventory and production control, fixed assets, investments, and others. In each instance, the objective is to apply systems theory to arrive at the practical solution to a systems problem.

The appendices are of special assistance to the student of systems. The internal control questionnaire in Appendix A provides a check list of considerations in a systems investigation. Reference to the questionnaire in the solution of questions, problems, and cases could be most helpful. The Industrial Parts Company Case, Appendix B, can be used optionally for special study and illustration. A Model Evaluation Report, Appendix C, affords the student the opportunity to view the special way in which the analyst may report his preliminary findings.

The theory of systems presented in this book enables the mature student to reconcile the traditional theories of accounting, management, and other business areas presented in the classroom with the realistic and practical business world. To go from the theoretical to the practical is often a difficult transition for a student. An understanding of organization structure, human behavior, and procedural and control difficulties in the context of a system is certain to enable the student to "bridge the gap" with greater ease.

Many changes are occurring in business today. Traditional ways of doing many things are disappearing. Modern auditing includes a major element of systems review. The development of a systems theory is especially important to auditing. More and more consulting engagements are, in fact, systems studies.

One of the unique characteristics of the work of the systems analyst is that his work cuts across the various organizational units. He must deal with organization structure and basic business functions as they exist, with his success often related to his effectiveness in implementing change when different organization units, and thus people with all of their differences, are involved.

It is notable that in many situations in which the analyst works, the correct decision is not always clear—there may be trade-offs of one objective for another. He usually will know whether or not an adequate system has been designed and installed, but he is seldom sure that his system is an optimum one. There is always the challenge of improving on what exists.

This book is designed for the student, whether he is in a systems class at the collegiate level or a prospective systems analyst in a business concern with the need to learn the conceptual framework within which the system functions. The detail of machine operation and other such mechanics are not included.

Many individuals and business firms deserve recognition for their willing and constructive contributions to this work. Their interest and encouragement in the development of this new approach to systems design is greatly appreciated. Our sincere appreciation is extended to all of those who made major contributions to this book. While there is a danger in singling out a few from the many who were helpful, special thanks are extended to J. Bruce

Sefert for his work in assisting with the development of original material on human factors in systems design and Professor William Thomas, who deserves special recognition for permitting the use of his Industrial Parts Company case. Business equipment manufacturers have been most generous. Several firms of certified public accountants have made substantial contributions, but have requested that materials drawn from their files not be identified.

Finally, the authors take full responsibility for the content of the book. Much of the material is produced for the first time in the structure of a systems theory—we expect the systems theory to become more refined over the years. The authors are convinced that the theory approach to systems design is most productive and, if once used, will be used over and over again in the design of systems.

JBB, RES, and *CTZ*

CONTENTS

Unit 1—A Systems Theory

Unit 2—Systems Investigations

Unit 3—Extensions of Systems Theory

Unit 4—Systems Problems and Cases

Unit 1

A Systems Theory

otherwise it would fail to collect what is due, or fail to make timely payment of its debt.

5. Those responsible for the custody of property would have no means of discharging their custodianship without knowing the value associated with the property, its quantity, and its location.

The business information system includes the records and processing structure by which the above and other objectives requiring quantitative information can be accomplished. A well-designed business information system is essential to successful management planning and control. Without adequate information neither function could be accomplished with economy or efficiency. The management of a medium-sized or large business may be limited in effectiveness without the availability of a steady flow of accurate and reliable information.

The usual business information system is highly complex, yet extremely practical and logical. It consists of a combination of sub-systems and procedures, with the components of each interrelated to provide appropriate information and control measures for every segment of the business.

Early business information systems were limited to the information processed through accounting systems. Until recently such systems were designed almost exclusively for the processing of historical facts necessary for traditional financial statements. For example, in processing sales transactions it was adequate to accumulate only the summary information necessary for debiting accounts receivable and crediting sales, providing the basic information for traditional financial statements. The modern business information system must provide for many needs. It provides information for the various traditional accounting reports and statements, but, in addition, it provides a great variety of detailed statistical information. The total amount of sales as the basis for debiting accounts receivable and crediting sales is no longer adequate; information is required concerning sales by product, by territory, by salesman, by discount class, and the like. Data beyond the usual dollar amounts are accumulated. The number of units, pounds, or gallons are commonly provided.

The detailed and statistical nature of the information needed by modern management is causing a re-examination of the role of its information-producing system. There is also considerable emphasis on the availability of projected and estimated planning information. In recent years business information systems have been designed to provide more and more quantitative information, including detailed facts about markets, production, and financial matters. Business managers in the past have often considered the system as a necessary evil, and did not utilize it as a useful tool to accomplish their own function of managing the business. For modern management, a broadly based, efficient, and effective system is essential.

Systems Contribution

A business information system should be justified by the contributions that it makes to enable effective management. It should furnish timely information to management, setting the stage for good decision making. A successful business information system contributes materially to better service and better management, and provides a vigorous environment for the accomplishment of business goals and objectives.

Management expects its business information system to provide the information and control facts and procedures necessary for the accomplishment of its objectives. The system must provide information concerning historical costs and profitability. Periodic performance reports, covering all areas of responsibility, must be available. Such reports provide identification of strengths or weaknesses in the present position, and the magnitude and priorities of *future* tasks.

The availability of information that is useful in anticipating the future is especially important. The information system should provide the structure and substantial detail for the compilation of an orderly set of short-run and long-run budgets, indicating anticipated profit and investment results. In addition, detailed analyses of the profit and investment consequences that are likely to flow from specific decisions should be obtainable.

Relationship to Data Processing

Business information systems are designed to accomplish many routine procedural objectives, but of most importance they provide management and others with information for planning and control, and the structure in which internal control duties can be effective. These objectives are accomplished through the processing of data utilizing different types of machines and equipment, communication media, reports, and by the activities of many individuals.

In recent years the term data processing has become commonplace. Business machine and office forms companies have described almost any procedure or method using their product as data processing. *Data processing* consists of the operations needed to capture and transform data into useful managerial information and the transmission of this information to management or other specific individuals or groups. The term *data* denotes unorganized facts, while *information* results from the capture and organization of data. Thus customer data are being transformed into meaningful sales and customer information which can help management operate the business effectively.

The term integrated data processing is also common. *Integrated data processing* refers to the processing of information in a continuous sequence with a minimum of transformation or change after initial recording so as to optimize accuracy and control through subsequent data handling. For example, the automatic preparation of a punched card or paper tape as a by-product of the initial handling of a customer's order, and the sequence of steps that follows in which the data are handled automatically in each additional processing step, is integrated data processing. Each step of integrated data processing follows the prior step without recopying, and is designed to make a specific contribution to the objective of the system. *Electronic data processing* is data processing or integrated data processing that includes the utilization of equipment with electronic capabilities, such as an electronic computer. A basic discussion of electronic computers is to be found in Chapters 16 and 17.

Complexity of the System

The complexity of a business information system depends on the needs of management. The needs of management for information and internal control are a function of the size, geographical diversification, and the nature of the business activity. In the small business with a single proprietor, the needs of management for custodial or planning and control information can be satisfied with a simple system. In the large business a more extensive system is needed. The difference in systems complexity necessary to provide management with needed information lies in the fact that most events occurring in the small business are within the range of personal knowledge and direct control of the owner-manager. In the small business, for example, the owner-manager checks out the cash register daily, signs all checks, and may be personally involved in each transaction. Thus the owner-manager is in possession of the information that he needs to make business decisions and to plan and control operations. He is his own processor, and does not need a complex system. As the business grows larger, the personal contact of management with all phases of the operation becomes more limited, until in the large business, management is almost completely dependent on the information system for the facts it needs to manage the business effectively.

The "Total Information System" Concept

Modern businesses are moving toward adoption of business information systems that function as a total information system. The *total information system* concept is based on the premise that each business is a complete system in itself. It is a highly interrelated and complex maze of sub-systems and procedures. Ideally, each sub-system or procedure processes data and provides internal control[1] in such a manner as to require the input of specific data into the system but once. Thereafter, the system can be called upon to provide the original data and/or information from subsequent processing, depending on the particular needs. The inefficiency of bringing the same data or information into the system more than once is avoided, and the advantages of multiple data and information use and of the automatic sequencing of signals for action can be realized.

Prior to the advent of the computer, the great volume of business detail and the many variables involved in each type of business activity encouraged compartmentalization of business processes. Computers brought about the ability to handle volumes of detail automatically and with relative ease. They brought an immediate need for precise description of the variables involved in each business situation along with need for identification of specific organizational relationships. When such information became available, more informed decisions could be made, and mathematical techniques related to scientific management could be used with greater effectiveness. In the background of the managerial needs, many variables have been identified, and relationships confirmed or established. From the viewpoint of the "total information system" many of the customary compartments or areas into which business is organized are artificial. There is growing evidence that the "total information system" will change organization structures to reduce compartmenting as the slow process of evolution in business continues.

The modern business information system is to some extent a reflection of the "total information system" concept. In larger organizations, electronic computers provide the focal point for such a system. To oversimplify an illustration, visualize the information from each order received from a customer being placed into a business information system. The data needed for a complete analysis of sales by customer, salesman, product, how the order is to be processed, for invoicing, and for accounts receivable, are immediately available through the system. In addition, the system has some of the information needed for inventory control. By the introduction of beginning inventory data, acquisition data, inventory requirements, and the like, inventory control information can automatically be obtained. When all order and inventory data are in the system, only a modest amount of additional data are needed to enable production scheduling and control. The introduction of payroll data could be the next step. And so the system grows until all information needs are satisfied. The "total information system" concept is an accurate and efficient approach to information needs. It is being developed rapidly in many businesses today. There are limitations, of course, the major one being the complexity and inflexibility of such a system. Nevertheless, there is little doubt that the future will see greater and greater recognition and utilization of "total information systems."

---

[1] Internal control is defined and discussed on pages 20 and 21, later in this chapter.

Universal Applicability

The need for information and internal control is not limited to business organizations. While the various service, retail, wholesale, and manufacturing businesses have major requirements for economical and effective information systems, other types of organizations have comparable needs. Regulated businesses, governmental units, fraternal organizations, clubs, charitable organizations, and others require specially adapted information systems. The system principles that apply to business information systems also have application to these other organizations.

It has been noted that the need for information and internal control exists in all types of organizations. In addition, many special types of information and internal controls are required to serve the varying needs of specific businesses. The need exists for qualitative as well as quantitative data. Competitor information, market information, customer information, and technical data alike are all required. Most business information systems are more closely identified with the processing of financial data than with other types. This does not always apply, and the evolution of business information systems indicates that the need to expand the scope of the business information system is having an effect. As modern executives review their systems, more and more information is being sought. Large amounts of all types of information must be expressed and evaluated without excessive difficulty. An effective information system is vital.

This book will emphasize, but not be limited to, the narrower financial information system portion of the business information system that processes accounting, statistical, and other quantitative data and information almost exclusively. At this writing the distinction between the financial information system and business information system is still clear, but as evolution continues in the direction of the "total information system," the distinctions between the business information system and the financial information system will become blurred or disappear.

THE FINANCIAL INFORMATION SYSTEM

The financial information system is the focal point of this book. The systems theory and practice presented and discussed herein will explain the many vague and hidden relationships of such a system. The *financial information system* is a combination of systems components that function within the business organization to process data and to provide the information and internal control needed by management to carry out its responsibilities of stewardship over the assets, of control over operations, and to plan future enterprise activities. It functions within the scope of systems principles and limitations of systems standards.

The structure of the financial information system often reflects the design of a previous accounting system. The financial information system is usually broader, and includes more extensive accumulations of statistical data than would be the case in a traditional accounting system. The accounting system has traditionally been designed to emphasize the detail associated with financial input data, its preparation, control, processing, and eventual output. The restricting influence of traditional techniques is often notable. The distinctions between a modern financial information system and an accounting system are important. More detailed data, unit information, decision limits, and accumulations of special significance to internal management are typical in a well-designed financial information system.

The financial information system is an aggregate that includes the sub-systems within a business organization designed to provide the necessary managerial information and internal control. A *sub-system* (or system when only one exists) includes the procedures, methods, and operations designed to accomplish specific objectives within a specified segment of a business. For example, the Ford Motor Company has a sub-system to provide managerial information and internal control for the Ford Division, another for the Tractor Division, and the like. *Procedures* within the broader system and sub-system are the methods and operations designed to process recurring business transactions. For example, separate procedures should exist within a manufacturing company to process cash receipts, sales orders, purchases, cash disbursements, and the payroll. Procedures reflect the *what* and *why* of processing methods and operations and ideally are described in writing. *Methods* and *operations* relate to *how* processing is accomplished. For example, several methods could be used in a cash receiving procedure. One method could be used by a truck driver receiving cash from a customer, and another method by a central cashier. Either method could consist of a number of operations.

Need for a Financial Information System

Every business must have a financial information system to fulfill three specific needs. First, the system must provide for the internal informational needs of management. Second, the system must provide management with a means of measuring and controlling business activity. Lastly, the system must provide for the external informational needs of management.

INTERNAL INFORMATION NEED. Information should be available internally to disclose what has happened in the *past*. The need for historical information relates closely to the housekeeping need to record and process routine and

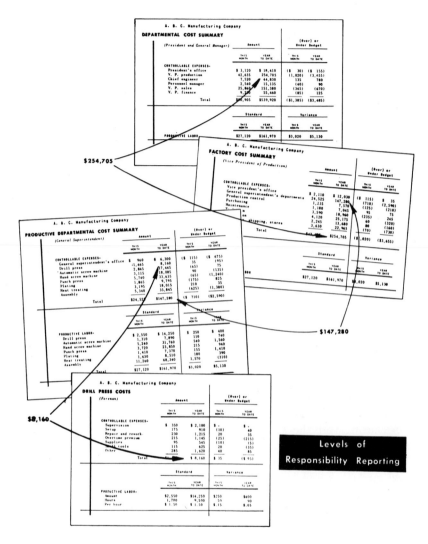

From *The Arthur Andersen Chronicle*, page 105, April, 1952.

FIGURE 1-1.   Responsibility Accounting Reporting System

daily business events. Then, too, the future is often similar to the past, and the events of the past become the starting point in projecting the future.

Management must also be fully informed about the *present*. It is necessary to know who has responsibility for the various assets, where each is located, how much should be on hand, and the events that are in the process of occurring. Current information may be especially meaningful when compared with information from other periods, budgets, or standards, enabling management to act when necessary.

Lastly, information relative to plans for the *future* should be available and cast in the structure dictated by the financial information system.

MEASUREMENT AND CONTROL NEED. One of the great challenges of the financial manager is the design of a financial information system that will serve his many and varying measurement and control needs. In a sense this need is a part of management's internal information need, yet it differs since the measurement and control system is dependent upon such factors as assignment of duties and organizational relationships. The timely and daily information that is necessary to operate the business effectively on a day-to-day and week-to-week basis must flow from the system. It does not flow from ledger balances exclusively, but is accumulated by many methods and at many points within the organization. A systems structure to enable management to be effective, to be informed, and to measure and motivate performance has always been and will continue to be vital to managers. Higgins, for example, developed a system designed to control expenditures at all levels of management by relating directly the reporting of expenditures (*see* Figure 1-1) to the individuals in the company organization responsible for their control.[2] This reporting system has become known as responsibility accounting, and conceptually is designed into most information systems to some extent.

EXTERNAL REPORTING NEED. The need of management for information to report for external purposes is substantial in magnitude. Many of the external needs can be fulfilled with data that flows from the system to meet internal needs. The needs of stockholders and other absentee owners, the government, bankers, and others require a major and costly effort on the part of the business.

The different contributions of a financial information system have often been presented separately, but seldom have they been brought together and integrated into a system. One of the more successful efforts to describe an integrated system has been by Robert Beyer. He suggested the concept of Profitability Accounting as an integrated management information system capable of meeting the requirements of custodial accounting, performance accounting, and decision accounting.[3] Figure 1-2 illustrates the functions and techniques Beyer would include in a comprehensive management information system. An adequate financial information system must meet the varying needs of management for information and provide the basis for control in much the same manner.

---

[2] Higgins, John A., "Responsibility Accounting," *The Arthur Andersen Chronicle*, April, 1952, p. 105.

[3] Beyer, Robert, *Profitability Accounting for Planning and Control* (New York: The Ronald Press Company, 1963), p. 7.

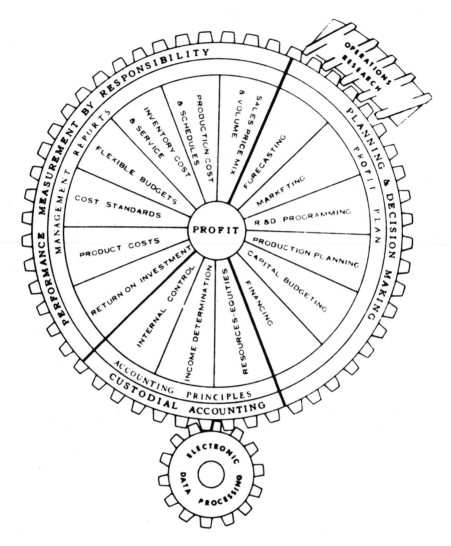

Robert Beyer, *Profitability Accounting for Planning and Control*,
Copyright © 1963, The Ronald Press Co., New York.

FIGURE 1-2.   Functions and Techniques Integrated in Profitability Accounting

The System

The financial information system is relevant to all business organizations, both large and small, and regardless of processing devices or methods used within the system. Either pen or pencil, simple machine, punched card, or computer systems are applicable within the same basic structure, using only different methods and devices to accomplish objectives. When pen or pencil methods are replaced or supplemented with machines, the devices of the financial information system have changed, but the structure of the system is basically the same. There may be significant changes in specific procedures or in sequencing and complexity, yet the theory of data and information flow, around which the financial information is structured, is conceptually constant.

A model of a financial information system, showing the theoretical structure, is graphically illustrated in Figure 1-3. The discussions that follow

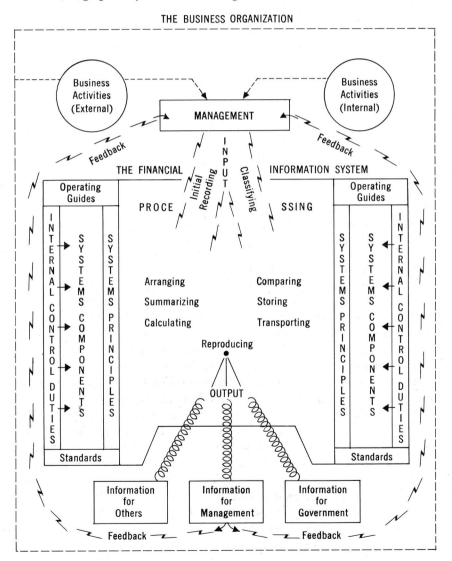

FIGURE 1-3. The Financial Information System

in this chapter introduce and summarize the theoretical structure of a financial information system. Throughout the remaining chapters of the book, the theory of the financial information system and its many ramifications, alternatives, and complexities, will be illustrated and developed in detail.

Business Organization

Business organization is the structure within which the financial information system must function. It consists of people, and of a maze of relationships between people and the varied activities for which they are responsible. The ability or lack of ability of the people within an organization makes a substantial difference in the method of application and effectiveness of the financial information system. The company executives and employees, their attitudes and relationships, all have an effect on the functioning of the system. The business organization represents the environment within which the financial information system operates. Although not independent of outside pressures and influences, the structure of the business organization provides the boundaries within which the financial information system functions.

Data and Information Flow

The data and information which flow through a financial information system are from three sources: (1) *business activities* with individuals or organizations *external* to the business, such as sales, purchases, payments of cash, or receipts of cash; (2) *internal business activities*, such as placing raw material in process, using direct labor, transfers; or (3) the *feedback* resulting from output information and managerial decisions, such as the need to place orders for materials when the inventory reaches the order point, the need for or utilization of equipment, authorizations for overtime work, or the decision to write off an account or obsolete inventory. Feedback, resulting from the processing of data and information, should inform management of the direction in which the business is moving. As a result of evaluating the information, management makes the necessary decisions to facilitate the accomplishment of its plans. These decisions have a stabilizing effect on the business, and are designed to compensate when actual operations are off target.

Business is a continuing and complex activity. It is not static. Each managerial decision and business transaction affects operations and is important to future activities. *Feedback* is the return of a portion of information output to input. Its function is to permit compensation for variations from the plan. The function of feedback can be compared to the function of a captain when his ship is off course. If a ship is off course, or if conditions warrant, the captain will note the situation and correct the course of the ship. By the same process, when operations vary from the plan, the condition is signaled, and through feedback, the system provides the information for management to make the necessary adjustment to maintain steady progress toward business goals.

Feedback also functions as a *closed loop of control*. The closed loop of control can be compared to a thermostat. If the water in a boiler is too cold, the thermostat will turn on the heating element. When the water is as hot as desired, the thermostat will turn the heating element off. In the financial information system, for example, an inventory control procedure may provide control information. Whenever the reorder point is reached for a specific item the system will signal for a purchase. With the order and acquisition of an item, the total inventory available and on order changes. If sufficient quantities are on hand or on order when the item is again needed, no further order will be signaled. In a closed loop of control, information about the item being controlled can control the item further through feedback.

It can be noted that all data or information are channeled through *management*. Management at all levels—top, middle, and supervisory—is involved. Management must provide judgment and has full responsibility for perceiving the events that have occurred, for reviewing input into the system, and for completeness. Valid and complete input are essential for accurate, timely, and factual data and information processing and output. Adequate internal control must be established and maintained.

The flow of data and information in a financial information system is often through channels originally designed for accounting purposes alone. The three phases of data and information flow are *input, processing,* and *output*. They are universal to all systems and relate to the total system as well as to each of the sub-systems and procedures of which it is made up. Each of the phases will be discussed in sequence.

INPUT. Input into the financial information system includes initial recording and classifying. *Initial recording* is the placing of data into the system for the first time. An essential of effective data flow is the placement of data into the system as early as possible. Once in the system, data can be utilized, controls can be established, and significance determined. As financial data become available, they must be introduced into the system immediately.

The adequacy of the entire system is often related to the validity of data entered on the initial recording. At the point of initial recording, data are processed through the human mind. Data incorrectly recorded or omitted may result in misleading or inadequate information output. No systems output can be any better than its initial input data.

Initial recording includes both the *collecting* of data and the *making of a record*. Either the collecting or the recording of data can start the sequence of data and information flow in the system. They can be separated, or they can be accomplished simultaneously. For example, collecting and recording are separate operations when a cash register collects data as to the different sources from which cash is received in mechanical accumulators without a written notation. The data in the accumulators (totaling devices) can then be recorded in a summary form report at the end of each day or some other given period. Collecting and recording may also be accomplished simultaneously. For example, at the time a business event occurs, such as a credit sale, the facts may be collected and recorded in writing on a sales ticket.

Data that are initially collected and recorded on a conventional source document, such as the sales ticket, must be further transferred to some other media or special form for processing within the financial information system. In a manual system, the data from source documents are extracted and prepared for processing by summary in a journal entry. In many machine systems, the data are extracted from the source documents and punched into a card, paper tape, or magnetic tape, and through these media are ready for further processing within the system.

Great progress is being made in methods of collecting and recording data so they will be ready for processing with fewer preliminary steps. Punched cards or paper tape can be created as a by-product of an original transaction such as writing up an order, or ringing up a transaction on a cash register. In such systems the input for the system, the card or tape, is completed at the time of writing up the original order or ringing up the transaction.

Before data are ready for processing within the system, they must be classified. The *classifying* of data relates to the identification scheme that is necessary so that the data can be channeled properly within the system and processed in accordance with a given plan.

The steps of data input include those necessary to bring data into the appropriate form to permit processing within the system. As a result information often becomes available to management through the steps of input. Data or information for many key daily reports are obtained during the input phase. Such data or information can be either a by-product of initial recording, collecting, making the record, or classifying by summarization of data extracted at points during input at which specific operations occur. Specific data processing operations are sometimes necessary as a part of input.

PROCESSSING. Essentially processing includes the *operations* which transform business data into intelligible managerial information. There are many variations to the sequence in which data may be processed within a financial information system. Data that have been introduced into the system and are in the proper form can sometimes be channeled through the system with little or no processing. In other instances, numerous processing steps are necessary. In most instances, one or more processing steps are necessary. Processing includes arranging, summarizing, calculating, comparing, storing, transporting, and reproducing.

The *arranging* of data relates to bringing data together according to a specific grouping or sequence. In more complex and efficient financial information systems, data can be entered in random order, and arranged in the desired grouping and sequence internal to the system. For example, order data could be entered into the system in the sequence in which orders are received. Internal to the system, order data can be grouped according to types of product, data required, or the like. In simpler systems, arranging merely consists of grouping similar data.

The financial information system enables *summarizing* the data into meaningful and useful information. Information systems can produce so much information that sheer volume may make evaluation difficult. Good summary information is essential to eliminate unnecessary detail and to allow emphasis to be placed on interpretation.

Calculating is an important part of processing. When new data are entered in the system, they are often added to or deducted from old information to obtain up-dated amounts as a normal part of the processing procedure. In addition, the more complex systems enable multiplication and division. For example, invoice amounts may be extended, straight time hours multiplied by straight time rates, payroll deductions subtracted, and so on.

The *comparing* feature of a financial information system is also important. It enables decisions, in which the factors can be identified in advance, to be accomplished automatically within the system. Only exceptions needing managerial action are brought to the attention of management through the system. Managerial effort can then be focused on important items. For example, actual expenses can be compared to budgeted expenses, and the amounts over budget identified. In processing incoming orders the price quoted by a salesman can be compared to a price list or range of prices, and exceptions noted for sales department consideration. In inventory control, actual balances can be compared to ordering levels, and items requiring reorder can be signaled.

The *storing* of data and information is a passive operation. During the processing steps it is often necessary to hold certain data and information until other operations have been completed or until output of the system is required. The storing operation is an important part of processing. The form in which data and information are stored varies considerably, as does the length of the time that storing is necessary.

Transporting relates to the physical movement of data and information within the system. Communication media, records, tapes, and other systems components that contain data and information must be transported from one location to the other. The data or information from initial records must be transported from the point at which they were collected, recorded, and possibly classified to the next step in the processing sequence. Transporting operations are a part of smooth and efficient information flow.

The transferring or duplicating data or information within the system is the *reproducing* operation. It is common to maintain permanent files of data or information within a system which can then be transferred from the file to a calculation or to output, or that can be duplicated whenever the processing system needs the facts involved to complete the processing of certain data or information.

It is important to note that the seven processing operations identified above may not relate exclusively to the data processing phase of data and information flow. These operations may also be a part of input or output.

OUTPUT. The output of the financial information system must be carefully planned to communicate to management the information necessary for planning and controlling the business. Such information, properly *communicated*, should justify the system. Unless the information is in such form that it is useful and understood, the system will not be fulfilling its function adequately.

With the great volume of information in the system, it is usually desirable to communicate only the information needed for a specific purpose in a given tabulation. Information that is in the system may be communicated many times without having to be withdrawn from the system. It is possible to use the same information for managerial reports, for the annual report to stockholders, or for governmental reports such as income tax returns. The versatility of the financial information system output can be compared to a television program in which several television cameras are focused on the same event from different positions. What is seen on the television screen can be selected by the director at the control. By the same token, the information that is to become output of the financial information system can be selected. The information selected may be from the point of view that best communicates to those for whom the information is intended. Unlike television, however, it *is* possible to extract *information for management*, and still extract the same *information for government* or *for others*, even though the information is reported in different sequences, degrees of completeness, and context for varying purposes.

Systems Principles

The financial information system should be designed consistent with systems principles. Systems principles are not absolute laws that cannot be violated; rather they are guides to systems design that have been proved by experience and that are essential to the design of an economical and effective financial information system. In a given situation one principle may be only partially relevant, and other principles may also be partially relevant. In such instances, the principles are applicable and each should be applied to the extent appropriate.

The financial information system must function within certain tolerances or it will go out of control. These tolerances can be observed through compliance with systems principles. When a systems principle is violated, the system involved cannot be expected to accomplish its objectives adequately.

The functioning of systems within tolerances can be compared to operating a boat on a river. The range within which the boat may operate is specific yet not always obvious to the eye. The edge of the river is clear, yet outside of the channel, the water can be shallow and cover many obstacles that could cause trouble if short cuts are attempted or if the course is miscalculated. If the boat leaves the channel and travels close to the edge of the river, obstacles are more likely to be encountered.

Principles of financial information system design are as follows:

1. *Reasonable Cost.* The system should be designed to provide information and internal control, consistent with the needs of management, at a reasonable cost.

2. *Report.* The system should be designed to permit effective reporting, both internally and externally, since reports are a primary systems product.

3. *Human Factors.* The system should be designed consistent with applicable human factors, since people are responsible for the effectiveness of the system.

4. *Organization Structure.* The system should be designed to function in a specific, clearly defined, organization structure, since the system should be tailored for the organization to satisfy particular information and control needs.

5. *Reliability.* The system should be designed to check the reliability and accuracy of financial data, minimize error, safeguard assets, and prevent fraud or other irregularity.

6. *Flexible, Yet Uniform and Consistent.* The system should be designed to be flexible, yet insure reasonable uniformity and consistency of application in order to facilitate the dynamics of business.

7. *Audit Trail.* The system should be designed to facilitate the tracing of procedural steps in order to permit the analysis of detail underlying summarized information.

8. *Data Accumulation.* The system should be designed to enable the rapid and efficient recording and classification of data in order to process it into information for planning, control, and the accomplishment of administrative routine.

9. *Data Processing.* The system should be designed to provide a meaningful, continuous, and controlled flow of data being processed in order to produce reliable information and facilitate control.

Systems Components

The components of a system are its tangible parts. These parts, the ingredients of a procedure, can be put together in many different combinations so as to accomplish systems objectives with varying degrees of economy and effectiveness. In each instance the way in which systems components are combined will make a significant difference in the internal control that can be obtained through the system. Systems components are as follows:

1. *Personnel.* People are required to make a system work. They are directly involved with each of the phases of data and information flow and are the most important components in a system. No system has been designed that will work if the people involved don't cooperate to make it work.

2. *Communication Media.* Communication media can be classified as original transaction documents, record documents, and discharge of duty documents. They consist of the forms and records that are necessary to store and transmit data and information. *Forms* are source documents or original media used for recurring transactions in accounting and other procedures. Included are such media as invoices, requisitions, time tickets, and the like. *Records*, as a systems component, relate to the books, ledgers, and summaries usually associated with permanence.

   Communication media provide *data and information storage* that are essential to every system. In a manual information system, data and information are stored in source documents and records. In conventional machine systems, data and information are stored in a comparable manner. In punched card, integrated or electronic data processing systems, the punched card, paper tape, magnetic tape, or internal processing mechanism also provide storage. Adequate data and information storage and ready access are special features necessary to financial information systems.

3. *Reports.* Reports are the output of a system designed to provide information without further processing. Included are daily cash and sales summaries, customer statements, periodic financial statements, and special studies. The flow of reports is often an important part of a system.

4. *Data Originating, Processing, and Control Devices.* Data originating, processing, and control devices are the machines and equipment utilized in the system. Included are such items as cash registers, accounting machines, files, and time clocks that are necessary to perform systems operations effectively and to insure accuracy and protection against internal pilferage. Also included are items such as safes, alarm systems, and special containers used to protect against destruction or pilferage.

Internal Control Duties

Internal control has been defined by the Committee on Auditing Procedure of the American Institute of Certified Public Accountants as follows:

Internal control comprises the plan of organization and all of the coordinate methods and measures adopted within a business to safeguard its assets, check the accuracy and reliability of its accounting data, promote operational efficiency, and encourage adherence to prescribed managerial policies.[4]

The AICPA definition is classic and, while intended for auditors, is especially appropriate for the systems practitioner. The definition notes that internal control has two parts: (1) a plan of organization and (2) all coordinate methods and measures adopted within a business. The definition continues to indicate that these two parts are to accomplish four specific objectives, namely to (1) safeguard assets, (2) check the accuracy and reliability of accounting data, (3) promote operational efficiency, and (4) to encourage adherence to prescribed managerial policies. To understand internal control, it is necessary to examine the two parts of internal control. First, consider the plan of organization. Organization consists of people. The plan of organization is the grouping of people and the assignment of duties and responsibilities. Second, the coordinate methods and measures adopted within a business relate to the accomplishment of procedures through appropriate methods and operations. Internal control is good when the systems components of a procedure, namely the people, communication media, reports, and data originating, processing, and control devices, are brought together in such a manner that the four objectives of internal control can be readily and efficiently accomplished.

Internal control duties are those duties that must be added to a system to provide internal control. The internal control duties are as follows:

1. Supervision.
2. Clerical proof.
3. Acknowledging performance.
4. Transferring responsibility.
5. Protective measures.
6. Review.
7. Verification and evaluation.

The components of a system, improperly used or not used at all, provide no control or assurance of accurate and complete data and information. Internal control duties provide such assurances.

It should be noted that internal control duties keep the systems components in the data and information flow of the financial information system under constant pressure. The pressure should cause frequent change to bring processing into line with good control and effective, economical, and efficient processing.

---

[4] *Internal Control.* Committee on Auditing Procedure, American Institute of Certified Public Accountants, 1949, p. 6. Reaffirmed in *Auditing Standards and Procedures,* Committee on Auditing Procedure Statement, No. 33, American Institute of Certified Public Accountants, 1963, p. 27.

Operating Guides

Operating guides are essential to the reliable and effective operation of a system. The manner in which the systems components are related and utilized should be reflected through written and illustrated operating guides. Included are such items as organization charts, operating manuals, and flow charts and diagrams. Accounting methodology is set forth.

Standards

Systems *standards* are the minimum acceptable level of attainment. They are the benchmarks that indicate the point beyond which it is unsafe to proceed. Systems standards apply to principles, components, and internal control duties alike. In the application of the reasonable cost principle, there is an applicable standard—a point beyond which no further costs can be justified and still have the system acceptable. For example, the double verification of each cash receipt may be a degree of control that cannot be justified. The minimum acceptable level of verification may be a limited verification by internal auditors combined with other control measures.

The Systems Study

One of the primary objectives of students learning about the total systems concept, the purpose and components of the financial information system, and the other aspects of the financial information system, is to permit them to engage in and/or supervise systems studies. There is much to be learned about the technique of organizing and performing complete or partial systems studies.

Ordinarily, a systems study consists of three phases: analysis, synthesis, and implementation and follow-up. In the *analysis* phase, facts are gathered by the systems analyst about the system of an existing business unit or about the proposed organization and objectives of a new business unit. In the *synthesis* phase, the systems analyst must take into account what was learned in the analysis phase and design or redesign, as the case may be, an efficient and economical financial information system for his employer or client. *Implementation* and *follow-up* is the phase in which the revised or newly designed procedures and methods are put into effect, and verified as to whether they function as planned.

The chapters that follow in this book explore the structure of the financial information system in considerable detail. Systems principles and standards are developed and expanded, system components are presented in detail and arranged in typical procedures, and internal control duties are further illustrated, and the techniques, procedures, and methods used in professional systems studies are expanded. All that follows fits into the theoretical structure of the financial information system.

QUESTIONS, PROBLEMS, AND CASES

1. Differentiate between data processing, integrated data processing, and electronic data processing.

2. Does the owner-manager of a small business need as much information to operate his business as the management of a large business? Is a business information system as complex as that needed for the large buisness necessary? Explain.

3. Name and briefly discuss some of the inherent *systems* differences in each of the following situations between:
   a. A city with a population of 15,000 and 200 employees, and a department store having 25,000 customers and 250 employees.
   b. A furniture factory employing 60 persons and a radio-TV station with the same size payroll.
   c. A shoe store employing 40 persons and a chain of ten shoe stores employing four persons each.
   d. A casualty insurance agency with eight persons on the payroll and a theater with a similar size payroll.

4. What is the "total information system" concept?

5. Is the need for information systems restricted to business organizations? Explain.

6. How does a business information system differ from a financial information system?

7. What are the three specific needs for a financial information system?

8. What is the most essential feature of effective data and information flow?

9. What are the sources of data or information that provide input into the financial information system?

10. What special operations are involved in input into the financial information system? Explain.

11. What are the three phases of data and information flow? Explain each.

12. What are the operations included in processing? Give an illustration of each.

13. What feature of output makes it possible to use the same information for more than one purpose?

14. What is feedback? Give specific examples of *feedback* involving:
    a. Credit granting.
    b. Production control.
    c. Budgeting.
    d. Advertising.
    e. Purchasing.

15. Distinguish between an accounting system, sub-system, procedure, method, and operation.

16. What are the components of an accounting procedure? Which is the most important and why?

17. Explain what is meant by internal control. What do internal control duties seek to accomplish?

18. Explain why you feel each of the following statements is either true or false.
    a. There is absolutely no conflict between any of the system principles postulated in Chapter 1; they are independent and mutually exclusive.
    b. The machines and physical environment in which operations are conducted are all important; the fact that certain individuals are there to "make it tick" does not make much difference—if they leave, they will be replaced.
    c. Integrated data processing has more to do with input than with output.
    d. You cannot have electronic data processing without integrated data processing.

19. The D & R Supermarket is located at 155 Main Street. Its present operation involves only one store, which is divided into five departments—dairy, produce, meat, grocery, and bakery. The owners of the store are now considering the acquisition of three additional stores. In examining the stores to be acquired you note that only two have meat departments, and only one has a bakery department. The owners of D & R Supermarket intend that all stores be comparable in operation and service to the present store. All stores operate along the usual supermarket pattern, with checkout counters and cash registers near the exit. Identify the changes that would be necessary if the existing D & R Supermarket financial information system is to be used for the combined operation of all four stores.

20. What relationship exists between the concept of internal control and the financial information system?

21. Look up the word "servo-mechanism" in a modern dictionary or encyclopedia. Is a financial information system related or comparable to such a mechanism?

22. What systems component distinguishes the financial information system from any other information processing system?

23. Select a not-for-profit organization, such as a Country Club, Fraternal Organization, Municipality, Research Foundation, or the like. Indicate whether a financial information system would be needed in the successful operation

of the organization, stating your reasons and giving specific illustrations where appropriate.

24. Show your knowledge of systems theory by identifying, explaining, and relating the following:
    a. Information flow.
    b. Systems components.
    c. Internal control duties.
    d. Principles of systems design.
    e. Systems standards.
    f. Operating guides.

CHAPTER 2

Systems Principles

A SYSTEM PRINCIPLE IS THE BASIS OF DESIGN FOR A SYSTEM THAT WILL PRO-duce a satisfactory or better result. It is a settled ground upon which a system can be designed with the expectation of good achievement. If a system is to provide management with information and a means of planning, coordinating, and controlling effectively, the applicable systems principles will be operative as a guide to practice or action. By the application of systems principles in a given systems design situation, an optimum system can result.

Accountants have for many years devoted their attention to stating *principles of accounting*. In many respects the systems principles can be compared to principles of accounting. Like accounting principles, the systems principles have been postulated by practitioners over the years. They are of equal force in situations involving different industries, size of operation, production processes, and/or distribution methods. They are applicable in systems designed for manual methods as well as those designed for machine methods. Many systems principles are now *generally accepted* as contrasted to others that have only been postulated and are in the process of being proven.

Constructive systems work is difficult because of the seeming conflict that arises in determining which of the various systems principles are applicable in any given situation and the extent to which each applies. *All* systems principles will apply in the optimum design of a system. The major difficulty for the systems analyst is to determine the desired extent of applicability of the principles. The extent of applicability is often governed by a set of values and the judgment of the managers involved in the systems decisions; thus values and judgment often become important variables. For example, in the design of a system the *reasonable cost* principle and the *reliability* principle are both applicable. The systems design problem is to determine the relative emphasis to be placed on each of the principles. In most systems both cost and reliability are important considerations. It then becomes a matter of judgment for the managers to determine the amount of reliability to be designed into the system and the cost that is to be incurred to achieve that degree of reliability. A system could have perfect reliability if cost is no object. The exercise of judgment by individual managers will determine the amount that will be paid to obtain a specific degree of reliability. The system design varies according to the values and judgment held by the manager.

Nine principles of systems design are apparent. Each of the principles is broad and has a depth of meaning covering major aspects of systems analysis, synthesis, and implementation and follow-up. Careful interpretation of each principle is important in establishing its breadth of applicability. Some principles are sufficiently broad to suggest the possibility of being divided. While division is possible, the principles set forth in this chapter are not considered to be broad enough to divide and still be treated as principles in their own right. Nevertheless, knowledge of the detailed parts of each principle is of great value in understanding the principle and in establishing its validity.

REASONABLE COST PRINCIPLE

> The system should be designed to provide information and internal control, consistent with the needs of management, at a reasonable cost.

The reasonable cost principle is the most important of the principles of systems design. Each of the terms used in the principle has a depth of meaning, and the relationships that govern its application are specific. Figure 2-1 summarizes the relationships between the needs of management and the reasonable cost of a system. Conceptually, it can be noted that the needs of management for information and internal control must always outweigh the reasonable cost required to provide the information and/or control. Any system that cannot pass the test of the reasonable cost principle is doomed to failure.

Needs of Management for Information and Internal Control

Management has two types of systems "needs" for information and internal control. The first need is for *required procedures,* and the second is for *optional features* designed to provide more *effective internal control* or *other benefits.* The two systems needs cannot always be separated completely in distinct parts of a system, but are provided together in the system adopted.

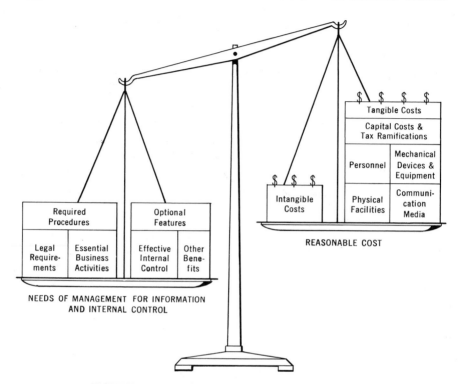

FIGURE 2-1.   Needs of Management *vs.* Reasonable Cost

Required procedures are necessary regardless while optional features can be selected or ignored, depending on the desires and judgment of management.

REQUIRED PROCEDURES. Required procedures enable compliance with the legal record keeping and reporting requirements of federal, state, and local governmental agencies, as well as requirements for essential business activities. They are procedures that must exist for the continued operation of the business.

1. *Legal requirements.* There is extensive legislation establishing the minimum records that must be maintained or reports that must be made to governmental or other agencies. For example, certain records are required for wage payments by employers. Reports are required for federal and state income taxes, sales taxes, social security taxes, unemployment insurance, the Securities and Exchange Commission, wage regulating agencies, Federal Trade Commission, census of manufacturers, and the like. Every information system must provide the means for complying with the legal responsibilities of the business.

2. *Essential business activities.* The system must be adequate to provide for the accomplishment of essential business activities. A means must exist to bill customers, receive payments, pay creditors, compute and pay the

payroll, and to accomplish other fundamental business operations. Such procedures are essential to the business and must always be accomplished. In a well-designed system, the procedures being followed for essential business activities provide the record or information for most legal requirements.

OPTIONAL FEATURES. In the design of a system there are many variations that are possible to accomplish a given required procedure. Such variations are often a reflection of management's philosophy, expectations, or performance standards. An optional feature may be only a small addition to a required procedure; in other instances it is a major addition or departure to achieve a specific objective. In either case it provides additional information or control that is not required of the system.

People, not records or reports, control. Records and reports provide information so people know what to control, why to control, when to control, whom to control, and where to control, but the controlling is done by an individual or individuals and judgments or values are involved. In the design of a system there are often procedural variations from which to choose, with each providing a different amount of information and internal control or other benefits. The optional features can be selected and utilized if desired. They can be adopted or rejected at the decision of management, and are the cause of many difficult systems decisions.

1. *Effective internal control.* The need for effective internal control goes beyond the need for information, and is an important consideration in systems design. Controls can be extensive or almost nonexistent and are often not essential to the operation in the sense that the business could not operate without them. The need for effective internal control involves internal control duties designed to facilitate accuracy, safeguard assets, promote operational efficiency, and encourage adherence to managerial policy. In a well-designed system, effective internal control should be of sufficient value to management to justify the system. A system dependent on required procedures exclusively for its justification is probably not well-designed nor is management taking advantage of effective tools that are waiting to be used.

Some managers feel a greater need for information and control because of their own past experiences or personal preferences, while other managers express little concern for information and many types of control. Controls judged necessary may differ in comparable procedures because of the philosophy of the individual manager as to the *relative risk* that is to be assumed. The need for control does not change from small businesses to large, only the means of obtaining control changes, and the necessity for management to assume differing risks. Management must always make decisions concerning the extent of the risk it is willing to assume. In almost every system the risk of employee embezzlement, error, robbery, and the like must be evaluated before a good systems decision can be made.

2. *Other benefits.* Whenever a system is designed the analyst must decide on other benefits to be provided through the system. These benefits should be designed into the basic system configuration. When selected, management has measured the need as being of sufficient magnitude to justify the additional cost. Such benefits often include provision for the following:

    a. Future systems requirements.

    b. Future cost reductions.

    c. Improved employee morale.

    d. Safeguarding the integrity of employees.

    e. Good public image.

    f. Improved services.

The design of a system requires the decision as to whether optional features are sufficiently important to management to make the necessary provision in the system. It can be noted that management is not required to obtain other benefits from the system. Other benefits are available if in the judgment of management they are important enough to justify their cost. Consider briefly each of the benefits given above and the systems ramification.

Does The System Provide For Future Needs? Should additional capacity be designed into the system? Will there be future benefits in having employees with experience with new equipment and in new methods? What will be the probable future demands upon the system? Will sales volume increase or decrease, and how will processing be affected? What are the system's implications of long-range planning? Will technological change alter the system requirements?

Can Future Operating Costs Be Reduced? The design and specifications of a system can change the total cost of the system. In addition it may shift costs between current periods and the future. Larger capital expenditures may reduce future operating costs and vice versa. The selection of an inexpensive machine with an expensive maintenance contract, technical operating personnel, or special supplies, etc., could reduce the initial expenditures for the system, but increase future annual operating costs. Full knowledge of cost behavior could alter a system decision.

Operating costs are often related by the efficiency of personnel. Whether employees must be skilled, trained, or efficient in a given systems situation affects both present and future operating costs.

To What Extent Does a Systems Decision Affect The Morale Of Employees? In an efficient, smooth, and trouble-free operation there is seldom a problem with employee morale that can be traced to the system. If a system breaks down or is not functioning adequately, there is usually an internal crisis accompanied by a search for the cause of the trouble and the disruption of correcting the difficulty. Employees are under pressure and morale can suffer. Employee morale is not a constant, and is affected by many things other than the system, yet the system can contribute or take away from morale too. For example, a system designed to utilize a machine that is inadequate or cannot be repaired immediately could cause a major morale problem. Operating personnel may become discouraged. A failure by the machine might cause a payroll to be late, billing to fall behind and thus cash shortages, or a breakdown of information for management. How much additional money should an employer be willing to pay for a system that would preclude the types of problem suggested above and the resulting effect on employee morale? What would be the effect on employee morale if a payroll were late? What would be the true cost to a business with low morale in terms of output and efficiency?

WHAT IS THE EMPLOYER'S RESPONSIBILITY FOR THE INTEGRITY OF HIS EMPLOYEES? Should an employer provide sufficient safeguards and control to remove the opportunity of embezzlement? Without such safeguards and controls, the employer may practically be inviting an employee to steal. In such a situation the employer is not completely free from blame if his invitation is accepted. If precautionary measures by an employer can save an employee's life from ruin, does he not have a great moral obligation to provide such precautions? Popular belief that employees are basically honest has been rejected by studies on employee embezzlement. It has been concluded that many employees refrain from dishonest acts because of fear of being caught. People cannot be classified according to whether they are honest or dishonest with exact precision. Under certain pressures and situations many individuals reach a point at which they no longer resist dishonesty. Dishonesty is often explained as "temporary borrowing" by the employee seeking to rationalize his unauthorized act. How far is the employer obligated to go in providing safeguards and controls? The employer cannot make a proper decision without weighing his responsibility to protect the integrity of his employees by removing temptation.

CAN THE DESIGN OF A SYSTEM HELP TO CREATE A GOOD PUBLIC IMAGE? What is the cost to an employer of unfavorable publicity if there is an employee fraud with the resulting newspaper headlines? Neither the owners of a business nor the customers like the implications associated with dishonest employees. Many employee frauds are never prosecuted to avoid publicity. Should it be worth something to an employer to have the type of system that would reduce the probability of an employee embezzlement and the resulting unfavorable publicity? How much should an employer be willing to pay for a good image? The presence or absence of a good image could result in continued business with a customer or the loss of his business.

DOES THE SYSTEM PROVIDE GOOD, EFFICIENT SERVICE TO EMPLOYEES AND THE CUSTOMER? Must a customer wait to pay his bill? Are there mistakes on his monthly statement? Are employee withholding statements correct? Inadequate proof techniques or poor methods often result in errors and record mistakes. Customer and employee service provides goodwill which is elusive and a valuable asset that must be safeguarded even at additional cost. Inefficiency, errors, and lack of dependability are by themselves costly and should not be tolerated for long.

Reasonable Costs

The *reasonable costs* of a system are the amounts (or equivalent amounts) paid, given, or charged for a specific procedure or control. There are two types of reasonable costs. The first are tangible costs capable of monetary measurement. The second are intangible costs for which monetary amounts cannot adequately be estimated. There is a necessity for considering intangible cost equivalents in the application of the reasonable cost principle.

TANGIBLE COSTS. Tangible costs can be expressed in monetary terms and determined with reasonable accuracy in a given situation. The determination of the cost is merely a matter of computation. For example, if a company is considering a change from a given billing procedure to a new billing procedure, the tangible cost differential from one billing procedure to the other could be computed. The computation of tangible costs would require the pricing of basic systems components, namely, (1) personnel, (2) communication media, (3) reports, and (4) mechanical devices and equipment, including physical facilities under each alternative. In addition the capital costs and tax ramifications must be considered. The total cost for the old procedure is determined and compared to the total cost for the new procedure and the specific, tangible cost differential would be known.

Tangible costs must be computed with regard to appropriate time periods. Either the technological life of the system or the life of the major systems elements would determine the span for which costs should be computed. These total costs must then be converted to annual or periodic amounts for comparative decision purposes. The longer the period of time in total, the more difficult a systems decision since the probability of incorrect projection increases rapidly.

Tangible costs must be determined for systems components at specific ability or performance levels. It is necessary to consider personnel with specific abilities and qualifications, equipment with specific capabilities, specific facilities, or specific types of communication media. It should be noted that in any system a major cost of the system will be the cost of personnel. An adequate determination of cost differences for personnel at various ability and performance levels is especially important.

INTANGIBLE COSTS. The intangible costs of a system cannot be measured easily in monetary terms, yet their consideration is critical to an informed systems decision.

Regardless of the difficulty in any systems decision, a minimal dollar value is in fact placed on intangible considerations. In the final analysis the dollar value of an acceptable system will reflect the amount management will pay, including intangible costs. When a system is designed and implemented the actual costs incurred are tangible costs. The intangible costs may be incurred along with tangible costs, but they cannot be measured with precision.

Consideration of intangible costs—such as the loss of future business, the additional costs of working capital if billings are late, costs of production stoppages because of purchasing or inventory control shortcomings, or the additional costs of systems-caused mistakes by untrained, misinformed or uncontrolled employees—is important. In the context of practical systems decisions, the intangible costs, if recognized in time, may not result in "out-of-pocket" tangible costs. For example, if it is recognized that customers are disturbed because of billing errors or having to wait for service or out-of-stock situations, and there is a loss of future business as a result, management could add appropriate optional features to the system to correct the problem or problems. While lost business cannot always be regained, it may be possible to eliminate future "out-of-pocket" tangible costs that are the result of system failure.

The reasonable cost principle is of sufficient importance *to cause a proposed system to be vetoed.* A proposed system must stand the test of the reasonable cost principle. The information and internal control that is consistent with needs as determined by management must be available at a reasonable cost or the system is not acceptable.

REPORT PRINCIPLE

> The system should be designed to permit effective reporting, both internally and externally, since reports are a primary systems product.

A major objective of every system is to provide information. Therefore it follows that every system should be designed for effective reporting to enable the communication of information. Attempts to design a system that will provide internal reports only or external reports only would not be realistic except in unusual or extraordinary situations. Information used in both internal and external reports should normally flow from the same system. Much of the information that was the basis for internal management reports will eventually appear in external reports. The design of a system so that the flow of reported information will be for internal planning and control as well as external use is an important implication of the report principle.

Businessmen wishing to obtain or communicate information or to control an activity are often dependent on reports to accomplish their objective. Significant information must be available to management as well as for reporting to individuals or agencies external to the company. The *starting point in the design of a system* is to determine the form and content of the reports that are to be produced by the system. The system must provide a steady flow of information for both internal and external reporting. Timely and accurate reporting are pertinent factors.

Reports Defined

Reports serve many functions. In systems work, reports are designed to provide information without further processing. They are *the output of the system.* When a report is considered as the output of the system, the difference between communication media and reports becomes clear.

Communication media are used for internal processing and are not output of the system. It is true that communication media can become reports. In general, communication media as discussed in Chapter 4 are as follows:

1. Original transaction (source) documents.
2. Record documents.
3. Discharge of duty documents.

Reports, on the other hand, are output of the system designed to:

1. Measure fulfillment of responsibility.
2. Provide information.
3. Become the basis for action.

Internal Reports

Internal management reports may be grouped under each of the three categories above. Reports designed to *measure fulfillment of responsibility* are essential where authority is delegated. They provide a means of knowing the success or lack of success with which delegated authority is used, and results obtained. *Information reports* are intended to provide the information necessary for planning, determining policy, or for an overview of a given situation. Special study reports are of this nature. They tend to include trend comparisons over a specific period of time, and are not designed to generate direct management action as is the case of control reports. Reports that are the *basis for action* (control reports) are intended to highlight areas in which corrective action is required. They are designed to emphasize variation from planned, budgeted, or standard performance, and should permit timely and effective control.

The report principle implies a design of internal reports to serve specific management needs. The form in which reports are prepared is determined to a large extent by the purpose of the report and the need of those that are to use it for information or control. The report presentation should be such that the user can comprehend it easily and so that it is within his specific background of technical knowledge. Internal reporting must be extremely flexible. Guides to good reporting are discussed in Chapter 9.

External Reports

External reports, like internal reports, should be prepared only for specific reasons. They are usually designed to keep persons outside of management informed about some phase of the business in which there is a special interest. With a properly designed system, most external reports can flow directly from information generated within the system for internal purposes. External reports must often conform to third party specifications. In such instances external reporting can be very bothersome. For example, cost reports on government contracts, where classification and allocation are substantially different from information regularly generated by the system, will require extensive special handling.

HUMAN FACTORS PRINCIPLE

> The system should be designed consistent with applicable human factors, since people are responsible for the effectiveness of the system.

There is probably no part of systems work that causes more difficulty than do human factors. The human factors involved in the design of a system always require special attention in the development of an efficient system. Business machine salesmen are often frustrated in their approach to selling because of delicate problems involving individuals instead of the equipment they are trying to sell. The interest, support, and competence of the people who will be a part of the system and making it work, their behavior, reactions, personality, experience, ability to get along, need for training, and other such factors, are vital considerations.

There are two types of systems engagements—*original design* and *revision design*. The difference in the applicability of human factors in the two types of systems engagements is especially notable, and is important in considering human factors in the proper perspective. Systems design work is a continuous process in most companies with modifications and improvements coming often. The phases of a systems engagement, namely analysis, synthesis, and implementation and follow-up, are similar in both original design and revision design as noted in Figure 2-2, yet the applicable human factors are quite different when each type of design is considered.

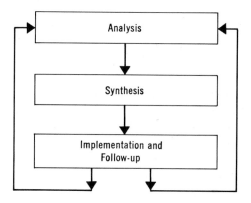

FIGURE 2-2.   Phases of Systems Engagements for Either Original
or Revision Design

Original Design

Original systems design engagements are applicable when there is no existing system in operation. In such situations the design can be theoretical and largely independent of major human relations problems. The analytical phase of the engagement is relatively simple. Problems with people are first encountered as a part of planning for personnel to man the system and for training and installation after the system has been designed. Original design represents a relatively small part of all systems design work. When applicable, original design work usually relates to the systems work necessary to provide for a new operation, division, or product.

Revision Design

Revision design requires a detailed analysis of the existing system. In the analysis phase of the engagement, the people performing in existing jobs, their abilities, strengths, and limitations, are often important considerations. Revision design must deal with the individuals actually performing or supervising existing procedures, and constitutes a large part of all systems work performed.

The human factors principle has far reaching implications. It encompasses all the problems that a systems analyst encounters with people. The philosophy and attitudes of key managers; the approach of employees to change and new methods; behavior, ability, and reactions of people; the screening and hiring, training, and testing; concern for displaced people; and availability of competent personnel to bridge procedural gaps where judgment is required at important systems control points—all are a part of the human factors principle.

ORGANIZATION STRUCTURE PRINCIPLE

> The system should be designed to function in a specific, clearly defined, organization structure, since the system should be tailored for the organization to satisfy particular information and control needs.

An organization is made up of people working in different activities within organization units. The organization structure principle is concerned with organizational units and the way in which these units are interrelated to accomplish the business objectives. The human factors principle, in comparison, is concerned with the individual and his ability, behavior, personal characteristics, etc.

Clearly Defined Organization

The requirement that organization structure be clearly defined does not imply that the existing organization structure is the "best" organization structure possible in a given situation. It merely alludes to the fact that the structure, whether good or bad, must be clear to the designer of the system so that it is appropriate to meet the need for which it was designed. The organization structure is a vital factor in determining the control potential built into a system. For example, the credit department could be the responsibility of the Sales Vice-President. The objectives of sales are in conflict with the objectives of the credit department. The success of the selling function is measured by the amount that is sold, while the credit department is concerned with collectibility of receivables and provides a reasonable balance for the aggressive sales department whose only concern is selling. To cite another example, an organization unit or key procedure may be dominated by an individual or group who has not been able to assume successfully the functions for which they are responsible. Management must make the decision as to whether this individual is to continue in the existing role within the organization. If no change is made, the system must be designed so that it will function within the structure and under conditions dictated by management, as undesirable as the structure or conditions may be from a theoretical point of view. A systems analyst must recognize the organizational relationships within which the system must function.

The organization structure must be crystal clear, even though not formally recorded or recognized by management in the form of an approved organization chart. Anything less than a clear understanding of the actual organization structure would preclude the design of the optimum system, tailor-made to the organization. The effective system cannot be designed without knowing organizational relationships and delegations. For example, if a clerk is making important decisions in the name of a responsible executive, the systems analyst must know about it or he may not recommend a system that would work effectively when jobs and responsibilities are reassigned.

The system should function within the organization structure established and approved by management. A major contribution of systems design is that it requires an analysis of organization structure. As a result of systems analysis, informal as well as formal organization structure is often strengthened and/or altered.

Organizational Independence

One of the important control criteria of a system is the extent to which it provides organizational independence between operating, custodial, and record functions. Organizational independence does not imply that personnel in each department proceed on an independent course of action or that barriers are erected that prevent consultation between departments or that personnel in a specific department can interrupt the smooth flow of procedures. Rather, it relates to the division of duties in such a way that specialization will preclude any individual from performing more than one of operating, control, or record functions. For example, different individuals should be responsible for the use, custody, and record of the material in the inventory. Where organizational independence exists the system can be designed so that error and fraud are at a minimum.

Organizational Relationships

The relationships between the people that make up an organization govern the efficient and effective flow of information and internal control.

A system will function efficiently only when organizational relationships are good.

DELEGATION OF AUTHORITY. Delegation is the process whereby a manager releases certain authority to a designated subordinate. The manager cannot be relieved of his responsibility by the act of delegating, but he is able to obtain some advantage by the delegation of authority to provide assistance with his work load. The extent of delegation of authority is an important consideration in the basic framework in which the system functions. The need for fixing responsibility and authority provides the basis for internal reporting, measuring efficiency, and control. The extent of delegation to every level in the organization structure must be known for the design of an effective system. Without such knowledge the information needed cannot be determined or the appropriate method of control identified.

SUPPORT OF KEY MANAGERS. Managers are people and are subject to human limitations. Their thinking reflects their own experiences, education, and preferences. Logically it is important in their approach to problem solving and means of communicating. Top management executives are responsible for the nature of the system and for the success of the system once it is installed. The support and use of a system by a key manager can be noted rapidly throughout an organization. Investigations have shown that lower levels of management tend to view a system or management tool in the same light as their superiors. If top level managers are lackadaisical, inconsistent, and do not use the information provided by the system to advantage, their subordinates will not use the information or controls available through the system either. The active and wholehearted support and use of a system by management at all levels within the organization structure is a key implication of the organization structure principle.

CENTRALIZATION VS. DECENTRALIZATION. The extent of centralization or decentralization of management within an organization structure, and especially within the accounting function, has a direct bearing on the way in which a system should be designed. Management is decentralized to the extent that decisions are made on a low organizational level, and centralized to the extent decisions are made on a high organizational level. It is interesting to note that management can be decentralized, while the accounting function is centralized. For example, it is possible for managerial decisions to be decentralized to department or division levels, but to have the accounting function centralized in the home office to obtain the economies possible with large-scale computer processing. The systems need for information and internal control on the level at which decisions are made and to which profit responsibility is delegated is obvious. The organization level at which accounting work is performed can also be an important variable in systems design, but the organizational level at which the accounting work is performed does not necessarily have to be the same level at which data and information are used.

RELIABILITY PRINCIPLE

> The system should be designed to check the
> reliability and accuracy of financial data, mini-
> mize error, safeguard assets, and prevent fraud
> or other irregularity.

The reliability principle encompases the proofs and controls that should
be designed into every system. These proofs and controls can include the
balancing features of double entry, prelisting techniques, machine proofs, and
other measures to insure prompt and accurate records, and the safeguarding
of assets.

Internal Check

The reliability principle provides for internal check. *Internal check*,
being much narrower than internal control, includes the processing of data
to provide automatic proof or verification through the sequence of operations
performed. It is one of the important tools available for management to eliminate or reduce the opportunity for error or fraud. It may be described as the
accounting or statistical controls which protect against error, fraud, or other
similar irregularity.

Processing of data in the system should be effective for both the prevention and control of fraud and similar irregularity, and for the prevention and
control of error. For example, an accounting procedure could require comparison by someone (such as the general ledger bookkeeper) of total cash
collections posted to customers' accounts with the independently determined
amount of cash received from customers on account. Such a procedure is
designed to make certain that all customer collections are deposited, but it also
tends to insure the total postings to customers' accounts were made without
error in amount.

Physical Control of Assets

Many of the usual facilities or devices used to control assets physically,
such as watchmen, storerooms, toolrooms, vaults, cash registers, safety deposit
boxes, alarm systems, and the like are integral parts of the system. It can be
noted that control over external forces such as burglary which are provided by
watchmen, alarm systems, safes, and the like, do not normally change the
basic structure of a system. Control over internal forces, such as error or
employee dishonesty, will usually have a major effect on the structure of the

system. Nonetheless, a reliable system must provide the means for external protection as well as procedures and devices for internal protection.

There are many important specifications for the physical control of assets. Individual responsibility for assets is essential. Periodic verification of assets is for the detection of error or the discovery and prevention of fraud and can be designed into the system. For example, an inventory system can be designed to require the actual count of items when the number is at the lowest level, or a cash procedure can be designed to verify cash each day, or supervisors can be required to verify cash funds periodically.

Services, such as Brink's armored cars and checking accounts, or techniques such as using imprest cash funds or depositing receipts intact each day, are also important in the physical control of assets.

Customer Protection

The reliability principle applies to protection of the customer as well as to the owners of the business. For example, a customer could be short-changed in cash or merchandise. The employee, as an agent of the employer, will usually make good on such shortages even though customers may not have good evidence to support a claim. A properly designed system would minimize the occurrence of such an event, and aid in disclosing the validity of customer claims.

Other Controls

There are other controls designed to prevent irregularity in a system and to safeguard the assets. These controls are usually designed to be active where the regular controls are ineffective. For example, measures such as requiring key officers and employees to post bonds are routine procedures to provide adequate protection to the business where the original screening of employees has been unsuccessful or controls inadequate. The use of shopping services provides a check on the activities of clerks at the point of employee contact where assets are not under control of the system. Reliability principle controls that are operative in their own right include internal and external audit.

FLEXIBLE, YET UNIFORM AND CONSISTENT PRINCIPLE

The system should be designed to be flexible, yet insure reasonable uniformity and consistency of application in order to facilitate the dynamics of business.

The flexible yet uniform and consistent principle seems to be a paradox. *Flexibility* is thought to mean not rigid or capable of being modified or adapted while *uniformity* means that separate units operate in a parallel fashion within a given period. *Consistency* is continued uniformity from one period to another. Actually the principle is not paradoxical. The system must be easy to modify or adopt, yet it must also insure reasonable uniformity and consistency in classifying the data to enable effective control to help insure the validity of the information being accumulated within the system.

The flexibility of a system can be obtained by careful design to permit contraction or expansion as needed. Expansion should be possible without altering excessively, if at all, the basic structure of the system. For example, the chart of accounts or code should be designed to permit the addition or elimination of classifications without destroying the significance and usefulness of the structure.

The increase in volume of business created a demand for a greater degree of uniformity—that there should be similar treatment of the same item occurring in many cases. The implication is that different individuals working independently would perform in the same manner or reach the same conclusion. Thus different individuals, classifying a charge for a specific salesmen's expense, would each charge the appropriate selling expense account. In the development of the system, uniformity and consistency are related and both must be considered. Thus the salesmen's expense must also be charged to the appropriate selling expense account with consistency every month.

Uniformity may mean that others are doing the same thing. Thus we have "uniform" systems available in some industries. Uniform systems, especially for costs, have enabled more effective comparisons and control. Such systems have both advantages and disadvantages.

Systems Manuals and Guides

One of the greatest needs for uniformity is reflected in the number of clerical operations in many procedures. Untrained individuals are sometimes expected to initiate source documents or process information in a similar manner. Uniformity in such a situation is most advantageous and underlies the accuracy of the information that flows from the system. Untrained people should, by the use of systems manuals and guides, obtain uniform and consistent results.

Systems manuals and guides arise from the application of the flexible yet uniform and consistent principle and are used in different ways and organized according to different patterns. Nonetheless, manuals provide the basis for building the necessary uniformity and consistency into any system and are described in detail in Chapter 13.

AUDIT TRAIL PRINCIPLE

> The system should be designed to facilitate the tracing of procedural steps in order to permit the analysis of detail underlying summarized information.

Audit trails are essential in the design of a system. Since the system is the prime source of managerial information, there must be a means to ferret out factual data and permit the analysis of summarized totals. Audit trails are not primarily for the use of auditors as the word "audit" would seem to imply. Rather they are tools that are designed to help management in four ways:

1. To provide access to information in order to answer inquiries of customers and others;
2. To provide a means to trace and verify transaction detail involving asset control, such as disbursements;
3. To provide a means to analyze and compare summarized operating results compiled within the structure of the system;
4. To provide proof of the facts required to establish validity of accounting transactions to meet tax and other legal requirements through trails to communication media and other records or studies.

The auditor uses audit trails which management has found necessary for internal purposes. Management would resist modification of its system exclusively for the purpose of providing the auditor with an audit trail. The auditor is expected to go into a business and work with what he finds. If audit trails are inadequate, the examination must be adapted to the records that exist. For example, where audit trails are inadequate, a more time consuming, detailed examination must be performed. In the design of a system, the need of management justifies audit trails and the need of the auditor is served incidentally.

Relation to the Bookkeeping Cycle

The audit trail principle, as it relates to the bookkeeping cycle, requires system design so that it would be possible to start with communication media and trace procedural steps to the amount summarized in the reports, to retrace procedural steps from reports back to communication media, or to start at any point in the procedural sequence and trace procedural steps either to communication media or to the report.

Modern business management has caused the basic procedural steps that are visualized in the traditional bookkeeping cycle to be modified. In modern systems, the efficiency of the system is related to the number of traditional bookkeeping steps that have been eliminated. Where possible, the efficient system goes from communication media directly to the amount accumulated in the report, thus eliminating all intervening procedural steps. The audit trail principle relates to the ability of management to use such a system and is satisfied if information that is accumulated is readily available and capable of analysis. It is especially important to notice that audit trails are such items as dates, numbers on communication media, names and addresses, as well as ledger and journal folios.

DATA ACCUMULATION PRINCIPLE

> The system should be designed to enable the rapid and efficient recording and classification of data in order to process it into information for planning, control, and the accomplishment of administrative routine.

The data accumulation principle governs the initial recording of data and provides a criterion for determining the number of parts into which units of information should be divided at the time of the initial record. It has to do with the collection of data and amount and type of detail that the system is designed to accumulate. At one extreme would be a system with too little detail and broad, meaningless classifications. At the other extreme would be excess detail and equally meaningless categories. Neither extreme is practical nor meaningful for managerial purposes. Thus there is need for a broad guide to action or a principle to point the way toward meaningful data accumulation for information and control.

Initial Record

Information generated in a system is seldom better than the initial record. The amount of detail and accuracy of the initial record is an important factor in establishing the usefulness and reliability of the system. Information not captured, or captured inaccurately or in inadequate detail at the time an event occurs, places a serious limitation on the system. In a job cost system, for example, the labor costs charged to jobs can be no more reliable than the initial time records. If a supervisor estimates time on jobs and prepares cost records at the end of the week, the labor costs of each job will be far less reliable than had working time been recorded on a time clock. Data not captured at the time of the event or its initial recording may be lost forever.

Units of the Least Common Denominator

Data should be recorded in units of the least common denominator to permit flexibility in the subsequent use of the resulting information. *Units of the least common denominator* are units of data combined as much as possible without reaching the point at which combined data will later have to be separated. Data should be recorded initially in such a manner and in sufficient detail as to enable the accumulation of a pool of data or information that is readily available for various managerial needs. It should be accumulated in such form that it can be used in different combinations, depending on the needs of management. Thus the extent of detail in units of the least common denominator differs from business to business according to needs. For example, advertising expense could be accumulated in three types of units: one for radio and television advertising, one for newspaper advertising, and a third for other advertising. The three types of advertising units would provide adequate information for management in a specific business. In this instance the data that were accumulated in three types of units, each of which are units of the least common denominator, would provide information needed by management. In some other business, management could be concerned only with total advertising—thus advertising would be the unit of least common denominator. In still other businesses, management might want detailed information about advertising and many different units of the least common denominator would be necessary to accumulate the detail desired. Figure 2-3 illustrates the manner in which units of the least common denominator provide a pool of data or information in units of the least common denominator for various needs.

The original recording or summarizing of transactions should be in such detail that additional analysis is unnecessary to obtain needed managerial information. If information on the three types of advertising illustrated above was needed, the detailed amounts for each would have to be recorded initially to enable proper accumulation. Then the totals for each type could be reported to the advertising manager to facilitate control over each type of advertising. The same information could also be used for preparing the tax return or the income statement by adding the three types together and obtaining one total. The accumulation of data according to units of the least common denominator gives flexibility in obtaining information for the various needs of management. It permits ready access to the required detail yet serves reporting needs for information when units of the least common denominator are combined.

The data accumulation principle also has to do with the classification

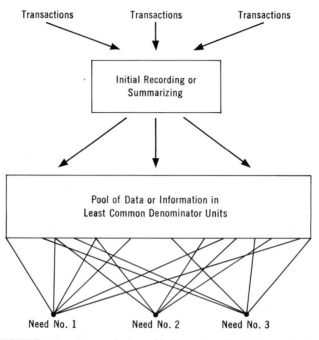

FIGURE 2-3.   **Accumulation of Information for Various Needs**
in Least Common Denominator Units

or coding of information. For example, data should be accumulated in sufficient detail to show clearly such relevant information as efficiency, abnormal
losses or expenses, responsibility, and the like.

The system must be designed to accumulate data that are valid, meaningful, and that can be used to meet the needs of management. At the time
of initial recording, the detail should be established with care. Amounts should
be summarized to the extent that they will not have to be separated later, but
not beyond that point. Once basic units of the least common denominator are
available in a proper record, they can be sorted and re-sorted either within or
outside of the record structure and in accordance with the many and varied
needs of management. The initial recording and accumulating should produce
a pool of data and information that will be available in such form that, regardless of need, data and information are available without undue analysis
directly from the system.

Allocations

In the initial recording of data, allocations, if made at all, should be made
direct to specific object classifications to increase the validity and usefulness of
the data. For example, the amount of a voucher for the repair of a building

should be recorded initially and charged direct to the "building repair expense" account. If more than one building repair expense account is used, allocation should be made direct to the appropriate building repair account. The needs of management dictate the amount of detail to be reflected in units of the least common denominator. If allocations are made other than *direct* at the time of *initial recording* it would not result in the most meaningful or useful management information, and would not result in units of the least common denominator. Allocations other than direct at the time of initial recording may result in two conditions—either the identity of the object of the amount being allocated is lost or the amount of the allocation is on a questionable or arbitrary basis that invalidates the effective use of information in some managerial situations. An example of an initial allocation in other than a direct manner is a voucher for building repairs being distributed between "occupancy, office" and "occupancy, store." Occupancy accounts are used to accumulate all cost of occupancy, thus the identity of building repair could be lost forever. Had the charge been between "building repairs, office" and "building repairs, store" the object of the units of the least common denominator could be identified, and later combined to obtain total occupancy cost if desired. An example of an arbitrary allocation of an amount is to charge "occupancy, store" equally to each income producing department of a retail store, regardless of space occupied or location. The data accumulation principle covers all types of allocations.

Unit Information

The data accumulation principle relates to the type of data that are accumulated. In addition to dollar amounts the system should provide unit information or be designed to make full use of the unit information accumulated at key points in the production or distribution process. Unit information includes such items as the number of items in an inventory, production runs, sales, or billings. Numerical counts should be established at points where items can easily be identified. Measurement should normally be at the end of a process, not in the middle.

Other

Included under the data accumulation principle would be consideration of such subjects as whole-dollar accounting. The distinction between *whole-dollar accounting* and *whole-dollar reporting* is important since the concepts may be interchanged erroneously. Whole-dollar reporting is widely used and consists of reporting on a whole-dollar basis, thus eliminating cents values on reports, but does not relate to the record-keeping process. Whole-dollar accounting has not received as much acceptance as whole-dollar reporting because it cannot be readily adapted to cash, accounts receivable, accounts payable, salaries and wages, or certain other type of data. Such items as depreciation, bad debts, and accruals are readily adaptable.

DATA PROCESSING PRINCIPLE

> The system should be designed to provide a meaningful, continuous, and controlled flow of data being processed in order to produce reliable information and facilitate control.

The data processing principle relates to the efficient and economical flow of data and information through a controlled system and to the way in which the components of the system operate together. It establishes the basis for design of the processing system and governs the data processing operation such as arranging, summarizing, calculating, comparing, storing, transporting, and reproducing data.

The processing system must be designed just as forms and records must be designed. It is important to note that the data processing principle does not imply a difference between manual, mechanical, or electronic systems. It applies with equal force to any system and highlights the processing operations and the *continuous flow of data and information* concept. In an "integrated non-electronic data processing system" or in an "integrated electronic data processing system" the continuous flow of data and information is essential. In both instances the data must be captured initially and processed through sequential steps until available in final form for control or planning use.

Relationships of Principles

Systems principles provide guides to practice or action. They are settled ground upon which a system can be designed with the expectation of good results. The most important is the *reasonable cost* principle. A system must meet the test of this principle or it is not acceptable.

The three principles of *reliability, organization structure,* and *human factors* serve as the primary basis for internal control. In the design or evaluation of internal control they are fundamental.

In addition to the vital reasonable cost principle and those principles which govern internal control, the principles of *data accumulation, data processing,* and *report* govern data and information flow (input, processing, and output).

The final two principles—*flexible, yet uniform and consistent* and *audit trail*—have to do with the actual design of the system to provide utility.

The proper application of systems principles will produce an optimum system.

QUESTIONS, PROBLEMS, AND CASES

1. Are systems principles absolute laws that cannot be violated? Explain.

2. Can more than one systems principle be applicable in a given situation? Explain.

3. How are systems principles related to the financial information system?

4. Which system principle do you think is the most important? Why?

5. You have been called in to review the financial information system of the Bolton Manufacturing Company. After the necessary study you make the following observations:
   a. There is a backlog of inquiries from customers about the status of their accounts.
   b. Factory foremen have been objecting to the items of cost charged to their departments.
   c. There has been difficulty in getting the accounts receivable subsidiary ledger to agree with the accounts receivable control account. In fact, they have not been in agreement for two months.
   d. The payroll section was one day late with payroll checks on the last payday. In addition, you discover that there have been many errors in copying payroll information on employee earnings records and that the reconciliations for quarterly payroll tax returns and annual payroll tax reporting have been an extremely difficult and time consuming task.

   From the brief information above it is obvious that some of the principles of financial information system design are being violated in the Bolton Manufacturing Company. Explain how each of the observations listed above might reflect violation of systems principles.

6. Distinguish between the role of communication media and reports in the financial information system. How is each related to the report principle?

7. Which systems principle or principles may be violated by the following?
   a. "It doesn't matter whether this new computer will be idle 40% of the time or not, it will get me the information faster won't it?"
   b. "We've done it this way for 18 years, why change now?"
   c. "Joe has a good memory, we'll let him tell the auditors about it when they arrive."
   d. "True, few of our accounting department people have much formal

training. But they are loyal employees and I feel confident their loyalty
and hard work will make this new computer system work."
e. "Every one of our employees is honest. We don't need all that red tape."
f. "We hired you to redesign our accounting system, not to advise us on
   who reports to whom."

8. You have been asked to study the possibility of changing the procedure for
   receiving cash in a restaurant. At the present time each of six waitresses
   collects cash from customers after the food has been served and rings it up
   on one of three cash registers located at places convenient to the waitresses.
   The guest check is imprinted by the amount rung up and is then placed on
   a spindle by the cash register. It has been suggested that the system be
   changed to one of a central cashier with all payments being made by customers to the cashier as they leave. State some of the considerations in the
   systems decision in terms of the following principles of system design:
   a. Reasonable cost.
   b. Reliability.
   c. Human factors.
   d. Data accumulation.

9. It has been stated that the human factors principle of systems design relates to
   the philosophy and attitudes of key managers; the approach of employees
   to change and new methods; behavior, abilities, and reactions of people;
   screening, hiring, training, and testing; concern for displaced people; and the
   availability of competent personnel to bridge procedural gaps where judgment is required at important systems control points.
       You have been asked to design a budget control system for a manufac-
   turing company. Indicate how each of the above human factors considerations
   could apply to the design of an adequate budget control system.

10. Does the organization structure principle of system design imply the fol-
    lowing:
    a. That the existing organization is the "best" organization structure possible
       in a given situation? Discuss.
    b. That there should be organizational independence? What is organiza-
       tional independence as it relates to the organization structure principle?
       Give several illustrations of situations in which organizational independ-
       ence would be important in the design of a system.

11. Differentiate between internal check and internal control. How are both
    related to systems principles and to the financial information system?

12. The data processing principle governs the flow of data and information
    through a controlled system. Give several illustrations of procedures you have
    observed that have been installed in their present form to encompass the
    continuous flow of data and information concept of the data processing
    principle.

13. In applying the reasonable cost principle to a system design problem, the
    needs of management must outweigh the cost of providing the necessary

information or internal control. Make the necessary assumptions to explain the way in which the reasonable cost principle would apply to the following situations in which systems decisions must be made:

a. The decision in a department store to change from a five-cycle-per-month customer billing system to a six-cycle-per-month system.

b. The decision in a manufacturing concern to change from a manual posting system for customer accounts to a machine posting system.

c. The decision in a drug store to change from a cash receiving operation using only a cash drawer, to a cash receiving operation using a cash register.

d. The decision that would follow from step c., above, as to the type of cash register to purchase.

14. The reliability principle is a key principle in that it relates to minimizing error, safeguarding assets, preventing frauds, and other irregularities. Explain and give illustrations of the application of the reliability principle in connection with each of the following:

a. Internal check.

b. Control of assets against internal pilferage.

c. Control of assets against external pilferage.

d. Customer protection.

15. In the design of a system there should be uniformity and consistency, yet flexibility should be maintained. It has been argued that the required "uniform systems of accounts" prescribed for public utilities maintains uniformity and consistency, but that flexibility is lost. Comment.

16. The data accumulation principle provides a guide to action in several respects. In this connection answer the following:

a. What are units of the least common denominator? Explain their significance in relation to the accumulation of sales data and information.

b. In what way are allocations of special importance in the application of the data accumulation principle to the design of a system?

c. The data accumulation principle supports the contention that it is not the role of the financial information system to accumulate unit information. Comment.

17. It has been argued that the system analyst should not be concerned with the audit trail principle. After all, the system should not be designed for the convenience of the external auditor, the auditor from the internal revenue service, or other auditors, but should be designed to be economical and effective and to provide for the needs of internal management. Comment.

CHAPTER 3

Organization Structure

THE ORGANIZATION STRUCTURE PRINCIPLE OF SYSTEMS DESIGN WAS BRIEFLY discussed in Chapter 2 as follows:

> The system should be designed to function in a specific, clearly defined, organization structure, since the system should be tailored for the organization to satisfy a particular information and control need.

Every financial information system must function within the existing organization structure. The organizational units and the way in which they are interrelated must be known by a systems analyst if he is to be effective in his work. The organization structure provides the boundaries within which the system must function, the direct lines of authority, the delegation of specific duties, the recognition of responsibilities, and the separation of incompatible duties.

The system should be designed for the organization rather than requiring the organization to adjust or conform to the system. Whatever the peculiarities of the organization, the system must be responsive. The study of organization structure is a part of the analysis phase of a systems engagement and the design of an *optimum* system may require modification of the organization structure. It is essential that the system analyst understand the actual organization structure functioning within a business early in his investigation. Without such information he would have great difficulty diagnosing any problem, and would often be unable to prescribe an appropriate and effective systems solution.

ORGANIZATION

A *business organization* is the structure established to enable the business to accomplish its objectives. It consists of people with specific responsibilities and duties, usually related to one of the business functions. The relationships between individuals and their duties often determines the manner in which a system is designed. The functions within a business are interrelated and complicated, and individuals, with all of their problems, make up the functions. Good systems design requires that the individuals within each function have duties assigned according to plan and that the functions themselves be well-organized.

Business management has formulated and placed into operation a great variety of different organization structures for a host of varying reasons. Major differences are found in the organization structure of businesses within the same industry, yet all are designed to bring individuals together into an efficient operating team with objectives that are quite similar.

Formal vs. Informal Organization

Experience has shown that there are a number of different ways for managers to obtain results within an organization. They can be accomplished by working through a *formal organization* structure; in other instances working through an *informal organization* structure is the practice. Business managers, especially at higher levels, tend to work through the formal organization structure. The informal organization usually develops either in response to a need of the business or objective of an individual or group, and may reflect vital and key relationships. In formal organization structure, the individuals charged with responsibility for accomplishment do in fact direct the operation and are held for performance. In informal organization structure someone other than the individual formally charged with responsibility is making decisions. Informal organization structure often evolves when authority relationships have not been established clearly or when personalities or necessity causes formal channels to be bypassed. For example, if a department head will not act or is thought to be a bottleneck, an informal structure to get things done or bypass the individual can arise. It is also notable that the formal organization structure tends to develop around and bypass such an individual.

Informal organization structure must receive the full attention of the systems analyst along with the formal structure. Informal organization patterns must be recognized when they exist, and the system designed either to correct or to take into account the situation. A system that does not reflect the actual power structure within a business will not be an optimum system.

Responsibility and Authority

The organization structure of a business should provide (1) clearly established levels of responsibility, (2) appropriate delegation of duties commensurate with the levels of responsibilities, and (3) the proper authority to carry out duties at each level of responsibility.

Responsibility, duties, and authority are closely related. However, they are not identical terms, and each must be given consideration. Responsibility is synonymous with accountability. Although duties may be delegated by someone at a higher level of responsibility to someone at a lower level, responsibility cannot be delegated. For example, the president of a corporation may delegate certain duties in connection with sales to the vice-president of sales. The vice-president of sales is thus responsible for performing these duties, but this does not make the president any less responsible for sales of the corporation. When duties are delegated in this way, the subordinate must be given adequate authority so that he may fulfill the obligations entrusted to him.

Each member of a business organization should know his responsibilities and the duties delegated to him. He should know to whom he is responsible for the performance of these duties as well as how his performance is to be reported. Those actions that are beyond the scope of his duties, as well as those that are within, should also be known. Without knowledge of the responsibility and authority relationships, an adequate system would be difficult or impossible to design.

Organization Charts

An organizaiton chart graphically portrays the structural relationship—the formal relationship—of the functions within the business as well as the delegation of authority. It is a static reflection of responsibility for activities within the major functions and the established structure through which the business operates and is controlled.

Every business should maintain a series of up-to-date organization charts. The charts can show the executive functions, their relationship to each other, and some detail of the staff departments and operating divisions. The detailed functions and activities of each staff department and operating division can be shown as a part of the chart or in separate charts that can be related to each other. The top-level organization charts for Monsanto Company are shown in Figures 3-1A through 3-1C.

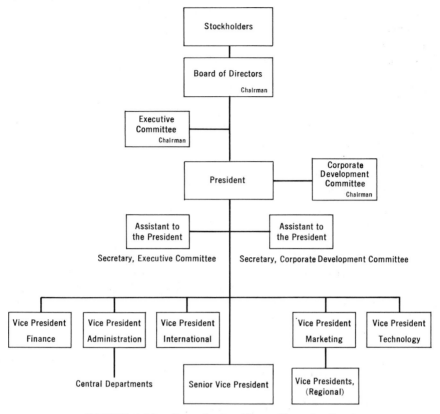

FIGURE 3-1A.   Organization Chart—Executive Level

An organization chart has a number of features that should be noted. There is a *pyramid pattern* caused by the spans of the various levels of responsibility and control. The lines on the chart extend from *top to bottom*—from the stockholders at the top of the pyramid, through the board of directors and the president, and finally to the operating divisions at the bottom. A complete organization chart could provide adequate detail to identify each organization unit within the business, with lines on the chart extending downward until each employee has been included in the structure. The operating employee provides the broad base for the organization structure reflected in a complete organization chart.

The *title* of the individual responsible for each office, department, or operating division can be shown on a chart. Some organization charts are prepared to include the names of each individual or his picture, although such a chart becomes obsolete rapidly.

The levels of management may be shown by an organization chart along with an indication as to whether the organization unit is a part of a line function or a staff function. The manager responsible for a *line function* and his subordinates carry out the major objectives of the business, such as selling or production. Line managers direct the operation and are working to accomplish the primary goals of the firm or organization unit. The manager responsible for a *staff function* and his subordinates will analyze, study, coordinate, recommend, plan, and advise the line manager on the various phases of the operation. A staff manager does not have direct authority in line operations. He usually provides the specialized technical services and makes studies and investigations to free operating personnel to perform their primary function. Staff executives may have line authority within their own function. For example, the Controller (responsible for the staff function of accounting) may have line authority for the billing operations, or for maintaining accounts receivable.

The line and staff relationships that exist within the organization structure must be recognized by the systems analyst. The systems analyst himself is a staff man, with no authority to direct others outside of his own organization. In the final analysis the information produced by the system must be beneficial to the line executive or the system cannot be justified. The financial information system must meet the test of providing for the needs of line executives, as these needs pre-empt all others. The line and staff relationships

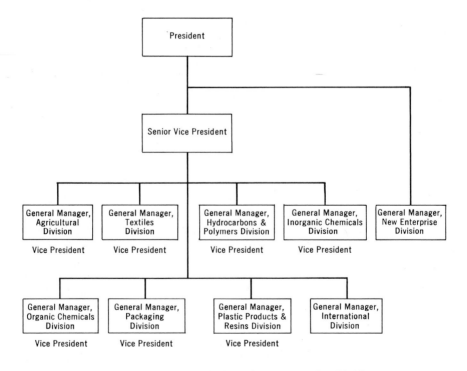

FIGURE 3-1B.   Organization Chart—Operative Divisions

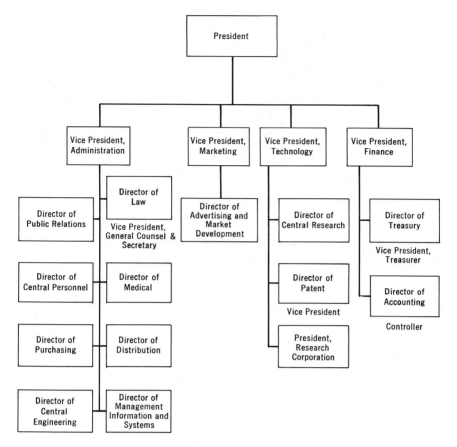

FIGURE 3-1C.   Organization Chart—Central Departments

within the organization units through which communication media and reports flow must always be in the foreground for the effective design of a system. To ignore them or try to design around them could be disastrous.

When the detail of each organization unit is available to the systems designer through accurate, up-to-date organization charts, an important part of his systems study has been completed.

Organization Study

When the organization structure is not clearly defined or is out of control, an organization study may be necessary. In general, there are four steps in the type of organization study needed to establish an adequate structure.

The *preparation of an organization chart* is the first step in an organization study. Separate charts are usually prepared for each organization unit in every department or division and are, in turn, brought together to form the complete chart. They may be constructed to show the name and position of all key personnel. Organization units should be shown even though key positions within the unit are not filled. The structure of the chart can be obtained from actual operations by determining to whom each individual reports, then arranging the structure according to levels of management and supervision, with authority relationships starting from the top and flowing downward.

The second step is to *define in writing the departmental or divisional responsibilities.* By defining the functional responsibilities for each major segment of the business, any undesirable duplication or unnecessary function will be noted and possibly eliminated. In addition, all necessary functions are specifically assigned to the proper organization unit. This requires that the subordinate units within each department or division be identified appropriately.

Third, a *job description* should be prepared for each position within each organizational unit. Careful determination of job descriptions, in view of the functional responsibility previously established, should again enable the elimination of unnecessary duplication, provide completeness, and streamline the operation to essentials only.

As the final step, *an organization manual* should be prepared. It should include the materials assembled in steps one through three above. It would also contain front material such as a brief history of the company, structural evolution, major policies, and procedures for maintaining the manual on a current basis. Job descriptions are often coded to the organization charts in the manual to provide ready reference.

Organizational Change

Changes in the organizational structure of a business must be planned with great care or internal work flow and control procedures can be disrupted. Changes in an existing organization cannot normally be placed into effect over the resistance and best judgment of those whose duties are being altered if the same individuals are to be a part of or responsible for the operation of the new organization. Reorganizations are often necessary and must be accomplished, but they should be undertaken only after there has been a careful study to make certain that the advantages to be gained from the change outweigh the disadvantages. It should be remembered that change for the sake of change is usually unwise. Most individuals tend to resist change, thus it is vital that necessary change be so implemented that the reasons for the change and the advantages of the change are fully understood, and in such a way that maximum cooperation is obtained from everyone.

Organizational changes are normally placed into operation by some type of directive. The need for informing those affected by the change, and for explaining the relative advantage of the change before the directive is issued, is important. Failure to do so can cause internal misunderstanding and affect the factors that are important to an organization, but difficult to direct, such as cooperation, enthusiasm, attitude, and the desire of the individuals responsible to perform at a high level, and to make the revised organization function effectively.

Relationships of Systems Design to the Organization Structure

One of the first steps in the design of a system is to analyze the existing organization structure. The systems analyst must study and analyze the organization and the relationships that individuals responsible for organization units have to each other. An organization chart should be obtained as early as possible in the engagement. Often there are differences between the actual organization and the organization shown on the chart, but it does provide a starting point for the study. The need for the type of information shown by an organization chart is most apparent when the systems design implications of organization structure are considered. Knowledge of this structure is vital to the systems analyst for the reasons that follow:

1. *The chart of accounts* or code provides the framework in which information is accumulated. It should reflect the basic organization structure and be designed so that planning and control information flows readily from the system by cost centers, departments, product, etc. It must be structured to reflect the organization and enable measurement if the financial information system is to be of optimum usefulness.

2. *The flow of reports* is in part, at least, along the lines of the organization chart. Whenever duties and authority are delegated to a subordinate, a report is necessary to communicate the success or failure of the subordinate in the exercise of the authority. These reports flow along organizational lines which reflect the delegation of authority.

3. *Identification of responsibility* is possible. Responsibility must be established to enable the specific identification of successful attainment and accomplishment, or of failure. Entire responsibility reporting systems have been based on the concept of holding individuals responsible for costs over which they have control. When the organization structure has been clearly defined, not only can responsibility be identified, but also the major lines of authority and delegation and separation of duties can be recognized.

4. *Communication media* flow throughout the organization structure. One of the unique aspects of a system is that communication media flow across organization lines without resistance. The design of a plan for the flow of communication media must reflect the organization structure.

5. Knowledge of the extent of *centralization vs. decentralization* of management as well as the accounting function can be partially reflected through organization structure. The relationship between the functions can be most revealing.

6. *Standards of organization structure*, as identified below, can be evaluated. As standards reflect the minimum acceptable levels of attainment, they are the key to the solution of many systems design problems.

Standards of Organization Structure

It is not possible to establish an ironclad set of standards that automatically will result in an adequate organization in which a system will function effectively. The organization structure required for efficient operation will vary with the type of business, size, number of operating branches, products, subsidiaries, geographical location of operations, needs of individual managers, and other factors. There are, however, a group of organization structure standards that are extremely helpful as guides to the minimum acceptable organization structure, and that serve the systems analyst well in his work. These standards are discussed below.

AUTHORITY DELEGATION MUST BE KNOWN. Clear lines of authority should extend from the top level of the organization as far down into each function as possible. Authority definitely fixed can be a motivating factor at every level of the organization. The individual who knows he will receive recognition for good performance and that it will not be possible to "pass-the-buck" when performance is substandard will have an incentive to take the initiative and perform in an outstanding manner. The lines on the organization chart should be drawn to reflect clearly the delegation. An advertising manager with direct authority over each of three organizational units would appear on an organization chart as shown in Figure 3-2. An incorrect reflection of authority relationships would be as shown in Figure 3-3. Authority flows along the lines of the organization chart, and from top to bottom. In Figure 3-3 the authority extends from the advertising manager to radio and television advertising, to general advertising, and finally to newspaper and magazine advertising. The lines on the organization chart should have meaning, and Figure 3-2 expresses the correct relationships. Figure 3-3, in our

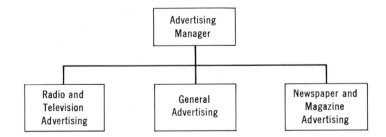

FIGURE 3-2. Organization of Advertising Function—Illustrating Delegation of Authority

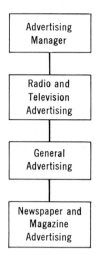

FIGURE 3-3. Incorrect Reflection of Delegation of Authority

assumption, is incorrect, as the lines on the organization chart do not reflect the actual delegation of authority.

SINGLE RESPONSIBILITY. Every individual should be responsible to only one person. If an individual has two bosses, the outcome is certain to be misunderstanding and internal friction about such things as priority of work, emphasis of reports, or in worse situations, conflicting work assignments or procedural instructions.

On high organization levels, dual responsibility can often be justified in theory. In some companies, for example, the internal auditor is responsible to both the controller or the president and the board of directors in accordance with company bylaws. Such a relationship is designed as a control to permit direct reporting to the Board should there be disagreement between the responsible officer and the internal auditor on matters of extreme importance, such as disclosure of significant facts. As a practical matter, however, the internal auditor does not report to the Board. Should such a report outside of usual channels be necessary, the internal auditor would be bypassing his superior. As the Board would probably back one or the other, the prospects for continued employment would not be good for the loser.

OBJECTIVES SHOULD BE CONSIDERED. Each unit in the organization structure should have a definite purpose for its existence in accomplishing the objectives of the business. All functions that are necessary to fulfill the objectives of the business should be included in the organizational plan, and the objectives clearly defined so as not to duplicate, overlap, or be in undesirable conflict with other organization units.

ORGANIZATION SHOULD BE SIMPLE. Complex organizations are difficult to control and in some instances leave question as to the lines of authority that must be definite if control is to be effective. Organizations that have been operating for a number of years tend to become complex as the company expands or as operational requirements change. Simplicity should be maintained except in the few instances where the economy of the operation requires that functions be combined.

ORGANIZATION SHOULD BE FLEXIBLE. Factors such as expansion or contraction in sales or production, or any change in conditions, should not materially disrupt or disorganize the organizational structure. Such variations should normally be possible within the existing organization structure without requiring major functional shifts.

SPAN OF CONTROL SHOULD BE REASONABLE. The number of persons that report to any executive or supervisor should not be so great as to complicate control or cause an excessive number of individual contacts. The levels within the organization often provide a clue as to the appropriate span of control. The lower the level, the greater the span that normally would be appropriate. For example, a supervisor of accounting machine operators could effectively supervise more persons than could the vice president in charge of an operating division. Accounting machine operators perform postings that involve a large volume of similar transactions, while persons reporting to the vice president in charge of an operating division would be concerned with policy matters, production schedules, trouble-shooting, and a great variety of items each requiring individual consultation, differences of opinion, and major planning decisions.

The work of management is to plan and control. Some management authors subdivide the functions of management to include more detailed functions such as coordinating, directing, and organizing. By broad definition and for purposes of systems design, the work of management will be considered as planning and control. Figure 3-4 illustrates the magnitude of the planning and control work at the various managerial levels. The top management level spends most of its time in planning, while managers on the lower levels are more concerned with control. While situations differ, the span of control on top management levels will usually vary from three to eight persons. The span of control for routine operating supervisors is considerably higher.

LEVELS OF SUPERVISION SHOULD BE LIMITED. The greater the number of levels of supervision, the greater the number of people between top management and the operating level. The flow of information downward through the organization is relatively unimpaired; however, when information moves from the lower levels up through the organization, it is often screened, reviewed, and condensed at every level. Screening, reviewing, and condensing information that is moving upward through the organization has the advantage of limiting the information that reaches top management to only the important matters. It reduces the volume to the point where it is possible for management to grasp the important facts quickly. There are situations, however, where information filtered through too many levels has the negative

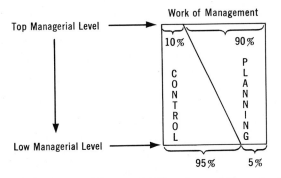

FIGURE 3-4. **Extent of Managerial Planning and Control at Various Managerial Levels**

effect of cutting management off without information that is necessary in making decisions. In the flow of information upward, duplication should be eliminated, and in some instances information should be summarized, but all relevant information should flow through. Direct channels of control are ordinarily faster, more accurate, and easier to coordinate.

ORGANIZATIONAL INDEPENDENCE SHOULD BE REQUIRED. There must be a separation of the operating, custodial, and record functions. This organizational independence makes it possible for a system of automatic checks and verifications to exist that will either detect errors and/or fraud or make it extremely difficult for either to go undetected.

Within every enterprise there are certain functions which, if combined under the control of one person, would increase the possibility of errors and/or irregularities. From the control point of view, such duties should be regarded as incompatible. For example, if the inventory storekeeper also maintains the only record of inventory quantities, any shortages, for whatever reasons, can be concealed through manipulation of the records. If one person prepares payrolls and also signs payroll checks, the opportunity for unauthorized payroll disbursements is increased. If one person records cash receipts and also has control over the cash, errors or manipulation can be concealed. If the custody of cash and the record of cash are separated, any error or manipulation of the record would be detected by the person with the cash; conversely, an error or fraud in handling the cash would be detected by the person keeping the record. The separation of the operating, custodial, and record functions provides an automatic check and effective control procedure.

As a general rule, the following should be considered incompatible duties:

1. Performance of an act or operation and authorization or recording of that act or operation.
2. Custodianship or access to property and the keeping of records of that property.

3. Authorization of an act or operation and the recording of that act or operation.

The recording referred to in this list of incompatible duties means the entry in the enterprise records and books of account. Obviously, a memorandum record kept by the storekeeper does not in itself weaken the system providing there is also an "official" record kept elsewhere.

RELATED ACTIVITIES SHOULD BE ORGANIZATIONALLY AS CLOSE AS POSSIBLE. Activities that are dependent on each other, performed in sequence, or otherwise related should be organizationally close together. For example, the processing of incoming material involves a number of separate steps— namely counting and examination, testing and inspection, and movement to the storeroom or yards where inventory control is maintained. Even though a number of separate activities are involved, the smooth flow of materials requires that there be maximum coordination and cooperation. If the activities are close organizationally, coordination and cooperation are more easily obtained.

SIMILAR ACTIVITIES SHOULD BE GROUPED TOGETHER. Activities that are similar should be grouped together as they tend to be more efficient and to have greater strength when combined. For example, all sales activities can be grouped under a sales executive. Purchasing activities for basic materials, indirect supplies, office supplies, and equipment can be combined under a purchasing executive. Clerical activities can often be pooled to provide an economical, efficient pattern of organization.

DUTIES SHOULD NOT BE SHOWN. An organization chart should show only organization units. If duties are shown, they should be shown only as adjuncts. For example, an advertising manager could be responsible for three organization units as shown in Figure 3-2. The structure of the chart can be modified to show duties as an adjunct, but they should not be incorporated in the chart in such a way that they could be mistaken for organization units. A modified chart showing duties as an adjunct is shown in Figure 3-5.

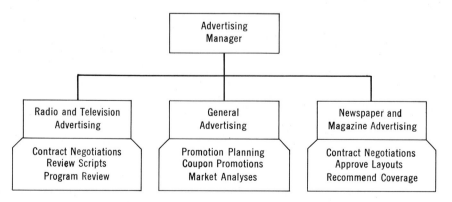

FIGURE 3-5. Organization Units with Duties as an Adjunct

HUMAN ELEMENT SHOULD BE CONSIDERED. An efficient organization must have the right individual for each job. A good organizational plan should be established in which individual abilities, desires, and interests can be integrated according to predetermined specifications. Provision in the organization for individuals with exceptional abilities, and for indvduals no longer able to perform the job for which they were originally hired, should be made with extreme caution since, structurally, the organization may not function well. In general, *consider the function first*, then the individual needed to perform the function. Individuals with exceptional ability soon move to executive positions where work load and duties require their full initiative and ability. Those unable to perform according to the functional plan, due to lack of ability, age, and the like, should be replaced, or, if desired, be given assistance to enable adequate performance. The human element is most difficult to control as it is seldom consistent. The function that is being adequately performed at present might not be adequately performed by the same individual in the near future. The changing human element is a continual source of difficulty in the design of an efficient and effective system.

FUNCTIONS WITH CONFLICTING OBJECTIVES SHOULD BE SEPARATED. Each function should have a definite objective and contribution to make to the over-all operating plan. Functions that are in conflict with each other should not be the responsibility of the same manager, but should be separated. For example, the success of the sales manager is measured by his selling record. By the same token, the success of the credit manager is measured by his record for keeping credit losses at a minimum and his ability to collect past-due accounts. Quite obviously the sales manager will be more successful if credit policies are lax, while the credit manager will be more successful if credit is difficult to obtain. The objectives are in conflict. The separation of the functions organizationally should result normally in performance according to established policy with little opportunity for coloring results of one function at the expense of the other.

RETAINED SERVICES ARE NOT A PART OF THE ORGANIZATION. Retained independent services are not a part of the organization structure. Independent services such as rendered by the certified public accountant, legal counsel, or management consultant for a fee, are not a part of the entity, and should not be shown on an organization chart.

THE FINANCE FUNCTION

Every business organization has three organic functions—selling, production (or purchasing), and finance. (*See* Figure 3-6.) These functions must exist regardless of the number of individuals in the business or the title of the

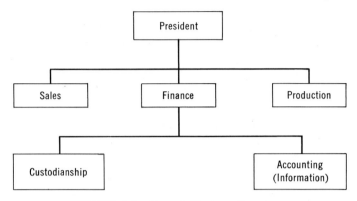

FIGURE 3-6.   Organic Business Functions

person who has been delegated authority for performing these functions. The finance function consists of two distinct parts—the custodianship function and the accounting (information) function. The mechanics of information processing are being separated in some organizations from accounting analysis and the use of information. Both are vital to the work of the systems analyst and are in general considered in this text as though controlled in one function.

Definition

In the evaluation of organization structure for systems design, the title of the individual delegated authority is of little importance—it is the function that must be identified and evaluated. Whether the title of the person responsible for the finance function is vice-president of finance, controller, treasurer, vice-president of data processing, or vice-president of administration is really not important. The function exists and the problem for the systems analyst is to communicate in such a way that all concerned consider the function and not be misled by the title of a given position. For purposes of communication, in this text the title of the top level financial executive is assumed to be the vice-president of finance. The individual responsible for the accounting (information) function is assumed to have the title of controller. The custodial function is assumed to be the responsibility of an individual with the title of treasurer, who is also a legal officer of the company. It is important to emphasize that this text *is not* concerned with the titles of men occupying positions. Our definitions are for communication purposes. In viewing any actual business organization, the title of the individual occupying a specific position and responsible for a specific function is immaterial to the systems analyst; the function being performed by the individual is the important consideration.

The Financial Executive

The Financial Executives Institute requires every membership applicant to perform the duties and responsibilities of a financial executive. They have developed the duties and responsibilities of both the treasurer (treasurership) and controller (controllership) as given in Figure 3-7. In considering the Institute's concept of a financial executive, it is important to note that reference is made to the controller as being "an integral part of management" and that there is responsibility "to establish, coordinate and administer an adequate plan for the control of operations." It should be noted also that the function requires the projection of data and information into the future. It requires the comparison of "performance with operating plans and standards, and to report and interpret the results of operations to all levels of management and to the owners of the business." The controller is also responsible for the "coordination of systems and procedures." It seems clear that the controller has the major responsibility for the financial information system.

The Accounting (Information) Function

The top management executive responsible for the accounting (information) function is the controller who is vitally concerned with systems design. Within his area of responsibility is the constructive development of a comprehensive financial information system. Responsibility for this system is unique in that all of the functions of the business are involved. The output of the information system is dependent upon data that must be obtained and processed in other functional areas. The financial information system does not know the organization boundaries of some other areas. For example, the system for processing a sales order involves the Sales Department, Inventory Control and Warehousing, the Shipping Department, the Credit Department, the Billing Department, Accounts Receivable, and the like. The order must be processed through different departments before the data necessary for the information system are accumulated and reported. The need for systems design to be implemented throughout the organization, not just within the controller's own department, is a unique requirement that calls for a depth of understanding and experience for the controller, and for a systems analyst.

SINGLE-PLANT COMPANY. In a single-plant company the activities performed within the Controller's Department will generally fall into the same line and staff relationships as exist for the company as a whole. The complete Controller's Department is a staff department, yet within the department the line and staff activities are most apparent. The line activities are those relating to the accomplishment of the major objectives of the department, while the

The first formal official statement of the responsibilities of the corporate treasurership function was approved in 1962 by the Board of Directors of Financial Executives Institute (established in 1931 as Controllers Institute of America). For many years the Institute and its predecessor body had published an established list of functions of con-

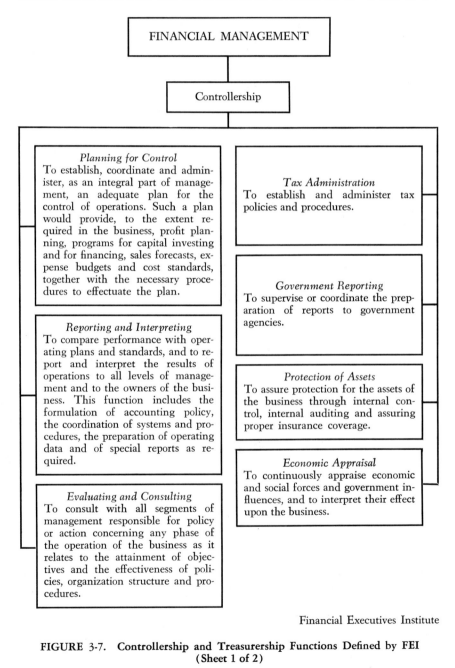

Financial Executives Institute

FIGURE 3-7. Controllership and Treasurership Functions Defined by FEI
(Sheet 1 of 2)

trollership. The newly approved list of treasurership functions was developed coincident with the change of scope and name of the Institute from Controllers Institute to Financial Executives Institute.

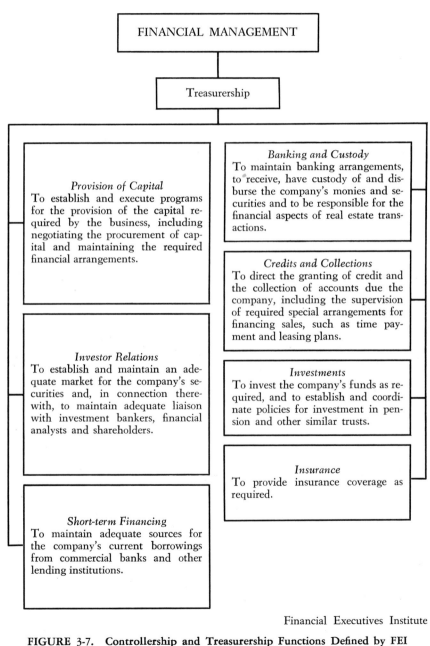

FINANCIAL MANAGEMENT

Treasurership

Provision of Capital
To establish and execute programs for the provision of the capital required by the business, including negotiating the procurement of capital and maintaining the required financial arrangements.

Investor Relations
To establish and maintain an adequate market for the company's securities and, in connection therewith, to maintain adequate liaison with investment bankers, financial analysts and shareholders.

Short-term Financing
To maintain adequate sources for the company's current borrowings from commercial banks and other lending institutions.

Banking and Custody
To maintain banking arrangements, to receive, have custody of and disburse the company's monies and securities and to be responsible for the financial aspects of real estate transactions.

Credits and Collections
To direct the granting of credit and the collection of accounts due the company, including the supervision of required special arrangements for financing sales, such as time payment and leasing plans.

Investments
To invest the company's funds as required, and to establish and coordinate policies for investment in pension and other similar trusts.

Insurance
To provide insurance coverage as required.

Financial Executives Institute

FIGURE 3-7. Controllership and Treasurership Functions Defined by FEI
(Sheet 2 of 2)

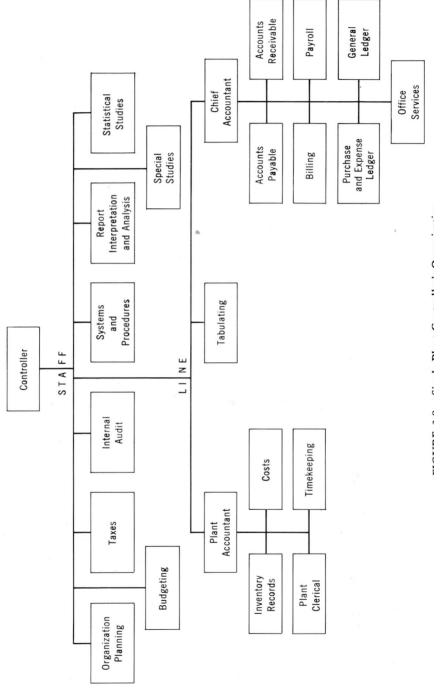

FIGURE 3-8. Single-Plant Controller's Organization

staff activities are those that are advisory in nature or that provide general service to the controller. In the typical single-plant controller's organization, the staff functions that exist are dependent upon the needs of the business concerned. A Controller's Department in a single-plant concern is as shown in Figure 3-8. More staff functions are shown in the illustration than ordinarily would exist in a single-plant concern to show the type of activity that could be accomplished in a given situation. The staff activities that exist in a specific situation would depend on the need of the concern.

MULTI-DIVISION COMPANIES. In multi-division companies, normally there will be several levels of controllership. For example, in a company such as Ford Motor Company there are a number of divisions such as the Ford Division, the Tractor Division, and the Lincoln-Mercury Division. Within each division there are a number of separate manufacturing and/or assembly plants. At each level, controllership activities are performed.

The various levels of controllership work could be organized according to a number of different patterns. Three such patterns are illustrated in Figure 3-9. It can be noted that the authority relationships differ in the three illustrative organizations. Each of the relationships can be found in actual business organizations, plus many others. In Figure 3-9*a* each controller is responsible to the line management at each level for his work load, salary determination, and promotional opportunities. In Figure 3-9*b* such determinations are made through the controller's department, while Figure 3-9*c* is a combination of *a.* and *b.* It seems obvious that the use of the staff services by

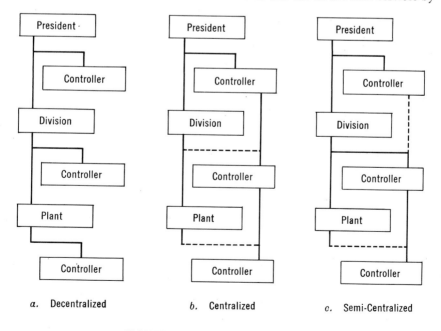

FIGURE 3-9. Controllership Function

each level of management would be different, and that the development of the information system would also be different.

The dotted lines on an organization chart, such as illustrated in Figures 3-9a and 3-9b, usually represent functional relationships rather than the delegation of authority. For example, in Figure 3-9c the top level controller may have functional responsibility for accounting matters, yet the authority delegation is from the president to the division manager to the plant manager. No authority is delegated direct from the top level controller to the division controller. The functional responsibility for such items as the structure of the accounting system, the chart of accounts and the reporting system, deadlines for providing data and information, and the like may be with the top level controller. Although there is no direct authority relationship, such functional relationships can be shown with dotted lines if desired. One of the unfortunate characteristics of an organization chart is that it portrays an organization as having compartments without any interchange or cooperation between organization units. An interchange and cooperation is essential in any organization and must exist. If all functional relationships were expressed on an organization chart with dotted lines, there would be such a maze that the chart would lose its meaning. The functional relationships within an organition normally are not reflected on an organization chart unless they are especially strong or have special significance in the situation for which the organization chart is being prepared.

The problems of the system analyst are further complicated in a multi-division company since it is necessary to determine the level within the company at which a specific activity is to be performed. In this connection, it is possible to have a highly centralized or a highly decentralized type of organization structure.

CENTRALIZATION VS. DECENTRALIZATION. The extent to which *management* is centralized is governed by the level at which decisions are made. If decisions are made at the high level, there is a high degree of centralization. If decisions are made at the lower level, there is decentralization. By the same token, if decisions within a controller's department are made at a high level, the system is highly centralized, while if the decisions are made at the lower level, it is decentralized. There is a seeming paradox that has come into the organization of the controllership function. There has been a tendency for the controller's department, responsible for the financial information system, to become more centralized, while management has often become more decentralized. This development is due to computers being used for major segments of processing and the combining of the facility in which work is actually performed. This means that instead of information processing being performed at the lower level, it is performed at a higher level where the advantages of large scale and more expensive equipment can be fully realized. Thus the controllership function can be centralized while management is, in fact, being decentralized.

There is no standard that can be used to determine the level within a multi-division company at which the various information processing procedures should be accomplished. Generally speaking, however, the major processing installation should be at the *lowest level to which authority for profits has been delegated.* The managers with profit responsibility must have complete information with which to plan and control. Information must be in the context and of the quality that will suit them. For example, assume that in Figure 3-9a profit responsibility is at division level. The division level is sufficiently high so that a major processing center is economically possible, thus the major accounting installation would exist there. With data transmission systems available to obtain the necessary data from plants each day, such a system could be efficient and adequate. It should be noted that in such instances the only processing done at the plant level would be that amount necessary to obtain the data to send to division. The activity at the home office level would be to provide staff coordination, to establish a reporting structure, to enable information consolidation and interpretation, and to provide such other staff services as might be necessary in the situation to service each division. For example, the tax and internal audit functions may be at the home office level.

Standards of Organization Structure for Controllership

Standards for the organization of the Controller's Department provide an excellent basis for measuring the adequacy of its structure. Standards for the organization of the Controller's Department are as follows:

PLANNING AND IMPROVEMENT ACTIVITIES SHOULD BE SEPARATED FROM LINE ACTIVITIES. Such activities as organization planning, systems and procedures, special studies, and budgeting are for the purpose of establishing and improving systems, controls, and administrative procedures. When responsibilities for these areas are delegated to line activities, they almost automatically become secondary duties. The day-to-day operations must be completed and up-to-date before personnel are placed on planning and improvement projects. If planning and improvement activities are to receive the attention necessary, they should be divorced from operations.

If the size of the organization does not warrant full-time personnel for planning and improvement activities, special provision should be made to free a qualified person or persons from their operating duties at specific periods during each year to make certain that the planning and improvement activity receives the proper attention.

USE AND INTERPRETATION ACTIVITIES SHOULD BE SEPARATED FROM LINE ACTIVITIES. Such activities as statistical studies, report analysis, and interpretation are organized to use and interpret records and reports. As in the case of the planning and improvement activities, use and interpretation is of such importance that proper performance cannot be left to the chance that the press of operating activities will preclude the necessary activity. The appropriate use and interpretation of data and information flowing from the system is the difference between an efficient management service and just another overhead cost of management.

The controller is in a key position; he has the choice of limiting his service to performing the clerical activity of compiling data or he can provide a dynamic service in which he not only compiles, but interprets and presents his findings in nontechnical language to other executives with constructive comments and, often, recommendations. He must be more than a figure accumulator. No individual is in a more advantageous position than the controller to provide an outstanding information service to others in management, including the interpretation of the information that is in the reports that flow from his system.

The highly mechanical nature of operating activities within parts of the Controller's Department serves to facilitate the application of this standard. Machine operators are becoming specialists in their own right, and many are technicians in machine methods. Their concern is often with machine problems and concepts as compared to the use and interpretation of data produced.

CLERICAL ACTIVITIES SHOULD BE GROUPED TOGETHER. Major amounts of clerical help are necessary to process the large volume of media passing through the Controller's Department. Just a few of the volume jobs that must be accomplished are accounts receivable, billing, disbursements, accounts payable, and payroll. The control of large volumes of media and posting large numbers of accounts are clerical activities similar in nature. Such activities are usually performed on machines. The technical aspect of performing the job is relatively simple, but an efficient routine to process and control the large volume must be established. Supervision of the operators who actually perform routine jobs is the major problem in accomplishing the activity once the procedure has been established. Problems of supervision are the same in all of the activities, thus grouping under one operating head is effective.

Clerical activities often misunderstood by students in their study of the controller's organization structure are those in a Billing Section as contrasted to those in an Accounts Receivable Section. In most companies the Billing Section is charged with the preparation of the customer's invoice for each sale, for issuing credit memorandums, and similar activities. At least one copy of each document (invoice) is sent from the Billing to the Accounts Receivable Section where the customer's account is posted, or where the copy becomes a part of the receivable record. The Billing Section is responsible for the preparation and mailing of invoices, credit memorandums, etc., while the Accounts Receivable Section is responsible for maintaining receivable records and preparing and sending out periodic statements of account.

CUSTODIANSHIP ACTIVITIES SHOULD NOT BE UNDER THE JURISDICTION OF THE CONTROLLER. Physical control of assets such as cash, inventories, machinery, equipment, and the like should be charged to an activity or function other than controllership. This organizational independence removes the asset being controlled from the function that is charged with the responsibility of providing the information for control.

INTERNAL AUDITING SHOULD BE A HIGH LEVEL, SEPARATE ACTIVITY. The internal auditing activity must be assigned high enough in the organization structure so that audit recommendations can be implemented. If internal auditing is to be effective, and include special investigation and management audit type work, it must have a separate identity.

QUESTIONS, PROBLEMS, AND CASES

1. In what ways is knowledge of the organization structure important to the systems analyst?

2. What type of work should be the most important to the controller—planning or control? Why?

3. What is the significance of the lines on an organization chart?

4. The trade association for your industry has designed a uniform system that is being considered for use within your business. Would you recommend that the system be adopted? Explain.

5. Distinguish between formal and informal organization structure and give illustrations of each.

6. Why should the systems analyst be fully informed concerning the informal organization structure?

7. What are the standards of organization structure, and how do they relate to the organization structure principle and the financial information system?

8. Can responsibility be delegated to a subordinate? Duties? Authority? Explain.

9. Distinguish between line and staff functions. Why are line and staff distinctions so important in the design of a system?

10. A study is being conducted to reorganize an accounts receivable section in connection with a change from a bookkeeping machine system to a punch card installation. What are some of the machine considerations that are associated with an organizational change of this type?

11. In your review of a cash receiving procedure, you discover that organizational independence does not exist. Explain, indicating the duties in the procedure that could be considered incompatible.

12. Where within the organization structure should authority for the financial information system be located? The accounting (information) function? What should be the title of the individual charged with the responsibility for each? Explain.

13. How would you be able to distinguish the extent to which management has been decentralized within a company?

14. Indicate whether you consider the following to be desirable or undesirable. Explain.
    a. Short span of control.
    b. Dual responsibility.
    c. Grouping similar functions.
    d. Organizational independence.
    e. Complex organization.

15. You have been asked to review the design of the system for the REM Company. The first day you ask the controller for a copy of the company organization chart. You are furnished an organization chart dated two weeks ago. The controller appeared to be surprised about your request for the organization chart, and has asked in what way the organization chart was related to your review.
    a. Why is an accurate and complete organization chart important in the design of a system?
    b. In commenting on the organization chart you make several observations as follows:
       (1) The span of control is too long.
       (2) The system should enable automatic checks.
       (3) Duties should not be shown.
       (4) Consider the human element.
       (5) Functions with conflicting objectives should be separated.
       (6) Activities performed in sequence should be organizationally close.
       Explain each of the above observations, giving a specific illustration not given in the text.

16. The Walsh Manufacturing Company produces steel tanks, containers, boilers, and other steel tank-type products of standard design as well as to specification. Work made to specification requires a high degree of engineering skill, and some of the tanks and containers are quite intricate. The company was organized during the latter part of 1966 and began quite modestly during the first several years. Since early 1968 it has undergone a rapid expansion.
    Mr. K. M. Walsh, the president and chairman of the board of directors, who started the business, has supervised the firm's affairs since its inception. As the business grew larger, and more people became involved, reponsibility and authority were delegated to various people in the firm. In reviewing recent operating data, Mr. Walsh has been alarmed by the fact that, while sales have been increasing along with expanded production, credit losses have grown disproportionally large. He has also noticed that the profit margins, especially on many standard items in the line, have decreased. An inquiry revealed that this was caused principally by the increased cost of reworking a large amount of products returned by dissatisfied customers and by the more costly materials specified by the purchasing agent in an effort to reach a higher standard of technical excellence. Mr. Walsh thinks that

this is a paradox, and has the feeling that his personnel are working at cross purposes.

Mr. Walsh has assigned you to investigate the situation and to make whatever recommendations you think necessary to correct the situation. You discover that the firm has no organization chart and that no formal listing of duties, responsibilities or authority is available, but that this has usually been accomplished by understandings reached at meetings of the executives, staff, and supervisory personnel. Through inquiry you obtain the following general picture of the organization of the company and the individuals performing the key functions.

Secretary-Treasurer: Mr. Graham, the secretary-treasurer, is a good friend of Mr. Walsh and was a top sales engineer with a similar firm. He has been with the company for about five years. Mr. Graham is credited with the great expansion in sales during the period he has been with the company. He owns 10% of the company's stock and is a vice president.

Assistant Secretary-Treasurer: Mr. Johnson, the assistant secretary-treasurer, has been with the company six years. He is a very capable man, with a sound background in finance and accounting. Along with his other duties, Mr. Johnson supervises and is responsible for the preparation of cash budgets, cash receipts and disbursements functions, and credit and collections.

Controller: Mr. Strong, the controller, reports to the secretary-treasurer. Mr. Brown, the cost accountant, and Mr. Adams, the chief financial account-ant, work under Mr. Strong. Major functions under the supervision of Mr. Adams are accounts receivable, accounts payable, general ledger, and billing, while those under Mr. Brown are cost records and expense distribution, time-keeping, inventory records, and payroll. Cost information provided by Mr. Brown is usually forwarded by Mr. Strong to the sales division for pricing purposes.

Sales: A general sales manager, Mr. Jason, reports to Mr. Graham. Mr. Jason governs the activities of eight sales engineers and ten salesmen. The advertising function, which is also supervised by Mr. Jason, consists mainly of placing advertisements in trade publications and magazines.

Manufacturing: Mr. Dodd, who soon expects to be named a vice president, is in charge of manufacturing. He reports directly to the president who devotes a good deal of time to this end of the business. The major functions include four producing departments (three fabricating departments and a machine shop), engineering, purchasing, production control, maintenance, receiving and stores, and shipping.

The general factory superintendent under Mr. Dodd is Mr. Wendt, whose major responsibility is maintaining production schedules in keeping with the expanding sales. He devotes most of his time to supervising the producing departments, production control, and inspection. Until three years ago, the purchasing function had been supervised by the president, Mr. Walsh, whose background is in engineering. In recent years the purchasing agent has been reporting to the products engineer, Mr. Hayes, because of the technical specifications inherent in this type of manufacturing.

a. Prepare an organization chart in proper form showing the organization structure of the Walsh Manufacturing Company as it now exists.

b. In a brief paragraph, state your analysis of the organization structure. List the changes that you would recommend in the organization and state the reason or reasons for each.

c. Prepare an organization chart in proper form, showing the organization structure after your recommendations have been placed into effect.

17. Mr. R. L. James, the sales manager of the M. N. Dunn Company, is an extremely competent and successful man 62 years old. The company policy is that all personnel, including executives, must retire at the age of 65. In anticipation of the retirement of Mr. James, Mr. H. K. Lee, 38 years old, one of the most promising young sales executives in the company with an outstanding record of performance, was transferred one year ago to Mr. James as the assistant sales manager.

Mr. K. L. Hughes, the assistant sales manager at the time of the transfer, was assigned as manager of the territory in which the home office was located and has continued to work out of the home office to help Mr. Lee become acquainted with his new position. Mr. Hughes is an excellent salesman and competent sales manager; however, he would be 59 years of age at the time Mr. James retires, and has had some minor difficulties in getting along with a few branch managers and top management executives. The difficulties were not considered serious, but when combined with the age factor, it was decided that he would not be promoted. This was explained to Mr. Hughes by Mr. James at the time Mr. Lee was assigned as assistant sales manager, and he agreed that the plan being followed was to the best interest of all concerned.

During the past six months Mr. James has been on an extended business trip to all of the branches, and has been in the office for only a few days each month. During his absence Mr. Lee was designated as the acting sales manager. While he was acting in this capacity there were several rather important contracts lost, and Mr. James stated to the president that the responsibility for the poor performance belonged to Mr. Lee who had been acting for him. He has also told Mr. Lee of his opinion in no uncertain terms. Mr. James had assigned the actual handling of the contracts lost directly to Mr. Hughes, who during Mr. James' absence, had discussed the contracts with Mr. Lee on several occasions.

Mr. Lee has requested to the president that he be transferred back to his former position as sales manager for one of the large and successful districts. The president is aware of the full situation as stated above.

Prepare a memorandum from the president to Mr. James stating his action on Mr. Lee's request. The memorandum should state all of the reasons for the decision.

18. The K. K. Kaul Tool Corporation produces a line of high quality small tools. During recent years five new products have been added to the line, all of which has been successful beyond original estimates. This factor, together with increased volume in regular lines, has increased production and sales to the extent that a large wing has been added to the plant and two branch factories have been acquired and are in full production. Distribution channels have been expanded proportionally.

Management has discovered that communications with operating functions have become increasingly difficult and that overhead costs are increasing more rapidly than expected. Certain functions within the organization do not seem to have the direction that is desired. You have been requested to study the organization and make any recommendations necessary for reorganization or better control.

List the manner in which you would proceed, step by step, to study the organization as it is presently functioning, and the reason for each step in your plan. How would you proceed to change the plan now in operation?

19. The organization structure of the Speedee Motor Truck Corporation is shown by the following organization chart:

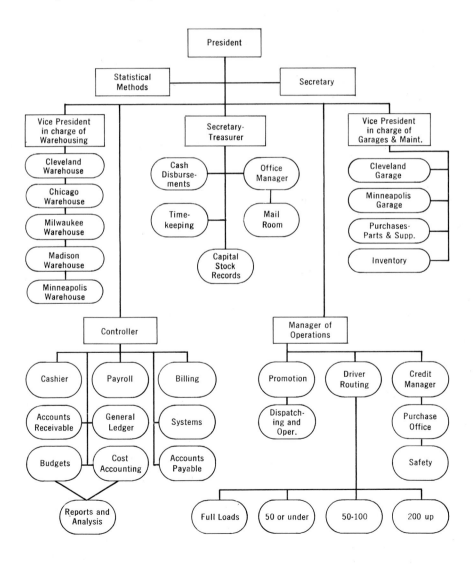

The Speedee Motor Truck Corporation is a large closely held organization. All stock is controlled by twenty persons, of whom ten are on the board of directors. There has been no stock transferred for the past two years.

The board of directors function through an executive committee. The executive committee has three subcommittees—operations, audit, and finance.

Warehouse facilities are operated in Cleveland, Chicago, Milwaukee, Madison, and Minneapolis. In the Cleveland and Minneapolis terminals extensive garage facilities for major as well as for minor repairs and overhauls are maintained.

The plan of operation is to dispatch trucks to local destinations only when the complete capacity of a truck is utilized. All other shipments are between warehouses from which local deliveries within assigned territories are dispatched. Individual shipments of less than a truck load are divided at the warehouses into three groups: shipments from 50 pounds and under, 50 to 200 pounds, and 200 pounds and up. Drivers are permanently assigned to vehicles under this plan. When a load is accumulated, or at specific intervals, a truck is dispatched to the warehouses nearest to the destinations, and the individual shipments are finally delivered to the destination by local dispatch according to the weight breakdown.

Recast the organization chart for the Speedee Motor Truck Corporation according to sound standards of organization to provide better control and more efficient operation. List each change from the organization chart shown above and state specifically the reason or reasons for the changes.

20. Should the organization chart of a Controller's Department of a single-plant manufacturing company show the following, and why?
   a. Budgeting.
   b. Internal audit.
   c. External audit.
   d. Bank reconciliation.
   e. Credit and collection.
   f. Organization planning.

21. Distinguish between the duties of the treasurer and those of the controller.

22. The recommendation has been made that the Internal Auditing Department be assigned to the Chief Bookkeeper. Can you see any difficulty with the delegation of this duty? Discuss.

23. The controller has suggested that the duty for developing a budget system be delegated to Mr. Harold K. Johnson, the cost accountant. Mr. Johnson is a competent man who has been able to perform every assignment to date in an excellent manner. Can you see any problem in the delegation of this duty? Discuss.

24. The controller of the Harrisonberg Corporation, a multi-plant business, has recently become alarmed at the cost of his own operation. As a result of a study he noted that the cost of controllership has increased steadily while sales volume of the company has been relatively stable.

There are two levels of controllership in the Harrisonberg Corporation— the top level with responsibility directly to the president, and the plant level. Plant managers have been delegated authority for plant controllership, while functional authority is charged to the top level controller. All actual accounting records are kept at the plants located in six different cities in the state of Illinois.

The controller has assigned the matter of increased costs to a special studies unit for investigation, with the comment that he is of the opinion that costs could be reduced by having all accounting work performed at fewer geographical locations. After receiving the report from the special studies group, he asked for a clarification of the following statements:

"Accounting activities can be geographically centralized, yet the accounting function can be very decentralized."

"Authority over plant controllership is not as efficient when delegated to plant managers as when delegated to the top level controller."

"The profit contribution of each plant is difficult to determine when there is a high degree of centralization."

Prepare a memorandum to the controller including at least one paragraph to clarify each of the above statements.

25. The Sweeney Manufacturing Company was organized several years ago for the purpose of producing plastic products, with the main product line high quality dishes for commercial use. Since then the company has been following a program of local expansion by construction as well as purchase. The board of directors now feel that the program has been carried to the point where facilities are adequate and production goals are within sight.

The president, desiring to establish more definite responsibility and to improve the control over operations of the company, has requested all top level executives to review the activities for which they are responsible and present an organization chart outlining functional responsibility as it exists at the present time. An organization planning section has been authorized under the controller to coordinate the organizational review.

Responsibilities had not been clearly defined prior to this time, and in reviewing his function the controller determined the following:

A cost accounting system is in operation, designed to determine the cost of production and measure the results of operations. Perpetual inventory and timekeeping records are maintained. Special attention is given to the accounting distribution of materials, labor, and manufacturing expenses.

A staff is employed to design and review the system, methods, and procedures. Budgets are prepared and compared to operating results.

In addition to the outside auditors called in to certify statements each year, the company provides for an internal auditor who reports directly to the executive vice president. A general ledger is used to control all subsidiary ledger accounts by accumulating totals from independent sources. Subsidiary ledgers are kept for accounts receivable, accounts payable, purchases, and expenses. Payroll and billing are separate activities.

Prepare an organization chart showing the organization structure of the Controller's Department.

26. The organization structure of the Danial Corporation, a single-plant manufacturing concern, includes the usual basic functions for such a business. The finance function is performed by a controller and a treasurer, both of whom are responsible directly to the president. Some of the activities performed within the company, most of which are performed within the finance function, are as follows:

Accounts payable	Inventory control
Accounts receivable	Organization planning
Analysis and interpretation	Payroll
Billing	Personnel administration
Budgets	Procedures and methods
Cashier	Production control
Communication services	Property records
Cost accounting	Purchasing
Credit and collections	Sales analysis
Economic studies	Special studies
External auditor	Statistical studies
General accounting	Tabulating
Insurance	Taxes
Internal audit	Timekeeping

a. Prepare an organization chart, in proper form, for the Danial Corporation, showing all portions of the organization for which information is provided above.

b. *Briefly* state why the following activities were placed as indicated in your organization structure:

Analysis and interpretation
Budgets
Credit and collections
Economic studies
Insurance
Organization planning
Payroll
Statistical studies
Timekeeping

27. The Readi-Roller Company, Cleveland, Ohio, produces and markets a number of motor propelled units, namely lawn mowers, cultivators, motor scooters, and golf buggies. The company management has a typical organization structure, which includes a controller who reports directly to the president.

The company has three major operating divisions—the motor division, accessories and parts division, and the assembly division. The assembly division is responsible for the assembly plant located in Cleveland in conjunction with home office facilities. The motor division is responsible for the operation of four separate factories, while the accessories and parts division is responsible for the operation of six separate factories. The majority of the production of all plants is transferred to Cleveland and assembled into products bearing the company trade-mark; however, in each instance, some of the production is for outside vendees. The organization structure is the same for all ten factories and the assembly plant. Full profit responsibility has been delegated by management to each operating division.

a. Prepare a memorandum from the controller of the company to the president recommending the extent to which the accounting function should be decentralized, with appropriate reasons for your position.

b. Draw an organization chart or charts that shows the formal responsibility for all levels of controllership in accordance with the controller's recommendation to the president prepared under step a. above. Include as a minimum the following:

Internal auditing	Tabulating
Organization planning	General ledger
Payroll	Timekeeping
Accounts receivable	Inventory control
Accounts payable	Cost distribution
Billing	Budgeting
Purchase and expense ledger	Taxes
Special studies	

28. What is the difference between a Billing Section and an Accounts Receivable Section?

29. In a company with multi-level controllership, at which level would you expect to find the major accounting organization?

30. The Modern Manufacturing Corporating, a large company, has three levels of controllership in the company organization as indicated in the chart below.

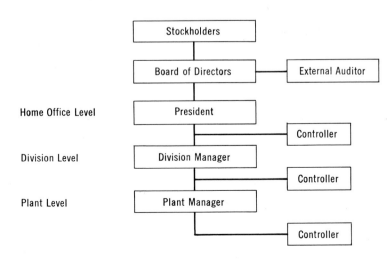

Each of the two divisions of the company has four plants. The president has delegated profit responsibility to division managers; however, plant managers have responsibility only for performance and cost control.

a. Prepare an organization chart that reflects good organization of the accounting function for the Modern Manufacturing Corporation. Assume that the organization of each division and plant is the same. Show as a minimum the appropriate organization shown above plus the organization units that should be shown on an organization chart from those listed below. Indicate the reason why any unit is omitted.

V.P. sales	Credits and collections
V.P. manufacturing	General ledger
Secretary-treasurer	Cashier
Accounts receivable	Budgets
Billing	Purchase and expense ledger
Bank reconciliation	Inventory control
Tabulating	Timekeeping
Internal auditing	Payroll
Taxes	Mailroom
Special studies	Systems and procedures
Cost accounting	Chief accountant

b. Is the management of the above corporation centralized or decentralized? How can you tell?

c. Is the accounting (information) function in the above company centralized or decentralized? Explain.

d. How would the organization chart, prepared in requirement a., differ if the three levels of controllership had been organized as shown in the chart below.

e. What are the meanings of the dotted lines between the various levels of controllership on the chart below? Explain the specific relationships between the home office controller and the division controller. For what part of the accounting function is the home office controller responsible?

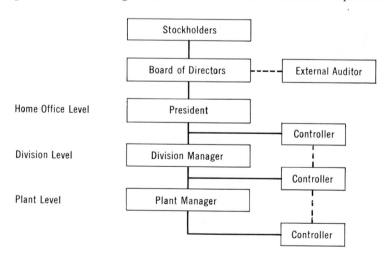

31. In a multiple-level (three level) company, where profit responsibility has been delegated to the second or divisional level, but not to the third or plant level, what is the implication insofar as the system is concerned?

32. The MNO Company, whose home office and factory is in Madison, manufactures and sells plastic household items. Items manufactured are sold from the factory directly to independent wholesalers, and also to retailers through two company-owned wholesale sales outlets, one in Milwaukee and the other in Omaha. Company sales outlets carry a balanced inventory of all items, with transfers from the factory being at the same price paid by independent wholesalers. Management of the company has delegated profit responsibility to the manager of the factory and to the manager of each company sales outlet. Responsibility for the accounting function is as shown below (other functions omitted).

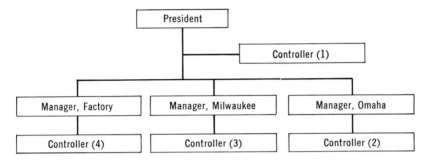

Indicate the number of the controller who would be assigned responsibility for performing the following activities. If the activity is not performed by a controller, use the number (5).

a. Budgeting.
b. Internal audit.
c. Accounts receivable.
d. Inventory control.
e. Cashier.
f. Economic analysis.
g. Systems and procedures.
h. Timekeeping.
i. Factory accounting.
j. External auditor.

k. General ledger.
l. Purchase and expense ledger.
m. Billing.
n. Special studies.
o. Taxes.
p. Production control.
q. Testing and inspection.
r. Vouchers payable.
s. Payroll.
t. Stockholder records.

33. The All Products Corporation has grown rapidly in the past ten years. A number of smaller companies have been brought into the organization through purchase and merger to complicate the problems caused by growth. In the current year, sales volume has leveled off and there are indications that total volume will be below previous years for the first time this year. Management is undertaking a review of the company organization, with special emphasis on the Controller's Department, in hopes of increasing efficiency and control procedures, and thus help relieve the present profit pinch. The organization chart is as shown on the next page.

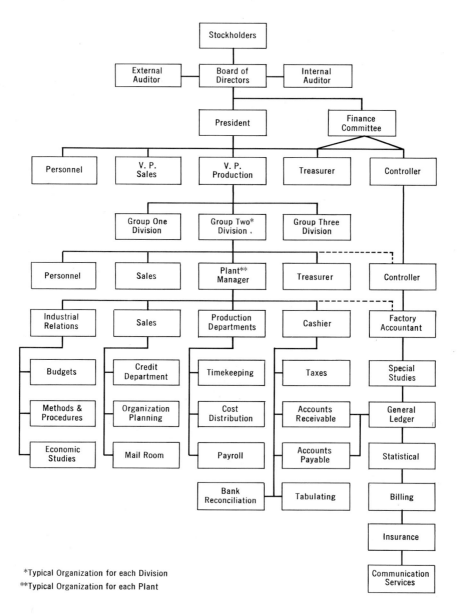

*Typical Organization for each Division
**Typical Organization for each Plant

About 60 different products are now being manufactured, all of which can be classified into one of three basic groups. Each group is managed through a Division. There are eight plants in each of the three Divisions, all located within a radius of 40 miles of the Division Office.

Management has deliberately followed a policy of what they term "decentralization." Responsibility for work performance and cost control has been delegated as far into the organization as possible. Top management has a bonus plan based on profits earned.

Your study of the allocation of functions within the present organization resulted in the organization chart that follows. This chart was reviewed by management, at your request, and the following statements of policy approved:

"Full profit responsibility is to be delegated to the Division level; plants are to be responsible primarily for meeting budgets and cost control."

"All executives reporting to the president are to be members of the finance committee."

Prepare an organization chart or charts for the All Products Corporation that will reflect good organization and the managerial policies set forth above. Show *exactly* the same detail as reflected in the chart on the facing page, or *state specifically* why any section was omitted or added.

CHAPTER 4

Communication Media

THE COMPONENTS OF A SYSTEM ARE ITS TANGIBLE PARTS. INCLUDED ARE personnel, communication media, reports, and data originating, processing, and control devices. Detailed knowledge about systems components is essential to a systems analyst if he is to select and bring together the components in an optimum, efficient, and effective system. In this chapter the most common of the systems components—communication media—will be studied. Data originating, processing, and control devices will be studied in Chapter 5, personnel in Chapter 6, and reports in Chapter 9.

All of the systems principles can be related directly to communication media. The reasonable cost, reliability, human factors, data accumulation and data processing principles are especially applicable. When the role of communication media in the system is studied in the context of the standards of communication media design, the full significance and application of each of the principles is easily recognized.

THE NEED FOR COMMUNICATION MEDIA

It was pointed out that communication media are an essential component of any financial information system. The pertinent question, "Why is this so?" should be answered here. Since the primary purpose of a financial information system is to collect and process business transaction data of a particular business enterprise so that useful financial and other information can be produced for its management, some means must be found to enable facts about the myriad of business transactions, which affect the enterprise daily, to be collected and processed efficiently.

One of the first conclusions that is reached in this search is that it is far more efficient to use some physical medium to store and transmit data rather than to rely on mental storage and verbal transmission. Even in the operation of a small craft guild during the Middle Ages, the owner found it necessary to record the names of his customers in a book along with the description or specifications of the product and the quoted price so that the right product would be delivered to the right customer for the correct price. Think of the problems that would be encountered today if the financial, statistical, and other data concerning enterprise transactions and events were not represented on some physical medium independent of the person who first caused or came into contact with the transactions or events. Think of the problems of computing the total sales for the day for Macy's, or Gimbel's, or of remembering how much each of their charge account customers owe with none of the data about either of these situations represented apart from the persons who first encountered the facts. The impossibility of this task is evident.

In addition to providing a *physical medium to store and transmit data,* communication media are essential in situations in which *repetitive* elements are involved, where *inexperienced employees are responsible for a proven procedure,* and when an individual is to be *charged or relieved of responsibility.*

Communication media are especially effective in situations in which repetitive elements are involved. Sales, for example, occur over and over again in any given day. By the design of the sales ticket, a repetitive operation is facilitated, saving time and making the job of recording uniform and comparatively easy.

The use of communication media, in situations in which inexperienced employees are responsible for a proven procedure and for which a well-defined requirement and method has been established by experienced employees, holds considerable advantage. Data collection is reduced to the simplest level by the necessity of recording only the variable portion of the well-defined event, as the fixed information is printed or already available on the media. The data that are necessary and the methods of collecting them are well established by experienced employees, thus the demands on inexperienced employees are at a minimum and accuracy, completeness, and effectiveness maximized when communication media are used.

Communication media effectively provide evidence that an individual is charged or relieved from a given responsibility. Whenever cash changes hands within a business, for example, communication media should relieve one party of responsibility and charge another. To cite another example, a signed voucher should have the signature of a number of individuals to establish that they have assumed responsibility for the specific verifications that are necessary before a payment of company funds is authorized. Nothing establishes or relieves an individual of responsibility as clearly as signed communication media.

Kinds of Communication Media

Basically, there are three kinds of communication media used in financial information systems, namely, original transaction (source) documents, record documents, and discharge of duty documents.

ORIGINAL TRANSACTION (SOURCE) DOCUMENTS. The facts surrounding a particular transaction, or event, are first represented on original transaction (source) documents. Such documents then serve as a device which permits data to be transmitted to other parts of the business or through additional processing steps. Vendors' invoices, purchase orders, purchase requisitions, sales invoices, and deposit slips are some common original transaction documents. Usually, these documents request, or direct, some particular employee to perform some operation. For example, a notification of employment received in the payroll department from the personnel department directs the payroll department to place a new employee on the payroll, and supplies the necessary information. A purchase order is a request to a vendor for certain merchandise or services.

In addition to requesting or directing performance, original transaction documents are often required to be in the possession of certain employees before further processing of the data can continue. For example, a copy of the purchase order is often required to be in the hands of a voucher clerk before he is permitted to voucher a vendor's invoice for payment. Job time tickets should be sent to the appropriate section to be reconciled with the clock card before being sent to payroll where the pay check is prepared.

In summary, we can say that original transaction documents are used to serve as a medium on which data are represented. The data can be transmitted to other areas of the enterprise or through additional processing steps to request or direct performance of some operation. They may also provide data which must be received before further processing can continue.

Although the word document is used to describe this and the other classes of communication media, the word paper is not implied. The specific medium upon which data are represented could be paper, but it could also be punched cards, punched paper tape, magnetic tape, or any other substance upon which data could be represented effectively.

RECORD DOCUMENTS. This type of communication media can be described as media which contain data, or information, which will be subject to interpretive reuse. Records are used to assemble and arrange data that were initially represented on original transaction documents. Books of original entry and the various ledgers used in an accounting system are record documents. It should be pointed out that original transaction documents can become record documents. Many business enterprises use a copy of the sales invoice as the customer's ledger. The total amount owed by a customer would be a total of his unpaid invoices. Using the copy of the sales invoice in this way obviates the need for a formal subsidiary ledger. The copy of the sales invoice became a record. Voucher copies also can serve as a record, eliminating the need for a vendor's ledger. Data in records are always subject to reuse. Management must see to it that customers pay their bills regularly and, as a result, must continually use the data preserved in the accounts receivable subsidiary ledger. The general ledger is constantly used for statement purposes and special analyses. Books of original entry are often used to summarize much transaction data and must be relied upon to furnish details if needed for subsequent data analyses.

DISCHARGE OF DUTY DOCUMENTS. These documents are submitted to inform others in the financial information system that certain operations have been carried out, and that further processing of data can continue. A receiving report is a separate, formal document which informs interested parties of the quality and quantity of goods received. Original transaction documents are often converted into discharge of duty documents. For example, a box is often stamped upon a vendor's invoice containing spaces in which clerks can acknowledge that they have performed certain operations with regard to the invoice and to facilitate further processing. Figure 4-1 shows a vendor's invoice with a stamp which is signed to indicate that materials or services were received. The invoice was refooted and extended, prices and quantities were approved, transportation charges were checked, and coding completed for the processing of the payment.

The three types of communication media discussed above are the types which must be considered by anyone responsible for the design of a financial information system. It is not our purpose here to exhaust the topic of communication media. Chapters 10 through 18 will illustrate how communication media as well as the other components of a financial information system are combined in more specific situations. Prior to the discussion as to how communication media are used in specific situations, it is important to consider some of the standards of media design which are applicable regardless of the specific requirements in any given situation.

The following discussion on media design will use the word "form" to mean "document with printing or writing on it and blank spaces to be filled in," which is an inclusive term applicable to original transaction documents, record documents, and discharge of duty documents. Reports which are products of the financial information system are not communication media, although a given document can have a dual function. For example, a daily summary of cash received taken off the cash register at the end of the day may be an original transaction document from which the cash receipts journal entry is taken in further processing. It could also be a discharge of duty document, one copy of which would relieve the cashier of responsibility for the

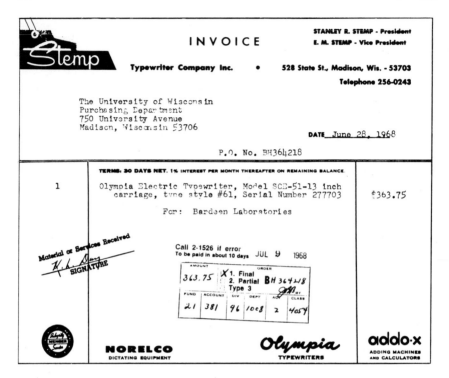

FIGURE 4-1.   Original Transaction Document Converted to Discharge
of Duty Document

cash cleared from the cash register. It could also be a report to the treasurer, who may need the information provided to make certain decisions involving cash. The use of a given document as both a communication medium and a report does not cause difficulty; however, the role of the document must be understood and recognized to be brought into the design of the system appropriately. Reports will be discussed in detail in Chapter 9.

STANDARDS OF FORM DESIGN

There are five major standards that are applicable to the design of forms:

1. The form must create a favorable mental attitude in the user.
2. The form must afford the easiest possible method of entering data.
3. The form must afford the easiest possible method of using the data.
4. The form must reduce the tendency to error in entering or using the data.

5. The form must make for paper and printing economy within limits for efficient clerical use.[1]

FAVORABLE MENTAL ATTITUDE. As long as people are responsible for placing data on forms or using the data already there, it is only logical that the form itself should not be repulsive to the user. The form designer must know quite a bit about the user and about human nature in general. One approach to form design, which seems to create a favorable mental attitude in users, is to consult the user of a proposed new, or revised, form *before* asking him to use it. This will give the user an opportunity to express objections and opinions, and will enable the designer to explain away objections and incorporate user suggestions into the final design. Users who feel that they have had a part in the design of a new, or improved, form are far more disposed to see to it that it is used effectively.

The educational level of the users of a new, or revised, form has a direct bearing on attitude. The use of different colors, where a multiple copy form is being used, may be more acceptable for certain employees since less mental effort is needed to route the copies properly. Often employees are asked to complete certain forms under adverse conditions. A situation, such as requiring that a time ticket be completed for each job an employee works on during the day, may be more acceptable to the employee if care has been used in the design of the form which keeps writing to a minimum. Consider Figure 4-2 which illustrates a time ticket upon which the employee need only write the job number and circle the time spent. Such "minimum of effort" forms find far greater acceptance among production line people who, as a group, are generally opposed to forms in the first place.

ENTERING DATA. Efficiency of processing is hampered when employees cannot enter data or otherwise complete a form easily. If insufficient space is allowed for the data to be inserted, the data are often illegible and/or incomplete. In either case, unnecessary time must be spent to correct the situation. Figure 4-3 contains the Hospital Admittance Sheet of the Barnes Hospital, St. Louis, Missouri. This form was designed so that it could be completed on a typewriter. Any attempts to complete this form manually would require that the data be placed in an area too small for normal writing. In specific instances when this form was completed manually, the data were often illegible or omitted. An evident conclusion is that less space is necessary on a form for data entered by machine than by data entered manually.

Preprinted lines under the data to be entered in spaces is another factor to consider. Lines on a form which will be completed on a typewriter, or other machine, unless precisely calibrated to the proper machine spacing, often cause the typed data to be imprinted over the lines, decreasing legibility.

---

[1] Frank M. Knox, "Design and Control of Business Forms," in J. K. Lasser, (ed.) *Handbook for Accountants* (New York: McGraw-Hill Book Company, Inc., 1956), pp. 4–152.

```
┌─────────────────────────────────────────┐
│                                         │
│            XY Manufacturing Co.         │
│                                         │
│             Finishing Dept.             │
│                                         │
│        Empl. No. 841                    │
│                                         │
│        Empl. Name   John Doe            │
│                                         │
├──────────────────┬──────────────────────┤
│                  │        Time          │
│   Job No.        │    .5   1   1.5   2  │
│                  │   2.5   3   3.5   4  │
├──────────────────┼──────────────────────┤
│   Job No.        │    .5   1   1.5   2  │
│                  │   2.5   3   3.5   4  │
├──────────────────┼──────────────────────┤
│   Job No.        │    .5   1   1.5   2  │
│                  │   2.5   3   3.5   4  │
├──────────────────┼──────────────────────┤
│   Job No.        │    .5   1   1.5   2  │
│                  │   2.5   3   3.5   4  │
├──────────────────┼──────────────────────┤
│   Job No.        │    .5   1   1.5   2  │
│                  │   2.5   3   3.5   4  │
├──────────────────┴──────────────────────┤
│   Foreman                               │
│   Signature   _____  │
└─────────────────────────────────────────┘
```

FIGURE 4-2.   "Minimum of Effort" Time Ticket

Employees who are typing a lined form may recognize that unless adjustments are periodically made, they will type over a line instead of on it, and they will make the necessary adjustments. The recipient of the form will now be able to read it, but production efficiency of the typists will slip. When a form is to be filled in by pencil or ink, preprinted lines should be used.

Space coordination, among related forms, is still another factor which can affect the ease of entering data onto a form. Sales clerks, for example, may be required to complete three or four types of forms, depending on the type of customer service they were rendering. Assume that a different form is needed to be prepared in order to initially record a cash sale, charge sale, credit on account, or debit memo. All of these forms have space for data which should be identical on all forms. Customer name and clerk number would be two examples. There should also be space on all of these forms for a description of the merchandise sold, returned, or for which there is a correction of a previous error. Clerks become confused when they are required to put the customer's name at the top of one form but at the bottom of another; or if the space for his number is located at one place on the charge sales ticket but at a

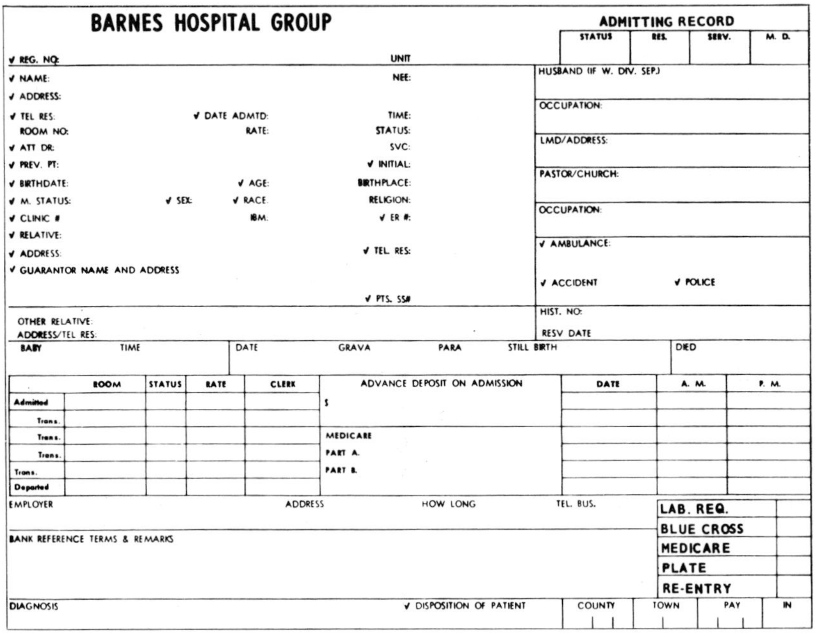
BARNES HOSPITAL GROUP

ADMITTING RECORD

STATUS	RES.	SERV.	M. D.

✓ REG. NO: UNIT
✓ NAME: NEE:
✓ ADDRESS:
✓ TEL RES: ✓ DATE ADMTD: TIME:
ROOM NO: RATE: STATUS:
✓ ATT DR: SVC:
✓ PREV. PT: ✓ INITIAL:
✓ BIRTHDATE: ✓ AGE: BIRTHPLACE:
✓ M. STATUS: ✓ SEX: ✓ RACE: RELIGION:
✓ CLINIC # IBM: ✓ ER #:
✓ RELATIVE:
✓ ADDRESS: ✓ TEL RES:
✓ GUARANTOR NAME AND ADDRESS
✓ PTS. SS#
OTHER RELATIVE:
ADDRESS/TEL RES:

HUSBAND (IF W. DIV. SEP.)
OCCUPATION:
LMD/ADDRESS:
PASTOR/CHURCH:
OCCUPATION:
✓ AMBULANCE:
✓ ACCIDENT ✓ POLICE
HIST. NO:
RESV DATE

BABY TIME DATE GRAVA PARA STILL BIRTH DIED

	ROOM	STATUS	RATE	CLERK	ADVANCE DEPOSIT ON ADMISSION	DATE	A. M.	P. M.
Admitted					$			
Trans.								
Trans.					MEDICARE			
Trans.					PART A.			
Trans.					PART B.			
Departed								

EMPLOYER ADDRESS HOW LONG TEL. BUS.
BANK REFERENCE TERMS & REMARKS

LAB. REQ.
BLUE CROSS
MEDICARE
PLATE
RE-ENTRY

DIAGNOSIS ✓ DISPOSITION OF PATIENT COUNTY TOWN PAY IN

FIGURE 4-3. Admittance Sheet Designed to be Completed on a Typewriter

different place on a credit memorandum. Careful space coordination will eliminate tendency to error. Consider Figure 4-4 which illustrates two different original documents, but which are coordinated concerning similar or related spaces. The forms in Figure 4-4 are two of about 14 forms which were used by the laboratory department of a large medical clinic. Note that the forms are identical, except for the name of the laboratory test group, down to the space for the date and doctor name. The total cost of the tests indicated on each form is placed in the upper left corner. The box in the upper right corner contains the abbreviations of the various sections of the clinic to which this form could be routed. The blank space below the test cost and test group name was imprinted with the patient's name and clinic number through the use of addressograph plates. Clerks and laboratory technicians who prepared these forms did not have to concern themselves with 14 different ways to insert data common to all forms.

Using Data. Figure 4-4 was chosen to illustrate space coordination which contributes to ease in entering data on related forms. Space coordination also assists the users of related forms. Key punch operators, for example, who must transcribe the data on cash sales tickets, charge sales tickets, debit memos, credit memos, and cash receipt tickets, find two types of coordination helpful to them. First, space coordination among related forms as described in the section above and illustrated in Figure 4-4. Second, *data coordination* between the document from which data are being transcribed and the punched card.

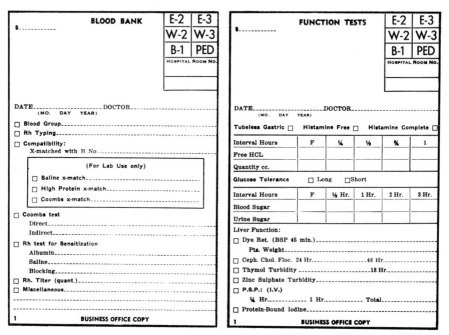

FIGURE 4-4. Coordinated Original Documents

If customer number is the first item to be punched into the card, it is far more efficient from a key punch operator's viewpoint to have the customer number in the same position on related forms and in a location which will logically be noticed first by the key punch operator. More errors in key punching seem to occur when the operator must read the data on a source document in a different order than the data being punched into the cards, and when data on related source documents are not in similar sequence. It could be said that any transcription operations would be governed by the same considerations as in the example above.

Appropriate color contrast is another factor affecting the ease of using data on forms. Using different colors to make up a set of a multiple copy form may assist in the distribution of the copies, but it may also make further use of particular copies more difficult. For example, if the fourth or fifth copy in a customer invoice set is to be used as a packing ticket in the warehouse, a blue invoice copy with either blue or black carbon is less contrasting than a white copy with the same color carbon. Quite often, such lack of contrast causes 5's to be read as 8's or 7's to be read as 9's. Even though errors are caught before shipment is made, these errors cause the order filling operation to be less efficient than it should be.

In a recent systems study, a number of systems analysts recommended against using color alone to indicate the proper distribution of a form, noting that a surprising number of individuals are color blind.

REDUCE TENDENCY TO ERROR. Factors which promote the ease with which data are entered on or used from a form are also important in reducing the tendency to error. If it is difficult for an employee to complete a form because of cramped spacing, it is conceivable that his attitude toward the form may become antagonistic; he may omit essential data from the form; his cramped writing may make it very difficult for another employee to use the data the first employee was to have put on the form; and it may cause the written data to be misinterpreted by the second employee.

Two factors seem to stand out, however, when considering the reduction of tendency to error: (1) transcription errors and (2) the mental effort required to use a particular form. When data must be copied from one form to another, the data processing system is confronted with a possible transcription error. The problem of transcription brings into focus for the first time the importance of the *one-writing technique* in the design of communication media. This technique requires that communication media be designed to facilitate the initial capture of data in such a manner that it will not have to be recopied. In essence it requires that an adequate number of copies of each document be prepared to preclude the recopying of the information, or that the information be captured in such a manner that it will be available again without recopying, and that the errors of transcription, therefore, will be minimized or eliminated.

Good form design requires that the problems of transcription be recognized and that the designer do all in his power to reduce the probability of error. The designer is often limited in his considerations by the degree of mechanization in the system, but transcription errors can be reduced through methods ranging from carbon paper, through mechanized duplicating and copying, to media capable of being processed by machines. The specifics of such methods are covered in more detail in Chapter 5.

A second important factor which reduces the tendency to error is the facility with which the form can be used, in other words, the degree of mental effort required to complete or use the data on the form. The use of different colors in multiple copy form sets requires less thought as to where they should be routed and, as a result, promotes accuracy as well. Shaded areas, or areas blocked with a heavy black ink, tend to make these areas stand out, which helps the correct piece of data to be put in the right place on the form. Pre-printed data which only needs to be circled, or otherwise marked, reduces errors caused by illegible entry, and helps the correct data to be placed on the form because the correct answer need only be chosen from a group. The time ticket in Figure 4-2 would be a good example of how the mental effort needed to complete a form can be reduced. In this requirement, as in the others, the designer must be familiar with and must be "psychologically cognizant" of form users.

PAPER AND PRINTING ECONOMY. This requirement for good form design often works at cross purposes from some of the methods used to accomplish the other requirements. The use of multicolored ink, or the use of various colors for a multiple copy form set, is more expensive than one color of ink on a single color for all the copies in the form set. *Prenumbering* documents is more costly than not prenumbering. *Number control,* namely the assignment of a number at a control point during processing, is an alternative to prenumbering if document control is needed. Indiscriminate choice of form size may also influence form cost. Printers cut documents into the desired sizes from larger stocks of paper. If the size specification of a particular form is such that it cannot be cut evenly from a standard commercial paper size, waste occurs which increases the cost per form. As important, however, is the processing and filing equipment that will be used for the forms when they are being processed through the organization and stored. It obviously doesn't make much sense to order forms that cannot be used or filed in the available equipment. Also important is the grade and weight of paper. A heavier paper may be necessary for use in machines. Better quality is desirable for forms that circulate externally. Also basic is the number of handlings expected for a given document, and the length of time that the form or record is to be retained. The quantity in which forms are purchased from a supplier is still another factor. Usually the larger the order, the less cost per form.

The design of a form requires many decisions by the systems analyst. These decisions have a direct bearing on the data collection function and on the cost of the procedure involved. It is necessary, for example, to decide whether there will be any difference between the first copy of a form and other copies. It is not uncommon to have the name of the department or purpose for each additional copy of a form printed on each copy as identification of the disposition required. In some instances there is a special overprint that is placed on certain copies but not on others. The differences in copies of a form should be prescribed when the form is designed and with a specific reason to justify the additional cost.

It is necessary for the systems analyst to decide whether all of the information entered on the original copy of a form is to be reproduced on each of the copies when the form is being filled in. When copies are routed to a number of departments, control may be improved if all data on the original are not duplicated on certain copies. For example, the number of items ordered should not be known by the individuals counting incoming materials in order to force them to count each item received and to verify the receipt of everything for which payment is to be authorized. Thus any of the purchase documents available to the counters should not have the quantity ordered noted. It may be desirable, in some systems, not to indicate the number of items ordered on the receiving department copy of a purchase order. There are a number of ways in which the designer of the form can provide for this "blind" copy. One such method would be to design the form with "short carbons." For the receiving department copy there would be no carbon under the column in which the number of units is printed. Thus, on the receiving department copy the amounts would not duplicate. Another technique to accomplish the same objective is to print a cross-hatched design in the amount column of the receiving department copy. Such a design can be printed so that amounts duplicated on the cross-hatched design cannot be read.

The number of copies of a form is important to the systems analyst. The distribution of the form governs the control, processing, and information patterns to be followed. It can also preclude the necessity of recopying data or information at a later time. If the preparation of an additional copy of a form will make it unnecessary to incur the cost of labor to copy data or information in another department, the cost of the extra copy of the form will be more than saved by the reduced labor to do the recopy work and increased accuracy.

The manner in which forms are packaged is also an important factor in the design of the form and its cost. For example, when forms are ordered they can be packaged in pads, unit sets, continuous forms for constant feed into a machine, or in separate sheets. The manner in which they are packaged is related directly to the way in which they are to be used in the equipment on which they are to be processed, and the way in which they are to be filed. The cost of labor in processing is often the governing factor in determining the way in which a form is packaged.

All of the above factors and more affect form costs. How then can economy be achieved in form design? Before any aspect of form costs need be considered, the *use* for a specific form must be completely analyzed. Systems analysts quite often use a very lengthy form analysis sheet to accumulate facts they need to know about a particular form. In lieu of a detailed analysis sheet, the analyst should try to keep in mind the relatively small number of standards discussed above which can be adapted to suit specific situations. This is where professional judgment must be used.

A forms manufacturer needs to know at least seven things about a form, in addition to quantities, in order to quote a price:

1. The method of reproduction—printing, offset, stencil, etc.
2. The form layout.
3. The form size.
4. The type and color of paper.
5. The way in which the forms are to be bound, punched, etc., if at all.
6. The different colors of ink.
7. Direction concerning multiple form sets.

The analyst must know the effect on form usage and form cost that his decision in each of the above areas will cause. His decision, however, in any of the areas is never simple. Even though stencil reproduction is less expensive than printing, all forms in the financial information system are not stencil reproduced. Forms are often the chief contact a business has with a customer or creditor, and the need to create a good impression should be considered. Forms must be handled by people and by machines, and the systems analyst must be aware that the *form's preparing and handling costs are usually far greater than the most expensively produced form.* Some analysts maintain that for every dollar spent on the cost of a form itself, from $10 to $100 is spent by the firm to process this form. The analyst, therefore, must blend the factors that affect the cost of the form itself with form handling cost in order to effect real paper and printing economy.

A few examples should dramatize this point more effectively. If a new customer subsidiary ledger sheet is being designed to be used with a multiple-purpose accounting machine, the weight and grain direction of paper chosen must be such that it will endure machine processing, and that it will stand upright in a posting ledger tray. To select a light paper stock because it could be purchased for less money would be pseudo-economy because it could not be used effectively in processing. Ledger sheets, which will be filed upright in trays between posting runs, should be cut from vertically grained paper stock. If the grain were horizontal, there would be a tendency for the ledger sheets to bend or droop more easily.

As was mentioned above, the use of multiple color inks and paper increase form costs. A decision may be made to use multiple color paper in a multi-copy form, because the ease with which an employee can correctly use a multiple color form set counterbalances the increased cost of the form set. Similarly, more than one color ink may be used on a form to attract the user's attention to important instructions or warranties. Forms going to customers may be imprinted with short advertisements in a different color of ink than the rest of the form.

The decision to use a multi-copy form with one-time disposable carbon paper inserted by the factory must be weighed against the cost of labor to insert and align carbon paper and the saving from the use of the carbon paper more than once. The cost of labor is sufficiently high so that it is often less expensive to purchase the costly form sets with the one-time carbons than to incur the additional clerical costs.

In summary, paper and printing economy can only be achieved if the systems analyst is aware of the use that is to be made of a specific form, and he must correlate this use to the factors that affect form cost. He must ever be aware of the cost of processing forms and must never be guilty of pseudo-economy whereby a few dollars are saved in the purchase of the forms themselves, but many dollars are lost because they cannot be processed efficiently.

FORM CHECK LIST. In the design of a form it is helpful to have a means of appraising a new or revised form. The Hammermill Paper Company suggests the use of a "5-Minute Form Check List" as shown in Figure 4-5 after the form has been laid out and printing specifications determined to help in working out and testing the best working arrangement and copy. If items are checked "OK" the design can be considered as adequate; if the "?" is checked,

A 5 MINUTE FORM CHECK LIST (A quick and easy method of checking the efficiency and economy of any form — new or old — before placing your printing order.)

NECESSITY	OK	?	WORDING	OK	?
1 Has the entire system been checked and would a written procedure for the use of this form help put it into more efficient operation?			17 Does the form, by title and arrangement, clearly indicate its purpose?		
2 Are all copies of the form or report necessary?			18 Is there a proper space for the date?		
3 Have the actual users of this form been consulted for suggested improvements, additional requirements and possible eliminations?			19 Is the form identified by company name and firm name or code number to aid reordering?		
4 Can the data furnished by this form be combined with some other form or can some other form be eliminated or consolidated with it?			20 If this is a revised form, can it be distinguished from the previous form?		
5 Has everyone responsible for the form or the form system approved it?			**PAPER AND PRINTING** (SPECIFICATIONS)	OK	?
PURPOSE	OK	?	21 Should the form be on colored paper to speed up writing, distribution, sorting and filing; to designate departments or branch offices; to indicate days, months or years; to distinguish manifold copies; to identify rush orders?		
6 If form is to be sent from one person to another, are proper spaces for "to" and "from" provided?			22 Have we specified paper which will be thoroughly satisfactory, economical enough for form use, consistent in performance and surely available for later reorders?		
7 Will routing or handling instructions printed on each copy be helpful?			23 Is proper weight of paper used for original and each carbon copy? (Bond Substances 13, 16, 20 and 24. Ledger Substances 24, 28, 32 and 36. Mimeo-Bond Substances 16, 20 and 24. Spirit and Gelatin Duplicator Substances 16, 20 and 24.)		
8 Should this form be consecutively numbered, or have a place for inserting a number?					
9 If this is an Outside Contact Form, should it be designed to mail in a window envelope?			24 Are detailed specifications complete? (Paper, type, ink, rules, punch, perforate, score, fold, gather, pad, carbon sheet, stitch, etc.)		
10 If this form is to take information from or pass information to, another form, do both have the same sequence of items?			25 Can other forms, printed on the same paper as this one, be ordered now to reduce production costs?		
11 Have we taken into consideration the number of forms which will be used in a given time (4 to 12 months)—the possibility of changes, and how long the form will remain in use?			26 Have requirements been estimated correctly and is the quantity to be ordered most economical? (Consider probability of revision and rate of use.)		
SIZE AND ARRANGEMENT	OK	?	Pt. #	**REMARKS on points questioned (?)**	
12 Is the size right for filing, attention value, ample room for information and to cut without waste?					
13 Is all recurring information being printed, so that only variable items need be filled in?					
14 Has space been provided for a signature?					
15 Is spacing correct for handwriting or typing? Handwriting should be allowed double the space of typewriting.					
16 Are the most important items, which should be seen first, prominently placed? (Near the top, if practicable.)					

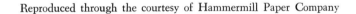

Reproduced through the courtesy of Hammermill Paper Company

FIGURE 4-5.   Hammermill Five-Minute Form Check List

further study and work with those who are to use the form regularly would be in order. Note that there is provision for a signature of the person accepting the adequacy of the design. The check list would be filed with a copy of the Printing Specifications and Form Approval Sheet in the Media Control Unit file.

CENTRALIZED MEDIA CONTROL

Many firms interested in good form design have recognized the balance which must be achieved between the cost of forms and the cost of using them. Not only must skill be exercised in the design of a form so that it will fulfill its purpose efficiently, but also skill must be exercised in the coordination of a particular form with the firm's entire forms family. Rarely is the accomplishment of both these objectives achieved unless control over the design and coordination of forms used in the firm's data processing systems is centralized in one individual or unit within the business.

Centralized media control is usually a responsibility of a Media Control Unit. The functions of a Media Control Unit are:

1. Obtaining approval for all requests for new and revised forms;
2. The technical aspects of form design—printing specifications, weight of paper, quality, size, etc.;
3. Form inventory control;
4. Form identification; and
5. Form review.

Approval. Just as in any other area of the business, someone or some group, who is in a position to know the broad effects certain procedural changes will cause, must approve the use of a new or revised business form. It is quite conceivable that a particular shop foreman may develop a better time ticket for use in reporting time spent on specific jobs on which his men work. This new time ticket may be wholly unacceptable to the men in another department. Only two choices seem available. Either departments report time on different kinds of time tickets, or a compromise ticket must be worked out so that all departments use the same kind of time ticket, even though all are not completely satisfied with it. A choice in favor of the former may increase the cost of processing the time tickets more than the latter or vice-versa. It is a question of whether the using departments can make this decision effectively. If the responsibility for approving the use of all new or revised forms is given to a specific unit, it is expected to maintain a broad perspective and to be in a position to intelligently decide if the proposed new or revised form will contribute positively to efficient data processing.

A Central Media Control Unit can function with one individual being given major responsibility, or it can work through a Forms Committee. Wisconsin Telephone Company, for example, requires all forms requests, both for new forms and forms changes, to be channeled through a Forms Committee with representation from each major segment of the organization. For each request a Form Approval Sheet such as shown in Figure 4-6 must be prepared and approved. Note that the type of information required by the sheet includes such facts as departments concerned, to be used by, approximate annual usage, and disposition of present stock. The company has developed an Administrative Bulletin to govern its forms procedure. Included are sections on general (scope, control, definition), forms committee, preparation and approval, numbering, reproduction, stocking, ordering, revision and cancellation, catalog, index, and definitions of terminology.

Responsibility for considering problems related to retention requirements and destruction classification must also be considered in form design.

Technical Aspects. There are usually two parties responsible for the design of a new or revised form, the author and the designer. The author of a new or revised form is considered to be the "idea" man. It is he who sketched the new sales ticket, working out in rough fashion the space coordination needed between it and other related forms. The designer is conversant with all of the factors which make up form cost and with the features of the

FORM APPROVAL SHEET

W.T.CO.
ADM. BULL. NO. 22

FORM 433
(12-67)
F.C.C. 86F

Title of Form   Form No.

Dept. Originating Form   Area No.   Acct. No.

Reason   Adopt ☐   Revise ☐   Stop Print ☐   Cancel ☐   Replaced By / Replaces   Form No.

To be filled in by: Pencil ☐   Pen ☐   Typewriter ☐   Number Carbon Copies -

PAGE NO.	SIZE			PAPER SPECIFICATIONS		COLOR PRINTING		F.C.C. NUMBER
	Width	Length	Weight	Color	Kind of Paper	Front	Back	

Approx. Annual Usage   Ordering Multiple

DEPARTMENTS CONCERNED   **TO BE USED BY**

Authorized Stock | Ltd. Auth. Stock | Job Lot | Stock Job Lot

Accounting ☐   Executive ☐   Gen. Off. ☐   Exch. Off. ☐
Commercial ☐   Plant ☐   Div. Off. ☐   Field ☐
Engineer ☐   Traffic ☐   Dist. Off. ☐   Public ☐

Initial Supply   Will Last   Requisition No.

Yearly ☐   Quarterly ☐   Monthly ☐   Weekly ☐   Daily ☐

Send Initial Supply To:

Form To Be Ordered By: Dept.

Stocked By: W.E.Co. ☐   S.B. ☐   Other ☐   Explain

DISPOSITION OF OLD COMPOSITION OR MASTER | Hold ☐ Destroy ☐ Return ☐ | DISPOSITION OF PRESENT STOCK | Hold ☐ Use ☐ Junk ☐

Type of Turn   Book ☐   Tumble ☐   Other ☐

Form Instructions In:

Punching: Left or Top _____   No. of Holes _____
            Size & Style _____   Centers _____

Prepared By: _____   Date _____

Perforating: No ☐   Yes ☐   Explain

Approved: _____   Date _____

Registration: Commercial ☐   Exact ☐

Sec'y. Approval: _____   Date _____

Collating: No ☐   Yes ☐   Explain

DEPT	FORMS COMMITTEE REPRESENTATIVE	DATE

Binding: Sheets ☐   Sets ☐   per unit _____   Padded ☐   Banded ☐   at   Top ☐   Left ☐

Packaging: Units per package _____   Special ☐   Packaging   Explain in Remarks

Printing Process

ENVELOPES

Flap Edge   Top ☐   Bottom ☐   Left ☐   Right ☐

Dimensions: Flapedge _____ " Otheredge _____ "

Flap Fastening

Face   Open Window ☐   Closed Window ☐   Regular ☐

Window (Inches) | From Bottom " | From Left " | Left to Right " | Top to Bottom "

Master or Proofs To Be Approved By:

REMARKS: (Use reverse if necessary) estimate the number of employees using form, annual costs, savings, etc.

FIGURE 4-6.   Wisconsin Telephone Form Approval Sheet

existing media control program. Quite frequently, authorship occurs in the operational areas where forms are being used. It is the responsibility of the Media Control Unit to furnish the technical assistance which will allow a new or revised form that will contribute to improved processing to proceed smoothly from a rough idea to a finished product. Help is given authors, such as drawing the new form to scale, advising on the size, keeping cost in mind, and the relationship of this form to other forms; advising on the weight of paper, which should be most satisfactory considering the use to be made of the form; advising on the differences between interleaved carbons or carbon-less paper versus inserting carbons each time the form set is to be used; and so on. Proficiency in matters such as this is rarely achieved on a part-time basis. Small companies that do not feel that they can justify centralized media control often seek professional assistance on a part-time basis when the need arises.

Implied in the technical assistance, which should be provided by the Media Control Unit, is forms standardization. In most accounting contexts, the word standardization is not in good repute. Nevertheless, forms standardization is imperative to effective forms control.

"Standardization" is not synonymous with "static." Forms standardization is an attempt to bring organization into the family of forms used by a particular enterprise. For example, during a forms study it was discovered that many different sizes and styles of envelopes were in use. Careful analysis of the need, review of envelopes, and redesign of forms, reduced the number of different envelopes needed substantially. A relatively small number of standard envelopes were adopted for use with a significant cost reduction.

Quite frequently, a particular department will ask for a special labor report, not knowing that a similar report is already being prepared for another department. The Media Control Unit is in a position to review this possibility and to work out a solution which would keep duplication of forms at a minimum.

Another aspect of standardization which is important, particularly in larger organizations, is the facility with which employees from different departments, plants, or divisions can step into new positions outside of their own departments. Paper work will always be a part of everyone's workday. It is reassuring to employees who know that a "whole new world of paper" will not have to be mastered in the new positions.

The technical aspects of form design that are related to the type of information needed by a printer to reproduce the form should be carefully determined and retained as a part of a Printing Specification Sheet. Ordering quantities would be established on the Printing Specification Sheet and a form history accumulated. When a form is reordered the Printing Specification Sheet would be withdrawn from the file and the technical information obtained. When forms are ordered there is always the possibility that a substitution will be necessary. The Printing Specifications will preclude the possibility of having a substitution perpetuated when the quality is either more or less than required. Printing specifications can be maintained as a separate sheet, or as a part of a Form Layout Sheet or Form Approval Sheet. All should be in the form file record of the Media Control Unit.

INVENTORY CONTROL. Nothing is more frustrating than running out of invoices during a customer billing operation, nor more exasperating than wanting to revise a form and to find that a five year supply of the old form is on hand. It is only through forms inventory control that such situations can be prevented or acceptably reduced. It is only logical that this responsibility be given to the Media Control Unit. Policies must be established with regard to the economic order quantity of each form, suppliers, storage space, distribution procedures, and others. Although not as critical nor involving as much money, forms inventory control has all of the problems of reports control. See Chapter 9 for a discussion of reports control.

FORM IDENTIFICATION. As soon as a centralized media control program is begun, form identification becomes an essential part of it. The need for form identification is twofold. First, efficient inventory control demands some form identification scheme so that forms may be reordered with a minimum of effort. Normally, once a form is approved, it is assigned a form number. In addition, the complete specifications of the form, its standard order quantity, names of acceptable forms manufacturers, method of reproduction, and any other pertinent data about the form are incorporated into a *form file record.* Each form is assigned an official forms number which is coded on the corner of each form and identifies the form file record. In requesting additional forms from the storeroom or in requesting that additional forms be ordered, the requestor merely needs to refer to the official forms number. The Media Control Unit can then refer to the file record for all pertinent information. The second need for forms identification lies in the relationship of forms to manufacturing processes and business systems. Systems manuals are common both in the operating and business information systems. A more detailed discussion of systems manuals can be found in Chapter 13, but it is important to note here that when references are made to specific forms that must be used in specific procedures, it is far easier to refer to them by number than by name. Many forms are known by different names to different people, and the name is often lengthy. In the interest of brevity and of correct reference, the use of form numbers instead of name in procedure manuals has gained widespread acceptance. Since form inventory control is a primary responsibility of the Media Control Unit and that this unit often assists in the preparation of systems manuals, it is only logical that forms identification is also a responsibility of this unit.

FORM REVIEW. If management assigns responsibility for form approval, design, inventory control, and identification to a Media Control Unit, effective control cannot be achieved unless the Unit is constantly reviewing the forms that are used by the company. Each time approval is sought for a new or revised form, a certain amount of form review must take place to ascertain whether the new form will fit efficiently into the forms family.

A Media Control Unit, since it is specializing in media control, is in a better position to recognize that a form, or series of forms, may be affected by changes in company policy, changes in the productive process, changes in government regulation, etc. This unit, therefore, is given the responsibility to maintain a constant review over forms in use and to recommend changes whenever they seem apparent.

SUMMARY

It has been the purpose of this chapter to point out the need for some physical medium upon which data could be represented so that it could be preserved and processed apart from the individual who first came into contact with the facts. The communication media in use in a financial information system can be grouped into three classes (1) original transaction documents, (2) record documents, and (3) discharge of duty documents. Original transaction documents are the media upon which transaction data are first represented and serve as devices for transmitting data to other parts of the business or through additional processing steps. Record documents are media which contain data, or information, which will be subject to interpretive reuse. Discharge of duty documents are an integral part of the financial information system used principally to inform others in the financial information system that certain operations have been performed and further processing of the data can continue.

The word "form" was chosen to refer to all classes of communication media when discussing the basic requirements for good media design. In brief, these requirements were:

1. Favorable mental attitude.
2. Ease of entering data.
3. Ease of using data.
4. Reduce tendency to error.
5. Paper and printing economy.

Consideration was also given to the problem of media control. A Centralized Media Control Unit was advocated where the size of the enterprise could justify such specialization. A Centralized Media Control Unit is normally responsible for:

1. New or revised form approval.
2. The technical aspects of form design.
3. Form inventory control.

4. Form identification.

5. Form review.

With this background, it is hoped that the student will be able to solve most of the simulated business problems concerning this essential element of a financial information system contained in the following questions, problems, and cases. But, it is also hoped that the experience gained in solving these problems will assist in the development of the professional judgment which is so important to a professional person.

QUESTIONS, PROBLEMS, AND CASES

1. Are communication media essential to the operation of a financial information system? Discuss.

2. Describe and distinguish between the kinds of communication media used in a financial information system.

3. Give five examples illustrating how original transaction documents also serve as record documents. (Do not use any of the examples cited in this chapter.)

4. Describe four situations in which original transaction documents and/or record documents could be converted to or otherwise utilized as discharge of duty documents. (Do not use any of the examples cited in this chapter.)

5. Visit a business firm of your choice and obtain a sufficient number of forms of all types to construct a display which (*a.*) illustrates adherence to standards of form design, and/or (*b.*) illustrates violations of standards of form design.

6. Reproduced below is an accounts receivable charge card used by a large midwestern hospital. After examining the punched card, you are to *design* a charge ticket which would be completed by the hospital floor nurse, or clerk, from which the card below would be keypunched in the data processing department. Justify your design by reference to the standards of form design.

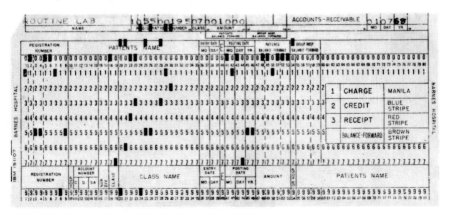

7. In the accounts receivable processing of the same hospital referred in item 6 above, noncash credit and cash receipt cards must be punched from credit memorandums and cash receipt slips. Discuss and illustrate the factors you would consider in designing the appropriate credit memorandums and cash receipt slips.

8. Discuss why the decision regarding the size, paper stock, form layout, etc. is rarely simple. What are several factors which enter into this decision?

9. What is meant by pseudo-economy in form cost savings?

10. What are the major responsibilities of a Centralized Media Control department? Discuss each briefly.

11. Distinguish between an author of a form and its designer.

12. In conjunction with your assignment in item 5, obtain from the company you visited their most recent forms cost saving project. Describe it, and indicate the amount of savings achieved.

13. Does a systems analyst equate "forms standardization" with "uniformity" and/or with "no change?" Explain.

14. Discuss several factors which should be considered in the design of a forms identification scheme. Set up a brief illustration of your scheme.

15. Review of one's own work is considered to be poor internal control. Yet, it is standard practice for the Centralized Media Control department to be responsible for forms review. Is this good? Discuss.

16. Give some specific illustrations of communication media. Distinguish between communication media, forms, and reports.

17. How do record documents differ from original transaction documents? Give a number of illustrations of record documents.

18. It has been said that a system can be no more accurate than the data originally captured. Correct data must be placed into the system before it can be extracted from the system. Which of the standards of form design govern the capture of data accurately?

19. Standards of form design are the minimum levels of attainment acceptable in the design of a given form. You are in the process of designing a customer's invoice form. It has been agreed that the form is to be in four copies, the first to be sent to the customer, the second to Accounts Receivable, the third to a numerical file, and the fourth to an alphabetic file.
    a. What factors would be important in the design of the invoice so as to meet each of the following standards of form design?
       (1) Favorable mental attitude.
       (2) Entering data.
       (3) Using data.
       (4) Reduce tendency to error.
       (5) Paper and printing economy.

b. What are the advantages of both a numerical and an alphabetical file of invoices, or is this unnecessary duplication?

c. It has been suggested that the invoice use white for the first copy, pink for the second, yellow for the third, and blue for the fourth. Give the reasons both for and against the use of color for copies. Would there be any difference in copies other than color. Which of the standards of form design govern color?

d. Would the same quality of paper be used for each copy? Explain.

20. In the design of a purchase order it has been suggested that preprinted horizontal lines be used where data are to be filled in. Would you recommend that the suggestion be followed? Indicate your reason(s) and explain.

21. Distinguish between space coordination and data coordination as the terms relate to the design of a form.

22. How does the one-writing technique relate to form design? Give an example of the application of the one-writing technique, and relate to the standard of form design that governs it.

23. Distinguish between prenumbering and number control. Indicate and give an example of a situation in which each would be the most appropriate.

24. The use of multicolored ink for a form is more expensive than only one color. Why might it be advisable to use more than one color of ink? Which of the standards of form design would govern your decision?

25. Principles of systems design also relate to the design of a form inasmuch as forms are components of the system. You are in the process of designing a receiving report which is to be prepared in four copies. The original copy is to be sent to the purchase office, and the duplicate and triplicate are routed with the incoming materials to Stores. In Stores the duplicate copy is stamped to acknowledge the receipt of material and that material is under accounting control. The duplicate is then forwarded by Stores to Accounts Payable to support the voucher authorizing payment. The fourth copy remains in a numerical file in the Receiving Office.

    Indicate how each of the principles of systems design relate to the receiving report form.

26. You are designing a form to be used to enter the data extracted from each of 12 cash registers in a retail store each day. It has been suggested that stencil reproduction of the form would be adequate. Would you use stencil reproduction, printing, or some other method of reproduction? Explain.

27. During recent years your company has almost doubled its sales volume. Every aspect of the organization has been under strain, and administrative costs have gone up out of proportion to sales volume. It has been suggested that an analysis of forms being used might provide a clue to the problem of runaway costs. Do you agree? Why?

28. Obtain an invoice form that has been sent to you for a recent purchase. Using the forms check list as shown in Figure 4-5 on Page 101, evaluate the adequacy of the form design. Have any standards been violated? Explain.

29. You have been asked to structure a media control plan for your company.
    a. State the organization that would be necessary to place your plan in operation.
    b. Step by step trace the procedure that would be necessary to obtain a new form in the Treasurer's Department. The form is to be used by plant managers located in areas a considerable distance from the home office to request the transfer of cash into banks where it would be subject to plant withdrawal for local expenses. Start with the need for the form and follow the necessary steps through the organization recommended in step a. above to the receipt of the printed form for distribution to plants.

30. What would be the function of a Forms Committee in a media control plan? Would you favor such a committee? Explain.

31. Printing specifications are an important part of media control. Explain.

32. What is a form file record? Where would it be kept, and what types of data and information would it include?

33. The Middleton Manufacturing Company was organized three years ago to manufacture a patented product. The past three years have been expansion years and management now expects that production will taper off at the present output. Because administrative costs have run high, the controller has assigned to you the task of making an analysis of the forms being used, and to evaluate the existing forms control program.

    Your investigation reveals that in connection with the materials stores organization, the company has a stationery stores department through which all printing orders are cleared. The stationery stores department stocks all forms and originates the purchase order for forms whenever the inventory gets to a minimum position. Anyone wishing to change an existing form or to procure a new one brings a sketch to the stationery department where a purchase request is originated. No attempt is made to determine how the form will be used, how long it will be on file, or how many should be ordered at one time. The stationery stores department is in charge of a clerk who has no training in writing printing specifications.
    a. Evaluate the forms control program now in operation and list the effect on the business of the continued use of the present plan.
    b. Outline what you would consider to be a good program of forms control and list the possible achievements of the program.
    c. How would you go about the installation of an adequate system of forms control in the Middleton Manufacturing Company?
    d. State specifically some of the common sources of waste in connection with the design, printing, and maintenance of forms that could be eliminated to reduce costs.

34. The Oldstown Sheet and Tube Company discovered that 25 per cent of their purchase orders (20,000) were for minor single-shipment orders. The cost of paper work for each order was as great for these orders averaging five dollars as for a much larger order. What are the possibilities for reducing costs? How could cost reduction be related to communication media design?

35. What are three general types of situations in which communication media should be used? Do not name specific procedures.

36. When communication media are designed, what is the most significant cost to be considered?

37. What is "document control"? Give an illustration and indicate the factors that would cause document control to grow in importance.

38. When preparing a preassembled set of communication media to be used in a system, what are five adjustments or arrangements (differences in copies) that could be made?

39. Unit accounting can be accomplished through the use of multiple or continuous forms. Explain.

40. Do you see any justification for the purchase of low grade paper for communication media? Discuss briefly.

41. Comment on the following statement: "Bond paper (rag content) should be used for forms that must be durable and have some degree of permanency."

42. A form should permit the right thing to be done at the right time. What form would you want as proper authorization to perform the tasks named below?
    a. To assemble the items ordered by a customer and prepare them for delivery.
    b. To arrange for the purchase of goods for your company at the best price.
    c. To write a check in payment of a company bill except for signature.
    d. To assign work to factory operators in your department.
    e. To issue materials and supplies to employees for use in their work.
    f. To post charges (debits) to customers' accounts.
    g. To make out the payroll summary each week.
    h. To disburse petty cash.
    i. To repair equipment that is not functioning properly.
    j. To release operators of cash registers at the end of their shift.

43. You are designing a form consisting of an original and some carbon copies and you do not want certain information written on the original to appear on the copies. What are some of the means by which this could be accomplished?

44. On what basis is each of the following characteristics of a business form decided?
    a. Grade and weight of paper.
    b. Size of the form.
    c. Padded, unit sets, continuous, or single sheets.
    d. Amount of space allowed for blanks to be filled in.
    e. Color of paper.
    f. Copy to be printed on the form.
    g. Identification of the form.

45. Forms are designed to perform one of two general functions: (1) to request or order a specific action, or (2) to record or advise of action already performed. Which of the following forms are designed for objective (1) and which for objective (2)? Explain.
    a. Purchase requisition.
    b. Shipping order.
    c. Sales invoice.
    d. Purchase order.
    e. Check.

46. What are the advantages to be gained by the use of a well-designed form? (Hint: *See* the standards.)

47. In the design of an invoice form, space or provision has to be made for the filling in of many diverse types of information. Aside from certain obvious things such as customer's name and address, for which items would blanks have to be provided?

48. When should printed forms be used?

49. Draw (in pencil) a form suitable for use as a journal voucher by a medium-sized or large business.

50. The Purchasing Agent of the Seesaw Manufacturing Company has approved the design of the following purchase requisition. All requisitions originate in the Stores Department.
    List and explain your criticisms of the design of the purchase requisition below. Limit your criticisms to the original copy below.

THE SEESAW MANUFACTURING COMPANY
Madison, Wisconsin

To: Purchasing Agent   No. _____

Quantity Required	Description	Amount

CHAPTER 5

Data Originating,

Processing, and Control Devices

INTRODUCTION

A FINANCIAL INFORMATION SYSTEM IS CONCERNED WITH DATA INPUT, processing data, and output of financial, statistical, and other data and information. All of these collecting, processing, and communicating steps can be performed manually, but as administrative units become larger and more complex, manual methods impede the flow of work. It is not feasible to "put more men on the job" in order to accomplish the processing tasks. A point of "diminishing returns" is eventually reached as to both cost and physical output. For a solution to this problem, ways to mechanize data processing operations have been sought.

Basic Advantages of Mechanization

In general, financial information systems, which in whole or in part have been mechanized, have certain advantages over manual systems. A mechanized system can: (1) produce more legible records; (2) reduce transcription error probability; (3) reduce the number of calculation errors; (4) process data more rapidly, with fewer people and in less space than a manual system, provided a certain minimum volume of processing exists; (5) reduce unauthorized system changes because of the more formal nature of mechanized procedures; (6) accumulate check totals to be posted to control accounts as an automatic by-product of initial registration or writing; and (7) facilitate putting the collecting, processing, and communicating of business data and information on an assembly line basis, much as in a factory where machines are used.

It is reasonable to assume that the *more legible characters* and *figures* produced by machines are less likely to be misinterpreted than are handwritten data. A sales invoice, for example, is used as a basis for recording debits to accounts receivable, credits to various sales categories, reductions in inventory amounts, and in various types of sales analyses. Invoice legibility is important to the accuracy of the records and analyses based on the invoice.

Machine systems *reduce the need for manual transcriptions* and, hence, reduce transcription error probability. Multiple-purpose accounting machines utilize the "one-writing technique" (discussed more fully later in this chapter) where through carbonization several records are prepared simultaneously. Punched card and electronic data processing systems accomplish the same result by utilizing unit records governed by the data processing principle. (*See* Chapters 15 and 16.)

The automatic features of machines serve to *reduce calculation errors*. In the preparation of a customer's statement while posting the subsidiary accounts receivable ledger, for example, the extension of the beginning balance plus charges minus payments or adjustments is automatic. In electronic data processing systems the machines can perform not only a single calculation, but can perform a series of calculations automatically. The accuracy enabled by automatic calculation of machines is especially important in that the hours of time often required to locate errors associated with records in a manual system are substantially reduced or eliminated.

The advantage that a *mechanized system will process data more rapidly*, while valid, must be qualified. In a machine system, data can be processed more rapidly with fewer people and in less space than by a manual system, provided a certain volume of processing exists. A primary advantage of a machine system over a manual system is speed. If a sufficient volume of processing does not exist, speed is not an important factor. However, the volume necessary to begin using machines in the data processing system is much less than one might surmise. Corner grocery stores utilize cash registers and adding machines, as do service stations and other small retail businesses. As these small enterprises grow, the financial information system must grow with them. Increased system mechanization becomes desirable when increased volume of data cannot be processed rapidly enough by hand to permit efficient use of the information generated. As businesses grow, mechanization can also be a factor which would improve manpower utilization as well as more efficient processing. Where these data, if processed manually, might require two or three people, a mechanized system may only require a machine and one operator. The two employees formerly employed as clerks could now be used more effectively as part of the sales or production work force. Savings could result in both speed of processing and cost of processing.

Machine systems and *procedures are more rigid* and, therefore, are less subject to change without permission by employees performing specific operations. Mechanized systems, because of the machines themselves, demand operational sequencing. When billing is being done mechanically, it would be extremely inefficient to interrupt the operation to prepare a check or a journal voucher on the same machine. Work must be done in batches and, for greatest efficiency, in a selected sequence. Manual systems are difficult to control in two respects. First, individuals can deviate from instructions in the manner of performance of a certain procedure, and second, because of this, job descriptions are difficult to formalize in a procedures manual. As a result, the data may not be processed as efficiently as possible and certain internal control duties may not be functioning. It is more difficult to deviate from prescribed methods in a machine system. This system rigidity helps maintain control activities and permits job descriptions to be properly established. The use of job descriptions in turn helps to improve employee effectiveness, training, and classification.

Machine systems, in general, are designed to provide routine proof of processing accuracy. Most machine systems *accumulate totals* and check figures that are verified at various points in the processing operation as control amounts. The total of credit sales, for example, can be accumulated in a cash register by imprinting each credit sales ticket in the selling department at the time of the transactions, thus accumulating a control total of all credit sales in the cash register accumulating mechanism. The total can be used to control the accuracy of further processing of the batch of credit sales tickets coming from the sales department. Each time the batch of sales tickets is processed, the total of individual sales tickets processed must agree with the control total.

As businesses grow in size, the volume of paper processing increases and becomes a major systems problem. More people must be involved in paper processing, and often at the minimum clerical skill level. With machine systems the accuracy of processing can be established, and routines can reduce paper processing to a *controlled* assembly line basis. While such an operation has disadvantages, they are far outweighed by the advantages of uniformity, accuracy, lower cost, and increased efficiency.

Economic Justification

Machines, whether they are simple adding machines or other more complicated and expensive mechanical devices, should be used whenever they can be economically justified in keeping with the systems principles discussed in Chapter 2. There is more to economic justification of the use of machines in an information system than the labor-saving features most often quoted by various manufacturers of systems equipment. In the discussion of the reasonable cost principle, it was noted that it is difficult to quantify intangible costs such as loss of future business, costs of production stoppages, or additional costs of working capital. Nevertheless, the labor saving features can be more easily quantified and serve the systems analyst with an indicative guide to assist in systems decisions. Figure 5-1 is a chart that is helpful in equating potential equipment outlays and the necessary labor hours per day saving (at various wage levels) necessary to justify the equipment costs. This chart can be used effectively as a rule of thumb device except at the more sophisticated punched card and electronic computer system levels. It is only when machine configurations become more complex that additional factors need to be quantified and a more complete economic justification study need be made.

Levels of Mechanization

A systems analyst seldom needs to possess a high degree of technical knowledge about specific models of machines and devices which assist in the input, processing, and output of data and information. It is necessary for the analyst to be sufficiently familiar with the kinds of machines and devices that are available and their various capabilities so that he is able to recommend a configuration of machines and devices in keeping with the systems principles, particularly the reasonable cost and data processing principles.

In order to make the necessary professional judgments concerning machines and devices, the analyst must be aware that there are levels of mechanization and he must be able to ascertain which level (or levels of mechanization) is suitable in specific instances. These are (1) general office machines, (2) multiple-purpose accounting machines, (3) punched card machines, and (4) electronic computers and related equipment. The remaining sections of this chapter will introduce the reader to the first two levels. Since the latter two levels are more complex, discussion of them appears in Chapters 15, 16, and 17.

GENERAL OFFICE MACHINES

Machines which fall into the category of general office machines are used for single or dual steps in carrying out the chain of data collection, processing, and communication operations. (*See* Chapters 8 and 9.) Typewriters, for example, are used principally in recording and/or classifying; desk calculators in calculation; adding machines in summarizing and/or recording; and various kinds of duplicating equipment in recording and/or communicating. It is not

DAILY TIME SAVING NEEDED TO JUSTIFY EQUIPMENT COST
(Assumes Estimated Useful Life of 10 Years)

Hourly Rate:	$1.00	$1.25	$1.50	$1.75	$2.00	$2.25	$2.50	$2.75
Annual Salary:	$2000	$2500	$3000	$3500	$4000	$4500	$5000	$5500
Equipment Cost	Necessary Hours Per Day Saving to Justify Expense							
$ 100	.1	.1	.1	.1	.1	.1	.1	.1
200	.1	.1	.1	.1	.1	.1	.1	.1
300	.1	.1	.1	.1	.1	.1	.1	.1
400	.2	.1	.1	.1	.1	.1	.1	.1
500	.2	.2	.1	.1	.1	.1	.1	.1
600	.2	.2	.2	.1	.1	.1	.1	.1
700	.3	.2	.2	.2	.1	.1	.1	.1
800	.3	.3	.2	.2	.2	.2	.1	.1
900	.4	.3	.2	.2	.2	.2	.2	.1
1000	.4	.3	.3	.2	.2	.2	.2	.2
1100	.5	.4	.3	.3	.2	.2	.2	.2
1200	.5	.4	.3	.3	.2	.2	.2	.2
1300	.5	.4	.4	.3	.3	.2	.2	.2
1400	.6	.5	.4	.3	.3	.3	.2	.2
1500	.6	.5	.4	.4	.3	.3	.2	.2
1600	.6	.5	.4	.4	.3	.3	.3	.2
1700	.7	.6	.5	.4	.3	.3	.3	.3
1800	.7	.6	.5	.4	.4	.3	.3	.3
1900	.8	.6	.5	.4	.4	.3	.3	.3
2000	.8	.6	.5	.5	.4	.4	.3	.3
3000	1.2	1.0	.8	.7	.6	.5	.5	.5
4000	1.6	1.3	1.1	.9	.8	.7	.6	.6
5000	2.0	1.6	1.3	1.1	1.0	.9	.8	.8
6000	2.4	1.9	1.6	1.4	1.2	1.1	1.0	.9
7000	2.8	2.2	1.9	1.6	1.4	1.2	1.1	1.1
8000	3.2	2.5	2.1	1.8	1.6	1.4	1.3	1.2
9000	3.6	2.9	2.4	2.0	1.8	1.6	1.4	1.4
10000	4.0	3.2	2.7	2.3	2.0	1.8	1.6	1.5
11000	4.4	3.5	2.9	2.5	2.2	1.9	1.8	1.7
12000	4.8	3.8	3.2	2.7	2.4	2.1	1.9	1.8
13000	5.2	4.1	3.5	2.9	2.6	2.3	2.1	2.0
14000	5.6	4.4	3.6	3.2	2.8	2.5	2.2	2.1
15000	6.0	4.8	4.0	3.4	3.0	2.6	2.4	2.3
16000	6.4	5.1	4.3	3.6	3.2	2.8	2.5	2.4
17000	6.8	5.4	4.5	3.8	3.4	3.0	2.7	2.6
18000	7.2	5.7	4.8	4.1	3.6	3.2	2.9	2.7
19000	7.6	6.0	5.1	4.3	3.8	3.3	3.0	2.9
20000	8.0	6.3	5.3	4.5	4.0	3.5	3.2	3.0

FIGURE 5-1. Chart of Daily Time-Saving Needed to Justify Equipment Cost

feasible to exhaust this machine classification here, but some of the major categories of machines in this group are discussed below.

It is extremely important for systems analysts to be aware of the various devices available for use short of acquiring full technical knowledge of machines in mechanization levels 2, 3, and 4. Figure 5-2 is a fairly complete chart of machines normally classified as general office machines and their relationship to the various system operations. A system analyst must select machines, as well as coordinate the other components of the financial information system in accordance with the nine systems principles set forth in Chapter 2.

Equipment	*Systems Operations*
Typewriters	Recording (Transcription and Duplication)
Adding Machines	Recording and Summarizing
Calculators	Calculating
Autographic Registers	Recording and Classifying
Cash Registers	Recording, Classifying, and Summarizing
Duplication	Recording and Communicating
Addressing	Classifying

FIGURE 5-2.   Chart of General Office Machines with Systems Operations

Adding Machines

The first practical adding machine (adding-subtracting-listing machine), which simultaneously listed the numbers on a visible tape as its internal mechanism was summing the figures listed, was produced by Felt in 1889 and W. S. Burroughs in 1892. (This concept of summarization is the foundation for several other office machines.)

Today, adding machines are either electrically or manually driven and have either a full-keyboard (Figure 5-3) or a ten-keyboard. (*See* Figure 5-4.) The principal advantage of the ten-keyboard machine over the full-keyboard machine is the amount of learning time needed to become proficient in its use. Utilizing a touch system which encompasses only ten keys, it is generally easier for a beginner to master than the full-keyboard machine with ten digit banks of eight or ten columns. However, advocates of the full-keyboard machine maintain that once the technique for operating a full-keyboard machine is learned, a much faster rate of input can be achieved than on a ten-key machine. Another advantage claimed for the full-keyboard machine

Courtesy of Burroughs Corporation

FIGURE 5-3.   Full-Keyboard Adding Machine

is that it is not necessary to depress a key to register zeroes which must be done on a ten-keyboard machine. Any adding-listing of numbers containing terminal zeros, the numbers 1,000.00, 2,000.00, 2,500.00 for example, or numbers with several internal zeroes such as 2,005.07 or 4,006.00, normally are more quickly indexed on a full-keyboard machine. However, certain manufacturers of ten-keyboard machines are installing keys that will register one, two, or three zeros with a single key depression partially to offset this advantage claimed for full-keyboard machines.

Modifications of the adding machine permit other business functions to be performed in addition to the basic functions of adding and subtracting. *Cash registers*, for example, summarize various types of cash receipts by using several adding registers and also provide for the physical control of cash. (*See* Figure 5-5.) A *receipting machine* (Figure 5-6) combines the listing function

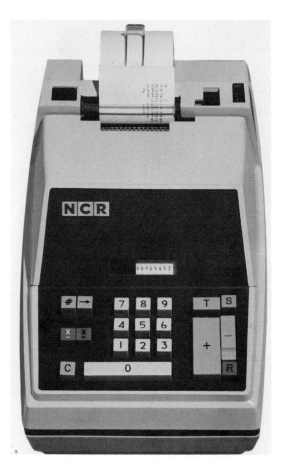

Courtesy of NCR

FIGURE 5-4.   Ten-Keyboard Adding Machine

with validating receipts for customers. Multiple-purpose accounting machines (see discussion below) using several adding registers combine in various ways recording, sorting, summarizing, and calculating.

Calculators

A calculator or calculating machine is classified here as a machine capable of performing the four mathematical processes of addition, subtraction, multiplication, and division. It is generally accepted today that the word calculator is more closely associated with four-process machines that are small enough to

Courtesy of NCR

FIGURE 5-5. Cash Register

be placed on a desk. Larger and more complex electronic calculators will be discussed in other sections.

History traces the origin of the first successful four-process calculator to Charles Thomas who invented his machine in 1820. From this beginning two families of calculators emerged and today desk calculators are classified as either "rotary" or "key-driven" machines. A *key-driven calculator,* as shown in Figure 5-7, is operated by depressing keys which cause the numbers on the keys depressed to show on a dial visible to the operator. Basically, this machine adds only. Subtraction is accomplished through the use of complements; multiplication by repeated addition; and division by repeated subtraction. Manual dexterity is important in the efficient use of this type calculator. The key-driven calculator is a very high speed device (in the hands of a skilled operator) for such things as invoice extension checking, payroll computations, etc.

The *rotary calculator,* through rotating gears in its mechanism, actually performs each of the four mathematical processes in separate operations.

Courtesy of NCR

FIGURE 5-6.   Receipting Machine

Today most rotary calculators are electrically powered. A fairly recent development has made it possible for this type calculator to be purchased as a listing
or non-listing machine and with a full-keyboard or with a ten-keyboard.
Before the development of a listing rotary calculator, answers were given only
on dials which had to be cleared prior to each new calculation. Desk calculators are used almost exclusively in calculating or summarizing operations at
the first two levels of mechanization.

Autographic Registers

The *autographic register* is a device designed to control initial record
documents. The autographic register is usually a metal container through
which forms can be cranked, such as shown in Figure 5-8. A continuous
form is exposed through the opening on the top of the register. When the
exposed document has been completed, the original and second copies are
cranked out of the register for the recipient, and the third copy is locked inside

Courtesy of Victor Comptometer Corporation

FIGURE 5-7. Key-Driven Calculator

the container. The autographic register employs the one-writing technique to produce the necessary documents. In such a system control over the documents is obtained by using prenumbering and the *"locked-in"* copy.

An autographic register can be mounted on a cash drawer for a simple "cash receiving" configuration. For example, when a customer makes a cash purchase or payment on account, a cash receipt can be written upon the autographic register, and the cash placed in the drawer. The original copy is given to the customer as his receipt. The duplicate and triplicate are "locked-in" the register where they are not subject to alteration or destruction after the customer leaves. When the "locked-in" copies are withdrawn they are prelisted and the total verified to the amount that had been withdrawn from the cash drawer. The duplicate becomes the accounting copy, while the triplicate can be returned to the customer with his monthly statement. By a simple "charge" code that can be checked on the document, the same system can also record credit sales.

Autographic registers have many uses. Portable registers are useful for service station work orders, at points where incoming materials are received

Courtesy of Standard Register Company

FIGURE 5-8.   Electric Carbomatic Register

such as in a locker plant, or merely to write a sales ticket. In each instance the chief advantage is the prenumbered, locked-in copy, that provides the systems basis for control.

Duplicating Equipment

One of the most important but often ignored groups of machines used in business is duplicating equipment. For discussion purposes, duplication equipment is considered to be devices which are designed to facilitate the recording operation, which includes duplication and transcription as discussed in Chapter 8. To the systems analyst, however, it is more important to know the advantages and disadvantages of the various processes of duplication rather than to have a commanding knowledge of the specific features of particular machines used in the various processes. Duplication of communication medium is necessary in a system because single sources are often the basis for many business documents. If some form of duplication were not available, multiple recording of the same information could only be accomplished by recopying.

CARBONIZATION. One of the oldest and most widely used methods of duplication is the use of carbon paper. This paper can be interleaved between sheets of the form to be duplicated and as pressure is exerted upon the original document with a pen, pencil, or mechanical writing aid, such as a typewriter, similar impressions are made on the sheets under the carbon paper. Business forms are often prepared in sets utilizing very thin carbon (one-time carbon) which is to be discarded after the form has been prepared. A sales invoice is an example where the one-time carbon is used often. Sales information is needed by the customer, by the accounts receivable ledger clerk, by the Shipping Department and by the Selling Department to name but a few interested in sales information. Quite often as the invoice is prepared, duplicates of the invoice utilizing one-time carbons, are distributed to the interested parties. The original and copies are interleaved with one-time carbons by the forms manufacturer, permitting the typist to insert a set of forms without taking the time to interleave carbon paper. A recent development in the manufacture of paper permits ink nodules to be incorporated into the texture of the paper itself, and as pressure is applied through a writing aid, the ink nodules break and permit the original data to be duplicated on the additional sheets under the original. This type of paper is called commonly "no-carbon required paper."

An important disadvantage of the carbon method of duplication is that the number of copies that can be made with one writing is very limited. Even with power driven equipment, such as an electric typewriter, it is very difficult to produce more than ten or twelve legible copies. It should be evident, therefore, that carbonization in any form can only be used efficiently where the number of copies needed does not normally exceed the number of copies that can be made in one writing.

THE HECTOGRAPH PROCESS. This process of duplicating derives its name Hecto (100)-graph (a writing) from the fact that the process is not too effective when more than 100 copies are needed. To use this process a "master" must be prepared on special paper. This "master" must contain all of the data that are to be reproduced. It is also recommended that a typewriter be used to prepare the "master," but it is possible to prepare the "master" manually by using a pencil or stylus. The information on the "master" is transferred to the copy either through a gelatin process or a fluid process. If the gelatin process is used, the information on the "master" is transferred to a gelatin bed in a special piece of equipment. When the copy paper is brought into contact with the gelatin bed, the data on the bed are transferred to the copy paper completing the reproduction.

If the fluid process is used, the "master" itself is the duplicating medium. Fluid is brought into contact with the special copy paper and as the "master" is brought into contact with the special copy paper a transfer is made. (*See* Figure 5-9.)

In order to put this discussion into an appropriate perspective, consider the following application which is being used by a mid-western hospital. As patients are admitted to the hospital, pertinent personal data are typed on a hectograph master. After the patient has been taken to his hospital room, the

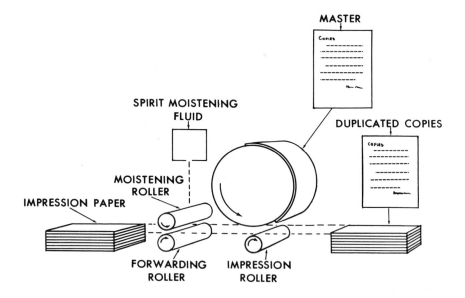

THE SPIRIT PROCESS

Courtesy of A. B. Dick Company

FIGURE 5-9.   Fluid Process Duplicating

following records are originated for him in the Admitting Department by transferring selected data from the master:

1. Accounts receivable ledger card.
2. A six part medical record.
3. Name and address cards for:
   (a) the house directory,
   (b) the mail and delivery directory,
   (c) bed identification,
   (d) the admitting department directory.

Before the installation of the above system, each document had to be inserted into a typewriter and the information pertinent to the document copied from the admittance sheet.

THE STENCIL PROCESS. In situations where more than 100 copies are desired and a quality of product below that found in printing is acceptable, the stencil process of duplicating can be used. With the aid of a typewriter or stylus, the copy to be reproduced is cut into a special master called a stencil. This stencil is placed on the drum of a special machine which permits ink to seep through the cuts in the stencil. When paper is brought into contact with the drum, reproductions of the copy placed on the stencil result. The practical limit to the number of copies which may be made in this way is between 4,000 and 5,000. This method is used frequently to reproduce internal reports that are distributed widely.

OFFSET PROCESS. Still another duplication process which is similar to the hectograph and stencil methods is called the offset process or more commonly "multilith." This particular process utilizes the fact that oil and water repel each other. A master must be prepared (special paper or a very thin metal plate) by placing the text to be copied on the master utilizing a water repellant material. A typewriter is most often used to prepare the master but a pen, pencil, brush, or crayon could be used.[1] Next, a moistening agent is brought into contact with the master. Since the moistening agent will not adhere to the text copy, which is water repellent, the oil base ink rolled over the master will ink the text copy but will be repelled from the remainder of the master. The master is then brought into contact with a rubber blanket or "mat" which in turn is brought into contact with the copy paper completing the transfer process. (*See* Figure 5-10.)

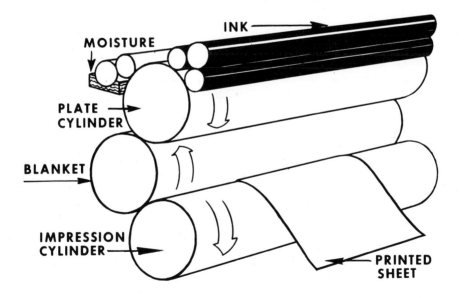

Courtesy of Addressograph Multigraph Corporation

FIGURE 5-10. Offset Lithography

---

[1] In more elaborate circumstances, photography can be used to prepare masters. Photographs of the text to be copied are developed on the metal or paper masters using a special developer.

The principal advantages of the offset method are the excellent quality of the copy obtained, the practically unlimited quantity which can be obtained from one master, and the colors that can be reproduced effectively. Many public accounting firms use this method to reproduce audit and management advisory service reports. On the other hand, this method costs more to operate and maintain than either hectograph or stencil duplication.

PHOTOCOPYING. Numerous photographic processes are in existence for use in reproducing various kinds of copy, but all of them, essentially, photograph the text to be copied and print the photograph rapidly in a one or two step operation. Photocopying methods do not photograph copy to be reproduced through the use of a camera. Copies are made by bringing the data to be copied into direct contact with sensitized paper and exposed to beams of light. Some methods produce a usable positive print after the sensitized paper is "developed," while other methods require a second sheet of sensitized paper to be brought into contact with the first exposure or "negative." A schematic illustration of a typical two step photocopying process is shown in Figure 5-11. Unlike camera exposed negatives, few photocopying methods permit enlargements or reductions in print sizes. Most methods, on the other hand, can produce a usable copy in less than one minute which is considerably faster than most camera-produced prints.

The principal advantages in all photographic processes are accuracy and, because a photograph is made, it is not possible for transcription errors to occur. However, an extra burden is placed on the person responsible for the original copy because errors photograph as well as correct copy. The principal disadvantage is that photocopy methods are not economical for a large number of copies.

THERMOGRAPHY. Utilizing the fact that dark objects absorb more heat than light objects do, the thermographic process, using infra red light and special paper, literally burn the data to be copied into the special copy paper. This process is being used widely in physicians' offices in billing operations. When a statement is to be sent to a patient, a copy of the patient's ledger account is made using a thermographic machine. This eliminates the need of typing or otherwise preparing a statement and, in addition, gives the patient a resumé of his account for several months.

One disadvantage of this process is that all inks and dyes are not compatible with the thermographic process. Inks or dyes with a carbon base as well as pencil copy are most usable in the process.

Addressing Equipment

One of the important systems needs is a means of addressing. Each active customer is billed at least once each month. Employees must be paid at least every month and often every two weeks. Materials are purchased from the

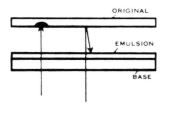

1. EXPOSURE

This diagram shows how light rays capture the image on the matrix paper. Light rays pass through the matrix paper base and emulsion, and strike (1) the dark image area of the original, where they are absorbed. Light rays (2) striking the original in white, or non-image, areas are reflected back to the matrix paper and form an invisible image on it. It becomes visible when placed in activator.

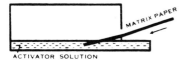

2. ACTIVATION

The exposed matrix paper is put into activator solution for 20 seconds. The gelatin in the image area is softened, and dye is formed, so that the image will transfer to copy paper. In the non-image areas, the gelatin is hardened so that non-image areas will not transfer to the copy paper. Thus, the exposed matrix paper has become a matrix.

3. FINISHED COPIES

After the activation cycle, copy paper is placed in contact with the matrix and drawn out between a roller and squeegee. This pressure deposits a thin layer of the softened and dyed gelatin from the image area onto the copy paper, which remains when the matrix is stripped from the copy paper. To make more copies, slide the matrix back into the activator and repeat the process. The image on the finished copy is the result of an actual physical transfer of gelatin softened by the activator. The copies are as permanent as a normal typewritten document. They're made on bond-type sulfite paper which lasts as well as, or better than, many other office papers.

Courtesy of Eastman Kodak Company

FIGURE 5-11.   Photocopying Process of Duplication

same supplier often within each year. It becomes obvious then that there can be a worthwhile systems efficiency in being able to reproduce the name and address of an individual or company automatically, without the need of special typing or entering. Once such an addressing system is available, it can also be used for advertising and other comparable business purposes.

Companies whose information system is still either at the first or second level of mechanization must make special provision for addressing. In some instances an addressograph system is used. Such a system consists of metal plates on which a name, address, and other relevant information is punched. Plates can be used over and over again and can be coded according to the different addressing uses. When a need arises for which the plates can be used, they can be run and those with the indicated code designation will be used to imprint the desired media.

In most of the systems in operation today the addressing or imprinting of name or alphabetical information on media is a separate operation. In a payroll procedure, for example, using a multiple-purpose accounting machine, the time clock cards and payroll checks will normally have the name of the payee printed on the check before the payroll writing procedure starts. In an accounts receivable system, the customer's statement will normally have the name imprinted in a separate operation before any amounts are entered.

Integrated data processing systems have made great strides toward the solution of the name and address problem. Punched paper tape files, punched card files, and other media files are commonplace.

MULTIPLE-PURPOSE ACCOUNTING MACHINES

Basic accounting methodology dictates that business transactions must be recorded (journalized), posted to ledger accounts, and periodically summarized and reported to management. In this typically manual system, the subject of most introductory accounting instruction, a bookkeeper is visualized as doing all of the book work and having responsibility for the system. In businesses with sufficient volume to justify a multiple-purpose accounting machine the configuration of the system is modified by the establishment of separate procedures. The operations of the different procedures are often the responsibility of different organization units. The results of the procedures are periodically transferred via journal voucher to the General Ledger Section where the financial accounts are maintained, statements summarized, and formal management reports prepared. Figure 5-12 illustrates a simple system in which five procedures, namely sales, cash receipts, purchases, payroll, and cash disbursements, each provide data via journal voucher to the General Ledger Section. The emphasis in such a multiple-purpose accounting machine system focuses on the separate procedures. It is important to recognize that daily management reports will flow directly from the procedures in such a system. For example, the daily sales figure can be reported as a result of the processing in the sales procedure, and it is not necessary for management to wait for the information until it comes from the balance of the ledger account maintained in the General Ledger Section. The systems analyst in an industrial company in his day-to-day work normally approaches his redesign problems through the study of procedures. Redesign problems relating to the entire

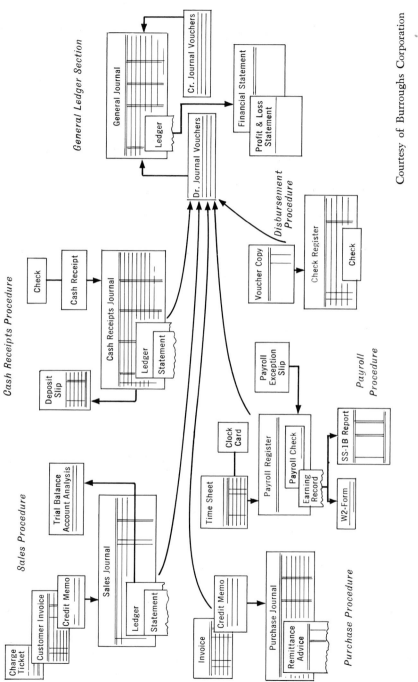

General Ledger Section

Cash Receipts Procedure

Sales Procedure

Payroll Procedure

Purchase Procedure

Disbursement Procedure

Courtesy of Burroughs Corporation

FIGURE 5-12. Procedures in a Simplified Multiple-Purpose Accounting Machine System

system, such as those created by the major change from a multiple-purpose accounting machine system to a punched card system, occur infrequently.

Types of Multiple-Purpose Accounting Machines

Multiple-purpose accounting machines are often divided into two classifications—*front-feed* and *flat-bed* machines. This classification is based on the way in which the various media handled by the machine are inserted for processing. Posting media in the "front-feed" type are inserted in front of a rounded platen as shown in Figure 5-13. Media are inserted into the "flat-bed" machine via a slot which positions the media over a flat platen as shown in Figure 5-14. The "flat-bed" machine is often called a "window-posting" machine because of the way in which it is most commonly used. This machine is usually found in situations where there is little or no time lag between the event to be recorded and the actual recording. Savings account deposits and withdrawals are examples. Most banks deem it necessary to post a deposit or withdrawal immediately to the customer's savings account and, as a by-product, post the activity simultaneously to the customer's pass book. This is done at the teller's window, hence the name "window-posting." Hotels often

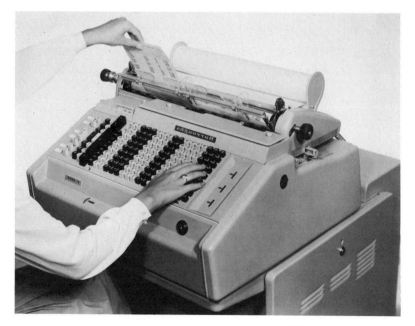

Courtesy of Burroughs Corporation

FIGURE 5-13.   Front-Feed Multiple-Purpose Accounting Machine

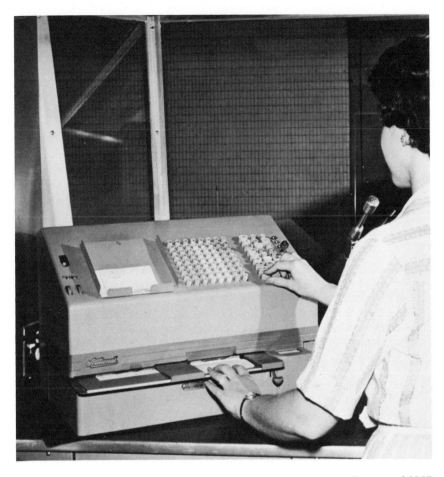

Courtesy of NCR

FIGURE 5-14.   Flat-Bed Multiple-Purpose Accounting Machine

find the window-posting machine appropriate for their use. The trend, how-ever, seems to be away from the use of a "flat-bed" machine in most industrial companies.

Machine Features and Terminology

Both the front-feed or flat-bed accounting machines, while different in appearance and in mode of operation, have several common features. In order to facilitate the discussion of these features, the front-feed accounting machine will be used as a basis for describing them. However, specific examples will be given of how both types of machines make use of these features.

There is considerable new terminology that is used in connection with multiple-purpose accounting machines and the systems in which they are used. A number of these terms are listed below.

Activity. The frequency with which an account is posted or the percentage of accounts affected during a given period of time, as for example, during a posting run, a day, or a week.

Batching. The grouping of communication media for a given period of time, or from a given operation or department, into managable lots for control during processing.

Control Account. A summary account representing the total of balances on all accounts in the ledger or section.

Cross-footer. The cross-footer is the computing mechanism used to calculate the new balance on a ledger account. As the term implies, it cross-foots (adds or subtracts) the account as the entries are made in the various columns across the sheet. The cross-footer is normally cleared when the balance of the account is printed.

Collation. The positioning of two or more related forms together for simultaneous posting so that the beginning of the next blank writing line on each form will be at the same printing point.

Localizing an Error. The procedure of analyzing the machine records, in case the results do not immediately prove to be correct, in order to determine in what operation and on what account the error was made.

Offsetting. The movement of a ledger or statement sheet to the right or left of its normal position in the binder. Accounts are offset to facilitate their location when posting, to localize errors in proving, to apply certain methods of proof, or for special attention.

Pickup. The previous balance of an account which is entered in the bookkeeping machine so that a debit may be added to it or a credit subtracted from it to obtain the current new balance.

Pre-list. A total of the media which is obtained for proof purposes before they are posted. When different kinds of items are to be posted, as for example, debits and credits, a separate total is obtained for each. They should agree with the register accumulations resulting from posting.

Progressive Posting. The posting of accounts in the order in which they occur in the ledger, for example, alphabetically or numerically. The media would be arranged in the same order as the ledger accounts.

Pulling. The removal of accounts from a binder, tray, or file. Sometimes all accounts to be posted are "pulled" before any are posted so they can be posted without repeated interruption for locating the accounts individually.

Random Posting. The posting of items in the order in which they appear on the media rather than in the order in which the accounts are filed in the ledger.

Registers. The accumulating mechanisms in which columnar totals are accumulated. The totals may represent the sums of debits, credits, balances, etc., on numerous accounts, or differences between debits and credits. Registers are usually cleared at the end of a batch of postings. In some applications, registers may be used as additional cross-footers.

Skeleton Record. A condensed record to which totals only are posted rather than individual items. Thus, by eliminating detail, both posting time and space on the account are saved.

Stuffing. The placement of posting media in the ledger in front of or behind the account affected. This routine combines the locating of accounts and the arranging of media in account order prior to posting.

The One-Writing Technique

Although the one-writing technique is not unique with multiple-purpose accounting machines, it is probably the feature most systems analysts would agree is indispensable. Through the use of carbon paper and the proper collation of forms, several business records can receive data with one operation of the machine. Figure 5-12, for example, illustrates that in conjunction with preparing a weekly pay check for an employee, the payroll check, the employee's earning record, and the payroll register (journal) can be prepared in one operation. In manual systems not utilizing a "writing board," each one of the forms above would have to be prepared individually. Because three forms are prepared or entered into separately from one source, the possibility of a transcription error is three times as great compared to the one-writing operation done on an accounting machine.

Distribution Registers

The posting operation in accounting is the transferring of amounts from the journals to their appropriate ledger accounts. Columnar journals are used in manual systems in order to reduce the time spent on this operation. If columns are used in a cash disbursement book for cash credits and accounts payable, purchases, supplies, and several other active expense account debits, it is possible to accumulate column totals which can be posted daily or monthly in lieu of posting each debit and credit after each transaction has been journalized. Multiple-purpose accounting machine manufacturers incorporate this idea into their machine systems. The multiple-purpose accounting machine is really only a group of adding machine type mechanisms or registers built into a single case with several extra features peculiar to the model of machine. One or more of these registers can be activated by the machine operator by depressing one key or group of keys and the operating bar. It is therefore possible to accumulate automatically the total postings for active accounts in much the same manner as columnar totals are accumulated in a manual system. For example, a $100 cash merchandise purchase can be added into a totaling register for cash disbursements and at the same time into another register for purchases. As additional purchase transactions are entered, the amounts are entered in both the cash disbursement and purchases registers, where the total is accumulated. For each active account such as purchases, a separate accumulating register is necessary. For comparatively inactive accounts, such as rent expense, one totaling register is used to accumulate the total of these sundry amounts. During the posting run, the operator will select each such inactive account from the tray, insert it into the machine, and permit the posting to be done simultaneously with the journalizing operation. The active ledger accounts, such as cash and purchases, need to be inserted into the machine only at the end of each posting run to post the total accumulated in the special register.

Machines can be purchased that contain as many as 25 accumulating registers. It is possible, when more totals are needed, to split some or all of the basic registers. If a totaling register, which normally could accumulate a twelve-digit number was split into two six-digit registers, the systems analyst must be absolutely certain that neither split register will exceed 9,999.99.

It is possible to obtain a multiple-purpose accounting machine containing only one totaling register. Distribution and proof methods (see below) are not as effective with a one-register machine, but the advantages of record legibility, one-writing, etc., are present. Naturally, as more totaling registers are added, the cost of the machine increases somewhat proportionately. The differences between a single-register, multiple-purpose accounting machine, and an adding-subtracting-listing machine are primarily the control features present in the accounting machine as described below in the section on machine control.

Alphanumeric Features

Multiple-purpose accounting machines are either numeric (nondescriptive) or alphanumeric (descriptive). Numeric machines have specific keys that can print limited alphabetic information such as the month, i.e. "Jan." for January and "Dis" for discount. In general, however, only the special bits of information on special printing slugs can be used. The alphanumeric or descriptive machines include a typewriter keyboard as an integral part of the machine. This feature enables the typing of alphabetic data at any place in the sequence of operations making up the machine procedure. For example, a description of an item being billed can be typed on an invoice or on a statement. The name of the employee can be typed on a pay check. The typewriter feature on a multiple-purpose accounting machine is expensive and is not too common in practical industrial systems work since acceptable alternatives are available. For example, instead of typing a description of the items being billed on a statement, the invoice number can be indicated and a copy of the invoice or sales ticket enclosed with the statement; instead of typing the name on the pay check when the check is being written, the name can be put on the check with addressograph or typed with a regular typewriter before the writing of the check occurs. In such payroll systems the employee is identified in preliminary processing by his clock number. The advantage of using a three-digit or four-digit clock number in terms of reduced machine work is obvious when compared to the number of letters in the average name.

Machine Posting in General

Before considering the nature of proof methods and specific examples of several posting-proof methods, it may be well to consider the mechanics of machine posting in general. Assume charges and credits are to be posted to accounts receivable subsidiary accounts on a multiple register "front-feed" posting machine. The operator must select the proper account from the ledger file and pick up the old balance from the account by indexing the old balance amount on the machine keyboard, inserting the account in the machine, and depressing the proper operating bar. Once the old balance has been picked up, the operator selects the charge and credit media which affect the account in the machine, indexes the proper amounts on the keyboard and, in each case, depresses the proper operating bar. At the conclusion of posting individual charges and credits, the operator will depress a balance bar, the new balance of the account will be computed and printed on the account card, and the carriage of the machine will open so that the ledger card can be removed and another card inserted. As an additional control a total of the charges and credits can be obtained in a vertical register.

Proof Methods

One of the advantages of machines over manual accounting is that a higher degree of accuracy can be achieved in a machine system. Nevertheless, at least six kinds of errors are possible in machine posting:

1. The incorrect entry of any of the detail items.
2. The omission of any of the detail items.
3. Posting to the wrong account.
4. The pickup of an incorrect old balance.
5. The computation of an incorrect new balance.
6. Those caused by improper positioning of media inserted into the machine.

Many proof methods are used to eliminate errors in machine posting. Most proof methods are based on prelists and batching media before processing, repetition (the theory that if an item is handled twice and the two operations are in agreement, then the posting has been accomplished correctly), or on balancing procedures.

A number of specific proof methods are based on repetition. For example, consider the use of *multiple-register proof*. In this method, the old balances of all accounts are picked up twice and the second pickup is accumulated in a separate register. At the end of the posting run, the second old balance pick-up total is subtracted from the total of all new balances. If the difference agrees with the net charges and credits posted, then one is confident that no incorrect balances have been picked up. Also, if net charges and credits agree with a batch prelisting of charges and credits, then all items have been posted. One disadvantage of this method is that errors are not discovered until the end of a posting run, although batching reduces the area of error search.

In situations where it is inadvisable to wait until the end of a posting run to find and correct errors, a line proof method can be used. There are many variations to line proof. Assume, for example, the posting of a sale of $200, $150 from department number one and $50 from department number two, to the account receivable of a customer already owing $400. In the *media proof method* the old balance of $400 is first entered in a cross-footer. The total charge of $200 is then added to the balance in the cross-footer, and also into another totaling register at the same time. The cross-footer is subtotaled and the new balance of $600 is printed out without clearing the cross-footer. The old balance of $400 is again picked up and entered in the cross-footer as a deduction. The cross-footer is then cleared by printing out the $200 amount of the media that had been posted. The amount is printed on a proof sheet and can be visually compared to the original posting media to insure accuracy. If a register had been available to accumulate charges, the total of the amounts accumulated in the register could have been cleared at the end of the run, and the total checked to the prelist total of media processed.

Using the *zero* or *distribution proof method*, the old balance of $400 is first entered in the cross-footer. The charge of $200 is entered in the cross-footer and also in a second register used to accumulate the total of all charges. The cross-footer is then subtotaled and the new balance of $600 is printed out but not cleared. The old balance of $400 is picked up again in the cross-footer as a subtraction, leaving the amount of the charge of $200 in the cross-footer. The department number one sale of $150 would be entered into register number three and printed on the debit distribution as well as deducted from the amount in the cross-footer. The department number two sale of $50 would then be entered into register number four and printed on the debit distribution as well as deducted from the amount in the cross-footer. The balance in the cross-footer of zero would be printed out on a proof sheet. Any balance other than zero would indicate an error.

Still another line proof method compares the old balance pickup with the second old balance pickup and prints a zero in the proof column if the two items agree and either locks the machine or prints the difference if the items do not agree. The operator must wait until the posting run is completed, as in the multiple-register method, before a check can be made of the total of individual items posted to the prelist tape to determine if all items have been posted.

It can be noted that neither of the above proof methods provides for proving that each item has been posted to the correct account. This type of error is not as common nor as costly as the others and, in many instances, businesses rely on their customers, vendors, auditors, and others dealing with the enterprise to discover these errors for them. Customers, for example, will notify the company if they have been overcharged, and quite often will notify the company of undercharges. When it is important that proof of posting to the correct account be accomplished, it is possible to pre-list the account numbers to which certain items are to be posted. When the posting run is made, one of the registers is used to accumulate account numbers. If the register total agrees with the pre-list of account numbers, reasonable certainty is achieved that all items were posted to the correct account.

A second method often used to prove that amounts have been posted to the correct account is known as *direct or detailed* proof. Essentially, this method compares the amount posted to a particular account with the original medium. The technique used most often to accomplish this check is to utilize a proof sheet. The proof sheet is covered by a carbon and fed continuously over the platen of the multiple-purpose accounting machine. As each account is inserted and postings made to it, the carbon permits a copy of each amount posted, along with its classification, to be made on the continuous proof sheet. When the posting run is completed, the operator can compare the amount posted from the posting medium, a sales invoice for example, to the proof sheet and determine whether the postings were made to the correct account. The use of a proof sheet does away with the necessity of actually referring to each account a second time.

In some instances the proof of old-balance pickup is combined with proof of posting to the correct account. Such a technique is often referred to as package proof. *Package proof* requires that the ledger card contain a special column in which the sum of the new balance and the account number will appear after each posting. Assume, for example, that the account of M. L. Richards has a balance of $325.10 and that the account number is 110. On line with the last posting would be the amount $326.20, the sum of 325.10 and 110. When the next posting to the account is made the old balance of $325.10 is first picked up in a cross-footer. Next the account number from the posting medium is picked up of 110. The package proof figure from the last posting of $326.20 is then picked up from the ledger card as a negative amount in the cross-footer. If the cross-footer clears, the posting is to the correct account and the old balance was picked up correctly. The posting of the current transaction then continues and a new package proof figure determined to be used in the next posting. It can be seen that the package proof method requires that the number of the account or customer be on the posting medium. Such a condition exists more commonly in Credit Unions, Savings and Loan Associations, and comparable organizations.

The improper positioning of media in the machine can result in a difficult-to-discover overprint. The last item being posted prints higher on the ledger card than the prior posting. In such a situation the bottom amount on the ledger is not the correct balance of the account. Periodic trial balances will disclose such overprints. They can also be eliminated by electronic multiple-purpose accounting machines with provision for automatic form positioning as discussed below.

More examples of proof methods and techniques to reduce or eliminate errors could be described, but it is more important for the systems analyst to recognize the need for proof methods and techniques to insure accuracy than to know the nature of each method or technique. Manufacturers' representatives are well equipped to determine the specific proof method for given applications. It is the obligation of the analyst to see to it that adequate proof methods are incorporated into each system utilizing mutliple-purpose accounting machines in order to comply with the "reliability principle." Adequacy must be judged by the analyst after weighing the machine cost of the various types of proof methods and the clerical work necessary in each case against the caliber of results. It would seem reasonable that in an application where a large volume of posting is done, it might be better to utilize a line proof method rather than the multiple-register proof method. This judgment, however, must be made by the analyst in each individual case. No set rule is applicable. The application of the "reliability principle" must be made in conjunction with the "reasonable cost principle."

Machine Control

Multiple-purpose accounting machines are electrically driven and have a carriage control mechanism similar to the tab control on a typewriter. Through the use of control panels (Figure 5-15) or control bars (Figure 5-16), front-feed machines can be programmed to move the carriage automatically through much of the data processing application, which would include mathematical processes, carriage spacing, printing, repeating, and the opening and closing of the carriage. These automatic machine controls permit the operator to spend most of the operating time selecting the proper media to be inserted, depressing the amount keys, and refiling updated media.

The control bar or panel gives the multiple-purpose accounting machine its great flexibility in changing from one procedure to another. Applications can be changed in a few seconds by removing one control panel or bar and inserting another. With the control panel the application can be changed by turning the knob on the panel to "engage" the appropriate control bar selected from the four bars built into each panel.

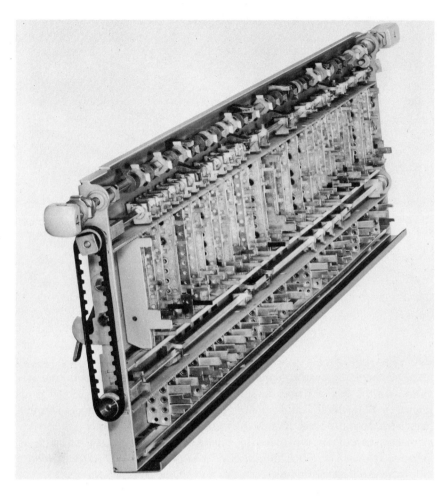

Courtesy of Burroughs Corporation

FIGURE 5-15.   Control Panel

Electronic Features

Manufacturers have recognized that certain phases of multiple-purpose accounting machine operations were neither as rapid nor as accurate as they might be. In large volume applications, the positioning of forms, the second old balance pickup, trial balancing, etc., consumed a substantial percentage of an operator's time. To overcome the problems and to make multiple-purpose accounting machines more compatible to larger electronic systems (Chapters 15 through 17) certain electronic features were incorporated into the electrically driven, but mechanical, multiple-purpose accounting machines.

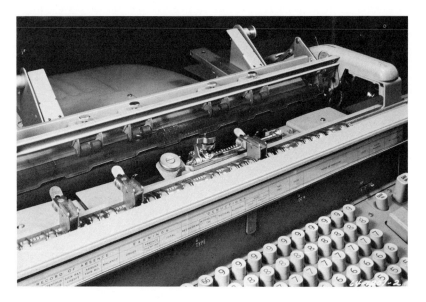

Courtesy of NCR

FIGURE 5-16.   Control Bar

The major innovation applied to the multiple-purpose accounting machines was the use of stripes in special ink on the back of the ledger cards (Figure 5-17) which could contain coded information in magnetic pulse (magnetized spots) form that is electronically accessible. Some forms have a broader stripe than illustrated in Figure 5-17; however, the principle of operation is the same. Such information as account number, account balance with its appropriate arithmetic sign, the line of last posting, and other special codes can be placed on the stripes. Utilizing this information as the operator inserts the posting medium, the machine automatically positions the form correctly and picks up old balances, and during the posting operation verifies postings to the proper account. After the proper amounts have been posted, the new balance is encoded on the magnetic stripes and the form is ejected into the hand of the operator. Manufacturers' representatives have stated that this feature permits the form to be inserted and made ready for posting in about four seconds. If it took approximately 34 seconds, utilizing mechanical form alignment and old balance pickup, a saving of over eight hours in posting time could result in every 1,000 forms handled.

To facilitate trial balancing and balance transfer operations, an automatic reading machine can be used in conjunction with one or more electronic accounting machines. The reader (Figure 5-18) automatically feeds the ledger cards, reads the balances, and transfers the balance to a new ledger card, or

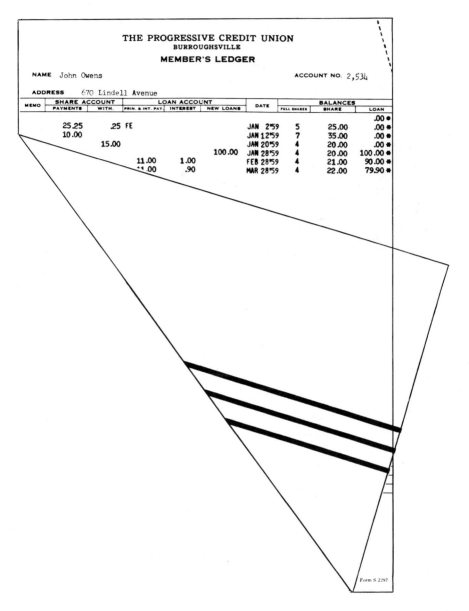

THE PROGRESSIVE CREDIT UNION
BURROUGHSVILLE
MEMBER'S LEDGER

NAME   John Owens   ACCOUNT NO. 2,534

ADDRESS   670 Lindell Avenue

| MEMO | SHARE ACCOUNT | | LOAN ACCOUNT | | | DATE | BALANCES | | |
	PAYMENTS	WITH.	PRIN. & INT. PAY.	INTEREST	NEW LOANS		FULL SHARES	SHARE	LOAN
									.00 ●
	25.25	.25 FE				JAN 2'59	5	25.00	.00 ✳
	10.00					JAN 12'59	7	35.00	.00 ✳
		15.00				JAN 20'59	4	20.00	.00 ✳
					100.00	JAN 28'59	4	20.00	100.00 ✳
			11.00	1.00		FEB 28'59	4	21.00	90.00 ✳
			11.00	.90		MAR 28'59	4	22.00	79.90 ✳

Form S 2297

Courtesy of Burroughs Corporation

**FIGURE 5-17.   Form Illustrating Stripe on Back—Used in Machine
with Electronic Features**

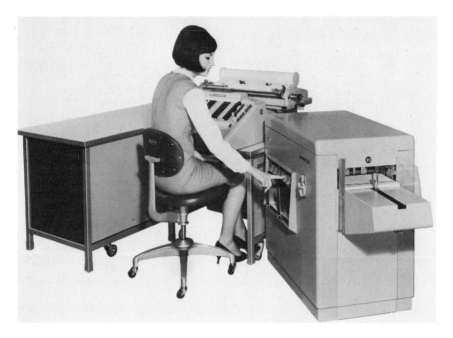

Courtesy of Burroughs Corporation

FIGURE 5-18.   Reading Machine

accumulates the trial balance total. Transcription errors are nonexistent, except those caused by machine failure. The latter type, according to various experience reports, is extremely rare.

OTHER DEVICES AND TECHNIQUES

Many different relatively simple devices are used in certain procedures to enable more efficient or effective systems operations. Devices to aid in sorting, to facilitate filing, to assist in summarization, or to speed up a needed operation are common and are all a part of the components of a system. It is not the purpose of this text to introduce and discuss in detail these simple but necessary devices that are in reality more technique than anything else. Later in the text a few of these device-technique systems aids, such as peg-boards and edge-notched cards, will be presented. At this time only writing boards and devices for external protection will be discussed.

Writing Boards

There is a time during the early growth of a business when its information needs cannot be adequately met by its existing manual data processing system. Neither is it justifiable to install a new system which would require a higher degree of mechanization, such as moving from the use of manual methods to the use of a multiple-purpose accounting machine. Usually, certain applications could justify the use of a multiple-purpose accounting machine, others do not, and overall sufficient justification cannot be given for a complete change.

In order to bridge this gap and to enable partial progress toward the next level of mechanization, it is possible to use certain transition devices and machine configurations. In a manual system, for example, which does not collect, process, and communicate a sufficient volume of data and information to justify a multiple-purpose accounting machine, devices such as writing boards are very useful.

A writing board is designed to permit more than one input or processing operation to be performed simultaneously. In the preparation of a payroll, for example, it is necessary to prepare an earnings statement and check for each employee, a payroll register, and an individual earnings record. Through the use of a writing board, as illustrated in Figure 5-19, it is possible to prepare all three items, which contain identical data, in one writing. The payroll register is placed over the pegs on the writing board first and is covered with carbon paper. Next, a group of pay checks and earnings statements are placed on the pegs over the carbon paper and payroll register. The appropriate earnings record for the first employee is selected from a tub file and inserted between the first check and the payroll register. When the payroll clerk fills in the earnings statement, the data, due to the appropriately placed carbon, is simultaneously recorded on the earnings record and the payroll register. This one-writing technique eliminates the need to transcribe the same data into two additional records. The one-writing technique can be used wherever it is operationally feasible to do so. Other possibilities include (1) invoicing, where the invoice and sales journal are prepared; (2) accounts payable, where the voucher and voucher register are prepared; (3) cash receipts, where the accounts receivable, credit, and the cash receipts journal are prepared; (4) cash disbursements, where the check and the check register are prepared; and many more. The analyst must be aware that such writing boards are available and must be able to recognize when they can be used effectively.

Devices for External Protection

No control system that is designed to safeguard assets is complete without provision for the many devices that provide protection in the event of external

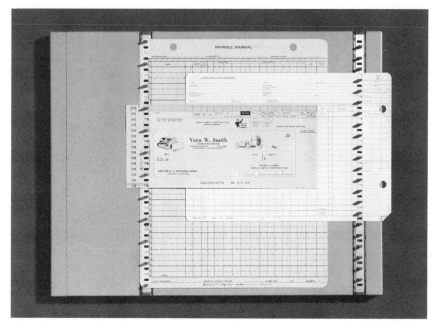

Courtesy of Burroughs Corporation

FIGURE 5-19. Writing Board

threat. The provision for a safe, burglar alarm, fire proof file, sprinkler system, and locked storeroom, when appropriate, is important in systems design. While such devices will not be studied in this text, they are integral components of the system, and a system which lacks them may be unacceptable.

QUESTIONS, PROBLEMS, AND CASES

1. Seven principal advantages of mechanization were discussed in this chapter. Are there any other advantages or disadvantages inherent in system mechanization? Confine your discussion to the first two levels of machine classifications.

2. Briefly describe the basic difference between the flat-bed and front-feed-posting machines, and illustrate the types of applications best suited for each machine.

3. What is it about the combination of several adding machines and, in some cases, a typewriter in a front-feed accounting machine, that makes this particular piece of equipment useful in a system?

4. What are the factors that must be considered by the systems analyst before a particular duplicating process can be selected?

5. Outline a procedure or group of procedures illustrating the use of both general office machines and multiple-purpose accounting machines.

6. Using the outline developed in item 5 above, describe in detail the operations that must be performed before the procedure(s) can be completed.

7. In addition to the capital outlay necessary for the purchase of office machines, what other factors must be considered by management before a decision to purchase can be made?

8. In a system utilizing a multiple-purpose accounting machine for vouchering and paying all invoices, what are the processing controls necessary and how can the machine provide these controls?

9. In a system utilizing a multiple-purpose accounting machine for posting to accounts receivable subsidiary ledgers, what are the processing controls necessary and how can the machine provide these controls?

10. What are the processing controls necessary in a payroll procedure? How can a multiple-purpose accounting machine provide these controls?

11. Distinguish between a single-register posting machine and a simple adding machine.

12. List the specific ways in which pen-and-ink posting is likely to differ from machine posting.

13. Discuss why it may be easier to detect errors made by machine posting than those made when pen-and-ink methods are used.

14. Comment on the following statement: "Because machine posting involves the simultaneous writing on two or more documents, if the amounts are correct, it is not possible to make posting errors."

15. How long would it take a posting machine to "pay for itself" through labor savings under these conditions?

Cost	$1,200
Annual service contract	80
Imputed interest	8%
Scrap value	200
Useful life	8 years
Property taxes and insurance per annum	30
Average clerical salaries per annum	4,500
Fringe benefit costs for clerical employees	15%
Time saved per week by machine	3 clerical hours

Clerical employees get a two week paid vacation, cost of which is included in the fringe benefit figure. The work week is 36 hours.

16. How much could be paid for a posting machine which would save two hours per week of clerical time based on all figures set out in problem 15 above, except for the $1,200 cost and $200 scrap value amounts? In this connection, assume scrap value is 1/6 of cost as in problem 15.

17. As between a single-register posting machine and a two-register machine, what extra steps would have to be taken in posting to accounts receivable if the simpler machine were used? (Hint: consider proof procedures.)

18. The Jackson Corporation is a metal fabricating company that has been undergoing rapid growth during the past five years. There has been considerable difficulty in meeting deadlines for completion of accounting work. Customer billings were 12 days behind at one time during the past month, and only recently the payroll was late. The cost of accounting work has been increasing at a rate greater than that of the growth of the entire company. Management has been concerned about the effect of late customer billings on the working capital position, and was also embarrassed by the reaction of employees when pay checks were late. You have now been given authority to investigate the possibility of streamlining procedures and the necessity for multiple-purpose accounting machines to accomplish accounting work with the maximum efficiency and minimum cost.
    a. What would be an important source of information about accounting machines and the related procedures?
    b. What are the principal advantages of a machine system over a hand system?
    c. What are the basic considerations in the decision to install a multiple-purpose accounting machine?
    d. What are some of the characteristics of a machine system that could enable greater efficiency or better control?
    e. How is it possible to use the same multiple-purpose accounting machine for several different procedures, i.e., accounts receivable and payroll?

19. Comment on the following statement: "Machine systems are rigid and less subject to change. Such systems are often not appropriate in a dynamic business."

20. In what way would a receipting machine be important to a cash receiving system? Which of the principles of systems design has the most significant application in this instance? Explain.

21. Give an illustration of a financial information system (not procedure) in which a cash register, autographic register, writing board, and addressing equipment would all seem appropriate.

22. You have been asked to provide a systems report in 20 copies for distribution to the Board of Directors of the Jefferson Manufacturing Company before you present your findings. Which duplicating process would you use to obtain 20 copies, and why?

23. Which of the duplicating processes would you use for each of the following? Explain.

a. The accounting copy of an invoice.
b. 50 copies of a production order.
c. 400 letters to customers.
d. 10,000 checks.
e. Two copies of a tax return.
f. 2,000 daily cash reports (internal use).

24. Would you recommend the purchase of an alphanumeric multiple-purpose accounting machine for a payroll procedure? Explain.

25. How can distribution registers provide line proof of posting accuracy? Explain.

26. How can a system utilizing a multiple-purpose accounting machine prevent the following errors?
a. The posting of a sales ticket of $44.50 as $45.40.
b. Failure to post a sales ticket of $25.
c. Posting a sales ticket of $5 to James R. Henry instead of James S. Henry.
d. Picking up an old balance of $150 instead of $510.
e. Computing the old balance pickup of $400 plus the sales ticket of $50 to be $540.
f. Overprinting the old balance of an account of $530 with a cash receipt of $130 leaving a balance of $400 printed above the balance of $530.

27. What are the relative advantages of media proof as contrasted to zero proof?

28. What are the major advantages of the multiple-purpose accounting machine with electronic features as contrasted to the electrically driven but mechanical machine?

29. How large would a payroll have to become and what other factors should be studied to determine whether a payroll system on a writing board should be changed to a system with a higher level of mechanization?

30. You have been asked to design a system for control of cash receipts at the central cashier's operation in a large department store. What devices should be included in the system as protection against external pilferage?

31. Between a ten key and full keyboard adding or posting machine, what are some of the considerations which would lead you to select one over the other?

32. Describe the main features of posting accomplished by means of a multiple-purpose accounting machine.

33. Indicate some of the means by which "proof" is accomplished with machine posting and tell, in general, what the "proofs" prove and do not prove.

34. State whether each of the following relates to the writing board, and explain why or why not.
a. Accumulates automatic subtotals for control purposes.
b. Provides a locked-in copy for control purposes.
c. Eliminates need for prenumbered forms.
d. Permits writing up several documents simultaneously.
e. Needs to be used only at the close of a fiscal period.

35. Name three procedures in which the writing board can be used besides payroll.

36. You are recommending that a client purchase a new machine to process data. A statistical analysis of the present system yields the following information: the machine now in use cost $2,500 three years ago and is being depreciated at the rate of $400 per year for five years; the second-hand value is now about $600; supplies cost about $20 per month and power $10 per month; four people are now working in the procedure, representing a $1,600 per month payroll.

    The new machine costs $5,000, with a five-year life and salvage value of $1,000. One employee can be transferred to other work. Supplies are expected to run $30 per month and power costs are to double. How would you present these data on your report to assist in convincing a client to make the change?

37. Design a customer's statement and ledger form for use on a multiple-purpose accounting machine. Enter the following transactions reflected in a manual posting situation onto your statement form. Fill in all data.

Jerry Farr, 321 Oak St., Bay City, Iowa

Feb. 29	Balance		$30.00	Mar. 8	SR1	$10.00
Mar. 5		S1	50.00	Mar. 15	CR1	25.00
Mar. 18		S3	70.00			

38. Blank Wholesalers has a limited number of accounts receivable customers, most of whose accounts are fairly active. Posting to their accounts is done on a multiple-purpose accounting machine. Media are accumulated for a week and then posted at one time. Commonly about one-half of the accounts in the ledger are affected on a typical posting run. The system was designed to use a trial balance proof to verify posting. A trial balance of the subsidiary ledger is taken Friday afternoon of each week. This proof method is used even though certain changes in the pattern of customer activity have evolved. Do you recommend continued use of this proof method? If not, why and what alternate plan would you suggest? Give reasons to support your choice.

39. Define or explain briefly the following terms as they relate to machine accounting:
    a. Stuffing.
    b. Random posting.
    c. Offsetting.
    d. Registers.
    e. Cross-footer.
    f. Pre-list.

40. What are three advantages claimed for the autographic register?

41. List the important factors that could be considered when deciding between two specific machines, if the cost of both machines is competitive.

42. Explain what is accomplished by having and making use of each of two registers in a multiple-purpose accounting machine, and cite one thing that is not assured by having used the two registers.

43. Contrast the concepts involved in "direct proof" to those in "zero proof."

44. What is "package proof" and what is its special function?

45. The posting cycle for a two register listing-adding machine is shown after posting the second document of a batch of 50 February 4 charges to the account of Mr. Lee Jones:

Account   Tape

Lee Jones		624 North Street South					
Old Balance	Date	Folio	Debits	Credits	New Balance		
	Feb. 1		800.00		800.00s	423.60—	23.60
800.00	Feb. 4	2111	28.00		828.00s	800.00—	28.00

a. Identify the posting cycle.
b. How would the above system differ if a single register listing-adding machine had been used?
c. What special machine feature is used when the folio is entered? To enable the separate tape?
d. What proof method is used in the above illustration and how does it apply to the above illustration?
e. How would an error be located if discovered after posting the entire batch?
f. State the two things the proof method really proves in the above illustration.
g. State what the proof method does not prove in the above illustration.

CHAPTER 6

Human Factors in Systems Design

INTRODUCTION

THE PEOPLE COMPONENT OF A FINANCIAL INFORMATION SYSTEM IS THE ONLY essential component. People alone are able to collect, process, and communicate data and information without the assistance of communication media, data originating and processing devices, or reports. Nevertheless, due to the complexity of even the smallest business, a situation where a person is the sole component of a financial information system is rarely found. Not only are people the only essential component, they are the most difficult component for the systems analyst to work with and control. Their behavior, personalities, experiences, ability to get along, need for training, willingness to work, and other such factors determine to a large extent the manner in which a system will function. Thus it is obvious that people must be a basic factor in the design of a system. People must bridge procedural gaps at systems control and decision points. It is pointless to design an outstanding system if it won't work in the situation or with the people whom management has decreed.

The human factors principle of systems design governs the people component of the financial information system as follows:

> The system should be designed consistent with applicable human factors, since people are responsible for the effectiveness of the system.

What are the "applicable human factors" that must be considered in the design of a system? Can they be identified? If identified, can a system be designed so they can be taken into account adequately? The variable of people—with their weaknesses and strengths—must be considered in the design of a system. The people problems of systems design are the most difficult. Finding solutions to the people problems clearly separates the outstanding systems analyst from others.

The design of a system is an art that is increasingly complex and strewn with pitfalls. This is especially true when a major systems overhaul is to be undertaken. The human factors principle has far-reaching implications on design. The term *human factors* includes all of those personality traits which consciously or subconsciously shape the actions and reactions of the people who must use the system as finally designed, as well as those same traits reflected in the systems analyst himself and which may affect his own ability to achieve objectively an efficient and successful design. The traits which affect the behavior of human beings are many and varied and only the more significant ones can be explored here as they particularly affect systems design. Some factors such as competence and the related selection and training, resistance to the new and strange, desire for job security, concern for displaced employees, tendency to be influenced by the opinions of others, and preference for familiar work habits are basic in all employees at all levels, but may apply with more force or in a different way with certain types of employees. Other factors become a problem only with certain groups.

ORIGINAL VS. REVISION DESIGN

In Chapter 2, when the human factors principle was introduced, it was noted that there was a difference in applicability of human factors between original design engagements and revision design engagements. In original design the systems analyst can be theoretical and independent of major human relations problems until such time as the system has to be implemented. Problems with people are first encountered as a part of planning for personnel to man the system and for their training to implement the system. Original design represents a relatively small part of all system design work. Revision design is different in many respects from the highly theoretical original design. In revision design people are already at work performing in existing positions, and their abilities, strengths, and limitations are not theoretical considerations, but are facts that must be considered. Revision design must deal with the individual actually performing or supervising existing procedures, and constitutes an important part of a systems engagement. Most systems design work is revision to some extent. Realistic design cannot proceed far without answers to the people problems.

THE DIFFERING IMPACT OF SYSTEMS CHANGES

Systems changes involve people and, consequently, changes do not always have the same effect. Sometimes they may be beneficial to one or a group of the people involved, while at other times they may be harmful. In some instances all seems well in the aftermath of the wholesale revamping of data processing methods, and in some situations it is reported that on the whole the employees are happy with their new jobs, feel that they have generally benefited themselves and the system, and that no hardship of any duration was visited upon anyone.[1] In other instances there appears to be employee disillusionment with the new jobs because the revised system caused the elimination of many promotional opportunities formerly available; complaints of being "chained to the machine" and empire building by a new elite of EDP; stagnation of middle-management; and other adverse effects.[2]

In recent economic recessions many of the trade unions, and in some instances the public itself, have tended to project the image of automation and other data processing methods as being one of the principal causes for unemployment. Some have even proposed that automation and data processing revisions be stopped altogether in order to prevent the resulting unemployment.[3] Congressional hearings have given both proponents and opponents of automation a sounding board, but seem to have resulted in no satisfactory answer.

Within the ranks of management, including systems analysts and personnel managers, there is a division of opinion as to the actual effect on employee wage levels, job security, advancement, and morale of the many changes which are taking place in both factory and office as a result of changes in procedures, work simplification, elimination of manual methods of data handling, and the advent of high-speed communication. These changes are not confined to those companies installing computers but are merely magnified and made more apparent in the latter case.

There is a need for extensive advance planning for any major procedural or data processing change. Advance provision should be made for combating

---

[1] Hardin, Einar, "The Reaction of Employees to Office Automation," *Monthly Labor Review*, September, 1960, p. 925.

[2] Blum, Albert A., "Electronic Data Processing and the Office Worker," *Data Processing*, June, 1961, p. 11. *Also see* Hoos, Ida R., "When the Computer Takes Over the Office," *The Harvard Business Review*, July, 1960, pp. 102–112.

[3] Carlos, William G., "Automation in Theory and Practice," *Business Topics*, Autumn, 1960, p. 7. *Also see Automation and Unemployment*, Washington: Economic Research Department, Chamber of Commerce of the United States, 1961; and "Saved Labor: Union Management Powder Keg With Lighted Fuse," *Factory*, October, 1960, p. 102.

any harmful impact of systems change on the people affected, as well as to take into account in the design the effect of human factors upon the operation of an economical and efficient system.

One of the greatest challenges to the effectiveness of the work of the systems analyst is the potential conflict between the need for change by the business and the resistance to change by its employees. As the business tries to adapt to changing conditions, its employees are required to accept new patterns of thought, new work routines, and new social relationships. Frequently, the psychological discomforts created by the new conditions cause good employees, regardless of position, to resist necessary changes. One of the major tasks of a systems analyst is to reduce this resistance by bringing order and understanding to the process of change. To do this successfully, an analyst must have not only a grasp of the technical needs and resources of the business, but also a sound understanding of the basic principles of psychology and the current focus of human factors as well. More specifically the analyst must understand people and must be able to develop good human relations.

While there is no general agreement as to what constitutes an adequate understanding of psychology, there are two concepts which can bring the area into focus. These concepts are *motivation* and *learning*.

Motivation

The concept of motivation is that every human experience involves a causation factor and an effect from that cause. Cause-and-effect relationships in human behavior imply that every motive produces some effect and that every response or effect is preceded by a motive. Motivation, as an activating force, affects every area of human behavior. Its field of influence ranges from the directing of a simple act, the motive of which is obvious, to a complex, formal activity pattern, e.g., career behavior, which represents numerous detailed aspects of motivation.[4]

One list of essential motivating causes includes the following: (1) the urge arising from bodily needs; (2) the urge to succeed and to achieve; (3) the urge to avoid failure and disappointment; (4) the urge for recognition and approval; (5) the urge for sympathy and affection; (6) the urge for security; (7) the urge to experience the new and the different; and (8) the sex urge.[5]

The systems analyst must be aware of these motivating forces and should use the knowledge of these forces in carrying out his assignments. Each one

---

[4] Lester D. and Alice Crow, *Understanding Our Behavior* (New York: Alfred Knopf Publishing Co., 1956), pp. 53–54.

[5] *Ibid.*, pp. 60–67.

of the motivating forces above can play a part in carrying through a systems engagement to a successful conclusion. To emphasize this point consider the following situations in which a systems analyst had to give some thought to these forces.

CONFLICT OF MOTIVATION. In order to increase the efficiency of processing receiving reports a systems analyst recommended, among other things, that the receiving departments be relocated nearer the receiving dock and the inspection department. The recommendation was accepted and the receiving department was relocated in the receiving dock area. Within a short time after the move the supervisor of the receiving department complained that he could not see much improvement in efficiency. He also expressed his concern over the morale of his employees. It seemed to be much lower at the new location. In looking into the problem the systems analyst discovered that the womens' rest room was located a good distance from the new receiving department quarters and to get there the ladies in the department had to run a "gauntlet" of men in the inspection department and in one factory department. Discomfiture caused by this arrangement was the root of the morale problem. Once rest room facilities were provided adjacent to the receiving department the morale problem disappeared and efficiency reached the level expected when the move was approved. In this instance the analyst either overlooked or failed to weigh sufficiently the human factors problem. It can be seen too that the problem arose from a conflict of motivating forces, the urge arising from bodily needs on the one hand and the urge for sympathy and affection on the other. The ladies could not avoid the use of rest room facilities and they did not like the lack of sympathy and understanding on the part of the "gauntlet" of men through which they passed to reach the facilities.

FRUSTRATION. Everyone possesses the motivating urge to succeed and to avoid failure. In redesigning a system in whole or in part the systems analyst must be aware of these forces. His efforts would be seriously jeopardized if suggested changes reflected unduly on the competence of certain employees, and if these same employees were to be expected to carry out the revised operations. The systems analyst can avoid frustrating these basic motivating urges if he is aware of their existence and adjusts his approach when dealing with employees. For example, a systems analyst discovered, while on an assignment involving the investigation of the entire accounting system for a moving van company, that the normal journalizing and posting of transactions and manual preparation of payroll data was extremely inefficient. In recommending that a multiple-purpose bookkeeping machine be installed with all of the attendant changes in forms and procedures, he neglected to discuss this with the bookkeeper who had been with the company for several years and had been considered a very competent person. The bookkeeper reacted vigorously in opposing the recommendation chiefly because he had assumed that the recommendation made by the analyst was a direct disparagement of his ability. The urge to succeed and to avoid failure was being frustrated.

USING MOTIVATIONS. One of the principle motivating forces with which a systems analyst must deal is the urge for recognition and approval. Invariably when personnel are consulted and their opinions given thoughtful consideration, changes to be effected by the systems analyst become joint projects. A very effective approach which utilizes this urge and the urge to experience the new and the different in a positive way could be called the *team approach*. In most systems modification, more than one person and more than one department are involved. In lieu of attempting to make the complete systems analysis, synthesis, and implementation and follow-up himself, a systems analyst will often enlist the help of a representative from each department to be affected. This is the team approach. Results from the group will be workable compromises which help in the acceptance of changes by all departments involved because one of their representatives helped draft the solution. It can be safely said that this approach can assist in offsetting deleterious affects from all of the motivating forces. By using this approach the analyst is permitting various human urges to be expressed and solutions found, rather than ignoring the psychological reaction of the people in a system and in most instances dooming his efforts to failure.

Learning

Two sources define learning as follows:

(1) . . . a process of adaptation. Through the process of learning, men acquire new ways of behaving or performing in order that they can make better adjustment to the demands of life.[6]

(2) . . . learning is shown by a change in behavior as a result of experience.[7]

In most assignments undertaken by a systems analyst, the degree of success experienced by him is directly dependent on how well the personnel understand the new procedures and methods which have been installed. Effective teaching can only be accomplished if the teacher understands the concept of learning.

Lee J. Cronbach discusses "seven elements in behavior." If we are to accept Professor Cronbach's definition, (2) above, that learning is a change in behavior, careful consideration of these "seven elements in behavior" is most appropriate.

---

[6] G. Lester Anderson and Arthur I. Gates, "The General Nature of Learning," *National Society for the Study of Education—Forty-Ninth Yearbook, Part I, Learning and Instruction* (Chicago: University of Chicago Press, 1950), p. 16.

[7] Lee J. Cronbach, *Educational Psychology*, (2nd. ed.), in consultation with Ernest R. Hilgard and Willard R. Spalding, (New York: Harcourt, Brace & World, Inc., 1963), p. 71.

The elements in behavior are as follows:

1. *Situation.* The situation presents alternatives requiring choice.

2. *Personal characteristics.* A person's abilities and attitudes limit the ways in which he can respond.

3. *Goal.* The person sees some possibility of acting on the situation so as to gain satisfaction.

4. *Interpretation.* The person interprets the situation.

5. *Action.* The person takes whatever action he expects will lead to the greatest net satisfaction.

6. *Consequence: confirmation or contradiction.* The response is followed by consequences which confirm or contradict the person's interpretation.

7. *Reaction to thwarting.* If a response does not satisfy the person's wants, we say that he is blocked or thwarted. He may reinterpret and try a new response. He may decide that his goal cannot be reached. If he doubts that he can reach his goal, he is likely to become emotionally upset.[8]

At this point, the intimate relationship between the concept of motivation and the concept of learning should be obvious. The concept of motivation contains the urges that spur individuals toward goals. The concept of learning is the change in behavior that results from experiences. Consider further some of the elements of behavior as they relate to systems design.

SITUATION. *"The situation consists of all the objects, persons, and symbols in the learner's environment. Experience in one situation prepares a person to respond to similar situations in the future."*[9] If a systems analyst is aware that the situation in which certain employees have found themselves during their normal working hours has an affect on their behavior patterns both currently and with those patterns the analyst would like to see them move toward, the analyst is in a better position to judge what affect new or revised data processing procedures will have on these employees. Employees, who have been taught that systems changes are good and that there is a vicarious thrill in experiencing new and more efficient data processing procedures, will choose the new and the different when they are confronted with the new or revised set of procedures. Employees who have been encouraged to resist change, either actually or implicitly by their employer, normally resist systems changes before listening to the merits of the proposal. The systems analyst must recognize or discover the experience level that he must work with during his engagement.

During a systems investigation at a fairly large medical clinic in the midwestern part of the United States a systems analyst recognized that employees were not reluctant to try new and different procedures. The reason for this stemmed from the fact that the clinic management did an excellent

---

[8] *Ibid.,* p. 69.

[9] *Ibid.*

job of employee training. Employee goals were very effectively tied to company goals. Due to the fact that the employees had been exposed many times to new and different situations and had been expected to choose alternatives which advanced their own goals as well as the company's, one could say that these employees were in a personal state of readiness for the new procedures recommended. Unfortunately, this type of situation exists in too few organizations.

PERSONAL CHARACTERISTICS. Personal characteristics refer to *"all the abilities and all the typical responses that the person brings to the situation."*[10] Personal characteristics actually relate to a frame of mind of the individual and to what he has already learned from previous experience.

The approach that the systems analyst used in the example given under "Goals," below, in which he convinced the laborers through their supervisors that the new labor reporting procedure was necessary, would have been doomed to failure had not the men in each department learned through prior experience that cooperation with their boss was far more beneficial than opposition or disobedience. These men were *ready* to be convinced by their foremen that the new procedure was necessary.

Quite frequently the systems analyst must study the personnel in a department which is to be affected by a new or revised procedure and to determine if their personal characteristics place them in a state of readiness to accept the suggested change. In some cases he will be required to create certain experiences for the employees in order to get them into the necessary state of readiness.

The element of personal characteristics in human behavior often needs special attention by the systems analyst in situations where increased mechanization of the data processing system is being recommended. Employees who have not been sufficiently introduced to the idea of working in a data processing system centered around an electronic computer, for example, often resist the proposed innovation because they are not personally ready to embrace the new concepts and the new approach to data processing made possible by the computer. A major portion of the work of the systems analyst is to get employees ready to accept the highly mechanized system so that they can learn to operate the system properly. Many system revisions or new installations have been set back or could not be effected because the systems analyst did not recognize personal characteristics as an element of human behavior and failed to give sufficient weight to the human factor in a systems engagement.

GOALS. Goals can either be proximate or remote. To an employee, a proximate goal may be the finishing of a particular work assignment. A remote goal may be self-advancement. The employee has been led to believe that good works will be rewarded by professional advancement. Another proximate

---

[10] *Ibid.*, p. 73.

goal may be the employee's desire to finish so that he could leave early to attend a twilight double-header baseball game.

The systems analyst, if he is to initiate and maintain effective employee learning processes, must be able to create attainable goals for the employees involved in the data processing system. For example, in a job shop manufacturing plant it is imperative that the time spent on each job be accurately reported if the direct labor cost per job is to be computed. If direct laborers are being asked to report their time in this way for the first time something more than just instructions must be issued to them. A goal must be created. They must see in their own way that a worthwhile goal is being reached. In one manufacturing plant the systems analyst talked first with the foremen of the various direct labor departments involved, convincing them that his request would lead to more meaningful information that would not only help general management but would have beneficial results for the foremen as well. Those foremen who were convinced that their ultimate goal of self-advancement would be helped by this change in procedure became staunch allies of the systems analyst. Those that could not translate this change immediately into a worthwhile personal goal had to be approached differently by the analyst. He had to probe and to find the correct argument which would convince these foremen that the proposed change was necessary and worthwhile. Once the immediate on-line supervisors of the direct laborers had accepted the new procedure some time was given to them so that they could convince the men under them that the change was necessary. Many of the foremen relied quite heavily on the urge to succeed and to avoid failure. Once the men became aware that the successful completion of accurate time tickets was a means to success most resistance to the new procedure ceased. The new procedure became a worthwhile goal.

INTERPRETATION. *"Interpretation is a process of directing attention to parts of the situation, relating them to past experience, and predicting what can be expected to happen if various actions are taken."*[11] It is important to know that once the learner is confronted with a situation he will make certain interpretations based on previous experience while trying to predict what he can expect to happen if certain alternatives are taken. In any systems engagement, changes in routine will be proposed to certain employees. Depending on how the employees interpret these changes, they will either be convinced that the changes are worthwhile or they will be opposed to them. If the systems analyst has a sufficient depth of understanding human behavior, his presentation of proposed changes will permit favorable interpretation of the proposals.

On one systems engagement the analyst discovered that a certain department supervisor interpreted most problems or situations by asking himself

---

[11] *Ibid.*

this question: "Which alternative will make me look the best—to my boss and to my people?" Upon discovering this outlook the systems analyst utilized an interesting approach. One problem which had to be solved in this part of the engagement was the redesign of a customer charge ticket which could be used more effectively by the accounts receivable clerks and accounting machine operators. The analyst spent most of his time helping the supervisor redesign this document. When the task was completed *all* of the credit for the new form design was given to the supervisor. There was no question about the acceptance of this form when the new procedures were installed. The supervisor convinced his people that far more benefits would accrue to the department through the new procedure than through the continuation of the old. In this instance the analyst is credited with presenting the situation properly so that the desired interpretation was made from it.

ACTION. *"The person's actions include movements and statements; they are observable responses. A person chooses whatever action he expects to give him the greatest satisfaction."*[12] In the example above both interpretation and action were illustrated. The supervisor not only interpreted the use of the new form properly but also responded to or acted on an alternative in the situation by convincing his subordinates that this was a desirable change.

In some respects the element of action in human behavior is dependent on the other elements. If certain facts are known about the status of the other elements with regard to a particular individual the kind of action that he will take can quite often be predicted. In recommending a proposed systems innovation the analyst can be reasonably sure that it will be received favorably if he has done a good job in preparing the individuals affected by this innovation. If acceptable goals have been outlined for them; if they have a proper state of personal readiness to accept this change; and if the situation has been presented properly so that the desired interpretations will be made, the systems analyst should be able to expect a favorable response.

CONSEQUENCES. *"Some events that follow the action are regarded by the learner as the consequence of it."*[13] This element, too, is contributory to being able to predict or expect certain actions. The learner inevitably predicts consequences of certain actions that he is about to take. When consequences are favorable this assists the learner in choosing alternative courses of action when a similar situation is presented to him. Employees who have had favorable experiences when working with a systems analyst are far more willing to work again with him. Employees who have had no experience in this regard tend to be a bit hesitant and "standoffish" until they are motivated and willing to accept this new experience as part of their learning process.

An absolute must for a successful systems analyst is to see to it that the

---

[12] *Ibid.*, p. 74.
[13] *Ibid.*

consequences of his proposals are salutary. To be assured of this result the analyst must have the support of top management. Employees must see that they have the support of management and from past experience they should be able to see that cooperation is far more beneficial to them than opposition or rejection of new proposals. New proposals must be beneficial in terms of the employees' long- and short-run goals.

REACTION TO THWARTING. *"Thwarting occurs when the person fails to attain his goals."*[14] Up to this point in the discussion of the elements of human behavior little doubt has been expressed that the systems analyst could, in every instance, create proper goals, induce a proper state of personal characteristics, and present the situation so that the proper interpretation will be made and desired action will be taken. Unfortunately this is not always the case. Systems analysts are as imperfect as anyone else in properly utilizing the various elements of human behavior. All actions do not result in favorable consequences for the employees who must accept new procedures and must be taught how to use them nor are consequences always favorable for the analyst himself.

Usually when an individual is thwarted one of two reactions takes place. If his first response has been thwarted, he may reassess the situation and try another action or he may give up and refuse to respond at all (nonadaptive). A successful systems analyst should never be guilty of the latter reaction to thwarting. He should believe "that the mountain can be moved," and act accordingly.

Another problem presents itself, however, when a nonadaptive action is encountered by the systems analyst in dealing with individuals who will be responsible for effecting the new or revised procedures which are being recommended. How should this be handled? In the final analysis, if the new procedures have been approved by management, nonadaptive employees must be reassigned in, or separated from, the company. By all means this should be resorted to only if the individual's reaction to thwarting is definitely nonadaptive.

One systems analyst related the following situation. He had been asked by the owners of a small trucking company to review the system to see if a more mechanized system were feasible. After doing everything that he could from a human relations point of view, he was not able to convince the bookkeeper that she could learn to operate a general purpose accounting machine. When this person realized that her employer was convinced that the more mechanized procedures should be installed and that her resistance would not forestall the change, she asked to be relieved of her duties. The company was sorry to see her react this way but was instrumental in placing here in another firm in the same city.

---

[14] *Ibid.*

FOCUSING ON HUMAN FACTORS
IN THE ENTERPRISE

In addition to a basic understanding of motivating urges and the elements of learning behavior, the systems analyst must investigate and determine the human relations climate that will affect the system or part of a system that is being studied. This investigation is essential if he is to apply what he knows about motivation and learning. Figure 6-1 is a fairly complete *check list of various human factors* which affect three levels of company employees. It has always been recognized that during the implementation of a new or revised financial information system, adaptations and revisions were often necessary to accommodate problems not previously foreseen, including some problems caused by human factors. This will continue to be true. But by applying the human factors principle of system design the analyst has an opportunity to take into account any such adaptations prior to the implementation stage. Proper consideration of the human factors in the company should assure a better design, greater acceptance by the employees, and a more efficient operation when the new system is in use.

Utilization of the human factors check list in Figure 6-1 can be very beneficial to the systems analyst at each step in a systems investigation. In using the check list, it should be noted that the division of points among top management, middle management, and nonsupervisory employees does not mean that a particular point applies only to the level of employee under which it is listed. "Resistance to the new and strange" is under nonsupervisory employees. This does not mean that top or middle management cannot be afflicted with this human factor. Sound use of the checklist demands that the points in each column be considered to apply more directly to the level of employee described at the top of the column, but should not be ignored when examining the human factors for other employee levels.

After completing the check list and the system design to reach conclusions about the human factors which seem to be apropos to the three levels of management, it is necessary to implement the system. Once implemented, the performance of the individual in each position that will be held by an employee in the new system must be determined. This more particular consideration of human factors is called personnel evaluation.

Personnel Evaluation

The systems analyst must be familiar with the concepts of motivation and learning in order to do a good job of dealing with the people from whom

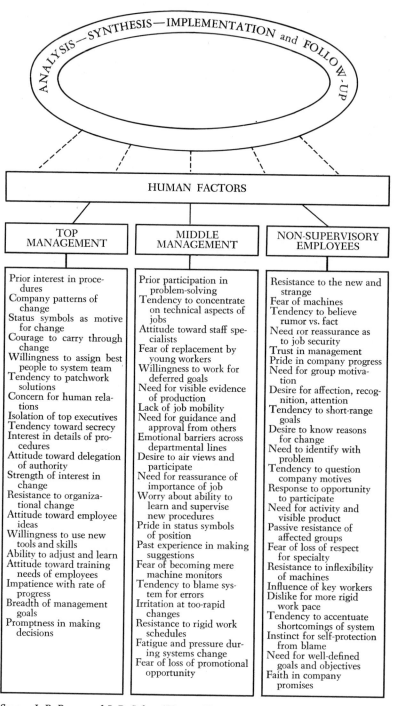

HUMAN FACTORS

TOP MANAGEMENT	MIDDLE MANAGEMENT	NON-SUPERVISORY EMPLOYEES
Prior interest in procedures	Prior participation in problem-solving	Resistance to the new and strange
Company patterns of change	Tendency to concentrate on technical aspects of jobs	Fear of machines
Status symbols as motive for change	Attitude toward staff specialists	Tendency to believe rumor vs. fact
Courage to carry through change	Fear of replacement by young workers	Need for reassurance as to job security
Willingness to assign best people to system team	Willingness to work for deferred goals	Trust in management
Tendency to patchwork solutions	Need for visible evidence of production	Pride in company progress
Concern for human relations	Lack of job mobility	Need for group motivation
Isolation of top executives	Need for guidance and approval from others	Desire for affection, recognition, attention
Tendency toward secrecy	Emotional barriers across departmental lines	Tendency to short-range goals
Interest in details of procedures	Desire to air views and participate	Desire to know reasons for change
Attitude toward delegation of authority	Need for reassurance of importance of job	Need to identify with problem
Strength of interest in change	Worry about ability to learn and supervise new procedures	Tendency to question company motives
Resistance to organizational change	Pride in status symbols of position	Response to opportunity to participate
Attitude toward employee ideas	Past experience in making suggestions	Need for activity and visible product
Willingness to use new tools and skills	Fear of becoming mere machine monitors	Passive resistance of affected groups
Ability to adjust and learn	Tendency to blame system for errors	Fear of loss of respect for specialty
Attitude toward training needs of employees	Irritation at too-rapid changes	Resistance to inflexibility of machines
Impatience with rate of progress	Resistance to rigid work schedules	Influence of key workers
Breadth of management goals	Fatigue and pressure during systems change	Dislike for more rigid work pace
Promptness in making decisions	Fear of loss of promotional opportunity	Tendency to accentuate shortcomings of system
		Instinct for self-protection from blame
		Need for well-defined goals and objectives
		Faith in company promises

Source: J. B. Bower and J. B. Sefert, "Human Factors in Systems Design," *Management Services* (November–December, 1965).

FIGURE 6-1. Focusing on Human Factors—A Check List

he must get much of his information about the current system under review in the *analysis* phase of a systems investigation. The concepts of motivation and learning also contribute to the work that the analyst must do in the *synthesis, implementation, and follow-up* phases of his assignment. The ability to convince employees that new methods are better than old and to be able to instruct employees properly in new assignments is extremely important.

During the analysis or fact-finding stage of a systems investigation the analyst must make certain value judgments about individual employees as to their ability to carry out their present work assignments and to rate each employee on his potential ability. Potential ability of employees cannot help but affect certain considerations of the analyst during the design or synthesis phase of his assignment. In a situation when employees may not have the ability to handle proposed procedures, it may not be possible to recommend the installation of the new procedures unless suitable employees can be found.

DESCRIPTION. The personnel evaluation which must be done by the systems analyst has two aspects. First, the job which is being done and which is under review must be described properly. Some thought must also be given to possible changes in the current job description and to new jobs which may be introduced as part of the revised system. Second, present employees must be evaluated with regard to how well they carry out the jobs currently assigned to them and as to their potential ability. These two aspects must be approached in that order.

It is difficult to evaluate employee performance or potential ability until existing and potential job descriptions have been carefully prepared. A job *description* is a summary of the results of a job analysis. A job analysis, in turn, is an intensive investigation of the parameters and composition of a particular job for which an employee will be given the responsibility to perform. More specifically:

> *Job analysis* is defined as the process of determining, by observation and study, and reporting pertinent information relating to the nature of a specific job. It is the determination of the tasks which comprise the job and of the skills, knowledge, abilities, and responsibilities required of the worker for successful performance and which differentiate the job from all others. . . .
>
> Basically there are but three parts to the analysis of any job: (1) The job must be completely and accurately identified; (2) the tasks of the job must be completely and accurately described; (3) the requirements the job makes upon the worker for successful performance must be indicated.[15]

---

[15] War Manpower Commission, *Training and Reference Manual for Job Analysis* (Washington: Government Printing Office, Bureau of Manpower Utilization, June, 1944), pp. 1–2.

Many times job descriptions are available to the systems analyst from the company's personnel department or from existing procedures manuals. However, it is often necessary for the analyst to prepare his own job descriptions.

EVALUATION AND DESIGN. Job descriptions are essential so the analyst can proceed to observe the job being performed, interview job supervisors, and to interview the employees themselves in order to determine for himself the extent to which the descriptions are being followed and to attempt to project the potential abilities of the employees under review.

Based on the ability potential determined in the fact-finding phase of his assignment, the analyst should be able to devise new or revised procedures, methods, and operations which are compatible with the abilities of the employees who will be assigned to carry out an improved system. To do this he must first work out revised job specifications and to fit employees into these revised jobs based on the ability level, both mental and physical, which was determined in the personnel evaluation made during the fact-finding phase of his engagement.

It is naive to think that the only objective that a systems analyst must work toward is the most efficient system possible for a compatible cost. Just as it is naive to think that old employees, who are not able to adjust to new skills necessary in revised systems, will be fired and new employees possessing the desired skills will be hired. If for no other reason (and there are many more) qualified employees are not always available for hire if old employees cannot handle the new procedures. Many times systems analysts are confronted with very large retraining jobs and even with the fact that a very efficiently conceived system must be modified to comply with restrictive personnel capabilities.

For example, a large midwestern hospital installed a complete punched card data processing system to handle almost all phases of their data processing needs. It was decided when the system was originally designed, that pre-punched and mark-sensed cards would be utilized as charge media and that these cards would be available at each nurse's station in the hospital. It was to be the nurses' responsibility to select the proper charge card when services were rendered to a patient, mark in a special way on the card the patient's identification number and the amount of the charge, and forward the charge cards to the data processing center. So many mistakes were made by the nurses, such as selecting the wrong charge card or improperly recording the patient's identification number, that the punched cards were removed from the nurses' stations and the nurses were asked to report charges as they had done prior to the new system. Once the manually produced charge slips were received in the data processing center, cards were punched and verified in a very extensive conversion operation from the media received from the nursing floors.

For one reason or another the personnel in the above example could not or would not cope with the new procedures. The systems analyst has a chance if the employees tend to resist the proposed change by embracing a "would not" attitude. If employees do not embrace new procedures an alternative open to an analyst may be procedure revision to coincide with the characteristics or ability level of the employees who will be responsible for operating the proposed procedures.

Systems Analysts are Human Too

Given an opportunity to comment, employees have accused systems men variously of having a narrow perspective, a tendency toward isolation, talking in a language incomprehensible to the ordinary person, cutting across lines of authority, empire building, and of stirring up jurisdictional disputes.[16] Some are said to be automatically against any methods in use before they arrived on the scene and to set themselves by instinct against the *old* in favor of the *new*.

The natural suspicion with which an *expert* is often viewed as he comes into a department to begin an analysis of work flows and procedures, makes it all the more necessary that he handle his job in a manner which will establish, as quickly as possible, a relationship of cooperation which will lead to later acceptance and support of any changes he proposes. Among the more important desirable qualities in a systems analyst are humility, a realization that his mission is one of service and not an end in itself, and a genuine interest in people. He should be a good listener, be willing to accept suggestions and to analyze them objectively, and to give due credit to the employee for any ideas adopted.

The advent of electronic data processing and the necessity of combining together, in management and operating teams, persons of technical training and scientific background with those having only operating experience, has compounded the problems of human relations in the systems field. Often the specialized and scientific personnel are accused of setting themselves apart from the regular organization, of adopting a tough attitude, and of showing a tendency toward a philosophy that human frailties are a nuisance and are best handled by the installation of more equipment.[17] These allegations have brought quick denials from systems people, machine accountants, and the scientists, who counter with evidence of their concern for the human being in the machine age. Emotionalism has entered the picture and made an objective determination of the facts more difficult.

The fact that the systems analyst himself recognizes the problem which human factors in others cause in his work makes it all the more important for

---

[16] Davis, Keith, *Human Relations in Business* (New York: McGraw-Hill Book Company, Inc., 1957), pp. 81–84.

[17] Hoos, *loc. cit.*

him to analyze critically his own methods. He must determine if any of the difficulties he may encounter in securing cooperation and acceptance from employees may stem from his own failure to practice good human relations. Like Caesar's wife, he should be above reproach.

SUMMARY

People are an essential part of any data processing system. No matter how heavily mechanized data processing systems become, people will be part of these systems and will present a series of problems to systems analysts far different from those they must ponder and solve regarding communication media and machines, which are also essential physical elements of a data processing system.

The systems analyst must be aware of and understand two important concepts of psychology—the concept of motivation and the concept of learning. The concept of motivation embraces the idea that every human experience involves a causation factor and an effect from that cause. One source maintains that there are eight essential motivating causes: (1) the urge arising from bodily needs; (2) the urge to succeed and to achieve; (3) the urge to avoid failure and disappointment; (4) the urge for recognition and approval; (5) the urge for sympathy and affection; (6) the urge for security; (7) the urge to experience the new and different; and (8) the sex urge. The systems analyst must be aware of these motivating forces and should use the knowledge of these forces in carrying out his assignments.

The concept of learning centers around the idea that ". . . learning is shown by a change in behavior as a result of experience." Since a good deal of the effort put forth by a systems analyst is in the area of teaching, it is imperative for the systems analyst to understand the various elements of human behavior which are the basic aspects of learning. These seven aspects of learning as conceived by one eminent educational psychologist are: (1) situation; (2) personal characteristics; (3) goals; (4) interpretation; (5) action; (6) consequences—confirmation or contradiction; and (7) reaction to thwarting. The seven aspects function in this way—every individual strives for goals. His previous experience has prepared him in certain ways to be personally ready for new experiences. When new situations are presented to him, he will interpret this new situation and respond in such a way that he concluded he should respond based on the consequences that he has experienced in similar situations before. Previous consequences in similar situations brought him closer to his goals and thereby increased his personal readiness to accept the new situation. However, favorable consequences do not always result and the individual is said to be thwarted.

The systems analyst must concentrate on teaching employees to accept and to operate new procedures in such a way that none of them feels that he has been thwarted. He must also be realistic enough to know that this ideal cannot always be attained and should give sufficient thought of ways to turn employees away from nonadaptive behavior.

In addition to a working knowledge of the concepts of motivation and learning, the systems analyst must also be able to evaluate effectively the employees who are operating the system under review. He must be able to envision the types of people that he will need in the revised system. Extensive job analyses, accompanied by appropriate job descriptions, must be obtained for the old system and for the new system. Once the analyst has established the ability levels necessary to operate the existing system and projected, somewhat, personnel needs for planned revisions, he is in a position to judge the limits which he must work within, which have been placed there by personnel constraints. It is not possible to operate a data processing system without people.

QUESTIONS, PROBLEMS, AND CASES

1. A part of the human factors principle of systems design is the availability of competent personnel to bridge procedural gaps at systems control points where judgment is required. Explain and give an example.

2. The majority of systems work is revision design. Of what significance is this in relation to the human factors principle?

3. Two motivating causes are the urge to succeed and to achieve and the urge for recognition and approval. What is the impact of these motivations on the work of a systems analyst?

4. Three elements of behavior are interpretation, consequences, and reaction to thwarting. What is the significance of behavior to the systems analyst? Explain and illustrate for each element.

5. It has been said that most established companies have patterns of activities which determine their approach to new ideas and innovations. Discuss.

6. You are on a systems investigation that requires a great amount of work. You have asked top management for more help on the investigation, and have been assigned a new employee as an assistant. You have also requested a project team to work along as needed. Due to several apparently valid reasons, you have been told to work with the executive vice-president. Discuss the implication of the situation in which a new employee is assigned to your investigation, and the denial of a project team. Would you take any action by way of discussing either your new assistant or failure to obtain a project team with the president? Explain.

7. Go to Figure 6-1 and select three of the human factors at each organization level. Explain and illustrate how each relates to the design of a system.

8. Explain and illustrate the way in which the following personality traits relate to the design of a system:
   a. Resistance to the new and strange.
   b. Desire for job security.
   c. Concern for displaced employees.
   d. Tendency to be influenced by the opinions of others.
   e. Ability to get along with others.
   f. Willingness to work.

9. It has been stated that automation and other data processing methods are one of the principal causes for unemployment. Comment. What is the implication in the design of a specific system?

10. As a systems analyst it is necessary to design and implement a system that will resolve the conflict between the need for change and the resistance to change by employees. How can the problem be approached by the systems analyst? Discuss.

11. There are often conflicts of motivations arising in the design of a new procedure or system. Give several examples other than the one in the text of the way in which motivations may be in conflict so as to affect the design of a system.

12. The urge to succeed and to avoid failure is often a strong motivating force in a system. Discuss and give examples of the way in which the design of the system can be affected by this motivating force.

13. The situation or situations within the learning experiences of an individual are important in the application of the human factors principle. Discuss and illustrate.

14. Personal characterstics in human behavior are especially important when increased automation is being recommended. Discuss and illustrate.

15. You are in the process of the design of a payroll procedure in a manufacturing concern. You plan to design a system that will provide both proximate and remote goals for the employees who will be responsible for the functioning of the system. Explain your intent and illustrate how both proximate and remote goals can be relevant.

16. Interpretation has an important role in the design of a system. Discuss and illustrate.

17. Explain and contrast action and consequences as they relate to systems design.

18. What are the ramifications of thwarting to the systems analyst? Explain.

19. As a systems analyst you are in the process of designing a system involving the use of a management tool, namely the tool of return on investment. Use

Figure 6-1 and relate how top management human factors are applicable to your investigation.

20. As a systems analyst you are in the process of designing a new customer cycle billing procedure. Use Figure 6-1 and relate how the middle management human factors are applicable to your investigation.

21. As a systems analyst you are in the process of designing a system involving the control of tools as they are drawn from the tool crib by workers. Use Figure 6-1 and relate how the non-supervisory employee human factors are applicable to your investigation.

22. How does personnel evaluation relate to the design of a system?

23. It has been stated that the only objective of a systems analyst is to work toward the most efficient system compatible with reasonable cost. Discuss.

24. Mr. Bruce Bowman, a systems consultant, had been called in by the Meanwell Manufacturing Company to supervise the installation of a high speed accounting machine recently purchased for Accounts Receivable, Payroll, and Disbursements.

    The Meanwell Manufacturing Company has been in successful operation for twenty years as a manufacturer of a wide variety of finely machined products; pocket and table cigarette lighters, fishing reels, camera accessories, and gauges. For the past few years the company had devoted about 20 per cent of its capacity to a sub-contract for component parts of aircraft control systems.

    Mr. Harvey Arnold had founded the Meanwell Manufacturing Company and was still majority stockholder and president of the firm. In recent years he had slowly passed effective control to his son-in-law, Robert Tredwell, who carried the title of Vice-President in Charge of Operations. Mr. Arnold was proud of the company's record in the community as a "good place to work" and kept an open door for all employees of the firm.

    Mr. Tredwell had been responsible for the purchase of the accounting machine and was a personal friend of Bruce Bowman. Just prior to the following interview, Mr. Tredwell and Bruce Bowman had discussed at some length Mr. Bowman's suggestion that the company improve its system of internal control. Mr. Tredwell agreed that something should be done along this line but said that any decision regarding a better program of internal control would have to be made by Mr. Arnold.

    Accordingly, Bruce Bowman had the following conversation with Mr. Arnold in the latter's office.

    Bruce Bowman: "Mr. Arnold, in the course of the accounting machine installation which we are just now completing, I happened to notice many places in your operations where the system of internal control was not up to par."

    Mr. Arnold: "Internal Control? This is a new term to me, Mr. Bowman. What do you mean by 'Internal Control.'"

    Mr. Bowman: "Oh, its just a standard way of referring to some of the techniques that almost all companies use to make sure—as sure as possible, that is—that employees do not steal any of the money or merchandise they handle every day. It also involves ways of minimizing unintentional errors in the records."

Mr. Arnold: "And in what respects do you think our 'Internal Control' fails to do the job, Mr. Bowman?"

Mr. Bowman: "Well, I could give you several instances. For example, did you know that your accounting department authorizes credit memos on customers' accounts instead of the credit manager?" (Pause—Mr. Arnold nods his head slightly without making comment.) "Also, just yesterday while I was watching the issuance of payroll checks, I noticed that several of the factory employees walked right out of the back door to the parking lot without having their lunch boxes and coats checked by the guard at the main gate. They could have been taking home————"

Mr. Arnold: "I see what you are driving at now, Mr. Bowman, but I think you have the wrong slant on things. Most of our employees have been with us a long time, some since we started way back in 1946. A lot of them are personal friends of mine. I don't think any of them would steal from me."

Mr. Bowman: "Statistics show that most employees who are caught embezzling or stealing have worked for their victims for several years. In fact, the fellow who embezzles money would usually have to have been employed by the company for some time before he would be put in the position of trust where he *could* take advantage of the firm."

Mr. Arnold: "Well, I'll take my chances on the people we have working here. I have too much respect for most of them to insult them by looking through their lunchboxes or briefcases before they go home. Anyway, from a dollar-and-cents standpoint, it would probably be cheaper to let the factory people take something now and then—if it makes them feel better. Again, I don't think they would. I'm certainly not going to the expense of having a fence built around the parking lot and having another guard on duty there."

Mr. Bowman, getting up to leave: "Well, I wanted to meet you anyway. I really wasn't directly concerned with these things in the job I did for your company. I just felt it my duty to tell you about them before I left. (Pause) I hope the new machine works out for you. Please let me know if I can be of service to you again."

Mr. Arnold: "Good day, Mr. Bowman."

Discuss the human factors that relate to the above situation from the viewpoint of Mr. Harvey Arnold, Mr. Bruce Bowman, and Mr. Robert Tredwell.

CHAPTER 7

Internal Control*

INTRODUCTION

In 1949 the Committee on Auditing Procedure of the American Institute of Certified Public Accountants defined *internal control* in a pamphlet entitled, *Special Report on Internal Control*. This definition was reaffirmed in 1963 as follows:

> Internal control comprises the plan of organization and all of the co-ordinate methods and measures adopted within a business to safeguard its assets, check the accuracy and reliability of its accounting data, promote operational efficiency, and encourage adherence to prescribed managerial policies.[1]

Systems men have accepted this definition of internal control as being accurate and adequately descriptive. The auditor has not been well satisfied. The last two phrases of the internal control definition caused him difficulty from the start. The phrase to "promote operational efficiency, and encourage adherence to prescribed managerial policies" created many problems of interpretation. This was especially true in the light of one of the standards of audit field work which stipulates:

---

* Major portions of this chapter are based on the article by J. B. Bower and R. E. Schlosser, "Internal Control—Its True Nature," *The Accounting Review* (April, 1965).

[1] Committee on Auditing Procedure, *Auditing Standards and Procedures*, Statements on Auditing Procedure No. 33, American Institute of Certified Public Accountants, 1963, p. 27.

> There is to be a proper study and evaluation of the existing internal control as a basis for reliance thereon and for the determination of the resultant extent of the tests to which auditing procedures are to be restricted.[2]

If auditors were to be responsible for "a proper study and evaluation of existing internal control," exactly what and how much had to be done to preclude any legal liability? What was the responsibility for evaluation of internal control that was to promote operational efficiency and encourage adherence to prescribed managerial policies? While the definition of internal control was not to change, it seemed apparent that clarification was necessary if the auditor's responsibility was to be identified. Statement on Auditing Procedure No. 29, reaffirmed in Statement on Auditing Procedure No. 33, attempted to clarify the definition of internal control by identifying "accounting control" and "administrative control" as follows:

> In the broad sense, internal control includes, therefore, controls which may be characterized as either accounting or administrative, as follows:
>
> a. *Accounting controls* comprise the plan of organization and all methods and procedures that are concerned mainly with, and relate directly to, safeguarding of assets and the reliability of the financial records. They generally include such controls as the systems of authorization and approval, separation of duties concerned with record keeping and accounting reports from those concerned with operations or asset custody, physical controls over assets, and internal auditing.
>
> b. *Administrative controls* comprise the plan of organization and all methods and procedures that are concerned mainly with operational efficiency and adherence to managerial policies and usually relate only indirectly to the financial records. They generally include such controls as statistical analyses, time and motion studies, performance reports, employee training programs, and quality controls.[3]

Having differentiated between accounting controls and administrative controls, it could then be stated that the independent auditor is primarily concerned with the accounting controls because they bear directly on the reliability of financial records.

The concept of internal control needs still further refinement and a more specific identification of its true nature. The mild controversy which arose out of the 1949 definition and the later dichotomy of "internal control" into accounting controls and administrative controls has only clouded the issue. Re-examination of the original 1949 definition of internal control leads to the conclusion that it is sound and can be accepted by the systems analyst without modification or distinguishing between accounting and administrative controls.

---

[2] *Ibid.*

[3] *Ibid.*, p. 28.

Only the words *promote* and *encourage* in the last two phrases require explanation. Operational efficiency is "promoted" through the flow of adequate and appropriate reports from the financial information system to enable management to plan and take control action. Internal control does not encompass the managerial acts of either planning or control. Adherence to prescribed managerial policies is "encouraged" through a similar flow of adequate and appropriate management reports from the financial information system. The encouragement comes through full disclosure and reporting to emphasize adherence to policy. With these interpretations it seems evident that the AICPA-defined administrative controls are themselves not a part of internal control, although internal control contributes materially to them.

INTERNAL CONTROL AND THE FINANCIAL INFORMATION SYSTEM

The basic purposes of internal control are to bring *reliability* into the financial information system and to safeguard assets. Such a financial information system provides management with reliable and accurate financial information so necessary in business operations.

The true nature of internal control can be identified and observed in the setting of the financial information system. It is generally accepted that a financial information system can exist with little or no internal control. Nevertheless, it is often stated that the financial system can be strengthened by the addition of internal control. What must be done to strengthen the system in a situation in which internal control has not previously existed? The strengthening of a system is the direct result of adding internal control duties. *Internal control duties* are duties prescribed to safeguard assets and to make the system more reliable. Such duties reduce to a minimum the opportunities for people to make errors or to perpetrate various types of fraud and other improper actions.

Internal control duties are necessary because of the mental, moral and physical weaknesses inherent in people. Although not all persons are mentally, morally, or physically inept, they may suffer lapses. Internal control duties are, therefore, designed to protect against inadvertent or willful lapses on the part of people who have a role in the functioning of the financial information system. These duties are also designed to assist in the efficient and trustworthy discharge of stewardship. Management, stockholders, government, and others rely upon the information produced by the financial information system in their decision-making processes. Such information must be as reliable as possible, since business decisions are often only as good as information upon which they are based.

Without altering the meaning of the 1949 definition, we would suggest that the concept of internal control is more clearly expressed as follows:

Internal control comprises the plan of organization and all of the co-ordinate methods and measures adopted within a business to safeguard its assets *and* check the accuracy and reliability of *the information produced by the financial information system.*

The concept of internal control exists in the context of the financial information system, and should not be confused with other management controls embodied in the final phrases of the Institute's definition. It is evident that the financial information system contributes to effective *administrative control.* Such tools of administrative control as statistics, responsibility reports, and cost and budget variances are vital. It should be noted that the financial information system provides data and information necessary for the construction or use of many such tools. Internal control is involved to the extent of providing accurate and reliable data and information for planning and control, but does not include the managerial action that follows its use. Internal control relates to the financial information system and its components. To take effective action, management must also have information about internal factors not normally provided through the financial information system such as employee morale and individual abilities, as well as external factors such as products of competitors, conditions in the industry, and the economy as a whole.

All of the principles of systems design must be considered in the design of a system with good internal control, yet the three principles that are of the greatest importance are the reliability, organization structure, and human factors principles. The "plan of organization" and "co-ordinate methods and measures" that comprise internal control and that are effective through internal control duties draw primarily on these three principles.

The work of the systems analyst is to bring together the components of the system in the most effective manner possible to accomplish the systems objectives. The reliability principle governs the vital internal check feature of the system. *Internal check* is the assignment of duties so that accuracy and reliability are obtained through proof methods and controls at each step of the information flow. The organization structure principle governs the relationships between organization units and the assignment of duties between and within organization units to enable organizational independence, proper authority-responsibility relationships, and other control advantages. The human factors principle governs the role of the individual and such factors as his actions, ability, behavior, personal characteristics, learning, and motivation. The other principles relate to cost, the sequence and flow of information, and the design of the system to be useful and easy to work with; yet they highlight aspects of systems design other than reliability and accuracy. As principles of systems design are universal, none of them can be ignored in any context, yet in the design of the internal control features of a system, the reliability, organization structure, and human factors principles are of the greatest importance.

INTERNAL CONTROL DUTIES

The physical components of the financial information system, namely people, communications media, machines and devices, and reports are combined by processing operations and internal control duties to facilitate the collection and transformation of data into useful information. Regardless of how efficiently the system components and data processing operations were combined, a prudent person would not place much faith in the information produced by the system unless he could be certain that an acceptable minimum number of internal control duties are part of the system. Without internal control duties present in the system, there can be no internal control. There are seven basic internal control duties:

1. Supervision.
2. Clerical proof.
3. Acknowledging performance.
4. Transferring responsibility.
5. Protective measures.
6. Review.
7. Verification and evaluation.

It should be noted in the following discussion that internal control duties relate to the action of individuals and do not relate to components of the system themselves. A cash register as a component of a system, for example, contributes to internal control only when accumulators are used, or totals cleared by key, or when processing is in proper sequence. When internal control duties are added to use properly the devices that are a part of the financial information system, the optimum opportunity will exist to safeguard assets and provide accurate and reliable data and information.

On close examination, it is notable that internal control duties provide the plan of organization and co-ordinate methods and measures adopted within the business insofar as the financial information system is concerned. Each of the internal control duties is discussed below.

Supervision

Supervision is composed of all of the methods and measures normally used in direct surveillance of personnel and of the assets of the company.

In most cases supervising internal control duties are additional safeguarding measures. It is standard practice to recommend that the responsibility for opening mail receipts be given to a responsible mail clerk who is expected to list the name of the customer remitting and the amount. The list is turned over to the bookkeeper and the cash is turned over to the cashier, along with a copy of the list. The cash recorded by the bookkeeper must agree with the cash deposited by the cashier. In situations where mail receipts from customers are predominantly coin or currency an additional internal control activity may be warranted—supervision. If mail receipts consisting of coin and currency were opened in the presence of other employees and under the surveillance of a mail room supervisor, an additional measure of internal control is present.

A similar but more extreme example is the use of supervision as the only internal control duty. In the situation above cash or currency received on account can indirectly be controlled by the customer. If the proper amount has not been credited to a particular customer's account, the customer will usually call attention to the error. Coin or currency received via the mails for cash purchases, such as promotion items offered by the various breakfast cereal manufacturers, does not lend itself to indirect control. The supervisory employees in the mail room are responsible for the prime internal control activity over these receipts. Although supervision can be used effectively as the only internal control duty in a particular situation, it is more often used as an additional control activity. Other examples of supervision as an internal control duty are the collecting and counting of cash from parking meters, vending machines, telephones, etc., as a part of establishing the initial accounting control.

In smaller businesses supervisory measures must suffice as a primary form of internal control because it is often not feasible to divide duties which, for internal control purposes, would be deemed incompatible. For example, where all of the finance and treasury functions are performed by two individuals, reliance on supervision for internal control is far greater than in the case where the financial and treasury functions are carried out by separate departments, each containing many individuals.

Clerical Proof

Duties which are incorporated into data processing operations aimed at maintaining numerical accuracy can be called "clerical proof" duties. Double entry bookkeeping itself is considered to be an effective clerical proof measure. However, it is quite ineffective unless periodic trial balances and other proof measures are taken to make the bookkeeping procedures reliable.

In utilizing a manual cash disbursements journal, a bookkeeper normally foots the columns on each page and checks to see that the total of all debit columns equals the total of all credit columns prior to moving to the second page or to posting various column totals to general ledger accounts. If no discrepancy is found, further processing of this data can continue with assurance that the data up to this point in the system are in balance.

Batch proof used in conjunction with a multiple-purpose accounting machine is still another example of a clerical proof. Charges to customer accounts are often posted to these accounts—via an accounting machine—in batches. An adding machine tape of the total charges in a batch (pre-list) is prepared prior to delivering the group of charges to the machine operator. With proper machine procedures, total charges can be accumulated automatically as the batch is posted. At the end of the posting run, the total charges as accumulated by the machine should agree with the batch total prepared prior to posting. Clerical proofs should be installed wherever the cost of providing the proof is less than the cost of the undiscovered errors which would likely otherwise occur.

Acknowledging Performance

Another internal control duty is called acknowledging performance. In all data processing systems, people are responsible for the performance of the various operations which must be completed in order to collect, process, and communicate data and information. It has been pointed out many times in this text that the data and information communicated to management and to other interested parties are useful only if it is reliably accurate. Improper information will lead to improper decisions. It is reasonable, therefore, to require that responsible persons who collect or process data at earlier stages in the system *acknowledge* that their operations have been completed as prescribed.

A few examples of acknowledging performance may be helpful. It is standard practice to require that a clerk, who has been assigned the job of re-extending and refooting vendor invoices, initial each invoice as it is completed. A receiving report indicates that certain merchandise has been received and that it has been properly counted. An inspection ticket acknowledges that the goods received complied with specifications. Many times both of the latter documents are necessary before payments to vendors can be authorized.

Transferring Responsibility

Just as there is need in a complex information system for individuals to acknowledge formally that specific operations have been performed, it is also necessary to transfer formally responsibility for the custodianship of certain assets as these assets move through the enterprise. It was pointed out above that a receiving report is used to acknowledge performance. It also can be an effective device to transfer responsibility for assets. When the receiving clerk turns over the goods received to the storekeeper, the storekeeper is expected to sign two (or more) copies of the receiving report. By doing this the storekeeper formally acknowledges the receipt into his custody of the goods as described on the receiving report. If this were not done, subsequent discovery of shortages in this shipment could be traced either to the receiving clerk or to the storekeeper, but it could not readily be pinpointed to either of them.

Another example is in the handling and custodianship of cash. When a deliveryman, who is expected to collect for C.O.D. parcels, turns over his collections and undelivered parcels to his dispatcher, the dispatcher is expected to give the driver a receipt for the transfer.

Where large computer systems are in operation, a common use of transferring responsibility duties is in the handling of magnetic tape reels. Usually all program, transaction, and file tapes are under the custody of a "tape librarian." When the computer operators need certain tapes, they must go to the library and sign out for their use. When they are finished with the tapes, they must be returned to the library and checked in.

Protective Measures

It is assumed many times that the presence of locks, burglar alarm systems, security forces and the like, *ipso facto*, contribute to internal control. No physical device or security force itself can protect assets. A lock, for example, if never used does not give protection. Watchmen who do not patrol the premises are ineffective. For the raw materials of protection to be effective it is necessary to devise certain protective measures which govern their use. The measures surrounding their use and not the devices themselves constitute the essence of this internal control duty.

Again, an example may be helpful. A cash register is usually equipped with a continuous tape upon which all "rings" of the cash register are recorded. Access to this tape is only possible by key. Common sense should tell us that this key should not be given to one of the cashiers for safe keeping. If the key were given to a cashier it would be possible for that cashier to circumvent all of the protection which can be given by the proper use of a cash register.

Similarly ineffective would be the erection of a special tools storeroom which is accessible to everyone in the factory. Suitable protective measures would require that access to the storeroom be limited and that tools can be obtained only through a properly authorized request.

Review

The tendency of people to prefer their "own way" of doing things, to circumvent prescribed control duties, to omit or modify established procedures all require that some provision be included in the framework of internal control to discover whether various job assignments are performed satisfactorily. This essential duty of internal control is called *review*. Many would probably claim that *review* is merely a form of *supervision*. The authors submit there is a difference and that the regularity with which this internal control duty is performed and the specific attention given to it warrants special consideration.

KINDS OF REVIEW. Review which takes place before action is taken is *pre-view*. For example, the examination and correlation of documents supporting an accounts payable voucher is a form of *pre-review*. Review which takes place after an action has been taken is *post-review*. Examination of checks paid and returned by the bank and comparison with the documents supporting the disbursement is an example of *post-review*. The reader should note that review duties within a specific processing procedure usually contain both kinds of review. The voucher clerk in the example above performed *post-review* over the accurate processing of the documents up to his station, but was performing *pre-review* in regard to disbursement actions sequenced after his station.

Pre-review is useful as a means of preventing or stopping improper and/or unauthorized enterprise activities; it gives the enterprise an opportunity to veto or modify actions and/or transactions before they have been completed. Post-review, on the other hand, has only an indirect effect toward preventing transactions, but offers an excellent means of uncovering unauthorized or otherwise improper actions actually performed. The indirect influence of post-review toward preventing unauthorized transactions lies in the fact that one of the most effective deterrents to improper activities is knowledge that such activities will surely be discovered.

Regardless whether one is concerned with pre-review or post-review, two standards are common to both. The first standard is that the review be sufficiently thorough and complete to disclose errors, omissions, and other irregularities. This means that those who perform review functions must know the purpose of the review and must perform the activity conscientiously. The second standard is that the review must be independent. That is, the reviewer must (1) be free of any kind of control or other retaliatory action from the person reviewed, and (2) be free of any bias or self-interest, as far as practically possible, that might influence him to overlook errors or irregularities discovered. Unless these standards govern, reviews cannot be considered to contribute fully to internal control.

Verification and Evaluation

Verification and evaluation consist of the duties designed to substantiate the effectiveness of the various internal control duties. It is not enough merely to prescribe suitable internal control duties. Provisions must be made to insure that the duties themselves are functioning properly and are necessary. At this point the reader may be questioning the difference between the internal control duties "review" and "verification and evaluation." Although the duties are similar, the authors feel that sufficient difference exists to warrant a separate classification. By and large, "verification and evaluation" duties can be equated with "post-review." Nevertheless, the authors would limit the post-review duties to those performed as a part of the continuous processing of business data currently in the system. All other post-review duties, such as internal audit examination to establish the fact that procedures are followed as designed, would be part of verification and evaluation.

Effective internal control is predicated on the fact that internal control duties are being performed and that these prescribed duties are suitable to the circumstances. Whether performed by the internal audit department or by another unit of the company, verification and evaluation are an essential part of working internal control. For example, invoices are often batch totaled before being sent to a key punch section where sales analysis and/or accounts receivable cards are to be punched from the invoices. Clerical proof often requires that all cards punched should be run through an accounting machine (punched card tabulator) where the total sales for the batch are accumulated. This total must agree with the batch total run prior to punching before further processing should continue. Verification and evaluation duties are assigned to test this clerical proof duty to determine if the clerical proofs are being performed as prescribed. Prescribing an internal control duty is only one phase of the problem—the key is whether the internal control duty is actually performed as prescribed.

An invoice clerk is usually required to refoot and extend each vendor invoice prior to approving it for payment. The work of this employee is often tested in order to verify that the prescribed clerical proof duty is being performed conscientiously.

In addition to the verification of internal control duty, evaluation is also present. Rarely would one of the other internal control duties be tested for accuracy and compliance without being evaluated at the same time. Business conditions change, data processing procedures change, and frequently internal control duties should be modified accordingly. For example, it had been the policy of a certain department store to make a fairly extensive credit check on each new charge account customer. The firm's internal audit department during a routine test of this *pre-view* activity noted that none of the credit requests tested had been refused. Upon inquiry into the credit granting policies, it was discovered that credit policies had become liberal to the extent that almost no one would ever be refused credit. Since management decided that the liberal credit granting policies should not be changed—because losses were fully justified by resulting sales volume and profit—a recommendation was made to eliminate the useless review of credit applications. As is the case with most of the various kinds of internal control duties, verification and evaluation activities should be incorporated whenever the cost of carrying out these activities is less than potential losses which could result if the duty were omitted.

STANDARDS OF INTERNAL CONTROL

In the sections above, an endless string of examples could have been enumerated. For each example cited, an experienced systems analyst could have cited many more. A student will not remember many specific examples nor will his early business need for devising certain internal control duties often fit into these example situations. More important than examples are a set of *standards* against which the novice as well as the experienced analyst may measure his performance. Standards of internal control are minimum levels of achievement designed to assist in the determination of the acceptable degree of internal control activities. The authors contend that the following are acceptable statements of these standards:

1. Authority for the performance of all activities essential to internal control and responsibility for performance of such activities should be clearly established and specifically prescribed.

2. Proof measures should be incorporated into data processing operations whenever the cost of the proof measure is less than the effect of probable potential losses through errors or other irregularities.

3. Measures requiring acknowledgment of performance should be incorporated in data input and processing operations whenever material misstatements and frauds could arise if prior operations had not been performed properly.

4. Protective devices should be governed by measures which contribute to the effective use of the devices.

5. Transferring responsibility over custodianship of assets should be formally effected whenever material fraud or error is possible.

6. Actions, events, and transactions, both projected and completed, should be reviewed sufficiently to give reasonable assurance that transactions essential to enterprise objectives are effected and that unauthorized and otherwise irregular transactions are prevented or discovered.

7. The various kinds of internal control activities incorporated into a data processing system should be verified and evaluated periodically in order to provide the most effective internal control possible.

A first reaction, on reviewing these standards, may be that they are too general and too brief. Certainly they do not provide a check list of detailed internal control duties necessary in every set of circumstances. Yet in this very fact lies their chief usefulness. They apply to any enterprise of any size or degree of complexity. Thus they provide something of a universal standard. By omitting detail and restraining the phraseology to fundamentals, they aid in understanding the nature and purpose of internal control. They are not intended as an aid to memory but rather as a stimulant to the imagination. It is the task of the individual systems analyst, accountant, or manager to apply them in specific situations.

A Most Important Aspect of Standards. Not only is a standard a minimum level of achievement, but also it should be "a point of departure when variation is justifiable by the circumstances."[4] This idea is quite frequently overlooked by skeptics who maintain standards are not useful because they are set too high. If it could be established (which the writers strongly doubt) that minimum levels of achievement could not be designed and phrased properly so that they would be attainable universally, immeasurable assistance would still be possible for various managements not able for various reasons to comply with one or more of the internal control standards. All that would be necessary is a report simply to permit these managements to visualize the extent of their deviations from standards. Consider, for example, a hypothetical company which has a dynamic president. Formal organization charts define levels of responsibility. But, because of the dynamic quality of its president, certain acts of this individual override or impinge upon the authority and supervisory duties of certain subordinates. A properly informed board of directors will weigh the costs of permitting this infringement on a proper functioning of internal control with the benefits gained by the dynamic qualities of this individual. The board cannot make this decision unless it is using some kind of standard as a point of departure.

EVALUATING INTERNAL CONTROL

A good system requires provision for good internal control. This entails both (1) the design of an adequate system and (2) the system functioning as designed. The latter is often the most difficult to determine, and if the system is functioning, periodic assurance is necessary to make certain that there has been no change.

It is easy to understand why "internal control duties," which must be accomplished by individuals, could be designed into a system but fail to be operative as designed in actual practice. New employees are sometimes not

---

[4] A. C. Littleton, *Structure of Accounting Theory*, American Accounting Association, 1953, p. 143.

oriented properly, the pressure of getting a job done could cause a proof procedure to be skipped to save time and effort, or there could be a misunderstanding as to the purpose of an activity and an individual employee might take it upon himself to short-cut or ignore the control entirely. There are many reasons why well-designed systems involving internal control duties do not function as planned, even though the system design is adequate.

In the analysis phase of a systems engagement, the analyst must determine the specific nature of the system that is being followed, and whether the internal controls thought to be operative are in fact functioning. The internal auditor and external auditors have much the same problem in conducting their examinations. All must place reliance on the adequacy and effectiveness of internal control duties to determine the extent of the procedures it will be necessary for them to follow to satisfy themselves that the output of the system is reliable.

There are two tools that are used frequently in the analysis phase of a systems engagement to evaluate the existence or adequacy of internal control duties. The tools are (1) the internal control questionnaire and (2) the internal control write-up. Both tools serve a similar function. They assist the analyst to determine the adequacy of the functioning of the existing system by producing the factual basis of what is being done, and thus through analysis, disclose internal control weaknesses. In some instances, both internal control questionnaires and internal control write-ups can be used to advantage.

THE INTERNAL CONTROL QUESTIONNAIRE. The internal control questionnaire is designed to provide a comprehensive guide for the systems analyst or auditor to follow in determining the adequacy or inadequacy of internal control. Questionnaires are usually designed so that an affirmative answer indicates an adequate degree of internal control, while a negative answer indicates the need for further information or a weakness in the internal control. It is possible in the evaluation of responses to a questionnaire to find one control violated, but a compensating control existing to negate the violation. For example, the cashier in the savings department of a bank often handles cash and also posts the ledger and passbook record, thus performing incompatible duties. By the use of a window-posting machine, however, the posting of the records involves a locked-in control. Even though the cashier does post the record, the compensating locked-in record control negates the violation.

The use of an internal control questionnaire serves only to provide a starting point in the evaluation of the internal control. It is a means to an end, and not an end in itself, and must be used accordingly.

The manner in which the questionnaire is used on an engagement is extremely important. The questionnaire should be filled in by the analyst based on his observations and the information obtained in discussions with the client. It is usually poor procedure to take a questionnaire to the in-charge individual, and to sit across a desk asking him each question on the questionnaire in sequence. There is usually a negative reaction to having someone write down everything being said. Information should be recorded on working papers, but not necessarily at the time of a client discussion.

The analyst must ask questions to find out what he doesn't know, of course, yet actually filling in the questionnaire can be deferred until a time when the client is not present. The questionnaire in this context serves as a comprehensive guide to assure that major areas have not been overlooked, and that all important investigations have been made.

Some analysts and auditors do not like to use internal control questionnaires, especially if it is necessary for the less experienced staff members to fill them in. There are instances in which some of the questions on a standard questionnaire do not fit the situation, and the mere asking of the question places the analyst in the light of not being well informed. Inexperienced staff are inclined to take a questionnaire and go down the page asking each question in sequence just to complete their assignment.

A detailed internal control questionnaire is provided in Appendix A of this text. It will be especially helpful during the study of specific systems problems and cases in Chapters 19 and 20. It provides a comprehensive guide as to the effectiveness of internal control duties for specific procedures to be studied.

INTERNAL CONTROL WRITE-UP. Many systems analysts and auditors prefer to use the internal control write-up method of evaluating internal control duties. They consider the write-up method to be more direct and to the point.

The write-up of internal control duties is usually in the context of a specific procedure, although certain parts of a procedure can be studied by themselves. There is no specific form to be followed for an internal control write-up, except that it must be complete and descriptive of the internal control duties. Most systems analysts and auditors have developed their own patterns.

An internal control write-up usually includes information concerning the components of the system (people, media, machines, and reports) and their functions and/or duties. It will include a flow diagram (see Chapter 10) and a narrative description of the control characteristics of the procedure. It is a detailed reflection of the exact situation that exists, and should be designed to provide the analyst with a factual base to provide the optimum opportunity for critical and constructive analysis.

EVIDENCE. In an engagement to evaluate the adequacy or functioning of internal control, there are various sources of information that evidence the nature of internal control duties and whether they are operative. A systems manual, for example, will furnish evidence about duties, information flow, and systems components. An organization chart is also included in the systems manual and could be obtained to provide evidence of organizational independence. Inspection of the chart of accounts, communication media, and reports will disclose information about control techniques and devices. Inquiry can be made of responsible officers, personnel in the accounting department, department heads and others in key positions.

The functioning of procedures can be observed for evidence as to the manner in which they are actually operating. The work and operation of the internal audit section can be investigated and observed. If an external auditor is employed, any internal control memoranda or special systems reports can be examined. There is substantial evidence reflecting or measuring internal control duties available throughout any company.

INTERNAL CONTROL FOR SMALL BUSINESS

The need for good internal control to safeguard assets and check the accuracy and reliability of the information produced by the financial information system in the small business is as great as the need for good internal control in a medium-sized or large business. Systems instructors are often accused of being concerned only with internal control in the medium-sized or large businesses where there are many people and theoretically ideal internal control duties can be designed into systems. They are accused of not discussing the problems of the small businessman. While it is true that the application of internal control duties can be illustrated more easily in the larger company, it should not be true that there is greater emphasis on one than the other. In fact, the internal control duties as given above are identical for all businesses, large or small. The only difference is that the small businessman has more difficult problems of safeguarding assets, and a lesser concern for the accuracy and reliability of information.

In the discussion of the internal control duty of supervision above, it was noted that in the smaller business it was necessary to rely on supervision to a greater extent than in larger businesses. There are relatively few employees in a small business, thus there are fewer individuals to share the duties and enable organizational independence. In the small business it is almost certain that incompatible duties will be assigned to some of the employees. The owner will prefer to assign them in this way rather than assume more duties himself, or incur the cost of hiring others, and he will have to extend his own supervisory activity.

In a small retail store the owner-manager plus several employees are often all of the people available to assume internal control duties. If internal control duties are divided to be compatible with adequate control, it becomes crystal clear that the *owner himself will have to assume all of the key duties* in each procedure. For example, he would open all incoming mail, sign all checks, clear the cash register daily, prepare the daily deposit, receive and reconcile the bank statement, approve all entries other than routine operations such as returns and the write-off of bad accounts, test and mail customers' statements, place all orders, etc. There is usually no other acceptable way to establish internal control.

Safeguarding the assets is the primary internal control concern of the owner of a small business. He has excellent first-hand information about his business, and is, therefore, not as concerned about the financial information system as managers in big business. He is interested to the extent that day-to-day routines are accomplished and the legal requirements, for such purposes as tax returns and other government reports, are met. In these situations, if the owner of a small business is not personally willing to assume the internal control duties, then he must accept the fact of greater exposure to loss.

The Industrial Parts Company Case

The Industrial Parts Company case is included in Appendix B in order to illustrate how the standards of internal control may be applied in actual practice to illustrate the relationships between the standards of internal control and internal control duties. The Industrial Parts Company case has been compiled from an actual situation.

QUESTIONS, PROBLEMS, AND CASES

1. "Internal control comprises the plan of organization and all of the co-ordinate methods and measures adopted within a business to . . ." What is meant by the "plan of organization" and "methods and measures"?

2. Does internal control promote operational efficiency and encourage adherence to prescribed managerial policies? Explain.

3. Distinguish between and give examples of accounting controls and administrative controls.

4. What is the function of internal control duties in relation to the components of the financial information system?

5. When a system has inadequate internal control, what must be added to result in good internal control? Explain.

6. You have been asked to design a system for the control of cash received from municipal parking meters. Your system should be designed to follow the money from the time it is inserted in the parking meter until it has been deposited in the bank and has been acknowledged by an authenticated deposit ticket.

    a. In outline form describe the system you have designed.

    b. Identify each of the internal control duties in your system, and indicate the contribution of each if appropriate.

7. Define briefly each of the internal control duties, and give an illustration of the application of each in a situation not mentioned in the text.

8. Describe the following internal control duties as they relate to the application indicated by the same letter in the second column.

a. Supervision.	a. Collections through the mail in a "box top" promotion.
b. Clerical proof.	b. Administrative expense control.
c. Acknowledging performance.	c. Approval of a voucher.
d. Transferring responsibility.	d. Transfer of cash register receipts to the central cashier.
e. Protective measures.	e. A locked "walk-in" vault for cash and securities.
f. Review.	f. Approval of the return of merchandise returns.
g. Verification and evaluation.	g. Receiving procedure.

9. Distinguish between the internal control duties of review, supervision, and verification and evaluation.

10. Explain the role of review as an internal control duty in a functioning system.

11. Relate the internal control duties to internal control standards. Why are they important to the systems analyst?

12. It has been said that the design of a system with appropriate internal control duties can assure good internal control, but the objective is only half attained. Assuming that a system has been designed with good internal control, what additional assurance is needed? Explain.

13. What reasonable explanations might exist for well-designed internal control duties being ignored or modified in a functioning system? What can be done to make certain that the system is functioning as designed?

14. What is the contribution of the internal control questionnaire to the systems analyst? The internal control write-up? Contrast the use of the questionnaire to the write-up for a specific systems engagement.

15. Mr. Gilbert Showman is the owner of a small retail clothing business. He has three clerks working in the store, one of whom assists with the records. It has been pointed out to Mr. Showman that his internal control is poor. Which of the internal control duties should be added if his internal control is to be improved? Explain.

16. Standards of field work include the statement that *there is to be a proper study and evaluation of the existing internal control as a basis for reliance thereon and for the determination of the resultant extent of the tests to which*

auditing procedures are to be restricted. Another standard of field work states that *sufficient competent evidential matter is to be obtained.* . . .

    a. What are the major characteristics of a satisfactory system of internal control?

    b. List six sources of evidence about a given system of internal control which are available to an auditor, and state briefly how the evidence from each source can be used in evaluating the system of internal control. (AICPA Examination)

17. Internal control, in the broad sense, includes controls which may be characterized as either administrative or accounting.

    a. What comprises and is generally included in:

        (1) administrative controls

        (2) accounting controls?

    b. What bearing would these controls have on the work of the independent auditor? The systems analyst? (Adapted AICPA Examination)

18. a. You are asked by a client, a medium-sized manufacturing company, to evaluate its internal control system. State the purpose of an internal control system and mention some of the factors and procedures to look for in determining the effective operation of such a system.

    b. Another client, the sole owner of a small business, believes mistakenly that because he has few employees a system of internal control is not practicable for his business. List ten control measures which can be instituted in such a business to provide some degree of internal control. (AICPA Examination)

19. The Y Company, a client of your firm, has come to you with the following problem:

    It has three clerical employees who must perform the following functions:

        (1) Maintain general ledger;

        (2) Maintain accounts payable ledger;

        (3) Maintain accounts receivable ledger;

        (4) Prepare checks for signature;

        (5) Maintain disbursements journal;

        (6) Issue credits on returns and allowances;

        (7) Reconcile the bank account;

        (8) Handle and deposit cash receipts.

Assuming that there is no problem as to the ability of any of the employees, the company requests that you assign the above functions to the three employees in such a manner as to achieve the highest degree of internal control. It may be assumed that these employees will perform no other accounting functions than the ones listed and that any accounting functions not listed will be performed by persons other than these three employees.

    a. State how you would distribute the above functions among the three employees. Assume that with the exception of the nominal jobs of the bank reconciliation and the issuance of credits on returns and allowances, all functions require an equal amount of time.

b. List four possible unsatisfactory combinations of the above listed functions. (AICPA Examination)

20. An internal control questionnaire includes the following items. For each item, explain what is accomplished by the existence of the controls involved.
   a. Are costs and expenses under budgetary control?
   b. Is a postage meter machine used?
   c. Are monthly statements of account mailed to all customers?
   d. In reconciling bank accounts do employees of the client examine endorsements?
   e. Has the bank (or banks) been instructed not to cash checks payable to the company? (AICPA Examination)

21. You have been assigned to review the internal control in a manufacturing company. It has been suggested that great benefit could be obtained by studying several case studies in internal control. The following have been recommended:
   a. Case Studies in Internal Control Number 1, *The Textile Company*, American Institute of Certified Public Accountants, 1950.
   b. Case Studies in Internal Control Number 2, *The Machine Manufacturing Company*, American Institute of Certified Public Accountants, 1950.
   Obtain the case studies listed above. Indicate the special features of each that contribute in a special manner to the understanding of internal control and internal control investigations.

22. The Kellog Wholesale Company was organized on January 1, 1938, with an authorized capital stock of $1,000,000. All stock is now outstanding in the hands of 754 different stockholders, the largest being Mr. J. J. Jay, the President of the company and Chairman of the Board of Directors. Capital stock records are maintained by the chief bookkeeper.

   The company had a sales volume last year of $10,000,000. It has an administrative office and main warehouse located in Madison, Wisconsin, and branch warehouses in Minneapolis, Duluth, and Milwaukee. The company has decentralized its records insofar as stock records for inventory control are maintained at each of the four warehouses by the shipping clerks. When warehouse quantities reach a minimum level, a purchase requisition is sent from the warehouse to a central purchasing office. The central purchasing office is under the supervision of the vice-president in charge of purchases. This section prepares the purchase order, based on warehouse requisitions, to replenish the warehouse stock. The central purchase office also is responsible for maintenance of the voucher register, for cost analysis, and for the purchase return journal (all purchase returns must be approved by the vice-president in charge of purchases).

   Each warehouse has a manager who is directly responsible to the vice-president in charge of distribution for the successful operation of the warehouse. In addition to the manager each warehouse employs a petty cashier and shipping clerks.

   Sales are the responsibility of the vice-president in charge of distribution. Sales orders are received at the home office from salesmen who cover specific routes and also through the mail direct from retailers. These orders are sorted and sent to the warehouse nearest to the customer for filling by the shipping clerks, thus reducing shipping charges to the minimum. The sales journal, customer billing, accounts receivable ledger, and credit department are a part of the home office organization in this section.

Cash is received from customers through the mail, through direct payments to salesmen at the time the order is placed, or through payments to the petty cashier at any warehouse. Each warehouse has an imprest petty cash fund from which to make small disbursements. All cash received by the petty cashier at a warehouse is added to the petty cash fund. At the end of the week the petty cashier reports all collections, from cash sales and collections on account, and certifies all disbursements for the week to the home office. The report is the basis for a weekly settlement to maintain the petty cash fund at a $200 balance. All other payments are made by the home office by check or, if the amount is less than $10, from customer receipts in possession of the home office cashier.

The Controller of the company is J. J. Jay, Jr., the president's son. As is the case in many companies, his primary duty and responsibility is accounting. The assistant controller is also the cashier who is responsible for all cash receipts and cash disbursements. He is required to sign all checks. In addition, he maintains the cash receipts journal, check register, accounts payable ledger, and prepares the monthly bank reconciliation. Another assistant controller is in charge of the budget and system sections. He is also responsible for payroll, including timekeeping, preparation of pay envelopes (cash is paid), and distribution of pay to employees. The chief bookkeeper is responsible for the general journal, general ledger, accounts receivable, and the preparation and interpretation of financial statements.

The president, who believes in the complete utilization of statistical information, has the tabulation and statistical section directly under his supervision. The company employs an internal auditor who is responsible directly to the president. The external auditor reports directly to the board of directors.

The organization as it exists at the time of your investigation is as reflected on the organization chart that follows:

a. Draw an organization chart for the Kellog Wholesale Company, *reallocating responsibilities* to reflect *good organization* and to enable the *maximum amount* of internal control. Show as a *minimum* the same amount of detail as shown on the chart on the facing page.

b. List every change (addition, elimination, or reallocation) from the existing organization that you recommend and state *very briefly* the reason for each change directly after the change suggested.

c. List *briefly* the violations of good internal control that exist in the Kellog Wholesale Company.

23. You are the proprietor of a small retail business. You employ a clerk, a cashier, and a part-time bookkeeper. The cashier must also assist as a clerk. If you as the proprietor are to have adequate internal control, what are the duties that you must personally perform? *Briefly* state why these specific duties would not be assigned to other employees.

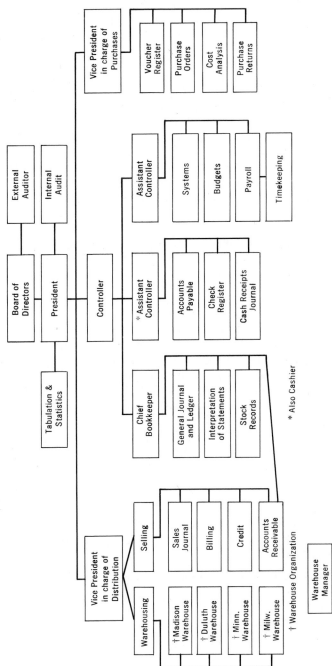
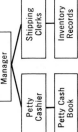

24. Mr. Henry R. Meyers owns and operates a small store at 622 Portage Avenue,
     Madison, Wisconsin. He employs the following persons:
          Mrs. John Kelly, bookkeeper, cashier, and clerical
          Mrs. Jack Johnson, clerk
          Mr. Carl Smith, clerk
     The business sells merchandise over the counter for cash, which is rung
     up on a cash register at the time of the sale. It also sells on credit, at which
     time a sales ticket in duplicate is prepared, the original (white) is placed on
     a spindle and the customer is given the duplicate (yellow).
          Charge customers are billed at the end of each month, and remittance
     is made to the business through the mail or over-the-counter. For over-the-
     counter remittances, a sales ticket in duplicate is prepared with the comment,
     "cash credit" and the customer is given the original (white) and the dupli-
     cate (yellow) is placed on the spindle and the cash rung up as "received on
     account." Mrs. Kelly prepares tickets for cash received through the mail and
     after ringing up the amount on the cash register, places the duplicate slips
     on the spindle.
          Mrs. Kelly posts to the subsidiary accounts receivable ledger direct from
     the sales tickets and credit slips collected on the spindle. She enters the total
     sales tickets and cash register totals in the combined journal daily, clears the
     cash register at the end of each day, and prepares the daily deposit.
          Mr. Meyers does all purchasing and manages the store. He approves all
     invoices for payment, after which Mrs. Kelly writes, signs, and mails the
     checks.
          Small disbursements are made from the cash register, with cash being
     replaced by a receipted bill. While Mr. Meyers makes most such disburse-
     ments, clerks are authorized to pay out small amounts for necessary expenses,
     i.e., express charges, refunds, etc. Receipted bills are removed from the cash
     register by Mrs. Kelly when she clears totals each night. Mrs. Kelly reconciles
     the bank statement.
          What internal controls might Mr. Meyers install in order to safeguard
     the assets of the business without increasing the personnel in the present
     organization?

25. A window-posting machine enables the violation of good internal control.
     State how internal control is violated and why it is not a control problem.

26. In implementing internal control, what three functions are vested in separate
     persons to the maximum extent practicable? Illustrate by applying to a cash
     payments procedure.

27. Define the following terms as they relate to a system:
     a. Embezzlement.
     b. Collusion.
     c. Defalcation.
     d. Kiting.
     e. Lapping.
     f. Peculation.

CHAPTER 8

Systems Input and Processing

INTRODUCTION

IT HAS BEEN POINTED OUT THAT THE PRIMARY OBJECTIVE OF A FINANCIAL information system is to produce financial, statistical, and other information for use by management. The inputs, or raw materials of the system, are financial, statistical, and other data.[1] The basic operations of a financial information system are those which transform pieces of data into useful information. Refer once again to Figure 1-3, the diagram of a financial information system, on Page 13. Conceptually, Figure 1-3 illustrates a total systems theory, including data and information flow. When considering the financial information system as a vehicle which processes data and produces information, the data and information flow can be summarized graphically as shown in Figure 8-1.

In a financial information system, there are basically three phases of data and information flow, namely input, processing, and output. Data and information flow are governed by the data accumulation, data processing, and report principles. The data accumulation principle governs input, the data processing principle governs processing, and the report principle governs output.

---

[1] Data, in this sense, means a series of unorganized facts, while information is a set of facts organized in a meaningful way.

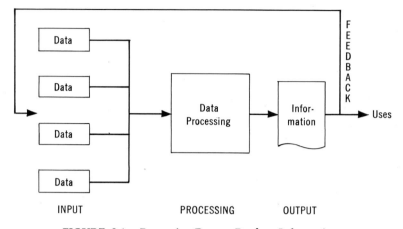

FIGURE 8-1.   Processing Data to Produce Information

Within the three phases of data and information flow there are eleven specific operations which function within the system as follows:

1. Input:
   a. Initial recording
   b. Classifying
2. Data Processing:
   a. Arranging
   b. Summarizing
   c. Calculating
   d. Comparing
   e. Storing
   f. Transporting
   g. Reproducing
3. Output:
   a. Reporting
   b. Feedback

The remaining sections of this chapter will explore the first two major phases of data and information flow, and the related operations. The third phase, output, will be covered in Chapter 9.

INPUT

Input into a system consists of the initial record and classification of data that are placed into the system. It includes all of the steps of data collection and handling necessary to bring the data into appropriate form for processing within the system. Input of good quality is often the key to accuracy and adequacy of the information flowing from the systems. Once the data are in the system, the processing steps can often be automated to produce the desired output. Controls over data can be established during input phases, and the potential of the system can be realized.

Initial Recording

Because the financial information system is a data processing system, it is essential that a description of each significant event or transaction occurring within a business be preserved in some finite manner. Humans are not capable of retaining each fact they learn nor is it possible, even if all facts introduced to man could be retained for this data to be arranged and re-arranged easily. Initial recording, therefore, is the expression of a business event or transaction on some physical medium so that this fact will be preserved in a form that can be processed independently of the individuals who first come into contact with the event. It is placing the data into the system for the first time. The concept of initial recording includes the initial transcription of the data.

Initial recording is the collection of the needed data. The most common recording or collecting medium is paper upon which alphabetic and Arabic numerical symbols are used to represent a business transaction or event. By no means is the manual recording of data on paper the only way of giving physical expression to pieces of data. Data can be collected on cards or paper tape through the systematic arrangement of punched holes. Magnetic spots on plastic tape or characters printed in magnetizable ink are further examples of collecting media. Initial recording can be done manually (by pen and ink), mechanically (by cash register, time clocks), or electronically (by equipment that reads special inks). There are various kinds of devices used to assist in the recording operation. Specific details are given about many such devices in other chapters.

It should be evident that a good initial record is required if the system is to be adequate. For example, the A.B.C. Construction Company owned two supporting subsidiary companies: The D.E.F. Masonry Company and the G.H.I. Carpentry Contractors. Customers contracting principally with the A.B.C. Company frequently order a deeper basement or additional concrete work or some other modification of the original house plan. A.B.C. immediately billed the customer for the additional work required. No provision was made, however, for the subsidiary companies to bill the parent for the extra work they were to do. As a result, subsidiary revenue was understated and parent costs understated. This situation was rectified by instructing the clerk responsible for the extra billings to customers to bill the additional work from the corresponding subsidiary to the parent company at the same time—thus establishing a vital initial record.

IMMEDIATE RECORD. It is necessary for the systems analyst to be aware of the nature of initial recording and to be able to design a system in which the recording operation will be performed at the first opportunity so that valid data are collected. Basically, the following input standard for initial recording should be used in all situations.

> Initial recording should be performed as soon as possible after the occurrence of the actual event or transaction so that the risks of omission or erroneous recording are minimized.

The amount and quality of data are established at the time the data are captured. Such data become available through the system because they were a part of the initial recording. The output of the system can include no more data or no better data than were originally recorded. Erroneous data going into the system that are not discovered result in erroneous output.

ALL DATA NECESSARY. It should be noted that the initial record is not restricted to dollar amounts. There are many instances in which unit or other data are collected. Such managerial needs as unit data for production scheduling, inventory control, and sales analysis illustrate the type of data other than dollar amounts that are necessary.

UNITS OF THE LEAST COMMON DENOMINATOR. It is vital that the initial recording be in *units of the least common denominator*. Units of the least common denominator were discussed in detail in Chapter 2 in connection with the data accumulation principle. Such units are not identical from one business to another, as the needs of various managements differ. They provide the great flexibility possible in systems output by making possible different types of output to meet varying needs. A second input standard for initial recording also applies to all situations:

> Initial recording should be in units of data combined as much as possible without reaching the point at which combined data will later have to be separated so that additional analysis will not be necessary to provide information for the varying needs of management.

Classifying

There are two distinct aspects to data classification: (1) identification, and (2) coding. Classification is defined as:

> The identification of each item and the systematic placement of like items together according to their common features. Items grouped together under common heads are further defined according to their fundamental differences.[2]

---

[2] *Classification and Coding Techniques to Facilitate Accounting Operations*, National Association of Accountants Research Report 34, (New York: National Association of Accountants, April, 1959), p. 3.

Classification is a matter of establishing specific categories into which financial and statistical data can be grouped. Unless data are grouped according to some kind of order, it would be impossible for such data to be of assistance to management.

IDENTIFICATION. The needs of management are the criteria governing the choice of categories to be used in a data processing system. The identification of the category appropriate for given data is important in arriving at meaningful information in each category.

The number $438.50, for example, could refer to a cash receipt, a sale on account, a cash disbursement, a purchase, or any one of a thousand possibilities. If the $438.50 was the amount of a sale of a food freezer on account to Mr. Hiram Spot, the following steps to identify the amount could have been taken. The clerk:

1. Used a sale on account ticket book;
2. Wrote in the name and address of the purchaser;
3. Wrote in the description of the item sold and the price $438.50;
4. Inserted his (clerk's) name on the ticket;
5. Inserted the name of his department on the ticket.

Such identification would permit the categorization of this sale by product class, by department or by salesman. In addition it is possible to add this amount to previous sales and due from customers, and to identify the particular customer from whom payment is to be received.

The identification of appropriate units of the least common denominator is often one of the most difficult of the data and information flow steps. One means of distorting systems output is to design a system of data and information identification in such a way that *arbitrary allocations* are made at the time of the initial recording. Such arbitrary allocations are often the result of an effort to accumulate smaller units of the least common denominator than are natural. Meaningful units of the least common denominator are the result of *direct* identification of the object for which data are being accumulated. The arbitrary allocation of amounts to several categories can either result in the identity of the object being lost or the accumulated information being of questionable validity. Allocations other than direct should be avoided. The input standard for initial recording and identification is as follows:

> Initial recording should be direct to specific object groups so that the identity of the object directly associated is not lost through allocation and valid data are accumulated.

CODING. Having identified the units of data and information needed by management for various reports, schedules, and analyses, an appropriate classification must be devised. A coding plan is also needed to facilitate the processing steps and to accumulate the data according to the desired management information groupings.

Coding is the *assignment of numbers, letters, or other symbols according to a systematic plan for distinguishing the classifications to which each item belongs and for distinguishing items within a given classification from each other*.[3] Coding is essential to modern data processing systems. In such systems, data can be processed manually, mechanically or electronically. Disregarding the method of processing, it has been demonstrated that the shorter the identifying words on a piece of data, the easier and faster the processing. Codes are used, therefore, after the categories into which data are to be grouped have been selected, to shorten the category title, and to facilitate the data processing necessary to accumulate like items. For example, it is easier to place the number 1234 on a sales invoice to identify the product sold than writing out the full product name.

The input standard for classifying data is as follows:

> Codes should be designed to provide symbolic representations of classifications reflecting the needs of management to provide for the appropriate accumulation and arrangement of data and to assist in rapid and efficient processing.

Traditionally, systems analysts contrived a *Chart of Accounts* which consisted of the categories used to present financial information in the Balance Sheet and Income Statement. This approach is useful, but it is also important for the systems analyst to keep in mind that financial statement preparation is not the exclusive justification for the existence of a system or specific classification method. Attention must be given to all of management's needs for information. The traditional *Chart of Accounts* is often expanded in the more complex machine systems to a *Company Code*.

Consider the Balance Sheet and Income Statement shown in Figures 8-2 and 8-3 of the Mason Stone Company. This company is engaged in all forms of masonry work and also operates a stoneyard which sells various kinds of raw and polished stone, mortar, sand, and other masonry supplies to its own mason crews and to outside contractors.

Utilizing the financial statements as a guide, the chart of accounts in Figure 8-4 was designed. Shortly after the new chart of accounts was installed, the accountant and the other officers of the company realized that information which they felt was needed for management purposes was not being accumulated. An analysis proved that it was not sufficient to merely identify data by account number. Masonry Job Receipts, for example, needed further categorization into Revenue from Concrete Work, Laying Concrete Block, and Laying Brick Veneers. Stoneyard Sales, Cost of Masonry Jobs Finished, Cost of Stone Sold, Inventory—Stone, and Jobs in Process—

---

[3] *Ibid.*

MASON STONE COMPANY
BALANCE SHEET
AS OF DECEMBER 31, 1968

ASSETS

Current Assets:

Cash		$ 463.45
Accounts Receivable	$ 9,663.39	
Less Provision for Doubtful Accounts	1,450.00	8,213.39
Inventory—Stone		8,291.87
Total Current Assets		$16,968.71

Investments:

Hard Rock Concrete Products Company		16,242.76

Fixed Assets:

Land		$ 2,000.00	
Building and Equipment	$57,070.71		
Less Accumulated Depreciation	30,991.76	26,078.95	28,078.95
Total Assets			$61,290.42

LIABILITIES AND STOCKHOLDERS' EQUITY

Current Liabilities:

Accounts Payable	$ 6,929.03
Notes Payable—Bank	8,000.00
Due to V.L. Good	651.58
Accrued State U. C. Taxes Payable	47.59
Accrued Federal U. C. Taxes Payable	82.72
Accrued Withholding Taxes Payable	508.09
Accrued Interest on Mortgages Payable	1,160.60
Accrued Interest Payable	494.76
Accrued Real Estate Taxes Payable	370.00
Total Current Liabilities	$18,245.17

Fixed Liabilities:

Mortgages Payable	$10,560.63	
Installments Payable	5,798.25	
Due R. Roe	9,576.00	
Total Fixed Liabilities		25,934.88
Total Liabilities		$44,180.05

Stockholders' Equity:

Common Stock	$10,000.00	
Retained Earnings	7,110.37	
Total Stockholders' Equity		17,110.37
Total Liabilities and Stockholders' Equity		$61,290.42

FIGURE 8-2. Mason Stone Company Balance Sheet

MASON STONE COMPANY
INCOME STATEMENT
FOR THE YEAR ENDED DECEMBER 31, 1968

Revenue:

	Masonry	*Stoneyard*	*Total*
Sales	$ 111,238.11	$34,907.10	$146,145.21
Less Cost of Sales	79,897.15	18,283.36	98,180.51
Gross Margin on Sales	$ 31,340.96	$16,623.74	$ 47,964.70

Operating Expenses:

Stoneyard Labor	$ 5,663.20	
Supplies	3,021.72	
Truck Expenses	4,485.10	
General Office Expenses	1,527.47	
Office Salary Expense	2,750.00	
Small Tool Expense	406.07	
Equipment Repairs and		
Stone Saw Blades	366.20	
Heat, Light, and Water	723.84	
Insurance Expense	2,236.17	
Depreciation Expense	9,471.07	
Bad Debt Expense	2,780.00	
State U. C. Tax Expense	763.09	
Federal U. C. Tax Expense	84.79	
Employer's F.I.C.A. Tax Expense	1,058.89	
Real Estate Taxes	472.14	
Advertising	712.95	
Travel Expenses	359.14	
Airplane Expenses	112.59	
Dues, Subscriptions, and Donations	303.50	
Business Entertainment	293.46	
Miscellaneous Expense	165.78	
Total Operating Expenses		37,757.17

Net Operating Profit $ 10,207.53

Other Income:
Rent Income   1,125.00

                                                         $ 11,332.53

Other Expenses:

Interest Expense	$ 2,503.44	
Federal Income Taxes	2,648.73	5,152.17

Net Income for the Year $ 6,180.36

FIGURE 8-3.   Mason Stone Company Income Statement

MASON STONE COMPANY
CHART OF ACCOUNTS

Account Number	Account Title
1-10	**Current Assets:**
1	Cash
2	Accounts Receivable
2(a)	Provision for Doubtful Accounts
3	Inventory—Stone
4	Jobs in Process—Masonry
11-15	**Investments:**
11	Investment in Hard Rock Concrete Products Co.
16-20	**Fixed Assets:**
16	Land
17	Building—Warehouse
18	Equipment
18(a)	Accumulated Depreciation—Building and Equipment
21-35	**Current Liabilities:**
21	Accounts Payable
22	Notes Payable—Bank
23	Due V. L. Good
24	Accrued State U. C. Tax Payable
25	Accrued Federal U. C. Tax Payable
26	Accrued FICA and Withholding Taxes Payable
27	Accrued Real Estate Taxes Payable
28	Accrued Interest on Mortgages Payable
29	Accrued Interest Payable
30	Accrued Federal Income Taxes Payable
36-40	**Fixed Liabilities:**
36	Installments Payable
37	Due R. Roe
38	Mortgages Payable

Account Number	Account Title
41-42	**Stockholders' Equity:**
41	Common Stock
42	Retained Earnings
43	Profit and Loss Summary
43-50	**Income:**
43	Masonry Job Receipts
44	Stoneyard Sales
45	Rent Income
51-80	**Expenses:**
51	Cost of Masonry Jobs Finished
52	Cost of Stone Sold
53	Stoneyard Labor
54	Supplies
55	Truck Expenses
56	General Office Expense
57	Office Salary Expense
58	Small Tool Expense
59	Equipment Repairs and Stone Saw Blades
60	Heat, Light, and Water
61	Depreciation Expense
62	Insurance Expense
63	Bad Debt Expense
64	State U. C. Tax Expense
65	Federal U. C. Tax Expense
66	Employer's FICA Tax Expense
67	Real Estate Taxes
68	Advertising
69	Travel Expense
70	Airplane Expense
71	Dues, Subscriptions, and Donations
72	Business Entertainment
73	Miscellaneous Expense
74	Interest Expense
75	Federal Income Taxes

FIGURE 8-4.   Mason Stone Company Chart of Accounts

Masonry, were other accounts needing additional classification breakdowns. Figure 8-5 illustrates the revised chart of accounts incorporating the changes deemed necessary to comply with management needs. If this sample illustration is magnified hundreds of times, and expanded to include statistical data needed, the extent of the coding problem in medium-sized and large companies can be understood.

TYPES OF CODES. There are many types of codes and they are usually identified according to the manner in which the symbols are arranged. Some common types of codes are sequence codes, block codes, group codes, and decimal codes.

Practical business situations tend to combine the features of several types of codes to provide the structure that best meets the specific requirements of the business. Briefly, some of the types of codes are as follows:

(1) *Sequence Code.* In a sequence code, items are numbered consecutively. Applications are found in the numbering of purchase orders, checks, and sales orders which are assigned numbers in the order in which issued or received. This practice facilitates control by making it possible to account for all copies of these documents. Sequence codes are also used for assigning numbers to employees (clock numbers).

Sequence coding provides only one basis of classification, and so long as the numerical sequence is maintained, items can be added only at the end of the list. Inactive numbers in a sequence code are sometimes reassigned when maintenance of the original sequence is not important as, for example, in assigning numbers to employees. However, the assignment of code numbers is then made in arbitrary order rather than in sequence.

(2) *Block Code.* A block code is designed by reserving blocks of numbers in sequence for each classification of items to be coded. For example, balance sheet accounts might be coded as follows:

Code Numbers	Descriptions
01-49	Assets
50-79	Liabilities
80-99	Stockholders' Equity

Unassigned numbers are left in each block to permit the future addition of items in each classification. The number of digits needed in a block code depends upon the number of items to be coded and the extent to which provision is made for future expansion.

Block coding provides more groups with fewer digits than does the group coding plan below.

(3) *Group Code.* In a group code, successive digits are arranged in groups or fields to designate the several classifications to which a coded item belongs. Digits at the left denote major classifications and, moving from left to right, successive groups of digits in the number denote subclassifications.

MASON STONE COMPANY
REVISED CHART OF ACCOUNTS

100-199	*Current Assets*
101	Cash
102	Accounts Payable
102-1	Provision for Doubtful Accounts
103	Inventory—Stoneyard
104	Jobs in Process—Masonry
200-299	*Investments*
201	Investments in Hard Rock Concrete Products Co.
300-399	*Fixed Assets*
301	Land
302	Building—Warehouse
302-1	Accumulated Depreciation— Building
303	Masonry Equipment
303-1	Accumulated Depreciation— Masonry Equipment
304	Stoneyard Equipment
304-1	Accumulated Depreciation— Stoneyard Equipment
400-499	*Current Liabilities*
401	Accounts Payable
402	Notes Payable—Bank
403	Notes Payable—V. L. Good
404	State U.C. Tax Payable
405	Federal U.C. Tax Payable
406	Withholding Taxes Payable
407	Real Estate Taxes Payable
408	Interest on Mortgages Payable
409	Federal Income Taxes Payable
500-599	*Fixed Liabilities*
501	Installment Notes Payable
502	Mortgages Payable
600-699	*Stockholders' Equity*
601	Common Stock
602	Retained Earnings
603	Profit and Loss Summary
700-709	*Masonry Revenue*
701	Brick Work
702	Concrete Work
703	Concrete Block Work

710-749	*Masonry Expenses—Construction Overhead*
711	Cost of Brick Completed
712	Cost of Concrete Work Finished
713	Cost of Concrete Block Work Finished
714	Supplies
715	Truck Expenses
716	Small Tool Expense
717	Equipment Repairs
718	Depreciation—Equipment
750-759	*Stoneyard Revenue*
751	Crab Orchard Stone Sales
752	Limestone Sales
753	Masonry Supply Sales
760-799	*Stoneyard Expenses—Yard Overhead*
761	Cost of Crab Orchard Stone Sold
762	Cost of Limestone Sold
763	Cost of Masonry Supplies Sold
764	Supplies
765	Truck Expenses
766	Small Tool Expenses
767	Equipment Repair and Stone Saw Blade
768	Depreciation—Equipment
769	Depreciation—Warehouse
770	Stoneyard Labor
771	Heat, Light, and Water
800-899	*Selling and Administrative Expenses*
801	Office Salaries
802	Insurance Expense
803	Depreciation Expense—Equipment
804	Depreciation Expense—Building
805	Bad Debt Expense
806	State U.C. Tax Expense
807	Federal U.C. Tax Expense
808	Real Estate Taxes Expense
809	Employer's FICA Tax Expense
810	Advertising Expense
811	Travel Expense
812	Airplane Expense
813	Dues, Subscriptions, and Donations
814	Business Entertainment
815	Miscellaneous Expenses
900-999	*Other Revenue and Expense*
901	Rent Income
951	Interest Expense
952	Federal Income Tax Expense

FIGURE 8-5. Mason Stone Company Revised Chart of Accounts

Since the position of a digit is significant in classification of coded items, the number of digits in each field is limited to a pre-established number and consistency must be observed in a sequence of the several fields. For example, one company's accounting code consists of sixteen digits (000-00000-00-000-000) in which, reading from left to right, the fields denote the following classifications:

Field	Digit	Classification
1	1-3	Corporation, division, plant
2	4-8	Account
3	9-10	Department
4	11-13	Work center, office, or section
5	14-16	Nature of expense

Group codes are well suited to machine data processing because items can readily be sorted and tabulated by any classification provided in the code. They are readily memorized because of the significance possessed by numbers in each position. Provision for future expansion is made by leaving unused numbers in the various groups.

In practice, some items may not require coding in all fields. For example, when transactions affect only the accounts of a single division, it is unnecessary to include the division code number in coding account titles. However, it is necessary to maintain consistency in position of the fields so that interpretation of the data is not changed.

(4) *Decimal Code.* Decimal coding is best known for its use in libraries, although it is equally well adapted to coding of correspondence and similar material where classification on the basis of subject matter is desired. In a decimal code, major classifications are represented by groups of numbers to the left of the decimal point while digits to the right of the decimal point are used to provide subclassifications. Unlimited expansion is possible, for any number of digits can be added. However, decimal coding is not well adapted to machine data processing becausing code numbers are of varying length. Furthermore, decimal code numbers are often longer than group code numbers.[4]

CHOICE OF CODING METHODS. Four factors are considered important influences on the specific coding method to be selected in a particular situation.[5] These factors are (1) the materials to be coded, (2) uses to be made of coded data, (3) clerical economy, and (4) acceptability to personnel. Each factor is presented in the following paragraphs.

In establishing a specific coding plan one of the most important factors to consider is the *material to be coded*. If the subject is simple in its basic nature, a simple coding system is naturally in order. If, however, the subject to be coded is a customer file, for example, comprised of several hundred

---

[4] *Ibid.,* pp. 10–11.

[5] *Ibid.,* pp. 11–13.

customers, in various locations, serviced by several salesmen, the data to be arranged according to customer may well be subsequently arranged by salesmen, by territory, by product, etc. In the latter case, a more complex identification system would be in order than in the former.

Since machines and people are used to arrange data according to various categories, just *how the coded data are to be used* is of great importance to the systems analysts. Machines, whether they be mechanical or electronic, rarely handle alphabetic or alpha-numeric codes efficiently. People, on the other hand, find a mnemonic code, such as the three letter code used by the airline and telegraph companies to identify the cities of the United States, e.g., CHI = Chicago, MKE = Milwaukee, MSP = Minneapolis-St. Paul, easy to use and to memorize.

If data will eventually be arranged under several categories, a more complicated code will be necessary than would be needed if only a single use of the data is to be made. In bookstores, for example, the cost price of the book is often written under the retail price in alphabetic code. A book which sold for $10 could have the letters HAA written under the retail price. When decoded HAA = $8.00. If further processing is to be done with the cost price, such as its removal from inventory, clerks will decode the amount so that the numeric translation can be used in further processing.

Clerical economy is necessary if a code is to be acceptable. Common sense dictates that if one set of symbols is going to be used to represent a fact normally expressed in another set of symbols, it would not aid data arrangement if the former symbols were more difficult to use than the latter. Again, as in considering uses to be made of the data, the systems analyst must know whether machines or people are going to arrange the data physically. Lengthy, complicated codes may be easily handled by an electronic computer. The same coded data processed manually might take longer to process than would have been the case had the data not been coded at all. If the code selected does not contribute to clerical economy, it must be considered a defective code.

Regardless of whether machines or people will process coded data, people are responsible for the coding of data, and the code must be *acceptable to the personnel*. If codes were chosen that confused rather than helped coding or processing personnel, it would be extremely difficult to be sure that correct codes have been assigned. Whether processed manually or by machines, incorrectly coded data will result in fallacious information. Where several types of codes can be used, the systems analyst should choose the code that is able to be understood by, and that is acceptable to, the employees who will be using the code. In a highly mechanized system of data processing, less choice is often present. Often the systems analyst must shift or acquire personnel who are mentally equipped to use the codes that must be used because of the nature of the system. For example, where extensive cost analysis is desirable and a punched card system is used, field codes of ten digits or more are often used, such as the group code previously illustrated.

DATA PROCESSING

The second phase of data and information flow is data processing. It includes the arranging, summarizing, calculating, comparing, storing, transporting, and reproducing of data and information. These operations are designed to receive data and to perform the activities necessary to arrive at the output needed by management.

Arranging

Many systems analysts refer to the activity of data arranging as sorting. In essence, sorting is the process of taking the data recorded and identified and physically putting related items together. The arrangement is usually a numerical or alphabetical sequence, or an arrangement where a common characteristic determines the categories for data to be grouped, i.e., sales, purchases, etc. There are several types of data arranging, however, which are included in the concept of sorting.

MERGING. Merging is the process of bringing two groups of data together. For example, in order to send monthly statements to customers, the old balances (if any) must be modified according to the purchases and payments on account made by the customers since the last billing. The old balance file, in alphabetical order, is often merged with the file of transactions for the month so that the new accounts receivable balance can be ascertained easily.

SELECTING. Another aspect of data arrangement is selecting. Selecting is the process whereby certain items in a particular file are removed from the main file. In the illustration of merging, for example, the operation of selecting probably preceded the merging operation. If only 20 per cent of the accounts receivable were affected by this month's transactions, it would be less cumbersome to handle only the 20 per cent that were affected by the transactions in lieu of the entire file. By selection, the active 20 per cent of the main file can be selected, modified, and merged back into the main file at the completion of the operation.

COLUMNARIZATION. Probably one of the most often used data arranging devices is the columnar journal. It is possible to recall from elementary accounting that a columnar journal was used to accumulate like transactions. Columnarization, or data arranging by the use of columnar distributions, is illustrated in Figure 8-6, a typical columnar Sales Journal. The only transactions recorded in this journal are sales on account. Each amount, therefore, must be placed in the first column. It is evident, however, that sales have been subclassified, and that each sale can be grouped into one of five subclasses.

ACME CORPORATION

SALES JOURNAL

Date	Customer	Terms	Accounts Receivable	Sales				
				Product A	Product B	Product C	Product D	Product E
10/4/68	Black Corp.	2/10, N/30	$ 800.00	$ 200.00		$ 300.00	$ 100.00	$ 200.00
10/7/68	Wyatt Arthur Co.	N/30	300.00		$ 300.00			
10/10/68	Excello Co.	1/10, N/30	500.00	100.00	200.00		200.00	
10/15/68	Black Corp.	2/10, N/30	200.00		200.00			
10/17/68	Roper, Inc.	N/30	400.00			300.00		100.00
10/29/68	White Co.	2/10, N/30	800.00	400.00			300.00	100.00
	TOTALS		$37,200.00	$8,500.00	$9,700.00	$6,700.00	$9,600.00	$2,700.00

FIGURE 8-6. Columnar Sales Journal

The columnar Sales Journal permits the sales data to be arranged so that at
the end of each month not only can the total sales on accounts be determined
but also the total of each subclassification. Columnar Journals also facilitate
the summarizing operation discussed below.

COLLATING. Collating is often considered to be solely associated with
punched card accounting equipment. In reality collating also plays an important part in manual data arrangement situations. Figure 8-7 depicts four

Courtesy of Thomas Collators, Subsidiary of Pitney-Bowes, Inc.

FIGURE 8-7A. The Thomas Gathermatic. A Twelve-Station Automatic Collator

Courtesy of Thomas Collators, Subsidiary of Pitney-Bowes, Inc.

FIGURE 8-7B.   The Thomas Rotomatic. A Fifty-Bin High-Speed Collator

different types of collators. For example, prior to posting charges to customers' accounts, and more than one charge per customer is not unusual, it is advisable to arrange the charges in the same order as the accounts receivable file. The vertical multi-sort device illustrated would be ideal. Sorting with this device permits all charges for a period to be brought together so they can all be posted to a particular customer's account. If charge data were not arranged in this manner, individual customers' accounts would have to be handled as many times as there were charges to be made to the account. Other collating devices illustrated have special uses to bring data together in the proper sequence.

Systems analysts should rely on the following data processing standard for arranging:

> The specific method of data arranging selected should tend to maximize efficiency of operation in keeping with the principles of reasonable cost and data processing.

As systems develop the importance of data arranging changes. In many computer systems, for example, data may be processed in random order. The elimination of manual arranging data for processing is an important advantage of such systems.

Courtesy of Thomas Collators, Subsidiary of Pitney-Bowes, Inc.

FIGURE 8-7C.   The Thomas Thirty-two-Bin Semi-Automatic Collator

Summarizing

Summarizing is the data processing operation which assembles a mass of financial or statistical data and expresses it as new data or information in a more concise form, i.e., sales invoices for the day represented as a total sales figure, or individual cash receipts for the day represented as total cash received. Even though data have been classified and arranged, results are often meaningless unless they are summarized. Specific equipment aids in the summarizing operation are discussed in other chapters.

It was pointed out in the section on "arranging" that columnar journals play a vital part in summarizing. Complementing journals are ledger accounts. Journals assist summarizing of data most often on a monthly basis,

Courtesy of Remington Rand Office Systems Division, Sperry Rand Corporation

FIGURE 8-7D. Multisort ®

while ledger accounts are used to summarize data over a longer period of time. The following data processing standard of summarizing is applicable:

> Summarizing and the methods to achieve this operation should assist in the accumulation of the type of additional data or information needed by management.

Summarizing results in the elimination of excess detail, making it possible for management to consider complete data. With more and better data available to interpret, the probability of better decisions is increased.

Calculating

An important and easily understood data processing operation is mathematical calculation. Included are adding, subtracting, multiplying, and dividing. The calculating operation is the process of applying the basic rules of mathematics to two or more pieces of data in order to create more usable pieces of data than were in existence prior to the mathematical process. For example, if it is known that five units of a product which cost $5 had been sold for $10 each, the total cost of this sale and the total sales price are usable pieces of data. By applying basic rules of mathematics, extensions can be made resulting in a total cost figure of $25 and a total sales price of $50.

Systems analysts must consider *when* and *how* this operation will be performed. Chapter 5 illustrates mechanical means of computation and Chapters 15 and 16 illustrate additional mechanical and electronic methods of calculation. People, however, are capable of performing calculations in their minds and manually symbolizing the answer. In many instances, this is the most economical and the most efficient way to perform mathematical calculations.

People in certain situations can be assisted by precalculated charts and tables. Figure 8-8 illustrates a table for precalculated interest. Many other tables and charts are used in systems work. Commonly used precalculated charts include payroll withholding tables, etc.

When calculations should be made cannot specifically be set forth. Experience and common sense play an important role in the systems analyst's decision. The data processing standard that relates to calculating is as follows:

> Mathematical calculations in a data processing system should be made when the combination of data through calculation will be more useful than the original data.

Comparing

The data processing operation of comparing is necessary to determine whether additional processing or managerial consideration is to follow, or whether prior processing was correct. The use of the comparing operation to signal the possible need for managerial consideration is an important contribution of comparing. When material is withdrawn from the storeroom, for example, the balance of stock on hand must be compared to the minimum inventory level. If the level is above minimum, no further action is necessary. If the balance is below minimum, the system should automatically signal the processing necessary for management to determine whether another order should be placed. The type of comparing that signals a needed purchase, and in which the factors can be specifically identified, has been the work of middle management in the past. With the advent of the computer, this type of comparing (or decision), is being automated.

The data processing standard for comparing is as follows:

> Comparing should be done whenever the factors affecting a specific decision or amount can be identified with actual data, enabling the appropriate steps of additional processing, managerial consideration, or control.

2½%

9000	6.25	900	.63	90	.06	9	.01
8000	5.56	800	.56	80	.06	8	.01
7000	4.86	700	.49	70	.05	7	.00
6000	4.17	600	.42	60	.04	6	.00
5000	3.47	500	.35	50	.03	5	.00
4000	2.78	400	.28	40	.03	4	.00
3000	2.08	300	.21	30	.02	3	.00
2000	1.39	200	.14	20	.01	2	.00
1000	.69	100	.07	10	.01	1	.00

3%

9000	7.50	900	.75	90	.08	9	.01
8000	6.67	800	.67	80	.07	8	.01
7000	5.83	700	.58	70	.06	7	.01
6000	5.00	600	.50	60	.05	6	.01
5000	4.17	500	.42	50	.04	5	.00
4000	3.33	400	.33	40	.03	4	.00
3000	2.50	300	.25	30	.03	3	.00
2000	1.67	200	.17	20	.02	2	.00
1000	.83	100	.08	10	.01	1	.00

3½%

9000	8.75	900	.88	90	.09	9	.01
8000	7.78	800	.78	80	.08	8	.01
7000	6.81	700	.68	70	.07	7	.01
6000	5.83	600	.58	60	.06	6	.01
5000	4.86	500	.49	50	.05	5	.00
4000	3.89	400	.39	40	.04	4	.00
3000	2.92	300	.29	30	.03	3	.00
2000	1.94	200	.19	20	.02	2.	.00
1000	.97	100	.10	10	.01	1	.00

4%

9000	10.00	900	1.00	90	.10	9	.01
8000	8.89	800	.89	80	.09	8	.01
7000	7.78	700	.78	70	.08	7	.01
6000	6.67	600	.67	60	.07	6	.01
5000	5.56	500	.56	50	.06	5	.01
4000	4.44	400	.44	40	.04	4	.00
3000	3.33	300	.33	30	.03	3	.00
2000	2.22	200	.22	20	.02	2	.00
1000	1.11	100	.11	10	.01	1	.00

4½%

9000	11.25	900	1.13	90	.11	9	.01
8000	10.00	800	1.00	80	.10	8	.01
7000	8.75	700	.88	70	.09	7	.01
6000	7.50	600	.75	60	.08	6	.01
5000	6.25	500	.63	50	.06	5	.01
4000	5.00	400	.50	40	.05	4	.01
3000	3.75	300	.38	30	.04	3	.00
2000	2.50	200	.25	20	.03	2	.00
1000	1.25	100	.13	10	.01	1	.00

5%

9000	12.50	900	1.25	90	.13	9	.01
8000	11.11	800	1.11	80	.11	8	.01
7000	9.72	700	.97	70	.10	7	.01
6000	8.33	600	.83	60	.08	6	.01
5000	6.94	500	.69	50	.07	5	.01
4000	5.56	400	.56	40	.06	4	.01
3000	4.17	300	.42	30	.04	3	.00
2000	2.78	200	.28	20	.03	2	.00
1000	1.39	100	.14	10	.01	1	.00

5½%

9000	13.75	900	1.38	90	.14	9	.01
8000	12.22	800	1.22	80	.12	8	.01
7000	10.69	700	1.07	70	.11	7	.01
6000	9.17	600	.92	60	.09	6	.01
5000	7.64	500	.76	50	.08	5	.01
4000	6.11	400	.61	40	.06	4	.01
3000	4.58	300	.46	30	.05	3	.00
2000	3.06	200	.31	20	.03	2	.00
1000	1.53	100	.15	10	.02	1	.00

6%

9000	15.00	900	1.50	90	.15	9	.02
8000	13.33	800	1.33	80	.13	8	.01
7000	11.67	700	1.17	70	.12	7	.01
6000	10.00	600	1.00	60	.10	6	.01
5000	8.33	500	.83	50	.08	5	.01
4000	6.67	400	.67	40	.07	4	.01
3000	5.00	300	.50	30	.05	3	.01
2000	3.33	200	.33	20	.03	2	.00
1000	1.67	100	.17	10	.02	1	.00

6½%

9000	16.25	900	1.63	90	.16	9	.02
8000	14.44	800	1.44	80	.14	8	.01
7000	12.64	700	1.26	70	.13	7	.01
6000	10.83	600	1.08	60	.11	6	.01
5000	9.03	500	.90	50	.09	5	.01
4000	7.22	400	.72	40	.07	4	.01
3000	5.42	300	.54	30	.05	3	.01
2000	3.61	200	.36	20	.04	2	.00
1000	1.81	100	.18	10	.02	1	.00

7%

9000	17.50	900	1.75	90	.18	9	.02
8000	15.56	800	1.56	80	.16	8	.02
7000	13.61	700	1.36	70	.14	7	.01
6000	11.67	600	1.17	60	.12	6	.01
5000	9.72	500	.97	50	.10	5	.01
4000	7.78	400	.78	40	.08	4	.01
3000	5.83	300	.58	30	.06	3	.01
2000	3.89	200	.39	20	.04	2	.00
1000	1.94	100	.19	10	.02	1	.00

8%

9000	20.00	900	2.00	90	.20	9	.02
8000	17.78	800	1.78	80	.18	8	.02
7000	15.56	700	1.56	70	.16	7	.02
6000	13.33	600	1.33	60	.13	6	.01
5000	11.11	500	1.11	50	.11	5	.01
4000	8.89	400	.89	40	.09	4	.01
3000	6.67	300	.67	30	.07	3	.01
2000	4.44	200	.44	20	.04	2	.00
1000	2.22	100	.22	10	.02	1	.00

9%

9000	22.50	900	2.25	90	.23	9	.02
8000	20.00	800	2.00	80	.20	8	.02
7000	17.50	700	1.75	70	.18	7	.02
6000	15.00	600	1.50	60	.15	6	.02
5000	12.50	500	1.25	50	.13	5	.01
4000	10.00	400	1.00	40	.10	4	.01
3000	7.50	300	.75	30	.08	3	.01
2000	5.00	200	.50	20	.05	2	.00
1000	2.50	100	.25	10	.03	1	.00

Source: E-Z Interest Tables, The Twentieth Century Company,
542 So. Dearborn St., Chicago, Ill.

FIGURE 8-8. Precalculated Interest Chart

There are many instances in which comparing plays an important role in control. Provision for matching, quantitative comparisons, and reconciling illustrate some of the applications common in systems design. An example of matching is the comparison of a receiving report to the invoice before a disbursement is made. Quantitative comparisons are illustrated by the comparison of control accounts to the total of amounts in a subsidiary ledger. Reconciliation is illustrated by the comparison of bank balance to the company balance to account for differences. All are a part of the comparing operation.

Storing

Unlike the connotation that the word operation implies, storing is a passive operation. Nevertheless, it is an important step in data processing. The time may come but, at present, it is not logical to assume that data can be converted into useful information in an unbroken chain from recording to communication. Many temporary storage locations must be used for recording data before processing can be completed. A systems analyst must be able to see to it that this operation is used effectively. Similar to the other operations, the underuse or overuse of this operation tends to hamper the efficient transformation of data into information.

Data can be stored on communication media, punched cards, paper or magnetic tapes, in special files, and in other ways. The data processing standard for storing is as follows:

Data should be stored in a secure form to be available readily when further processing steps are appropriate.

The storing of data is costly after the immediate information and control needs have been satisfied. Many important systems questions are raised concerning the storing of data and information after the probability of further processing steps has passed. These questions relate to the record retention policy. Provision must be made for the orderly disposal of records after their information flow function has been accomplished. The record retention policy can often change the design of a system. For example, the retention period for a purchase requisition, a purchase order, a receiving report, and an invoice differ. In the design of a voucher system the requisition is often stored separately instead of with the voucher as it can be disposed of much earlier than the remainder of the data in support of the voucher.

Transporting

The transporting operation includes all of the physical movement of recorded data for whatever reason. In order for the record of sales for the day to be made, the individual sales slips must be transported from the sales department to the accounting department. Whenever transportation of data or information is necessary, the systems analyst must recommend the method of transportation which will comply with almost all of the systems principles described in Chapter 2. It is necessary for the analyst, therefore, to be familiar with all of the modes of data transportation. Data transportation methods range from hand-carrying data to the transmission of data via teletype, telephone, and microwave systems. Further discussion of various methods will be covered in subsequent chapters.

The data processing standard for transporting data is as follows:

> Data should be transported from one step of information flow to the next in the most effective and direct manner possible to insure a complete and current flow of information to management.

Reproducing

Reproducing is the operation of transferring or duplicating data or information within the system to facilitate further steps in data processing. Reproducing differs between initial recording in that the data or information is not being brought into the system for the first time. For example, data in the system can include a master name and address file or a price list. When a customer order is received, the data from the master name and address file or price list can be transferred to the order as a part of the processing operation. There are many examples of duplicating data to make it available for further processing operations.

QUESTIONS, PROBLEMS, AND CASES

1. What are the phases of data and information flow and conceptually explain each? What are the operations within each phase in all financial information systems, and what is the contribution of each operation?

2. From your experience, or as a result of a visit to a business, describe the initial record and its characteristics for each of the following:
   a. Sale on credit in a department store.
   b. Cash sale in a newsstand.
   c. Cash sale in a supermarket.
   d. Deposit of cash in a bank savings account.
   e. Receipt of cash from a customer through the mail.
   f. Scrapping of a machine.

3. Your company has received $50 in full payment of the amount owed by a customer, Jackson M. Turner. Indicate the manner in which the eight operations of input and data processing relate to the event.

4. Initial recording is one of the important input operations. Explain the application of the various input standards for initial recording to a labor timekeeping situation.

5. Units of the least common denominator should be the input into a system. Explain the importance of units of the least common denominator in terms of depreciation charges about to be recorded, and why they are important in systems design.

6. Distinguish between data classification, identification, and coding.

7. What relationship does a chart of accounts have to data identification?

8. The Merchant Manufacturing Company has decided to change its code from a block code to a group code. Distinguish between the two types of code, and indicate some of the valid reasons why such a change might be made.

9. Distinguish between a sequence code, decimal code, and mnemonic code. Might all three codes be used in the same company? Explain.

10. You have been asked to design a code for the Des Moines Wholesale Hardware Company. All sales are made by salesmen assigned to 30 districts that cover the United States. Approximately 20,500 items are in the inventory. What are the factors that should be considered by the Des Moines Wholesale Hardware Company in choosing a specific coding method? Explain. Which coding method would appear to be best suited to the company?

11. How does merging differ from selecting? Give an illustration of a situation in which each would be used.

12. Why is data arranging so important in machine systems? Explain.

13. The comparing operation often requires a decision about the magnitude of amounts. Explain why comparing is an important data processing operation in this and other situations. Illustrate situations, other than those in the text, in which the different comparing operations are important.

14. Select a particular subsystem or procedure, and illustrate how the data processing operation of storing is vital to successful data processing.

15. Solve question 14 again substituting transporting for storing.

16. A manufacturer of electrical appliances stocks 2,000 items of materials and 500 subassemblies for 100 different products. Some of the small items are kept in the departments where used; the rest are stored in a central location. What code would you devise for control of this inventory? Illustrate and explain.

17. Who should code transaction documents in a manufacturing company—the person who prepares the document originally, or one person in the account-

ing department through whom all documents would be routed? Explain. Would your answer be the same for a municipality?

18. You have been requested to illustrate a code for classification of the expenditures of a large state university. Illustrate the code you would recommend.

19. The Mildred Manufacturing Company receives orders from customers through the mail. Customer orders are all sent from the mail room to Miss Roberts at the order desk who checks credit histories and writes up the order form to be used internally within the company. Two copies of the order are sent to the finished goods warehouse. One of the copies sent to the warehouse is included with the merchandise as a packing slip. The second copy is stamped with a "delivered" stamp and sent back to the order desk. When the copy marked "delivered" is received it is placed in a customer history file, and the original copy that had been held at the order desk is sent to the Billing Department.

    Comment on the above system, indicating some of the problems that are obvious. What control could be established to make certain all orders are shipped and billed? Where would the calculating operation be performed? Why?

20. Explain the operation of summarizing as it relates to the cash receiving system of the Ajax Oil Company. Fourteen service stations are located in the community. Daily sales and cash reports are submitted to the main office where centralized records are maintained.

21. What are four advantages of using codes?

22. You have submitted a tentative draft of a chart of accounts and pro forma statements for the approval of a client whose system you are revising. The following excerpts from your draft particularly caused his comment:

10	Cash	23	Equipment
11	Accounts Receivable	24	Allowance for Depreciation
12	Allowance for Bad Debts		of Building
13	Inventory	30-39	Intangibles (details omitted)
14	Supplies in Hand	50-59	Liabilities (details omitted)
15	Prepaid Expenses	60-69	Capital (details omitted)
20	Land	70-79	Sales and Cost of Sales
21	Building		Accounts
22	Allowance for	80-89	Expenses
	Depreciation of Building	90-99	Miscellaneous Profit and Loss

    Your client's first comment was to inquire about the "double identification" of each account. He also commented, "If you must use these numbers, why all of the gaps; it's like building a skyscraper and finishing the interior of every other floor," and "Why use meaningless numbers to identify accounts? Why not use letters or a combination of letters and numbers?"

    a. Would you defend the "double identification" or scrap the code for something better? Explain.

    b. What would be your response to your client's other questions?

c. What type of code did you use? By inference what type did your client suggest? Which code do you prefer, and why?

23. How does initial recording differ from reproducing? You are designing a payroll procedure in which a payroll register is to be prepared. Explain the role of initial recording as contrasted to reproducing in this procedure.

24. Can the classifying operation be automated? Explain.

25. What are the ideal specifications for a good classification scheme? Do the specifications differ for a good code? Explain.

26. What is meant by *validating* or *authenticating* a sales ticket? How does the operation fit into data and information flow?

27. What is meant by *distribution* of expenses and how does the operation fit into data and information flow?

28. What are unit tickets and why are they important in data and information flow?

29. Is the traditional accounting cycle descriptive of the data and information flow of the financial information system of a medium-sized or large business today? Explain.

30. Since so much depends on the accuracy and completeness of the initial record, why are nonaccounting personnel allowed to create communication media?

31. From your experience, or as a result of a visit to a business, describe the initial record and its characteristics for each of the following:
    a. Cash sale of a box of popcorn in a theater.
    b. Write-off of an account receivable.
    c. Redemption for cash of a book of trading stamps.
    d. Cash placed in the church collection plate.
    e. Refund of a bottle deposit.
    f. Payment of 20¢ bus fare.
    g. Delivery of ten gallons of gasoline.

32. What are the important variables that the systems analyst must consider in the design of a chart of accounts?

33. What are the tests of a satisfactory code? For each test of a satisfactory code, indicate the name of the code which probably best meets each of your tests and explain why. In terms of a particular test, the code should be superior to most if not all others, although in other respects the code you select may not be satisfactory.

34. Discuss the significance of coding in connection with processing accounting information by machines.

35. Besides accounts, what are some of the things commonly identified by code numbers in a code?

36. Identify the type of code exemplified by each of the following, and its principal advantages and disadvantages.

   a.

No.	Name
1	Brown, Charles
2	Adam, William
3	Cunningham, Fred
4	Davis, Wilson
5	Thomas, Harris

   b. A code where, say 1-19, is used to designate current assets, 20-29 for prepaid expenses, 30-59 for fixed assets, etc.

   c.

Symbol	Description
7.24	Front wheel assembly
7.241	Discs
7.242	Tire
7.243	Bearing assembly
7.2431	Bearings

   d.

Symbol	Description
7	#7 Wagon Complete
7T	Top assembly—
7TS	sides
7TB	bottom
7TBR	brake
7FBA	Front bolster assembly
7FBAA	front axle
7FBABO	front bolster

   e.

Symbol	Description
070000	#7 Wagon Complete
070100	Top assembly—
070101	sides
070102	bottom
070103	brake
070200	Front bolster assembly
070201	front axle
070202	front bolster

CHAPTER 9

Systems Output

INTRODUCTION

REPORTS ARE THE OUTPUT OF THE INFORMATION SYSTEM. THEY PROVIDE information without further processing. Information from reports is the basis for management's planning, coordination, and controlling effort. Information can be read out of a system and stored in cards or on tape temporarily, but is not the output of the system unless it is in usable form. To the extent that reports, the output of a system, are adequate, the work of management can become more precise and effective.

The report principle of systems design requires:

The system should be designed to permit effective reporting, both internally and externally, since reports are a primary systems product.

The design of a system so that there is a flow of accurate information for effective internal as well as external reporting purposes is vital. It has been noted that the output of a system governs its design. Thus, the *starting point in the design of a system* is to determine the output required. The output can then be planned so that it will be accurate and in appropriate detail and the system developed accordingly. Thus, the adequacy of the system is in direct relation to the quality of the systems output.

Adequate communication of data and information are dependent on good reporting. Facts must be known. Operating personnel and executives must have timely and complete information if they are to perform their functions efficiently and expeditiously. Operations must be controlled and actual performance measured against forecasts or standards. Thus reports are the neck of the funnel through which management keeps informed and the business operates. Reports are the *life blood of the business.* They present facts, provide the basis for decisions, direct attention to efficiencies as well as inefficiencies, and provide a measuring device that is the basis for all control tools. *Systems should be justified primarily because they are the basis for informative reports and enable management to perform its functions adequately.*

COMMUNICATION

All business activities center around the actions of people dealing with the business as customers, employees, owners, or interested third parties. In order for any of these groups to be informed and make intelligent decisions and to act on them, information about the business must be available. *Communication* is the transmission of data and/or information to individuals within or associated with the enterprise. This activity has a dual dimension. Not only does information need to be disseminated within the enterprise, but also to interested parties outside the business. It is important for the systems analyst to know the basic objectives of communication which are valid regardless of whether the communication problem is internal or external, or whether communication media or reports contain the solution to a specific problem.

The systems analyst's concept of communication must be more inclusive than the narrow area of written reports. He must seek to achieve the basic objectives of communication in every phase of his work. In any situation where information and/or data are transmitted, the basic objectives of communication discussed below are applicable.

1. Intelligible message.
2. Consistency in preparation.
3. Completeness.
4. Timing and timeliness.
5. Effective transmission.
6. Interest and acceptance.

INTELLIGIBLE MESSAGE. In order for the message transmitted in any type of communication to be understood by the recipient so that prompt and efficient action can be taken with regard to the message, clarity of language in the message must be achieved. If recipients of data and/or information do not understand the message sent to them, inefficient or erroneous actions may be taken as a result. In communication, therefore, the systems analyst must know the level of competence of the recipients and/or originators of any business communications to determine the type and level of language that must be used. Sales, for example, recorded on unmarked forms which are sent to the accounting department for proper recording could well be mis-recorded. Financial reports to production foremen may be unsuitable because the financial jargon used is unintelligible.

CONSISTENCY IN PREPARATION. Consistency in preparation of any type of communication supports and facilitates effectiveness of clear language. Communication accomplished in the same way each time is more understandable to operating personnel than unique and varying communications. It is evident that mistakes would occur in the processing of data and misunderstandings increase if the format of communication media used to record sales on account was changed frequently.

COMPLETENESS. Completeness is an objective of communication which means that the message transmitted must contain neither too little nor too much data or information. Production foremen, for example, have little need for instructions that do not relate to their operation. Conversely, all instructions that relate to their operation must be known. Inadequate or excess information may hamper rather than help them to manage their crews more efficiently.

TIMING AND TIMELINESS. Timing is of great importance to good communication. Not only must information be available when needed, but it must be current and accurate enough to enable the recipient to take any necessary actions. Communication implies that some type of action is expected of the recipient. The transmission of data or information that is incapable of being acted upon because it is received too late is inefficient. Inefficiency is also fostered due to ill-timed data transmission about operational problems when action is still possible, but the problem has not been corrected as quickly as it should have been. Unless communications with the data processing system and to interested outsiders are timely, the data processing operation is malfunctioning.

EFFECTIVE TRANSMISSION. The most direct method of transmission should be selected if this method is to be compatible with the reasonable cost principle. Many types of messages transmitted within or without the enterprise lose their effectiveness because the wrong mode of transmission was selected. One company, for example, was not satisfied with the results that should have been forthcoming from monthly reports prepared for department managers. Top management felt that much of the material in the reports was not understood and, therefore, was ignored. The executive vice-president instructed the accounting department to prepare graphic reports for the next month which were interpreted for the managers in a special report meeting. During this meeting the managers had ample opportunity to question the accountants as well as to grasp the interrelationships existing among their various departments. This mode of communication worked so effectively that it became a firm policy to encourage graphic report presentations.

INTEREST AND ACCEPTANCE. Communication is essential to provide needed information so that individuals or groups of individuals may perform certain actions effectively. If employees and other interested parties are to act properly when a particular type of communication is received, some means of motivation must be present. It is not the authors' contention that a well-conceived communication method will furnish the motivating force to bring about required action. It is our belief, however, that communication can be accomplished to arouse the interest of recipients and to encourage their acceptance.

At every organizational level, a major concern is communication. Only through communicating ideas or the result of certain transactions is it possible for the affairs of a business to be understood or directed. Internally, we have noted that communication media provide an important function. These are the business papers that flow through the organization to accomplish the intermediary steps in procedures. They are different from systems output or reports in that they are not considered to be the end output of the system. Sales tickets, for example, are communication media. This can be contrasted to the total of all sales tickets that are summarized in the report of sales.

In attempting to communicate, it is often difficult to know the means of communication that would be most effective. Communication in business is usually oral, in writing, by visual presentations, or by combining several methods. Overhead projectors, slides, tapes, charts, graphs, diagrams, and other means of communication are available and should be used whenever appropriate. At every level of management, a major objective is to let others know the relevant facts.

Need for Reports

As any business grows, management must rely to a greater extent on the information compiled, summarized, and interpreted through systems output. In the small business, the proprietor does not need a reporting system to be informed about day-to-day events. He personally signs all checks, helps place merchandise on the shelf, sells to customers, and checks out the cash register each night. It is no wonder that the small businessman is not concerned with the development of reports. To him, reports are merely documenting the obvious and not worthy of any expenditure of time or money. The reporting system for a small business will be only those reports necessary to comply with external needs. If a banker requires a report, the small business owner will reluctantly produce it. As a business grows in size, the owners or top managers are no longer as well able to supervise and witness each transaction personally. It thus becomes more and more important that the reporting system provide the necessary information for managerial and other purposes. In the large company, management is often expected to be familiar with occurrences thousands of miles away. They can fulfill their responsibilities only through an efficient and effective reporting system.

Business reports can be classified according to whether designed for an internal or external need. Internal reports, the major justification for an information system, can be further classified according to the systems purpose for which they are designed as follows:

1. Internal reports:
   a. Measure fulfillment of responsibility.
   b. Information.
   c. Basis for action.
2. External reports.

The classification of internal reports has special significance because it reflects areas where management can expect major contributions from the information system. The design of the report, at the very least, must be to fulfill the basic objectives of the user. In the discussion that follows, it can be noted that a report may be in one classification for one party, and in another for a different party. For example, a report that is a basis for action report to a factory foreman, may be an information report for a sales supervisor.

INTERNAL REPORTS

Internal reports are essential to the operation of businesses when the owners cannot personally supervise all activities. They are the information tools—designed to provide information at the time and place where it is needed—that keep management informed and able to make intelligent decisions, solve problems, and control operations. All levels of management must be given the information necessary for constructive action.

MEASURE FULFILLMENT OF RESPONSIBILITY. Managers have many occasions in which it is necessary to delegate authority. Information should flow from the system to each responsible manager so that he knows the degree of success or failure of those to whom authority is delegated. For example, a sales manager should receive a report of sales for each district sales manager, and the district sales manager should have a report of the sales of each salesman. Such reports enable the manager to evaluate the performance of his subordinates.

INFORMATION. Reports are necessary to provide all types of information to management. Many accounting reports drawn from ledger balances, such as the Income Statement, are information reports, and serve internally only to confirm the daily operating reports. Most special studies are also information reports and are a vital part of systems output. It is usually designed to provide all information in a given situation for planning, policy determination, or decision making.

BASIS OF ACTION. Reports designed to provide information for control are the basis of action reports. Their purpose is to focus attention on a given area or special problem in which action is needed. Such reports must be timely and highlight variations from predetermined amounts to enable effective action. Basis-of-action reports would include comparative budgets, inventory status reports, etc.

Effective Use of Internal Reports

Reports are of practical value to a business organization only if they are used properly. Many of the control reports that flow through the business are accounting-based reports, and it is essential that they be used by operating personnel as intended, or their preparation is not justified. One of the main considerations in authorizing the preparation of a report is to determine that it will be used constructively.

The effective use of reports depends on a number of factors. *First, the further from actual operations, the more likely the use of reports.* High level executives use reports to a greater extent than operating supervisors. Operating supervisors are close enough to their jobs that many factors relating to operations are known prior to the time that reports can be prepared. Higher executives, on the other hand, are more dependent upon reports for the great variety of information they must have. *Second, operating personnel who are familiar with the data or information are more apt to use reports than those that do not fully understand their significance.* Most golfers have a favorite club; gardeners, carpenters, and other craftsmen have their favorite tools. In each case, the club or tool is used because it is familiar and will produce the desired results. By the same token, reports are tools that will be used by those who are familiar with them and can use them to obtain results. *Third, use of reports by subordinate levels of supervision is more often than not correlated with the use made of the report by higher levels.* If, for example, an operating executive regularly inquires of a subordinate the reason for a variance shown in a certain report, that subordinate is going to be watching variances carefully, in the future, in order to be able to answer inquiries that he might receive. In situations such as this, reports are very effective. If explanations are not required, even though reports reveal the situations they were designed to disclose, then the purpose of reporting can be defeated. *Lastly, reports will be used if they help the user to perform his job better, and if he has confidence in their accuracy.* Much is to be gained by using a report that will help in job performance when accuracy is assured.

The use of reports is directly related to the communication that is established with operating departments. Simon illustrates the point for the controller's department. He indicates that if reports *are not used* to the satisfaction of all, there are some specific steps that can be taken to establish the desired contacts and communications as follows: [1]

> 1. Give Controller's Department personnel definite assignments which require working with operating men. The simplest device of this kind is to require accounting personnel, with the cooperation of operating men, to prepare explanations of variances from performance standards.
>
> 2. Give these assignments high priority. Insure that they will not be neglected under the pressure of report deadlines or other duties.
>
> 3. Locate the Controller's staffman as close as possible to his counterpart in the operating department.
>
> 4. Place contact responsibilities at a high enough level in the Controller's Department so that the gap in status between this man and his counterpart in operations will not be too great.
>
> 5. In every possible way, try to staff contact positions with personnel who have a thorough understanding of operations.

All personnel should strive to improve the usefulness and effectiveness of their reports. When the same information is being entered on different reports, there is a possibility that the reports can be combined to serve both purposes, thus eliminating duplication. If adequate information is not available on reports, every effort should be made to see that it is included. Information from informal tabulations should be incorporated into regular reports. When there is no need for information in separate informal records, internal reporting will be serving its purpose in a superior manner.

Channels of Internal Reporting

Whenever a report is designed, the flow or distribution of the report through the organization structure, as well as the objectives and purpose of the report, must be definitely established. Reports can be prepared in any number of copies by using the appropriate duplicating process. Planning the report flow is a basic part of the design of a systems output. The channels of reporting are both vertical and horizontal, and in some instances a combination of both horizontal and vertical is appropriate.

The flow of reports is important and should reflect the philosophy behind the information need or control technique. For example, budget control can be accomplished in a number of ways, each requiring a different flow of reports. The foreman of an operating department, his immediate supervisor, the production manager, and the budget officer could each be sent budget

---

[1] Simon, H. A., Guetzkow, H., Kozmetsky, G., and Tyndall, G., *Centralization vs. Decentralization in Organizing the Controller's Department*, A Research Study and Report Prepared for Controllership Foundation, Inc. (New York: Controllership Foundation, Inc., August, 1954), p. 54.

reports simultaneously, with regular evaluation conferences scheduled at a later date. A different flow would direct all copies to the budget director who would distribute them at an evaluation conference. Still another plan would be to send all reports to the production manager who would use them or not, according to his best judgment. Any number of plans can exist for budget control and in each instance, the control pattern is revealed by the flow of reports.

Reports often flow along the lines of an organization chart to reflect the discharge of authority. Thus, if a production department has authority for the manufacture of certain types of items, a report should go to the production supervisor to show how well the job is being done. There should be a fairly direct relationship between organization structure and the flow of reports.

EXTERNAL REPORTS

External reports have special purposes as do internal reports. They are designed to keep those interested persons outside of management informed about phases of the business in which they are especially interested. There are four groupings into which external reports that are prepared as a regular part of doing business can be classified. They are reports to owners, to governmental and regulatory units, to financial institutions, and to others. These reports are generally prepared, at least in part, from the regular systems output.

REPORTS TO OWNERS. The annual report to owners (shareholders) is one of the common external reports. It contains an Income Statement, Balance Sheet, and a considerable amount of additional data and information about the company, such as a letter from the president, current developments in the industry and company, new products, consolidated statements, and statistical tabulations. It is not the purpose of this text to discuss the preparation of annual reports, as separate volumes have been written on the subject. It should be pointed out, however, that the basic statements around which the annual report is constructed are a product of the system. The amounts that are included are usually certified by an independent accountant and can be traced to the records of the company reporting. An excellent source of information concerning annual reports and analysis of accounting trends, as reflected in annual reports, is published each year by the American Institute of Certified Public Accountants.[2]

REPORTS TO GOVERNMENTAL AND REGULATORY UNITS. Most businessmen are required by law to submit a tremendous amount of information to

---

[2] *Accounting Trends and Techniques in Published Corporate Annual Reports*, American Institute of Certified Public Accountants, New York. Published annually.

governmental agencies and regulatory groups. Such information is expensive to obtain and accumulate, yet there is no alternative. Typical of such reports are income tax returns, payroll and sales tax returns and related records and reports, statements for registration of securities, and the like.

REPORTS TO FINANCIAL INSTITUTIONS. Businessmen deal with banks, insurance companies, or other financial institutions that make it their business to furnish capital and provide financial services. Such institutions request and receive reports, and work closely with management.

OTHERS. There seems to be no end of the reporting required of businessmen. Vendors need reports to determine if credit should be extended. Customers, business research organizations, trade associations, and others request reports and information for their own special purposes.

External reports are often taken from information that is used internally by management. They usually contain the minimum amount of information necessary to satisfy the need for which the report is being prepared. Management would, for example, have the sales figures divided into sales by each department or product line for their own internal use, yet for external reporting purposes, only the total sales figure is normally given. The same factual data are presented in many different ways and are geared to the many different levels of understanding, yet all facts are, in the aggregate, the same.

REPORTS TO MANAGEMENT

Top Management

The design of different types of reports for the various levels of management is extremely important. It can be noted that a special type of report is required by top management to perform their function. Generally speaking, reports to top management are not in great detail, although they are often well documented. Reports to top management fall into four general categories:

1. Reports for long-range planning.
2. Reports for short-range planning.
3. Special reports for nonrepetitive decisions.
4. Reports for reviewing current progress.

Top management reports are normally for key executives, and relate primarily to information necessary for planning and policy formulation. In reporting to top management, it is important to know that the major concern is for planning the future. This means that most reports are projections or planning documents, and relate to what will happen in the future rather than what has already happened. For example, one of the projections that is most meaningful is the budget which is fundamentally a planning document, but also an important control tool.

The number of figures that top executives follow on a regular basis is usually few. These figures too often are from a "little black book" or are under the glass on the desk top. In the design of top management reports, it is most important that information be obtained so that key information usually followed by management is produced on a regular basis as part of the formal reporting structure.

It should be noted that the source of information for most internal reports, including reports for top management, is not from ledger balances. Key totals are reported from different points in the information system. While these totals are accurate, they are often days away from the ledger. For example, daily cash register summaries of sales in a department store provide an excellent basis for a report to management, yet sales may actually be posted to the ledger only once each month.

Middle Management

Middle management in many large companies has authority approximating that of the president in a small company. Middle managers will be more concerned with operating detail than top management since they have direct responsibility for activities such as sales, production, cost control and inventory control as well as profit performance. Middle management will often require balance sheet information as a part of being able to control their own operations. Middle management also includes major department heads. The further down the chain of command toward major department heads, the greater should be the detail built into middle management reports.

Supervisors and Foremen

There is no great uniformity in belief as to the amount of information that should be reported to supervisors and foremen. Many companies have taken the position that the purpose of their supervisors and foremen is to direct the workers. Such a philosophy gives rise to the need for an individual who might be called a cost analyst who represents the controller, yet works in production departments. The cost analyst assists in clerical activities, budget preparation, and does the necessary data gathering. He makes it possible for the supervisors and foremen to spend their time in line work. Some, however, say the supervisors and foremen are logically a part of the control process and should be expected to do their share of paper work.

Where supervisors and foremen are to receive reports, the question arises as to the type of reports that are appropriate. Many will argue that only the controllable portion of the costs should be reported to lower managerial levels. The basis for such a position is that any other costs are really not relevant since foremen can do nothing about them. Others will argue that all costs should be reported. They contend a foreman should be fully informed of the amount that has been invested and the costs that are incurred to make the jobs possible in his department. While costs would be divided between controllable and noncontrollable, there would be no question as to the fact that they were incurred in his operation.

Instances exist where it is appropriate to report physical units as well as dollars. If communication or control can be facilitated, the system should be designed so that both units and dollars can be reported. At the lower level, as is true with the higher level, reports should be designed to focus attention on items that are not according to plan or that require action.

REPORTING STANDARDS

Internal reporting must be flexible to meet the great variety of needs found in various businesses. Modern reporting is an art not mastered by many. Individuals skilled in internal report preparation find that standards of reporting provide a minimum level of attainment for effective communication. Standards of reporting helpful in the design of reports are as follows:

ONE SUBJECT. Different subjects or problems require different actions, solutions and decisions. Internal reports that are limited to a specific subject or problem can be analyzed, distributed to individuals in departments concerned, or studied without being revised or rewritten. Organization and presentation can be aimed at a specific subject or problem and the objective of the report can be accomplished with less difficulty.

KNOW THE RECIPIENT. Whenever there is need for a report, that report cannot have optimum effectiveness unless the person preparing it knows something about the individual or individuals to whom the report is directed. Knowledge of the group to whom a report is being submitted is vital. For example, the president of a business who is not finance oriented may prefer not to have the quantitative type summary that a treasurer or controller might prefer. Some executives prefer graphic presentations as contrasted to written tabular presentations. Whenever the preferances or strong or weak points of the individual or groups to whom a report is submitted are known, they should be carefully considered so that effective communication is possible.

ACCURACY. Confidence in the accuracy of a report makes it an effective tool for the user. Lack of confidence may undermine the entire reporting procedure. Minor errors often detract, disproportionately, from the real significance of a report. For example, a misspelled word causes the reader of a report to wonder how many other errors are included.

Data or information used in internal reports should be obtained at points in the procedure at which the possibility of error is at a minimum. For example, data obtained and verified by machine or meter at the end of a process are collected at an ideal point. The validity of the data is certain. Partial information or data obtained at the midpoint of a process or procedure are often incorrect. For example, if a liquid is being processed, quantity data should be obtained for reporting when the liquid is metered into or out of the process as conclusions at this point are warranted. If a quality report is being prepared, it should be extracted at a point where quality can be measured so that data are accurate.

Accountants are sometimes guilty of giving a false impression of the accuracy of data and information that they have collected and are reporting. By carrying figures to the closest penny, the implication is that amounts are absolutely accurate. In the case of bad debts, inventories, or depreciation, for example, the amounts that are used include estimates and certainly differ from actual figures. Nothing is accomplished by carrying many figures to the nearest penny in reports, implying accuracy that is a fiction.

TIMELINESS. Effective reporting must be timely. Knowledge that requires action or is needed for decisions but is not received until it is too late to act or to be used is not much better than no knowledge at all, and its receipt is a source of considerable irritation to responsible executives. Reports must reach the designated recipients when events are fresh in their mind, when interest is high, and when action based on the information would be timely.

Standards such as accuracy and timeliness are sometimes in conflict, and specific facts in the case will have to govern the extent to which one takes precedence over the other. For example, it is often better to use informed estimates in timely reports than to have completely accurate reports too late to be of value. All reports should, of course, show the date or period covered.

REDUCE BULK. Effective internal reports must be short and to the point. Where possible, all major points should be established and conclusions and recommendations presented in no more than a page or two. Detailed explanations and tabulations in support of the summarized facts contained in the report can be attached for use if the reader so desires.

Managers are busy people and are inclined to set aside lengthy reports until a block of time is available to study the information. It is essential then that every long report have a summary not exceeding one-half to three-quarters of a page in length. The summary should state the major points in the overall report. If the manager feels that a detailed study is appropriate, this can always be undertaken. In the meantime, the point or points that are vital in the total report will have been considered by the manager.

Management does not weigh in reports to determine how good they are. On the contrary, good reports are those that establish the pertinent facts in as few words as possible.

CLARITY. Reports should be clear and complete. If the report does not clearly state its purpose, or what is expected of the recipient, the desired results will not be accomplished. Reports must be written so as to prevent misunderstandings.

IDENTIFY ORIGINATOR. The person who originates a report should acknowledge responsibility for its preparation. In some instances, responsibility is designated by the originating individual placing his initials or signature on the report. In other instances, the reporting responsibility is designated through a reports control plan or in the procedures manual. Written information can be traced to its source, and is, therefore, sent forward only after it has been properly verified and given appropriate consideration by the person responsible for its preparation.

A report that is distributed over a manager's signature reflects the quality of the work for which the person signing the report becomes known. Good construction is a mark of quality and instills confidence in users.

COMPARISONS. Comparative information should be included in the design of reports whenever it permits more informed conclusions or will facilitate control. Comparisons to budget, standard, previous experience, established trends, or the like provide more meaningful information. Comparisons effectively establish the direction in which a given activity is moving. It is, however, essential that information being compared be similar. For example, comparison of the amount of sales in one year to the amount of sales in the previous year may be misleading. Not only is price per unit a factor in the dollar amount, but product mix can also change. There could be an increase in the amount of sales with fewer units sold. Also if sales in the first year were of products A and B, while sales in the second year were products C and D, the dollar comparison could have little meaning. The comparison of what *should have been done* to what *was done* is often the most meaningful.

Statistical comparisons are also misleading in some instances. When percentages are compared, the magnitude of raw data should be considered so that small numbers do not detract from the meaning. For example, if sales had increased from one dollar to five dollars in a given department, there has been a 400 per cent increase. Yet if sales increase from one million to two million dollars in another department, there has been only a 100 per cent increase.

DISCLOSURE. Reports should be designed to include all relevant facts. The system can provide a useful service as long as all relevant facts are included in the reporting procedure and presented in such a way as to not distort situations by disclosing half complete information. Good judgment and diplomacy must be used in some reports to prevent offending unnecessarily. Facts can be disclosed and responsibility identified without rubbing in unfortunate results, and creating ill-will unnecessarily. Both positive and negative facts should be revealed.

ELIMINATION OF DUPLICATION. When the same information is being entered on different reports, there is a possibility that the reports can be redesigned to serve both purposes, thus eliminating costly duplication.

POSITIVE REPORTING. Reporting that is negative automatically causes resistance. Positive reporting accomplishes the desired objective and has the advantage of sounding helpful rather than critical. For example, a negative report could state, "Operating personnel did not complete satisfactorily one-fourth of the work for which they are responsible." A positive report could state, "Operating personnel completed satisfactorily three-fourths of the work for which they are responsible." The facts for managerial evaluation are exactly the same, but the implication is not negative nor does it imply that no good reason exists for the facts reported.

DEVICES TO EMPHASIZE SIGNIFICANT POINTS. Many different devices are helpful in emphasizing important points in reports. The use of arrows, marginal notes, or circling certain key figures is effective. Also effective are underscoring, the use of color, different style print, and varying margins.

APPEARANCE AND READABILITY. Appearance and readability are important factors relating to the acceptance of report contents. If reports are attractive, well prepared, and easy to read, it seems evident that they will be given consideration. If they are messy and difficult to read, they may not receive proper consideration from recipients.

ESTIMATES. Use of informed estimates in reports is proper. It is often more important to have information early than it is to have accurate information much later. Informed estimates can provide a contribution to a reporting system. Such estimates even though slightly inaccurate, can provide the basis for cost savings. They should be identified for what they are, however.

It is often worthwhile to develop a reporting system in which certain figures or statistics are communicated orally as preliminary estimates become available. This makes it possible for key executives to have information earlier than would otherwise be the case and they can presumably be more effective in their work. The use of machines to speed up the availability of preliminary information is also very important.

ANALYTICAL OR INTERPRETIVE COMMENTS. Reports that do not include analytical or interpretive comments are not optimum reports. In the process of accumulating information, there will often be inconsistent or unusual kinds of information disclosed. When such is the case, an explanation should be set forth and an interpretive comment added to the report. The people responsible for the financial information system must be more than figure accumulators. They should be able to explain the meaning of their figures on the reports and be ready to make recommendations if asked.

SIMPLICITY. Reports are intended to communicate information. To be effective, it is necessary that nontechnical language be used. This does not mean that the report has to be simplified to the extent that it is an insult to a person's intelligence, but it does mean that where it is possible to use a more descriptive term or a shorter word, it should be done.

Individuals are inclined to be vain, thus they are certain that others have the same interests, likes and dislikes, and methods of reasoning as their own.

Accountants, unfortunately, are no exception. Their technical training and basic approach to problems is through facts and figures analyzed and summarized in worksheets. Most people would agree that, as an approach to problem-solving, the factual approach, with thorough documentation and analysis, is essential. Yet reporting is entirely different from obtaining the answer to the problem. It is a matter of communicating with others. Tabulations of figures that are alive and meaningful to the accountant may be complicated, deadening, and meaningless to others. To report effectively, information must be presented simply and in such a manner as to be of interest to the individual or group of individuals that are to receive the report.

Reporting by Exception

The design of reports at the top level should be such that the significant items are highlighted, and the deviations from the plan are emphasized. Reporting in this manner is reporting on the *exception basis*. Reporting according to the exception basis does not imply that reports are condensed to the extent of reporting only exceptions to the plan. Carried to the extreme, when everything is going according to plans, such an interpretation would cause top management reports to be nothing more than blank sheets of paper. On the contrary, management is not to be cut off from information, but is to be fully informed. To accomplish objectives, top management need not be involved in controlling activities so long as they are within the scope of plans or policies already approved and in effect. It is when business activities are not according to plans and policies that management must initiate corrective action.

Reporting on the exception basis is reporting in such a way as to highlight variations from the plan. For example, the use of over- or under-budget or variances from standard could highlight a situation that is out of control.

The necessity for management to wade through mountains of information to discover whether or not exceptions exist is eliminated. Reporting by exception frees managers to plan and to handle problems that are important rather than to devote their time to reading and evaluating reports to discover if there are exceptions.

Reports Control

Unnecessary and costly reports are often prepared. Once authorized, a report can be prepared over and over again even though it is no longer used. Reports are usually initiated for a good reason, but with ever changing business situations the need for reports changes too. The reporting principle requires effective reporting. It follows that there must be control over reports being prepared. A systematic review of reports being prepared and their value should be scheduled periodically to establish and maintain control.

One method of determining whether or not a report is being used is to withhold distribution of the report for a period of time to see if anyone inquires as to why the report was not received. If there is no complaint the report can be discontinued after appropriate arrangement. If a complaint is received after the lapse of several weeks there is a good possibility that the inquiry was only for the purpose of keeping the file complete, thus the matter of continuing the report should still be considered carefully.

Reports are costly and require the expenditure of large amounts of time and effort. They should be prepared only when there is a good reason. A reports control system that provides for authorization of reports and their proposed distribution prior to preparation can be initiated. Such a plan will maintain control over existing reports, and proposed new reporting. The system must provide for numbering, periodic review, and the approval of changes to reports. The reports control program is frequently administered by the Media Control Unit discussed in Chapter 4.

QUESTIONS, PROBLEMS, AND CASES

1. At what stage in the design of a system is the output of the system planned? Explain.

2. Distinguish between, and give examples of, internal reports that can be classified as (*a*) measure fulfillment of responsibility, (*b*) information, and (*c*) basis for action reports.

3. Why are reports viewed differently by the small business owner than by the manager of a large corporation?

4. The president of the company has indicated that he does not believe that middle management is using reports properly. How would you determine whether there is anything to the president's hunch? Specifically, what are some of the factors that bear on the use of reports by subordinates?

5. Indicate why channels of internal reporting are so important in the design of a report. Illustrate, using an example of different flows of the same report that might be used. (Do not use a budget for your illustration.)

6. To what source would you go to determine how certain financial information is being reported in corporate annual reports? Go to this source in the library, and prepare a report concerning the current treatment of either contingent liabilities, leaseholds, or prepaid expenses. Your report should be designed as a memorandum from yourself to your instructor, and follow the appropriate standards of reporting.

7. In what way would a report of operations prepared for top management differ from such a report for middle management? For supervisors or foremen?

8. Reporting standards relating to accuracy and estimates seem to be in conflict. Are they in conflict? Explain.

9. One of the reporting standards is to know the recipient of a report. Explain and illustrate this standard. Does the standard mean that different facts would be reported to different groups?

10. Reporting standards relating to timeliness and disclosure seem to be in conflict. Are they in conflict? Explain.

11. In the design of a report, you are considering the presentation of some comparative information. For each of the following possibilities, indicate and explain whether the presentations might be misleading. Also indicate the advantages of the comparisons.
    a. This year's purchases to last year's purchases.
    b. This year's advertising expense to last year's advertising expense.
    c. This year's direct labor cost to the direct labor budget for this year.
    d. Percentage of rent expense to total sales this year to the percentage of rent expense to total sales last year.

12. Contrast and illustrate reporting that is positive to reporting that is negative. Which do you prefer, and why?

13. The standard of reporting that has the most to do with the management potential of accountants is the analytical or interpretive comments standard. Discuss.

14. What is the major problem encountered by companies using the exception basis of reporting? Discuss.

15. The Automatic Controls Company was established in 1941. Regular production schedules have been followed since that time, even through the product line is almost completely different than it was at the time the company was organized. Commercial-type machinery and equipment have constituted the majority of the sales volume during the past four years.
    The vice-president in charge of production has requested that one of the large machines used in production be overhauled, while the plant engineer insists that a new machine should be purchased. The president has referred the matter to the controller for study. In conference with other management executives and as a result of studies by his staff, the following facts were determined:
    a. The old machine had been acquired six years ago at a cost of $100,000. It had been depreciated at the rate of 10 per cent per year.
    b. The cost of the overhaul would be $65,500. The cost of the new machine, including removal of the old machine and installation of the new, would be $250,000.
    c. The new machine has been improved to the point that it will turn out approximately twice as many units as the old machine.
    d. It is estimated that it would take about the same amount of downtime

to repair the old machine as to remove the old machine and to install the new one.

e. The old machine, if run on two shifts, will be adequate for all foreseeable production. Present production on the old machine is accomplished in one shift and a half. Second shift personnel are used to advantage on other machines when time permits, thus running the machine for an extra half-shift presents no problem.

f. Both the old and new machines require a crew of three men for operation. Weekly salaries for a 40-hour week are $150, $130, and $90 respectively. A 5 per cent night shift premium is paid to men on the second shift. Time and one-half is paid for overtime.

g. The old machine would have to be sold as scrap. It is estimated that $600 would be received.

h. Money to purchase the new machine would have to be borrowed at 5 per cent interest, as working capital is all needed for operations at the present time. Money for overhauling the machine would also have to be borrowed.

i. The company is in the 50 per cent tax bracket for federal income taxes. Other taxes and the investment credit should be ignored.

j. The estimated future life of the old machine, if repaired and run for two shifts, is eight years, while the estimated life of the new machine, if run for one shift, is ten years. Machines would be scrapped at the end of their estimated life. Technological developments have been rapid in machines of this type, and are not considered in estimating the life of the machines.

Prepare a report in good form, from the controller to the president, with a recommendation as to whether the old machine should be repaired or the new machine purchased. Assume that any factors needed to make the report complete and not given above, apply equally to both the old and new machines, therefore, and do not affect the decision.

16. The Hollen Company manufactures and distributes directly to retail outlets a line of household utensils. The top level organization of the company is as follows:

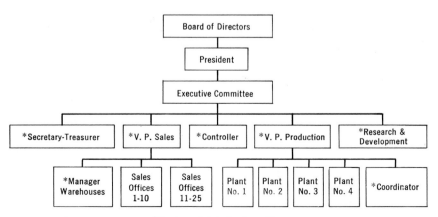

*Members of Executive Committee

Sales are made through 25 regional sales offices, with all shipments to customers direct from three warehouses, one in Baltimore, one in St. Louis, and the other in San Francisco. Regional sales offices carry a limited stock of merchandise for emergency orders, but as a general rule send orders to the warehouses who ship to customers via commercial carrier. Four factories produce about 500 different items for sale through company outlets and on contract for other companies. Production for sale through company outlets is shipped direct to warehouses. Another 700 items are purchased under contract from other companies, who also ship direct to warehouses.

Each warehouse maintains a full stock of all items. A perpetual inventory system is maintained based on number of units only. Each warehouse initiates requests to the coordinator for items to replenish their stocks. Warehouse managers complain that they sometimes receive items that are not ordered or larger quantities than ordered, and space and slow moving stocks present many difficulties. The coordinator admits that he often takes advantage of cheaper rates for quantity orders, and that items ordered from company-owned factories are always in economical production quantities. Additional quantities must be stored until sold. He can cite many profitable deals on this basis, and has a partial tabulation showing savings of $73,000.

During one of the recent executive committee meetings a number of subjects were discussed, one of which was the level of the inventory at the warehouses. Another was the increase in the number of orders that could not immediately be filled, and the necessity of costly emergency back orders. A special study, made by a staff section in the controller's division, revealed specifically that the dollar value of the inventory had been increasing at an alarming rate (from $2,000,000 to $2,700,000 in six months—after adjustment for price level increases, etc.) that the "balance" of items required to fill customer orders was abnormal, that the average orders from warehouses to the coordinator were decreasing in size as there was no place to store items, and that customer complaints were increasing.

The secretary-treasurer informed the executive committee that funds to finance the increase in inventory had been borrowed at interest of 5.5 per cent. The executive committee then recommended certain specific actions and that the controller design a periodic report that would provide continuing information about the level of the inventory, balance, and back orders.

a. What might be the specific recommendations of the executive committee?
b. Design a report to meet the need of the Hollen Company.
c. State specifically the channels of reporting to be used for the report designed in step b. above. Include such information as the number of copies, disposition of each copy, and the reason each copy is necessary.

17. The Hughes Distributing Company operates a fleet of trucks over 94 different routes selling a large number of food products such as nuts, special cheeses, potato chips, popcorn, and the like. Routes are centered around 22 distribution centers out of which from one to six trucks are dispatched. Distribution centers are serviced twice each week by semitrailer vans delivering items necessary to replenish the stock level of distribution centers from company plants and warehouses.

A request has been received from a former employee to establish a new distribution center at a location approximately 80 miles beyond the perimeter of present distribution coverage. Investigation of the former employee making the request reveals that he was a successful distribution center manager and could be expected to run an efficient center. The letter has been referred to the controller to study and report back to an executive meeting scheduled in one week.

Prepare an outline for the oral report to be made by the controller to the executive meeting, recommending either that a new distribution center be established, or that the request be denied. Assume such added facts as necessary to document your case. Outlines should be such that a ten minute talk is possible, with any devices to be used, i.e., blackboard illustrations, charts, etc., included in support of the outline.

18. The cash control procedures of the Kendall Company, a wholesale distributing company, are being revised. In the process of the revision a new daily cash report is to be designed. Cash procedures are as follows:
   a. All incoming cash is deposited intact in the First Federal Bank via the night depository on the day it is received.
   b. Three change funds of $100 each are maintained by the three cashiers, each of whom has responsibility for a cash register.
   c. The imprest petty cash fund of $300 is maintained by the chief cashier.
   d. All disbursements are either from the petty cash fund or by check.

   From the above information, (1) design a daily cash report that will provide all the information required for cash control, and (2) state the number of copies of the report that would be prepared and the distribution that would be made.

19. The controller of the Jordan Company, Mr. Jack A. Anderson, received the following report from the factory accountant, Mr. Robert R. Rand, of a recently-acquired subsidiary:

ABC MANUFACTURING COMPANY
Little Town, Kansas

Inter-Company Memo
Dear Jack:

I was glad to get your phone call last night. I have got the information that you requested, so here goes:

Cost estimates on contract #465 are off because of Department #1. Detail costs incurred in Department #1 were $6,340 as compared to the $5,200 estimated. Spoiled material of $490 was charged to the contract too. Overhead applied to the contract on the basis of direct labor was $5,850.

Department #1 variance was caused by John Kittle's wife. Last week she was taken to the hospital to have an emergency appendectomy and John has been home taking care of his kids. Harry Cane has been operating his machine since, and he doesn't know how too well yet. We expect John back tomorrow.

Be sure to give me a ring or write if I can give you any other information. Best regards to Hilda and the family.

Bob

P.S. We just got word that John Kittle won't be back for another week.

---

a. List any specific criticism of the above report.

b. Rewrite the report in proper form. Assume any facts that are not given, but are required to make the report complete.

20. The letter that follows, relating to internal control, was sent by an independent Certified Public Accountant to his client:

December 10, 1968

Board of Directors
The Allen-Brown Corporation
Madison, Wisconsin 53702

Gentlemen:

During the course of our examination, the following matters which came to our attention are, we believe, worthy of your consideration.

1. Petty cash fund ($25.00 in amount) is left unattended during the lunch period.

2. Receipts from gum machine are not removed in the presence of a second person.

3. The cashier maintains the accounts receivable ledger and the sales journal.

4. Receiving reports are not prepared when material is received and payment of invoices is made without any check as to the actual receipt of merchandise covered by the invoice.

5. The stamp fund was short two dollars at the time of our cash count.

6. In our review of payroll and personnel records it was noted that the cashier had not taken a vacation in seven years.

Sincerely yours,

John A. Student

John A. Student
Certified Public Accountant

---

a. Evaluate the above letter, with respect to (1) presentation and (2) subject matter, stating its strong points as well as weaknesses.

b. Would your evaluation be the same if the letter had been from the Internal Auditor to the Controller?

21. The president of your company, the Jones-Smith Manufacturing Company, has asked you to recommend a system of internal reporting for use throughout the organization. He has suggested that excellent material is available on the subject. A few specific references recommended are as follows:

> Doris, Lillian, *Corporate Treasurer's and Controller's Encyclopedia*, Prentice-Hall, Inc., 1958. (Volume III, Chapter 22).
>
> Heckert, J. B. and Willson, J. D., *Controllership (Second Edition)*, The Ronald Press Company, 1963. (Chapter 28).

Keller, Wayne, *Management Accounting for Profit Control*, McGraw-Hill Book Company, Inc., 1957. (Chapter 26).

Lasser, J. K., *Standard Handbook for Accountants*, McGraw-Hill Book Company, Inc., 1956. (Part 5).

Wixon, Rufus and Kell, W. G. (Editors), *Accountants' Handbook* (*Fourth Edition*), The Ronald Press Company, 1957. (Section 4).

Prepare a formal memorandum to the president on the subject of "Principles of Internal Reporting." Your solution will be evaluated partially on the basis of how well you have followed reporting standards in the preparation of your memorandum.

22. Assume that you are the controller of a large manufacturing company. The president is hazy about the effect of depreciation. He has asked you to (a) define depreciation, (b) explain why different methods of recording depreciation can be properly utilized, (c) explain if there is any money in the reserve for depreciation, (d) state the effect of depreciation on the accuracy of profits (especially in the recent periods of rising prices), and whether or not accountants should recognize price level fluctuations in the preparation of statements, and (e) any other ramifications that you deem important.

Prepare a *formal memorandum* to the president explaining depreciation, with emphasis on points (a) through (e) above. Your memorandum should not exceed one typewritten page single spaced, or two typewritten pages double spaced.

Excellent material for such a report is found in the references given below:

1. Committees on Accounting Procedure and Accounting Terminology, *Accounting Research and Terminology Bulletins* (Final Edition), American Institute of Certified Public Accountants, 1961. (Chapter 9 and Accounting Terminology Bulletin No. 1).

2. Becker, Morton (Editor), *Modern Accounting Theory*, Prentice-Hall, Inc., 1966. (Chapter 7).

3. Grady, Paul, *Inventory of Generally Accepted Accounting Principles for Business Enterprises*, Accounting Research Study No. 7, American Institute of Certified Public Accountants, 1965.

4. Welsch, Glenn A., Zlatkovich, Charles T., and White, John Arch, *Intermediate Accounting*, (Revised Edition) Richard D. Irwin, Inc., 1968. (Chapters 8, 9, and 23).

23. The controller of a large wholesale company was previously one of the company's top-line executives. He is being rotated through the top managerial positions as training that is to precede his assumption of the presidency. At a recent meeting attended by the controller the speaker implied that all corporate profits were overstated due to inflationary trends. The controller has asked you to explain the meaning of this statement.

Prepare a memorandum to the controller on the subject, "The Effect of Inflation on Profits." Observe standards of good internal reporting. Conclude your memorandum with a recommendation as to company accounting policy on inflation, and state specifically why your recommendation is being made.

(A suggested basis for your report is Chapter 9a, Committees on Accounting Procedure and Accounting Terminology, *Accounting Research and Terminology Bulletins* (Final Edition), American Institute of Certified Public Accountants, 1961. Recommend additional reading: Chapter 15 in *Modern Accounting Theory*, edited by Morton Backer, Prentice-Hall, Inc., 1966. AICPA Staff, *Reporting the Financial Effects of Price-Level Changes*, Accounting Research Study No. 6, American Institute of Certified Public Accountants, 1963. Grady, Paul, *Inventory of Generally Accepted Accounting Principles for Business Enterprises*, Accounting Research Study No. 7, American Institute of Certified Public Accountants, 1965. Extensive background reading can be obtained from the *Accountants' Index*.)

24. Management often prepares various reports involving financial data for internal use. Frequently these reports are quite different from those reported on by the CPA for the same company.
    a. Explain why these reports may differ as to the same basic information.
    b. Name two frequently used types of internal statements, other than the balance sheet and income statement and explain briefly the value of each to management. (AICPA Examination)

25. Accounting reports must be submitted to various levels of management. On what basis do you decide what to include and what not to include on the several reports?

26. Since most accounting facts are initially recorded by persons outside the accounting department, how can the systems analyst maximize the odds that the original record, from which reports are to be prepared, will be accurate and complete?

27. A system should provide information for management from sources other than ledger account balances. List three internal reports that do not come from ledger balances, and indicate the source of the data or information.

28. You are employed in the Management Services (System) Department of a national public accounting firm. At a recent professional meeting you were sitting next to the controller of the Paper Bag Manufacturing Company, a large company, who informs you that his company is reviewing their system of internal reporting. During the course of the evening, he made the following comments:

    "We are extremely pleased with our progress in revising internal reporting procedures. All reports are now channeled through a report analysis section headed by an assistant controller. He investigates unusual items and encloses an analysis of problem areas with reports being sent out. He is also responsible for follow-up on suggestions made in his reports. Duplication of effort is being eliminated by sending copies of detail reports to all organizational levels, removing the necessity for many summaries that did not reveal the full information anyway. All reports are now designed to compare current data to that of prior years, and are prepared directly by machine. Accuracy has been greatly improved due to the practice of verifying reports to the ledger at the time data are prepared."

At the close of the meeting the controller asked you to comment on the above reporting system in writing. Prepare a formal letter to the controller in which you evaluate the comments above.

29. Relate the organization of a general contractor's firm, primarily engaged in large scale construction projects, to an adequate reporting system. For each managerial level discuss the kind of information that should be useful at these levels.

30. Your accounting reports have been prepared from account balances in the past and have been subject to criticism because they are not of enough value for current operating decisions. For this reason you plan to initiate a new series of internal reports. Indicate the types of information useful in operations that would not be immediately available from account balances but that could be obtained through an adequate financial information system.

Unit 2

Systems Investigations

CHAPTER 10

Output Criteria and Analysis*

INTRODUCTION

THE FINANCIAL INFORMATION SYSTEM HAS BEEN DEFINED IN CHAPTER 1 AS "a combination of system components that function within the business organization to process data and to provide the information and internal controls needed by management to carry out its responsibilities of stewardship over the assets, of control over operations, and for planning future enterprise activities." A systems analyst or other individual performing his function is responsible for integrating the physical components—personnel, communication media, reports, and data originating, processing and control devices—along with appropriate internal control duties in such a way that his particular management receives information from reports which will help it carry out its responsibilities.

The work of the systems analyst requires that he understand systems theory and is able to make the necessary application of the theory in any of the many varied and different situations he investigates. The systems study, engagement, or investigation is the work of the systems analyst. Unit 2 of this volume is designed to consider the various phases of systems investigations, and to bring the necessary techniques into focus.

A systems investigation is important in both the design of a new system or the revision of an existing system, and normally consists of three phases, namely analysis, synthesis, and implementation and follow-up. The *analysis*

---

* Major portions of this chapter are based on Schlosser, R. E., "Accounting Systems Review Techniques," *The Journal of Accountancy* (December, 1962).

phase of a systems investigation is discussed in this chapter. In this phase the systems analyst determines how the organization functions and the way in which the existing system operates. He learns the facts necessary to understand what is occurring and why. One of the important aspects is to understand the output criteria and other characteristics of the existing system as well as the output needed or desired of the new system. In his effort to analyze and understand the existing organization and the way in which procedures are accomplished, the systems analyst must establish what kind, how many, and what form reports take that flow from the system. Such output criteria are the foundation for any useful and economical system to be designed later. The needs and demands of management for output must be known and understood. Output criteria are considered as a part of the analysis phase of a systems investigation since the output information required is obtained during analysis, and provides the basis for the second phase of the systems investigation—synthesis.

The *synthesis phase* of a systems investigation, presented in Chapter 11, follows naturally from the analysis phase. The creative work of the systems analyst is to take into account what was learned in the analysis phase and to design a system with the proper components and internal control duties to accomplish the objectives and requirements of an efficient and economical financial information system.

In Chapter 12 the *implementation and follow-up phase* of a systems investigation is discussed. This is the phase in which the new system is put into effect and tested to see that it is operating as designed. Unless a system is designed to be implemented and is followed, it is of little value.

The work of the systems analyst should be reported in written form. While the structure and content of such reports vary greatly in practice, Appendix C illustrates a model evaluation report such as those prepared by a systems analyst.

OUTPUT CRITERIA—DETERMINATION SCHEME

The most challenging task confronted by the systems analyst is the delineation of proper output criteria. It is overwhelming, particularly in medium-to-large businesses, because many levels of management must receive many and various kinds of information in order to perform their duties effectively. Before an analyst can suggest new or revised combinations of personnel, communication media, reports, and devices, he must establish clearly the kind of information output needed by management. Figure 10-1 is an example of a worksheet used by a national firm of certified public accountants to establish output criteria as part of the analysis phase of a systems investigation. (The worksheet has been modified slightly to fit the terminology used in this textbook.)

Column I in Figure 10-1 lists seven major control areas about which information is generated in most businesses. An eighth item is included—Other Areas—to permit the analyst to list other areas which may be peculiar to the business under review. In actual use each major area in column I should be separated from the next areas by sufficient space to permit the analyst to write in additional items under each heading—Over-all Operating Results, for example—which may be of special interest in the system under review.

Column II in Figure 10-1 describes in a general way whether information about each area is necessary for planning purposes. Part of this column is pre-printed for the analyst but statements should be added to correspond to the items added in column I.

Column III contains a brief description of the kind of stewardship and control information needed about each area. As with column II the analyst should add to this column, in each area, points which pertain to the individual business under review.

Column IV illustrates a description of the kinds of reports which are often used to fulfill the needs described in columns II and III. In an actual assignment the analyst would list in this column the kinds of reports in use by the company under review. He may note apparent holes in the reporting scheme which will bear further investigation but column IV is designed to be a list of the reports in use currently.

Column V (and other columns as needed) should be used to show how the reports named (or described) in column IV are being distributed.

Once the present information areas, reports about these areas, and to whom the reports are distributed have been completely delineated, the analyst in conference with the proper representative(s) of management must determine certain output criteria which will govern the systems assignments to be undertaken. Often the output criteria will take the form of a new worksheet developed from the first which will show the major areas about which information is to be produced, the kinds of reports needed, and the new distribution schedule. It is only after the analyst has determined, to his satisfaction, the present output of the system or subsystem and its form that he has been called upon to review and what the desired output and its form is to be, that he can proceed to the other phases of a systems investigation.

To facilitate the use of columns IV and V on the worksheet, two companion schedules are helpful. Figure 10-2 illustrates a two-page *Control Report Inventory Record*. This record serves as a subsidiary record to the brief description of each report given in column IV. Figure 10-3 illustrates a two-page *Control Report Users Record* which is used as a detailed subsidiary of the distribution schedule summarized in column V at the end of the worksheet. Note that figures 10-2 and 10-3 have been designed to provide for

MANAGEMENT CONTROL AND REPORT SCHEME

MAJOR CONTROL AREAS	PLANNING	ACCOUNTING	REPORTING	DISTRIBUTION
Overall Operating Results: Profits Return on investment Contribution to period costs and profit by product lines	Objectives determined and used in conjunction with the overall company profit plan	Actual sales and lease dollars Direct product costs Manufacturing, engineering, selling, general, and administrative expenses Capital expenditures	Monthly income statements comparing actual and planned results Percentages of earnings on assets employed Margins earned by product lines	Distribution of all reports tied to assignment of authority and responsibility under organization plan—only one position receives report for control purposes—others may receive for information and planning purposes if report is related to their assigned functions
Financial Position: Balance sheet Cash position and requirements Accounts receivable status Collection performance Inventory position and trend Capital projects and status Borrowed capital	Pro forma balance sheets developed to show results of planned operations and capital expenditures	Actual dollars by account, summarized by balance sheet classifications	Comparative balance sheets, statement of sources and application of funds	

FIGURE 10-1. Output Criterial Worksheet Data (Sheet 1 of 3)

Sales:			
Gross sales and lease dollars by product line and geographical area Volume Price Mix Profitability Adjustments and discounts	Forecasts of sales by type, kind, and responsibility area Plans and policies in regard to prices, discounts, allowances, advertising, commissions, etc. Conversion of planned sales to planned marginal contribution	Results accumulated in terms of— Units Dollars By product and product line By geographical and responsibility area	Actual sales and variations from forecasts Relationships of volumes to break-even points under same premises as used for budget development Effect of mix, price, and volume changes on marginal contribution of each class of sales

Product Costs:			
Material Productive labor Variable burden	Fabrication and assembly schedules developed to meet optimum requirements of inventory levels and customer demands Production plan extended at standard costs	Production activity recorded in terms of— Material receipts, issues, and prices Labor hours used and payroll distribution Expenditures for items classed as variable burden Variations from standard Units produced	Operating reports by accountability and cost centers Actual activity reported at standard costs, showing variation from standard— Material price and usage Scrappage and routing Labor rate and efficiency Expense spending and efficiency (Budget allowances determined by applying predetermined rates to actual hours)

FIGURE 10-1. Output Criterial Worksheet Data (Sheet 2 of 3)

MAJOR CONTROL AREAS	PLANNING	ACCOUNTING	REPORTING	DISTRIBUTION
Period Costs: Unused capacity costs Manufacturing expenses Engineering—Departmental expenses Project costs Sales department operating expenses General and administrative expenses	Budgets of expenses and project authorizations	Actual expenses recorded and distributed to proper accounts Supplementary records of research, development, and other project costs	Actual expenditures and variations from those planned	
Quality Control: Levels Costs	Standards developed to meet customer requirements and company cost objectives	Rejects recorded, showing location and cause	Rejects, rework, scrap, and customer returns	
Personnel: Requirements Turnover Promotability	Requirements determined based upon levels of planned activity Organization guides—job descriptions Periodic reviews and evaluation Retirement programs	Manpower/headcounts maintained in all functional areas Employment records History files	Actual numbers of persons vs. planned Labor turnover Retirements and disabilities	
Other Control Areas	As appropriate	As appropriate	As appropriate	

FIGURE 10-1. Output Criterial Worksheet Data (Sheet 3 of 3)

CONTROL REPORT INVENTORY RECORDS		
Report Title		
Known As		Report No.
Freq.	As of	Issue Date
Originated By		Requested By
Control Area		

GENERAL DESCRIPTION

Original Units And/Or Opns. Covered:

Type Information Shown:

Source of Data:

Other Reports Prepared From This Report:

Related Reports:

PURPOSES

Primary

Secondary

FIGURE 10-2. **Control Report Inventory Record (Sheet 1 of 2)**

DISTRIBUTION					
Name	Unit	√	Name	Unit	√

Remarks:

ESTIMATED COST			
Avg. No. Pgs.	No. Copies Run	Compilation Hrs.	Cost $
Sheet Size	Form No.	Typing Hrs.	Cost $
Type of Form		Reproduction Cost	$
Reproduction Method		Assembly Cost	$
		Cost Per Issue	$
		Total Annual Cost	$

FINAL RECOMMENDATION			
Not Control Report O No Change O Revise O Eliminate O			
No Change O Pending			
Combine O With			
Other:			
Contacted	Ext.	Contacted	Ext.
Contacted	Ext.	Contacted	Ext.
Prepared By	Date	Reviewed By	Date

FIGURE 10-2.   Control Report Inventory Record (Sheet 2 of 2)

CONTROL REPORT USER RECORD
Report Title
Known As　　　　　　　　　　　　　　Report No.
User's Name　　　　　　　　　Position
User's Org. Unit
How Used?　Control ○　Info ○　Future Ref. ○　Prepare Another Report ○
Other ○　Explain
Control Area
USER'S COMMENTS & EVALUATION
Examples of Use:
What is the Most Important Part?
How Much of Report is Used?
Time Required to Read and Analyze Report

FIGURE 10-3.　Control Report User Record (Sheet 1 of 2)

Comments as to Readability and Useability:
Is Time Lag Satisfactory?
Is Issue Interval Satisfactory?
Does Report Conflict with Other Reports or Data?
Is Necessary Info Available in any Other Form?
Supplemented By or Supplement to Other Reports?
Any Reason to Believe not Accurate or Reliable?
Is Report Considered Essential? In Present Form and Frequency?
How Long is Each Issue Retained? Why?
Do Subordinates Also Use Report?   Purpose?
Remarks:
Prepared By   Date   Reviewed By   Date

FIGURE 10-3.   Control Report User Record (Sheet 2 of 2)

written entries as well as the use of check marks to simplify response. Check marks are to be entered in the circles provided for possible "Final Recommendation" in Figure 10-2, and "How Used" in Figure 10-3, if the item is applicable. When used properly the information on these two supporting worksheets are invaluable to the analyst in determining the output criteria which will govern the balance of his assignment.

ANALYSIS TECHNIQUES

In order to establish output criteria, the systems analyst must make a thorough review or analysis of the existing system. The general nature of managerial planning and control must be established. The worksheets illustrated in Figures 10-1, 10-2, and 10-3 result from extensive systems analysis. In the relatively few investigations where a financial information system must be designed for a new company or division, the establishment of output criteria requires extensive analysis but the benefit and/or drag of the past system will be absent.

In the process of establishing output criteria and analyzing the present system, the systems analyst uses six effective techniques:

1. Data processing operation and flow analysis.
2. Data media analysis.
3. Inquiry.
4. Visual observation.
5. Personnel review.
6. Cost analysis.

The foregoing techniques are offered as the basic tools used by the systems analyst in the analysis phase of his work. They are similar to audit techniques and others in that they may be used in a variety of different ways and in an order and to a degree deemed suitable by the analyst. Professional judgment and technical competence permits this latitude. They are specific enough, however, to serve as an excellent teaching device. Teachers could probably use these techniques effectively with either students or on-the-job trainees as the center of instruction involving the analysis, design, and installation of systems. Neophytes, who are grounded in basic accounting theory, basic system theory, and the principles of financial and production management should be able to utilize these techniques effectively once their nature and importance is convincingly evident to them.

Analysis techniques are applicable in both original design or revision design

assignments. In order to simplify discussion a revision design investigation
will be assumed in the following paragraphs.

DATA PROCESSING OPERATION AND FLOW ANALYSIS. Systems analysts
often utilize a single flow chart which depicts both the data processing operations and the flow of data from one part of the organization to another as the
primary method of applying this technique. Clients are often skeptical when
viewing this technique being performed but it is axiomatic that an improved
design can rarely result unless the existing operations and data flow are understood by the analyst.

An important aspect of this technique, which is often overlooked when
flow charting is discussed, is the need to relate the various manual, mechanical, or electronic devices utilized in the performance of the procedure to the
steps on the flow chart. The flow charting of a sales analysis procedure being
performed on worksheets with the help of an adding machine, while customer
billing is done on a two-register posting machine, may be evidence enough
that a multiple register machine should be utilized appropriately.

Due to the complexity of the system even in a small company it is rarely
possible to develop a single flow chart for the entire system. Normally each
procedure is the subject of a separate flow chart. This is a minor defect in
flow charting which must be recognized by the analyst. So that flow charts
can assist the analyst effectively, the individual procedure charts must be
suitably coordinated. Often related procedures are grouped on a single chart
if they are not unduly complex. This is where experience and professional
judgment must be used by the analyst.

A *flow chart* is nothing more than a graphic representation of the activities being carried out in one or more of the phases of data and information
flow, namely input, processing, and output. The graphic representation can
stress document flow as data are being processed or it can stress the operations
performed on data as they are being processed. The former is called a *procedural flow chart* and the latter is called a *system flow chart*. Figure 10-4 is
a procedural flow chart illustrating a typical accounts receivable procedure.
Such flow charts lend themselves to thorough study by the systems analyst.
It is often possible to discover inefficiencies and control weaknesses in the
processing of accounts receivable data by studying a procedural flow chart
that may not have been discovered by either observation or interviewing techniques. Often the analyst can use the flow chart to communicate suggested
improvement in processing activities. To draw this type of flow chart, it is not
necessary to learn symbols or a graphic language. As you can see in Figure
10-4 the various divisions of the processing activities are given a vertical
column and the flow of data is represented by arrows and squares representing the documents being processed. The primary objective of such a flow chart
is to depict, ideally on one page, the flow of media and steps and control
measures taken as a result of processing data.

When a particular part of a system is being considered for mechanization

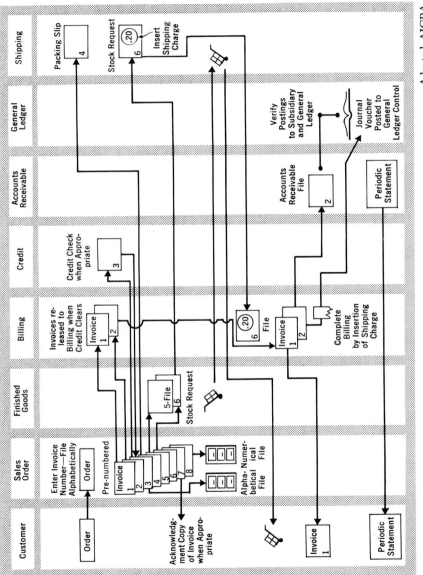

FIGURE 10-4. Procedural Flow Chart for Sales and Accounts Receivable

at the punched card or electronic computer level, the analyst finds the system flow chart very helpful. Not only does it depict the flow of data processing activities but, because distinctive symbols are used, it also depicts the various machine operations. While this type of flow chart can be used by an analyst to spot inefficient processing, it is most often used to assemble the processing steps necessary for a particular set of circumstances.

For the purpose of settling on one set of symbols when problems call for a systems flow chart, the symbols in Figure 10-5 should be used. These symbols were taken from a flow charting template produced by the International Business Machines Corporation. Other equipment manufacturers such as National Cash Register, Honeywell, Burroughs, and General Electric use somewhat similar charting templates. The symbols in Figure 10-5 relate to computer as well as punched card systems.

Figures 10-6, 10-7, and 10-8 illustrate how the symbols can be used to depict three phases of a punched card sales analysis procedure. Figure 10-6 is a chart of the daily routine and Figures 10-7 and 10-8 are charts of the monthly routine.

The use of flow charts for the "data processing operation and flow analysis" technique in the analysis phase of a systems investigation can also be helpful in the synthesis or design phase of a systems investigation as detailed in Chapter 11.

DATA MEDIA ANALYSIS. Often in the synthesis or design phase the product of the analyst's work does not resemble the original system or procedure. Improvements are obtained because of changes made in data flows or data media. In utilizing the technique of data media analysis, the analyst critically appraises the media under review to determine if requirements for good flow and design have been met.

Design requirements for communication media have previously been set forth in Chapter 4. Implied is the knowledge and experience which the analyst must have so that he may interpret these requirements in specific situations. For example, different media with similar data recorded thereon should be coordinated. If the customer's name must be written on a cash ticket, charge sale ticket, credit memorandum, and other media related to customer accounting, it is good practice to standardize the name area on all documents. If, as some individuals maintain, blue report covers encourage executive reading, a new series of reports with gaudy covers may not create a "favorable mental attitude in users." Handwritten data are not easily inserted on data media if the space allowed on the media is too small. Conversely, some of the advantages of typed data may be lost when lines on forms or reports are not coordinated with standard typewriter spacing. Adequate analysis of the data media should uncover most shortcomings and will lead to proper media design.

INQUIRY. In auditing, the technique of inquiry is not a primary source of information. Employee bias, fear, and many other factors cause evidence

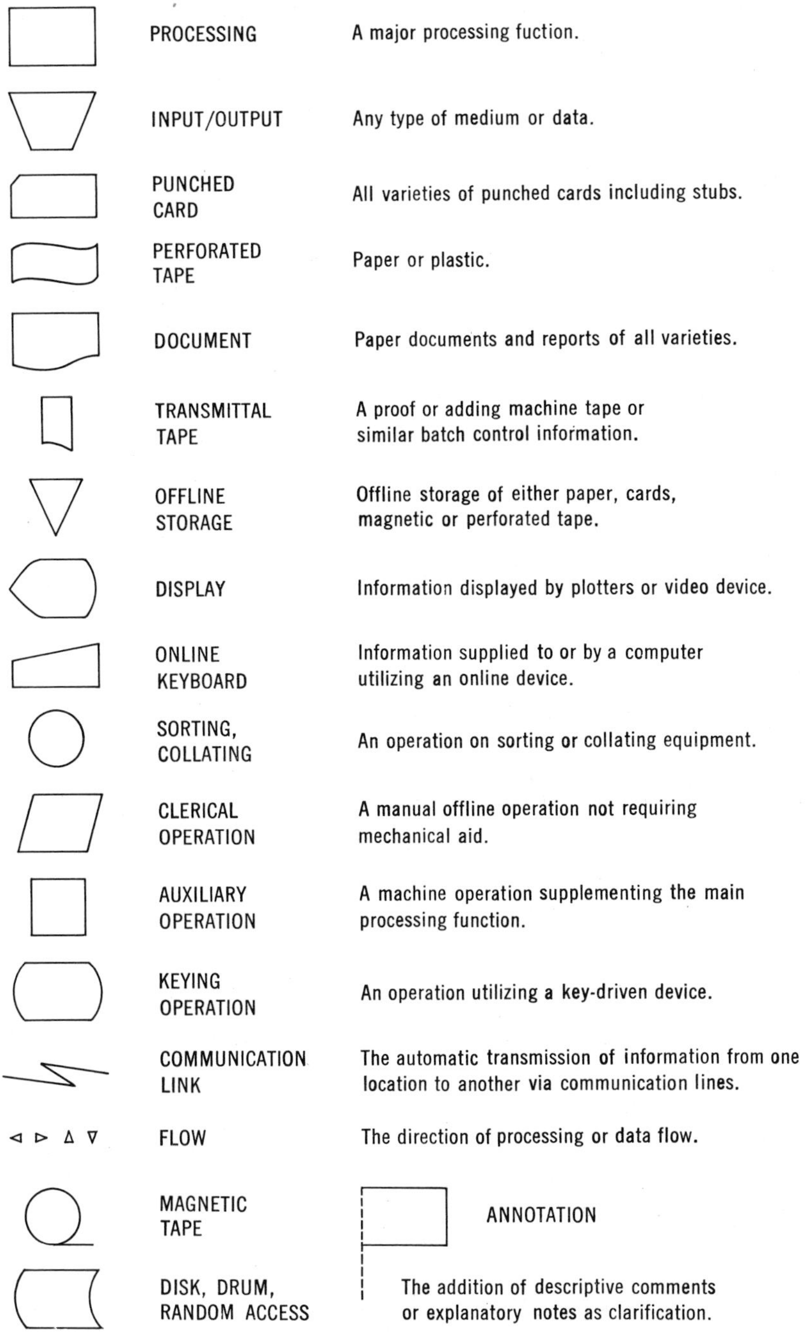

	PROCESSING	A major processing fuction.
	INPUT/OUTPUT	Any type of medium or data.
	PUNCHED CARD	All varieties of punched cards including stubs.
	PERFORATED TAPE	Paper or plastic.
	DOCUMENT	Paper documents and reports of all varieties.
	TRANSMITTAL TAPE	A proof or adding machine tape or similar batch control information.
	OFFLINE STORAGE	Offline storage of either paper, cards, magnetic or perforated tape.
	DISPLAY	Information displayed by plotters or video device.
	ONLINE KEYBOARD	Information supplied to or by a computer utilizing an online device.
	SORTING, COLLATING	An operation on sorting or collating equipment.
	CLERICAL OPERATION	A manual offline operation not requiring mechanical aid.
	AUXILIARY OPERATION	A machine operation supplementing the main processing function.
	KEYING OPERATION	An operation utilizing a key-driven device.
	COMMUNICATION LINK	The automatic transmission of information from one location to another via communication lines.
◁ ▷ △ ▽	FLOW	The direction of processing or data flow.
	MAGNETIC TAPE	ANNOTATION
	DISK, DRUM, RANDOM ACCESS	The addition of descriptive comments or explanatory notes as clarification.

Courtesy of IBM Corporation

FIGURE 10-5.   Symbols for a Systems Flow Chart

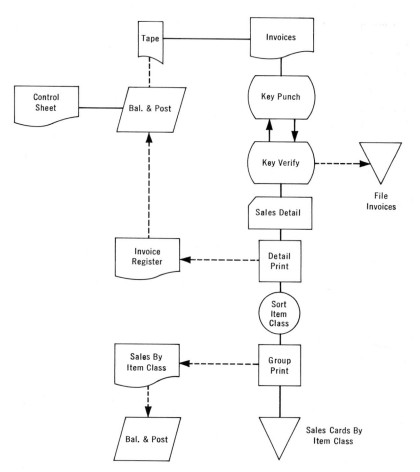

FIGURE 10-6.   Daily Sales Procedure

gained from this technique to be persuasive but not compelling evidence.[1] Inquiry as a system analysis technique is more reliable than inquiry in auditing. It is through conversation, interview, etc., that the systems analyst obtains information about company organization, goals, and policies which directly affect the system and its required output. Through the use of this technique, the analyst determines what executives think the system or parts thereof is or should be doing. It is invaluable in helping to establish the needs for data at all levels of management and for use in conjunction with many of the other review techniques. Data operation and flow analysis, for example, are heavily dependent on the results of inquiry.

---

[1] See Mautz, R. K. and Sharaf, H. A., *The Philosophy of Auditing,* American Accounting Association, 1961.

One of the vital characteristics of effective inquiry is the ability of the analyst to *listen*. People working with a procedure do not feel disposed to disclose their knowledge when the analyst is doing most of the talking or does not listen attentively.

VISUAL OBSERVATION. There is no substitute for first-hand information concerning the system under review. Visual observation consists of the personal examination of books, papers, processing, etc. It is also a technique that

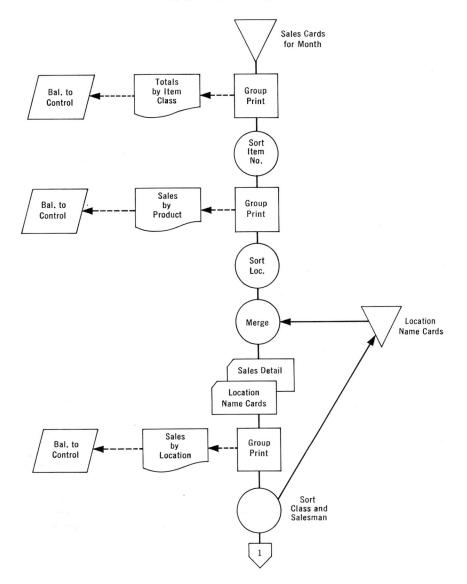

FIGURE 10-7. Monthly Sales Procedure

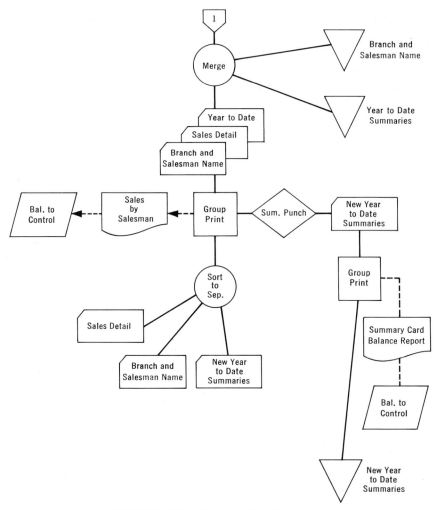

FIGURE 10-8. Monthly Sales Procedure

is used in conjunction with all of the other system review techniques. Often material for operation, data flow, or media analysis is obtained through inquiry. In these cases visual observation is used to corroborate verbal statements. In other situations visual observation becomes the sole source of information needed by the analyst. For example, it is often the only technique used to determine the ways in which several copies of a particular report or form are being distributed.

PERSONNEL REVIEW. If one were to classify system analysis techniques into primary and secondary categories, personnel review would be a primary technique because personnel determine the degree of sophistication possible in a system. Personnel not able to master the operation of a multiple-purpose accounting machine, for example, would render inoperative a system centered around such equipment. Personnel not capable of or who refuse to complete a card which is to be punched later by a mark sensing method render the use of the mark-sensed card impractical.

In every systems engagement, therefore, the analyst must make an extensive review of the existing personnel who will be expected to use various system output and to carry out revised methods and procedures. The analyst must also project the caliber of individuals needed if additional employees must be hired. The application of this technique is dependent on the analyst's knowledge of human nature as well as his ability to judge technical competence. An employee who possesses the necessary faculties to do a particular task may purposely fail or refuse to perform. While the basic human fears of (1) change itself, (2) loss of job, (3) demotion of current job status, or (4) that new duties may not be mastered, must be assuaged by the analyst during the design and installation phases, the analyst can isolate particular trouble spots through personnel examination during the analysis phase. The caliber of personnel in existing systems, or which can be obtained for new installations, cannot help but influence the analyst's work in the later phases of his assignment.

COST ANALYSIS. Realistically, new or revised procedures must be economically justifiable. The reasonable cost principle of systems design is applied in the analysis phase so that the cost to operate and maintain the present system or parts thereof may be weighed fairly against new or revised system recommendations. In addition, the cost analysis technique discloses the high volume, high cost, or both, parts of the existing system. As a matter of strategy it is more productive to examine those areas first since these types of areas are more often in need of improved methods and procedures.

This cost analysis technique is difficult to classify solely as a tool of the analysis phase. Cost analysis must be begun in the analysis phase since one aspect of its use is to determine the cost of operating and maintaining the present system, but the technique must be used in the synthesis or design phase as well. Many ideas are discarded in the synthesis phase before they are developed fully because the analyst is aware that these ideas cannot be justified economically.

The most cumbersome aspect in the application of cost analysis is the difficulty surrounding a quantitative evaluation of relatively intangible benefits—such things as more rapid reporting, "real time" inventory control versus delayed time controls, etc. One company claims to have justified the installation of a medium-sized computer solely on the fact that the computer inventory control system enabled the company to reduce its revolving base investment in inventory to the extent that the profit earned on the cash freed for an alternative use more than covered the annual cost of the new system. On the other hand, another company claimed that operating reports were out by the twelfth of the following month in a new system as compared to a report date of the twenty-sixth in the old system. They had not actually tried to quantify their savings. In any event, whether it be difficult or not, every effort should be made to quantify the intangible benefits that often accrue to system revisions as suggested in the discussion of the reasonable cost principle.

QUESTIONS, PROBLEMS, AND CASES

1. What is the relevance to the systems analyst of analysis, synthesis, and implementation and follow-up?

2. You have been assigned to assist in a systems engagement designed to study and recommend an improved billing procedure. In the existing procedure the sale invoice is prepared on a typewriter, with the original sent to the customer, one copy being used for the account receivable posting media, and the second copy used for a manual analysis of sales. A tabulation is made of sales by product line, sales area, and by salesman from the second copy. How would you perform the assignment? Note that you are being asked *how* to go about the assignment, not for a solution to the problem.

3. The controller of the Milford Axel Company has been aware of stress on his financial information system. There are many evidences that the time is close at hand when the traditional bookkeeping-machine-centered system will have to be replaced with punched cards or some other higher level of mechanization. As the systems analyst for the company, you have been asked to undertake a review of the existing system for the purpose of recommending the configuration of the new system, and the appropriate level of mechanization. What would be your greatest concerns in the recommendation? What would you do first? Explain in some detail the initial step.

4. You have been given a worksheet similar to Figure 10-1 to use in the analysis of a system. Why would the worksheet be useful, and what role should it assume in a systems engagement? What use would be made of a Control Report Inventory Record and a Control Report Users Record?

5. Distinguish between a procedural flow chart and system flow chart as to use by the systems analyst.

6. Prepare a procedural flow chart for a purchase procedure from the requisition through the issue of a purchase order. Prepare a systems flow chart for a phase of the same procedure.

7. Explain the systems analyst's use of data media analysis.

8. Inquiry is a technique that can be of vital importance in the analysis phase of a systems investigation. Explain and give several examples.

9. You have been assigned to a work simplification engagement. Your supervisor has asked that you do nothing but sit at a desk in the back of the office for several days and observe what goes on and watch for methods and measures of improving the operation and work flow in the office. What type of activities might you observe? What is the relationship between systems analysis and visual observation?

10. Why is it necessary for the systems analyst to review personnel during a systems investigation? Give several examples of situations in which the analysis phase of a systems investigation must consider existing personnel.

11. Give several illustrations of the manner in which cost analysis can be used as a tool of the systems analyst.

12. You have been asked to make a systems investigation for the Racine Distribution Company, a wholesale novelty concern. Items are stocked in a central warehouse from which mail orders are filled. Large orders from retail outlets are normally shipped by truck or express. All delivery charges are added to the billing price of the merchandise.
    a. What are the phases of the systems investigation that would be appropriate to recommend a new and improved financial information system for the company?
    b. Illustrate the major control area of sales as it could appear on a worksheet, as illustrated in Figure 10-1, that would be appropriate for the Racine Distribution Company engagement. Indicate the purpose of the specific information provided in the various columns of the worksheet.
    c. What are proper output criteria, and how do they relate to the systems investigation?
    d. Which of the analysis techniques would you recommend? Why would each be important?

13. Several months ago, the Ace Construction Company received a number of large contracts that will require a major expansion of the scope of company operations. One procedure in the company's financial information system that obviously is inadequate and will have to be revised is the payroll procedure and the related job cost system. You have been engaged as the analyst to review and redesign the payroll system, with specific instructions to limit your activities to payroll and the related job cost determination.
    a. Would the worksheet illustrated in Figure 10-1 be appropriate for this type of engagement? Explain.
    b. What method or methods of analysis would you use to determine the relevant output criteria? Why?
    c. How would you proceed with the investigation assuming you have two staff men to assist with the necessary work? (You should decide on the jobs to be assigned to each of the two staff men and what will be undertaken by yourself.)

14. During a recent systems investigation you were making an inquiry of a department head concerning the preparation of a report, the data for which

originated in his department. Discuss the analysis techniques that would be appropriate in the situation, stating the importance of each to the investigation.

15. In the preparation of a system flow chart you would like to use symbols to communicate certain meanings. What symbols should be used for each of the following:
    a. The addition of descriptive comments.
    b. A report.
    c. A punched card.
    d. The direction of data flow.
    e. Information displayed on video devices.
    f. Medium.

16. Go to a business or other organization with which you are acquainted and study a specific procedure that is in use and functioning properly. Prepare a procedural flow chart of the procedure.

17. Why is the determination scheme for output criteria so important to the systems analyst?

18. How does the approach of the systems analyst differ from the approach of an accountant using budgeting techniques in making a decision on the acquisition of a bookkeeping machine?

19. What is the relationship between output criteria and the components of a system?

20. Relate the principles of systems design to the analysis techniques of the systems analyst.

21. It is customary for a systems analyst to make inquiries of nonaccounting officers and responsible employees. State five different things about which the analyst might make inquiries that are not primarily aimed at determining the kind and degree of internal control. For each, explain the purpose of the inquiry and the title (or duties) of the person to whom the inquiry is addressed. (Adapted AICPA Examination)

22. Assume you are an established, practicing CPA and that you receive a telephone inquiry from a local businessman who is principal stockholder and president of a local medium-sized manufacturing concern. He wants to make an appointment with you immediately at his place of business relative to revision of his accounting system. Because you are busy winding up the tax season (and because you would like some time to prepare for the engagement), you set an appointment at his business for one week from today.

    This man has not been one of your clients and is engaged in a line of business different from that of any of your clients, past or present. By way of preparation for your first visit to his business what would you do?

23. The Redfern Manufacturing Company has been in operation for several years producing and selling a line of 14 different kitchen products such as flour sifters, can openers, condiment canisters, etc. Their general ledger consists of 78 accounts supported by (1) a plant ledger showing details of fixed assets, (2) a manufacturing ledger containing 170 separate cost accounts, (3) a ledgerless accounts receivable record of some 1,500 customer accounts, and (4) a "tickler" file of invoice due dates for purchases recorded in the voucher register.

You have been called in by the management of the Redfern Manufacturing Company to make a systems investigation with the emphasis on cost reduction.

a. What other aspects of the accounting function must you be concerned with in your basic analysis and final recommendations?

b. As you begin your analysis, you are cautioned by the vice-president in charge of operations—to whom you will make your final report—to "avoid disturbing old habits and sensitive spots."

(1) How would you respond to this? (Remember that this job is your bread and butter.)

(2) Is there any merit in what the vice-president has said?

c. After you have been oriented briefly in the firm's operations, you decide to start your analysis by surveying the 115 different reports which are prepared by the accounting department for the various levels of management. You find that the firm's accounting department has recently attempted to determine the utilization of these reports by sending a printed card along with each report asking the people on the circulation list to sign and return the card if they no longer wished to receive a specific report. While the accounting department's survey indicated that the circulation list of some of the reports could be cut down, it did not indicate that any of the 115 reports should be discontinued.

(1) Would you be satisfied that the information contained in all of these reports was important to the firm's management and therefore these reports contained the basic information around which the accounting system should be built?

(2) Why might the accounting department tend to be satisfied with the results of its survey while you are not?

(3) What specific steps might you take to make a more adequate survey of these reports and their actual usage? Name three. (These three steps need not all be taken in a particular situation.)

d. The general ledger accounts have been numbered with a block coding system which does not require change. This block code has been carried into the manufacturing ledger, however, resulting in a good deal of confusion and error in the handling of the cost accounts. The firm's controller says that he has been considering the use of a mnemonic code for the cost accounts and he suggests that now might be the time to design one. You have seen this word somewhere before and after stealing a look over the controller's shoulder to see how it is spelled you look it up in your text and proceed to design such a coding system. Describe the makeup of such a code for the manufacturing ledger, using a flour sifter—one of the company's products—as an example. Would your cost classification be broken down by (1) function, (2) object or (3) both?

e. After your analysis of the company's accounts receivable system you decide that it is probably the least expensive way of handling its receivables. The method the company uses, however, is prone to error and frequently makes it impossible to reconcile the monthly accounts receivable trial balance (the schedule of accounts receivable) with the control account. What most likely causes this difficulty in reconciliation?

f. As you continue your analysis you uncover many company practices which would make it easy for employees to steal cash, merchandise, and/or supplies. When you report this fact to the vice-president in charge of operations you find him quite sincerely interested in human relations and unwilling to "insult the employees with tighter internal control." "Besides," he says, "most of our employees have been here a long time and wouldn't think of taking anything." If you were still convinced that tighter controls were necessary, what line of reasoning might you use to induce him to accept such controls? (Remember again that this is your bread and butter and that future clients will measure your worth as a systems analyst on your record with this firm.)

g. In your talk with the guard at the gate through which the production employees pass, the guard asks your advice on something. He says that for a week or so one of the employees has been taking home wrapping waste each night in a wheelbarrow. The employee said that his foreman said that it was all right and that the waste would just be burned anyway. At first the guard said he was suspicious and carefully went through the waste to see if it concealed any stolen objects. The guard wants to know if he should report this man's actions to his superior. What is your advice?

24. Management does not order a systems investigation merely for a change in pace. Name three occurrences or situations which might spur management to direct a system or procedure to be reviewed and changed.

25. What working papers might you expect to prepare during the analysis phase of a systems investigation? Discuss briefly the purpose of each.

26. The Automotive Products Company is a wholly owned subsidiary of a large U. S. Corporation. James Bronson, Manager of the Systems and Data Processing Department, has been asked by the Vice-President for Sales, John Cogsworth, and the Vice-President and Controller, Robert Martin, to make an extensive analysis of the present Order-Billing Procedure currently being used by the Company.

As a first step in this project Mr. Bronson has asked you, a systems analyst in his department, to prepare a procedural flow chart of the existing procedure. Exhibit A that follows is a complete description of the current procedure. You are to confine yourself to the facts presented in Exhibit A. You may make any assumptions that you deem necessary and you may document your chart in any way you wish.

EXHIBIT A
AUTOMOTIVE PRODUCTS COMPANY

Title   Order and Billing

 I. *Introduction*
The following presents the procedure to be followed from the time
an order is received from a customer until it is shipped, billed and
payment received.

 II. *Departments Involved*
   a. Mail Desk
   b. Sales Department
   c. Treasurer
   d. Billing
   e. Cost
   f. Accounts Receivable
   g. Production Control
   h. Shipping Department
   i. Parts Stockroom
   j. Carburetor Repair Department
   k. Quality Control

III. *Forms Involved*
   a. Order from customer
   b. Customer Order and Invoice Set (Form 311)

Copy	Distribution	Color Paper
(order set)	Order Master	Master
1	Production Dept.	Canary
2	Shipping Sheet	Master
3	Packing Sheet	White
4	Shipping Dept.	Goldenrod
5	Sales Dept. Order Copy	Blue
6	Acknowledgment	White
7	Stock Copy	Green
(invoice set)		
8	Original Invoice	White
9	Invoice Copy	White
10	Accounts Receivable	Buff
11	Billing	Green
12	Distribution	Goldenrod
13	Sales Dept. Invoice Copy	Canary
14	Order Edit Sheet	White

   c. Packing Ticket (Form 306)
      1. Package Slip
      2. Government Inspector
      3. Billing—Customer
      4. Billing—File
      5. Production Control
      6. Quality Control
   d. Order Log
   e. Daily Report of Incoming Orders
   f. Daily Sales Report

EXHIBIT A (continued)

Title   Order and Billing

III. *Forms Involved (Continued)*
   g. Invoice Log
   h. Government Form DD 250
   i. Canadian Customs Invoice MA

IV. *Receipt of Customer Order at Mail Desk*
   a. Orders are opened by mail clerk, date stamped, and stamped with the order stamp. Deliver to the secretary to the treasurer.

V. *Receipt of Order by Telephone or Telegram*
   a. The sales administrator will complete an "Order Edit Sheet" and take the same steps as for those orders received through the mail as outlined in paragraph 7. The "Order Edit Sheet" will be forwarded to the Treasurer.

VI. *Credit Approval by Treasurer*
   a. The treasurer (or in his absence, an accountant) will give credit approval to the orders received from the Mail Desk or the "Order Edit Sheet" for telephone orders received from the Sales Department. The customer orders will be forwarded to the Sales Department or the Order Edit Sheet to the Billing Department.

VII. *Handling of Order from Customers in Sales Department*
   a. The Sales Manager will review all orders and forward them to the Sales Administrator.
   b. The Sales Administrator will edit all orders. If the order from the customer is illegible or requires so many changes that it is difficult to interpret the order, he will prepare an order edit sheet and attach the order from the customer to the back. He will examine the descriptions, part number, unit price, terms of payment, and delivery terms for correctness. He will obtain the shipping date from the Production Department. The Sales Administrator will indicate that date on the order unless it is the date specified by the customer in which case he will write "OK" after that date.

   The Sales Administrator will indicate any copies more or less than the normal Customer Order and Invoice Set (form 311) normally printed, consisting of copies 1 thru 6, copy 8, two copies of 9, and copies 10 thru 14. If it is a stock or repair order, this must be indicated so that copy 7 may be prepared.

   The Sales Administrator will initial the reviewed space in the Customer Order Stamp and forward it to the Billing Department.

VIII. *Preparation of Order in Billing Department*
   a. Reviewing Order. The order from the customer will be reviewed for proper price, terms of payment, and delivery terms. If any of these vary from established price lists of the Sales Department, the discrepancy will be called to the attention of the Sales Department for verification, unless previously initialled by the Sales Administrator. The account number will be indicated in the

EXHIBIT A (continued)

Title   Order and Billing

VIII. *Preparation of Order in Billing Department (Continued)*

Customer Order Stamp. If more than one account number is required for an order, this will be indicated for each item. Whether Government, Subcontract, Renegotiable or Intercompany Sale, will be indicated. The person auditing the order will initial it.

b. Typing Order. The order typist will type the orders on Order Master (form 312). Separate orders will be typed for each account number as indicated on the order from the customer. The typist will type the order number, which will be the next open number in the Order Log. Separate blocks of numbers will be used for Unit Orders and all other orders. The typist will list after the order number in the log, the customer name, customer purchase order number, and our other order numbers written from the same order from the customer. Write our order numbers on the order from the customer. Complete typing all of the information on the order master. Write at the bottom of the master with nonreproducing pencil the special copy requirements. Proofread the orders. Put order master in a "to be run" file. Put the order from the customer in a customer file.

c. Duplicating Order. Twice a day the orders will be taken from the "to be run" file. The masters will be put on the multilith machine. The normal order set, 1 thru 6, and any special requirements, will be collected and run. The copies will be placed in the mail for distribution. The following copies will be sent together to the Production Control Department: 1—Production Department; 2—Shipping Sheet; 3—Packing Sheet; 4—Shipping Department; 7—Stock Copy (if stock order; directly to repair department, if repair order). The Sales Department Order Copy 5, and Acknowledgment Copy 6, will be sent to the Sales Department. The master will be retained in the Billing Department.

d. Order Backlog. The Billing Clerk will make extensions on the master in order to obtain the value of the open orders. A daily tape of the orders will be taken by class so that the daily report of incoming orders may be prepared. The master will be filed alphabetically by customer and numerically within that group.

IX. *Handling of Our Order Copies in Sales Department*

a. Order Acknowledgment Copy 6. The Sales Administrator will examine the acknowledgment copy, sign it, and place it in outgoing mail.

b. Sales Department Order Copy 5. Make entries on records and file by customer.

X. *Handling by Production Control*

Make required entries on records from Production Copy 1, and file by date to ship. Follow up on this file one week prior to shipping date. Hold shipping sheet copy 2, packing sheet 3, shipping depart-

EXHIBIT A (continued)

Title   Order and Billing

X.   *Handling by Production Control (Continued)*
ment 4, and stock copy 7 (if required) with Production Copy until
several days prior to shipping date. Then distribute copies 2, 3, and
4 to the Shipping Department and the Stock copy 7 to the appropriate stock room.

XI.   *Handling of Copies in Stockroom*
Upon receipt of stock copy 7 in the Parts Stockroom, or Stockroom
in the Shipping Department, the stock will be drawn and the
material with the stock copy sent to the shipping room.

XII.   *Handling of Copies in Shipping Department*
Upon receipt of copies 2, 3, and 4, an investigation will be made
to see if the material ordered is in the shipping room. The shipment
will be made if it is. If all the material is not present, tag the material that is there for the order and indicate the items on the Shipping Department copy. File copies 2, 3, and 4 by shipping date.
Pull all orders to be shipped on a day and fill and ship the *complete*
order. If an order cannot be filled completely, send a memo of
the outstanding items to the Production Control Department for
follow-up, and if it is decided to make a partial shipment, the
revised shipping date for the balance of the items. The Production
Control Department will notify the Sales Department of any delays
of more than two days. The Production Control Department will
send a memo to the shipping department, telling whether to release
a partial shipment and giving the revised shipping date for whole or
part of the order.

XIII.   *Change or Cancellation of Orders*
a. The Sales Department will notify the Billing Department in
writing of any changes in orders except changes in shipping
dates of less than two weeks.
b. The Billing Department clerk will change the original order
master accordingly and run a new order set with the same distribution as the original set. Each copy of the new set will be
stamped with "Amended" or "Cancelled," whichever applies.
c. Each department that receives an amended order will make the
necessary changes on their records and replace the original copy
with the amendment. Cancelled orders will be taken from the
files.

XIV.   *Writing up the Shipment*
Upon the decision to ship items, the Shipping Department copy 4,
will be placed on a hard board with shipping sheet, copy 2 on top,
and the packing sheet, copy 3 on top of that. The information will
be written with a ballpoint pen and firm pressure. The "Quality
Shipped" for each item, "Shipped Via," shipped "date," "No. of
Packages," and "Total Weight," will be filled in for each item. The
Packing slip will be placed in the package, the shipping sheet will
be placed in the mail for the Billing Department, and the shipping

EXHIBIT A (continued)

Title   Order and Billing

XIV. *Writing up the Shipment (Continued)*
department copy will be filed alphabetically by customer and then by order number.

XV. *Shipments to Commercial Accounts Requiring Resident Government Inspection*
The shipping clerk will prepare the Packing Ticket (form 306) in six copies in addition to copies 2, 3, and 4 of the Order and Billing Set (form 311).
After preparation of form 306 and initialling by the government inspector, the copies will be distributed as follows:

1. In Package
2. Government Inspector
3. Billing (with shipping sheet) for forwarding to customer with invoice
4. Billing (with shipping sheet) for file
5. Production Control
6. Quality Control

XVI. *Duplicating Invoices*
Twice daily the invoices will be run on the multilith machine. The order master with shipping variable will be placed on the duplicator. Copies 8 through 14 with two copies of invoice copy 9 will be collated and printed. The order master with variable will be destroyed if there is no back order. The copies will be given to the Billing Clerk.

XVII. *Handling of Invoices in Billing Department*
The copies will be sorted, a daily tape taken of the totals on the Accounts Receivable copies, and the tape attached to that group. The total will be noted on the Sales Department invoice batch. The distribution copies will be sorted by account number and totals added. The total should agree with the total from the Accounts Receivable copies. The Daily Sales Report will be prepared from this tape. The tape will be attached to the Distribution copy group. The copies will be distributed as follows:

8	Invoice Original	⎫	
9	Invoice Copy	⎬	Mail to Customer
9	Invoice Copy	⎭	
10	Accounts Receivable		Accounts Receivable (with tape)
11	Billing		File by Invoice Number
12	Distribution		Cost Accounting (with tape)
13	Production Control		Production Control
14	Sales Department Invoice Copy		Sales Department (with control total)

XVIII. *Use of Invoice Copies*
a. Accounts Receivable. This copy will be filed in the customers open file until paid. Upon being paid, this copy will be held in daily groups until the month is balanced and closed. The month

EXHIBIT A (continued)

Title   Order and Billing

XVIII.   *Use of Invoice Copies (Continued)*

will be balanced by checking the tape of additions from the Billing Department, less a tape of withdrawals and journals, with the total of the open accounts. After the month is closed, the Accounts Receivable copy will be filed by customer and then by invoice number.

   b.   Distribution Copy. The Standard Cost will be entered on this copy. The costs will be recorded on Cost Accounting Records. Invoices with questionable gross profit will be called to the attention of the treasurer. The copies will be forwarded with tape to Accounts Receivable in the same daily groupings as they were received from billing. With the invoices sorted by account number, the Accounts Receivable Clerk will add the sales by account groupings with separate totals for excise tax and other miscellaneous items. The total of the sales and miscellaneous items should equal the total from the Accounts Receivable copy tape for that day. Daily totals of all the accounts will be posted to a summary. The distribution copy will be retained in daily account groups until the month is closed, when they will be filed by account within that month.

   c.   Production Control Copy. Entries of the shipment can be entered on the desired Production Control forms from this copy. If there is a back order indicated on the invoice copy, attach it to the order copy. Destroy the order and invoice copies when the closing invoice copy is received.

   d.   Sales Department Invoice Copy. From this copy the Sales Department personnel will make the required entries and analysis. Pull and destroy the order copy upon receipt of the closing invoice. File the Sales Department invoice copy by customer.

XIX.   *Back Orders*

   a.   Preparation of Forms. When there is a balance due on an order the duplicating machine operator will run two extra copies of the invoice on plain paper. The shipping variable will be taken off the order master and the following copies run and stamped "Back Order":

Shipping Sheet Master Copy	2
Packing Slip Copy	3
Shipping Dept. Copy	4

These copies, together with one extra copy of the invoice, will be sent to the Production Control Department. One of the extra copies will be retained in the Billing Department by order number for use in completing the next balance due when the back order is shipped.

   b.   Back orders in the Production Control Department. The revised shipping date will be written on the Shipping Department copy and the copies will be forwarded to the shipping department at the proper time.

   c.   Handling in Shipping Department. Back orders will be handled

EXHIBIT A (continued)

Title   Order and Billing

XIX.   *Back Orders (Continued)*
the same as regular orders except that the balance due on the extra copy of the invoice will be checked to see that there isn't an overshipment.
d.   Invoicing of Back Orders. Back Orders will be handled the same as the original shipment. For each successive back order the Balance due on the previous "extra copy" invoice will be used to compute the new balance due. Above the Invoice Number on the Shipping Variable will be written "Shipment No. 2" or whatever the number is.

XX.   *Shipment to Government—Inspection Required*
For orders subject to inspection in the plant or Export Packed elsewhere, Invoice copies No. 9 will not be duplicated. The original invoice will be marked "Memorandum." Copies of Government Form DD 250 will be prepared from the original invoice for plant inspected orders. For export packing elsewhere, the original invoice will be held for receipt of the partially prepared invoice from the government. Other copies of the invoice set will be handled in the normal manner.

XXI.   *Canadian Shipments*
Canadian Customs Invoice (form M.A.) will be prepared in addition to the regular invoice set.

XXII.   *Labels and Stencils*
Package labels and stencils will be prepared in Shipping Department when the packaging is determined.

XXIII.   *Shipping Receipts*
Bills of Lading, Express, and Mailing Forms will be prepared in the Shipping Department. The plant copies will be filed by customer and then by order number.

XXIV.   *Related Forms*
a.   The "Shipping Memorandum" (form 319) will be used to send things out of the plant that are not regular customer sales. For instance, when our material is sent out for processing and testing, supplying others with our equipment, sending material out for export packing, returning items to vendors, or shipping scrap.
b.   Credits to customers will be written on Credit Memorandum (form 312).
c.   Debits and Credits to vendors will be written on Debit Memorandum (form 320).

27.   The independent auditor must evaluate a client's system of internal control to determine the extent to which various auditing procedures must be employed. A client who uses a computer should provide the CPA with a flow chart of the information processing system so the CPA can evaluate the control features in the system. In the figure on the next page is a simplified flow chart,

FLOWCHART

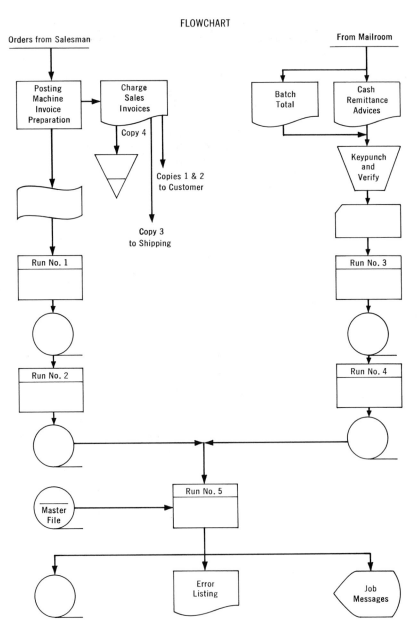

such as a client might provide. Unfortunately the client had only partially completed the flow chart when it was requested by you.

a. Complete the flow chart produced on the facing page.

b. Describe what each item in the flow chart indicates. When complete, your description should provide an explanation of the processing of the data involved. Your description should be in the following order:

   1. "Orders from Salesmen" to "Run No. 5."

   2. "From Mailroom" to "Run No. 5."

   3. "Run No. 5" through the remainder of the chart.

c. Name each of the "Flow Chart Symbols" below and describe what each represents. (AICPA Examination)

FLOWCHART SYMBOLS

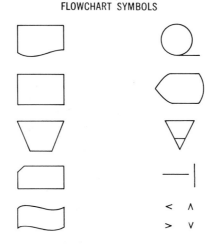

CHAPTER 11

Synthesis

AFTER THE SYSTEMS ANALYST HAS DEVELOPED PROPER OUTPUT CRITERIA AND thoroughly analyzed the system or subsystem under scrutiny, he must begin the next major phase of his engagement. He must organize the system components consisting of communication media, reports, people, and mechanical or electronic processing devices, including the establishment of sound internal control duties, into a functioning financial information system or subsystem which will achieve the desired output criteria. In most engagements the line between the analysis phase of a systems investigation and the synthesis phase is, at best, vague. Sometimes almost every aspect of the old system is reviewed before anything new is suggested. At other times the analyst is able to conduct both phases almost simultaneously. Exactly how one should proceed in a particular investigation is a function of experience.

TECHNIQUES OF SYSTEM SYNTHESIS

Just as the systems analyst is able to use certain techniques or tools to assist him in the analysis phase of his investigation, he is able to use certain techniques or tools in the synthesis phase as well. These techniques are:

1. Review of analysis data.
2. Data processing operation and flow design.
3. Data media design.
4. Testing.
5. Economic and aesthetic justification.

REVIEW OF ANALYSIS DATA. Prior to beginning the actual design of any part of a financial information system, the analyst subjects the results of his work in the analysis phase of his investigation to a critical review. This technique enables him to clarify vague or incomplete situations pertaining to the old system and to spot weak areas and specific problems which must be strengthened and solved in the new system. Often weak spots are difficult to identify for an individual close to a situation. To illustrate, "On the way to and from work in the mornings, most of us take a regular route. Aside from the general scene, we hardly notice anything specific. If, on a certain morning, we notice that a window in a house is broken it catches our eye immediately. If the window is not repaired, we no longer notice it—it simply becomes part of the scene."[1] Review of analysis data focuses attention on such "broken windows" and points out the obvious need for their mending.

The weak areas in a system being reviewed will be illuminated by the analyst's relating of the data to the theory of systems and systems principles, as discussed in Chapters 1 and 2, and the output criteria which he established in the analysis phase.

The data processing procedural flow chart shown in Figure 11-1 was prepared by a systems analyst, who had been engaged to review the purchasing function of a manufacturing enterprise, during the analysis phase of his investigation. After studying the chart briefly it was evident that an important control measure was missing. When merchandising was delivered to the storeroom clerk no official transfer was made. The material was merely delivered to the storeroom after being processed in the receiving room. Subsequent shortages of inventory could not be traced to either the receiving clerk or the storeroom clerk.

DATA PROCESSING OPERATION AND FLOW DESIGN. Once the systems analyst has reviewed the data collected in the analysis phase of his investigation, he must formulate a new or revised flow of data and data processing operations which will produce the output essential to the particular financial information system. In doing this the analyst is using the technique of data processing operation and flow design.

A common method of applying this technique is to develop a flow chart of the new system or subsystem. Flow charting not only is important to the analyst in his review of the data processing operations and data flow, but it is also an important method in applying this design technique as well. Specific flow charting methods have been discussed in Chapter 10.

Figure 11-1 illustrates a procedural flow chart which was developed in the analysis phase of a particular investigation. It helped the analyst discover a flaw in control. Figure 11-2 is the same procedural flow chart prepared during the synthesis phase of the investigation in which the control flaw is corrected.

---

[1] Esther R. Becker and Eugene F. Murphy, *The Office in Transition*, (New York: Harper and Brothers Publishers, 1957), p. 45.

To illustrate further, Figure 11-3 is the procedural flow chart of a payroll procedure as prepared during the analysis phase of the investigation. It had been decided that this application should be converted to punched card processing. After reviewing the chart in Figure 11-3 and other facts developed in the analysis phase, the analyst developed four systems flow charts illustrating how this procedure could be done on punched card data processing machines. Figure 11-4 illustrates the part of the procedure dealing with the preparation of weekly deductions and Figure 11-5 illustrates the major part of the payroll processing procedure. The other two charts are not shown but would be constructed in a manner similar to Figure 11-4 as they are concerned with the preparation of current earnings and adjustment cards.

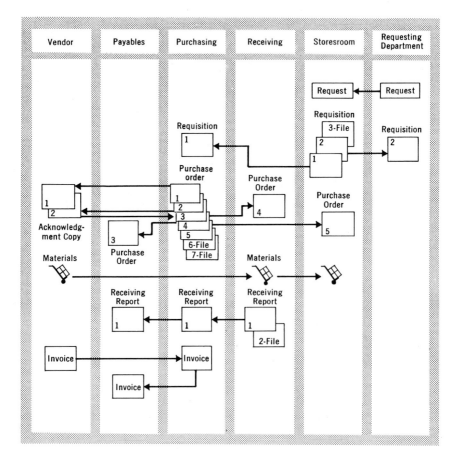

Adapted AICPA

FIGURE 11-1. Procedural Flow Chart for Purchasing Prepared During the Analysis Phase of a Systems Investigation

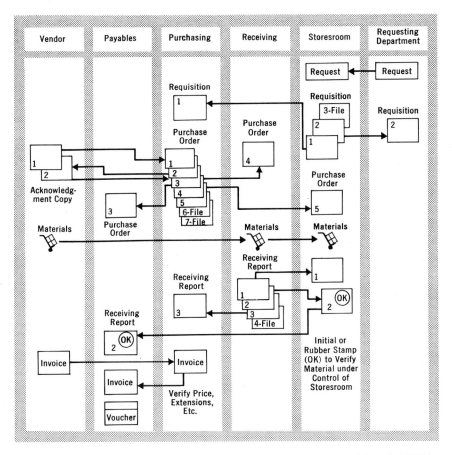

Adapted AICPA

FIGURE 11-2. Procedural Flow Chart for Purchasing Prepared During the Synthesis Phase of a Systems Investigation

DATA MEDIA DESIGN. A close companion to the technique of data processing operation and flow design is the technique, data media design. As its name implies, this technique is concerned with the design of data media which will facilitate data recording and processing operations and data flows in the systems being studied.

When using this technique the systems analyst is guided by the *data accumulation principle* which was discussed in detail in Chapter 2. Basically the data accumulation principle governs the initial recording of data and provides a criterion for determining the number of parts into which units of information should be divided at the time of the initial record.

If the data medium being designed in a particular situation consists of paper stock, the standards of design described in Chapter 4 should be

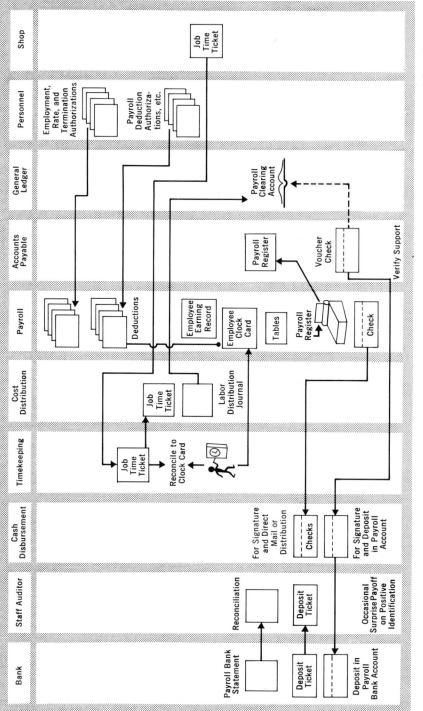

FIGURE 11-3. Procedural Flow Chart for Payroll Prepared During the Analysis Phase of a Systems Investigation

Adapted AICPA

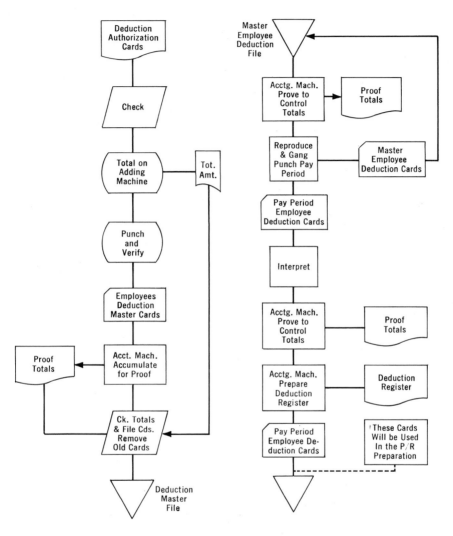

FIGURE 11-4. Systems Flow Chart Prepared During the Synthesis Phase of a Systems Investigation—Weekly Payroll Deduction

applied. These standards are helpful in the design of paper forms because they take into consideration the effect that the particular design of data medium have on the people in the system which must record data on this medium and may even subject the data to certain processing operations.

Over the years analysts have discovered that these same standards of form design, which were developed with only paper stock forms in mind, are valid no matter what data representation medium is used. For example, the fourth standard of form design listed on page 92 states, "The form must reduce

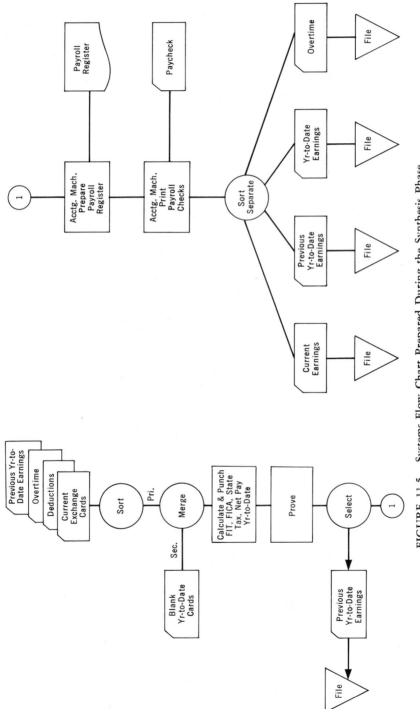

FIGURE 11-5. Systems Flow Chart Prepared During the Synthesis Phase of a Systems Investigation—Major Payroll Processing

the tendency to error in entering or using the data." In a data processing system using electronic processing methods few, if any, magnetic tape records are designed without a check channel. (See a further discussion of check channel on pages 440-442.) Too many undetected errors would occur when such a tape is read into a computer. A *person* is not using the data in this instance but the standard is valid.

In applying the data media design technique the analyst must also keep in mind the *data processing* principle. Although the data processing principle establishes the basis for design of the processing system and must be carefully considered when applying the technique of data processing operation and flow design, it cannot be ignored when the analyst is designing data media. As the standards of form design indicate, most data media will be subjected to processing operations. Improperly or illogically designed data media will not contribute to a "meaningful and controlled flow of data." For example, if a copy of the purchase order is to be used by the receiving clerk to record quantities received, provision should be made in the receiving clerk's copy of the purchase order for ease of entering received quantities. This scheme was used in a medium-size manufacturing plant but was not working smoothly because the voucher clerk could not readily read the receiving report quantities since they were often written over other data. Once the purchase order set was revised and space provided on the receiving report copy to insert quantities received, processing efficiency improved. It was data media design and not the flow concept which was at fault in this instance.

The techniques of data processing operation and flow design and data media design entail creativity on the part of the analyst. They are attempts to meet the needs for financial information by combining the specially designed elements of a financial information system in the proper quantities given to express needs of management.

TESTING. Testing is the technique applied in ascertaining the practicability of a newly synthesized system or subsystem. Regardless of the theoretical correctness of new data media, new data recording and processing operations, and new data flows designed for even the smallest part of a financial information system, a thorough test should be made of the new elements.

Up to this point in the synthesis phase of a systems engagement, primary emphasis has been placed on the theoretical aspects of the design. Subjecting the segment of a new system to simulated conditions of practice attempts to remove it from the theoretical drawing board and to examine it in the light of feasibility—will it work under real conditions?

Many different methods of testing are available with the choice of methods being a product of the surrounding circumstances. One method of testing a particular segment of a new system is to inquire of the person most directly in contact with it. For example, in the case of a report, does the person who will receive it accept it as fulfilling the expressed need? Does the report communicate the same information to him as it does to the analyst? If several data processing operations are to be performed by one operating person, does this person consider the work distribution to be feasible or is there a more acceptable procedure which could be incorporated?

Oral and written inquiry of this type is sometimes overlooked completely or fails to receive adequate attention from the analyst. Although he may be well-trained and experienced with many different systems, the analyst may not be as familiar with the workings of a particular operation as the person actually doing it. This knowledge can be profitably utilized by subjecting the segment to operating personnel's criticism and then deciding if the criticism is well-founded.

Another method of applying the testing technique is often used in mechanized operations. Old data can be taken from company files and re-processed by the revised data processing operations as a realistic test to determine if the new system will work. Results of the reprocessing can then be compared with the results of the first processing to determine the strengths and weaknesses of the new design. It is also often feasible to plan parallel operations with data being processed by both the old system and the proposed system. Such parallel work is not uncommon during major system changes.

Closely related to the reprocessing of old data is the use of fabricated data. The results can be examined in light of the applicable systems principles and a decision made regarding the acceptability of the revised system. Two physical tools which may be used in evaluating the reprocessing of old data or the processing of fabricated data, are *time and motion studies* and *work distribution tests*. These will aid in deciding if the job can be done within a stated time period with a certain degree of efficiency.

In today's age the computer can be used to apply the technique of testing. Systems or subsystems can be simulated mathematically and tested by the computer. Inventory control systems have been simulated by systems analysts and extensively tested by a computer. It is possible to change various conditions in the system and to compare the various results without risking the cost of lost time and confusion of actually using a condition that will not contribute to system efficiency in actual practice. Lead time, for example, is an important factor in any inventory reorder formula. One company used simulated inventory control models to test various lead times for different classes of inventory units. After establishing the lead time which made an optimum contribution to both inventory level and production schedules, the company set about obtaining suppliers who could meet required lead times. In the past companies have not been able to pin-point the effect of lead time and, as a result, merely accepted lead times common to customary suppliers.

When working on a particular segment of a system it is reasonable to assume that the analyst may subject his new ideas to other experts for constructive criticism. This is still another method of applying the technique of testing.

No matter what testing methods are chosen, subjecting the design to the most rigorous and diversified examination will serve to enhance the value of the finished product. The uncovering of weaknesses will permit changes to be made before costly installation begins. The uncovering of strengths will further convince the analyst that his design is the best in the circumstances.

ECONOMIC AND AESTHETIC JUSTIFICATION. This technique, although it is the final synthesis technique to be discussed, may be the most important tool of all. The synthesis phase of a systems engagement cannot be deemed successful unless the results are accepted by management. Management, in this case, would be the individuals, at whatever level, who are responsible for deciding whether to install the revised system.

The technique of economic and aesthetic justification encompasses all of the methods used by the systems analyst to convince management that the newly designed system is not only more economical than the preceding system, but that it is also aesthetically acceptable to overall management goals. It also includes the steps necessary to persuade management to initiate the installation phase of the investigation.

There are many rules which might be given to aid in the use of economic and aesthetic justification, but all of them center on sound human relations. Because no two people are alike it is important for the analyst to understand people—what motivates them and how they learn. (*See* Chapter 6.) It should go without saying that, regardless of the quality of human relations used by the analyst, he must have a good product for management.

Justifying a new system to management occurs at two general intervals: 1) during the synthesis phase and, 2) upon completion of the design. The first of these occurrences is probably more important than the latter. This is so because a management which has accepted the parts of a system design will most likely accept the whole.

Justification during the synthesis phase requires that management be kept aware of the progress being made and that they be asked for approval each step of the way. Presentation to management should be made after the analyst has tested a segment and co-ordinated it with the rest of the system.

Optimum use of management's constructive suggestions can be helpful in justifying the design. A person is much more willing to accept something he has helped to create. Management's objections to a proposed revision should also be taken into consideration. In cases of well-founded objections, the analyst should alter his proposed design. It is important that the analyst keep an open, unbiased mind so as to judge more fairly all suggestions—both his own and those of management. Only when management refuses to accept a revision which the analyst favors should an attempt be made to compromise in hopes of making the best of the situation.

The most effective means of convincing management that a new design is better than the old is to establish that the cost of the proposed new system is more reasonable than the old. No revised system or subsystem should be presented to management unless it is documented costwise.

There are times when the cost of a new system or subsystem will not be less than the existing system or subsystem it is replacing. At this point the intangible benefits of the new system must be pointed out. This is often difficult because of vague factors such as more accurate and more timely reports, impact on customers, and the extent to which profits increase. It is in this area that the reputation of the analyst will have an important effect. If a systems analyst has a reputation for not claiming intangible benefits which do not exist, management will be more inclined to place more weight on intangible benefits.

Economic and aesthetic justification to management can be accomplished by oral and visual and/or written presentations. The particular method of presentation should be exercised which the analyst can apply most proficiently and which will return the best results in the particular situation. The final report to management should include the following factors which may be applicable in particular circumstances:

1. Show what is being done now and the current problem existing.
2. Show an outline of suggested revisions.
3. Show economic data on reduced cost and reduced error.
4. Describe new information which could be available and its usefulness to management.
5. Show samples of new forms and their favorable traits.
6. Suggest whether to rent or buy new machines and the reasons therefor.

It cannot be overemphasized that systems recommendations are worthless if they never get past the synthesis phase and into the implementation and follow-up phase. For this reason, economic and aesthetic justification is a very important technique.

QUESTIONS, PROBLEMS, AND CASES

1. Contrast the synthesis phase of a systems investigation to the analysis phase.
2. In which of the phases of systems investigation might you find the procedural flow chart useful? Explain how it would be used with special emphasis on the synthesis phase.
3. Explain the review of analysis data technique, and its importance in synthesis.
4. What specifically is involved in the design of a new or revised flow of data and data processing operations during a systems investigation? Explain or illustrate.
5. The design of an effective and efficient system requires the proper recording and processing of data. What are some of the important considerations of data media design in this regard?

6. Why is the proper design of data media important to synthesis? Explain or give illustrations.

7. In the analysis phase of a systems investigation it was concluded that credit history information about many customers was not systematically checked and a number of losses were incurred. No credit check was normally made as a regular part of processing incoming orders. It was noted that when credit was checked, there was a delay of at least one week in the shipment of the order. You note that all orders come in by mail and are opened in the mail room. Having been identified as customer orders they are sent to the sales order section where they are edited for accuracy, pricing, and the like. An order form in four copies is prepared, one for shipping (packing slip), one for billing, one for the warehouse where the order will be filled, and one for file. Prebilling is not practicable. There is a separate credit department.

   Explain *how* you would go about the design of a system that would have the adequate credit check.

8. As a systems analyst you have designed a timekeeping, payroll, and labor cost system that you consider to be ready for installation. How would you go about testing the system?

9. As a test of a new system that has just been synthesized, it is possible to plan parallel operations of the old system and a new system. Is such duplication desirable? Explain.

10. During the synthesis phase of a systems investigation the system being designed should be justified more than once. Explain when the system being designed should be justified, to whom, and why.

11. What is one of the most convincing means of establishing a new system as being superior to the old system?

12. It has been suggested that the final report to management of a new system should describe new information which could be available and its usefulness to management. In the case of an inventory control system, what might such "new information" include that might be useful to management?

13. What is a major focal point for most of the rules which might be given to aid in the use of the economic and aesthetic technique?

14. Give an example of a situation in which a computer could be used to test a system being designed.

15. Two physical tools which may be used in evaluating the reprocessing of old data or the processing of fabricated data are time and motion studies and work distribution tests. Explain each and indicate a situation in which each might be used.

16. You have been called in as a systems analyst to study the internal control of the Black Biscuit Company. You have obtained the information that follows and have been asked to (1) comment on the existing internal control, point-

ing out weaknesses, and (2) make recommendations to correct or improve the situations causing the weaknesses noted.

The capital stock of the Black Biscuit Company is owned by two brothers, one of whom is president (in charge of sales and finance) and the other vice-president (in charge of production). Their wives and the secretary-treasurer each hold a qualifying share and act as directors.

This company owns a plant in a densely populated area and markets all of its biscuits within an area of 400 square miles, through fifteen salesmen who call on grocery, confectionery, and chain stores. Apart from miscellaneous income, all of its revenue is derived from the sale of biscuits.

The following statements indicate the relationship of costs and revenue in this company.

CONDENSED COMPARATIVE STATEMENTS
COST OF GOODS SOLD

	Dec. 31, 19A	Dec. 31, 19B
Raw materials	$1,802,500 (50%)	$1,871,595 (49¾%)
Packing materials	450,625 (12½%)	432,630 (11½%)
Direct labor	432,600 (12%)	451,440 (12%)
Overhead	180,250 (5%)	178,695 (4¾%)
	$2,865,975 (79½%)	$2,934,360 (78%)

OPERATING

Sales	$3,605,000 (100%)	$3,762,000 (100%)
Cost of goods sold	2,865,975 (79½%)	2,934,360 (78%)
Gross profit	739,025 (20½%)	827,640 (22%)
Selling expenses	290,200	299,300
General and administrative	184,300	186,500
Financial	58,000	65,000
Net operating profit	$ 206,525 (5.7%)	$ 276,840 (7.3%)

Comparative figures taken from the books are as follows:

Account No.	Assets	Jan. 1, 19A	Dec. 31, 19B
A-1	Cashier's office—cash	$ 3,540	$ 4,212
A-10	General bank account	215,403	249,321
A-15	Payroll bank account	7,328	10,209
A-16	Salary bank account	4,126	3,843
	Accounts receivable		
A-20	Salesmen's ledgers	308,114	341,225
A-30	House accounts	36,002	45,211

Account No.	Assets	Jan. 1, 19A	Dec. 31, 19B
A-40	Doubtful accounts	7,554	8,632
A-41	Advances to salesmen	2,500	3,000
	Inventories		
A-50	Raw materials	348,201	375,312
A-53	Packaging material	189,100	202,451
A-52	Finished goods	72,803	67,210
	Property accounts		
A-60	Land	30,000	30,000
A-61	Factory and office building	278,123	278,123
A-62	Machinery and equipment	566,921	623,212
A-63	Office furniture and equipment	60,410	65,420
A-62a	Machinery and equipment (fully depreciated)	63,418	50,312
A-64	Trucks	15,401	17,112
	Prepaid expenses and deferred charges		
A-70/74	Insurance, taxes, stationery, advertising, tools and maintenance supplies	38,150	40,554
		$2,247,094	$2,415,359

	Liabilities		
P-1	Accounts payable	$ 241,310	$ 208,420
P-2	Taxes payable	5,978	6,210
P-3	Commissions payable	16,220	18,450
P-5	Accrued wages payable	9,120	7,667
P-7	Bonus payable	32,000	38,500
P-10	Miscellaneous	1,519	2,142
P-20	Dividends payable—preferred shares	12,500	12,500
P-21	Dividends payable—common shares	15,000	15,000
P-25	Provision for Federal and state income taxes	96,842	138,216
P-40	Allowance for loss on accounts	7,554	8,632
P-41	Allowance for cash discounts	5,450	6,212
P-45	Allowance for possible inventory losses	10,000	15,000
P-61	Factory and office building depreciation	80,852	86,414
P-62	Machinery and equipment depreciation	169,776	250,196
P-62a	Machinery and equipment (fully depreciated)	63,418	50,312
P-63	Office furniture and equipment depreciation	19,095	24,301
P-64	Trucks—depreciation	10,551	4,223
P-90	5% preferred stock	500,000	500,000
P-91	No par value common stock	500,000	500,000
P-93	Retained earnings	449,909	522,964
		$2,247,094	$2,415,359

The major policies of the company are summarized as follows:

SALES AND REVENUES

1. The company operates under the Federal Pure Food and Drug Act and packages are labeled as to contents and weight.
2. Out-of-town sales are f.o.b. shipping point. Local deliveries are made by two trucks which the company owns.
3. Terms are 2 per cent ten days or net 30 days. There are no trade discounts but a yearly rebate based on dollar volume is credited to customers' accounts.
4. Sales are billed to customers on the date of bill of lading, or delivery receipt for local customers.
5. Comparative monthly sales statistics as to quantity and value are kept for each type of biscuit and each size of packaging, and by salesman. Comparative monthly dollar volume statistics are maintained for each customer.
6. Salesmen supply their own cars and are paid on a 5 per cent commission basis, plus car and traveling expenses. They are given advances against expenses for out-of-town traveling.
7. Freshness of product is a major sales policy. All stocks of biscuits over seven days old are sold to institutions (hospitals, etc.) at a 10 per cent or greater discount. These are house accounts handled by the president and no salesman's commission is paid.

PRODUCTION

Production is planned on Friday morning for the following week. The plant superintendent has prepared recipes, batches, instructions to production departments, and requisitions to raw material and packaging stores. This information is in the hands of interested parties by 4:00 P.M. on Friday.

Raw material stores deliver materials to production departments one-half hour before production starts each morning.

Production departments deliver biscuits to finished goods stores at the end of each morning and afternoon.

Production and stores reports of transactions are prepared in triplicate each day. The original goes to the cost department, the second copy to the vice-president, and the third copy to the plant superintendent.

Raw materials and packaging stores operate on *maximum/minimum* quantities. Requisitions are sent to the vice-president for approval and are then turned over to the purchasing department.

INTERNAL CONTROL AND ACCOUNTING PROCEDURES

The company maintains the following principal accounting records:
1. General ledger.
2. Journal voucher register (all journal entries are approved by the secretary-treasurer).
3. Cash receipts and disbursements records.
4. Payroll records.

   5. Accounts receivable subsidiary ledgers.
   6. Accounts payable subsidiary ledger.
   7. Cost accounting records.
   8. Perpetual inventory records.

There is no internal auditor. Original data are used for the recording of transactions wherever possible.

All prenumbered forms must be accounted for. If spoiled they are stamped *cancelled*. All multiple forms are printed *original, first copy*, etc.

Sales orders (prenumbered)

Sales orders are prepared in quadruplicate by salesmen, showing shipping and billing instructions. Quantities are shown under *ordered* section, opposite printed list of biscuits and packagings. Unit prices are also marked by salesmen. Three copies are mailed to the company.

The president reviews the orders and checks with the collection department concerning questionable credit risks, or asks the secretary-treasurer for a credit rating on new accounts. He approves the orders and turns them over to the order department to verify unit prices. The order department retains one copy and turns two over to the finished goods stores shipping department.

Goods are prepared for shipment and the quantities are entered under the *shipped* section of the order, one copy of which is included with the merchandise as a shipping memo. The other copy is entered on a daily summary sheet which forms the basis for deductions from the stock cards in the stores department (and later in the cost department) and is then returned to the order department.

The order department prepares back-order form in quadruplicate, if necessary. One copy is sent to the salesman.

A comptometer operator extends and adds the completed orders, which are turned over to the billing machine operator.

Telephone orders are handled in the same manner, with a copy mailed to the salesman.

Contacts with institutions are handled by the president. He, or his secretary, calls the institutions and advises them of items that are available and agrees on a price, if there is an excessive supply which the president believes will have to be reduced more than 10 per cent in price. The president has these orders written up in triplicate and at the same time prepares the invoice. He retains one copy of the order, sending two to the finished goods stores shipping department.

Invoices

Regular invoices are prepared in quadruplicate on prenumbered invoice forms by a billing machine operator, whose automatic calculations must agree with the comptometer operator's figures. Three copies are returned to the comptometer operator and the remaining copy is filed in a tray under customer's name (one tray for each salesman). These trays are the accounts receivable ledgers. The operator keeps control sheets for each tray on which she lists (in total) debits and credits each day. Each tray contains about one hundred active accounts. Trays are locked when the operator is not there and nothing can be extracted from a tray without her making a record on her control.

A copy of invoices to institutions that are prepared in the president's office are filed in a separate accounts receivable tray by the operator.

The comptometer operator compares regular invoices with orders for typographical errors, sends the original to the mailing department and one copy to the statistical department. The third copy is added, the total for the day entered in a sales summary which forms the basis of the posting to the general ledger, and is then filed in numerical order with the related order form attached.

The statistical department puts its copy of the invoice, by salesmen, on pegboards. Quantities, packagings, and values are cross-added and entered on sales summaries which balance with the total determined by the comptometer operator in the order department. Invoices are then filed by customers, the total dollar value for each customer is determined monthly and agreed in total with the sales summary. The former are the basis of commission calculations and the latter of rebate calculations.

CREDIT MEMOS

The receiving department prepares *returned goods* slips in quadruplicate. These are approved by the superintendent after inspecting the goods returned, and are then sent to the order department. The order, billing, and statistical departments handle receiving slips and credit memos in the same manner as orders and invoices.

Returned goods that cannot be sold to institutions at a special price are ground to form the base for a cheaper quality of biscuits or are scrapped entirely. In this last case, their cost is charged to a *scrap* account.

PURCHASE REQUISITIONS (PRENUMBERED)

These are prepared by the stores department heads, plant superintendent or office, and approved by the vice-president.

PURCHASE ORDERS (PRENUMBERED)

These are prepared in quadruplicate (last copy without prices). The original is mailed to the supplier; a copy goes to the accounting department; a copy without prices to the receiving department and one copy is filed by suppliers in the purchasing department.

RECEIVING SLIPS (PRENUMBERED)

These are prepared in duplicate in the receiving department. One copy goes to the accounting department and one copy to the stores department.

PURCHASE INVOICES (PRENUMBERED)

Suppliers are requested to use the invoice form supplied with the purchase order and to send an original and a copy. Most suppliers comply. The accounting department marks the distribution. The original is matched with the receiving slip and purchase order, and then sent to the purchasing department head for approval. Purchasing department retains the order and receiving slip, which are filed numerically. All numbers of the order and of the slip must be accounted for.

Original invoices form the basis of direct posting to the general ledger and to the voucher part of the check. Invoices and checks are filed in trays, by suppliers, under classification of due dates. On the due date, a check is completed on the bookkeeping machine and the total repeated by *check protectograph*. The check is then sent (with invoices attached) to the president or vice-president and secretary-treasurer for two signatures and initialing of invoices. Checks are turned over to the mailing department by the president's secretary, and invoices are returned to the accounting department where they are filed numerically. All numbers must be accounted for. The proof sheets of the posting of invoices to voucher part of check, and of posting of the amount on the body of check, form the voucher register and cash disbursements record respectively, and are the bases for posting to the general ledger.

The second copy of the invoice is sent to the cost department for individual machine posting to perpetual inventory cards and for total posting to the cost ledger. It is then filed in that department, under names of suppliers.

Where a supplier does not use the specified invoice form, the president must approve payment. He prepares memos to serve in lieu of the invoice form.

Salesmen's expense advances, commissions and other disbursements are recorded on *cash disbursement* forms in duplicate. The original is approved by the president, numbered consecutively with invoices and posted in the same manner. The duplicate is filed alphabetically in the accounting department.

CREDIT MEMOS FROM SUPPLIERS

These memos follow the same procedure as invoices.

FREIGHT BILLS

Bills for incoming freight are matched with bills of lading and sent to the purchasing department for comparison with receiving slips and for approval. They follow the same procedure as purchase invoices, with a copy going to the cost department. Outgoing freight is never *prepaid*.

INVENTORIES

Perpetual inventory records are maintained by the cost department for raw materials, packagings and finished goods. Units and values are posted to the cards. The FIFO method is in use in all stores. Complete physical inventories are taken at the year end, by teams composed of a member of the cost department and a member from the respective stores department. The cost department makes a weekly test of physical inventories against perpetual inventory records. All adjustments for shortages or overages are approved by the vice-president. The company values inventories at the lower of cost or market.

CASH RECEIPTS

Payment for cash sales is made to the cashier, who records it on a cash register. Cash is balanced with the locked tape by a member of the accounting staff. A separate deposit slip is made. The total for the day is entered in a cash summary and posted monthly to the general ledger. Cash sales invoices are prenumbered and all numbers must be accounted for. A copy is given to the statistical department and to the cost department.

Customer's checks are turned over to the collection department, which reports to the secretary-treasurer. They type deposit slips on special forms, in triplicate. The original serves as the customer's cash receipts record on which cash discounts, etc., are marked. The totals are posted to the general ledger. Matching invoices and credit memos are extracted from the trays and attached thereto. The duplicate deposit slip is retained by the bank and the triplicate is receipted and returned. Adjustment slips, in duplicate, may be approved by the secretary-treasurer, for accounts not balancing out. The original of such a slip is placed in the tray under the customer's name and the duplicate is attached to the cash receipts record.

Monthly open-item statements are prepared by the collection clerk for those accounts having past due accounts. Uncollectible or doubtful accounts are transferred to a separate tray and have their own general ledger control. The secretary-treasurer approves all accounts to be written off, except for accounts with institutions which are approved by the president. Trial balances of the accounts receivable trays are prepared and aged monthly.

FACTORY PAYROLL

Factory employees are paid weekly, by check, at fixed hourly rates. Checks are given out each Thursday for the prior week's earnings. Time cards are picked up by a member of the payroll department each Friday after the employees have checked out. Total hours are calculated and rechecked. Employees' names are entered on voucher checks from addressograph plates. Clock number, total hours, rate, gross pay, deductions and net pay are posted on the voucher part of the check and on the employee's cumulative record card in one operation, by an accounting machine which makes the calculations. The proof sheet forms the payroll record and is used for transfers to the payroll bank account and for posting the general ledger. It is approved by the personnel manager, who compares it with his record as to names and rates. The net amount is inscribed on the checks by *protectograph*. The payroll department is notified by the personnel department of all changes in employees or hourly rates. Prenumbered forms are used, which are approved by the vice-president.

OFFICE SALARIES

Officers, office employees and the plant superintendent are paid monthly by voucher check. They are not paid for overtime. The president's secretary prepares the checks and individual salary records on an accounting machine. The proof sheet is the monthly salary record, and is approved by the secretary-treasurer, who authorizes the transfer to the salary account.

DISTRIBUTION OF PAYROLL CHECKS

Factory payroll checks are turned over to the cashier in alphabetical order. Employees picking up their checks must wear their employment badges, the number on which the cashier compares with the employee's number shown on his check before handing it out.

Office payroll checks are distributed by the president's secretary.

(Adapted AICPA Examination)

CHAPTER 12

Implementation and Follow-Up*

IN THE PREVIOUS TWO CHAPTERS THE ANALYSIS AND SYNTHESIS PHASES OF A
systems investigation were examined. Some systems investigations stop at the
synthesis phase because the new system has not been justified to management
and will not be installed. In most systems, however, the responsibility of the
analyst does not stop until the new system, subsystem, or procedure is fully
operational. In other words, successful implementation will normally include
an adequate amount of planning and consulting by the systems analyst to
assure that the system is understood, installed properly, accepted, and operating smoothly. By all means the personnel responsible for the operation of the
new system or procedure should have the responsibility for actual implementation.

The implementation phase of most systems investigations involves, among
other things, planning and assisting in the ordering and testing of new equipment, the final design and printing of new communication media, debugging
the operation of new procedures, training employees in new methods, and
arranging new physical facilities. The analyst must recommend a systematic
approach to solving these problems in order to minimize confusion and to
insure that the new system is accepted and installed smoothly.

Implementation requires a change in the work being done by certain
people, in the skill required to perform, in responsibility, and in relationships
between groups. Throughout Chapter 12 the importance of the Human
Factors Principle of systems design will be evident. In addition, the need for
careful planning before the actual installation of the system is emphasized.

---

* Major portions of this chapter are based on J. B. Bower, and J. B. Sefert, "Human
Factors in Systems Designs," *Management Services* (November–December, 1965).

TECHNIQUES OF IMPLEMENTATION
AND FOLLOW-UP

Just as the analyst was able to use helpful techniques in the analysis and synthesis phases of his investigation, he can also apply certain techniques in the implementation and follow-up phase. These techniques are:

1. Scheduling.
2. Personnel selection and training.
3. Acquisition of equipment and communication media.
4. Testing.
5. Technical modification.
6. Reappraisal.

SCHEDULING. The implementation phase of a systems investigation involves the coordination of many diverse factors. The intricateness of this coordination is, of course, a function of the extent of the investigation itself. Nevertheless, in all systems investigations except those which affect only one of the system components, it is essential to use the scheduling technique. Scheduling is conceived as the technique in the implementation phase which must solve the problem of timing of installation components and steps so as to avoid bottlenecks, irritation, excessive cost and effort, and interim inefficiency.

A smooth introduction of the new system requires establishing priorities. Time lags in acquiring new equipment, hiring, transferring, and retraining employees, printing communication media, and the like must be taken into account. Factors such as the existence of pressing problems in one department may indicate that systems installation should start in this area. On the other hand, particularly favorable circumstances such as very effective administrative personnel or a good psychological response in a particular department may offer strong points from which to establish a new system. Management's desire to use up old supplies of communication media before a switchover should be considered. These are but a few random factors that are relevant to scheduling.

Until a few years ago systems analysts responsible for planning the implementation of the more complex system configuration used no methods more sophisticated than a Gantt Chart to help them in scheduling the entire implementation process. In 1958, the PERT technique was developed by the Navy. The letters in the word "PERT" stand for Program Evaluation and Review Technique. This technique was the application of statistical and mathematical methods to the planning, evaluation, and control of research and development effort. Primarily, PERT is used to define what must be done in order to accomplish program objectives on time. By using this method, areas of a particular project, such as the implementation of a financial information system, which require remedial decisions can be detected and corrected. In the implementation phase of any systems engagement, the implementor must "juggle" three factors—time, resources, and technical performance. PERT uses time as the common denominator to reflect planned resource application and performance specifications. Through the delineation of activities that must be performed in a project, the relative position in time of one activity to another, and the estimated time to complete each activity, an electronic computer can be used to determine the "critical path" of the project so that the project manager can concentrate his efforts on the activities which are crucial to the project's timetable.

It is not within the scope of this text to elaborate further on PERT or Gantt Charts or any other specific method of implementing the scheduling technique. Students will learn these methods in other courses of study. Individuals who have not been formally exposed to scheduling methods will certainly have difficulty implementing complex financial information systems.

PERSONNEL SELECTION AND TRAINING. A new or revised system or procedure implies that the personnel who will be required to carry out the new procedures must be selected and they must be trained. One of the techniques used in the analysis phase of a systems engagement is personnel review. Data about personnel which were accumulated by this technique should be valuable for use in the implementation phase to select the employees for specific job assignments who have both the ability to comply with job requirements and the desire to do a good job as well. In situations where substantial changes will be made in job contents, it may be necessary to use testing techniques as well as the judgment of company supervisors in order to place the right person in the right job. An individual, for example, may be well suited in his job as an operator of various punched card machines but may be unqualified to perform as a computer operator.

In any new system, personnel must not only be selected, but they must also be trained to operate effectively in the new environment. As new equipment, communication media, and procedures appear, supervisors, first, must be guided in their use and shown how each element is an integral part of the system. If the analyst has done his job during the synthesis phase of his engagement, much of his work with supervisors will center on details and not on essential concepts. It is the supervisor's responsibility for the training of subordinates. However, this responsibility is often willingly delegated to staff or other specialists in the case of major system revision.

The training of the employees who will actually operate the system is one of the most important aspects of implementation. In order for the system to operate efficiently, the employees must understand their duties as well as being capable of performing the tasks assigned and having sufficient company morale to keep following the prescribed procedures. Employees, generally, will do what is asked of them as long as they are capable, understand what is being asked, and understand why the particular job is needed. Employee training requires the teacher to instruct the employee in the who, what, when, where, why, and how of his new duties.

Depending on the complexity of the job many training aids can be used ranging from complete training manuals, including organization charts, flow charts, job descriptions and facility diagrams, to a simple blackboard. It is up to the teacher to select the methods most appropriate in the circumstances.

ACQUISITION OF EQUIPMENT AND COMMUNICATION MEDIA. The acquisition of the various types of communication media and equipment is another technique that can be used in the implementation phase of a systems investigation. When the synthesis or design phase of the investigation is completed, the type of equipment to be acquired, as well as the new or revised communication media to be used, have been established. It is necessary in the implementation phase to assist the client in the actual acquisition of both equipment and media. Not only is the selection of proper equipment and media important, but also the timing of the arrival of these items is essential to a smooth implementation.

For example, in the case of a large computer installation the computer and necessary peripheral equipment should be scheduled to arrive only after the training of programmers and the development of a basic complement of programs have been completed. Likewise, new communication media needed for the programmers or for the first programs to be run should be acquired and ready for use when needed. It should be quite evident that the technique of acquisition of equipment and communication media is closely linked to the technique of scheduling and to the technique of personnel selection and training.

In the synthesis phase of a systems investigation the technique of economic and aesthetic justification is utilized. However, it is necessary for the analyst to see to it that equipment, media, and any other cost elements in the new system are consistent with the estimates made earlier. Quite often the cost estimates need to be adjusted as contracts are let to acquire various components. For the analyst this is a very sensitive area. Most clients and most managements do not like to see the cost of a new system rise above the estimates that were made during synthesis and which may have been an important influence in decision making.

A particular method of implementing both the personnel selection and training and the acquisition of equipment and communication media techniques is the use of *implementation budgetary control*. Working from the detailed cost estimates made in the synthesis phase it is possible to compare actual costs as they are incurred with the estimates. Just as in the use of budgets in controlling manufacturing costs, the more detailed the budget the more control can be exercised. The analyst should be aware that the use of implementation budgetary control is more essential as the system being implemented becomes increasingly complex.

TESTING. The testing technique is used extensively in the synthesis phase of a systems investigation and it is also a very useful technique during implementation. Testing, as the name implies, is devoted to trying out the various components of a financial information system to see that they function properly.

Several different methods of applying the technique of testing were described in Chapter 11. These methods can also be used in the implementation phase. During synthesis the objective of testing was to establish the feasibility of the new system being designed and to the extent possible simulate the operations being conceived for the new system. Often during the synthesis phase small segments of the system are not tested because they are small segments and can be made to function properly only after implementation begins. During implementation the small segments, as well as the large, must be tested under realistic conditions. Often the small segment, if inoperative, will render the entire system inoperative.

New communication media designs are very difficult to test during the synthesis phase. A simulation may be attempted but rarely can it be done effectively. In most cases the new communication media are judged to be soundly conceived and are not tested until implementation. Such is the case with specific computer programs in a large data processing installation. The analyst knows that the particular parameters of an accounts receivable subsystem can be programmed on the particular computer that is being installed, but it is rarely practical to prepare the necessary programs until a decision has been made to install the computer. As a result of such situations and others that are similar, testing becomes a very important technique in the implementation phase.

TECHNICAL MODIFICATION. No matter how effectively a new system has been tested during synthesis, minor and in some cases major, technical imperfections are discovered as segments of a system are being tested in the implementation phase. It is often necessary to make certain technical modifications in order to produce a smoothly functioning system. A most vivid example of a major technical imperfection is a problem encountered during the installation of a punched card data processing system for a large midwestern hospital. It was decided during the synthesis phase to use cards in each department of the hospital to record various charges and credits to patient accounts. Floor nurses were expected to mark each card appropriately so that these cards could be punched by the mark-sensing method and could be introduced into the processing system without keypunching the cards. Preliminary tests were made and no problems were encountered. However, once the system was in full operation error upon error was discovered in the cards which were mark-sensed punched. In actual practice the nurses in the departments either were too busy to take the time to mark the cards properly or did not want to do it properly. Most likely both situations contributed to the error rate. A technical modification was made by using the old charge and credit tickets in place of the mark-sense cards and by keypunching cards from the tickets.

Many of the other techniques available in the various phases of an engagement have a finite number of methods of implementing them. Technical modification, however, has as many methods as potential problems that could be encountered in a particular system. The analyst must first encounter the difficulty during a test and then must adjust whatever elements of the system which are not functioning properly.

REAPPRAISAL. No system, particularly a system in which people play an integral role, can be put into operation and forgotten. Since a financial information system contains people as an essential component, it is absolutely necessary for the analyst to subject the newly installed system to critical reappraisal for a period of time after implementation is formally completed. The reappraisal technique amounts to a performance audit of the system, and can also be considered as the follow-up to see if the system is functioning. It seeks to find out if the system is accomplishing what was expected, if it has developed some unexpected advantages or disadvantages, if it is costing what was expected, if it is being operated according to plan or if "shortcuts" are appearing, and if systems changes should be considered.

One method of applying the reappraisal technique is to systematically compare the new system with each of the nine principles of system design. Has each one of the principles been applied successfully in the new system? Chapter 2 covered the nine principles in detail but it is appropriate to review them here to illustrate how well they can be used as an integral part of the reappraisal technique.

> *Reasonable Cost Principle.* The system should be designed to provide information and internal control, consistent with the needs of management, at a reasonable cost.

The analyst must judge whether the new system provides the information and internal control desired by management at a reasonable cost. If the effective budgetary control has been used to apply the implementation techniques of personnel selection and training and acquisition of equipment and communication media, the reasonable cost principle has most likely been achieved. In addition, however, a very critical reappraisal should be made of the internal control duties established in various parts of the system. More duties than necessary for effective control may violate the reasonable cost principle.

> *Report Principle.* The system should be designed to permit effective reporting, both internally and externally, since reports are a primary systems product.

In reviewing system compliance with this principle, effective use can be made of the worksheets described in Chapter 10 which were suggested aids in establishing output criteria. (*See* Figures 10-1, 10-2, and 10-3.) After completing these worksheets for the new system the analyst and his client should be convinced that the new system does permit effective reporting.

> *Human Factors Principle*. The system should be designed consistent with applicable human factors, since people are responsible for the effectiveness of the system.

Compliance with this principle is difficult to simulate in the synthesis phase of a systems engagement. Quite often the question of whether certain personnel can cope with a new assignment cannot be determined until the reappraisal technique is applied. Human factors are of such importance they are discussed separately and in some detail later in this chapter.

> *Organization Structure Principle*. The system should be designed to function in a specific, clearly defined, organization structure, since the system should be tailored for the organization to satisfy particular information and control needs.

A new organization chart coupled with the analysis techniques of inquiry and visual observation can be used by the analyst to judge systems compliance with this principle.

> *Reliability Principle*. The system should be designed to check the reliability and accuracy of financial data, minimize error, safeguard assets, and prevent fraud or other irregularity.

During reappraisal, again using the analysis techniques of inquiry and visual observation, the analyst must judge whether the error rate is acceptable at all points in the system. Managers want accurate and reliable information. Nothing will destroy confidence in the new system quicker than erroneous judgments made on the basis of inaccurate information produced by the system. Of course, a system which does not provide for asset safeguards fails to comply with the reliability principle.

> *Flexible Yet Uniform and Consistent Principle*. The system should be designed to be flexible yet insure reasonable uniformity and consistency of application in order to facilitate the dynamics of business.

Of all systems principles this one takes the most, in the way of professional judgment, to apply. It is the least quantifiable of the principles. For example, an analyst knows that the parameters of an accounts receivable subsystem can be set in any one of a myriad of ways. Once set for a particular class of receivables it would be a violation of the Flexible Yet Uniform and Consistent principle to permit various branches to establish different parameters. It becomes even more important to have common parameters for the receivable class if data processing is to be centralized.

> *Audit Trail Principle.* The system should be designed to facilitate the tracing of procedural steps in order to permit the analysis of detail underlying summarized information.

Without an audit trail in a financial information system management loses its ability to reconstruct the underlying parts of summarized data. Without an audit trail analysis is next to impossible. During the application of the reappraisal technique the analyst tests the system for possible gaps in the audit trail.

> *Data Accumulation Principle.* The system should be designed to enable the rapid and efficient recording and classification of data in order to process it into information for planning, control, and accomplishment of administrative routine.
>
> *Data Processing Principle.* The system should be designed to provide a meaningful continuous and controlled flow of data being processed in order to produce reliable information and facilitate control.

These two principles come under careful scrutiny during analysis, during synthesis, and again during implementation and follow-up. Unless the system complies with these two principles it is very doubtful that the system will be operating so that it can be subjected to reappraisal. It is possible during reappraisal to spot minor violations which may not impair operation but which, if corrected, would permit efficient and effective data and information flow.

EMPHASIS ON HUMAN FACTORS

During the actual implementation and follow-up of a new or revised financial information system, adaptations and revisions are often necessary to accommodate problems caused by human factors. By consideration of as many of these human factors as possible during the analysis and synthesis phases of the investigation, the analyst has an opportunity to take into account any adaptations necessary at an earlier stage, assuring a better design, greater acceptance by the employees, and a more efficient operation.

For convenience in examining and discussing the interaction of the various human factors on installation of a system, two levels of management will be distinguished as noted originally in Chapter 6 and Figure 6-1. *Top management* as a level includes those executives who participate in company-wide policy formulation, including the chief executive and those who report directly to him, such as vice-presidents, sales and production managers, and the treasurer and controller. *Middle management* includes not only the usual group of middle and junior executives such as division managers, department managers, and their staff functional advisers, but also operating supervisors and foremen. Since the human factors which affect this group as a whole are very similar they will be discussed concurrently.

Nonsupervisory employees will be treated separately since their actions and reactions to systems changes are normally different from those at the managerial levels.

The *systems analyst* is assumed to be either a member of an internal systems and procedures staff in a company or an outside specialist in this field who may represent an accounting or management services firm.

In the discussion which follows, the components of the human factors principle are examined as they apply in more detail to each of the three levels of personnel who are involved with the system.

Human Factors at the Top Management Level

It is axiomatic that an effective system requires the whole-hearted support of top management for the greatest degree of acceptance and success. The middle management and the nonsupervisory employees are quick to take their cue from the attitudes which flow downward. In the past, top management often considered work procedures and systems study as a specialized function to be concerned with only on a fire-fighting basis when a crisis arose. With the advent of costly mechanized or computer methods, which have to be justified to boards of directors or stockholders, or which in some cases have become status symbols worthy of discussion at the club, top management has become much more interested and involved in the problems of data processing. Whole-hearted support, not belated attention, is essential to the eventual success of the system. Top management must review interim findings, and approve or disapprove recommendation for further action at several points during the system project. Careful consideration and prompt decisions by the top executives are essential. If the system has the continuing interest of top management behind it, a desire on the part of all management to take action for the ultimate benefit of the company may be stimulated.

Mere interest and support by top management is not the whole answer, however. Many human factors at this level need to be taken into account in determining what the actual information needs of management are, in alerting top managers to the full implications of any large-scale revision of the data processing system, and in making certain that executives are aware of and can use the full range of benefits to be secured from a well-designed and integrated system.

COMPANY PATTERNS OF CHANGE. Most established companies have certain patterns of activity which determine their approach to new ideas and innovations. One systems analyst has likened these patterns to the tribal customs of a South Seas tribe with its rituals to drive out the evil spirits, complete with a dance around the totem pole.[1] Some managers may prefer to use devious and indirect methods of achieving results, others may be forceful and direct in ordering changes. The analyst must be alert to these differences of approach.

In some organizations there are well-defined duties and responsibilities assigned to each top manager: many small and close-knit firms prefer not to have duties and responsibilities too well-defined. In some situations top management is not prepared to make any substantial change in its organization or method of operation. In such situations it is necessary to decide whether to adapt the system design to accommodate the attitude, or whether to attempt to convince management of the necessity for organizational change or different approach concurrently with the building of an efficient system.

The pattern of change in a company may be dependent upon other predisposing factors which have operated in the past to mold the ideas of the top managers. A top executive may hold his present position because of some procedure or method he introduced many years ago and by virtue of which he has risen in the company. He is not likely to welcome any proposal which he feels may endanger his status or his own sense of value to the company. Special care will be needed to secure the participation of this executive in any new system planning so that he can identify with the new and feel that his own prior system contributed materially to the success of the new. Another top manager may have a pet project to which he gives special attention and which is part of his personal pattern of self-esteem. The analyst must alert himself to such "sacred cows." Another executive may be a so-called detail man who likes to have his hand in designing procedures himself. Another may be an idea man who is interested only in the broader aspects of the system. In each case the analyst adapts his approach accordingly, conferring much more often on details with the former type of executive, enlisting his support and ideas and securing his participation, but taking care to retain good

---

[1] Allen Y. Davis, "Gaining Acceptance of New Ideas," *Ideas for Management—1959* (Detroit: Systems and Procedures Association, 1959), p. 219.

design, and deftly guiding it so that it will not deviate from the best standards of an effective system.

If the past history of a company is one of orderly and considered attention to continued improvement in data handling, in contrast to a pattern of patchwork solutions to systems crises, the analyst will be able to determine whether the top management is *systems-oriented* and the degree to which he can expect support in designing and installing any new system.

STRENGTH OF DESIRE FOR IMPROVEMENT. If the systems analyst finds that top management has a *genuine concern in achieving a solution* for any systems problem found to exist, it is likely that he will also find the desire and courage present in management to make the changes necessary to implement the solution. The systems analyst needs to know how much support he can expect from management should organizational changes, or personnel displacements, or an addition or reduction in departments be found necessary.

Top management's willingness to *assign good people* to work with the analyst and to allow them to devote the necessary time to the project is one test of its real interest and concern. Too often the tendency has been to make such assignments on the basis of availability rather than suitability.[2] If there is an indication that this is likely to be done, the analyst needs to point out to management the importance of having outstanding people on the planning group and the later benefits which will outweigh the present outlay of time. The use of a project team made up of representatives from the various departments affected, operating with or under the analyst, is itself a concept of procedure and problem-solving that may be appropriate but new to top management in that particular company.

The extent to which *delegation of authority* to lower levels has previously existed is a factor which will affect the ability of those below to accept change and to participate in bringing it about. If all decisions have traditionally been made from above, the analyst is likely to find middle management, operating supervisors, and nonsupervisory employees alike hesitant to express opinions and make suggestions simply because their ideas have dried up from lack of encouragement. Top management needs, at this point, to give visible evidence of its desire for improvement by being willing to allow the best people to participate and to give them the time and authority needed to do a proper job.

A striking example of how differences in prior participation in planning and problem-solving affects the manner in which departments can contribute to and accept change is illustrated in a detailed study of fundamental systems changes made over a period of five years in a large light and power company.[3]

---

[2] Benjamin Conway, "Putting Electronic Data Processing to Work," *The Price Waterhouse Review* (September, 1958), p. 19.

[3] Floyd C. Mann and Lawrence K. Williams, "Observations on the Dynamics of Change to Electronic Data-Processing Equipment," *Administrative Science Quarterly* (September, 1960), p. 217.

In the accounting department over the years much effort had been spent in developing participation in management by intermediate and first-line supervisors. As a result a high degree of employee satisfaction, trust, and good will had been created which proved very valuable during the transition period. In the sales department, for a variety of reasons, the employees had never participated in management to this degree. Communication of information concerning the change was much more complete at all levels in the accounting department. In the sales department no attempt was made to present the new system in terms of significance to the sales employees in relation to their special interests and objectives, as contrasted to the different interests of the accounting employees. As a result the sales employees never understood the system as well, tended to lack confidence in it, and the problems of transition were made more difficult.

The strength of top management's desire for improvement will be further tested as it is alerted to the probable training time and costs of installation which will be involved in any large-scale revision of the system. A realistic appraisal of such factors during the synthesis phase will provide management with an opportunity to determine its step-by-step involvement. In this respect, if *cost-cutting* has been the principal factor in top management's motive for change, it may be desirable for the analyst to also orient the manager toward an appreciation of the benefits of *labor-saving* as a broad goal, with the use of saved labor to make possible improved and faster information for decision-making. The system will be of special value if it includes plans for the profitable use of saved labor to provide better tools for management. This shift in emphasis toward a broader goal will also serve to ease the fears of operating personnel as to labor displacement which may have been aggravated by over-emphasis on cost-cutting alone as a management motive.

Ability or inability to secure *prompt policy decisions* from top management as the designing and planning progresses will be an important factor of concern to the systems analyst. Procrastination in making difficult decisions is a basic human trait. The systems analyst must press firmly for such decisions while using every means available to demonstrate the logical basis of his proposals. In one instance of a manufacturing company the systems and procedures staff personnel were forced to spend 60 per cent of their time on attempts to obtain final decisions. In the words of one staff member, attempting to get a decision was "like trying to tie a rope around a pile of sand."[4] Decisions will be particularly difficult to secure if a basic change in organizational structure is involved or the proposed change will create an embarrassing personnel problem. If the organizational pattern of the company has tended to develop around personalities, rather than being based upon logical division of functions, the difficulties of change are magnified. If top manage-

---

[4] Richard F. Neuschel, *Management by System* (New York: McGraw-Hill Book Company, Inc., 1960), p. 91.

ment is adamant in refusing to make a certain indicated organizational or personnel change, the systems analyst may have to build around the existing structure or person, recognizing that a *good system* which has the support of management is to be preferred over the *best system* which will not be supported or used.

ATTITUDE TOWARD EMPLOYEES. Much of the recent experience with large-scale computer installations has demonstrated the fact that among the major factors contributing to a smooth transition and insuring a maximum acceptance of systems change by the employees involved has been the willingness of top management to make assurances concerning job security, retention of salary, opportunity for training, and definite rules to be followed in reassignment. The past practices of the company in this respect and its philosophy of social responsibility will be important factors to be studied and considered by the analyst.

In those companies where there has been a sincere concern for the employee as a human being, a trust in top management has been built up which is of great value later in gaining acceptance of change. If there has been a willingness in the past to use the ideas, imagination, and suggestions of the employees and to pay attention to workers' feelings in visible ways, the systems analyst will find his fact-finding and analysis task much easier. Experienced systems analysts place emphasis on the desirability for the analyst to appraise, as early as possible, the *management climate* of the organization and to take this into account in systems planning. If he finds this climate one of teamwork and understanding between departments, delegation of authority by management, and an atmosphere of stimulation and challenge to problem-solving, his work will be facilitated. If he finds a climate of top management isolation, rigid departmental barriers, little or no downward communication, and a reluctance to inform employees of company plans and policies, the analyst may need to demonstrate and emphasize the importance of *attention to people* in assuring the success of any proposed new system.

As the design and planning for a major systems change unfolds, top management for the first time may have to examine introspectively its future course of action in the field of human relations. What shall its attitude be toward displaced labor? Is it willing to assure to all employees affected the opportunity for continued employment regardless of the data processing changes and adjustments in departmental functions? Is it willing to bear the expense of retraining employees in former skills to enable them to perform different jobs? Is it willing to recognize the interdependence of the organization and the individual and give visible evidence of this in its concern for the self-respect and personal improvement of the employee during change and otherwise? The final proposals involve employee utilization. The representatives of the affected departments are needed to assist in alerting the analyst to any special human factor problems which are likely to arise in their area.

Ability to Adapt and Learn. Prior reluctance of top management to concern itself in the complexity of data processing and work procedures has been mentioned. The systems analyst needs to determine management's willingness and ability to adapt to a large-scale revision of its processing system. The managers of tomorrow must have a broad knowledge of the interdependence of each part of the business and the vastly greater potential for decision-making which can result from the increased variety of information made possible by a modern data system. The systems analyst should assist top management in understanding what the system can provide and how it can be of value and incorporated in planning and decision-making. Already there is being envisioned for the future a management decision-making room where all executives will function as a team, using information made immediately available on visual output display devices connected directly with the source of information. Department store shopping without sales slips, supermarkets with no checkout stations, dial phone payments to doctors, dentists, and other professional people, ticketless traveling, and electronically computed income tax returns are but a few of the developments which the next decade may bring and which management must be prepared to take advantage of.[5]

Human Factors at the Middle Management Level

It is becoming apparent that as more and more mechanization of data processing takes place, and in particular as routine decisions in which factors can be identified are programmed into computers, there is a decreasing need for the type of daily decision-making which has been one of the principal functions of middle management and supervisory personnel, particularly as it has related to the collection, analysis, and sorting of data. The necessary inflexibility of the program inherent in any large-scale system in order to insure uniform input, processing, and output reduces the need for frequent decision-making during the intermediate steps of a process. The job of work scheduling will also diminish. The eventual reduction in the total manpower needed for manual data handling likewise reduces the number of supervisors needed. Middle management senses this change in the financial information system and is instinctively fearful of it.

Traditionally, the systems analyst has found it necessary to work closely with middle management in analysis, synthesis, and finally implementation and follow-up because the personnel at this level can have in their hands the potential success or failure of a new system. Top management relies on them

---

[5] Lach, Edward L., "The Total Systems Concept," *Systems and Procedures*, (November, 1960), p. 6; and "Effects of Business Automation in the Sixties," *Management and Business Automation*, Part I (January, 1961), p. 18*ff*; and Part II, (February, 1961), p. 28*ff*.

for the everyday efficiency and the smooth operation of the organization, and from them the nonsupervisory employee takes his direction and sets his course. An understanding of the human factors at work in this group of managers and supervisors is especially important to the systems analyst since he must depend to a great extent upon the information the supervisors can furnish and also upon their later acceptance and implementation of any system he designs and installs.

INFLUENCES OF PAST EXPERIENCES. It is characteristic of most middle management that in the past it has concentrated its attention mainly on the technical aspects of the work and not enough on the administrative and human relations aspects of its job. Many managers and supervisors are unprepared, therefore, to visualize the broader range of a new system and the greater need for educating the employees under them to their part in the total operation. If necessary, the systems analyst should seek to overcome this narrowness of perspective and to build up in the supervisor a *feeling for the total job* which is being attempted. He will be aided in this if, in the past, top management has encouraged the participation of middle management in the discussion of problems and in decision-making. Another factor on the side of the analyst is that middle management is generally accustomed to working toward long-range goals such as future promotion, retirement, and providing for family education, and does not need the evidence of *immediate* advantage from a change to the degree that operating employees at lower levels normally do.

Nevertheless, *prior experience* of a manager or supervisor with system changes is a powerful determinant of his present attitude toward change. If his last experience with a staff specialist was unfortunate, he may now be convinced that all staff men are arrogant, opinionated, impractical, and that dealing with them is a waste of time taken from productive work. Perhaps he once made a suggested improvement in procedures which was not acknowledged, or which was adopted without giving credit to him. He has since nurtured his hurt and resolved never again to volunteer any ideas. In such cases the systems analyst has to bear the burden of overcoming the effects of prior unfavorable impressions and also convince the supervisor that systems analysts are genuinely interested in hearing his ideas and using them.

Another human factor of importance at the middle management level is the greater resistance to change that accompanies *higher age*. This is particularly true in large and stable organizations. Age brings greater resistance to change partly from dislike of altering established patterns of work which are familiar and comfortable and partly from the ever-present fear of not being able to compete with the younger people coming up in the organization. Instinctively, there is also the tendency to organize experience in a manner which will be minimally threatening and to believe what one wants to believe. This is why mental images formed by rumor and hearsay are so resistant to factual statements by the employer.

In dealing with these factors the systems analyst should take no pre-determined position for or against the question of the ability of older workers to adapt to change and to learn new techniques. There is a considerable amount of experience in companies installing automated data processing systems which indicates that there are factors in favor of training and using the older workers in the new jobs. Their greater sense of responsibility toward the job, their reliability, their care for details, and their mature judgment have been cited as significant factors weighing in their favor. Many persons over 45 have been trained to fill technical positions in the computer field and in many cases the training period for the older worker could be shortened, which also helped reduce anxiety during the transition.[6] The systems analyst who is aware of these facts can deal with the older employee in such a manner that fears and tensions are diminished rather than increased.

During all phases of synthesis the analyst must be continually alert to the deep-seated human factors which are operating to influence the people he deals with. He seeks by preplanning to take into account the effect which these factors will have on the ultimate operation of the system.

Special Announcement. It is difficult in any organization to get ahead of the rumor network in alerting employees to any impending change in their work procedure or status. For this reason experience in systems design has shown that the earlier a *definitive announcement* can be made by top management the better in order to substitute fact for rumor. Even though only a preliminary study is being made, the rumors begin to circulate immediately. At this stage, therefore, a definitive announcement by top management of the scope of the study will be very useful and will prepare the way for the later more detailed analysis. If this announcement can also contain management assurances of job security and such other measures for employment stabilization as might later be necessary the value of the advance notice will be increased.

Reasons for the changes would be stated, with emphasis upon the use of better tools for management and the eventual benefits to be derived by everyone. Where appropriate, better use of labor rather than cost-cutting can be stressed and an attempt made to build up employee pride in the progressiveness of the firm. Some companies planning computer installations have given employees as much as three years' notice of impending changes in order to accustom them to the idea. If management itself does not recognize the importance of informing the employees at an early date, the systems analyst should consider it his responsibility to point out the advantages of such a course of action and stand ready to recommend the timing and content of such announcements.

Subsequent interim reports to employees are desirable. These should be

---

[6] *Adjustments to the Introduction of Office Automation* (Washington: U. S. Department of Labor, Bulletin No. 1276, 1960).

as definite and factual as possible and continue to stress the positive benefits to be derived at all levels. Middle management especially needs to be kept continuously informed in order that it can answer questions from employees and interpret to them the aims and policies of top management. During this period of initial planning, and prior to the more extended period of individual contact with the analyst, middle management personnel will be especially beset by fears that they will be replaced by outsiders, that they will be downgraded, that the new positions will be difficult to learn, that they will lose status, and by many other disturbing rumors. Realizing his dependence upon this level of management for the later success of his system, the analyst tries to see that all of the channels of communication are kept open and that a carefully planned program of information is provided for the supervisors as well as for the nonsupervisory personnel.

DURING THE STUDY. When the systems analyst is gathering information on current procedures and work flows by interviewing, he has one of his best opportunities to secure simultaneously the support and cooperation he needs for the later acceptance and effective operation of any system he designs. How he conducts himself during this phase and the care which he uses in dealing with each individual justifies the most careful planning.

Managers and supervisors are often worried about their ability to learn any new techniques and their ability to keep ahead of their subordinates in this respect. Many will doubt their ability to supervise under the new methods. Even though the system is not yet designed, the analyst must be alert to such situations. By treating the supervisor as being intelligently competent to understand the discussion and the proposals, and by avoiding any sign of condescension, the designer can build up the confidence of the employee. Normally no assumption ought to be made nor the implication created at this stage that there is any question of the supervisor's ability to handle any new system which may result.

Opportunity to air his views on the present system and to participate in the planning for any improvements will give the supervisor an interest in the ultimate success of the new procedures. The analyst should recognize the experience of the manager and supervisor, remember to be a good listener, and whenever appropriate visibly record suggestions made so that later credit can be given if adopted. He should stress the mutuality of interest between middle and top management in building the very best system possible. Often it may be profitable to interview the supervisor away from the office atmosphere so that the pressures of the work do not compete with his objective consideration of the new proposals or where he may feel more free to discuss certain aspects of the present system.

The approach of the systems analyst has been likened to that of a doctor whose concern is essentially a preservative one. He adopts the view that the organization is basically sound and healthy and that he is not there to tinker for the sake of tinkering. In this way he will impress the supervisor that his concern is with people and problems and to pass on ideas which have survival value with the organization.[7]

This fear of the manager or supervisor that he is being replaced by a machine, resulting in a loss of self-esteem as well as status in the eyes of his co-workers, friends, and family, can be countered by stressing the increased importance of each manager and supervisor to top management through his having a part in supplying better information for decision-making at a higher level. The analyst can give a preview of the future uses to which this better material may be put. The increased need for the manager as a trainer of personnel can be stressed to compensate for any diminution of personal responsibility for decision-making. The substitution of new values for old can begin early and the systems analyst can play a vital role in the process.

Middle management will be anxious concerning any decrease in the number of top positions and about his possible loss of status as an adviser to top management. The systems analyst can stress the assurances previously given by top management as to job security, displacement policies, and retraining, and answer questions as to probable new positions and their duties. He can also point out that studies of the current trends in the types of office workers indicate that the professional and technical group will increase and that clerical and sales occupations will increase. He must be careful, however, not to encourage any overexpectation of upgrading which may not materialize.

If the human factors outlined above are to be taken into account, the role of the systems analyst in fact-finding calls for much more than a merely technical exchange confined to exploration of work flows and data handling. He uses the interview for a much broader purpose, engaging in open and frank discussion, and securing the trust and confidence of the manager and supervisor. The time spent in so doing will bring handsome returns during later phases of the new system.

PLANNING FOR HUMAN FACTORS. It seems appropriate that during the synthesis phase the analyst should also anticipate some of the human factor problems which may arise during implementation, and give consideration to what can be done by design or preplanning to minimize or affect them.

One of the job dissatisfactions found among workers and supervisors alike after the installation of highly mechanized or automated systems is the lack of visible evidence of the product of their labor. This stems from the basic need of a worker to *see* that his job is significant. A series of entries, a list prepared, a report are all visible evidence of accomplishment. In many new systems the supervisor sees no end product of his work. Closely allied to this is his feeling that to be producing he must be *doing*. Since the probable

---

[7] Davis, *op. cit.*, pp. 219–225.

future development of data processing indicates more and more programming of decision-making to machines and the eventual elimination of many original documents altogether, it is likely that the visibility of product will decrease rather than increase. The systems analyst should be alert to this trend and should begin to educate middle management during the analysis stage to other job satisfactions. This will not be easy since these satisfactions will tend to be more abstract than the old, and not always be immediately evident. Supervisors themselves will also have to plan to give more attention to the morale of their workers and provide new methods of praise and reward.

The systems analyst should make certain that plans for job training for middle management include training in understanding the changing nature of their positions and in awareness of the problems of human relations with their subordinates in promoting job satisfaction.

One of the changes for which middle management must be prepared is the greater inflexibility which will exist in any highly integrated data processing system. The supervisor is often disturbed to find that his section is being blamed for a delay further down the line because he was not sufficiently impressed with the importance of the interdependence of each part of the system. He will also be subjected to greater pressure for adherence to higher work standards and he will find that feedback of errors will pinpoint responsibility more surely than ever before. Unless he is properly alerted to these aspects of the new system he is likely to become resentful and resistant when caught off guard and this feeling may be transmitted to his subordinates. The systems analyst should plan for these possibilities by holding briefing sessions with both superviors and employees, and by planning a program of follow-up during implementation and thereafter with individual supervisors to check on their reaction to the system and on the morale of the employees.

When planning for implementation during the synthesis phase, the systems analyst should be alert to the resentment which unrealistic deadlines arouse in both supervisor and employee. If such deadlines are imposed by top management the designer should endeavor to get them as realistic as possible. If it becomes apparent that deadlines cannot be met through no fault of the supervisors or employees, they should be relieved of their anxiety and be assured that no blame attaches to them. The analyst also does everything possible to minimize the increased workload which will fall upon middle management during the entire synthesis and implementation period. Learning new procedures, training employees, supervising two parallel work processing systems during testing periods, attending meetings, and being interviewed can all combine to create tremendous pressures on middle management which are not conducive to a kindly feeling toward any new system. In view of this the systems analyst keeps a close watch over this aspect of design and implementation and by careful preplanning seeks to minimize such work pressures as much as possible.

Human Factors at the Nonsupervisory Level

The nonsupervisory employee is often affected by many of the same human factors which operate at the top management and middle management levels but, because of his different position in the organization and his normal lack of contact with top management plans and policies, the individual weight which these factors carry in his case will differ. They are usually the result of the same basic human drives but are manifested in ways which are unique to this level. The potency of these various factors for affecting employee reactions to a new system should not be underestimated. A group of nonsupervisory employees can just as effectively sabotage a system they do not accept as can a supervisor. In fact, it may be more difficult to pinpoint employee resistance since it may be more subtly applied through group action. Recognizing this, the systems analyst should be as anxious to enlist the understanding and support of the nonsupervisory employee as he is to secure management help.

BASIC HUMAN FEARS AND GOALS. Among the more important conditioning factors present at the nonsupervisory employee level are those related to the common human fear of machinery as a displacement of labor, coupled with the basic instinct of resistance to the strange, new, or unknown. Experience has shown that these factors are as strong today as they were three centuries ago even though the clerks of today may not be putting their spike heels into the gears of the tabulator or short-circuiting the computer, in emulation of the workers affected by the advent of machinery in earlier times who used their wooden shoes or *sabots* to sabotage the new threat of automation in their jobs. Recurrent periods of unemployment have kept alive a fear of the machine and currently there is evidence that automation has replaced the loom and the steam engine of former days as the public and trade union image of the *deus ex machina* operating against their interests.

Nonsupervisory workers, and particularly the younger workers, tend to have short-range goals as compared with the goals of middle and top management personnel. It is difficult to sell changes to them based upon some abstract general benefit. They demand an immediate personal advantage. Union agreements have usually tended to reinforce this human factor by the nature of their demands for specific additional benefits each year. The growth of unionism among clerical workers indicates the concern of white collar groups about their position in the world of change.

Coupled with the more visible and conscious human factors mentioned are those which are more obscure and subconscious but which, nevertheless, profoundly affect human conduct. Among these human factors are the desire to produce a visible product as evidence of work accomplished; a need for recognition, affection, and attention; the importance of standing and status among co-workers, friends, and family; a need for activity in work as contrasted with the inactivity associated with merely monitoring a machine; the motivation of working in groups; and the need to lean on others for support and encouragement. The greater isolation of the worker at his work place through automation comes at the very time when there has been a growing number of *other-directed* persons in our culture who look to others for guide lines and approval. The increased attention to the coffee break is said to indicate a compensation for the decrease in jobs where social involvement is present.[8]

Obviously, the systems analyst cannot hope to prevent the operation of these basic human factors nor eliminate them by his preplanning of design and implementation. Many of these factors will require the substitution of new values and new job satisfactions over a long period of time. However, *by being aware of the existence of these forces at work* and by being guided thereby, they can often minimize their effects or offset them in some cases by training and by emphasizing and developing equally strong counter-factors.

CONVERTING PASSIVE RESISTANCE INTO ACTIVE ASSISTANCE. Prey as he is to the interaction of his basic human fears and drives, the employee in a company undergoing systems change is likely to develop a core of passive resistance to these changes if left to his own inclination and to the influence of his co-workers. This may be so in spite of the fact that if he were confronted with a specific proposal he might in a moment of objectivity admit that the changes were good and probably needed. It is into this vacuum that the systems analyst should move promptly with logic and persuasion if he is to overcome any negative intentions on the part of the employees.

The importance of prompt and factual announcements of company plans during the preliminary study has already been stressed. Some companies have operated under the theory that such information should be withheld until the last possible moment lest it upset the employee and interfere with current work accomplishment. The experience of many companies with successful systems installations, however, indicates that early, complete, and continuous information is the method which has produced the most responsive acceptance and the least resistance. The employee needs reassurance concerning his job security, his opportunities under the new system, and a knowledge of what orderly process will be followed by the firm during reassignment. By a series of meetings, bulletins, newsletters, and other interim announcements these facts can be supplied and idle talk and rumor counteracted. Using the union as a channel of communication has proved effective.

As the systems analyst moves into the fact-finding and analysis phase of his work and begins to contact and interview individual employees he will meet many who will question the real motives of the company in making the

---

[8] Donald N. Michael, "The Social Environment," *Operations Research* (July, 1959), p. 506.

changes. By relating the general systems problem of the company to the individual's work experience and getting him to feel the need for improvement, the analyst attempts to break down this skepticism and pave the way for further active participation by the employee in making the change. The systems analyst should be sensitive to indications of who are the key employees in regard to worker influence in each section and seek to ensure the understanding and cooperation of these influential members of the group. By giving such employees an opportunity to air their views and by returning to them for further suggestions and criticisms as the design is developed, the systems man will secure the identification of these key people with the final system and they, in turn, will become salesmen to their fellow employees. Care must be used by the analyst to sell the ideas through merit, patient and clear explanation, and through understanding by the employee rather than by mere personality and salesmanship.

In counteracting the fears which employees will have that they are becoming secondary to machines and that they are losing status through loss of their specialty, the analyst can emphasize in his contact the new job values which will place a premium on responsibility and which will be as significant and valuable to the employer as the former job. Likewise, employees can be encouraged to apply and test for new positions as they are opened up, emphasizing that it is the company's policy to staff from within whenever possible. By showing that he is genuinely interested in the people he is interviewing, the analyst can do much to boost employee morale during a period of change.

As was true for middle management, the systems analyst should prepare the nonsupervisory employee for the greater rigidity of mechanical equipment and the necessity for teamwork between departments and sections to keep the work flow moving. He should point out that greater adherence to work standards will be necessary to insure high quality of input. If employee training is not designed to alert him to this fact, he will later be quick to blame the system for any delay or breakdown of the process rather than the human error which was the probable cause. This tendency to blame the system for errors can cause an undermining of confidence in a system and create a serious operating problem later. A loss of confidence in a system brings into play the human tendency to create additional records for self-protection to hedge against possible blame for error. Implementation planning should provide for continuous checking to disclose possible breakdowns and to eliminate trouble spots as quickly as possible.

One device of systems design which has proven effective in preventing later breakdown has been to build some *flexibility for limited self-adjustment* in the system. This allows the affected department to adjust for certain unforeseen contingencies without having to wait for a formal systems change and thus prevents an irritant from growing. The ability of the supervisor and employee working together to make these limited adjustments gives them a sense of identification with the system and insures their concern for its continued success.

In summary, the systems analyst in dealing with the nonsupervisory employee should be sensitive to the greater weight which certain human factors carry at this level as compared to the same factor at a higher level. The nonsupervisory employee is generally more group-oriented and less an individualist. He is more susceptible to rumors and to the influence of fellow-worker opinion. The ability of the system to meet with and take into account the various human factors at this level will be a further test of how well he succeeds in applying the human factor to his systems design.

Systems Analysts Are Human Too

In the preceding discussion of the human factors with which the systems analyst must deal in applying the human factor principle, we have by implication already noted some of the human factors which operate within the analyst himself to affect the way in which he does his job.

SUMMARY

In this chapter the reader has been introduced to the third phase of a typical systems investigation. It should be evident from this chapter and the two preceding it that the division of a systems investigation into phases is a vehicle of convenience. In an actual investigation the phases are very difficult to delineate and in some of the more complex situations the three phases are applied over and over again as the analyst attempts to solve his complex problem by breaking it down into more manageable parts and working on each part in turn.

During the implementation and follow-up phase of a systems investigation the analyst has at his disposal six techniques. These techniques are:

1. Scheduling.
2. Personnel selection and training.
3. Acquisition of equipment and communication media.
4. Testing.
5. Technical modification.
6. Reappraisal.

During analysis and synthesis and during earlier stages of implementation the analyst must constantly judge whether the new system being designed complies with the nine basic systems principles, including the vital human factors principle. He has one final chance to see if the new system passes these exacting tests. One by one as he is using the technique of reappraisal the new system must measure up to each of these principles.

QUESTIONS, PROBLEMS, AND CASES

1. Assume that you are the systems analyst assigned to an investigation to redesign and implement a voucher check system. Provide a brief description of a suggested system and indicate the manner in which you would utilize the techniques of implementation and follow-up in your engagement. Discuss the application of each technique of implementation and follow-up as it relates specifically to the system.

2. Why is the scheduling technique important? Explain and illustrate several methods that might be used in the scheduling technique, and indicate the reason or reasons for their importance.

3. Distinguish between the techniques of selecting and training, indicating the importance of both as well as the similarities and differences.

4. What is implementation budgetary control, and when should it be used?

5. Illustrate the manner in which the testing technique would apply to the implementation and follow-up phase of a systems investigation within the context of an inventory control system.

6. Distinguish between the objective of testing in the synthesis phase as compared to the implementation and follow-up phase of a systems investigation to revise a payroll system.

7. During a billing systems study now in the implementation and follow-up phase, you discover that the credit check is being omitted for a substantial number of orders received for processing. On investigation you discover that inexperienced employees are often used to process incoming orders, and the turnover of employees is great. Even when adequate help is available, the amount of time necessary for credit checks often has discouraged employees from attempting the processing since they are paid by the number of orders processed. What are your recommendations?

8. What can the systems analyst expect the performance audit of a system to accomplish? What is the relationship to the reappraisal technique and how might it be applicable to the implementation and follow-up phase of a systems investigation?

9. The implementation and follow-up phase of a systems investigation demands appropriate emphasis on human factors because they are so important. These techniques relate to each level of management, but with a differing impact.

Identify the various levels of management and indicate some of the human factor differences at each level.

10. In what way must top management become involved in a systems investigation to assure a system that will function economically and effectively?

11. What is there about the patterns of change within a company that could make a new system extremely difficult to implement?

12. What evidence might be found in a company to identify the strength of the desire on the part of management for systems change?

13. What is the common reaction of middle management to a proposed revision of the financial information system, and why?

14. Higher age has been given as a reason for middle management to show greater resistance to change. Is this true or not, and explain.

15. The "rumor network" in the ABC Company is usually very effective. You have designed a system that will result in a number of organization changes and that will take quite a period of time to install. You are ready to start on the installation phase but are concerned about the possible negative reaction of a number of employees. What would you do to make the implementation of the system as easy and smooth as possible?

16. In announcing a pending systems change you suspect that a number of middle managers are worried about their ability to keep ahead of their subordinates in the new system. As the systems analyst, what would you do about such a situation?

17. There is a basic need for an employee to see the results of his job and to be assured that it is important. With increased automation other job satisfactions must be found. Explain and expand.

18. Why is the understanding and support of nonsupervisory personnel important to the systems analyst in the implementation and follow-up phase of a systems investigation?

19. Are the goals of the typical nonsupervisory employee long range or short range? Give an illustration and explain why they are as indicated in the illustration.

20. Why is flexibility for limited self-adjustment important in implementation and follow-up? Give an illustration and discuss.

21. To what extent do the human factors of systems design relate to the systems analyst personally?

22. What is the effect of the tendency to blame a system for difficulties and errors? Discuss.

23. How can the passive resistance of an employee be converted into active assistance by the systems analyst? Explain and illustrate.

CHAPTER 13

Documentation

IN THE COMPLEX DATA PROCESSING SYSTEMS OF TODAY, THERE IS A NEED FOR more than just verbal instructions regarding the way in which communication media, personnel, and processing machines are combined with internal control duties to produce a functioning financial information system. A complete financial information system must provide for adequate documentation. *Documentation*, in this sense, means a detailed written description of the system supported by specimens of communication media—both input and output systems and program flow charts as needed—and anything else required to make the description of the system complete.

The documentation package can serve as the "official" system description against which the actual system can be compared from time to time. It can also serve as a manual to instruct new employees or other interested persons in the working of the system.

DOCUMENTATION OF ELECTRONIC (AUTOMATIC) DATA PROCESSING SYSTEMS

Documentation was difficult even before the introduction of electronic data processing systems. But with the introduction of computers having large internal record storage and extensive internal processing capabilities, a substantial problem of adequate documentation became evident. The Internal Revenue Service, for example, was concerned to such an extent that it published guidelines for records, audit trails, and procedural documentation.

Although the IRS gave recognition to the need for and desirability of systems that differ from business to business, a method was required for providing from punched cards or tapes certain visible and legible records that could be verified and which would include the necessary information to verify the taxpayer's tax liability. A system was considered acceptable when complying with the IRS *guidelines for records* as follows:

(1) *General and Subsidiary Books of Account.* A general ledger, with source references, should be written out to coincide with financial reports for tax reporting periods. In cases where subsidiary ledgers are used to support the general ledger accounts, the subsidiary ledgers should also be written out periodically.

(2) *Supporting Documents and Audit Trail.* The audit trail should be designed so that the details underlying the summary accounting data, such as invoices and vouchers, may be identified and made available to the Internal Revenue Service upon request.

(3) *Recorded or Reconstructible Data.* The records must provide the opportunity to trace any transaction back to the original source or forward to a final total. If print-outs are not made of transactions at the time they are processed, then the system must have the ability to reconstruct these transactions.

(4) *Data Storage Media.* Adequate record retention facilities must be available for storing tapes and print-outs as well as all applicable supporting documents. These records must be retained in accordance with the provisions of the Internal Revenue Code of 1954 and the regulations prescribed thereunder.

(5) *Program Documentation.* A description of the ADP portion of the accounting system should be available. The statements and illustrations as to the scope of operations should be sufficiently detailed to indicate (a) the application being performed, (b) the procedures employed in each application (which, for example, might be supported by flow charts, block diagrams or other satisfactory descriptions, of input or output procedures), and (c) the controls used to insure accurate and reliable processing. Important changes, together with their effective dates, should be noted in order to preserve an accurate chronological record.

TYPES OF DOCUMENTATION

Two types of documentation relate to a system. The first type, *record documentation*, includes the tangible evidence validating an event or group of events. Typical of record documentation are communication media evidencing specific transactions, ledgers, or daily reports evidencing the detail of a summary or statement total. The second type, *procedural documentation*, relates to the distribution and flow of communication media and reports, the assignment of internal control duties, and the processing operations and controls designed for the economical and effective functioning of the system.

Most organizations have found it desirable to formalize in writing the procedural documentation. Included are fundamentals of organization, procedures, and policies. While the amount of detail and degree of comprehensiveness vary substantially, the general practice has become almost universal. A written procedural documentation is generally in the form of a *manual*.[1]

THE SYSTEMS MANUAL

On a functional basis, documentation evidenced by manuals may be said to include organization, policy, procedures (including guide handbooks and work flow books), equipment, and various technical matters relating to specifications, processes, and maintenance of products. The financial information system, like important functions such as production, marketing, and personnel, is usually the subject of one or more separate manuals.

Basic Reference on All Systems Matters

The most important single function of the systems manual or manuals is to set out the basic systems and accounting policies and procedures which are to be followed throughout the entity. Some indication of the scope of manuals is to be gleaned by listing the typical contents.

1. Organization of the accounting, auditing, and systems departments.
2. Basic systems and accounting policies.
3. Charts of accounts or code.
4. Content and source of entries.
5. Statements and reports.
6. Standard journal entries.
7. Procedural and systems flow charts and descriptions.
8. Specimen communication media (usually filled-in illustrations).

---

[1] Strictly speaking, the *organization chart* is not a manual. It is, however, often an initial part of a manual and because of its static nature needs to be supplemented by the textual portions of the manual. This supplementation is necessary because titles do not mean the same thing in different entities, and because a chart alone does not indicate adequately the nature and extent of authority and responsibility of each incumbent of positions on the chart. Relationships between executives can be clarified when the organization chart is accompanied by textual material.

Ideally, it should be possible to resolve any question relating to the system, accounting principles, or procedures which arises within an organization by reference to its manual.

Uniformity Difficult Without Manuals

Any organization consisting of two or more operating units with essentially parallel functions must have uniform coding if its financial reports are to be useful or significant. The necessity for Branch A and Branch B or Department X and Department Y to account for similar transactions in parallel fashion is obvious. However, the likelihood they will do this without the guidance of a manual or of common and direct supervision is small. It is apparent that common supervision is often impractical; even where such supervision is feasible, the manual has the advantages of continuous availability and of saving the supervisor's time to perform other duties.

Consistency Depends on Manuals

Even if an entity consists of but a single operating unit, a manual is well-nigh essential if transactions are to be accounted for in the same way from one period to the next. Comparability of the statements of successive periods is impaired or destroyed unless there is assurance similar transactions were accounted for in the same way continuously.[2] Turnover of personnel doing the detailed work, forgetfulness, and other factors will almost surely lead to inadvertent changes in accounting treatment of similar transactions over time if a manual is not in use.

Manuals Save Supervisory Time and Serve As Texts

New employees need systems manuals in much the same way students in school need textbooks. While these employees may be well trained in the general principles and procedures of accounting and may have gained experience in other employment, they still need some means of learning the specifics of their new duties. Classes, indoctrination by the employees they are replacing, and on-the-job training all help, but are not a complete substitute for a manual to be studied and consulted after they have begun to assume responsibility for a job. If no manual is available it is apparent that the supervisors are going to have to spend much time on questions to which the answers would be found in a manual. A supervisor's efforts in instructing

---

[2] These remarks should not be construed as "freezing" practices when change is shown to be desirable. Manuals help implement deliberate change while guarding against inadvertent change.

new employees would be more fruitful if a manual were available as a text and reference.

Manuals Provide Standard Guideposts

Both internal and external auditors are in a better position to evaluate the adequacy of a system in organizations using systems manuals. Such matters as the safeguards provided by good internal control, conformity with generally accepted accounting principles, and methods by which procedures are carried out can be more readily evaluated through study of manuals. These will enable the auditors to judge whether, on paper, the system and procedures are adequate. Manuals also permit determination of whether what is actually done accords with what is supposed to be done.

CONTENT OF A SYSTEMS MANUAL

More or less standard elements are to be found in most systems manuals, though at the same time it must be noted that the manuals of two almost identical entities are likely to differ somewhat. The commonly recurring elements of manuals will now be described, and typical excerpts will be illustrated. The sequence in which the various manual parts appear varies somewhat from one manual to the next.

Organization of the Accounting, Auditing, and Systems Departments

The accounting function in a sizeable enterprise may require the full-time efforts of hundreds of employees and usage of millions of dollars worth of machines and equipment. Obviously, any such complex, or indeed even a modest accounting department employing but a dozen or even fewer persons, must be organized according to some plan for effective action. Depending principally on the nature of the enterprise and its products or services, but also on its physical diversification and arrangement, the accounting function may be organized into a few major components or into numerous segments, many of which may parallel one another. Whatever the organization might be, one or more manuals will set out the accounting structure and define its responsibilities, duties, and cognizance. The organization manual of the entire entity will describe all of its major components and structural segments, including accounting, and will indicate their functions. The systems manual will frequently repeat or perhaps elaborate on that part relating to accounting.

Typical components of a large accounting department will include the following:

Controller's Central Office

Regional Controllers' Offices

General Accounting Section

Accounts Receivable and Customer Billing Section

Payroll Section

Production Accounting Section

Plant Accounting Section

Reports Section

Tabulating and Computer Unit

Internal Auditing

Systems and Methods Staff

Records Management, Forms and Reports Control Unit

The manual serves to indicate the specific functions of each of these activities.

Basic Systems and Accounting Policies

A general description of accounting policies in effect will often appear in an early section of the systems manual. A general statement as to extent of usage of the accrual system or of some of the deviations therefrom is appropriate. An indication of internal pricing policies, such as whether interdepartment transfers of inventory items will be at cost or at marked-up amounts, typically would appear in this section. Practices as to preparation of consolidated or combined reports, type of cost accounting system in use, budgeting policies, imputation of cost and revenue items, inventory costing practices and procedures are but a few of the matters appropriately treated in a section on basic systems and accounting policies. If a business is regulated, some statement of conformity with the accounting prescriptions of cognizant regulatory agencies will appear. If the entity is a municipality, the manual may state that the system conforms to recommendations of the National Committee on Governmental Accounting.

Chart of Accounts or Code

Complete listings of the general ledger account numbers or codes and titles appear in any complete systems manual. Subsidiary ledger accounts may similarly be shown. Accounts usually appear in one of several sequences including code or numerical order, alphabetically, or in the sequence in which they appear in the trial balance, ledger, or statements. If the chart of accounts has been revised fairly recently a complete cross-classification of old-to-new and new-to-old accounts may appear. This is especially useful to veteran employees who have memorized large portions of an account structure which has been superseded. A cross-classification is similarly helpful when questions arise about transactions of prior periods such as the correction of past errors.

Content and Source of Entries

A complete textual discussion of the usual increases and decreases to each account may follow the section on chart of accounts. This would include criteria for making entries in a given account, source of entries, approvals necessary, summarization, disposition of the account balance, reconciliation with other data, etc. The text here needs to be explicit and complete. Accounting employees who code vouchers are likely to rely heavily on this portion of the manual in their day-to-day work. It is evident the accuracy of many accounting classifications is heavily dependent on the completeness and understandability of this material.

Statements and Reports

Specimen filled-out statements and reports are sometimes included in systems manuals. It is helpful to have a detailed guide for preparation of internal reports. Sources of data, timetables for report preparation, and routing and distribution of reports are but some of the matters covered. If a printed format is to be used in preparation of reports, form numbers and routing are specified in the manual.

Standard Journal Entries

Larger entities often prepare complete sets of standard journal entries. These provide a structure for the recording of all recurring transactions, adjustments, and closing entries. The accounts to be increased or decreased are set out in the *pro forma* entries. Amounts based on summarized data are filled in by accounting personnel according to a schedule or timetable set out in the manual. If an account is inactive, zeros or the word "none" are inserted. Thus, standard journal entries serve to remind persons charged with compiling the data and amounts for them not to overlook the accounts included in the entries. Where standard journal entries have been devised, the manual will usually contain complete instructions for making them.

When standard journal entry vouchers are preprinted and used by subsidiaries, branches, or departments having essentially parallel operations, work at the home office where consolidated or combined statements are prepared is greatly facilitated. All data affecting a single account are to be found in the same sequence and on the same line of each unit's journal vouchers with a resultant saving of time in the process of summarizing. It is amazing how much longer the same summarization would take if the data were found at the top of page 5 of one voucher set, at the center of page 2 on another, etc.

Brief excerpts from the procedure manual issued by the Department of Finance, City of San Antonio, will serve to illustrate standard journal entries and their authority and source.

ROUTINE RECURRING MONTHLY JOURNAL ENTRIES		
Schedule *Journal* *Entry* *Number*	*Type*	*Authority*
2	Record encumbering of budgeted operating funds by award of contract.	Ordinance
3	Record payments on contracts from budgeted operating funds.	Ordinance
4	Record appropriations from Bond and construction Funds.	Ordinance
5	Record net amount of payroll checks issued.	Payroll Summaries
6	Record gross payroll and payroll deduction.	Payroll Summaries
7	Record payroll deduction for social security taxes.	Payroll Summaries
8	Record bad checks charged back by the bank.	Bank debit memos

ROUTINE RECURRING MONTHLY JOURNAL ENTRIES			
Detail *Journal* *Entry* *Number*		*General* *Ledger* Debit	Credit
2	101 General Fund		
	Encumbrances	xx	
	Contracts Payable		xx
	To record encumbering of budgeted operating funds by award of contract.		
3	101 General Fund		
	Appropriation Expenditures	xx	
	Encumbrances		xx
	To record payments on contracts from budgeted operating funds.		

ROUTINE RECURRING MONTHLY JOURNAL ENTRIES			
Detail *Journal Entry Number*		*General Ledger* Debit	Credit
4	400 Bond and Construction Funds		
	Fund Balance Unappropriated	xx	
	Fund Balance Appropriated		xx
	Contracts in Progress	xx	
	Contracts Payable		xx
	Contingencies	xx	
	Reserve for Contingencies		xx
	To record appropriations from Bond and Construction Funds.		
5	600 Working Capital Fund 610 Payroll Account		
	Payroll Taxes and Deductions Payable	xx	
	Cash in Bank		xx
	To record net payroll checks issued.		
6	101 General Fund (and other funds)		
	Appropriation Expenditures	xx	
	Social Security Advance to Other Funds		xx
	Due to Other Funds		xx
	600 Working Capital Fund 610 Payroll Account #601		
	Due from Other Funds	xx	
	Payroll Taxes and Deductions Payable		xx
	To record gross payroll and payroll deductions.		
7	600 Working Capital Fund 610 Social Security Account		
	Social Security Advances from Other Funds	xx	
	Payroll Taxes and Deductions Payable		xx
	To record payroll deductions for social security taxes.		
8	101 General Fund		
	Accounts Receivable	xx	
	Cash in Bank		xx
	To record bad checks charged back by the bank.		

Procedural and Systems Flow Charts and Descriptions

Manuals usually contain graphic representations or descriptive material indicating the flow and distribution of communications media and the operations which occur at each point of processing. Both the procedural flow chart and the system flow chart are discussed and illustrated in Chapter 10.

To illustrate further the various types of flow chart documentation such as might appear in a systems manual, Figure 13-1 illustrates the documentation of a payroll application involving six machine runs. Each machine run would also be documented by a block diagram explanation of the run. Figure 13-2 illustrates the block diagram for Run 1 of the payroll application illustrated in Figure 13-1. Southern Union Gas Company uses still a different type of flow chart with descriptive comment to document the routing and filing of communication media copies. Figure 13-3 shows their flow chart for the Inter-Storeroom Transfer form.

Specimen Communications Media

Better systems manuals often include reproductions of communication media for which instructions are given. The old adage that "A picture is worth many words" was probably seldom truer than in connection with the instructions for filling out communication media. A simple but fairly typical example is shown in Figure 13-4.

PHYSICAL CHARACTERISTICS OF MANUALS

Loose-leaf Format

Unfortunately, a perfect manual (if one ever existed) would seldom remain perfect or even adequate if it were left alone very long. Changes in operations to be accounted for, regulations and laws under which businesses operate, new products and processes, and a host of other environmental conditions continually impose the necessity for revision of procedures. Since the manual is the guide to these procedures it must change at least concurrently if not in advance of the procedural changes. For this reason manuals are usually prepared in loose-leaf form. It is much simpler, cheaper, and faster to prepare replacement pages for those parts of the manual which have become obsolete than to produce an entire replacement manual.

Another reason for the widespread adoption of loose-leaf format is the fact that most individuals using manuals are concerned with only a small

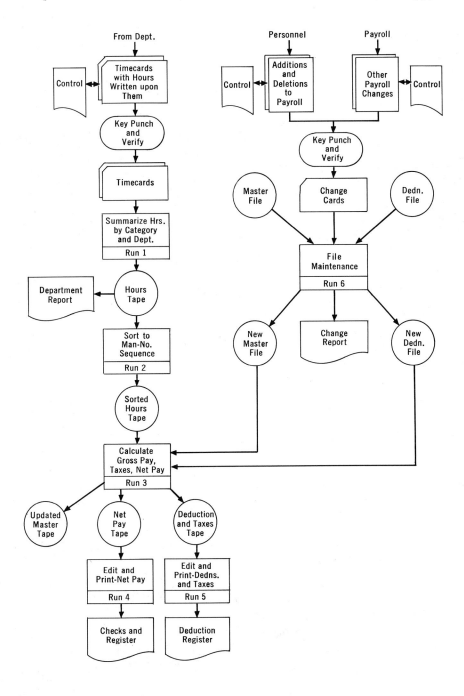

FIGURE 13-1. Flow Chart: Six-Run Payroll Application

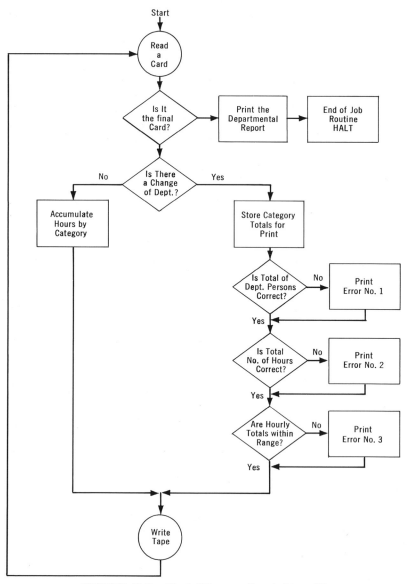

FIGURE 13-2. Block Diagram: Run 1 (Payroll)

segment of a procedure or system. For example, the individuals concerned
with customer billing and maintenance of the accounts receivable have no
need for a manual covering payroll preparation, cost accounting, or the like.
By supplying each individual or section with those parts of the entire manual

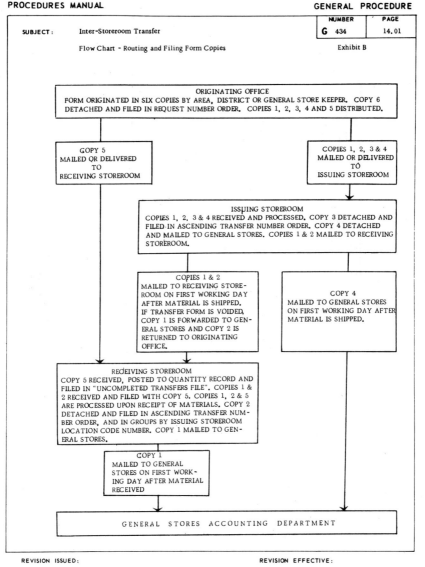

FIGURE 13-3. Flow Chart with Descriptive Comment

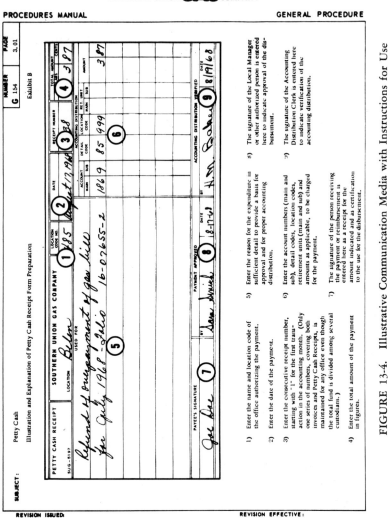

SUBJECT: Petty Cash

Illustration and Explanation of Petty Cash Receipt Form Preparation

Exhibit B

NUMBER G 154   **PAGE** 3.01

1) Enter the name and location code of the office authorizing the payment.

2) Enter the date of the payment.

3) Enter the consecutive receipt number, starting with "1" for the first transaction in the accounting month. (Only one series of numbers, covering both invoices and Petty Cash Receipts, is maintained for any office even though the total fund is divided among several custodians.)

4) Enter the total amount of the payment in figures.

5) Enter the reason for the expenditure in sufficient detail to provide a basis for approval and for proper accounting distribution.

6) Enter the account numbers (main and sub), detail codes, location codes, retirement units (main and sub) and amounts as applicable, to be charged for the payment.

7) The signature of the person receiving the payment or reimbursement is entered here as a receipt for the amount indicated and as certification to the use for the disbursement.

8) The signature of the Local Manager or other authorized person is entered here to indicate approval of the disbursement.

9) The signature of the Accounting Distribution Clerk is entered here to indicate verification of the accounting distribution.

FIGURE 13-4. Illustrative Communication Media with Instructions for Use

needed for guidance in its specific tasks, considerable savings are effected in the bulk of manuals and in their maintenance. The loose-leaf format is well adapted to this plan.

Numbering Plans

Because of the likelihood of expansion or the possibility of contraction of manuals, a flexible system of numbering pages and sections is usually adopted. Larger manuals are divided into sections in much the same way books are broken into chapters. Whole sections may be added or removed as the operations to be accounted for change. Within each section the number of subsections and pages may vary considerably with the passage of time. For these reasons a decimal numbering system is often adopted. Close examination of Figures 13-3 and 13-4 will reveal that sections of the source manual are identified by a three or four digit number and that pages are identified within each section by a decimal numbering system.

It is not uncommon for each manual or part of a manual separately maintained within an organization to be identified by a number (in much the same way each large machine has a plate with its distinct identifying number). These numbers are used to exercise physical control over manuals. When a manual is issued or transferred, the recipient supervisor signs a custody receipt for that particular manual. Revisions and revision instructions will be issued according to records showing who has custody of each manual. The confidential nature of portions of the content of almost any systems manual makes this custody system desirable, if not essential.

MANUAL REVISION AND CONTROL

We have already seen that any manual is subject to obsolescence. In complex and far-flung organizations the task of keeping the manual up to date is formidable and requires both an elaborate organization and procedure and considerable effort. Even in a comparatively small single-unit entity the task is somewhat greater than the uninitiated might expect. Though the implementation can be complex, a statement of the task in simple terms is fairly easy. As operations, methods, or procedures change, those parts of the manual relating to them must be changed. This may involve addition of new sections, deletions of sections or portions of sections, or modification of parts of sections already extant. Basically then the task is one of insertion, removal, or substitution of pages. Occasionally very minor changes (such as a word or sentence) are covered by "flyers"—sheets instructing custodians of manuals to change or add certain words, code numbers, or sentences.

Manual Revision and Control in a Large Company

The material which follows is based on an article, "An Introduction to Administering the Accounting Manual" by W. G. Cole, Administrative Assistant—Accounting, Bethlehem Steel Company.[3]

Both original writing and review for revision of the various manual sections at Bethlehem Steel are assigned through a manual control unit to administrative personnel responsible for the corresponding functions being accounted for. Responsibility for these manual assignments must be established at a sufficiently high organizational level to command respect, otherwise requests for original writing, review, and revision are not backed up by proper authority, and breakdowns will occur. An outline of the manual control and maintenance function appears below:

CONTROL AND MAINTENANCE FUNCTION FOR AN ACCOUNTING MANUAL

Introduction
  Scope
  Purpose
  Responsibility

Files maintained
  Functional purposes of files

Procedures
  General instructions
  Workfiles
  Historical file
  Revisions of sections
    Initiating the revision procedures
      Revision control
      Editing control
    Preparing copy for reviewer
    Editing copy (or draft) from
      reviewer

Sending draft to print shop for
  proofs
Checking proofs
Distributing printed matter
Partial revisions of sections
Indexing and index card files
Reference control files
Periodic check lists
Stock copies file

Editing and printing instructions
General
Editing instructions
General printing instructions
Typographical instructions
Proofreaders' marks
Examples of proof copy

Progress and status report

The workfiles referred to above consist of two groups, active and inactive. The active file consists of one copy of the current text of each section of the manual and subsequent related changes covered on "flyers." During revision all pertinent data, proofs, etc., not with the reviewer are retained in the workfiles. After a revised section has been released to the printer the contents of the active file folder are transferred to an inactive file for a reasonable period, then discarded.

---

[3] W. G. Cole, "An Introduction to Administering the Accounting Manual," *N.A.C.A. Bulletin,* February, 1957, pp. 799–807.

A historical file copy of each section and of partial changes to it is maintained indefinitely. Of course, operating units using manuals should be advised to discard all superseded sections, but the manual control unit must be in a position to provide copies of any superseded material.

An Editing Control Sheet such as illustrated in Figure 13-5 is designed to control, record, and follow each step in the process of revising a section of a manual. These sheets should be filed chronologically in a classified multi-

EDITING CONTROL

DISPOSAL DATE — DIV. / SEC.

PROCEDURE	COPY FOR REVISION	COPY FROM REVIEWER	PROOF FROM PRINTERY	PROOF FROM REVIEWER	SECOND PROOF FROM-PRINTERY
Date Revision Control & prepare Edit Control	1.				
Copy from Active Workfile	2.				
Stamp Copy(s) (Date received)	3.		1.		1.
Insert suggested changes	4.				
Proofread			2.		2.
Distribute: _____	5.	1.	3.	1.	
_____	5.	1.	3.	1.	
_____	5.	1.	3.	1.	
_____	5.	1.	3.	1.	
_____	5.	1.	3.	1.	
Verify: (a) paragraph numbers	2.			2.	
(b) changes & insert dots & footnotes	3.			3.	
(c) grammar & spelling	4.			4.	
(d) headings	5.			5.	
(e) legibility	6.			6.	
(f) x-ref. card - Div., sec. & par.	7.			7.	
- Forms	8.			8.	
- Accounts	9.			9.	
- Company names	10.			10.	
(g) table of contents	11.			11.	
Send to	12.			12.	3.

DATA RECALLED			PRINTED TEXT			WORKFILE
REQUESTED	RECEIVED	RETURNED	RECEIVED	DISTRIBUTED	INDEXED	TRANSF. TO INACT

Remarks _____

DIV. / SEC.

FIGURE 13-5. Editing Control Sheet

compartment folder with the following tabs: 1. With reviewer, 2. For proofs, 3. For printing, and 4. Being edited. Sheets are removed when the applicable section is printed and distributed.

Data accumulated for modification of a section during the period following the last printing should be withdrawn from the active workfile, suggested changes should be written in manual format, and the copy stamped "for revision" and forwarded to the proper cognizant section for this purpose. Adequate follow-up measures should be employed to insure return of the copy within a reasonable time.

Distribution of revised sections of the manual should be made in accordance with pre-established mailing lists. A simple columnar form will suffice here. It is, of course, necessary to revise the manual index from time to time. Generally speaking indexed material should be confined to text headings and side captions.

EDITING AND PRINTING INSTRUCTIONS
TABLE OF CONTENTS

In larger manuals it is necessary to compile a cross-reference index on cards. This card file includes (in manual sequence) every cross-reference in the manual. Its usefulness is obvious in the avoidance of both oversights and revisions that are not complete.

To insure that properly revised and complete copies of the manual are in the hands of recipients, check lists should be issued periodically which will enable them to check their manual copies for completeness and currency. The lists show the manual sectional and divisional numbers, titles, last printing date, and dates of any applicable flyers. At some decentralized locations it has been considered advisable to "call in" manuals from persons on the mailing lists. These are reviewed and brought up to date (if necessary) and reissued. This furnishes an excellent check on whether recipients are careless in maintaining their copies. It is advisable to maintain a stock of extra copies of each section of the manual so that needs for copies of sections or of complete manuals can be met without an added and expensive printing run.

Instructions should be prepared for the guidance of persons who contribute material to the manual. These include authors, originators of revised materials, compositors, proofreaders, and editors. The tabulation on the facing page indicates the contents of such instructions. From time to time, progress and status reports of manual control and maintenance work should be prepared for management.

RECORDS RETENTION

Records retention requirements should be considered in the design of a financial information system. Not only is record retention normally a responsibility of financial management, but record retention differences affect the flow and final disposition of communication media and internal reports. For example, the retention time for a purchase requisition, purchase order, and purchase invoice differs. The purchase invoice has the longest retention time, the purchase order retention time is not as long, and the purchase requisition the shortest retention time. If all three documents are filed together in a voucher to support the disbursement for a purchase, the retention time for the voucher with the group of documents enclosed or attached will have to be the longest time for any of the documents in the group. While policy differs from organization to organization, purchase requisitions are often retained for no longer than six months, while invoices supporting disbursements are seldom retained for less than six years. It follows logically from a record retention point of view (as well as for other reasons) that the purchase requisition should normally not be matched with the purchase order and the purchase invoice and filed in a voucher to support a disbursement.

Records Management

Management is faced with a bewildering variety of government requirements for record retention. Statutes and regulations are often precise, yet in
other instances they are ambiguous and even silent on the specific records that
an organization must keep, and/or the period for which they must be retained,
or both. There is a great need for a records management program to be coordinated with systems efforts within the financial information system. Each
organization should establish a records management program and a records
retention policy that is realistic and reasonable and within federal, state, or
other regulatory requirements denoting retention periods for at least general
business, taxation, labor, and securities records. Such a policy is most helpful
in the design of a system.

Storage

To be useful records must be stored in such a manner that they become
available readily when needed for reference. This requirement brings into
focus all of the problems of arranging (indexing) and filing communication
media and other records or reports as to provide ready access. The problems
of storage space, type of storage equipment, need for old records, legal retention requirements, and others should be considered and resolved either before
or during the design of a system. Record storage is costly, thus records no
longer useful or required should be thrown out as soon as possible. If appropriate, the most economical method of storage should be used.

Microfilming

In lieu of retaining original communication media or other records and
reports, it is sometimes cheaper and/or as desirable to retain microfilm records.
Thousands of records can be stored on a roll of film measuring only 3¾ inches
in diameter as shown in Figure 13-6. Microfilming of a document takes only
a fraction of a second, and if properly indexed before filming, specific records
can be located rapidly. As much as 98 per cent less filing space can be
required.

Microfilm records can be stored in a fireproof safe (or a duplicate security
roll may be stored in a separate location) in relatively little space. Using a
film reader, ready reference that is easy to read and transcribe is accomplished
easily. Enlarged facsimile prints can be obtained direct from the microfilm if
they are needed. A microfilm system is as illustrated in Figure 13-7.

A microfilmer, such as illustrated in Figure 13-8, automatically takes
care of illumination, exposure, and focus. Up to 100 letter-size documents per

Courtesy of Eastman Kodak Company

FIGURE 13-6. Microfilm Record

minute can be microfilmed by hand-feed, while as many as 600 check-size documents can be microfilmed with an automatic feed. Once the microfilm has been developed and the microfilmed records are available, the original records can often be legally destroyed. With a film reader such as reproduced in Figure 13-9, documents can be located quickly and read or transcribed from a projected film image, or exact facsimiles of any document can be printed in the reader in seconds.

While microfilm is often considered primarily as a record filing and storage media, its ability to enable low-cost facsimile prints and complete sequential recording of records can provide basic contributions to an operating system too. It is especially effective in establishing a record which takes the place of an additional copy. For example, Credit Unions and Savings and Loan Associations are required to report to their savers and borrowers periodically the activity in each individual's respective account. Rather than copy transactions or provide a periodic statement, the original ledger card

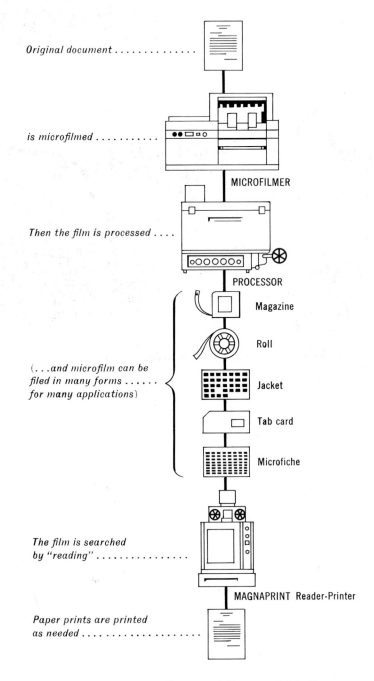

Original document . . . .

is microfilmed . . . .

MICROFILMER

Then the film is processed . . . .

PROCESSOR

Magazine

Roll

(*. . .and microfilm can be
filed in many forms* . . . . . .
for many applications)

Jacket

Tab card

Microfiche

*The film is searched
by "reading"* . . . .

MAGNAPRINT Reader-Printer

*Paper prints are printed
as needed* . . . .

Courtesy of Eastman Kodak Company

FIGURE 13-7. The Microfilm System

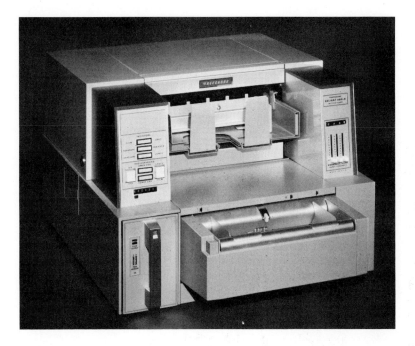

Courtesy of Eastman Kodak Company

FIGURE 13-8. Recordak Microfilmer

record can be microfilmed quarterly or semiannually. Not only is a microfilm record at the end of the period a documentation for each savings and/or loan account, but enlarged photo-accurate facsimiles, which can fit into a window envelope, can be mailed to individuals, eliminating the necessity for dual-posting or more expensive duplication at the end of the period or at other times. Another example of a systems contribution is the microfilming of communication media such as deposit or withdrawal slips for control. At the end of a given period, probably each day, the slips for the period are arranged in numerical order if numbered and by control batch. Not only is the chance of misfiling slips used in normal operations later eliminated, but the loss of any given slip cannot occur. More adequate and complete record documentation is assured, with the additional advantage of saving space when original communication media do not have to be retained for as long a period of time. Still another application is the microfilming of customer charge slips. Original slips can then be mailed to the customer as his billing, with the firm having a microfilm record of all that was sent out. Such a system is illustrated in Figure 13-10.

Microfilming does involve cost and has some limitations for use in an operating system. In the design of a system, roll microfilm should normally

Courtesy of Eastman Kodak Company

FIGURE 13-9.   Recordak Reader

not be used as the final form in situations in which additional entries must be
made on records after they have been microfilmed and stored or in which
new records are to be inserted in a special sequence with the old. In some
situations in which additional entries must be made, a "micro-thin jacket"
can be used effectively to hold microfilm images. The micro-thin jacket
permits separate images to be added, deleted, or rearranged and the rapid
retrieval, reference, and copying of information.

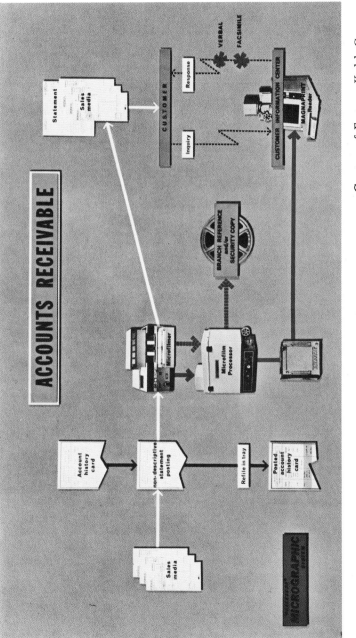

Courtesy of Eastman Kodak Company

FIGURE 13-10.   Accounts Receivable System with Microfilm

It is possible to mount individual microfilm frames in tab-card "apertures" which can then be processed for both filing and selection. Such a process is especially useful for engineering drawings.

QUESTIONS, PROBLEMS, AND CASES

1. Comment on the statement that "Manuals must be built around functions rather than individuals."

2. What is documentation and how does it relate to the design of a system?

3. Discuss the importance of a systems manual in relation to:
   a. The audit of an organization.
   b. Training new personnel.
   c. Uniformity and consistency of reports.
   d. The revision of a payroll procedure.

4. "It is necessary to have write-ups of procedures because many of them involve several sections and departments, some of which feed in information that others must process or act upon in performing their work."
   a. Discuss this general proposition.
   b. Specifically indicate some of the inter-department relationships the Controller who made the statement must have had in mind.

5. Prepare a sentence outline of that section of the systems manual of the Zee Wholesale Plumbing Supply Company relating to purchase discounts if:
   a. Discounts are accounted for as financial income.
   b. Purchases are recorded "net" and *lost* discounts are treated as expense.
   Hint: Deal with journalization, content of relevant accounts, summarization, and disposition.

6. The Oliver Branch of Rainbow Shoe Stores, Inc., is authorized to establish an imprest petty cash fund of $200. Write that portion of its systems manual governing the maintenance, replenishment, and accounting for this fund.

7. Nationwide Jewelers, Inc., is a holding company which owns all of the capital stock of 30 separately incorporated jewelry stores operating in shopping centers in 16 large cities in the midwest. Consolidated statements are prepared annually by the parent corporation.
   a. What would be some of the inherent differences in the systems manuals of the central office and of the stores if instead of consolidating statements the operation were conducted on a home-office and branch basis?
   b. Assuming individual stores operate in as nearly parallel fashion as possible, what are some inevitable differences that must be reflected in the systems manuals of the various stores?

8. Prepare a "flyer" to be sent to the subsidiaries of Nationwide Jewelers, Inc., (*see* problem 7 above) covering a change in the OASI (social security) tax

rate from 4.4 per cent to 4.9 per cent. Assume the change becomes effective January 1, 1969, and that seven different lines on four different pages in three separate sections of the manuals are involved.

9. Give reasons for your belief as to why an internal auditor should or should not examine the systems manuals of various branches and offices he visits in his official capacity. How might he go about determining the adequacy of manual maintenance?

10. The Tru-Rite Company, a medium-sized manufacturing concern, has just employed a controller. In becoming acquainted with the system, the new controller asked for the systems manual. He was told that the company did not have such a manual, but he was provided with copies of important reports, an organization chart, a chart of accounts, the tabulating room work-load summary of reports produced, and the like.

   Should the controller be concerned about the lack of a systems manual? Discuss the reason or reasons for your position.

11. The Monroe Wholesale Company has its home office in St. Louis. Products are distributed throughout the midwest area by 68 trucks on a route basis. Each truck covers a fixed route each two weeks. Trucks must return to the warehouse at least every other day.
    a. What are some of the accounting policies that you would suggest for inclusion in the systems manual of the Monroe Company that relate to control over the various routes?
    b. Prepare the most important of each type of standard journal entry that would be appropriate for the Monroe Wholesale Company.

12. The Jamesway Corporation prepared a systems manual six years ago. It was bound for durability, and was considered to be a superior job. In the past several months there have been complaints concerning the manual. On investigation, you discover that the employee charged with manual maintenance, Mr. Harold Johns, was retired six months ago. Changes and additions to the manual for the past year were distributed according to plan, with each custodian being expected to post his own copy. Prior to this time, Mr. Johns had been doing the posting personally. Manuals are now in many different stages of completeness.

   What steps would you take to eliminate complaints concerning the manual, and what should be done to assure an efficient maintenance system in the future?

13. "Systems manuals indicate the degree of adherence to generally accepted accounting principles." Comment.

14. To what extent do systems manuals implement or impede the functioning of internal accounting control? Administrative control?

15. The Schoppe Construction Company has just completed the preparation of a comprehensive systems manual. As a consultant to the company you have been requested to draft certain policies with regard to the maintenance and revision of the manual. This company is a rapidly growing company which

has recently established branches in several eastern cities where extensive slum clearance and reconstruction are underway. Outline your recommendations.

16. You have been engaged to survey the records handling, storage, and retention practices of a large client. Management proposes transferring all records over three years old to microfilm and then destroying the originals. What potential advantages do you see in this plan? What potential disadvantages?

17. If you were devising or redesigning a complete financial information system, what are some of the considerations which might lead you to prepare standard journal entries?

18. Why do businesses use microfilm in their financial information systems? What equipment units are needed? Explain. What are some of the disadvantages of microfilm?

19. What are standard journal entries, and under what conditions is it desirable for the systems analyst to draft a complete set of standard journal entries? What is the relationship of such entries to the systems manual?

20. You note that the Internal Revenue Service has established a guideline for records that include "supporting documents and audit trails." Explain this guideline.

21. You are designing that portion of a systems manual for The Fancy Restaurant that requires the inclusion of a specimen "guest check," and the instruction for filling it in. Prepare the necessary page or pages for the systems manual.

22. Explain why records retention policies are important to the systems analyst in the design of a procedure.

23. A systems analyst has suggested the use of microfilming for several purposes within your financial information system. State whether microfilming would be appropriate in the following procedures, and explain.
    a. Billing customers of a department store.
    b. Storage of cancelled checks and bank statements.
    c. Preparation of bank deposit.
    d. Control of withdrawal slips in a Savings and Loan Association.
    e. Maintenance of a customer credit history.
    f. Documenting a month-end trial balance.
    g. Filing name and address charges on a mailing list.

24. The chapter states that "it follows logically from a records retention point of view (as well as for other reasons) that the purchase requisition should normally not be matched with the purchase order and the purchase invoice and filed in a voucher to support a disbursement." Explain some of the "other reasons."

Unit 3

Extensions of Systems Theory

CHAPTER 14

Small Business Systems

INTRODUCTION

BUSINESSES OF EVERY SIZE MUST APPLY SYSTEMS THEORY TO THEIR OWN special situations. Theory does not differ for small businesses; the only modifications are the manner and extent to which principles and standards of systems design, especially for data and information flow, are applicable and the way in which systems components are combined. This chapter deals with the application and implementation of systems theory in the small business.

The "simplified" business system and systems that require "statements from incomplete records" are special adaptations of systems theory applied to small businesses. By starting our study of the application and implementation of systems theory in the context of the small business, it is possible to trace the evolution and development of systems configurations to parallel the growth of an enterprise from the simple to the more complex in this part of the text. The design of a system for a small business that provides effective control is more difficult than for the complicated larger business in which many devices, techniques, and a large number of people are available. It is often frustrating to attempt to design adequate procedures and a justified record system for a small business. Although the systems theory is relevant, the application and implementation differs from larger businesses.

What is a small business? Should the measure of size be number of employees, amount of investment, or some other factor? In amount of investment, for example, a high percentage of all American businesses represent an investment of less than $10,000. The term small business, as used in this text, would apply to such businesses. Small business is defined as a business or professional organization with limited capitalization and a small (less than ten) number of clerical employees. Most numerous would be the typical retail store, service businesses such as TV repair, garages, sheet metal shops, and the professional practices of accountants, doctors, and attorneys. In general, reference is to the situation in which the manager (owner) personally directs the majority of the operation.

SOURCES OF SYSTEMS INFORMATION

A systems analyst is often confronted with a request to design a system that is appropriate for a small business operating in a field in which he has little experience. In other situations he is asked to redesign a procedure within a system that requires certain mechanical devices or a combination of devices about which he has comparatively little knowledge. In situations such as these, where is the starting point? Where should a systems analyst turn for information and assistance?

As a starting point, the systems analyst must learn the fundamental characteristics and operating features of the business for which he is designing the system. He must be fully informed about the unique aspects of the business, if any, and the special practices that are customary in the field concerned.

LITERATURE. The analyst should follow the procedure of searching out the literature to determine whether anyone else has identified and/or solved some of the problems that will be encountered in the business for which he is designing the system. There are a number of special references explaining the nature of systems for particular businesses that can be used for this purpose.[1] In addition, standard guides to accounting references can be used to identify writings in current periodicals.[2]

TRADE ASSOCIATIONS. In addition to literature describing specialized businesses, a considerable amount of information can be obtained by writing to the trade association of a particular industry group. The amount and extent of information available through such associations differs substantially, yet trade associations have sufficient potential as a source of information that investigation is worthwhile. Even though the trade associations have nothing specific to offer that they have developed, they will usually be able to point

---

[1] See, for example, R. I. Williams and Lillian Doris, (Eds.), Encyclopedia of Accounting Systems (Englewood Cliffs, N. J.: Prentice-Hall, Inc., 1957), for a presentation of accounting systems for 67 diversified businesses (five volumes).

[2] See, for example, American Institute of Certified Public Accountants, Accountants Index (New York: American Institute Publishing Company), for a comprehensive index of accounting literature in the English language. The original index was published in 1920 and a supplement issued each four years or two years thereafter.

the way to the best information available. Trade associations can often refer the analyst to a leader in the industry with whom arrangements can be made to view a system that is considered to be a model.

A trade association may offer a "standard system" that would be adequate for a small business in the field concerned. In such situations the analyst must be certain that the "standard system" is appropriate for the business involved. Too often standard systems are used by a small business when the system doesn't fully apply. The system must be tailored to the business—the business should not be required to adjust to the system.

MANUFACTURER REPRESENTATIVES. Whenever specific information concerning mechanical devices is required, a manufacturer's representative from a business machine firm can be asked to study the system and recommend whether his equipment would be appropriate for the job at hand. One of the difficulties with requesting representatives to come into a firm and recommend a system is that they tend to design systems around their own mechanical devices, forcing the data flow into a structure that is dictated by the device. To the extent that manufacturers' representatives are consulted, the ground rules should be established well in advance. The systems analyst must state what he expects from the system. If the expectations of the system are well defined when the manufacturer's representative is brought in, his problem will be to propose a system that will accomplish the predetermined systems objectives. It will then be possible to compare systems proposed by different representatives in terms of how well they accomplish the objectives that are established for the system.

Manufacturers' representatives often prepare a "proposition" in which they compare the existing systems to the system that is proposed using their equipment. Such comparisons are revealing and can be a substantial contribution. The systems analyst can often use advantageously the technique of the manufacturer's representative in selling a proposed system.

The manufacturer's representative normally is interested in seeing that a system is satisfactory to the customer as business relationships usually continue over the years. Nonetheless, it must be remembered that the manufacturer's representative does not represent an unbiased opinion in many situations. The appropriate safeguards must exist to make certain that the talents of manufacturers' representatives are available to a firm, yet they should be available to a firm on their own conditions. The technical ability that a manufacturer's representative can provide is usually worthwhile.

COMPARABLE BUSINESSES. In a situation that is strange to an analyst, many excellent ideas can be obtained by seeking information and advice from business firms which have been struggling with systems problems relevant to the situation confronted by the analyst, or who may have discovered a solution that is acceptable in their situation. A discussion with the people responsible for the system in a business comparable to the one for which a system is being designed, can often enable the anticipation of specific difficulties and assist in the design of the system. While the design appropriate in a given instance may differ from the system reviewed, the design task is easier with knowledge about the experience and procedures of others.

SMALL BUSINESS SYSTEMS REQUIREMENTS

Like its large business counterpart, the manager (owner) of a small business needs a system to provide information and control. The information demands that will be made on the system in a larger business are greater than the demands in a smaller business, yet the control demands may be greater in the small business. In regard to control and safeguarding assets of a small business, for example, it is obvious that the proportionate exposure to loss is probably greater in the smaller business than it is in the larger business. Yet the need for information via systems output and reporting is usually less in the small business. The manager (owner) of a small business can be informed personally through his own observations and activities in a normal day, and thus does not need reports that have been formally drawn up. His closeness to the business eliminates some of the formal data and information requirements. In the control and safeguarding of assets the situation is reversed. With fewer people to share duties, the necessity of assigning incompatible duties to employees and the difficulties of supervision often cause the small business manager (owner) to choose less formal controls as a means of being able to get the work done economically.

To illustrate the systems requirements of the small business, the question, "What is the minimum systems configuration that could be used?" is relevant. What are the records that *must* be maintained as contrasted to those that are not absolutely required?

MINIMUM RECORDS. Most small business managers (owners) want a minimum records system. They have complete control over the business personally and do not need, to any great extent, records for information purposes inasmuch as most of the information needed is already a matter of personal knowledge. The records need of the small businessman are essentially for "must procedures" to keep the business in operation. The small business manager (owner) must focus his attention on operating the business and consequently looks upon his information system as a necessary evil that is forced upon him primarily by the government for income tax purposes, for payroll tax records, etc. A record of checks written, accounts receivable, and accounts payable *must* be maintained. Aside from such vital "must procedures," the small businessman often considers his information system of little value. The challenge to the analyst is to design a system of optimum value.

The minimum amount of basic information about a business that is required by the businessman can be obtained from a system with few records. The balance sheet, consisting of the items that a business owns and owes and the resulting owner's equity, can be obtained at any time with basic documents and using an inventory process. The amount of the net income can be determined by using a net worth technique. By comparing the equity section of two balance sheets, one obtained at the start and the other at the end of a period, and taking withdrawals and added investments into consideration, the net income for the period can be determined. Net worth measurements are dangerous and can be misleading when all information is not available. The point here, however, is that only a few documents and no formal ledger or journal records are needed if the only facts wanted are balance sheet and the amount of the net income. The net income figure on an income statement should only confirm what management already knows through daily reports. In this context, the detailed information necessary to arrive at the amount of net income is more important than the bottom figure on the income statement.

Even in the simplest system, it is necessary to make some provision for records of accounts receivable and accounts payable. Such records can be obtained by the utilization of a filing system for sales tickets and/or sales and purchase invoices. Cash receipts and disbursement records are also essential. It is said that the record system used by Thomas Edison was several nails on the wall, one for bills that were to be paid and another for those that had been paid. In many small businesses a drawer or file for paid bills and another for unpaid bills is an effective part of the record system. By the same token, properly filed sales tickets may evidence the amounts that customers owe to the business.

The use of a checking account can provide cash control and a minimum disbursement record when all receipts are deposited intact and all disbursements are made by check. The cash register is also a vital part of a control system in most cash-basis systems. Its role is dicussed in more detail later in the chapter.

It is little wonder that small businessmen rebel when a "trained accountant" designs a system that imposes a complete record system with five books of original entry, a ledger, and complicated adjusting and closing procedures such as taught in the usual college introductory accounting course. The theory and practice taught in such a course are essential, and the more complex record system is appropriate in some businesses. For the small business manager (owner) who must keep the records himself, however, complicated records are only an overhead cost and a burden. Complicated records require maintenance by an individual with accounting training to keep them straight and in balance. In most instances such a system is beyond the small business manager (owner), and even if it weren't, he does not want to take the time to keep elaborate records when he can see no real practical benefits. The small business system must be practical and meaningful, and simple to maintain. The small businessman often finds it necessary to do a substantial amount of his record work personally and, therefore, often seeks a "simplified system" to provide for his need.

CASH VERSUS ACCRUAL BASIS. The majority of small service or professional businesses utilize a cash-basis record system. In situations in which inventories are a factor in determining income, it is more common for the accrual basis to be used. There is only one basis of accounting that will accurately allocate income and expenses to the proper periods, the accrual basis. There are instances in which the cash basis and the accrual basis will give the same result. However, these instances are rare. The cash basis of accounting *recognizes revenue when cash is received and expenses when cash is paid*, while the accrual basis of accounting *recognizes revenue in the period in which revenue is earned regardless of when cash is received and expenses in the period in which expenses are incurred regardless of when cash is paid.*

The distinction between the cash basis of accounting and the accrual basis of accounting in systems for small businesses is vital. The small business manager (owner) is not a trained bookkeeper and usually does not have the technical background for maintaining a set of accrual-basis books. He can maintain proper and accurate records of cash received and cash disbursed. For this reason it is common for the small business manager (owner) to maintain records on a cash basis. At the end of the month or oftener, a trained accountant can use the cash-basis records to prepare accrual-basis statements. The conversion can be accomplished by using a work sheet and making simple adjustments so that accurate and meaningful accrual-basis statements are available even though the records are on the more practical cash basis. A cash-basis record system is often adequate, if for no other reason than the businessman understands the records he must keep personally. The usual bookkeeping or accounting service performed by the local accounting practitioner is often nothing more than converting cash-basis records to the accrual basis along with the appropriate adjustments to reflect properly revenue and expenses. Most "simplified" record systems or "single entry" systems are cash-basis systems.

When cash-basis records are maintained, management may choose to prepare cash-basis operating statements. In *strict* cash-basis operating statements, all amounts received are recognized as revenue and all amounts disbursed are recognized as expenditures of the period. For example, the acquisition for cash of a $40,000 building that is to last 50 years would be an expense for the full $40,000 in the year that the cash is paid for the building. Most municipalities recognize expenses on the strict cash basis. If, for example, a fire truck is purchased, it is recognized as an expense of the period in which the cash is paid. Revenues of the municipality are also frequently recognized in the period received on the cash basis.

It is unusual to find a strict cash-basis income statement in business. Most of the so-called cash-basis statements for businesses are in fact *modified* cash-basis statements. Accounting theory and the Internal Revenue Service both require that a business capitalize the acquisition cost of long-term assets. Such assets can then be depreciated over the estimated life of the asset by the appropriate charge to each accounting period. Any other treatment could destroy the measurement function of the cash-basis income statement for a business. Business statements prepared on the cash basis will recognize depreciation as an expense of the period rather than recognize the cash paid for an asset as an expense of the period.

Even in the instance of cash-basis statements, income for a business cannot be so materially distorted that the statements are misleading. The Internal Revenue Code, for example, will not permit the use of the cash basis in situations in which inventories are an income determining factor. The cash basis seldom will reflect income properly when inventories are involved. For example, a taxpayer purchasing a herd of steers to fatten for market can deduct the cost of the herd only in the period in which the herd or individual animals are sold. To deduct the cost of acquisition in one period, and claim the revenue from the sale in the next, only distorts the statements for each of the years to such an extent that they have little meaning. It seems clear that the cash basis is not appropriate when inventories are a material factor in determining income.

It has already been noted that the true income for a given period should be determined on an accrual basis, and that it is seldom indeed when the income is the same under both the cash basis and accrual basis. Differences in the time that revenue and expenses are recognized are notable. The write-off of a bad account, for example, is not an expense deduction on the cash basis because the revenue from the sale that resulted in the write-off of the account receivable had never been recognized. There is also the problem of recognition of the appropriate magnitude of amounts on cash-basis statements. Refunds, for example, should normally be deducted from the amount of the expense. For example, if $550 had been paid to repair a delivery truck, the cost of which was later reimbursed through an insurance claim, the amount of the insurance settlement should be recorded as a reduction to the repair expense account that had been charged for actual repairs. If no other expenses for repairs had been incurred during the period, the balance of repair expense would "zero out." The magnitude of repair expenses is zero, as the expenditure to repair the truck was incurred to return the delivery truck to the same condition that existed prior to the accident. The appropriate magnitude of repair expenses is disclosed.

DOUBLE-ENTRY VERSUS SINGLE-ENTRY. A double-entry system emphasizes the dual exchange elements (debits and credits) in each business transaction in such a way as to provide a self-balancing record system. Most accountants prefer records kept under a double-entry system and consider them superior to single-entry or incomplete records. Double-entry records are capable of being checked for accuracy and where discrepancies occur, they are likely to be noticed and corrected. Double-entry records enable the preparation of financial statements in a self-balancing and direct manner. Such records are usually associated with permanence and are considered to be available and acceptable as more adequate evidence in a case of litigation or settling controversies than single-entry records. Collegiate-level accounting education presupposes the utilization of self-balancing techniques associated with double-entry in practically all formal instruction. In a sense this is unfortunate as by far the greater number of businesses use single-entry systems, although double-entry records are used in businesses representing a majority of the sales volume. It should be noted that double-entry records are more complicated and require bookkeeping skill for proper maintenance.

For lack of any better criterion, a single-entry system will be considered to include all systems that are short of being double-entry systems. This would include all systems that are based on incomplete records and that require reconciliation to produce acceptable financial statements. Single-entry systems vary so greatly that it is practically impossible to describe such systems in detail. Nevertheless, there are certain characteristics that are evident as follows:

1. *A daybook or journal.* A columnar daybook or journal usually exists for the purpose of summarizing the events that occur within a business.

2. *No general ledger.* In most single-entry systems the columnar totals of the daybook are transferred directly to statements and are not summarized in a ledger. Columnar totals provide the summarizing device.

3. *Financial statements, especially the Balance Sheet, are more difficult to obtain.* Single-entry systems produce the income statement with little difficulty from amounts taken directly from the daybook. In the preparation of a Balance Sheet, it is necessary to reconcile items to obtain the amounts that are normally obtained from ledger balances in double-entry systems. For example, the balance of accounts receivable, fixed assets, and accounts payable would not flow automatically from single-entry records. Also, it is conceivable that the difference between the equity on one balance sheet and the equity on the next balance sheet may not tie into the net income as shown on the income statement. In these instances it is usually considered necessary to work until the differences can be accounted for in order that accuracy of the statements can be assured.

4. *The mathematical accuracy of a trial balance is not available.* The self-balancing feature of double-entry bookkeeping is not available through the preparation of a trial balance prior to preparing statements. There is no general ledger from which to obtain amounts.

5. *Inadequate legal evidence.* Comparatively speaking, single-entry records are not as good legal evidence as double-entry records. They are not self-balancing and by definition are not complete.

6. *Inadequate audit trails.* In single-entry systems there are generally inadequate audit trails to provide a useful system for management. The manager (owner) of the business may have difficulty in going from an amount on one of the financial statements to some of the detail underlying the amounts. Audit trails enable the manager (owner) to use the system. Inadequate audit trails are a reflection of the incomplete record aspect of a single-entry system.

In determining the adequacy of the single-entry system for the small businessman, the question must be asked as to whether the system provides for the information and control needs. If the answer is in the affirmative, the system should be used. Such systems are simple and can be operated without special bookkeeping skills. There are many situations in which single-entry or simplified record systems can be recommended with confidence. If they meet the information and control needs of the owner, they have passed the vital test. It should be obvious that information and control needs vary for small businessmen, thus the systems should differ too.

A SINGLE-ENTRY SYSTEM. There are many standard "simplified" single-entry systems.[3] Such systems usually require as a minimum a daybook, audit strip envelopes, and a cash register. The *daybook* is usually designed for one year's use, and is combined with other special records in one compact record book. Such a record book might include the daybook or summary record of sales, cash receipts, and cash disbursements, and special records such as (1) a distribution record if detailed departmental amounts are desired, (2) monthly profit and loss statements, (3) a record of loss on bad debts, (4) depreciation of fixtures and equipment, (5) prepaid taxes, licenses, and insurance, (6) record of invoices, and (7) payroll and social security records. The daybook or summary record of sales, cash receipts, and cash disbursements, such as shown in Figure 14-1, is the focal point of the system. One line is provided for each day, and weekly and monthly totals are obtained.

The heart of most single-entry systems is the cash register. At the end of each day the data accumulated in the cash register can be cleared and a summary tape of totals from the different type of transactions that were "rung up" can be obtained. Data from the summary tape are entered on the front of an audit strip envelope such as shown in Figure 14-2. The summary tape can be placed in the envelope and retained as a part of the evidence provided by the record system. The audit strip envelope also has provision for summarizing disbursements by cash and check on the back as shown in Figure 14-3. It can be seen that the source of information for entry in the daybook or summary of sales, cash receipts, and cash disbursements is the audit strip envelope.

Cash-basis statements and single-entry records usually go together. From

---

[3] Typical is the *National Cash Register Simplified System,* The National Cash Register Company, Dayton, Ohio. The illustrations in this section are drawn primarily from this system.

	Total Sales	Charge Sales	Cash Sales	Received on Account	Other Cash Receipts	Cash Over	Cash Paid Out	Bank Deposits	Cash Short	Checks Drawn
Date	(1)	(2)	(3)	(4)	(5)	(6)	(7)	(8)	(9)	(10)
Forwarded										
Sun.										
Mon.										
Tues.										
Wed.										
Thurs.										
Fri.										
Sat.										
Week's Total										
Sun.										
Mon.										
Tues.										

Date	Merchandise Purchase	Miscellaneous			Expenses				Other Expense		Outstanding Charges
		Personal	Fixtures and Equipment	Other Disbursement	Salaries	Rent	Light, Fuel Phone, Water		Explanation	Amount	
	(11)	(12)	(13)	(14)	(15)	(16)	(17)	(18)	(19)		(20)
Fwd											
Sun											
Mon											
Tues											
Wed											
Thurs											
Fri											
Sat											
Total											
Sun											
Mon											
Tues											

Courtesy of NCR

FIGURE 14-1. A Twenty-Column Summary Record of Sales, Cash Receipts, and Cash Disbursements

the summary record of sales, cash receipts, and disbursements, a monthly cash-basis income statement can be prepared. Figure 14-4 shows such an income (profit and loss) statement. Note that the statement refers to "where found." The amounts on the statement are taken directly from columnar totals obtained in the daybook or in one of the other special records.

In addition to the other information entered in the record book, accounts receivable files must be maintained if applicable. The difficulty in obtaining Balance Sheet information is obvious, as the asset, liability, and equity information does not flow automatically from the system as in the case of double-entry records.

Role of the Cash Register

A cash register, like a multiple-purpose accounting machine, includes the appropriate adding, subtracting, and totaling mechanisms that are designed to collect and summarize information. In addition, a cash drawer(s) is pro-

Daily Balance Form   Date_____19.___

SALES RECORD					OUTSTANDING CHARGES			
	Register Total				Previous Outstanding			
	Less Refund				Net Charge Sales (Add)			
	Net Register Total				Total			
	Less Rec'd on Acct.				Rec'd on Acct.			
	Net Cash Sales				Loss on Bad Acct.			
	Charge Sales |No.				Total (Deduct)			
	Less Chg. Credit			A-20	Present Outstanding			
A-2	Net Charge Sales (Add)							
A-1	Total Sales - Cash & Charge			No. Cust.	No. No Sales		Reset No.	

CASH BALANCE								
A-3	Net Cash Sales |No.			A-7	Cash Paid Out |No.			
A-4	Received on Acct. |No.			A-8	Bank Deposits			
A-5	Other Cash Received							
	Cash Start of Day				Cash End of Day			
	Total				Total			
A-6	Cash Over			A-9	Cash Short			

Form 8502—Audit Strip Envelope and Balance Form Press of The National Cash Register Co., Dayton, Ohio

Courtesy of NCR

FIGURE 14-2. Front Audit Strip Envelope

Record of Cash and Check Paid Outs				(15-16-17 18-19)	This column used for additional distribution		Distribution Records			
Post these entries to section A, Column (11) (12-13-14)							Post these entries to section B			
To Whom Paid	Mdse.	Misc.	Expense		Row 8	Amount	Row 1	Gross Sales	Refund	Net Sales
					1		I			
					2		II			
					3		III			
					4		IV			
					5		V			
					6		VI			
					7		VII			
					8		VIII			
					9					
					Total		Total			

Record of Paid Outs			
	Cash	Check	Total
Mdse.			
Misc.			
Expense			
Total			

Total Total

Post Total Checks Drawn to Sec. A Col. K

Courtesy of NCR

FIGURE 14-3. Back Audit Strip Envelope

PROFIT AND LOSS STATEMENT

	Name of Account	Where Found	Month Ending ••• 19			Month Ending ••• 19		
			Amount	Total	%	Amount	Total	%
1	Total Sales	Sec. A Col. 1						
2								
3	Net Sales							
4	Inventory - First of Month							
5	Add Purchases	Sec. A Col. 11						
6	Total							
7	Less Inventory - End of Month							
8	Cost of Goods Sold							
9	Gross Profit on Sales							
10	Operating Expenses							
11	Salaries	Sec. A Col. 15						
12	Rent	Sec. A Col. 16						
13	Light, Fuel, Phone, Water	Sec. A Col. 17						
14		Sec. A Col. 18						
15	All Other Expense	Sec. A Col. 19						
16	Advertising							
17	Laundry	These expenses are a						
18	Repairs and Maintenance	breakdown of Col.						
19	Supplies	19 of Sec. A. The						
20		total of these ex-						
21								
22		penses must equal						
23		the total of Col. 19						
24		Sec. A						
25	Miscellaneous							
26	Cash Shortage	Sec. A Col. 9						
27	Loss on Bad Accounts	Sec. D						
28	Deprec. on Fixtures and Equipment	Sec. E						
29	Deprec. on Auto Equipment	Sec. E						
30	Taxes, License, Insurance	Sec. F						
31	Total Expenses							
32	Net Operating Profit							
33	Cash Overages	Sec. A Col. 6						
34								
35	Other Income	Sec. A Col. 5						
36	Total							
37	Total Net Profit and Income							
38	Proprietor's Withdrawals	Sec. A Col. 12						
39								
40	Net Profit After Withdrawals							
41	Total Net Profit To Date							
42								

Courtesy of NCR

FIGURE 14-4.　Cash Basis Profit and Loss Statement

vided to safeguard the cash that has been collected. Many mechanical and special features can be acquired to contribute to control. Cash registers contribute in a substantial way to the financial information system and to internal control of cash and other assets when adequate internal control duties are designed into a system. A cash register with automatic change maker attachment is illustrated in Figure 14-5.

PROPER RECORD OF SALES. The cash register tends to provide assurance that all sales are recorded and that they are recorded properly at the time of the transaction. Cash registers can provide for the automatic issuance of a customer's receipt. The receipt is a record of the identical amount recorded by the cash register and is given to the customer or placed with his purchase to make the customer an inspector of the amounts that have been "rung up." Figure 14-6 illustrates cash register tapes, including a customer's receipt, a tape showing control totals cleared from 17 departments, and a tape that can be "locked in" for audit purposes.

It is interesting to note the various procedures that are used by business-

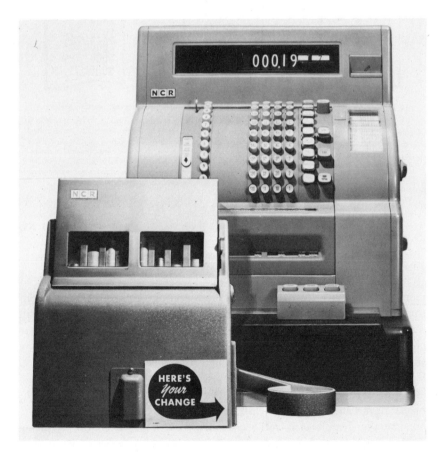

Courtesy of NCR

FIGURE 14-5. **Cash Register with Automatic Change Maker**

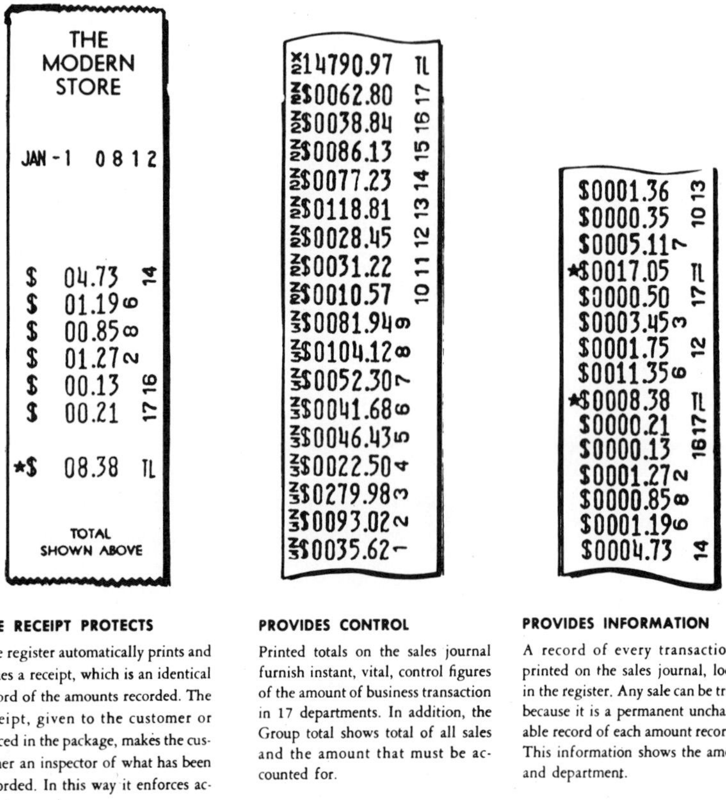

THE
MODERN
STORE

JAN - 1   0 8 1 2

```
$   04.73  14
$   01.19   6
$   00.85   8
$   01.27   2
$   00.13  16
$   00.21  17

*$  08.38  TL
```

TOTAL
SHOWN ABOVE

```
$14790.97  TL
$$0062.80  17
$$0038.84  16
$$0086.13  15
$$0077.23  14
$$0118.81  13
$$0028.45  12
$$0031.22  11
$$0010.57  10
$$0081.94   9
$$0104.12   8
$$0052.30   7
$$0041.68   6
$$0046.43   5
$$0022.50   4
$$0279.98   3
$$0093.02   2
$$0035.62   1
```

```
 $0001.36  13
 $0000.35  10
 $0005.11   7
*$0017.05  TL
 $0000.50  17
 $0003.45   3
 $0001.75  12
 $0011.35   6
*$0008.38  TL
 $0000.21  17
 $0000.13  18
 $0001.27   2
 $0000.85   8
 $0001.19   6
 $0004.73  14
```

THE RECEIPT PROTECTS

The register automatically prints and issues a receipt, which is an identical record of the amounts recorded. The receipt, given to the customer or placed in the package, makes the customer an inspector of what has been recorded. In this way it enforces accurate records.

PROVIDES CONTROL

Printed totals on the sales journal furnish instant, vital, control figures of the amount of business transaction in 17 departments. In addition, the Group total shows total of all sales and the amount that must be accounted for.

PROVIDES INFORMATION

A record of every transaction is printed on the sales journal, locked in the register. Any sale can be traced because it is a permanent unchangeable record of each amount recorded. This information shows the amount and department.

Courtesy of NCR

FIGURE 14-6.   Cash Register Tapes

men to establish the initial record and accounting control over cash receipts through a cash register. In some stores there will be a notice posted that if a receipt isn't given within 60 seconds after a customer makes his payment, the entire purchase is free. In other stores, such as those serving hamburgers and snacks direct to customers in automobiles, the policy is to provide any order free if the customer's receipt is printed with a red star. All such plans are an effort to have the customer provide the necessary audit and to establish a proper record and control over cash receipts.

Another feature of a cash register that contributes to control by making certain of a proper record is the fact that each time the cash drawer opens a bell rings. By giving publicity to the opening of the cash register whenever an item is rung up and the cash drawer is opened, the manager (owner) or supervisor is aware that a transaction is occurring and can verify the transaction.

The customer audit feature of the cash register is also evidenced by the totals displayed in large numbers through a window at the top of the cash register. When a clerk rings up the amount of cash received, this amount registers and is flashed in large numbers in a window at the top of the cash register so that it can be seen by the customer or by a supervisor from some distance from the cash register.

ACCOUNTABILITY FOR CASH. A cash register can provide one drawer or several drawers for cash. Accumulating mechanisms internal to the cash register also accumulate the total that should be in each cash drawer. It thus becomes possible to count the cash and to verify not only the amount that is in the cash drawer but to determine the amount that should be in the cash drawer based on sales, collections on account, and other sources of receipts. In addition it is possible to determine the total amount of sales and to permit the proving out of cash at any time. Accountability for cash is established in much the same manner as in an imprest system for petty cash. The total accumulated in the cash register should be the amount in the appropriate cash drawer.

RELIABLE RECORD. All amounts rung up on a cash register are accumulated in totals within the cash register. These totals are concealed and under lock and key. The salesmen cannot tamper with the record accumulated in the cash register and accounting control is established over the amount of cash that should be on hand. A tape listing totals of transaction by classes is produced. This tape (Figure 14-6) is often used as the basis for transferring totals to an audit strip envelope and for retention as a record of the receipts coming into each cash register.

MECHANICAL CONTROLS. There are many basic models of cash registers available from which the businessman can choose the features that are essential to an adequate information and control system. If several salesmen are to use one cash register, it may be desirable to acquire a cash register with *more than one cash drawer*. It will be possible to accumulate totals by salesmen and to check out the amount for which each salesman is responsible.

Cash registers can also be obtained with a differing *number of accumulators*. In the collection of basic data, for example, it may be desirable to accumulate sales not only by salesmen but by departments. In a supermarket it is not unusual to accumulate the total sales for each of the grocery, dairy, meat, bakery, and produce departments. Provision for accumulating sales taxes or other such items must be made. The greater the number of totals, the more complicated and expensive the cash register.

Another cash register feature that is often worthwhile in situations where sales are made both on credit and for cash is to provide a cash register that *imprints* the amount of a credit sale across the top of a sales ticket. Cash sales can be accumulated as can credit sales. Credit sales can be accumulated to provide a control total of charge tickets for each cash register for each period of time. This control total is the basis for further processing control.

Cash registers are available that *compute the amount of change* that is to be given to a customer. This feature provides additional protection for the customer and reduces the possibility of errors in making change. Assume, for example, that a sale of $14.50 is made for which a clerk received a $20 bill. When the sale is recorded on the cash register the $14.50 will be accumulated when the detail is rung up. The clerk will then ring up the receipt of a $20 bill, and the amount of change of $5.50 will flash up in the window of the cash register.

Cash registers can be connected with a device for *automatic change dispensing*, with a device for the *preparation of punched paper tape* as input to future data processing operations, or with *transactions counters*. The use of such features all make the cash register more beneficial as a part of a system. Also included is mechanical subtraction. Remote control cash drawers also prevent congestion at a register during peak periods.

Mechanized Systems for Small Businesses

The cash register and possibly an adding machine are usually the basic devices acquired by the small businessman to implement his financial information system. As the business grows in size and as special problems arise in which other items of equipment are needed, there is usually a period of time during which the cost of additional mechanization cannot be justified, yet the old system is not entirely adequate. In the advance from one level of mechanization to another, the utilization of the services of a data processing service bureau can be the answer that will make it possible for the small businessman to enjoy the advantages of more complex equipment at a reasonable cost.

The *data processing service bureau* is . . .

> ". . . an organization whose services are those involving operations, performed on the premises of the vendor, requiring the utilization of such equipment as punched cards, punched and magnetic tapes and related pieces and activities."[4]

The role of the data processing service bureau is to provide services to businesses which cannot afford their own equipment because of the nature of their work or the lack of sufficient volume. Data processing service bureaus also can assume specific procedures such as payroll, inventory updating, or a sales analysis. A useful function can be performed during periods of business growth when there are regular peak loads that cannot be handled in the structure of the routine operation. Overloads may also occur during periods

---

[4] Association of Data Processing Service Organizations, *Manual*, Proceedings Management Symposium (New York, January, 1962), p. 7.

in which systems are being revised and when illness, vacation, or replacements disrupt usual procedures. Companies cannot pay for a level of mechanization that can be used efficiently only a small portion of the year. Thus even in well-mechanized offices, overloads might be more efficiently handled by a data processing service bureau than by expanding temporary staff. The services that can be provided by the data processing service bureau are extensive and often worthy of careful consideration.

In utilizing a data processing service bureau, one of the bottlenecks and expensive features is to provide the appropriate input data for the service bureau operation. When the bureau is required to create the input from communication media, the cost increases rapidly. If the data are captured to preclude the necessity for creating input media in the service bureau, the cost of the service can be greatly reduced, and accuracy and processing can be more easily controlled. Whenever possible, input media should be created automatically as a part of a "must procedure." For example, cash registers are now available that can capture data in punched paper tape as a result of the regular cash register operation. Punched paper tapes or punched cards can be produced automatically during a billing or payroll procedure. The automatic production of tapes or cards at the time of initial record insures accuracy and economy, and facilitates the problems of reconciliation between company records and reports and those produced within the data processing service bureau. Equipment as simple as an adapted tape adding machine can produce both a punched paper tape and a printed tape, and is relatively low in cost.

It seems obvious that the smaller company is able to pass the burden of heavy investment in equipment and skilled technicians to an outsider specializing in data processing and yet take full advantage of the more efficient machine accounting methods.[5] Punched paper tapes and similar data processing media and devices that are important to common language concepts are discussed in more detail later in the book.

Ledgerless Bookkeeping

A ledgerless bookkeeping system is one in which communication media are filed as records rather than being used as source documents from which to post to ledger accounts and other records. The theory of ledgerless bookkeeping has been extended to entire record systems, but such applications are very rare in practice. Ledgerless bookkeeping is usually found as a small part of a more complete system. The most common application is to accounts receivable or accounts payable procedures.

Ledgerless bookkeeping applied to accounts receivable requires that at the time a sales invoice is prepared, an adequate number of copies of the

---

[5] Donald A. Schwartz, "Punched Tape Accounting for Smaller Business," *The Journal of Accountancy*, May, 1959, p. 42.

invoice are made, including at least one accounts receivable copy. The accounts receivable copy is sent to the Accounts Receivable Section where it is filed in an alphabetical file by customer name. At any given time the unpaid invoices in the customer file can be totaled to determine the amount that customers owe to the company. When cash is received, the invoice is withdrawn and stamped paid, after which it is filed in a paid invoice file.

Ledgerless bookkeeping has both advantages and disadvantages. It can be used most effectively in situations in which the industry practice is to invoice and pay on receipt of the invoice rather than to pay on a receipt of a periodic statement of open invoices. Ledgerless bookkeeping functions best when each invoice is paid separately. It is awkward in situations in which partial shipments and back orders are common. It also has limitations when the majority of remittances received are not for the amount of the invoice. If a partial payment is received, the amount of the payment must be either entered on the face of the invoice as a deduction or a special partial payment slip prepared and stapled to the invoice in the open invoice file.

On the positive side, there is no more economical system than ledgerless bookkeeping. It is simple and can be effective.

One of the primary objections of most ledgerless bookkeeping procedures is in the area of control. No record has been posted and adequate audit trails do not exist to facilitate meaningful management use of data or to assist in locating errors. If the detail in the subsidiary accounts receivable file does not agree with the total in the control account, where is the error? Was an invoice lost or misfiled? Was the wrong invoice pulled when a payment was made, or were two invoices pulled by mistake? Did someone destroy an invoice? What is the reason for the difference? Control in ledgerless bookkeeping systems is difficult, at best, but not impossible. Division of the customer file, batching and prelisting techniques, prenumbering or number control of invoices, appropriate control—subsidiary proof techniques, etc.—can provide reasonable control.

Ledgerless bookkeeping is especially effective in situations in which the billing of small fixed amounts is done periodically. For example, a monthly magazine may bill subscribers for their annual subscription two months in advance of expiration. The billing can be prepared in several copies so that if remittance is not received in a few weeks, another copy of the original notice, designated as a follow-up notice, can be placed in the mail without additional addressing, etc. As renewal subscriptions come in, the copies that had been retained in the file can be pulled and the basic copy used as a unit ticket to support the deposit and to provide the basis for updating subscription records. If the expiration date arrives without a renewal, the basic copy can be used as a unit ticket for processing the cancellation of the subscription.

In some situations, communication media can be assembled or bound as an adequate substitute for a journal. For example, carbon copies of checks can be bound to provide a good cash disbursement journal.

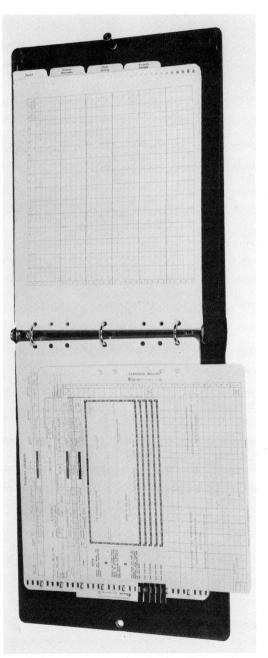

FIGURE 14-7. Pegboard Payroll System

Pegboards

Pegboards are devices to provide a simplified method of summarization. There are many business situations in which data are to be summarized and in which a pegboard can preclude the necessity for recopying. The pegboard is a hard surfaced board with pegs across the top or side as the need dictates. Communication media or reports used with such a board have holes designed across the top or side to facilitate alignment on the board when the holes are placed over the pegs. In this manner it is possible to have media or reports arranged in shingle fashion so that all similar items on each document can be read across a line or down a column.

The pegboard is a device that is designed to be used in much the same manner as a worksheet, enabling information from various sources to be summarized in two different directions. Pegboards are especially useful to summarize data and information being reported from similar operations. For example, a pegboard would be useful to summarize sales or cash receipts from a chain of service stations, restaurants, or drug stores. The report from each store can be placed on the pegboard with reports from other similar operations as illustrated in Figure 14-7. The shingled reports can then be used in much the same manner as a worksheet to provide information on all operations. Pegboards can also be used to compare actual operations with budget or comparative figures from preceding periods.

The design of communication media or reports for use with a pegboard requires placement of data to be summarized on the edge of the media or report. All of the edges can be used except the edge with the holes. When three sides are used for data, media or reports must be shingled three different times for complete utilization. Media and reports can also be designed so that they can be mailed to a central office without an envelope by providing for the name and address on the back in such a manner that the address will be exposed when the media or reports are folded for mailing. The data to be summarized on such media are usually entered only on the inside of the sheet to be folded for mailing.

QUESTIONS, PROBLEMS, AND CASES

1. For some time Mr. Friend has operated a small grocery. He has limited his accounts to single-entry records and has engaged outside assistance only for preparation of his tax return. He has never needed to obtain credit and does not expect to need to do so. Mr. Friend approaches you with the statement that he has heard of "double-entry" and would like to know what benefits, if any, he would derive from the use of such a system.

Prepare a brief statement of the advantages to Mr. Friend of using double-entry bookkeeping, and also indicate the disadvantages, if any. (AICPA Examination)

2. Mr. Harold K. Lins, an experienced manager of the hardware department in a large store, has purchased a small neighborhood hardware store. He has asked you to design a bookkeeping system appropriate for his new store. Mr. Lins has had no record keeping experience, and admits that he is mainly interested in the marketing and managerial aspects of the store. He will employ two sales clerks to assist with the operation of the store. Mr. Lins has recognized that good records must be maintained, and will do what is necessary to have such records.
   a. What are the minimum records necessary if Mr. Lins wanted to know *only* the amount of profit each month and his financial position?
   b. If your investigation indicates that a single-entry system is desirable, what would be the characteristics of such a system? Briefly describe the manner in which the system would operate.
   c. Would you recommend single-entry or double-entry records for Mr. Lins? Why?
   d. Would you recommend cash-basis or accrual-basis records? Why?
   e. If you are employed by Mr. Lins to come in at the end of each month to prepare accrual-basis financial statements, what changes, if any, would be required from the single-entry system visualized in requirement b., above? Discuss.

3. The X-All Drug Company sells drugs through 15 retail outlets. Cash is controlled in the central office, inventories are automatically replenished from a central warehouse, and customers are sent monthly statements from the central Accounts Receivable Section. Records are maintained in such a manner as to permit the preparation of statements for each store. The gross profit contribution of each store is determined.

   The X-All Drug Company has recently hired a systems analyst who has recommended the installation of pegboards to assist in summarization. In what situations could pegboards be used? Would you recommend their use? Why or why not?

4. Can ledgerless bookkeeping be used for a complete system? Explain, giving illustrations.

5. As systems analyst, you have recommended a ledgerless bookkeeping system for accounts receivable. The chief bookkeeper does not believe in ledgerless bookkeeping and has made the following statements. For each of his statements, explain whether your system deals adequately with his allegations.
   a. There is no general ledger control.
   b. An invoice might be lost or destroyed and there would be no way of knowing which document is missing.
   c. It is not an economical system.
   d. Customer statements are difficult to send out as they are not prepared automatically when posting to the accounts receivable ledger card.
   e. Partial payments are received occasionally, and are difficult to process.

    f. No audit trails are left to go back to check out individual customer records.

    g. Follow-up collection notices require extra work.

    h. When the accounts receivable file is not in balance, there is no way to find the error.

    i. There is no customer credit history.

6. Your client, the owner of the Corner Grocery Store, has become discouraged with the amount of record work that has been necessary to maintain his financial information system properly. He has heard about ledgerless bookkeeping and has inquired whether such a system would help.

    Your investigation discloses that a simplified system is now used, with data posted to a combination journal from a summary prepared from the totals accumulated in the cash register and cleared in summary form each night. A checkbook is used for all disbursements, and as a basis for combination journal entries. A general ledger is maintained. Sales are about 60 per cent for cash and 40 per cent on account. All sales tickets are validated and the amounts accumulated in the cash register. On the last day of each month the credit sales tickets for each customer are copied on a statement which is mailed to the customer. Customers usually pay the amount of the statement before the 15th of the following month.

    Would you recommend a ledgerless bookkeeping system for the Corner Grocery Store? Explain. How would you improve the present system?

7. Why might the manager (owner) of a small business utilize the services of a data processing service bureau? Under what special conditions might such services be purchased advantageously?

8. What is the role of punched paper tape or punched cards in a procedure using a data processing service bureau? Why are paper tapes and punched cards important when making the decision as to whether a specific job is to be done by a data processing service bureau?

9. The Verona Company has asked a manufacturer's representative to study the multiple-purpose accounting machine installation being used for the payroll and general ledger procedures in a small business. During the investigation he has commented that the ledgerless bookkeeping system did not provide control over accounts receivable, and has recommended that accounts receivable be put on the multiple-purpose accounting machine. Compare the control over accounts receivable using the multiple-purpose accounting machine as contrasted to the ledgerless bookkeeping procedure. Which would you recommend?

10. In what ways can the use of cash registers contribute to the effectiveness of internal control over receipts from cash sales? (AICPA Examination)

11. The owner of a local clothing store has asked you to design an accounting system in such a way that he will not be bothered with any more records than are absolutely necessary. He wants you to come in as his accountant and do whatever work is necessary once each month. He will need accrual-basis

statements. A cash register is used, and ledgerless accounts receivable records are maintained.
a. What books and records would you recommend? Why?
b. Would you recommend single- or double-entry bookkeeping? Why?
c. Should cash or accrual method of keeping records be used? Give your reason or reasons for each answer.

12. The Allen Company is a young, fast-growing company. All records are manually prepared by Mr. Harry Cain, the bookkeeper, and his assistant. Recently the volume of work has made it necessary for both Mr. Cain and his assistant to work on Saturday to stay current with daily transactions.

    In attempting to streamline the accounting system, Mr. Cain has been investigating the possibility of acquiring a cash register and a multiple-purpose accounting machine. The accounting system, after installing the accounting machine, would be as shown in Figure 5-12, page 131.
    a. How would a cash register contribute specifically to the bookkeeping processes? Explain.
    b. What are advantages of a cash register for other than bookkeeping purposes?
    c. What would be the advantages and disadvantages of the machine system over the present system?

13. How would the following items be reflected on a cash-basis operating statement of a business?
    a. Expense refund.
    b. Depreciation.
    c. Bad debts written off.
    d. Cash received on account.
    e. Purchase of a machine.
    f. Sale of a fully depreciated machine.
    g. Inventory of merchandise.
    h. Cash repaid on a loan to the bank.
    i. Amount owed on a machine.
    j. Cash paid for supplies still on hand.
    k. Payment of last year invoice for supplies now used.
    l. Collection of a bad account written off two years ago.

14. You have been asked to design a system for a business about which you have little knowledge. [You will be assigned one of the 67 businesses presented in R. I. Williams and Lillian Doris, (Eds.), *Encyclopedia of Accounting Systems* (Prentice-Hall, Inc., 1957), 5 volumes.]
    a. Prepare a brief outline of the system information presented in Williams and Doris for the business assigned to you. Note the characteristics of the business that require special consideration in the design of the system.
    b. Compare the extent and type of information in Williams and Doris for the business assigned to you, to the information in either of the following references:
    (1) Lasser, J. K. (Ed.), *Handbook of Accounting Methods*, (Second Edition; New York: D. Van Nostrand Company, Inc., 1954).

(2) Lasser, J. K. (Ed.), *Handbook of Cost Accounting Methods*, (New York: D. Van Nostrand Company, Inc., 1949).

In instances in which there is no system comparable to the system assigned for investigation in either of the above references, select a similar business of interest to you and indicate the characteristics of the business that require special consideration in the design of the system.

  c. List five references from the *Accountants Index* that would be helpful in the design of the accounting system assigned to you in step a., above. State the specific supplement or supplements from which the references were obtained. If no reference is made to the type of business to which you were assigned, look up some aspect of accounting that could relate to the business, i.e., depreciation, inventories, or internal control.

15. State the sources of information available to the systems analyst when he is required to design a system for a business with which he is unfamiliar. What would be the objective of the systems analyst in consulting each of the sources listed? Discuss.

16. Give three examples of circumstances in which documents may be bound as an adequate substitute for a journal.

17. Sailing, Inc., is a distributor of boats (Brand 1 and Brand 2), motors (25-HP, 50-HP, and 75-HP), and accessories (grouped into classes: parts, ski gear, miscellaneous).

      Three salesmen work in the store. They are paid a nominal salary plus a commission, which is a different percentage on boats, motors, and accessories.

      The owner wants the following reports:

  a. A weekly report of product sales by salesmen.

  b. A monthly report of product sales by salesmen.

  c. A monthly report of sales by salesmen for calculating commissions earned.

      Design forms for applying the pegboard method of furnishing the data for these reports.

18. Mr. Miles Away, of the Away Drug Store, keeps single-entry records. A summary of cash and charge sales, cash receipts, and paid-outs is accumulated from detailed audit strips taken from the cash register.

      Mr. Away has been handling the sales tax on cosmetics and other such items in the following fashion: whenever an item is sold on which the tax must be charged, only the net price is rung up on the cash register. The change made is distributed between the customer and the sales tax. Cash equal to the sales tax is placed in a box. The amount collected in the box is the amount forwarded to the government.

  a. Is Mr. Away's procedure adequate? Explain.

  b. Suggest an alternative procedure for controlling the sales tax and give the details for handling and recording the type of sale described above.

  c. A customer returns some merchandise for a refund. She submits a cash register receipt for $9.50. Indicate how this refund would be handled, both as to making the refund, and recording it, under (1) Away's procedure and (2) your procedure.

19. You are called in to prepare accrual accounting statements for the Milwaukee Store at the end of the month. Compute the amount of purchases for the period from the following data:
    a. Unpaid invoices for merchandise at the end of the period amount to $3,100.
    b. Payments on account made during the period:
       Paid-out from cash register .... $ 160
       Checks sent to suppliers 2,450
    c. Of those bills paid by check, 2 per cent discount had been taken in every case.
    d. The amount owed at the beginning of the period was $2,200.
    e. Cash purchases amounted to $140.

20. Mr. James Jones operates a business in which records are kept on a cash basis. His income statement for January, prepared on a cash basis, shows the following:

Revenue	
Cash sales	$21,400
Net collections on account	2,955
Total revenue	$24,355

    Unpaid customers' bills at the beginning of the period totaled $2,700. There were $2,000 in unpaid customers' bills in the unpaid file on January 31. During the month of January, $200 of unpaid bills had been removed from this file, inasmuch as they were considered uncollectible. During January a 3 per cent discount had been taken on one-half of the bills paid by customers.
    Calculate the total revenue for January on an accrual basis.

21. The following data are obtained from a single-entry set of books kept by James Halloway:

	Jan. 1	Dec. 31		Jan. 1	Dec. 31
Accounts receivable	$4,000	$6,000	Notes payable	$ —	$1,000
Inventories	3,500	4,000	Accounts payable	2,000	1,200
Prepaid expense	300	280	Accrued expenses	200	250
Store equipment	3,000	2,700			

    The cashbook shows the following:

Balance January 1		$1,500
Receipts:		
Collections on account		3,000
Borrowed by issuance of note		1,000
		$5,500
Disbursements:		
Withdrawals by owner	$ 500	
Purchase of store equipment	800	
Payments on account	3,400	
Payments of expenses	1,000	5,700
Cash overdraft		($ 200)

All accounts receivable and payable were for merchandise sales and purchases.

Compute the total accrual basis *expense* which would appear on Halloway's income statement.

22. Make the following computations incident to a single-entry system:
    a. Cash:

Cash on hand, start of month	$ 30.00
Cash on hand, end of month	229.50
Deposits	200.00
Received on account	190.75
Cash sales	281.20
Paid outs	73.00

What is the overage or shortage?

    b. Costs of Sales:

Purchase invoices unpaid, end of month	$ 300.00
Purchase invoices unpaid, start of month	170.00
Merchandise purchases paid in cash	1,100.00
Inventory, start of month	250.00
Inventory, end of month	225.00

What is the cost of goods sold?

    c. Accounts Receivable:

Accounts receivable, start of period	$ 320.00
Collections on account	1,600.00
Cash sales	420.00
Charge sales	1,710.00

What is the ending balance of accounts receivable?

23. It is assumed that you are familiar with the basic mechanics of ledgerless bookkeeping so do not discuss these. Discuss the special features or limitations of ledgerless bookkeeping such as the following:
    a. How are partial payments handled?
    b. How are proofs handled, especially in a large volume situation?
    c. To what types of business is the system suited? Unsuited? Why?
    d. What about statements?
    e. Discuss any other non-routine aspects of ledgerless bookkeeping which you think are important.

24. The Pearson Drug Store uses a simplified, single-entry set of records, from which it prepares financial statements monthly. At the close of each day's transactions, detailed audit tapes, taken from the cash registers, provide the basis for entries in a Record of Sales, Cash Receipts, and Disbursements. A breakdown of the disbursements made from the register is provided by receipted bills. Whenever sales are made on account, duplicate sales slips are prepared, the originals being kept in a file folder. When payments are received on account, the sales slips are removed from the accounts receivable if payment is in full. Partial payments are entered on the customers' sales slips and retained in the file until paid in full.

The record of Sales, Cash Receipts, and Disbursements for the month of January, 1968, shows the following totals:

Total Sales	Charge Sales	Cash Sales	Rec'd on Acct.	Cash Over	Cash Short	Summary of Cash Pd. Out	Bank Deposits
$4,200	$350	$3,850	$380	$10	—	$600	$3,540

Purchases for Cash	Freight In	Delivery Expense	Store Supplies	Other
$310	$20	$125	$100	$35—Withdrawal, Pearson 10—Misc. Expense

A recap of the checkbook stubs and deposit tickets reveals the following:

Cash in bank, January 1, 1968		$4,000
Deposits:		
From receipts	3,540	
From tenant for rental of upstairs	600	
Proceeds from sale of store equipment, 1/1/1968	300	
Proceeds from discounting of $5,000 note at bank on January 31	4,925	
		$13,365
Checks Written:		
Cash purchases	$2,000	
Payments on account	1,300	
Payments for salaries	1,000	
Freight on purchases	50	
Payments for supplies	125	
Purchase of store equipment 1/1/1968	450	
Payment to bank for notes payable	3,000	
Personal withdrawals	200	8,125
Cash in bank, January 31, 1968		$ 5,240

Pearson's Balance Sheet at January 1, 1968 includes:

Cash on hand	$ 100		Accounts payable	$ 5,000
Cash in bank	4,000		Notes payable	3,000
Accounts receivable	725		Accrued salaries	75
Merchandise inventory	14,000		Pearson, capital	14,670
Supplies on hand	300			
Prepaid interest	20			
Store equipment	$3,000			
Accumulated depreciation	600	2,400		
Delivery equipment	$2,000			
Accumulated depreciation	800	1,200		
		$22,745		$22,745

a. *Additional Information:*
  1. Merchandise inventory January 31st is estimated at $14,500.
  2. A customer's account for $30 proved uncollectible and his sales slip has been removed from the receivable file.
  3. Supplies on hand January 31st amounted to $400.
  4. All store equipment has a 15-year life, while all delivery equipment has a five-year life.
  5. Store equipment sold during the period originally cost $600 and was six years old.
  6. Accrued salaries January 31st amounted to $60.
  7. Rental received from the tenant was for the entire year of 1968.
  8. Unpaid invoices for merchandise purchased on account amount to $4,100 at January 31.
b. Prepare an accrual basis income statement for the month of January and a balance sheet as of January 31, 1968. Be sure to reconcile beginning and ending capital utilizing the net income or net loss figure obtained from the income statement.
c. How would the statements differ if they were prepared as cash basis statements? State the amount of net income on a cash basis.
d. Mr. Pearson would like to departmentalize his operations, using the following classifications: Prescriptions, Packaged Goods, Fountain, and Tobacco and Notions. Suggest a means for accomplishing this objective. Also suggest other improvements which might be made with respect to his record system.

25. The Bloom Florist Shops are owned and operated by Sumner Bloom in two separate locations. Mr. Bloom has called you in for assistance. He states that until two years ago he operated only a small card and flower shop in an adjoining town. At that time he opened a new and modern shop in the city and affiliated with the Florists Telegraph Delivery Association.

  Although he has had large gains in sales and profits in these last two years, Mr. Bloom has never effected any substantial improvement in his financial condition. He has looked into the problem from the personnel and physical standpoints and is satisfied with the honesty of the employees and the conformity of his product, service, and price with that of other florists. He asks that you look over the profit statement prepared for the prior fiscal year. *It is his intention that this should be on a cash basis.*

  Your initial inquiries develop the following facts:

  Each store makes a daily report of certain financial and other data to the administrative office. This report includes, but is not limited to, the following information: opening cash balance, cash sales, charge sales, cash received on account, amounts paid out, amounts deposited, and ending cash balance. In addition, the retail values of inbound and outbound F.T.D. transactions are listed.

  (F.T.D. is an association of florists providing florists' services in other cities and towns. The florist with whom the customer places an order retains 20 per cent of the retail value of the order, 80 per cent being credited to the florist in the city where the order is filled and delivery made. The remittance is not made directly, since all of these transactions are channeled through a central clearing house operated by F.T.D. Member florists receive a monthly statement showing inbound and outbound items, as well as service and advertising charges. A net credit balance is accompanied by a remittance from F.T.D.; a net debit balance is paid by the florist to F.T.D.)

All disbursements by Bloom's shops, except for minor expenses shown on daily reports, are paid by check at the office.

No journals or ledgers are kept. Income statements have been prepared by the "bookkeeper" by summarizing on columnar paper certain of the data provided on the daily reports and from the checkbook stubs.

The following is the income statement so prepared for the *fiscal year* ended July 31, 1968:

BLOOM FLORIST SHOPS

Income Statement

Year Ended July 31, 1968

Receipts

Cash sales	$100,000
Charge sales	120,000
Inbound F.T.D. orders received	25,000
20% of outbound F.T.D. orders sent	3,000
Miscellaneous	2,000
Total receipts	$250,000

Expenses

Purchases, flowers	$ 80,000
Purchases, other merchandise	5,000
Salaries and wages	75,000
Rent	7,200
Express and freight	7,000
Utilities	2,000
Telephone and telegraph	3,000
Delivery expense and repairs	5,500
Repairs and maintenance	3,000
Advertising	2,500
Discounts and refunds	2,000
Depreciation and amortization	2,500
F.T.D. discount on orders received	5,000
Payments to F.T.D.	4,000
Interest	1,500
Miscellaneous	4,000
Total expenses	$209,200
Net Profit	$ 40,800

The following additional accounting information is assembled by you:

1. Miscellaneous receipts include:

Refunds and freight claims	$ 200
Insurance proceeds reimbursing repair costs of delivery truck involved in accident	600
Federal income tax refund (prior year tax)	300
Sale of fully depreciated assets	700
Other items	200
	$ 2,000

2. Miscellaneous expenses include:

Donations	$ 1,200
Dues and subscriptions	800
Taxes and licenses	500
Insurance	800
Bad accounts considered uncollectible	500
Cash over	200
	$ 4,000

3. Cash payments to F.T.D. for the fiscal year were .... $ 4,000
4. Cash receipts from F.T.D. for the fiscal year were .... $ 7,500
5. F.T.D. charges for advertising and expense (included in advertising expense on the income statement) .... $ 1,500
6. Depreciation on delivery equipment is on a four-year basis. Included in the depreciation taken is $250 for a station wagon, purchased February of the current year. You find that $2,000 was paid in cash in addition to trade-in of $1,200 allowed for a family sedan which had not been used in the business. Mr. Bloom anticipates that 75 per cent of the station wagon usage is attributable to the business.
7. Cash received on account $115,000
8. Inventories are not material and the estimated difference between the opening and closing balance is only $100.
9. Cash and charge sales include amounts received from customers on outbound F.T.D. orders.

a. Prepare a worksheet showing adjustments to the income statement to reflect the results of Bloom's operation for the past fiscal year on the cash basis.

b. Give explanations for each adjustment, showing calculations where appropriate. Key the explanations to the adjustments in the worksheet.

c. Cite the more important advantages to be gained by Bloom in the installation of a simple set of books, using the facts in the problem as illustrations where possible. State the books or other records to be maintained. (Adapted AICPA Examination)

26. The Professional Men's Association of Middleton is made up of men in the various professions, including CPA's. From the start it has been tax exempt from federal income and excise taxes, other than payroll.

The dues for members are $40 a year, after an initiation fee of $100. The Association has had a consistent policy of operating on a cash basis. It does not deposit initiation fees received with applications and does not consider them as income until the membership committee has acted thereon. Then the successful applicants' fees are deposited and the unsuccessful applicants' checks are returned to them.

The fiscal year ends August 31. Each year the directors choose from the membership a CPA to make a thorough audit, and no one is allowed to audit two consecutive years. This year you have been selected for the first time, but you are solemnly warned that the directors will not tolerate any suggestion of putting the accounts on an accrual basis. You accept. An adequate fee is provided.

The secretary furnishes you with the following information:

Membership at September 1, 1968		2,980
Elected during the year	123	
Dropped for nonpayment of dues	15	
Died	37	
Expelled	1	53
Net gain		70

Your examination of records shows the following:

Notices that "dues are due" are sent out in August. Dues for a full year, not to be prorated, must be paid when elected to membership. Prior to the end of the preceding fiscal year 410 members had paid their dues and in the current fiscal year 457 members had paid their dues for the year beginning September 1, 1969. One of these had died very suddenly on August 30 and is included in the 37 above. No refunds are made for deaths taking place after the fiscal year begins; however, refunds of one-half the dues are made to expelled members. There were 36 applications pending at the end of the fiscal year. During the course of your audit, the committee met and approved of 34. You further find that at the *beginning* of the year there were 47 such applications and that 45 had been acted upon favorably and are included in the 123 above.

The directors are interested in learning if there is a substantial difference between the income from dues on a cash basis as compared to the accrual basis.

a. Prepare a schedule of income from membership showing:
   1. Changes in members.
   2. Income from initiation fees.
   3. Income from dues for the year, accrual basis.
   4. Income from dues for the year, cash basis.
   5. Total income from membership.
   6. Reconciliation of income from dues cash basis to the accrual basis.
b. What other audit procedures would you use to verify the income from membership? Give reasons. (AICPA Examination)

27. The owner of a store previously doing a cash-and-carry business decides to extend credit to selected customers. How will the sales procedures have to be amended or extended to enable the change?

28. What are the features of the cash register that serves each of the following objectives:
    a. Use of publicity to minimize error or fraud.
    b. Fixing of responsibility.
    c. Prevention of record alteration.
    d. Reporting significant information to management.
    e. Prevention of errors in making change.
    f. Good internal control.

CHAPTER 15

Punched Card Concepts

IN PREVIOUS CHAPTERS, PUNCHED CARDS AND PUNCHED CARD MACHINES HAVE been referred to as one of the ways in which an information system can be mechanized so that data could be transformed into information more rapidly and more effectively than by manual means. Punched card machines are not just another type of bookkeeping device. They are different, and actually a unique philosophy of data processing has developed as a result.

PUNCHED CARDS

Punched card systems are centered around the fact that every transaction can be broken down into data units of the least common denominator, and these can then be processed by machine. The punched card is the *unit record* into which data units of the least common denominator are entered. It is possible to represent data on a card of uniform size by means of holes arranged in a definite pattern. International Business Machines Corporation, one of the manufacturers of punched card equipment, utilizes the card and data coding system showing in Figure 15-1. The standard IBM card is 7⅜" x 3¼" in size and can represent 26 letters of the alphabet, ten numerical digits and standard symbols, such as the $, #, %, by means of the presence of holes punched appropriately in the card. Note that the card in Figure 15-1 has 80 vertical columns with 12 punching positions in each column. The ten numerical symbols 0-9 are represented by a single punch in any of the 80 columns. 0 on the card in Figure 15-1 is represented by a punch in column 2 at the 0 vertical position. Alphabetic characters are represented by using

389

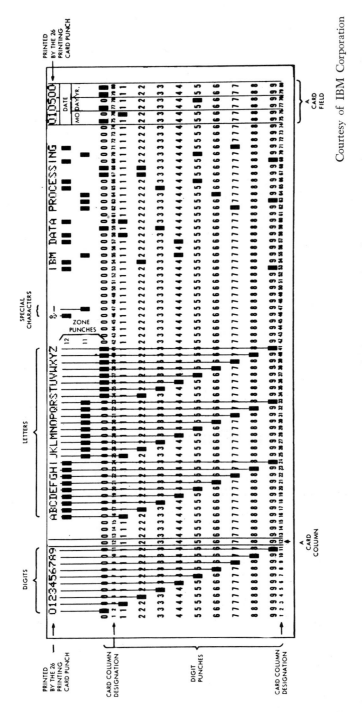

FIGURE 15-1. Standard IBM Punched Card

Courtesy of IBM Corporation

two punches in one of the 80 columns. The higher rows of punches, namely 0, 11, and 12, are called *zone punches*. The letters A through I are represented by combining a 12 zone punch with the digit punches 1-9, respectively; J through R utilizes an eleven zone punch and digit punches 1-9; and the letters S through Z combine a 0 zone punch with digit punches 2-9. Other characters, such as $, #, %, are represented by one, two, or three punches in a column.

Through the use of brushes, electricity, magnets, and other components to move the cards, the holes in the cards can activate the various machines in the ways to cause the results depicted in Figure 15-2.

It is possible, therefore, for a piece of data, once it is recorded and classified in a punched card, to sustain the remaining data processing operations of arranging, calculating, summarizing, comparing, storing and transporting without manual intervention in the actual processing operations. It is evident that this mode of mechanization is normally far more automated than a system using the conventional accounting machines described in Chapter 5.

Basic Types of Punched Cards

Although punched cards can be designed so that data can be punched into the card in many different formats and from many sources, the cards can be roughly classified into five groups: 1) transcript cards, 2) dual cards, 3) mark sensed cards, 4) Port-A-Punch cards, and 5) summary cards. *Transcript cards* are cards which are keypunched with data taken from another document. *Dual cards* contain the data on the cards which must be punched into the card. Quite frequently time data from the factory are reported on cards which are keypunched from the data written on the card. *Mark sensed cards* are automatically punched from pencil marks recorded in significant positions on the face of the card. Mark sensed procedures are discussed later in this chapter. *Port-A-Punch cards* are designed to enable the person recording data to "punch out" the digit or digits with a blunt instrument such as a ball point pen. Thus data are recorded originally in a card as holes, and are ready immediately for machine processing. A Port-A-Punch card is illustrated in Figure 15-3. *Summary cards* are punched with totals or new balances developed by the accounting machine. The actual punching is done by a reproducing punch which is connected to the accounting machine. (See sections later in this chapter.)

In the design of specific cards, the systems analyst should apply the prerequisites and the standards of good form design discussed in Chapter 4.

The Processing Machines

In this section, equipment of the International Business Machines Corporation has been selected to illustrate the basic pieces of equipment essential

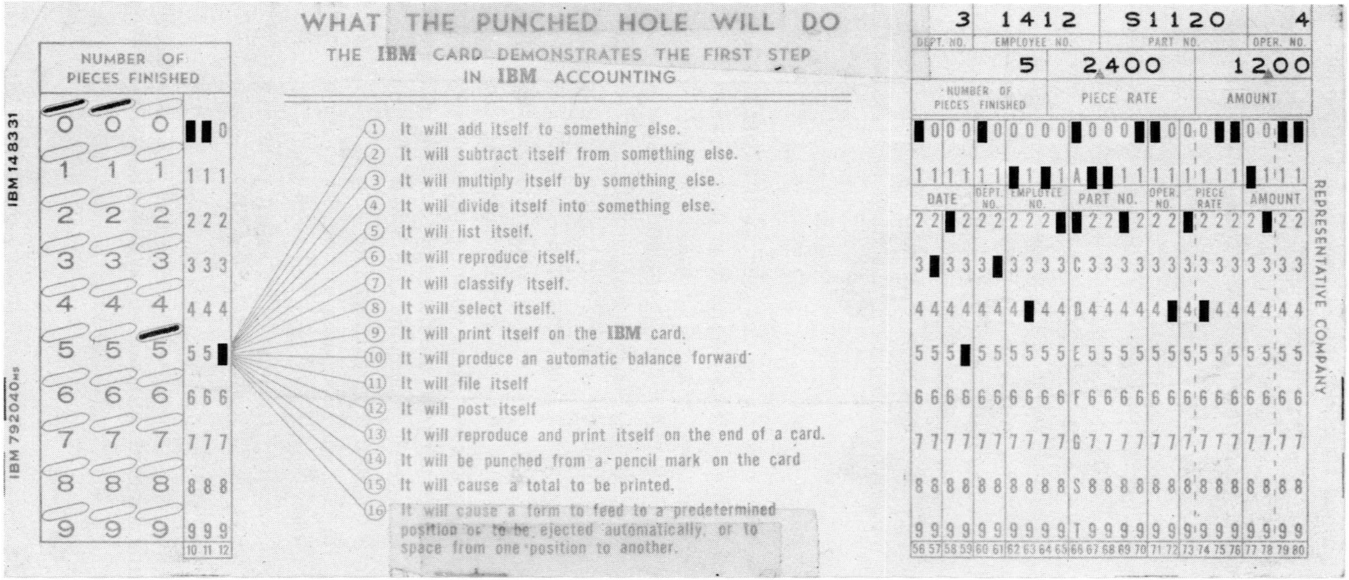

Courtesy of IBM Corporation

FIGURE 15-2. What Punched Holes Will Do

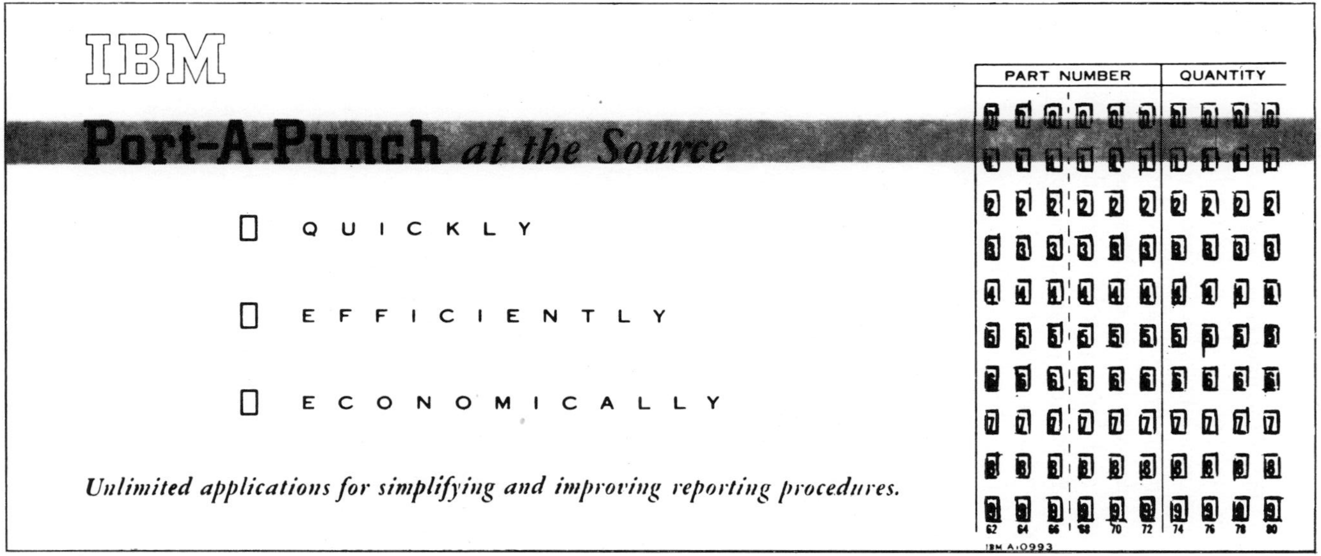

Courtesy of IBM Corporation

FIGURE 15-3. Port-A-Punch Card

to a punched card data processing system. The machines manufactured by other manufacturers differ somewhat in details of operation, but not in the theory of operation.

THE CARD PUNCH. One of the most essential pieces of equipment in the punched card line is the card punch. This is the machine that, through its operator, punches the appropriate holes in the cards. You can see in Figure 15-4 that this piece of equipment is similar in appearance to a standard typewriter. Instead of printing the letters, numbers, and miscellaneous business symbols on paper, the card punch puts holes into the cards. A particular model card punch also prints at the top edge of the column the digit, letter or symbol punched into a column. (See Figure 15-1.) As on a typewriter, certain columns on a card can be skipped through a "tab" arrangement. Unlike a typewriter, the cards can be automatically fed into the punching position and stacked after the punching has been completed. A unique feature

Courtesy of IBM Corporation

FIGURE 15-4. Card Punch

on the card punch is the reading station that each card must pass through after it has been punched. This reading station will permit data from one card to be duplicated automatically in the following card. For example, if today's date was to be placed in the first six columns of each card, it would be key punched by the operator in the first card, making six key depressions. Utilizing the tab set and the reading station, today's date would automatically be punched in each succeeding card without one further key depression on the part of the operator.

THE CARD VERIFIER. If all of the data processing operations subsequent to the recording and classification done in the card punch operation is automatic, it is imperative that the holes punched must be correct. Any numerical values, or alphabetic data, incorrectly punched will be further processed in error. If punched correctly, however, machine failure or willful fraud is the only type of error possible. Specific internal control duties can be designed to minimize these types of errors.

The inadvertent punching of an erroneous character, however, can be detected effectively through a special verification operation. The card verifier, shown in Figure 15-5, is the machine designed to help with the verification process. The principle utilized here is quite simple. If the key punch operation could be done twice, the cards compared, and no differences in the cards noted, it can be safely assumed that the first card was punched correctly. The card verifier is similar to a card punch, but instead of punching holes in cards, it tests to see if a hole is in a particular position. Cards punched in a punching operation are delivered to the key verifying machine operator along with the original documents from which the data originated that were punched into the cards. The punched cards are inserted into the verifier and the operator depresses the same character keys on the verifier as did the key punch operator. As each key is depressed, a brush tests to see if a hole is in the appropriate place on the card. If either the verifier operator or the key punch operator had struck the wrong key, the card will stop and a red light on the front of the verifier will tell the operator that some error exists. The operator will turn the light off, check the original document to see what was supposed to be punched into the column in question and depress the appropriate key. If the verifier operator had struck the wrong key in the first attempt to verify, the card will move to the next column. If the key punch operator had punched a different character in the column than was called for by the original document, the red light will come on again. The verifier operator must turn the light out a second time, check the original document a second time, and depress the appropriate key. If the error still persists, the verifying machine will notch the card over the column in error and permit the card to be moved to the next column. When each card has been verified, a notch is placed at the end of each card free of errors. The notches permit decks of cards to be inspected by the key punch supervisor or other machine operators before processing the data further.

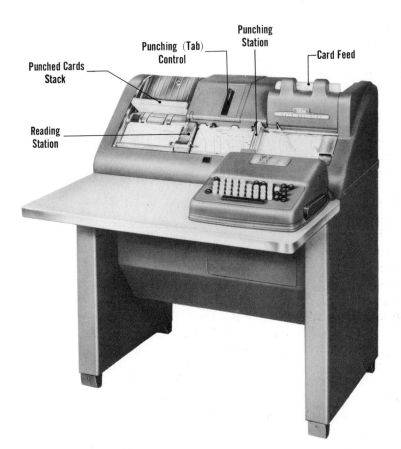

Courtesy of IBM Corporation

FIGURE 15-5.   Card Verifier

Neophytes to punched card accounting often wonder if the double work of punching and verifying is worth the effort. It is worth the effort, of course, because one must remember that the remaining processing steps are machine steps. Erroneous input causes erroneous output. Keep the fact in mind, also, that machine speeds can more than make up for the care taken during input preparation.

THE SORTER. Once data has been recorded and classified the next step in any data processing system is to arrange the data in some meaningful way. Sales on account, for example, need to be arranged by customer so that the proper posting can be made to the customers' accounts. Assume that as each sales card was punched a five-digit account number had been punched into the card. Five thousand such sales cards could be arranged in account number

Courtesy of IBM Corporation

FIGURE 15-6. Sorter

076
862
187
652
097
542
617
504
407
174
013
006
356
146
892
693
047
397
040
677
314
803

sequence (sorting on each of the five digits) in less than thirty minutes by one model of a sorting machine. Figure 15-6 shows the 1,000 card per minute sorter currently available from IBM.

Figure 15-7 is a schematic diagram of the sorting mechanism consisting of a brush, magnet, and rollers to move the cards. The brush "A" in Figure 15-7 has sensed a "4" punch in the card "C." The card acts as an insulator keeping magnets "D" from attracting the metal chute blades of digits 5, 6, 7, 8, and 9. By being able to attract and pull down blades 4, 3, 2, 1, 0, 11, and 12, the card is channeled into the "4" pocket where it will rest until removed by the operator. In order to arrange cards in sequence, the sorting brush would be placed over the low order (right) column of the customer account number during the first pass through the machine and then on the other four columns moving from right to left in four additional passes through the machine. Consider the series of three-digit numbers on cards illustrated at the left being sorted into ascending

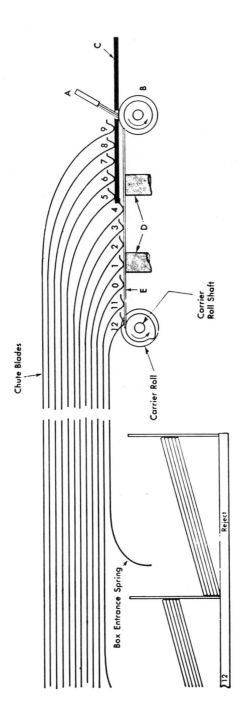

Courtesy of IBM Corporation

FIGURE 15-7. Sorting Mechanism

order. The cards were originally arranged and moved through the sorter on the first pass with the brush set on the far right column. The brush would be moved one column to the left on succeeding passes through the machine.

The results after each *sort* would be as follows. The numbers under each column show the order of input for the next pass:

First Sort (Rightmost Digit)

9	8	7	6	5	4	3	2	1	0
		187							
		097							
		617							
		407					862		
		047	076		504	013	652		
		397	006		174	693	542		
		677	356		314	803	892		040
		(6)	(5)		(4)	(3)	(2)		(1)

Second Sort (Middle Digit)

9	8	7	6	5	4	3	2	1	0
097									407
397		577			047			617	006
693		076		356	542			314	504
892	187	174	862	652	040			013	803
(8)	(7)	(6)	(5)	(4)	(3)			(2)	(1)

Third Sort (Leftmost Digit)

9	8	7	6	5	4	3	2	1	0
									097
									076
			693						047
	892		677			397		187	040
	862		652	542		356		174	013
	803		617	504	407	314		146	006
	(7)		(6)	(5)	(4)	(3)		(2)	(1)

To sort in descending sequence the various stacks of cards would be removed from the sorter from the leftmost pocket to the rightmost pocket instead of vice versa, as above.

Since it is possible to represent alphabetic data on punched cards as well as numeric, it is also possible to sort into alphabetic order. Alphabetic data, however, are represented by two punches in a column. In order to arrange such data, two passes must be made through the sorter for each alphabetic character. It takes twice as long, therefore, to arrange alphabetic data than numberic data. Systems analysts try to use numeric codes exclusively in punched card systems because of this fact and the need to economize in the number of columns used for specific data.

IBM Model 84 sorter uses a photoelectric method of card sensing in lieu of brushes. This model sorter can handle 2,000 cards per minute but the sorting principles described above are the same.

BLOCK SORTING. Refer again to the sorting example on page 399. Assume that instead of having an array of 21, three digit numbers the sorter operator had 10,000 cards containing a six digit account number to sort and that the cards are to be utilized in another operation as soon as possible after sorting. Using the straight sorting technique described above, it would take about one hour on a 1,000 card per minute sorter to sort the cards.

If the operator would set the sorting brush to the high order position (leftmost) during the first sorting pass, the ten numerical pockets would cause the 10,000 cards to be grouped as below:

Pocket	Account Numbers
0	000000 to 099999
1	100000 to 199999
2	200000 to 299999
⎰	⎰ ⎰ ⎰
9	900000 to 999999

Assuming that the 10,000 cards are spread evenly throughout the 1,000,000 possible numbers, about 1,000 cards would drop into the 0 pocket. These cards would then be sorted straight-forwardly to be put in ascending order from 000000 to 099999. When this block is in order they can be sent to the next operation without having to wait for the remaining 9,000 cards to be sorted. Even though punched card operations are rapid, much more processing time can be saved by proper sequencing of the machine operations.

THE COLLATOR. The verb "to collate" means to compare carefully and to check for correct arrangement. A punched card collator was designed to fulfill this definition. There are many times in the processing of data that certain items need to be selected from a larger group of items; that one group of items needs to be in exactly the same order as a companion group; or that the items extracted from the main group need to be returned. The updating of accounts receivable is a perfect example of a situation where all three of the above operations are performed. It is unlikely that any one day's activity (sales, receipts on account, etc.) would affect all of the existing accounts receivable. The old balance cards of the accounts which have been affected by the day's activity must be selected from the main file of accounts receivable balance cards in the same order as the transactions affecting the accounts, and new balance cards must be returned to the main file of accounts receivable balance cards once the updating process has been completed.

The punched card collator is so constructed that it will permit punched cards to be selected from an existing group of cards, matched with a deck of related cards, or merged into an existing group of cards. Figure 15-8 contains a picture and schematic diagram of a collator. Note that the collator has two feed hoppers and four card pockets. Assume that a merging or filing operation is to be performed and that none of the cards should possess the same identifying code. The two decks of cards are placed in the two feed hoppers, and when the first two cards reach the reading station, the machine compares the identifying account number code on each card. If the account number of the card from the main file is less in magnitude than the card from the group to be merged into the main file, the main file card is moved into the primary file pocket (2) and a second main file card is moved into the reading position. When the machine determines that the secondary file card account number is lower than the primary file card, it is the secondary card that is moved into the primary file pocket (2). In the event that two cards are compared, each having identical account numbers, one of the cards is out of place. In this event, the machine will move both cards to reject pockets (1) and (4).

THE TABULATOR. Prior sections have described machines which punch holes in cards, verify the punching operation, and arrange and/or collate cards in specific patterns. The information produced from the punched card data processing operation must be in some form that can be easily communicated to the interested recipients of this information. The tabulator or accounting machine, as it is often called, is the machine designed to convert the data stored in punched cards to "hard copy." In addition to merely reading the punched holes in cards and printing the alphabetic and numeric characters represented by these holes, the tabulator can accumulate totals by adding and/or subtracting appropriate numerical data in the cards. For example, in an end of the period accounts receivable billing operation, the tabulator can read and store in a numerical accumulator a customer's old balance in addition to printing the old balance on the statement. The current period's transaction cards, consisting of charges, receipts on account, etc., can be printed on the statement and added or subtracted in the accumulator. When the last of the transaction cards for this customer have been read, the new balance due is automatically printed. The tabulator, shown in Figure 15-9, has 120 type wheels, containing 47 alphabetic/numeric and special characters on each wheel. This model tabulator can add, subtract, and print at the rate of 150 lines per minute. A model of the tabulator has been developed called the calculating accounting machine or CAM, which, as its name implies, can carry out multiplication and division as well as addition and subtraction.

THE REPRODUCER. Historically, the first punched card machines developed were the card punch, card sorter, and tabulator. Even today these three machines are considered to be the minimum equipment necessary for a punched card system. A basic punched card system is not in use long before it becomes apparent that a machine is needed which could read certain data punched in one set of cards and punch this data into a second set of cards.

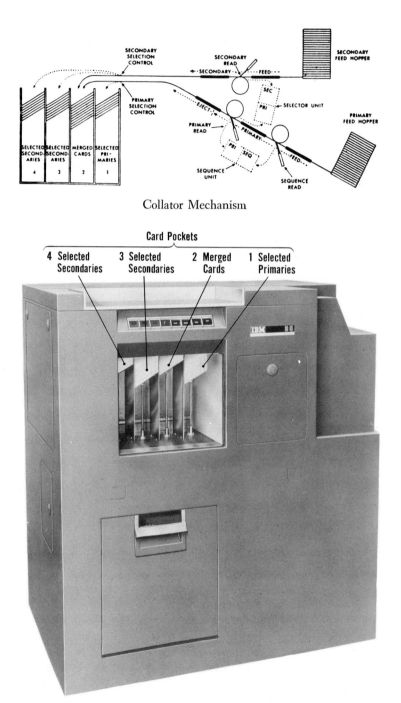

Collator Mechanism

Courtesy of IBM Corporation

FIGURE 15-8.   Collator

Courtesy of IBM Corporation

FIGURE 15-9. Tabulator

If such transfers could be accomplished, the need to use the key punch and the companion verification operation for these transfers could be eliminated. The reproducer was designed to fill this gap. Figure 15-10 consists of a picture and a schematic drawing of the reading and punch areas of a Reproducing Punch. Cards from which data are to be transferred are placed in the punch hopper. As each card is read, the data to be transferred to the second set of cards are punched into those cards.

In addition to routinely transferring data from one card to another, the reproducer can perform three additional functions: (1) gang punching, (2) summary punching, and (3) mark sense punching. *Gang punching* means that cards can be placed in the punch hopper of the reproducer; the machine will read certain data from the first card, and transfer this data to all or certain of the following cards in the deck. This feature can be used, for example, when a code, identifying a card as a sales card, needs to be punched in all sales cards.

Summary punching is an operation performed in conjunction with a tabulating machine. Refer to the example of preparing periodic statements for customers described above. Since old balance cards are used in this operation along with the transaction cards, it is obvious that these old balance cards must have been current balance cards at the end of the last period. Because the

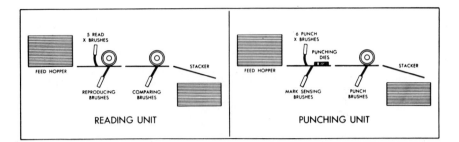

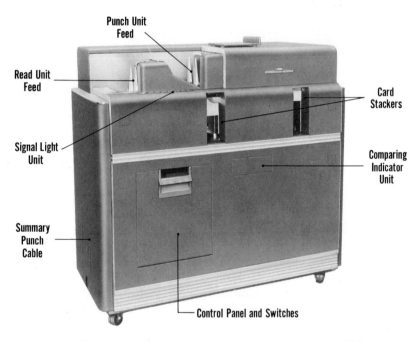

Courtesy of IBM Corporation

FIGURE 15-10. **Reproducing Punch**

reproducer can be connected by cable to the tabulator, it is possible to compute the new balance as described above and punch a new balance card on the reproducer. Since the tabulator can do no punching, the absence of such a connection between the tabulator and the reproducer would necessitate the use of the slower key punch to create the new balance cards.

The reproducer can also perform an operation called *mark sense punching* provided certain modifications are made in a standard model. It is possible to use a soft lead pencil to mark certain locations on a punched card. When fed into a reproducer capable of processing this type of card, the machine interprets the marks and punches holes in the card. In Figure 15-2, a mark sense card was utilized to illustrate the various ways a punched hole could activate different machines. Refer to this figure and note that the area for marking the card is to the left. A mark was made in the zero (0) position in the first two mark sense columns and in the five (5) position in the third mark sense column. In processing, the reproducer punched 0's in column 10 and 11, and a 5 in column 12. The drawback in this type of operation is the accuracy factor. Normally, mark sense cards are not key verified; therefore, any erroneous marks will be processed as marked. Mark sensing can be used effectively only where reliable employees who make few errors do the marking, and where the cost and magnitude of the errors that do result are not material.

THE PUNCHED CARD CALCULATOR. Until the announcement of the calculating accounting machine none of the machines discussed heretofore performed more than two mathematical processes. As more and more punched card systems were designed, a need arose for a machine which could multiply and divide as well as add and subtract factors punched in cards. The electronic calculator, shown in Figure 15-11, has the basic capacity for multiplying eight

Courtesy of IBM Corporation

FIGURE 15-11. Calculator

digits by five digits for a 13 digit product, and can divide 13 digits by eight digits for a five digit quotient.

THE INTERPRETER. From the examples given in this chapter, it should be apparent that a punched card can be a full-fledged business document as well as a processable data medium. Because machine operators and other employees must utilize punched cards as business documents, and because punched holes are not *easily* translatable by people, it is often necessary to print some of the data punched into cards on the face of the cards. The interpreter, Figure 15-12, at the speed of 60 cards per minute, can print up to two lines of data on each card containing a maximum of 60 characters per line. For example, the interpreter can be used to write punched card checks.

Courtesy of IBM Corporation

FIGURE 15-12.   Interpreter

Each of the machines discussed above are examples of the primary functions performed by the principal machine types and have at least one other model, while many of the machines have several models. These model differences involve such things as speed, printing, counter capacity, and the like. For example, an accumulating reproducer can accumulate totals as well as perform the regular reproducing operation. This is one reason even the most competent systems analyst should obtain the assistance of the manufacturers' representative to work out the final details of a punched card installation.

MACHINE CONTROL

In Figure 15-2 several ways were enumerated by which cards with holes punched into them could activate the various machines. This is possible through the use of electrical circuitry inside the machines activated in a controlled manner by the presence of holes appropriately punched into the cards. The card is actually an insulator. As it is moved through the machines at the various reading locations, the card breaks the electrical circuitry by separating wire brushes from rollers which complete the electrical circuits. The circuits are reunited according to where holes are in the card by permitting the brushes to again make contact with the roller. What is done with each character recognized by the machine in this way is determined by the way in which the other internal parts of each machine are activated.

Control panels, such as the collator panel shown in Figure 15-13, are used to connect the internal circuitry properly. The wires in Figure 15-13 are connected in such a way that if two decks of cards were fed into the machine they would be matched, placing cards not having a mate in the outside pockets and the matched cards in the two center pockets. By changing the wires in the control panel, the machine could have merged these two decks of cards. These control panels permit punched card machines to be "all purpose" machines, in that many different kinds of specific steps can be programmed on these panels. In one tabulator job, for example, only two totals may need to be accumulated, but in another job to be done four totals need to be accumulated and the printing is to be spaced differently than the first job. The interchange of the control panels will provide for this change in only a few seconds by replacing the control panel for the first job with the panel for the second job.

In order to be able to wire the control panels of the punched card machines efficiently, an individual must be taught basic wiring principles and then allowed to apply these principles to a wide range of problems. Practice in wiring panels and day-by-day association with wiring and operating the punched card machines is the only way in which proficient wiring techniques

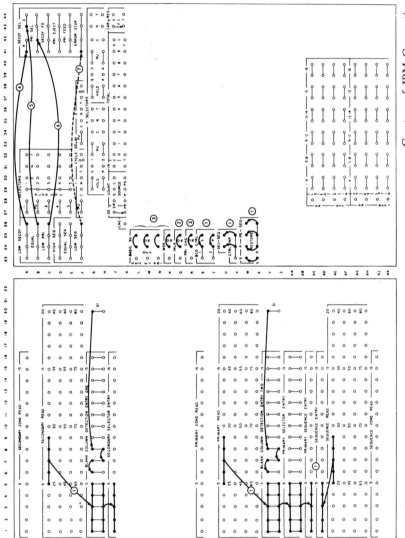

FIGURE 15-13. Control Panel Wiring

can be achieved. This fact is a second reason why systems analysts should rely on expert technical assistance when the details of control panel wiring must be worked out in specific situations.

Procedure Analysis

The foregoing description of the types of machines that can be utilized in a punched card installation should indicate that detailed procedure analysis is necessary in order to determine the correct processing sequence. As in any data processing system, the input operations of initial recording and classifying and the seven data processing operations of arranging, summarizing, calculating, comparing, storing, transporting, and reproducing must be part of a punched card data processing system. It is up to the systems analyst to determine which operations can be performed by the punched card machines. He must (1) determine the job steps necessary to bridge the gap between the source documents and the final report or document; (2) analyze the job steps and determine which can be performed mechanically; and (3) determine which machine operations and clerical functions will be applied to the various steps.[1]

PUNCHED CARD APPLICATIONS

It would be impossible to describe all of the procedures that have been put on punched card machines. Instead, consider these three: 1) accounts receivable accounting, 2) accounts payable recording and remittance, and 3) inventory and material accounting. After considering the semi-detailed flow charts and explanations of these three applications, it will be noted that there are striking similarities in all of the applications concerning the basic punched card processing operations performed.

APPLICATION NO. 1

Accounts Receivable (Modification)

This application is a description of the accounts receivable procedure used by a large midwestern hospital. It was the practice in the hospital to bill each in-patient weekly on the anniversary date of his admittance to the hos-

---

[1] *Accounting Management, Procedure Development*, IBM Department of Education, p. 7.

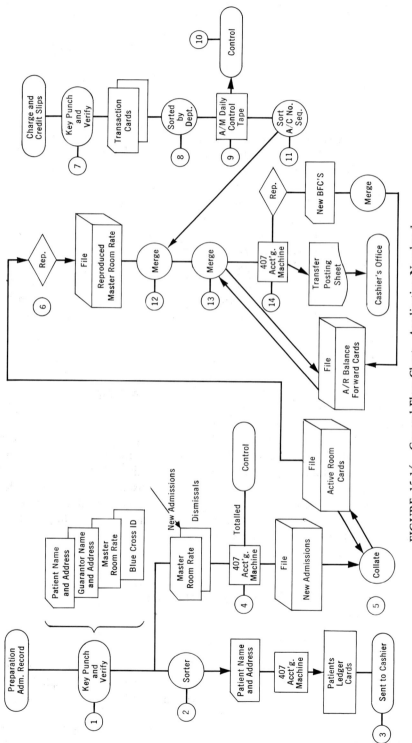

FIGURE 15-14. General Flow Chart—Application Number 1

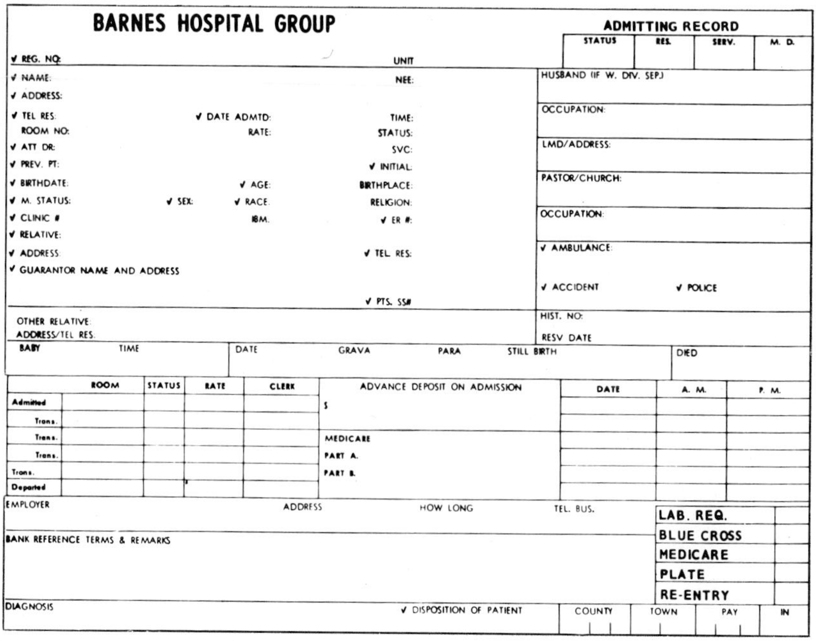

FIGURE 15-15. Admittance Sheet Designed to be Completed on a Typewriter

pital, and all other outstanding accounts once monthly. In-patient accounts receivable modification, however, was a daily operation. Figure 15-14 is a semi-detailed flow chart of this application. Details are described below and may be correlated by steps to the chart in Figure 15-14.

Upon admittance to the hospital, the admitting department prepares an admittance record for each patient. One copy of this record (*see* Figure 15-15) is sent to the key punch section of the data processing department. From this record four kinds of cards will be punched and verified (Step 1) as follows:

1. Patient name and address card. (*See* Figure 15-16.)
2. Guarantor name and address card. (*See* Figure 15-16.)
3. A master room rate card patient amount. (*See* Figure 15-17.)
4. A master room rate card insurance amount. (*See* Figure 15-18.)

After the new admission name and address cards are punched each day, they are sorted by patient account number and used to head patient ledger cards on the 407 accounting machine (Step 2). The ledger cards are then forwarded to the cashier's office (Step 3). You will note that the ledger pictured in Figure 15-19 is perforated in the center with identical information on both sides of the perforation. Upon discharge the right-hand portion is given to the patient with the left side being retained by the hospital.

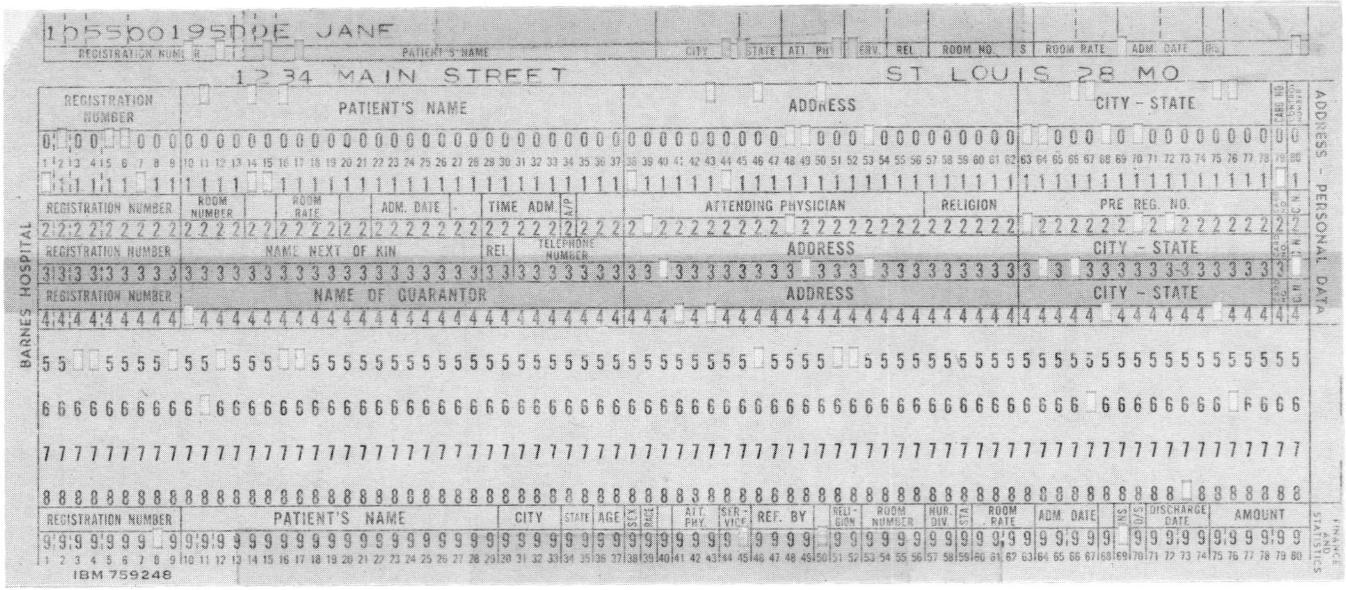

FIGURE 15-16. Patient Name and Address Card; Guarantor Name
and Address Card

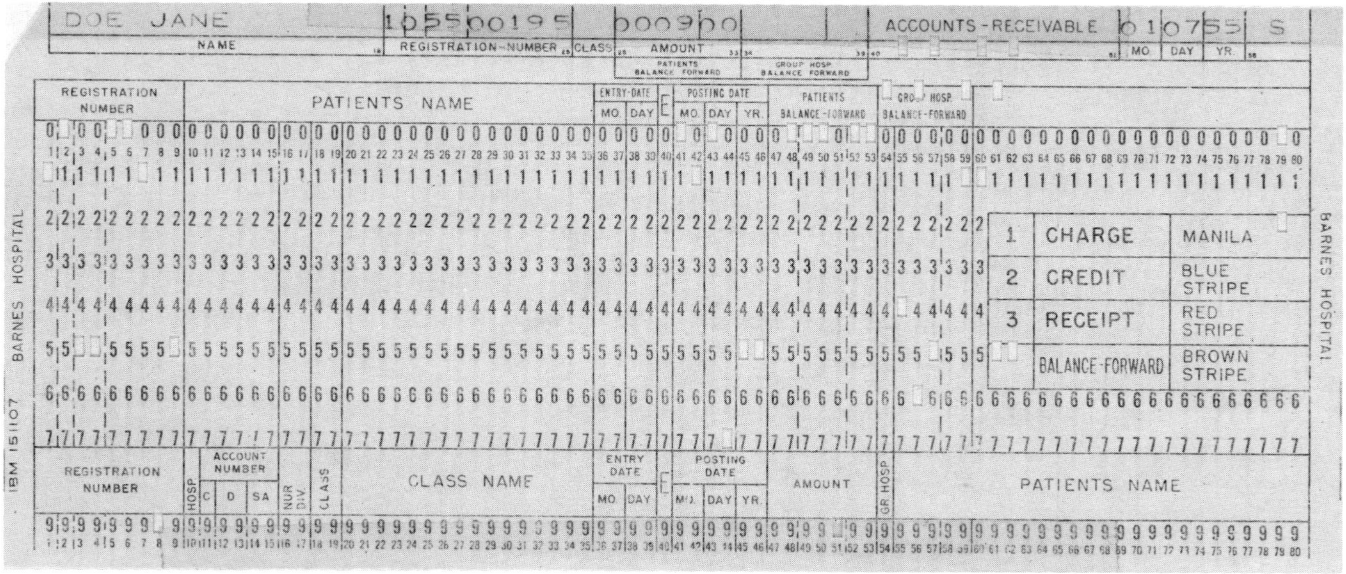

FIGURE 15-17. Master Room Rate Card Patient Amount

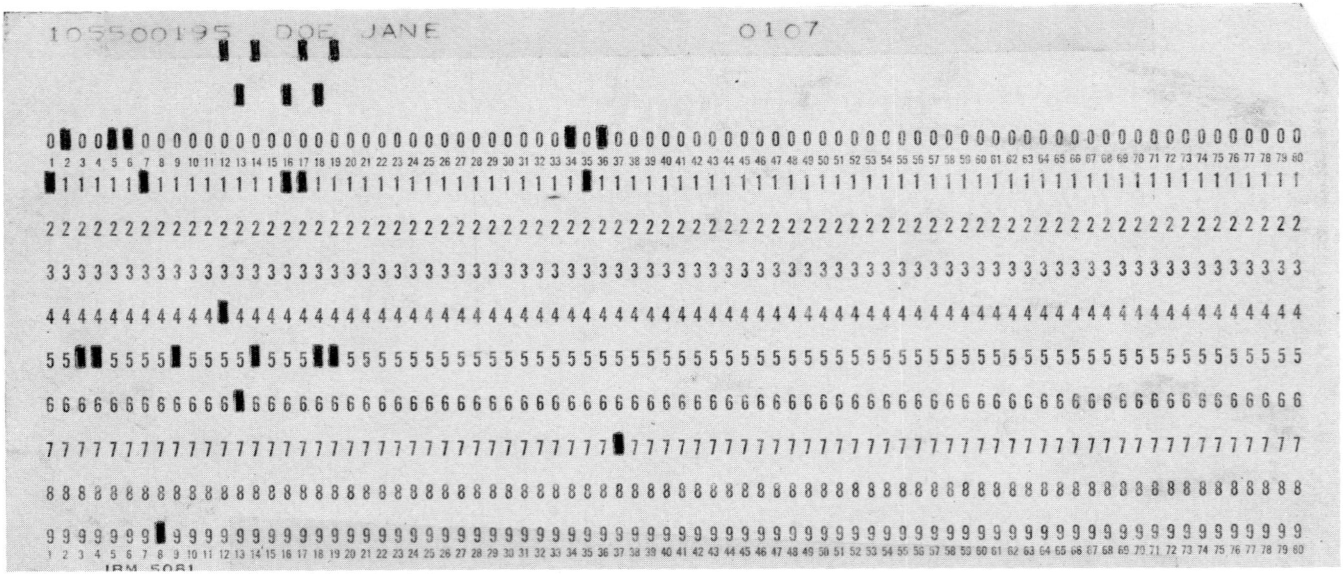

FIGURE 15-18. Master Room Rate Card Insurance Amount

The master room cards punched for new admissions are totaled on the 407 accounting machine (Step 4) as are all room cards of patients dismissed. These totals are entered into a room control book which gives the total room charges that are to be posted for the current day. Example: Previous day's total room charge + total of new admissions — total of dismissals = current day's total room charge (collator) (Step 5).

The new room charge cards are merged into the file of room cards remaining after the room cards of patients dismissed have been removed from the file. This gives a file of master room cards for both patient amounts and insurance amounts that must be posted to the in-patient accounts for the current day. The adjusted current day master room card file is reproduced (reproducing machine) so that the reproduced cards can be merged with the other transaction cards prior to posting (Step 6). (*See* paragraphs below.)

During the day, various services are being performed for the patients throughout the hospital. In these departments credits to patients' accounts also occur. Each department is responsible for the preparation of charge and credit slips which contain the name, patient account number, and the amount of the charge or credit. (*See* Figure 15-20.) The charge and credit slips are sent

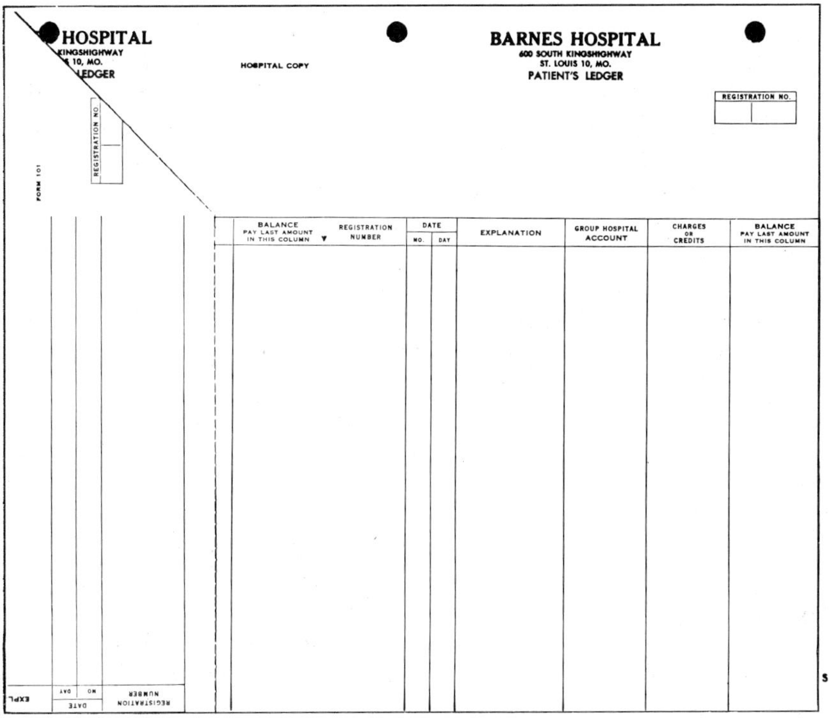

FIGURE 15-19. Patient's Ledger

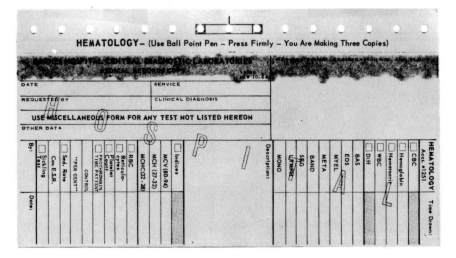

FIGURE 15-20.   Charge Slip

to the cashier's office where they, along with cash receipt slips prepared in the cashier's office, are checked against an alphabetic cross index file to insure that each slip has the correct account number written on it. The charge, credit, and cash receipt slips are then forwarded to the data processing department where a punched card is prepared for each slip (Step 7). After the verification operation, the cards are sorted by department, in the case of charge and credit cards, with all cash receipt cards grouped together (Step 8). When the cards are in order by department, a daily control tape is run on the 407 accounting machine showing class number, type of income, account number, account name, and daily amount (Step 9).

Total net postings are entered in the accounts receivable control book (Step 10). Example: Opening A/R balance ± daily net postings = ending A/R balance. The new file of A/R balance cards must total to the ending A/R balance in the control book.

The next operation is to sort the charge, credit, and receipt cards into patient account number sequence (Step 11) on the sorter and to use the collator to merge (Step 12) the room charge cards into this file to make it a complete transaction file.

In order to compute the amount due the hospital from each patient, it is necessary to add the charges and deduct the credits from the patient's previous day's balance, if any. The file of balance cards is merged with the transaction cards (Step 13). Any balance card which does not have any transaction cards is not merged in this operation. The procedure works in this way. The balance forward cards (BFC) in account number order are placed in the primary feed hopper of a collator and the transaction cards (TC), also in account number order, are placed in the secondary feed hopper. (*See* Figure 15-8.) As the cards are processed, the account number of the first BFC is compared with the first TC. If the account number of the BFC and TC match, the BFC is permitted to drop into pocket #2 with all matching TC's behind it. If the account numbers do not match, the machine tests to see if the BFC account number is higher or lower than the number of the TC. If BFC is lower, no TC are present today for this account, and the BFC is rejected into pocket #1. If the BFC is higher than the TC, then the TC's belong to a new account and are filed in pocket #2. This procedure is continued until the files have been processed.

At this point, the transaction amounts can be added to or subtracted from the old balance, if any, and the new accounts receivable balance computed (Step 14). Since a new BFC is also needed, an accounting machine and a reproducer must be connected and operated as a unit. The merged file of old BFC's and TC's are placed in the feed hopper of the accounting machine and unpunched BFC's are placed in the punch hopper of the reproducer. As the cards are run through the accounting machine, a transfer posting sheet is prepared.

When the last transaction card for a particular account is recognized by the accounting machine, the new balance forward is printed on the transfer posting sheet and simultaneously punched into a new BFC by the reproducer.

At this point, the new BFC's can be filed with the old BFC's not affected by today's transactions (Step 15). The transaction cards are filed by account number. The transaction cards for each in-patient are selected from the main file on the weekly anniversary date of the patient's entry to the hospital and a complete bill for the week is prepared.

The transfer posting sheet described above has a reverse carbon back-up sheet which causes the printing on the front to be duplicated in carbon on the back of the paper. A special machine called a transfer poster permits a *line* at a time to be posted to the patients' ledger cards kept in the cashier's office.

The transfer posting technique is not often recommended. Even though a line at a time can be posted, this slows the overall processing.

APPLICATION NO. 2

Accounts Payable and Expense Distribution

For the purpose of this example, assume that amounts due for the goods and services purchased by the company are all channeled through the accounts payable account. The procedure enables the accounts payable (control and subsidiary) account to be increased for each new item or service purchased and the same amount is distributed to the proper asset or expenses classification. Ancillary to the accounts payable and expense distribution phase is the payment of the accounts payable as they become due. Figure 15-21 is a flow chart of the accounts payable and expense distribution card preparation procedure described below. Figure 15-22 is a flow chart of the processing of the payables and expense cards, also described below. As you read the description follow the flow chart and the numbered steps carefully. The application described is not taken from a specific type business. It is a general procedure which could be adopted for use by many types of companies.

Accounts Payable and Expense Distribution Card Preparation

The source document for amounts due suppliers and the account(s) to which this amount must be distributed is usually the vendor's invoice which

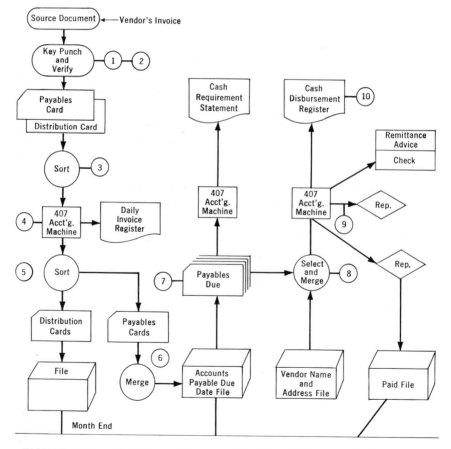

FIGURE 15-21. Flow Chart of Accounts Payable and Expense Distribution Card Preparation Procedure

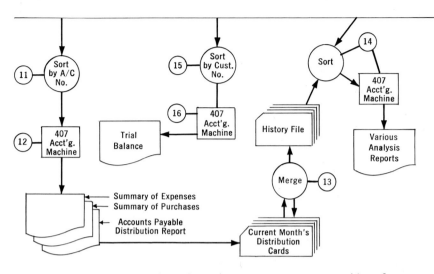

FIGURE 15-22. **Flow Chart of Processing Accounts Payable and Expense Distribution Card**

has been checked against the proper purchase order and receiving report, audited for mathematical accuracy, and notation made as to the account(s) and amounts to which the total is to be distributed. These source documents are given to the key punch operator who prepares a payables card and one or more distribution cards as seen in Figures 15-23 and 15-24 (Step 1). These cards are then verified (Step 2) and sorted into voucher number order (Step 3). The next step (4) in the procedure is to process the payable and distribution cards on the accounting machine to produce the invoice register. Two aspects of control are present in this procedure. (1) As a check that the total of the several distribution cards equals the payable card, both are used to prepare the invoice register. The accounting machine first lists the distribution cards and then the payables card. (*See* Figure 15-25.) Internally, the machine adds the amounts in the distribution card(s), subtracts the payables card, and prints the difference below the total invoice amount. If zero is the answer, as it should be, a symbol is used to denote this in lieu of printing zeros. (2) The second aspect of control is the manual posting of the grand total of invoices to the accounts payable control sheet which when modified by the cash disbursements for the day form the new accounts payable control amount.

Step 5 uses the sorter to separate the distribution cards from the payables cards. The payables cards in step 6 on the collator are merged into the accounts payable due file in vendor order by due date. The distribution cards are merely filed with the other distribution cards until the month end procedures (Steps 11 through 16 below).

Payable Card

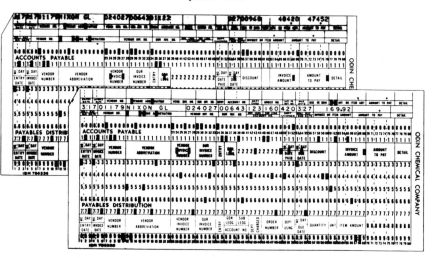

Courtesy of IBM Corporation

FIGURE 15-23.   Distribution Card

								ACCT. NO.	DEPT.			QUANTITY	ITEM AMOUNT	
ENTRY DATE	INV DATE	VENDOR	INVOICE NUMBER	VENDOR NUMBER	OUR VOUCHER NUMBER	ENTRY CODE		GEN. SUB	CHG.	ITEM NUMBER	DUE DATE	DISCOUNT •	INVOICE TOTAL •	NET PAYABLE
3/19	3/15	KESTON CASTINGS	42397	7604	46481	19	364-080		132	865	3/25	100	28.60	
3/19	3/15	KESTON CASTINGS	42397	7604	46481	19	364-410		132	1149⁸	3/25	1	32.97	
3/19	3/15	KESTON CASTINGS	42397	7604	46481	19	364-080		132	518	3/25	72	97.21	
3/19	3/15	KESTON CASTINGS	42397	7604	46481	19	211				3/25	3.18•5	158.78•5	155.60•
3/19	3/16	AMER REF PROD	12088	6620	46482	19	364-126		031	1242	3/26	50	675.95	
3/19	3/16	AMER REF PROD	12088	6620	46482	19	364-126		031	1633	3/26	50	195.15	
3/19	3/16	AMER REF PROD	12088	6620	46482	19	364-126		031	1040	3/26	10	310.52	
3/19	3/16	AMER REF PROD	12088	6620	46482	19	211				3/26	23.63•5	1,181.62•5	1,157.99•
3/19	3/15	OLONSON SUPPLY	8633	3642	46483	20	358-012		100		3/25	144	12.00	
3/19	3/15	OLONSON SUPPLY	8633	3642	46483	20	211				3/25	.24•5	12.00•5	11.76•
3/19	3/15	OLONSON SUPPLY	4290	7602	46484	27	358-012		100			12	3.00•	
3/19	3/15	OLONSON SUPPLY	4290	7602	46484	27	211					5	3.00•	3.00•
3/19	3/14	SUTLER MFG	55592	7731	46487	19	364-117		031	76428	3/24	48	12.38	
3/19	3/14	SUTLER MFG	55592	7731	46487	19	364-126		408	39117	3/24	144	53.05	
3/19	3/14	SUTLER MFG	55592	7731	46487	19	211				3/24	1.31•5	65.43•5	64.12•
3/19	3/15	CALHOUN & COLLS	18687	7755	46488	19	364-612		132	6677	3/25	50	32.77	
3/19	3/15	CALHOUN & COLLS	18687	7755	46488	19	364-525		391	10320	3/25	12	51.24	
3/19	3/15	CALHOUS & COLLS	18687	7755	46488	19	364-016		166	9117	3/25	1	27.25	
3/19	3/15	CALHOUN & COLLS	18687	7755	46488	27	358-525		391	10320		2	8.54•	
3/19	3/15	CALHOUN & COLLS	18687	7755	46488	19	211				3/25	2.05•5	102.72•5	100.67•
		CONTROL							5	62,106.47⊽✓		5 1,066.12•5	62,106.47•5	61,040.35

HENRY JOHN & CO.

DATE MAR 19 196-   DAILY INVOICE REGISTER   SHEET 4 OF 4

Courtesy of IBM Corporation

FIGURE 15-24.   Daily Invoice Register

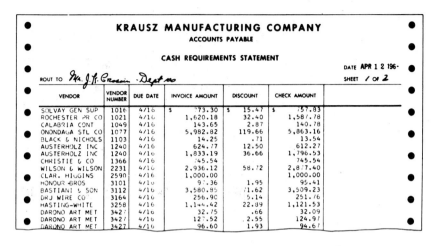

KRAUSZ MANUFACTURING COMPANY

ACCOUNTS PAYABLE

CASH REQUIREMENTS STATEMENT

DATE APR 1 2 196-

ROUT TO *Mr. J. K. Crossin · Dept no*

SHEET *1* OF *2*

VENDOR	VENDOR NUMBER	DUE DATE	INVOICE AMOUNT	DISCOUNT	CHECK AMOUNT
SOLVAY GEN SUP	1016	4/16	$ 773.30	$ 15.47	$ 757.83
ROCHESTER PR CO	1021	4/16	1,620.18	32.40	1,587.78
CALABRIA CONT	1049	4/16	143.65	2.87	140.78
ONONDAGA STL CO	1077	4/16	5,982.82	119.66	5,863.16
BLACK & NICHOLS	1103	4/16	14.25	.71	13.54
AUSTERHOLZ INC	1240	4/16	624.77	12.50	612.27
AUSTERHOLZ INC	1240	4/16	1,833.19	36.66	1,796.53
CHRISTIE & CO	1366	4/16	745.54		745.54
WILSON & WILSON	2231	4/16	2,936.12	58.72	2,877.40
CLAR. HIGGINS	2590	4/16	1,000.00		1,000.00
HONOUR BROS	3101	4/16	97.36	1.95	95.41
BASTIANI & SON	3112	4/16	3,580.85	71.62	3,509.23
DRJ WIRE CO	3164	4/16	256.90	5.14	251.76
HASTING-WHITE	3258	4/16	1,144.42	22.89	1,121.53
DARONO ART MET	3427	4/16	32.75	.66	32.09
DARONO ART MET	3427	4/16	127.52	2.55	124.97
DARONO ART MET	3427	4/16	96.60	1.93	94.67

Courtesy of IBM Corporation

FIGURE 15-25.   Cash Requirements Statement

The Cash Disbursement Procedure

There are three steps in the cash disbursement procedure: (1) the preparation of a cash requirements statement, (2) the preparation of checks and remittance advices, and (3) the preparation of a cash disbursements register.

THE PREPARATION OF A CASH REQUIREMENTS STATEMENT. Most companies prepare and remit checks to vendors only at certain times during the month. Prior to these days the treasurer needs to know the amounts to be disbursed each day. Shortly before the respective due date, payable cards of invoices that should be paid on this date are extracted from the payables due file and a cash requirement statement is run on the accounting machine (Step 7). (See Figure 15-26.)

THE PREPARATION OF CHECKS AND REMITTANCE ADVICES. Assuming that the treasurer approves the payables listed in step 7, the same accounts payable cards can be used to prepare the check. Vendor name and address cards are merged into the payables due and approved file in step 8. The vendor name and address cards can then be processed on the accounting machine to prepare the check and remittance advice. The accounting machine will detail the invoices being paid by number, accumulate the total amount being paid, and print it on the check. At this point a reproducer is usually attached to the accounting machine so that a summary card can be punched for each check written (Step 9). This summary card can be used for check reconciliation at a later date.

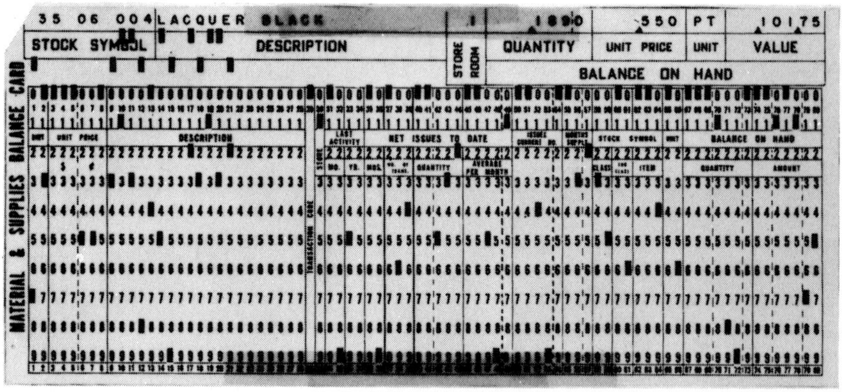

Courtesy of IBM Corporation

FIGURE 15-26.   Balance Forward Card

The cash disbursements register is prepared on the accounting machine in a second run (Step 10). The total of the cash disbursements is posted to the accounts payable control sheet as was the total of the invoice register.

After the checks and disbursements register has been prepared the accounts payable cards are processed by the reproducer which punches the payment date into the cards. (*See* Figure 15-23, columns 50, 51, and 52.) These cards are then merged by the collator into the paid invoice file which is kept in vendor order.

THE END OF THE MONTH PROCEDURES. At the month's end the distribution cards are sorted by account number from which a variety of reports and analyses can be prepared (Steps 11, 12, 13, and 14).

The remaining payable cards (unpaid) are sorted by customer number (Step 15) and a trial balance listed on the accounting machine (Step 16). The trial balance total should agree with the balance shown on the daily accounts payable control sheet for the last day of the month.

APPLICATION NO. 3

Inventory Control and Material Accounting

There are several specific ways in which punched card data processing can maintain perpetual inventory records. Out of these has been chosen the "balance forward method" of inventory control and material accounting. This method is used widely and can also furnish for examination a third punched card data processing application. Other specific procedures such as Unit Inventory Control, Inventory Control with Batch Billing, Automatic Reorder Systems, etc., are tailored to fit slightly different circumstances and management needs.

Basic Inputs

The balance forward method can best be described as a method which adheres to the following formula for each item in the inventory:

Opening balance + Receipts — Issues = Balance on Hand
Balance on Hand — Requirements + Units on Order = Units Available for Use

It is necessary, therefore, for two kinds of cards to be prepared: 1) a balance forward card (shown in Figure 15-27), and 2) a transaction card. (*See* Figure 15-24.) Note that the transaction card can be used for nine different transactions: 1) items on order, 2) receipts from vendors, 3) returns to vendors, 4) issues from stores, 5) returns to stores, 6) transfers in, 7) transfers out, 8) debit adjustment and 9) credit adjustment. Column 29, in the transaction card shown in Figure 15-24, is used to designate what kind of card it is being used for in specific instances. If the card in Figure 15-24 had a punch in the 4 position of column 29, the card would be for an issues from stores.

As the balance forward method is inaugurated, it is necessary to key punch a balance card for each item of inventory preferably from a physical inventory record. Subsequent to this initial operation, new balance forward cards will be produced in a summary punching operation described below. Transaction cards must be key punched and verified from appropriate source documents.

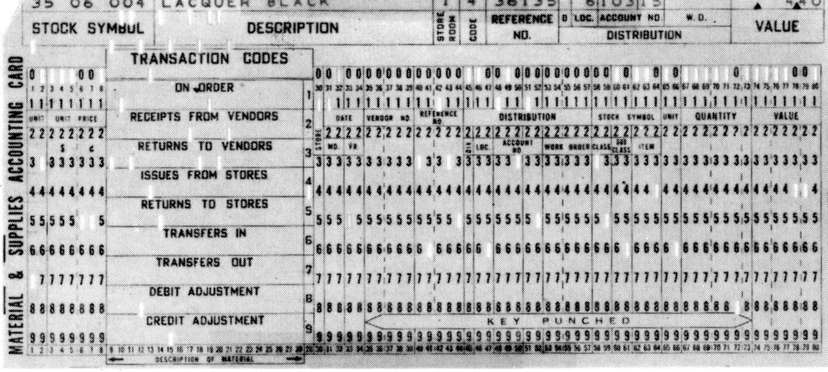

Courtesy of IBM Corporation

FIGURE 15-27. Transaction Card

The Processing Sequence

The flow chart in Figure 15-28 illustrates the processing after the balance cards and transaction cards have been prepared. The numbered steps on the chart are keyed to explanations below as in the previous application illustrations.

After the transaction cards for the period have been key punched and

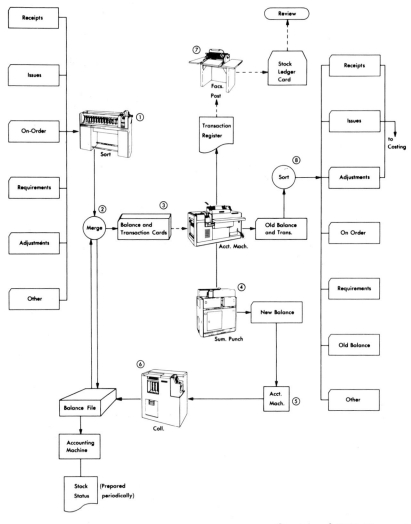

Courtesy of IBM Corporation

FIGURE 15-28. Processing Sequence

verified, the first operation (Step 1) is to sort these cards into ascending order by material class and stock number.

By means of the collator (Step 2) the sorted transaction cards are compared with the balance cards on file from the previous period's processing. The collator control panel is wired so that a merge and selection operation is performed. Those balance forward cards matching with transaction cards are merged with their respective transaction cards. The balance card is channelled into a pocket first and the transaction card(s) for this inventory number is filed on top of the balance cards. Balance cards for which there are no transaction cards are selected and filed in a separate pocket.

The next step (3) is to process the balance and transaction card file on an accounting machine which is connected to a reproducer. A transaction register is prepared on the accounting machine and a new balance card is punched by the reproducer.

For control purposes the new balance cards are checked for accuracy in step 5 by printing out the balance card information and permitting the accounting machine to do a zero balance check very similar to the check described in the payables application above.

After checking the accuracy of the new balance cards they are merged in step 6 with the balance cards which were selected in step 2. The balance card file is once more complete. From this file, stock status summary reports (Figure 15-29) can be prepared periodically on the accounting machine.

Step 7 is an auxiliary operation performed only when management is of the opinion that a stock ledger should be kept for each inventory item. If the transaction register prepared in step 3 were prepared on specially designed carbon backed paper, it is possible to post transactions to the stock ledger cards a line at a time using a transfer posting machine. Many firms are of the opinion that it is not necessary to maintain stock ledger cards. More frequent stock status summaries and other analyses are prepared in lieu of the stock ledger cards.

Finally, step 8, the transaction cards and old balance cards merged in step 2 are separated. The receipt, issues, and adjustment cards cannot be used in the material phase of cost accounting.

The foregoing example applications are but a sample of the myriad of ways the various punched card machines can be combined to process data for management. Although three different phases of processing accounting data were shown, all have a basic similarity. Note that a balance forward concept is present in all coupled with a merge and select operation. Systems analysts must familiarize themselves with the basic capabilities of the various machines so that when a procedure can be done effectively with punched card methods it will be recognized as such by the analyst. Wiring details can be worked out by a technician in the field.

Both punched cards and punched paper tape can be produced as a by-

STOCK STATUS REPORT

DETAIL

Code		Code	
0—BALANCE FWD		5—RETURNS TO STORES	
1—ON ORDER		6—TRANSFERS IN	
2—RECEIPTS FROM VENDORS		7—TRANSFERS OUT	
3—RETURNS TO VENDORS		8—DEBIT ADJUSTMENT	
4—ISSUES FROM STORES		9—CREDIT ADJUSTMENT	

STORE ROOM	DESCRIPTION	UNIT	REFERENCE NO.	TRANS. CODE	DATE	NET ISSUES			ON ORDER	BALANCE ON HAND		STOCK SYMBOL
						TO DATE	AVERAGE PER MONTH	CURRENT MONTH		MONTH'S SUPPLY	QUANTITY	
1	LACQUER BLACK	PT	361135	0	95	532	591		—	3.2	1890	35 06 004
1	LACQUER BLACK	PT	362436	4	05	8		80			800 —	
1	LACQUER BLACK	PT	362436	4	05	10		100			1000 —	
1	LACQUER BLACK	PT	363106	4	05	3		300			300 —	
1	LACQUER BLACK	PT	364051	4	05	14		1400			1400 —	
1	LACQUER BLACK	PT	364051	4	05	12		1200			1200 —	
1	LACQUER BLACK	PT	36491	4	05	584 ✻		520 ✻			1370 ✻	
1	LACQUER BRSHING WHITE	PT	121205	0	95	1015	1127	—		2.4	2760 —	35 06 005
1	LACQUER BRSHING WHITE	PT	361106	4	05	10		100	2000		100 —	
1	LACQUER BRSHING WHITE	PT	362016	4	05	25		250			250 —	
1	LACQUER BRSHING WHITE	PT	363391	4	05	20		200			200 —	
1	LACQUER BRSHING WHITE	PT	364381	4	05	15		150			150 —	
1	LACQUER BRSHING WHITE	PT	365902	4	05	32		320			320 —	
1	LACQUER BRSHING WHITE	PT	1512	5	05	1117 ✻		102 0 ✻	2000 0 ✻		1740 ✻	
1	LACQUER CLEAR	PT	118004	0	95	801	890		2000 0 ✻	.7	6100 —	35 06 00R
1	LACQUER CLEAR	PT	363081	2	05						2000 —	
1	LACQUER CLEAR	PT	363817	4	05	10		100			1500 —	
1	LACQUER CLEAR	PT	364071	4	05	15		150			300 —	
1	LACQUER CLEAR	PT	365101	4	05	3		300			370 —	
1	LACQUER CLEAR	PT	36541	7	05	37		370			1670 ✻	
1	LACQUER CLEAR	PT				895 ✻		940 ✻				

FIGURE 15-29. Stock Status Report

product from the posting operations of a general-purpose accounting machine and serve the second level of mechanization as transitional devices.

Edge-notched Cards

Edge-notched cards, such as the one shown in Figure 15-30, are most often used in transition periods between the first three levels of mechanization. In areas such as sales analysis, inventory, payroll, and labor distribution, certain data needed for managerial purposes must be analyzed more extensively than is possible at the present level of mechanization. Such data can be recorded on individual edge-notched cards, notched appropriately and arranged in the desired order for the analysis with the aid of a sorting needle (*see* Figure 15-30) much more rapidly than with the use of a worksheet and a pencil. For example, assume that a card is prepared for each item sold by company salesmen and that the holes at the top and other sides of the card are notched to indicate units sold, price, extension of total, salesman number, product number, and sales territory number. It would be possible to arrange these sales data in several ways—by product, by salesman, by territory, or by selected combinations, such as by product-by salesman, or by salesman-by product. Thus, a company is able to obtain more elaborate sales analyses without a substantial new investment in more elaborate equipment and

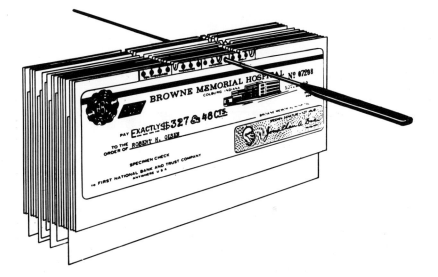

Courtesy of Royal McBee Corporation

FIGURE 15-30.   Edge-Notched Card

revised procedures which could not be justified by the sale information needs alone.

CODING. Data are coded on any or all four sides of an edge-notched card. The data must be coded to take the minimum space on the card and so that cards can be sorted with the aid of a needle with the minimum number of steps. Three types of coding, illustrated in Figure 15-31, are direct, numeric, and alphabetic.

Direct coding is notching data in a card according to a condition that exists. For example, in the illustration of direct coding in Figure 15-31 there are three salesmen, any one of whom might make a given sale. The card is notched for salesman two. A condition that exists has been notched direct, namely a sale made by salesman two.

Numeric coding has several advantages over direct coding when more than four possibilities for coding exist. In such situations the number of notching positions on the card may be reduced as are the number of sorts required in processing. Any digit from 0 through 9 can be coded into one field of the card with four notching positions designated 7-4-2-1 respectively. The illustration of numeric coding shown in Figure 15-31 has the number 4,467 notched into the card. Four notching positions are used for each of the four digits. In instances where 0 is to be coded, no position is notched.

When sorting a number of cards with a numeric code into numerical sequence, the needle is first inserted in the 1 position for the tens digit and lifted upward along with the cards not notched in that position. Cards with

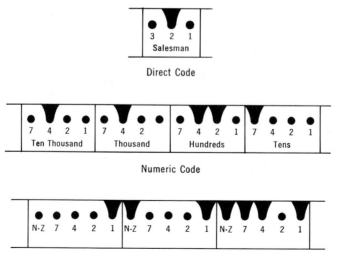

Direct Code

Numeric Code

Alphebetical Code

FIGURE 15-31. Coding

the 1 position notched will drop down and are placed at the back of the group of cards. This operation is repeated in positions 2, 4, and 7 for the tens digit. The operations are repeated again for the hundreds digit, etc. When completed the cards are in correct numerical sequence.

For *alphabetic coding*, a fifth N-Z notching position is added to enable an adequate number of combinations to accommodate the 26 letters of the alphabet. A through M are coded by using the regular positions according to the numeric code for 1 through 13. Thus a field notched with 1 is coded with the letter A. N through Z are coded by notching the fifth N-Z position along with the appropriate 1 through 13 code. Thus a field notched with both N-Z and 1 is coded with the letter N. The illustration of alphabetic coding in Figure 15-31 has been notched with the word *any*. Alphabetic data are seldom coded in edge-notched card procedures.

The corner of an edge-notched card is often clipped so that anyone working with the cards can see at a glance whether the cards are right side up. When the corner of cards used in a procedure are clipped, a header card or divider for different types of cards can be inserted that does not have the corner clipped, providing an excellent signal.

KEYSORT TABULATING PUNCH. In certain situations, edge-notched cards can be used in conjunction with a special keysort tabulating punch to improve processing efficiency. Such a system introduces additional punched holes in a special field of the card and does not utilize the notches on the edge of the card for tabulating. The additional tabulation feature would give a procedure some of the properties of a large punched card operation but at less cost. One model keysort tabulating punch can do the following

1. Automatically code-punch quantities and amounts in edge-notched cards—simultaneously accumulating and printing.
2. Read amounts punched in cards—automatically adding, subtracting, and printing.
3. Reproduce-punch cards from originals.
4. Automatically punch net accumulations in summary cards.
5. Provide tape for immediate visual verification of automatic code punching.

SUMMARY

In order to be able to achieve the level of competence necessary for the systems analyst, first, the basic philosophy of punched card accounting should be understood; second, the basic functions of the most commonly used punched card machines, such as those described in this chapter, should be learned; and third, the way in which a group of these machines can be utilized to accomplish the data processing operation of a particular procedure or group of procedures must become apparent from an understanding of the machine functions and the basic data processing operations. It is not necessary to be able to wire panels extensively or to be familiar with each model of every machine made by all manufacturers.

QUESTIONS, PROBLEMS, AND CASES

1. What special advantages does the punched card method afford for processing sales data?

2. Identify the differences between a mark-sensed card and a Port-A-Punch card.

3. Under what conditions might a punched card installation prove uneconomical?

4. What are the basic or essential machines in a punched card installation?

5. Distinguish between the punching operation and the verifying operation.

6. Describe the sorting operation as done by punched card machines. What is meant by "block sorting"?

7. Distinguish between gang punching and summary punching. Cite several examples of systems situations in which the summary punching feature of a tabulating machine would be important in a punched card system.

8. Describe the punched card equipment that would be appropriate for a small wholesale auto parts business with volume adequate to justify only a minimum installation.

9. A series of punched cards are in a deck to be sorted in ascending sequence. The cards are time cards in which the employee number has been punched. The cards are to be arranged in sequence by employee number prior to the preparation of the payroll. The employee number in cards in the deck are as shown in the sequence below:

(1)	364	(8)	147	(15)	025	(21)	046
(2)	260	(9)	001	(16)	416	(22)	114
(3)	149	(10)	188	(17)	721	(23)	167
(4)	333	(11)	254	(18)	543	(24)	010
(5)	222	(12)	218	(19)	609	(25)	131
(6)	039	(13)	162	(20)	811	(26)	181
(7)	040	(14)	155	(21)	012	(27)	368

    a. List the card in the sequence in which they would be arranged after one pass through the sorter. Two passes. Three passes.

    b. What procedures should be followed by the machine operator to be certain that there are no cards missing when the machine tabulation of the cards is accomplished?

    c. How might the punched card system for payroll utilize the time cards sorted above?

    d. What purpose might the summary punch serve in the payroll system?

10. The Milton Wholesale Drug Company handles several thousand items of merchandise with the inventory control system according to a "tub" file plan. When items are received in the inventory, they are made up into standard size packages and a separate inventory card punched for each standard unit of stock. These cards, each representing a standard unit of merchandise, are placed in a tub file representing the inventory in the warehouse. Inventory cards are end-printed with the merchandise code number.

    Design a system in which the inventory control card of the Milton Wholesale Drug Company will be used. Indicate how the orders will be filled, the customer billed, sales statistics prepared, accounts receivable records maintained, and the method of controlling inventory.

				Invoice No. 8390
The Adams Company Pleasant View, New York				Date Shipped
Customers Order	Date Entered	Salesman	Our Order	Feb. 12, 1968
				Prepaid or Collect
1599	2/10/68	38	7910	Collect
				How Shipped
Sold To: Smith & Co. Pittsburgh, Pa.				Erie Car 458
Shipped To: Same				
Shipping Instructions: Erie, Collect		Terms 2/10, N/30		

Quantity Ordered	Description	Price	Balance on Order	Shipped	Amount
200	10-Gal Carboys Amm. Sulph.	23.00	——	200	4,600.00
200	10-Gal Carboys Sod. Nit.	11.00	——	200	2,200.00
					6,800.00

11. The Adams Company wishes to utilize punched cards in sales analysis and in machine preparation of the sales journal. A typical sales invoice for the company is shown above. The largest quantity of any one commodity ever ordered amounted to 2,500 units; no partial units are sold. The highest price

per unit is $36.75. Each card should contain only a single kind of merchandise; therefore, several cards may be required for each invoice, but each card should contain full identification information.

    a. Identify the data to be punched into each of the 80-columns of an IBM punched card for this application.

    b. Do you consider this a good procedure? Discuss.

12. The R. O. Kamm Company, one of your clients, has employed you to design an edge-notched card to be used for sales analysis. Your investigation indicates that there are ten major product lines; 80 to 1,500 items within each product line; 30 salesmen; five geographical regions and distribution centers; and 5,000 customers, some of whom are subject to special quantity discounts and some who are not.

    a. Design or recommend the design of a card to provide for the necessary notching and sorting. Be certain to indicate the data to be written on the card.

    b. What is a major difficulty with the procedure and how might this be overcome?

13. The Witt Company is engaged in manufacturing. Certain features of its operations method are described below. You are to consider the procedure described and point out the existing deficiencies, if any, in internal control, including an explanation of the errors of manipulations which might occur in view of each weakness and your recommendations as to changes in procedure which could be made to correct the weakness.

    Time cards of employees are sent to a tabulating machine department which prepares punched cards for use in the preparation of payrolls, payroll checks, and labor cost distribution records. The payroll checks are compared with the payrolls and signed by an official of the company who returns them to the supervisor of the tabulating department for distribution to the employees. (Adapted AICPA Examination)

14. In punched card data processing, what is the most important operation? Why?

15. a. Design a procedural flow chart for one of the applications listed below:

    1. Accounts receivable.

    2. Accounts payable.

    3. Perpetual inventory.

    4. Payroll.

    b. Design a systems flow chart for the applications selected in step a., above, utilizing punched card equipment.

CHAPTER 16

Computer Concepts

INTRODUCTION

IN CHAPTER 15, FUNDAMENTAL CONCEPTS OF PUNCHED CARD DATA PROCESS-ing were discussed. The point was developed that if facts concerning a particular business could be reduced to their lowest possible denominator and represented on a uniform document, machines could be used to classify, calculate, and summarize data, and print results of the other processing activities. It is necessary, however, to use several different machines to accomplish various data recording and processing operations. Speed of processing is necessarily limited to the speeds of the machines and to the time needed to transfer cards from machine to machine. Although processing speeds were rapid compared to multiple-purpose accounting machines, the volume of data to be processed caused a need for even greater processing speeds. In addition to speed, the limited logical ability present in punched card processing machines, such as recognizing and printing credit balances or comparing established minimum levels of inventory with newly computed inventory balances, spawned a desire to have even greater logical ability and self-directive power in data processing equipment. Such a need has been fulfilled with the development of the electronic computer.

The Electronic Computer

Simply stated, an electronic computer is a machine which is capable of performing a long series of data processing operations under the control of an internal set of directions at speeds approaching the speed of light. In addition, the electronic computer is capable of making certain logical decisions based on simple rules set up by the individual who determined the computer directions (instructions). For example, in the area of payroll preparation, it is possible for the computer, as it is calculating the gross and net pay of an employee, to determine how much, if any, should be deducted for social security and other taxes.

Computer System Equipment

Figure 16-1 is a photograph of an IBM 360-30 card system. There are three pieces of equipment in this picture essential to an electronic computer system. In other computer systems, the specific pieces of equipment may look different or there may be several pieces of each kind in the system, but in every electronic computer system there must be provision for three essential types of equipment:

1. *Input Unit.* Some means by which data can be read or put into the processing mechanism.
2. *Central Processing Unit.* This consists of:
   a. Electronic storage—where data can be placed in coded form awaiting processing.

Courtesy of IBM Corporation

FIGURE 16-1.   IBM System/360 Model 30

    b. Arithmetic area—capable of performing the four arithmetic processes of addition, subtraction, multiplication, and division and certain logical operations.

    c. A control mechanism—that part of the processing unit which determines the flow and kind of activities to be performed on the data.

3. *Output Unit.* Some means by which the coded data which has been processed can be decoded and made intelligible to interested users.

COMPUTER MATHEMATICS

In sections below, a more detailed explanation will be given of various kinds of computer equipment; but first consider the mathematics system which permits calculations to be made so rapidly. In order to understand computer mathematics the reader must realize that there is nothing sacred about the decimal numbering system. Mathematicians, for ages, have used numbering systems other than decimal, but for the most part, exercises of this sort were restricted to trained mathematicians. The system of counting and performing the four mathematical processes is similar regardless of the number base used.

In the decimal system, there are ten symbols used, 0-9. The basic rule for counting can be stated as follows: After a count has been made from 0-9, to count higher it is necessary to set the symbol in the rightmost column to zero, move one place to the left and increase that symbol by one. For example:

```
01
02
03
04
05
06
07
08
09  (to go higher, the 9 is set back to 0 and
10   the 0 is advanced to 1)
```

When the count has reached 19, the 9 is set back to 0 and the 1 is increased to 2 to give us the number 20. When the count reaches 99, both places are set to 0 and the next place to the left is increased to 1 giving us the number 100. In effect, as we move to the left in this system, we are increasing our number by a power of ten. Each digit in a number can be multiplied by its corresponding place value, and the sum of these products equals the number that we want to represent. The place values in the decimal system are:

10^n	. . . . .	10^4	10^3	10^2	10^1	10^0
Place value		10000	1000	100	10	1

Another way of looking at the number 6483 would be to multiply each digit by its place value and sum—

$$
\begin{aligned}
3 \times 1 &= 3 \\
8 \times 10 &= 80 \\
4 \times 100 &= 400 \\
6 \times 1000 &= 6000 \\
\hline
&\ \ 6483
\end{aligned}
$$

Utilizing the same logic, any number of symbols or number base can be used for calculation purposes.

The *binary system* is a system of counting which is based on two symbols, zero (0) and one (1). Following the same rule for counting as described for the decimal system, the following schedule shows the binary system's symbol combinations which are equivalent to the decimal numbers zero through ten.

Decimal	Binary
0	0
1	1
2	10
3	11
4	100
5	101
6	110
7	111
8	1000
9	1001
10	1010

The binary system, as does the decimal system, utilizes the concept of place value. In the binary system, each digit position is a power of two (2). The binary place values from right to left are:

2^n	2^6	2^5	2^4	2^3	2^2	2^1	2^0
Place value decimal equivalent	64	32	16	8	4	2	1

The binary number 1011001 can be easily converted to its decimal equivalent by multiplying the symbol in each binary place by its corresponding place value. Starting with the rightmost symbol in the binary number, the decimal equivalent can be computed in the following way:

$$
\begin{aligned}
\text{Rightmost} \quad 1 \times 1 &= 1 \\
0 \times 2 &= 0 \\
0 \times 4 &= 0 \\
1 \times 8 &= 8 \\
1 \times 16 &= 16 \\
0 \times 32 &= 0 \\
\text{Leftmost} \quad 1 \times 64 &= 64 \\
\hline
\text{Decimal} \quad 89 &= 1011001 \text{ in binary}
\end{aligned}
$$

Electronic computers perform mathematical calculations in binary because successive electronic circuits can be used to perform mathematical calculations instead of mechanical wheels and gears as is the case in the familiar desk calculator. Since an electronic circuit can be in the *off* state representing a binary zero and in an *on* state representing a binary one, the following two binary numbers would be added in a computer as shown. Assume that each place in the binary numbers are electronic circuits that are in the off state if a zero is present and in the on state if a one is present:

Decimal	Binary
	c cc
89	1011001
90	1011010
179	10110011

c denotes a carry of one (1)

If the decimal system were used in an electronic computer, it would be necessary to have ten circuits for each decimal digit. It could be done, but calculation speeds would not be as great as with a binary system.

Some computer manufacturers utilize a *binary coded* system which is a combination of the binary system and the decimal system. One of the most common binary coded systems is the 8421 system. It works in this way. Each decimal digit is represented by four binary circuits. The addition problem worked above in binary would be done in binary coded decimal as follows:

Decimal	Binary Coded Decimal			
89	0000	1000	1001	
90	0000	1001	0000	
	0000	10001	1001	
	+0001	− 1010		correction factor
179	0001	0111	1001	
	1	7	9	

Extra circuitry is needed for a binary coded system because certain corrections must be made to the binary additions since each group of four binary circuits can represent only a decimal digit ranging from 0-9. In the example above, when binary coded eight (8) was added to binary coded nine (9), the sum of 17 was formed; but according to this scheme of a binary coded decimal system no binary coded number can be larger than nine (9). Therefore, it was necessary to subtract binary 10 from 17 in the second binary coded decimal position and add one (1) to the next leftmost position.

It is not essential for systems analysts to master the binary system or some coded form of binary. It is important to understand that all forms of mathematical calculation can be performed in a number system based on two symbols as well as in our familiar ten symbol system and to understand that a two based number system is very efficient to use in electronic computers. For the most part, only technicians such as computer programmers will need to concern themselves with the intricacies of binary number systems.

Data Representation—Input/Output Devices

Since a computer manipulates data in some form of binary code or number system, data which are to be processed by the computer must be introduced into the computer system in some sort of compatible code.

DATA RECORDING MEDIA. As is the case in punched card processing systems, whenever data are to be processed by machine some specially coded media must be used which the machine can read (interpret) and process the data thereon. Punched cards, punched paper tape, magnetic tape, and regular alphabetic and numeric characters printed in magnetic ink are the most common media in or on which data are represented so that the data can be efficiently introduced into computer systems for processing.

The code on a *punched card* in an electronic computer system is often no different than the code used in a strict punched card processing system. In some computer systems, data in the binary code must be punched on the card in lieu of the standard IBM (Hollerith) code as shown in Figure 15-1. Figure 16-2 illustrates how a standard 80 column card can be used to represent binary data. Although no punches have been made in the card, a no punch would represent a zero (0) and the existence of a punch would represent a one (1). The data are arranged in serial fashion from the left to the right of the card. The card in Figure 16-2 is compatible with several of the IBM computers. The data are punched into data segments or words which are 36 binary digits (bits) long. Using the 12 horizontal rows it would be possible to punch 24 thirty-six bit words into a single card.

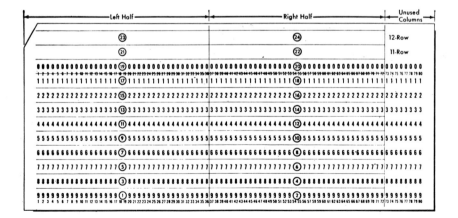

Courtesy of IBM Corporation

FIGURE 16-2. Card Used to Represent Binary Data

The *input and output devices* utilized to transmit data on punched cards to and from the computer are card readers and card punches. The machine on the left in Figure 16-1 is an IBM 360-30 model 2520 card read punch and is capable of both input and output function.

Punched paper tape utilizes the same basic principles for representing data as are used to represent data on punched cards. Each vertical column on a punched card utilizing the standard Hollerith code represents a single alphabetic, numeric, or special character. On punched paper tape, vertical columns are also used to represent a character of data. The difference between the two is the code used to represent characters and the fact that a punched card holds a maximum of 80-90 characters. The number of characters that can be punched in tandem on paper tape is limited only by the size of the feed or take-up spools on the tape reading or punching devices. Two common paper tape coding schemes are illustrated in Figure 16-3. You will note in the five channel tape that a shift character must be used prior to all alphabetic or numeric data. The tape reading devices must sense the shift character before interpreting whether a single punch in the first row from the top is supposed to be read as an "E" or as a "3." Such shifting is not necessary when an eight channel tape is used because a different combination of holes can be used for each character whether alphabetic or numeric.

Paper tape punches are the devices which create the paper tape so that the data thereon can be transmitted to the computer for processing. Tape punches also accept information processed from a computer and punch this information into the paper tape. *Paper tape readers* are the devices which examine the punching configurations on the paper tape and transmit this data to the computer. The examination of the holes in the tape is usually done photoelectrically instead of electromechanically as is often the case with the reading of punched cards. The reader will recall that punched card equipment utilize brushes which in effect feel the holes and make appropriate electrical contact. Figure 16-4 shows a paper tape reader.

A third media on which data are represented in computer systems is *magnetic tape*. This tape is not very different from the tape that is used in audio tape recording equipment. Characters are represented on the tape in vertical columns in the same way data are punched into paper tape. Magnetic tape is usually one-half inch to one inch wide and comes in reels up to 2500 feet long. Without doubt, magnetic tape is the most used medium to transmit data to and from a computer. The reason, of course, is speed. Data can be read into a computer system on magnetic tape at speeds exceeding 350,000 characters per second. This is as many characters as are contained in over 4300 punched cards. Figure 16-5 illustrates the very common seven track code used to represent data on magnetic tape. Six horizontal rows are used to represent up to 64 alphabetic, numeric, and special characters. The seventh horizontal row is used for check or accuracy purposes. For example, in the segment of tape shown in Figure 16-5, the character "A" is represented by a

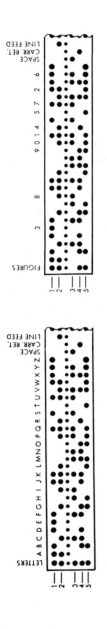

Five Channel Code

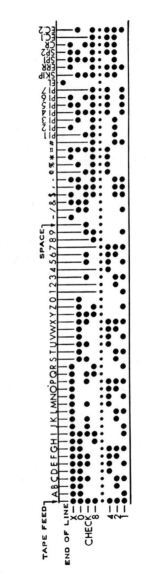

Eight Channel Code

FIGURE 16-3.   Five Channel and Eight Channel Codes

Courtesy of IBM Corporation

FIGURE 16-4. Paper Tape Recorder

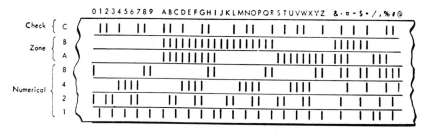

Magnetic Tape

Courtesy of IBM Corporation

FIGURE 16-5. Seven Channel Code

magnetic spot in the check row and in rows A, B, and 1. On the other hand, "C" is represented by spots in rows A, B, 4, and 1, but no spot is contained in the check row. To be read correctly into the computer, each character must contain an even number of spots in its respective vertical column. Therefore, the check row is used whenever it is needed to bring the complement of spots in a particular column up to an even number. Such a system of parity checks permits the tape reader to count the spots in each vertical column and to reject any character read from the tape that does not have an even spot or bit count. This is merely one step to assure that the data being read into the computer for processing are being read accurately. There are other coding

Courtesy of IBM Corporation

FIGURE 16-6. Magnetic Tape Unit

schemes for magnetic tape but all of them use the check-channel principal. Some manufacturers prefer "odd" parity checking as opposed to the "even" method illustrated.

Magnetic tape drives as the one shown in Figure 16-6 are the mechanisms used to read the data from the tape to the computer and to receive information or data from the computer and write it in coded form on the tape.

Still another method representing data for machine processing is the use of *magnetic ink* on standard paper. The magnetic ink characters are capable of being read by both men and machines. This mode of data representation is most commonly used in bank data processing since this industry can, to a large extent, regulate the media used in the industry for data processing purposes. Figure 16-7 shows a check which has been imprinted with magnetic ink characters at the bottom of the check. When a check of this sort is processed in a reader sorter (similar to the one pictured in Figure 16-8) the check passes under one reading head to receive a magnetic charge then passes under a second reading head to be interpreted and passed down the machine to rest in its appropriate pocket. Other machines can interpret the magnetic ink characters on the check for purposes of clearing the check to another bank or to automatically modify the account of the drawer of the check. Major computer manufacturers build special magnetic ink reading and writing devices which are used with the central processing unit of a computer as a special system or in conjunction with computer systems using other processing media as well.

Optical scanning equipment has been developed in recent years which permits regular numeric and alphabetic data as people read it to be processed. In addition to reading letters and numbers, most scanners can recognize cer-

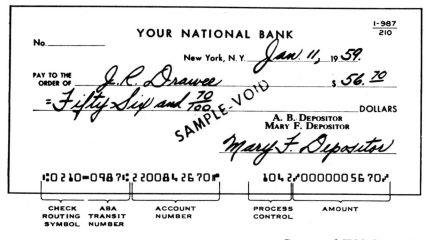

Courtesy of IBM Corporation

FIGURE 16-7.   Check with Magnetic Ink Characters

Courtesy of IBM Corporation

FIGURE 16-8. Magnetic Character Reader

tain pen or pencil marks on a document. For example, Figure 16-9 shows a municipal water works bill. All of the data, such as the account number, gross amount, net amount, etc., can be read by the scanner. When this bill is returned from the customer with a check for the proper amount, it can be used to machine post the cash credit to the customer's account. If a partial payment were received, the cashier would merely complete the left side on

Enter partial payment below	MUNICIPAL WATER WORKS			
o o o o o	Account Number	Gross Amount	Net Amount	Last Day To Pay Net
1 1 1 1 1				
2 2 2 2 2	RL45332	56 01	45 98	4 31 62
3 3 3 3 3				
4 4 4 4 4	DISCOUNT TERMS : 10 DAYS			
5 5 5 5 5	Present Reading	Previous Reading	Consumption Gals.	E D JONES
6 6 6 6 6				745 CHESTNUT ST
7 7 7 7 7	3255886	2369014	897	ANYTOWN USA
8 8 8 8 8				
9 9 9 9 9	PLEASE RETURN THIS WITH YOUR PAYMENT			

Courtesy of IBM Corporation

FIGURE 16-9. Optically Readable Characters

the bill for the amount received. When the bill is read by the scanner, only the amount recorded on the left of the bill would be recorded as a credit to the customer's account. Most scanners require that the data to be read be in a precise format and would reject manual script. However, extensive research and testing are being carried out in attempts to perfect devices which can read accurately any type of manual script.

Storage Devices

Any media on which data are represented can be called storage devices. But in this section a storage device will be restricted to mean only those devices which are connected to the central processing unit of a computer system and are considered to be the computer's central storage units.

Such storage devices are usually classified into primary and secondary units. A primary storage unit is the unit into which data are read from input and are directly available to the control and arithmetic units of the computer. Data in a secondary storage unit is available to the processing unit only through a primary storage unit. It is not possible to read data in or write data out of a secondary storage unit via an input/output device. Figure 16-10 illustrates the flow of data through a computer system and shows the relationship between primary and secondary storage.

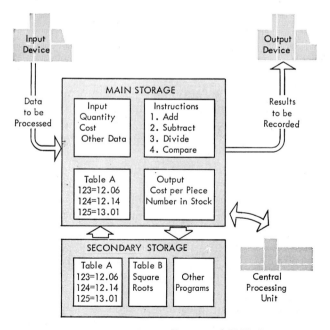

Courtesy of IBM Corporation

FIGURE 16-10.   Flow of Data Through a Computer System

Data are arranged in storage devices in a manner which can be compared to houses on a block. Each house on a block has a house number; these house numbers are assigned in some sort of orderly way, and there are people in these houses who are contacted by other people from time to time. Every electronic storage device is composed of units (houses); each unit has a location number (address); and each unit holds one or more pieces of datum (people). The express nature of the piece of datum at each address varies according to particular storage devices, but it can range from a single binary digit (bit) to a record consisting of several pieces of data.

A feature which is common to all electronic storage devices is often called "destructible read in, nondestructible read out." This means that data can be transferred from the storage device to the control unit, to the arithmetic unit, or to an output unit without altering the data in the storage unit. For example, if the number one was stored at storage location 4022, it could be transferred to the arithmetic unit but would still be available in location 4022 and could be retransferred to the arithmetic unit or to output at some later time. The "destructible read in" portion of the feature means that data read into a storage location where another piece of data is stored destroys the old data. The new piece of data, in effect, moves into the house and evicts the old data.

MAGNETIC CORES. A magnetic core is a doughnut shaped ring of ferromagnetic material only a few hundredths of an inch in diameter. Since these cores can be magnetized or demagnetized in a few millionths of a second, they are natural storage devices for use in an electronic computer. Their on-off states fit in well with the binary arithmetic performed by the computers.

In order to store coded data in magnetic cores, at least three very small wires must be threaded through each core. These cores are arranged in horizontal planes similar to the diagram in Figure 16-11. Note that two wires pass through each core perpendicular to each other. These are the *current wires*. Neither current wire is capable of magnetizing a core alone nor of demagnetizing a core alone. The diagram in Figure 16-11 illustrates that the core in the third core line from the right, five cores from the top can be magnetized only when current is passed through the third current wire from the right and the fifth current wire from the top. Any other combination of current wires would not have magnetized the core spotlighted in the plane.

The diagram in Figure 16-12 illustrates the positioning of seven-core planes and the scheme used to store data. Data can be stored in a magnetic core unit in strict binary code. However, the diagram shows a binary coded decimal arrangement which permits alphabetic and other special characters as well as decimal numbers to be stored in the cores. The seven-core planes can be considered as seven channels similar to seven channel magnetic tape. The top plane is the check plane and the others in descending order are the B, A, 8, 4, 2, 1 planes. To represent the letter A (as shown in Figure 16-12)

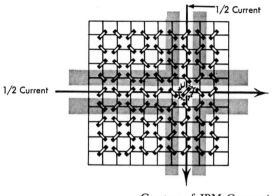

Courtesy of IBM Corporation

FIGURE 16-11. Magnetic Core Plane Being Magnetized

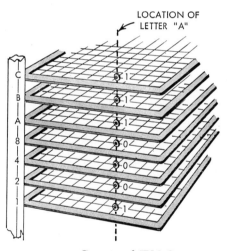

Courtesy of IBM Corporation

FIGURE 16-12. Positioning of Seven-Core Plane

the same relative core in the top three and the bottom planes would be positive and the other three cores would be negative. (*See* Figure 16-5).

A standard IBM core plane consists of 128 cores wide and 128 cores long, or a total of 16,384 cores in each plane. In seven-core planes arranged as in Figure 16-12, it would be possible to store 16,384 decimal digits, alphabetic, or special characters. Seventy- (70) core planes would hold 163,840 characters, Figure 16-13 is a schematic drawing of a unit comprised of seventy- (70) core planes.

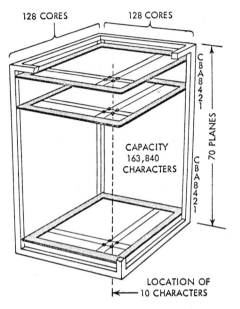

Courtesy of IBM Corporation

FIGURE 16-13.   Seventy-Core Planes Unit

Magnetic Drum. Another type of internal storage device is the magnetic drum. This device is a metal cylinder which is coated with a magnetic substance. The cylinder revolves at a high rate of speed under stationary read-and-write heads. The function of the write head is to magnetize the surface of the drum for the purpose of storing data in coded form thereon. The read head can sense the coded data which has been written on the drum and transfer it to some other part of the computer or, in some instance, to an output unit.

Some magnetic drums use the same binary coded decimal scheme as is used on magnetic tape and magnetic cores. For example, Figure 16-14 is a schematic drawing of a portion of a typical magnetic drum. Note that the drum is divided into channels and each channel contains seven tracks. This permits the storing of binary coded data along each channel on the surface of the drum. Depending on the coding system used, each character of coded data or groups of characters called words has a specific address on the drum. When the computer is instructed to utilize a piece of data, it needs to know only the address of the piece of data on the drum in order to obtain it.

Access time is the time needed between the call for a piece of data from storage and the readiness of this datum for use by the computer. Since the data stored on a magnetic drum cannot be read from or written into a specific

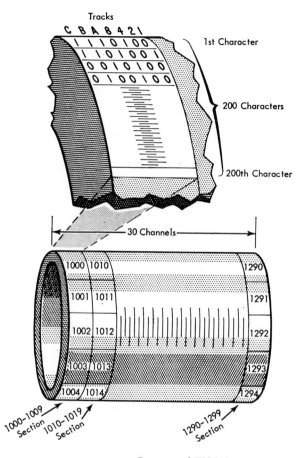

Courtesy of IBM Corporation

FIGURE 16-14.   Magnetic Drum

location until that location passes under the read-or-write heads, the actual reading or writing must often wait for the proper positioning of the drum. This feature causes the access time in a magnetic drum to be slower than the access time in a magnetic core unit which is limited only by the time necessary for current to pass through wires. Except on a few small computers, drum storage is usually auxiliary or secondary storage.

MAGNETIC DISKS. Utilizing the same principle as is used in phonograph records to store sounds, computer manufacturers found that a magnetic disk could be used to store digital and alphabetic data as well. One of the unique features of magnetic disks is the random availability of the data on the disks. Data are stored on each side of each disk in concentric circles divided into

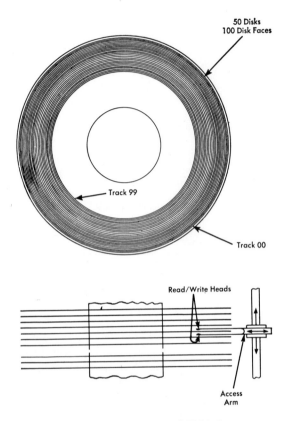

Courtesy of IBM Corporation

FIGURE 16-15. Magnetic Disk

areas and tracks. There can be a read-and-write head for each track, two or three heads which service a group of disks, or a single head assigned to service all the disks. The more read-and-write heads, of course, the less access time whether data is being sought serially or at random. To give the reader an idea of the size and shape of magnetic disks, the IBM 1301 disk storage contains one or two modules of disk assemblies. Each module consists of 25 magnetically coated disks, two feet in diameter, and an access mechanism with 24 access arms. Each disk surface has 250 tracks. The disks are mounted one-half inch apart on the rotating vertical shaft. Figure 16-15 is a schematic drawing of this unit.

CRAM Storage. This type of storage was developed by the National Cash Register Company primarily to serve as auxiliary storage capable of a high degree of random access. CRAM storage utilizes 256 cards fourteen

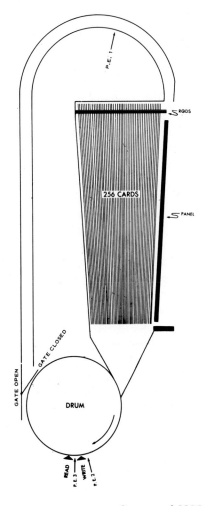

Courtesy of NCR

FIGURE 16-16. CRAM Unit

inches long and 3¼ inches wide which are placed when needed around a revolving drum to be read from or written on. Data can be placed in magnetic coded form on these cards which hang in a deck over a small revolving drum. When a specific card is called for by the control unit of the computer, it drops from the deck and is wrapped around the drum. When that particular card is no longer needed, it is taken from the drum and rehung with the other cards in the deck. Figure 16-16 is a schematic drawing of a CRAM unit.

ARITHMETIC AND CONTROL UNITS

Just as the names arithmetic and control imply, these parts of a computer system are the circuits which perform the arithmetic functions and control the flow and processing steps performed on data passing through the computer. As shown in Figure 16-1 the arithmetic and control units are part of the unit along with core storage. In other models of computers, the primary storage unit, the arithmetic unit, and the control unit may be separate pieces of hardware. Nevertheless, whether separate units or not, the functions these units perform in a data processing system are the same.

FUNCTIONAL UNITS. There are three functional parts which make up the arithmetic and control units: (1) registers, (2) counters, and (3) adders. "A *register* is a device capable of receiving *data or information*, holding it, and transferring it as directed by the control circuits. The electronic components used may be magnetic cores, transistors, or vacuum tubes.

"Registers are named according to their function: an accumulator accumulates results; a multiplier-quotient holds either multiplier or quotient; a storage register contains *data or information* taken from or being sent to storage; an address register holds the address of a storage location or device; and an instruction register contains the instruction being executed."[1]

Counters are similar to registers and perform many of the same functions. Unlike a register, a counter handles only numeric data and the content of the counter can be altered directly. This particular bit of circuitry is called a counter because it performs primarily a counting function. For example, if it were necessary to perform a particular computer instruction a certain number of times before moving on to the next instruction, a counter would be used to keep track of the number of times the instruction was carried out. Because of the close relationship between counters and registers, counters are often referred to as indexing registers.

"*Adders* are bits of circuitry which do the binary arithmetic common to most computers."[2] To illustrate how adders function, consider Figure 16-17. (Adders may function in series as is the case in Figure 16-17 or in parallel.) Note that the addition begins with the low order digit of both numbers to be added; a sum of these two digits is formed and placed in the third register; and a carry is forwarded for use when the next two digits of the numbers are added. This is called serial addition. Actually, one adder could be used to perform serial addition.

---

[1] General Information Manual Introduction to IBM Data Processing, International Business Machine Corp., p. 37. Italics have been added.

[2] *Ibid.*

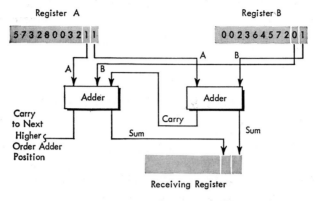

Courtesy of IBM Corporation

FIGURE 16-17.   Functioning of Adder

It is possible to speed up the addition process by performing parallel addition. In order to add numbers this way, it is necessary to have an adder for each digit position in the numbers to be added. A ten digit number would require ten adders. In parallel addition, the sum of each digit in the numbers to be added is formed simultaneously instead of singly as is the case in serial addition.

WORD LENGTHS. The mathematical calculations and other functions that can be performed by the arithmetic unit of a computer cannot be performed on any data regardless of their magnitude. Some of the early computers could handle only fixed numbers of digits or characters. This unit of data is called a word, and computers which could only process fixed units of data were called fixed word length computers. As the state of the art progressed, computers were developed which could store and process data which were not in a fixed length format. Logically, such computers were called variable word length computers. Practically, machines which can process and store data in variable lengths do have some finite limits that must be observed. For example, the IBM 360-30 computer is a variable word length computer, but it can develop a sum only as large as the number of digits in the addend.

The variable word length format is more significant in the storage of data. In the now obsolete IBM 650, data had to be stored in words that were ten decimal digits long. Although, in one model of the 650, 2,000 words or 20,000 decimal digits could be stored, effective digits stored were often much less. To store pay rates, which consisted of a maximum of four digits, it was necessary to utilize ten digit storage locations, thereby wasting six digits of storage space for each rate stored. There was a way to overcome this difficulty, at least partially, but it entailed considerable programming effort. In a variable word length format, it would be possible to place a three digit pay rate immediately adjacent to a four digit pay rate. In such storage, it is possible to use the available digits of storage more effectively.

THE STORED PROGRAM

An electric adding machine adds when an operator depresses appropriate keys; an electric desk calculator performs the various mathematical processes when its keys and control bars are depressed by its operator; and combining the keyboard operations performed by an operator and the typewriter tab principle, a general purpose accounting machine can perform a short series of operations of a data recording or processing nature. Punched card systems require that the punched cards in the systems be transferred from machine to machine as various data processing operations are performed on the data. Nowhere, except in an electronic data processing system, can data be entered into the system, taken through a long and uninterrupted series of data processing operations, and be removed from the system in the form of useful information for management.

INSTRUCTION. In the previous section, the control unit of the computer was described. The control unit is able to function because someone has worked out a long series of very minute instructions, which are stored in the primary storage unit of the computer. These instructions govern every aspect of the operations to be performed on the data being processed. These instructions, since they are in the magnetic storage unit of the computer, are available at electronic speed and in the required sequence when needed for interpretation and execution by the control unit.

Basically, there are only about nine types of operations that can be performed by a computer:

1. It can call for data to be *read* into its primary storage unit.
2. It can *write* data out of its primary storage unit onto appropriate data representation media.
3. It can *add* one number to another.
4. It can *subtract* one number from another.
5. It can *multiply* one number by another.
6. It can *divide* one number by another.
7. It can unconditionally *transfer* control over the program to an instruction which is out of the normal sequence.
8. It can *transfer* control on a conditional basis, e.g., when a certain condition occurs in the processing the computer would recognize it and trans-

fer control, but if the condition did not occur the regular processing sequence would be followed.

9. It can *shift data* after reading it from some input device, e.g., a number read as 4,500 can be shifted to be used in processing to 450,000.

The computer can also compare or test for position, or negative or zero condition. Other operations are usually either modifications or combinations of the above.

In order to perform the above operations, the computer must know the order in which to perform them and where the data are located on which the operations are to be performed. Therefore, a computer instruction must consist of an indication of the operation to be performed and an indication of the location of the data (operand) to be operated on, and the instructions which will process the data properly must be placed in the appropriate sequence. A number of instructions in sequence is called a *program*. An illustration of a program with the two parts of each instruction highlighted is contained in the Figure 16-18. The program illustrated in Figure 16-18 could actually be part of an inventory modification program. The part illustrated would be the subtraction of items issued or sold from the old balance to formulate a new balance.

Operation	Operand	Explanation
Rd	T-2 100	Read twenty words of data from tape unit 2 and store in consecutive locations beginning at #100.
CA	100	Clear the accumulator in the arithmetic unit and add the data contained in location 100 to the accumulator.
Sub	101	Subtract the data in location 101 from the contents of the accumulator.
St	200	Store the modified contents of the accumulator in location 200.
WR	T-1 200	Write 20 words of data on tape unit 1 from storage beginning at location 200.

FIGURE 16-18. Illustrative Program

STEPS IN PROGRAMMING. There are three important steps in the programming process:

1. Problem analysis.
2. Instruction arrangement.
3. Testing.

Before a programmer can formulate a program, he must be fully aware of what he wants to do with the data. Since the steps in processing particular data are often difficult to put into words, the programmer often uses graphic charts called *system flow charts* and *program flow charts*. A systems chart is a graphic representation of the data processing system, or a portion thereof, in which data are converted into information. "A system flow chart provides a picture of the data processing application from the standpoint of what is to be accomplished."[3] A program flow chart is a graphic representation of the specific operations which must be performed on data which will convert it into information in a specific circumstance. A discussion of flowcharting is contained in Chapter 10.

Usually, when a programmer has defined a particular problem to a point where he can put it into a program flowchart, he is able, then, to develop a sequence of instructions which should accomplish the objectives of his problem.

The final step in the programming process is to represent the specific instructions which have been developed by the programmer on some media which can be read by the computer so that the program can be tested. Whether this medium be punched cards, punched paper tape or magnetic tape, each instruction must be placed on the medium. When this is done, the program is read by the computer and placed in storage locations. Test data are then made available to the computer and the program started to see if the sequence of steps devised by the programmer will actually process the data as desired.

THE DEVELOPMENT OF PROGRAMMING LANGUAGES

In the early computers, programs were written in *machine language.* For example, if a computer was constructed to perform mathematical and other operations in the binary mode, computer instructions had to consist of binary numbers of a fixed or variable length. Computer programmers had to know the binary equivalents of all of the commands which the computer could execute. Obviously, it was very time consuming to write programs and to teach novices how to write them.

As experience was gained in programming, programmers learned to use the computer to assist in the difficult task of writing programs. If the computer could interpret the instruction Rd T-2 100 (as illustrated in Figure 16-18) and convert it to the appropriate binary number, it would be a great help to programmers. Instead of keeping in mind all of the binary numbers

---

[3] *Ibid.*, p. 62.

necessary to process a problem, the steps such as read, write, add, subtract, etc., could be used to describe how a problem should be processed and the computer could be used to translate commands such as the Rd T-2100 into the appropriate binary number. This type of programming language was called a *mnemonic language.*

Using a mnemonic language, programmers would list program commands as in Figure 16-18. In turn, these commands were punched into cards and read into a computer. The computer, using a special *assembly* program, would process the mnemonic language cards and produce a deck of cards with the corresponding machine language commands. The machine language deck could then be used to process the data for which the program was written. The mnemonic program is called a *source program* and the machine language program resulting from the assembly process is called an *object program.*

When mnemonic languages were first introduced, it was still necessary for the programmer to assign all of the computer's internal memory locations. This meant that if computer storage was limited to 4096 decimal digits of data, the programmer had to know where he would store each digit of his instruction list, data, processed data, or information, and any temporary data developed during processing. The next step in the development of special assembly programs to help the programmer was to write an assembly program which would not only translate mnemonic program commands into machine language commands but would also assign the computer's internal storage. Instead of writing the command Sub 101, as in Figure 16-18, and needing to know that the withdrawal from inventory amount was stored in location 101, the more powerful assembly programs would permit the programmer to assign a symbolic name such as "withd." to the data he wanted to subtract from the amount already in the arithmetic unit. He could write the command "Sub Withd." and not need to concern himself as to where the withdrawal amount should be stored.

With experience in the use of assembly programs, it was apparent that translator programs could be written which would take even more of the difficulty out of programming. By using more powerful translator programs, called *compilers*, programmers could write out their problems in languages that they were more familiar with. Engineers and various men of science often use mathematical notation to describe problems and would find programming very easy if the problems they wished solved could merely be put into mathematical notation with the computer doing the rest. FORTRAN, which is an acronym for FORmula TRANslating System, was designed to do this. The programmer, observing the basic rules of the system, writes the program in algebraic notation; it is punched into cards and introduced into the computer. The computer, under the control of the FORTRAN compiler, produces a deck of cards consisting of the appropriate machine language program commands. A person can learn to program FORTRAN in a few hours.

In 1961, another programming language was developed called Common Business Oriented Language or COBOL. Using this language, a programmer can write his program in English language sentences. For example, the command, "Multiply hours by rate giving gross pay," is analyzed by the computer and the appropriate machine commands necessary to perform this operation are developed and punched into cards by the computer which become the object program.

One should note that in either FORTRAN or COBOL source programs the instructions are called "macro" instructions. It is necessary to develop several "micro" or machine language instructions for each "macro" instruction. It is quite possible that 15 to 20 micro-instructions would be necessary to perform the COBOL macro-instruction—multiply hours by rate giving gross-pay. Programmers using FORTRAN, COBOL, or some other macro-instruction language are usually able to complete the writing of a program in far less time than those using micro-instruction or machine language.

SUMMARY

This chapter introduces the reader to basic computer concepts. If a systems analyst understands the way in which a computer performs mathematical calculations, has a working knowledge of the components of a computer system, and understands the concepts of programming and the use of various levels of programming languages, he is able to recognize when computer systems should be used in order to design the type of data processing system needed by particular managements.

QUESTIONS, PROBLEMS, AND CASES

1. Describe the basic equipment configuration essential to an electronic computer system.

2. In Chapter 1 a systems theory was presented. Relate a computer system to this theory with special attention to data and information flow and the systems components.

3. How would principles of systems design relate to a computer system? Discuss and illustrate.

4. Visit and study a computer installation. Respond briefly to each of the following as they relate to the system studied:

    a. Identify the equipment units of the system by model number and function.

    b. Determine the type of computer mathematics used in the system.

    c. Determine the data recording media used in the system and state the reason for selection of the particular media.

    d. Inquire into the reasons for acquiring the particular system and the nature of the study that was made prior to installation.

    e. Identify the type or types of storage devices used in the system, and in general the function of each.

    f. Determine the programming language used in the system, and the sequence of steps followed by a programmer in arriving at an object program.

5. a. List the data recording media that may be used to introduce data or information into a computer system and the characteristics of each. Assuming the availability of appropriate equipment, what would govern the selection of media to be used in a particular situation?

    b. Is there any way to get data or information into a computer system other than by the data recording media mentioned in your answer to step a., above?

6. Give the decimal number for each of the following binary numbers:

    a. 1000100   d. 0101010

    b. 0011101   e. 1011110

    c. 1110001   f. 0011001

7. Show the mathematics for each of the following in binary coded decimal:

a.	78		e.	4	
	86			3	
	164			7	
b.	15		f.	45	
	39			64	
	54			109	
c.	84		g.	34	
	96			90	
	180			124	
d.	19		h.	69	
	63			81	
	82			150	

8. a. Consult the data processing periodicals and references in your library for information about optical scanning and the progress being made toward total effectiveness. Write a brief descriptive statement about your findings.

    b. What is the major obstacle in perfecting optical scanning systems?

9. You are the systems analyst for a major oil company. You are designing a nationwide credit card system that is to provide for a centralized billing operation to be located in Kansas City. Would optical scanning equipment be a possibility for use within the system? Explain.

10. Magnetic tape coding schemes use a check-channel with either "odd" or "even" parity checking. Explain.

11. Explain why a magnetic core might play an important role in a computer system.

12. Distinguish between a magnetic drum and magnetic disks, and indicate their respective roles in a computer system.

13. Identify and discuss the three functional parts of an arithmetic and control unit in a computer system. What is the role of an indexing register?

14. Internal control duties are important in the design of major systems. Why might the internal control duties in a computer system differ from those in a lower level of mechanization system?

15. Magnetic ink characters are commonly used in bank processing of checks. Explain the use of magnetic ink characters in such a procedure, indicating when and by whom the magnetic ink characters would be used. State specifically if and/or how the account of the drawer can be modified from the information normally coded on the check in magnetic ink.

16. Distinguish between the following:
    a. Primary storage device and secondary storage device.
    b. CRAM storage and mangetic drum storage.
    c. Source program and object program.
    d. FORTRAN and COBOL.
    e. Macro-instructions and micro-instructions.

17. Discuss the computer system feature of "destructible read in, nondestructible read out." Might there be a problem with "destructible read in" in a computer system?

18. What is the advantage of the variable work length format in a computer system? Can mathematical calculations and other functions be performed on any data desired in a computer system?

19. You have been told that programmers for a specific system use FORTRAN. What is FORTRAN, does it take long to learn, and what is its relationship to the computer system?

20. Describe the operations that can be performed by a computer. How do they relate to instructions and the control unit?

21. Why is access time so important in a computer system?

22. Describe the steps in programming and the importance of each.

23. Indicate some of the systems applications for paper tape as a data recording media. Applications that are not a part of a computer system should be included.

24. Contrast machine language with mnemonic language.

25. What are compilers and how do they relate to a computer system?

26. What is the central processing unit of a computer system? Describe each of the components of the central processing unit.

27. Rather than punching data in a standard IBM punched card using the Hollerith code, it is often necessary to punch binary data into a card. Explain how this can be accomplished, and illustrate the manner in which the number 179 would be punched.

28. What is meant by "reducing facts concerning a particular business to their lowest common denominator?"

29. What feature in a computer based data processing system makes it unique among data processing systems?

30. What features in an electronic computer contribute to its speed of calculation?

31. Add the following sets of binary numbers:

a.	10010	d.	11000111
	1111		111011
b.	10101011	e.	10000001
	1101011		1000001
c.	101111	f.	1111001
	10001		1101

32. Subtract the sets of binary numbers given in problem 31, above.

33. Convert each number given in your solution to problem 31 above, to its decimal equivalent.

34. Explain the mechanics of the binary coded decimal mode of calculation used in some electronic computers.

35. What are three commonly used input media in computer systems? Which has the fastest input speed? Which is the most versatile?

36. a. Give the principal features of an electronic computer designed for business rather than scientific applications.
    b. Why does the computer have so much potential as an accounting tool and for financial information systems?

37. Describe five input situations which would be suitable for the use of optical scanning equipment.

38. What is a common feature in all primary electronic storage devices?

39. In choosing a particular kind of primary storage, what factors are important in the decision?

40. Why does a magnetic drum have slower access time than magnetic cores?

41. Differentiate a "field" and a "record" in usual computer usage.

42. With the present state of the art, what are the bottleneck components in computer systems?

43. Explain the ways in which direct dollar savings are possible with a computer system.

CHAPTER 17

Control of Computer Systems[1]

INTRODUCTION

In Chapter 7, the subject of internal control was discussed at some length. The concepts developed in that chapter are valid for any type of financial information system. In this chapter, our discussion will center on the internal control duties which are important to the functioning of an electronic-based data processing system. Not only must a systems analyst be aware of the basic computer concepts which were discussed in Chapter 16, but also he must be aware of the types of controls which are essential to an effective electronic data processing system.

The flow of data and information through a financial information system in which a computer is utilized is subject to the parameters resulting from the application of the principles of systems design. The relative importance of each principle must be determined in arriving at the extent of control to be designed into the system.

For the purpose of discussion in this chapter, various controls in an electronic data processing system will be discussed in three groups:

1. Input-output controls.
2. Processing controls.
3. Internal organization controls.

---

[1] Much of the material in this chapter is based on the IBM booklet, "Management Control in Electronic Data Processing." © 1964 by International Business Machines Corporation.

INPUT-OUTPUT CONTROLS

Need for Input Data Controls

Very early in the development of mechanized data processing, it was demonstrated that accurate processing of data was possible only if the data entered into the system was accurate. The acronym for "garbage-in, garbage-out"—GIGO—is classic. The speed of processing in computer systems and the integrated nature of many systems cause the effect of input errors to be more important and harder to correct than in any other type of data processing.

Kinds of Input Data Controls

A representative list of input controls would include the following:

1. Batching.
2. Data verification at conversion.
3. Turnaround documents.
4. List input for source department review.
5. Computer anticipation of needs.
6. Editing routines.

Concerning the input of data into a computer system, management as well as the systems analyst is interested in two things: (1) that data have been translated into machine language correctly, and (2) that the data have been read correctly by the computer. Rarely would all six of the controls which were enumerated above, or variations of them, be present in even a single run of an application. Nevertheless, it is the responsibility of the systems analyst to be aware of the kinds of input controls which can be used and to recommend use of those which are judged to be most appropriate in specific circumstances.

Batching is probably the first control technique to be used in any data processing system which, for practical reasons, must collect groups of like transactions before it can efficiently and economically convert the data to machine language and process it. Usually, a batch control is set up by the department which first comes into contact with the data. For example, sales transactions for a particular manufacturer of automotive parts are approved by the sales department. Batch control, in this case, was the daily dollar total of sales orders sent to the key punch department. It is common practice for the batch control total established in the originating department to be used as a control at each stage of processing that the batch is subject to.

Data verification at conversion, since the first use of punched card machines, has been one of the principle input controls techniques. Techniques of data verification at conversion vary from the familiar key verification of punched cards to a device which is available to key verify magnetic tapes. Behind all methods is the theory that the input data has been accurately converted to machine language if all input data has been converted to machine language twice—once when it was actually key stroked and again when these key strokes were compared to the original operation. When batch totals are used, we cannot assume that data verification at conversion is unnecessary. In the sales example used earlier, only the dollar total of sales was part of the batch control. Yet, much more data such as date, customer number, item name, number of units, and customer name were also converted into machine language. Key verification would be needed for certain other critical items if not for the sales figure.

Another version of data verification at conversion used in many systems today is *check digit verification.* Assume, for example, that a department store was equipped with cash registers which produced punched paper tape for each transaction recorded. The total sales punched into the tape can be verified with the cash and charge sale tickets in the register at the end of each day. Further verification would not be needed for these amounts. However, part of the data punched on the tape at the time each charge sale transaction was recorded was the customer number. If the clerk entered as much as one digit of the customer number in error, subsequent processing would result in a charge being made to the wrong customer or for an error condition to result if the number was not a valid customer number. To prevent errors of this type and to avoid some sort of key verification of the customer number, a small device can be attached to the cash register which will verify the accuracy of the customer number entered on the cash register before it is either punched into the tape or entered on the cash register tape. This device is called a check digit verifier. Each customer is assigned a number, let's say, five digits long. The digits of this number are submitted to a particular formula of calculation and a sixth digit in the low order position is produced. Whenever the sixth digit number is indexed on the cash register as part of the sale recording, the check digit verifier subjects the left-most five digits to the calculation formula and compares the answer to the sixth digit in the low order position. If the calculation answer agrees with the sixth digit, a correct customer number has been entered and the clerk may proceed to enter the amount of the sale.

The use of *turnaround documents* is a reliable way to reduce data conversion and, therefore, the need for verification. A turnaround document is any one which contains data in machine language. Oil companies and public utilities have used turnaround documents for years. An oil company might use a punched card as its statement to its customers for gasoline on other purchases. The customer is required to return a portion of the punched card statement with his remittance. This part of the card contains the customer's number, the amount of the statement balance, and possibly other data which has been punched into it before it was mailed to the customer. If the customer remits the amount due and returns the proper portion of the statement no data conversion operation is necessary. When such documents can be used conversion errors are usually reduced with less correction time necessary.

Sometimes, *input* data *are listed by the computer* or on auxiliary equipment and reviewed by the source department before any of the input data are processed. This type of input control is slow and often only as good as the person conducting the review. Usually, it is used on small volumes of very crucial data.

An extension of programmed controls can be made to give additional assurance that the data being read by the input device into the computer are being read correctly and are the correct data. Computer programs can be written to *anticipate needed data* and to call for it to be read into the computer from secondary storage or from a tape or cards mounted on an input device. Such programs virtually eliminate, for example, the possibility that last period's transaction tape can be mounted on a tape drive and reprocessed this period.

The segment of a computer program which is designed to test the accuracy and validity of input data is commonly referred to as an *edit routine*. Six commonly used tests in an edit routine are:

1. Limit checks.
2. Field checks.
3. Sign checks.
4. Validity checks.
5. Historical comparisons.
6. Logical relationships.

A lumber company in the midwest thinks that edit routines are so important that a special run is made of all input data, subjecting this data to a full series of tests prior to a formal input of data into the computer system.

A *limit check* is a fixed parameter written into the program and as data are being read by the computer they are compared to their related parameter. Any time data being read do not fall within these established parameters, an error condition may exist. Usually, these data are read a second time and if the condition remains the data are written on a special output tape or punched into cards for manual review. In one weekly payroll application, for example, a limit check was made on hours worked. If the hours worked exceeded sixty, the entire pay data were extracted from the file, written on an exception tape from which they were printed off line, and investigated.

A *field check* is an investigation of data within a particular field of the input record. In a particular record, for example, the second data item should always contain numeric data. A field check would reject a record which contained alphabetic data in this field.

Certain data in a particular application, to be valid data, should always contain a positive numeric sign. A *sign check* would reject any piece of data of this particular kind which was read as containing a negative sign. An invoice number in a billing run would usually be entered as a positive number. A sign check on this number would turn up errors of conversion or of reading.

A *validity check* is usually a comparison which the programmer includes before permitting a file to be altered by a transaction. Normally, a sales transaction affecting a particular customer's account would not be posted to that account by the computer unless the account number in the receivables file agreed with the customer's number contained in the sales record which is about to be posted to the customer's account. In applications where certain data are communicated to the computer from input stations, such as those used to transmit labor data in a manufacturing company or to transmit seat sales in an airlines system, the program often contains validity checks which will not permit any transaction except labor used or seats sold to be entered into the computer from input stations.

A good example of the use of *historical comparisons* as a programmed input control is the high-low check used in many utility applications. As the current meter reading is being read by the computer it is compared to high-low average amounts established in prior months. If the current meter reading is above the high limit or below the low limit, this reading is tagged for further investigation after the run has been completed. This is a reasonableness test applied to input data.

Logical relationships exist among most data being read by a computer and can be tested by it. For example, an employee current payroll record with income tax withheld but with zero hours worked this pay period is an illogical relationship and should be investigated.

Data User Controls—Output

Above, it was pointed out that a frequently used control over input was some sort of batch control total established by the department which originated the data or accumulated it for transmission to data processing. Just as the department which transmits data to be processed has responsibility to use suitable controls to insure that the data transmitted are accurate and complete, the department using the information produced by the processing of data has a responsibility to use appropriate control measures to assure it that the information that has been received is accurate and complete. A user of information, in effect, must approve the information which he receives from data processing. The importance of user controls as well as the responsibility of the user in this regard is expressed very well in the booklet footnoted earlier, "Management Control of Electronic Data Processing." The booklet states as follows:

> The responsibility of the users for the reliability of the EDP system is a significant departure from the responsibilities of the operating units (which originated the data) the systems development unit (which created the system and programs) and the data processing group (which processed the data received). The responsibility of each of these units is for a particular phase of the data processing system. The users, on the other hand, must pass upon the end result. This is a significant responsibility and one for which there may exist no further or timely control. It often represents the last chance to detect any errors introduced in prior stages before issuance of important reports, disbursing of checks to employees or suppliers, issuance of bills to customers, etc.

> In meeting this responsibility the users must be aware of and be able to appraise the controls practiced in the preceding phases of the system. However, while this knowledge influences the extent and type of checking and other controls which the user will perform, it is usually not given full weight by them. This recognizes the limitations of any control procedures, the possibility of unanticipated conditions for which controls were not previously provided, and the danger of fraudulent manipulation. Accordingly, users will often and should seek to base their acceptance of the processed data on their independent application of control procedures and standards of reasonableness which, even if other control procedures were to falter, would still ensure that no major inaccuracy exists in the process data.[2]

Generally speaking, data user controls fall into three categories:

1. Comparing computer output to pre-established input control totals.
2. Programmed controls designed for the user.
3. Review of output for reasonableness.

Although the three categories listed above use the words "computer" and "programmed," the essence of these types of user controls was used in many data processing systems before the advent of computers. With computer systems, however, and their tremendous processing speeds and capacity to handle data, control measures can be installed which were not practical in any other processing system.

Comparing computer output to pre-established input control totals is actually the other side of the coin to various input control measures. At input, the control figure or element is often established which is used by the output or user department to verify information transmitted to it from data process-

---

[2] *Ibid.*, p. 19.

ing. It should be pointed out that the originating department could be one of the data users. Such a department would have no less a responsibility for proper output review and control. This category of control would include (1) comparing record counts or hash totals of output to totals established prior to or at input, (2) comparing output totals from one run with input or output from a related but separate run, and (3) comparing output totals with totals that were generated outside of the application. Total hours worked, for example, per clock card can be compared to the total of the time tickets turned in by each employee to insure that the same amount of time clocked in and out was actually reported via the time tickets.

An example of programmed controls designed for the user would be as follows:

1. A programmed loop which compares a data element such as the unit cost of an inventory item with the average of this particular data element developed over several cycles of processing. Using inventory as a specific example, if the unit cost of a new shipment of an item were 10 per cent larger or smaller than the average cost of several past shipments, an exception record could be prepared which could be used by the user department to investigate a possible error situation.

2. Computer-generated totals can function as a data user control. Often it is impractical to generate a hash total of account numbers prior to input. However, when account numbers are introduced in the first run of an application, a hash total may be generated by the computer at input which can be used in succeeding runs.

3. Data elements for statistically selected transactions along with related master file data can be extracted from a particular master file transaction so that the selected data can be processed manually and compared with computer generated results for the same accounts.

Examples of the third category of user control *review of output for reasonableness* would be: (1) a reasonableness test of the cost of sales figure can be made by using average markup percentages and working back to cost on the total sales amounts of various product lines; (2) various kinds of statistical analyses can be made and data processed by using the computer to select the sample data and to extrapolate from this data.

Control of Exceptions

Just as in any non-computer system, when an exception or out-of-balance situation is found as the result of a control measure, a follow up is necessary in computer systems. Good control procedures should provide that the department using the data or the department where the control measure was applied and the error discovered should control the correction procedures.

Review of Master File Data

One aspect of user control which is often not included because it does not pertain particularly to output is the concern which data users must have for the quality of the data contained in the master files. There is need for these files to be subjected to more than routine processing controls. Often certain data in master files are not subjected to any sort of control step and such data kept on machinable media can deteriorate. It is good practice in many installations to require that master file data be printed on hard copy from time to time and subjected to intensive review.

PROCESSING CONTROLS

Just as it was difficult to separate specific controls designed for input and output, it is difficult to state specifically that certain controls are used only during processing. Certain of the edit routines which were very useful in controlling input are also very useful in the actual processing of data. If edit routines such as limit checks, field checks, sign checks, validity checks, historical comparisons, and logical relationships were used to control the input of data, these same controls are almost sure to be used as the processing of data is carried out. In the generation of gross pay, for example, a limit check could be made on each employee which would flag as an exception any gross pay in excess of $300. There are a few controls, however, which can be associated primarily with processing data. All of these controls consist of program instructions which are inserted into the main program to take care of specific situations.

One example of such control subroutines would be *overflow procedures*. Physical components of the arithmetic unit of an electronic computer have finite limits. Therefore, as computations, totals, etc., are being developed, it is quite possible that an amount being generated is larger than the finite limit of this particular arithmetic limit. When the particular calculation reaches this point, a computer will usually stop processing operations unless certain instructions are included in the program to tell the computer what to do when such a situation arises. On some data it would be appropriate to stop the computer; on other data alternate processing steps could be taken. Another type of program subroutine is called a *scuttle procedure*. This part of the program tells the computer what to do in the event that an error situation is detected. For example, what should be done if the gross pay of an employee is in excess of $500? Usually, the processing of this particular payroll record is continued but the computer is instructed to write a particular message on the typewriter console of the computer to bring this situation to the attention of the operator. Most programs today provide for an overflow condition and other error situations to be flagged in some way so that they can be investigated after processing has been completed. The objective of such procedures, of course, is to keep the program from stopping.

Many programs are written which prohibit any sort of program intervention without activating the console typewriter. This provides for a written *intervention record* which can later be reviewed by supervisory personnel. Some companies carry this control procedure one step farther and pre-number typewriter console sheets. This permits supervisory employees to account for all the sheets that have been used on the console typewriter on a given working day.

INTERNAL ORGANIZATIONAL CONTROLS

Introduction

Internal organization controls in an electronic data processing system are the activities and procedures which are necessary to insure the accurate receipt, processing, and disposition of data handled by the data processing department. Just as in any other department, this department must have the following basic ingredients necessary for a functioning system of internal control:

1. A plan of organization which provides for appropriate segregation of functional responsibilities.
2. A system of authorization and record procedures adequate to provide documentary control over data entering, within, and leaving the department.
3. Sound practices to be followed in the performance of duties within the department.
4. Qualified personnel commensurate with responsibilities assigned.[3]

Departmental Organization

Ideally, the organization of the data processing department should resemble the chart in Figure 17-1. Realistically, only parts of the division of duties shown may ever be used in practice. A systems analyst should work

---

[3] The above four ingredients have been paraphrased from the American Institute of Certified Public Accountants' bulletin, "Internal Control," 1949.

ORGANIZATION FLOW CHART

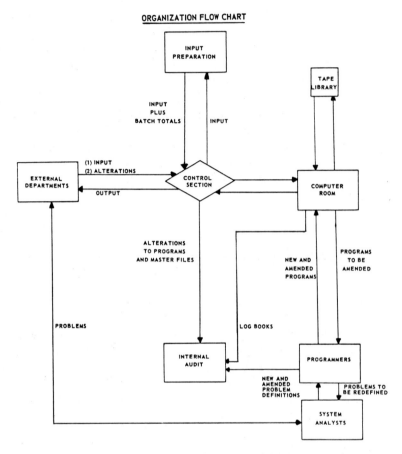

Reprinted by permission from *The Impact of Computers on Accounting*
by T. W. McRae © 1964 by John Wiley and Sons, Ltd.

FIGURE 17-1.   Organization Flow Chart

from the ideal situation to achieve the best organizational lines for a particular
set of circumstances. Some companies may be too small to organize effectively
according to the diagram, and others may be so large with decentralized computer locations that a more complex arrangement would be necessary. The
important thing, of course, is for each internal control configuration to contain
the elements essential to an adequate system of internal control.

The organization chart in Figure 17-1 provides for a separation of duties
among systems analysts, programmers, machine operators, tape librarians,
input preparers, and the control section.

Systems analysts are concerned with problem definitions and act as
specialists to work with the operating departments. A common type of output
from this group would be a systems flow chart which can be used by the

programmers. *Programmers* are responsible for writing instructions which the computer must have to process data properly. Their duties include individual testing of programs, preparation of operating instructions, and complete documentation of each program. *Machine operators* are responsible for all production runs as distinguished from test runs (of the computer in accordance with the operating instructions detailed for each program). The *tape librarian* is charged with the custodianship of tape files when they are not required by the operators. These tape files would include program, master file, and transaction tapes. As the name implies, the *input preparation section* is responsible for the translation of non-processible data to processible form such as converting vendor's invoices into punched cards. The *control section* monitors and controls the flow of items between sections. In effect, it is the production control section for data processing activities.

Authorization, Record Procedures, and Sound Practices

Although we have discussed control measures which are built into the equipment and incorporated into the programs themselves, it is also necessary for the data processing department to design control measures for the physical protection and efficient use of programs which are in every stage of development and use. Management must insist on procedures which will give it reasonable assurance that errors are not occurring through improper use of programs; that only properly approved programs are being used; that program changes can be made only if proper approval has been obtained; and that the programs are physically safeguarded. Consider three areas where internal control duties are necessary.

1. Program documentation.
2. Program changes.
3. Inventory control of programs.

Program Documentation

A computer program, as discussed in Chapter 16, is composed of machine instructions which govern the processing of data by the computer. In order for the machine to interpret these instructions they must be in machine sensible form such as magnetic tape or punched cards. Also, these same instructions must be in a form which is legible to a programmer and to the person responsible for approving the program. In order for knowledgeable approval of a program to be given, the entire program must be adequately documented just as any other segment of an information processing system. A typical documentation package for a computer program would include a series of system and program flow charts, block diagrams, a hard-copy printout of the machine instructions and a set of operating instructions which the machine operators must follow in order to run the program properly. At the time that the program is formally approved, a copy of the documentation package should be deposited for safekeeping with someone outside of the programming group. Many companies deposit a copy of each program with their internal auditors.

Program Changes

Changes to an official program should require a certain amount of approval before going into effect. An acceptable procedure provides for a contemplated change to be submitted to the chief programmer and to the department supervisor for review and approval. This gives reasonable assurance that only authorized changes are being made to the programs. Of course, any accepted change requires that the documentation of the original program be revised and that the revised program be sufficiently tested prior to official use. Another factor which must be considered by the supervisor of data processing is the timing of the change. Sometimes a program change is minor and it does not affect anyone except the operator. Other changes are major and not only affect the operator but people in the departments where the data originates and the media they must use to transmit this data to the computer room as well. In the latter case, the timing of change is very important to the continued accuracy and efficiency of the processing operation. This responsibility rests with the data processing department's staff who undoubtedly should act in consort with the other departments involved.

Inventory Control of Programs

In most medium-to-large scale electronic data processing installations, programs are usually quite numerous. Good control requires that only programs which are needed for the particular job being run on the computer are available to the operators; that obsolete programs be destroyed or stored separately from active programs; and that reasonable procedures be installed to physically safeguard the program from wanton or accidental destruction or alteration. A program library with appropriate library procedures is often used to provide this control. One large company operates a tape library as follows: The contents of the library include all of the operating programs transaction file tapes and master file tapes of the company. In addition, blank tapes and other supplies are also on hand in the library. Tape programs which have been superseded are kept until the new programs have been thoroughly tested by the operating or programming groups. After new programs are accepted the old program tapes are erased and reused. It is the responsibility of the tape librarian and his staff to supply machine operators with tapes when it is the proper time for a particular operation to be run on the computer. The company has a schedule from which neither librarian nor the operator can deviate unless written approval is obtained from the department supervisor. The librarian is required to maintain a log in which a complete chronological record is kept of the various tapes which have been issued and received by the library. This log provides space for the name of the operator checking the tape in or out; for the name and ID number of each tape reel; for the time and date of the issue or receipt; and for the initials of the operator and the librarian. The log, in addition to being an accountability record, can also be used to accumulate usage statistics. These statistics caused the company to rearrange the entire library so that the distance from the issuing and receiving window was in inverse proportion to the usage of various programs and files.

Another responsibility of the librarian is to inaugurate and maintain proper labeling of all tapes. Programmers are usually required to write a suitable label for each program tape and to provide for adequate machine labeling of every master file that results from processing. This procedure is complemented by requiring that each tape in use, for whatever reason, also be equipped with a descriptive external label. It is essential to the success of this requirement that the librarian be present when the internal tape label is printed out so that the external label will be identical with the language of the internal machine.

Although the policy is not often set by the librarian as to the retention period of certain tapes, he is the custodian of this policy. This policy is another aspect of data processing internal organization controls. Much of the business data processing today is application oriented in that it processes certain transactions against a master file to produce a new master file. Some applications are a bit more complex and may involve several transaction tapes and several master files on different media. In any case, minimum control procedures call for the retention of master file transaction tapes to the third generation. This is often referred to as the "grandfather-father-son" principle. This can be illustrated by the diagram in Figure 17-2. This policy provides a safeguard against inadvertent or willful destruction of data maintained on tape.

Another area of possible loss of data which is not covered by a tape retention policy is random access media. Many systems today use disks and cards to store file data. A common control policy, in this case, is to provide for a periodic printout of the data on the disk or card file. In the event the data on these files are destroyed, it would be possible to reconstruct the file from the last print-out for reprocessing.

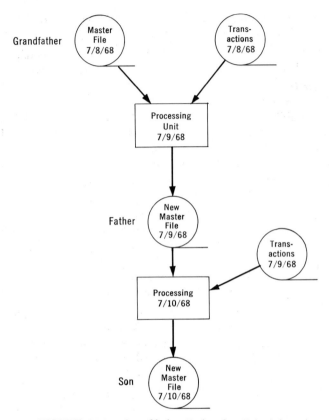

FIGURE 17-2.   Grandfather-Father-Son Principle

SUMMARY

This chapter has been devoted to a discussion of three areas of control which are important to the functioning of an electronic data processing system. The area of control was divided into the following:

1. Input-output controls.
2. Processing controls.
3. Internal organization controls.

In order to be effective in the design of an information processing system, which is centered on one or more electronic computers, the systems analyst must insist, as in any other system, that sufficiently appropriate internal control measures and activities are incorporated into the system. The control measures discussed in this chapter will furnish the systems analyst with the fundamentals necessary for good system design. Experience will add to this foundation.

QUESTIONS, PROBLEMS, AND CASES

1. Draw a diagram similar to Figure 17-1 which depicts an organization which has not been able to divide duties as finely as in Figure 17-1 but which would have acceptable division of duties. Describe any changes you would recommend in the assignment of internal control duties.

2. How does the organization of a data processing department relate to a machine shop?

3. In designing processing controls, what should the programmer strive to achieve?

4. Describe three input controls which would also be effective processing controls.

5. Describe briefly the three control areas in an electronic data processing system.

6. List and define the various types of input controls.

7. For each of the controls listed in 17-6 above, describe a situation in a business data processing system where each control would be appropriate. (Do not use the examples from the text.)

8. a. How does check digit verification work?
   b. Describe a situation in business where it could be used. (Do not use the example given in the text.)

9. Select four of the six edit routine tests and describe a systems situation in which the tests selected might be used. (Do not use examples from the text.)

10. What are data user controls? Why are they necessary?

11. Why is it essential to review master file data periodically?

12. Take each category of data user controls and describe a business situation in which each control category could be used. (Do not use examples given in the text.)

13. Distinguish between the following:
    a. Turnaround documents and intervention record.
    b. Limit checks and field checks.
    c. Logical relationships and validity checks.
    d. Historical comparisons and overflow procedures.

14. Explain the approach that should be taken within the data processing department to control exceptions.

15. What are internal organization controls and what is there about a computer system that makes them especially important?

16. How is it possible to control programs to be assured of physical protection and efficient use at each stage of development and use?

17. What would be included in a typical documentation package for a computer program?

18. What should be the responsibilities of the tape librarian and his staff?

19. It has been said that in some companies the Vice-President of Data Processing or the Vice-President of Administration has assumed responsibility for the financial information system. What change is this causing in corporate organization structure and the financial management function?

20. Where should the Data Processing Department be located in a large multiple-division manufacturing company? To whom should the department head report and why?

21. An effective data processing system should include the appropriate processing controls. Explain.

22. The audit of the financial statements of a client that utilizes the services of a computer for accounting functions compels the CPA to understand the operation of his client's electronic data processing (EDP) system.
    a. The first requirement of an effective system of internal control is a satisfactory plan of organization. List the characteristics of a satisfactory plan of organization for an EDP department, including the relationship between the department and the rest of the organization.
    b. An effective system of internal control also requires a sound system of records control of operations and transactions (source data and its flow) and of classification of data within the accounts. For an' EDP system, these controls include input controls, processing controls, and output controls. List the characteristics of a satisfactory system of input controls. (Confine your comments to a batch-controlled system employing punched cards and to the steps that occur prior to the processing of the input cards in the computer.) (AICPA Examination)

Unit 4

Systems Problems and Cases

CHAPTER 18

Functional Procedures—1

INTRODUCTION

IN MAKING GOOD APPLICATION OF PRINCIPLES OF SYSTEMS DESIGN AND REC-
ommending the assignment of internal control duties, the systems analyst
must examine the data and information flow as it relates to specific procedures.
When there is a volume of similar operations to reflect essential business
activities, to meet legal requirements, or to provide effective internal control,
a special procedure evolves as a sub-system within the total system. Examples
of such procedures are purchases, payables, sales, receivables, cash receipts,
cash disbursements, payroll, and many others often less obvious. Each procedure includes sub-procedures.

Chapter 18 and 19 of this text are designed to provide an understanding
of the elements of a few selected typical procedures. With a little imagination
it should be possible to adapt the basic elements of the typical procedures
to be appropriate for the many specialized situations and conditions that
exist in specific businesses and other organizations. A number of problems
and cases are included to provide an opportunity to adapt the typical procedure to a situation in which the facts are different. One of the fundamental
purposes of practice problems and cases is to illustrate and discuss the
relationship between the system components and the manner in which
records and forms flow to accomplish given objectives. The equipment and
devices used in processing media will not be emphasized. Although equipment and devices may change the mechanical aspects of the configuration,
conceptually the procedures normally should accomplish the same systems
objectives.

Each of the sections in Chapters 18 and 19 includes a procedural flow chart for the typical procedure. The section briefly explains the typical procedure and the factors and control measures that are relevant in the design of the procedure. Chapters 18 and 19 are not intended to provide exhaustive discussions since their primary purpose is to furnish problems and cases to which the theories of systems design provided in this text can be applied.

PURCHASES AND PAYABLES

The Purchasing Function

Purchasing involves buying everything an organization needs except for employee services and certain other services and securities. It thus encompasses procurement of inventory items, supplies, fixed assets and, in some instances, such services as utilities, insurance, and transportation. Although in a sense the purchasing department does not decide *what* is purchased, it does largely decide when, where, and on what terms purchases are to be made. Other departments usually initiate requests as to what is to be purchased, but even here purchasing will probably decide from which supplier the item will be bought and on what terms and how to ship. For example, the storeroom may requisition a given number of size 7.50 x 14 tubeless tires, 4-ply, with a given tread at the request of an operating department. It is, however, up to the purchasing department to select a vendor, arrange deliveries, set terms, and decide whether a contract or "spot" purchase is best. When whatever is ordered is delivered, it usually also is incumbent on purchasing to approve the vendor's invoice for payment after verification that goods specified were received in the proper quantities and in good condition and that prices were as agreed. Purchasing will often code the invoice, thereby determining to what account the debit distribution is made. Coding may also be by the requesting department when a budget system is operative, or in the payable section of the accounting department.

In cooperation with other departments, the purchasing department attempts to buy in economical order lot quantities and to avoid overstocking and understocking. Purchasing assumes responsibility for following up on orders placed and corresponding with vendors about adjustments.

Purchasing must stay in close contact with sources of supply to keep abreast of new product developments and improvements and the supply and demand situation. Catalogs, price lists, and specifications data files are customarily maintained in the purchasing department. It is not uncommon for over 50 cents of each sales dollar to be accounted for by purchase costs; the importance of effective purchasing can be seen from this statistic.

Aspects of purchasing warranting special control procedures and a brief statement of the usual means of achieving control over them are detailed below.

Phase of purchasing	Control feature
1. Amount of purchases for each department.	1. Budget or "open to buy" allotments.
2. Prices to be paid.	2. Budget or standard cost system.
3. Whether speculative buying is to be done.	3. Policy as set by Board of Directors.
4. Centralization or decentralization of purchasing.	4. Organization chart and related organization manual.
5. Authorization for field or emergency purchases.	5. Policies set by Board of Directors.
6. Accommodation purchases for employees.	6. Policies set by Board of Directors.

Typical Purchase Procedure

Figure 18-1 illustrates the major flows of communication media combined to provide a typical purchase procedure. A systems analyst should be able to make the modifications necessary to adjust the basic flows illustrated in the typical procedure to provide for the changes and expansion of detail necessary to adjust the purchase procedure in a specific organization so as not to violate principles of systems design and to provide an optimum procedure.

Principles of systems design, systems standards, and internal control duties that are applicable to purchasing can be recognized in Figure 18-1. The unique systems feature of procedures crossing organization lines and the organizational independence resulting from assignment of duties so that no individual or organization unit is in complete control of any transaction is evident. Adequate protection is provided against error or embezzlement when there is no collusion. Note especially:

1. Personnel in the *receiving section* could not divert materials for their personal benefit as it would not be possible to obtain the acknowledgment of storeskeeping to indicate that the material is under accounting control. Material shortages could be traced to receiving.

2. *Storeskeeping* could not avoid assuming accounting control for materials purchased. A copy of the receiving report goes from receiving directly to the storesroom, is stamped to indicate receipt in the storesroom, and is sent to the payables section. The invoice to pay for the materials would not be released from accounts payable unless the necessary verifications had been

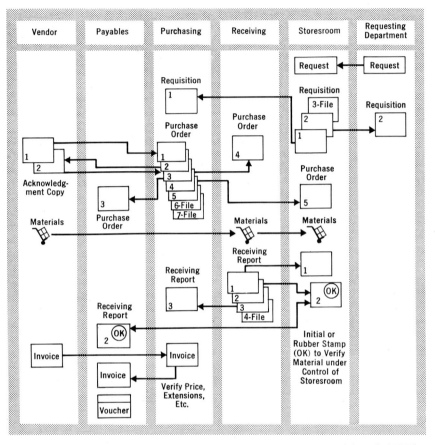

Adapted AICPA

FIGURE 18-1. Typical Purchase Procedure

made in purchasing, and materials were under accounting control. Material shortages could be traced to storeskeeping if a loss had occurred there.

3. *Purchasing* does not control the entire purchase transaction in that all materials received must be processed through the receiving room and storeskeeping, and approved receiving reports to verify receipt before payment is authorized comes from storeskeeping and not purchasing. Purchasing does not control the actual materials nor does it control the documents necessary to authorize payment. Nevertheless, the purchasing function is by far the most difficult to control. Purchasing enters into many price agreements and determines from which vendor purchases are to be made. Internal audit verifications and tests to provide protection where other controls are not applicable are a part of the control system.

Such controls and tests should be designed to test prices and the basis for agreements and for purchasing from specified vendors. The ethics of gifts to purchasing office employees and influential management also presents a problem. Kickbacks to purchasing personnel or others cannot be tolerated.

The purchasing procedure should provide for the approval of vendors periodically after consideration of such factors as financial soundness, reciprocity of trade relationships, reliability in past dealings, and avoidance of conflict of interests. Conflict of interest situations are exemplified by (a) company executives or employees (especially those in purchasing) having direct or indirect financial interests in vendor companies, and (b) receipt of gifts or other favors from vendors by purchasing personnel. The possibilities for personal gains in these situations are obvious. Policies should be adopted by the board of directors to minimize the risk of loss arising out of conflict of interest situations. Some specific measures which can be taken include (a) requiring purchasing and management personnel to supply data as to personal or family security holdings, and (b) requiring that all gifts from vendors be declined or allowing their acceptance only when their value is nominal.

4. *Accounts payable* personnel handle only records, and are not able to obtain either merchandise or cash independently. The necessary controls over disbursements are discussed later in this chapter.

Voucher Procedure

In studying Figure 18-1, it can be noted that the major control over amounts owed is in the payables section where a copy of the purchase order, receiving report, and invoice are assembled for review. The control over payments is obtained by review and authorization in the payables section, not through the signature on the check. Thus, the processing of communication media, prior to and in the payables section, is important as a part of the documentation to evidence the transaction and provide authorization for disbursement.

In the small business, a simplified method of controlling payables will probably be used. No formal record is made of invoices received at the time merchandise is delivered or service is performed. Instead, the invoice is received and placed in a file according to due date. In a small business the owner will have complete knowledge of each transaction and knows personally that the merchandise or service has been received and that it is proper to make payment. The first formal record is made at the time the invoice is paid, when the invoice for acquisition of material or services is entered directly in the record as a disbursement. Such a procedure anticipates the payment of all invoices when due or the accrual of any invoice in the unpaid file at the end of the accounting period if accrual statements are desired. The subsequent reversal of accruals is necessary on the first day of the following period.

A more formal payable procedure, designed to control subsidiary payables, is the voucher system. There are many variations of the voucher system, but the detailed control is centered around a *voucher jacket*. The voucher jacket is a form that can be controlled by either pre-numbering or number control, and provides a standard format for assembling the communication media and authorizations to document a disbursement. It can be a separate form printed for the purpose. In some procedures it can be printed on the reverse side of a duplicate copy of the voucher check or the purchase order.

Data on the voucher jacket include the date, to whom the payment is to be made, and the debit distribution with the account and amount being charged identified. The voucher jacket often shows disbursement information such as the check number, the amount of discount, and the net amount of the check. Stapled to the inside of the voucher jacket would be the invoice, a receiving report, and the purchase order if applicable. The necessary approvals and posting references would be required. Other documentation that may be relevant to the issuance of a check would also be included. The key authorization to approve a disbursement would be on the voucher. The signature of the individual approving each disbursement is evidence that the item for which payment is made was properly ordered, the materials were received, and that the calculations and items billed were correct. There has been a review of the entire transaction and, as a result, the amount is verified as due and payable and disbursement is therefore authorized. A procedure involving a voucher check that has a voucher jacket printed on the back of the account payable copy is illustrated later in the chapter as Figure 18-7.

The formal entry of an invoice into the record (voucher register) can be (a) at the time the invoice is received, (b) at the time documentation is complete, or (c) at the time of payment. In a voucher procedure there are usually at least three voucher files—a file of unpaid vouchers arranged by due date, a file of paid vouchers arranged by number, and a carbon copy of the voucher which becomes an alphabetical file to provide an audit trail to the proper voucher number and communication media documentation for a given disbursement. The alphabetical file is a means to find a given voucher located in either the unpaid or paid file by number.

The use of vouchers is not restricted to large businesses. The voucher concept is helpful in the disbursement procedure of any club or organization in which a basic record is desired and the proper authorization and control over disbursements is important. By requiring the signatures on the voucher jacket before disbursement, the treasurer of an organization and the president can each sign to indicate their knowledge and approval of the disbursement. Paid vouchers can be filed in strict numerical sequence to provide documentation for every amount paid. Such a procedure provides orderly records and good documentation and is advantageous in establishing good stewardship of cash.

Internal Control Over Purchases and Payables

Appendix A illustrates an internal control questionnaire with questions relating to purchases and payables. Each question is asked to lead an individual reviewing internal control to greater knowledge concerning the strengths and weaknesses of the procedure. A careful study of responses to an internal control questionnaire can provide an insight into the possible control strengths and weaknesses of a procedure. The use of the questionnaire as a check list to test a procedure is advantageous.

Purchases and Payables Questions, Problems, and Cases

1. It is your client's policy to have invoices and supporting documents accompany all checks presented for signature. The signing officer insists that the invoices and documents be marked "paid" before he will review them and sign the checks. His objective is to preclude resubmission of the same invoices and documents in support of another check. Do you believe this procedure is effective? Explain. (AICPA Examination)

2. The accounting and internal control procedures relating to purchases of materials by the Branden Company, a medium-sized concern manufacturing special machinery to order, have been described by your junior accountant in the following terms:

   > After approval by manufacturing department foremen, material purchase requisitions are forwarded to the purchasing department supervisor who distributes such requisitions to the several employees under his control. The latter employees prepare prenumbered purchase orders in triplicate, account for all numbers, and send the original purchase order to the vendor. One copy of the purchase order is sent to the receiving department where it is used as a receiving report. The other copy is filed in the purchasing department.

   > When the materials are received, they are moved directly to the storeroom and issued to the foremen on informal requests. The receiving department sends a receiving report (with its copy of the purchase order attached) to the purchasing department and sends copies of the receiving report to the storeroom and to the accounting department.

   > Vendors' invoices for material purchases, received in duplicate in the mailroom, are sent to the purchasing department and directed to the employee who placed the related order. The employee then compares the invoice with the copy of the purchase order on file in the purchasing department for price and terms and compares the invoice quantity with the quantity received as reported by the shipping and receiving department on its copy of the purchase order. The purchasing department employees also check discounts, footings, and extensions and initial the invoice to indicate approval for

payment. The invoice is then sent to the voucher section of the accounting department where it is coded for account distribution, assigned a voucher number, entered in the voucher register, and filed according to payment due date.

On payment dates prenumbered checks are requisitioned by the voucher section from the cashier and prepared except for signature. After the checks are prepared they are returned to the cashier, who puts them through a check signing machine, accounts for the sequence of numbers, and passes them to the cash disbursement bookkeeper for entry in the cash disbursements book. The cash disbursements bookkeeper then returns the checks to the voucher section which then notes payment dates in the voucher register, places the checks in envelopes, and sends them to the mail room. The vouchers are then filed in numerical sequence. At the end of each month one of the voucher clerks prepares an adding machine tape of unpaid items in the voucher register and compares the total thereof with the general ledger balance and investigates any difference disclosed by such comparison.

Required: Discuss the weaknesses, if any, in the internal control of Branden's purchasing and subsequent procedures and suggest supplementary or revised procedures for remedying each weakness with regard to (a) requisition of materials and (b) receipt and storage of materials. (AICPA Examination)

3. The Witt Company is engaged in manufacturing. Certain features of its operating methods are described below.

When materials are ordered, a duplicate of the purchase order is sent to the receiving department. When the materials are received, the receiving clerk records the receipt on the copy of the order, which is then sent to the accounting department to support the entry to accounts payable and material purchases. The materials are then taken to stores where the quantity is entered on bin records.

You are to consider the above procedure and point out the existing deficiencies, if any, in internal control, including an explanation of the errors or manipulations which might occur in view of the weakness and your recommendations as to changes which could be made to correct the weakness. (Adapted AICPA Examination)

4. The controller of the Garoville Company has assigned to you the task of revising the purchasing routine in a recently acquired subsidiary company. Your investigation reveals that purchases of $998,000 were made last year, $298,000 of which were placed locally. The procedure and media being used are adequate, with the exception of the purchase order.

Required: Prepare a report to the controller, including the following supporting data:

a. The purchase order, in at least quadruplicate, that you recommend. Either draw a purchase order or obtain a copy of one that is being used by some business. (If actual forms are used, the purchase order of a smaller business is adequate.)

b. A discussion of the purchase order procedure. Include or indicate clearly the full information, for example, the number of copies, the processing and disposition of each copy, color, size, type paper, etc. If actual forms are submitted, discuss the routine in which they are used and evaluate them.

c. The routine for local purchases. Indicate the special form or forms required, if any, and the purpose in the purchase procedure.

5. The Chicago Manufacturing Company, a manufacturer of plastic products, produces primarily for large chain outlets. The factory and warehouses are located in Chicago while the home office is in San Francisco.

The purchasing agent's office is now located at the home office in San Francisco. It has not been functioning efficiently for some time and has recently been the chief cause for some costly production stoppages. After an extensive investigation into purchasing procedures, the president made the following recommendations to the board of directors:

a. The purchasing agent's office and all allied records should be moved to the Chicago factory as soon as possible.

b. A complete new purchase routine should be established to replace the system being used.

c. A systems specialist should be employed to develop a system that will provide the necessary forms and records for the control of purchases. The system should be installed by the specialist.

The board of directors approved the recommendations and directed the president to take all necessary steps to place them in effect. In this connection, you have been called in to recommend the new purchase routine.

Your investigation disclosed that the system to be designed must be adequate to control the purchase of raw materials, supplies, and capital assets. Material Z must be purchased and stocked in the spring. Payment for this material is to be made in three equal monthly installments. Purchases for the past year were $1,500,000.

a. List the forms that you would recommend, including the number of copies, the routing of each, and its final disposition.

b. Prepare a procedural flow chart for the purchase procedure.

c. What books of original entry would be most logical for the system you recommend?

d. State specifically which forms in the purchasing routine are to be used as a basis for entries and what authority for entries is necessary.

e. What provision is to be made for the following items and how would they be treated in the accounting records?

(1) Purchase returns.

(2) Partially filled orders.

(3) Purchase of material Z.

(4) Discounts on the raw materials, supplies, and capital assets.

(5) Testing and inspecting materials received.

    f. What records and information will be kept in the purchasing agent's office?

6. How broad in scope is the purchasing function? What buying in large enterprises is commonly done by other personnel than purchasing employees?

7. Companies A and B are fairly similar as to products, geographic area served, and size. However, A's purchasing is centralized while B's is decentralized. Discuss the probable difference this would make insofar as the information system is concerned.

8. Indicate how budgetary control can be exercised over purchases.

9. What fixed, i.e., preprinted, data would appear on a purchase requisition form? In what respects would it differ from that appearing on a purchase order form?

10. How is a request for quotation form used? Explain its relationship to the price and quotation record.

11. What advantages, if any, can you see in use of receiving report forms which are not copies of the purchase order forms? What would be the advantage from an internal control standpoint of prenumbering receiving report forms?

12. What is the reason for distributing copies of the purchase order forms to the following departments or places?
    a. Receiving.
    b. Accounting.
    c. The requisitioning department.
    d. Vendor file in purchasing department.
    e. Numerical file in purchasing department.

13. What data should be deleted from the copy of the purchase order form sent to the receiving section and why? How can the receiving section be ready to receive materials if they do not know how much is to be received?

14. Under a situation in which purchase order forms are made out in quadruplicate, what distribution of copies would you expect was being made? Suppose instead that one additional copy was being prepared. What use would likely be made of it?

15. Distinguish between the functions of receiving and inspecting.

16. What data would be preprinted on a purchase invoice apron? Does use of an apron have any advantage over a rubber stamp?

17. Why is coding often performed by purchasing department personnel? Why is accuracy highly important in this function?

18. What is a debit memo? What steps should be taken in connection with debit memos to insure good control?

19. What are accommodation purchases? Discuss some problems they pose from a control standpoint.

20. Control over field purchasing is likely to be looser than over regular purchasing. Indicate why this is so and give some measures which can strengthen control over field purchases.

21. What evidence can be obtained that items ordered by us to be delivered to our customers directly were, in fact, delivered? Suggest some measures that would tend to insure that we bill our customers for all such shipments.

22. In approving vendor's invoices covering services rather than tangible items purchased, what evidence can be obtained that the services were actually received? Give specific examples.

23. In what respects should vendors and potential vendors be checked and why?

24. Describe several different plans for recording of purchase transactions in terms of debits and credits and the timing thereof.

25. In the order of their importance as you see them list five different internal control measures relevant to purchasing.

26. Look under "Purchasing" in any recent volume of *The Accountants' Index*. Find an article describing purchasing procedures in use in an organization. Summarize the article in approximately 800 words. Turn in three of the facsimile forms illustrated.

27. Design a form suitable for use as a traveling requisition. List the respects in which it differs from a conventional requisition.

28. In surveying the purchasing system of a company you find that no prices are entered on the purchase order forms when they are initially prepared. The wording "advise price" is typed in lieu of dollar amounts. Upon receipt of the vendor's invoice the amounts are recorded on the file copy of the purchase order form which is then processed for payment while the vendor invoice is retained in the files of the purchasing department. Evaluate this procedure.

29. A medium-sized furniture store with a weak internal control system had the misfortune to hire a dishonest employee as a buyer. He issued several purchase orders for direct shipments to his home and the homes of friends but, of course, had the furniture store pay the vendors' invoices which he approved for payment. His dishonesty was discovered more or less by accident. Bearing in mind the store is not large, and there are seven office employees including purchasing, accounting, and stenographic, what measures could be instituted to prevent a recurrence?

30. A privately conducted investigation revealed that the purchasing agent of a large sporting goods distributor had been given a boat worth $1,100 by one of the store's leading suppliers. This act is a clear violation of the store's policies and the purchasing agent was aware of the fact. Aside from the policy violation, of what other misdeeds would you suspect the purchasing agent? Assuming your suspicions are well founded, what steps might be taken in the future to avoid recurrences? (*Hint:* Do not assume any misdeed is confined to a single technique; several fraudulent possibilities exist here.)

31. Because vendors sometimes sent more than one copy of an invoice covering a single purchase, occasionally the same goods were being paid for twice by a local organization. What suggestions can you make for curing this problem?

32. The purchasing procedure is characteristically divided into at least four more detailed procedures. Identify and explain.

33. What special contribution can be made by a flexowriter in an order system?

34. A manufacturing company discovered that 25 per cent of their purchase orders (20,000 last year) were for minor single-shipment orders. The cost of paper work for each order was an great for a five dollar order as for a much larger order. Cost was reduced by combining a check with the purchase order. How was the solution related to form design? What are the control problems involved in such a system?

35. Prepare a questionnaire to be used by assistants on auditing engagements to determine whether or not the clients' systems of internal check are satisfactory with respect to (a) loans payable, (b) purchases, and the relative disbursements. (AICPA Examination)

36. The following questions relate to debit distribution:
    a. With what other procedure or procedures is debit distribution commonly associated?
    b. What balancing type of control can ordinarily be incorporated in a debit distribution procedure?
    c. In your opinion does debit distribution call for a relatively high order or low order of office personnel for its proper execution? Give reasons for your answer.
    d. Which is ordinarily more complex, debit distribution or credit distribution? Briefly, why?

37. A certain company uses a bookkeeping machine to prepare simultaneously a voucher, a check, and the voucher register. The purchase invoice is then forwarded to the key punch section where a card is punched for each line of the invoice. Suggest a method of getting distribution cards with fewer errors and greater speed.

38. The following communication media are used in a purchase and payable procedure. They are listed in random order. Rearrange the order of the communication on media to show their sequence in a single purchase and payable situation.
    a. Remittance advice.
    b. Purchase order.
    c. Request for quotation.
    d. Voucher.
    e. Apron.
    f. Request for purchase.
    g. Invoice.
    h. Receiving report.
    i. Check.

39. You have been asked to design a purchase requisition. Indicate the condition or conditions under which you would:
    a. Recommend prenumber control instead of number control.
    b. Recommend a different quality of paper for one of the copies.

    c. Recommend a different color for each copy.

    d. Recommend a different printing on various copies.

40. The Alpine Manufacturing Company maintains rigid inventory control over raw materials. All items required for production, including purchased parts, are recorded on perpetual inventory cards by the stock ledger clerks. When quantities are reduced to a predetermined ordering point, a requisition is forwarded by stock ledger clerks to the purchasing agent. In addition requisitions are initiated by stock ledger clerks when production schedules require materials not on hand or on order.

    The Alpine Manufacturing Company is a large company. You are asked to prepare a procedural flow chart showing the purchasing procedure, including the flow of forms and good internal control. Your chart should show the complete procedure through the preparation of the voucher for the payment of creditors for materials purchased.

41. The following relate to the subject of distribution of money amounts:

    a. Give two reasons debit distribution is more difficult and complex than credit distribution.

    b. By what physical or mechanical means is debit distribution frequently effected?

    c. What proof or control feature should be an integral part of any debit distribution procedure.

    d. Indicate the use of a "clearing account" in connection with debit distributions.

42. Prepare a diagram or flow chart of an entire purchase procedure of raw materials of a manufacturing concern. Your starting point should be the requisition and your ending point should be issuance of a combination voucher-check form. Take care to incorporate adequate internal control features. Some wording on your chart is desirable, but most of your ideas should be conveyed pictorially. Be careful that such details as distribution of multi-copy forms, posting to ledgers, etc., are indicated. You may assume any kind of organization structure of this manufacturing concern you wish so long as internal control is adequate.

43. The management of a department store has noticed a decrease in the percentage of purchase discounts (compared to purchases). Upon inquiry it is learned that substantially the same credit terms are in effect as when the discounts were relatively larger. There is no stringency of cash. Management is naturally anxious to correct the situation and calls on you to design a procedure (a) which will make it unlikely that available discounts will be overlooked (terms are 1/10, n/30), (b) which will avoid premature payments and duplicate payments (even though the latter will be refunded) and (c) which will show discounts available and discounts lost in the ledger. What would you do?

44. Name three kinds of volume statistics which you would obtain if you were converting a manual purchasing procedure to machines.

45. Whether the accounts payable or voucher payable plan is used, certain basic work must be done. Discuss briefly work preceding and including the recording of the liability.

SALES AND RECEIVABLES

The Selling Function

Selling is the life-blood of any business. It provides the focal point for customer contacts and the means of providing for customer needs with effectiveness and efficiency and in a manner that justifies the continuance of the business. The selling function has many aspects that are not discussed in this chapter but that are vital to business.

The detail of the selling function is a subject for study in its own right. This portion of Chapter 18 considers a typical sales and receivables procedure, a typical sales returns and allowance procedure, and a procedure for the write-off of worthless accounts. A number of the variations that are possible within each procedure will be discussed briefly in the context of the typical procedures.

Typical Sales and Receivables Procedure

Figure 18-2 illustrates the major flows of communication media within a typical sales and receivables procedure. The procedure illustrates a partial billing sequence in which orders are filled from a standard stock of finished goods. Study Figure 18-2 carefully, noting the following:

1. The *customer order* is received in the sales order department. Such orders can be received by telephone, directly from a customer by mail, or from a salesman who has called on a customer. Any sales procedure can be more effective when the order data are controlled to include appropriate description, stock numbers, sequencing of items and the like.

   On receipt of an order from a regular customer, a credit history check is made to determine whether the order is to be approved by the credit manager. In some businesses no credit checks are necessary since customers who have not established their credit will be shipped merchandise only on a C.O.D. basis. When a credit check is necessary, it is usually on a select basis, with regular customers having established their credit. Only orders from new or overextended customers will require approval. It is vital that the credit check does not delay the order-filling and shipping process, since customer service must be good.

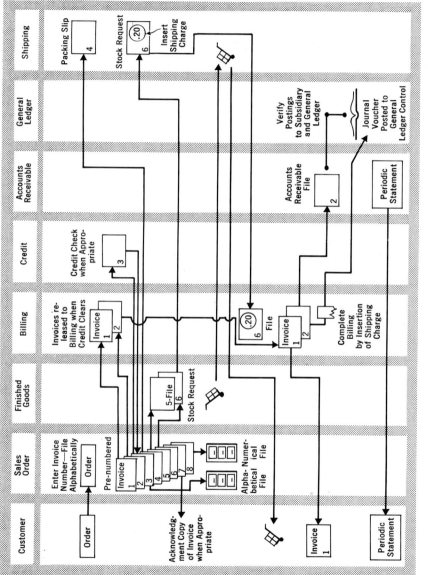

FIGURE 18-2. Typical Sales and Accounts Receivable Procedure

Adapted AICPA

2. In a procedure in which it is possible to prepare the complete customer's invoice when the order is received, the number of processing steps can be reduced. All of the clerical work of invoicing is done at one time. Such a procedure would not be appropriate when there are back orders, when freight or shipping charges are to be added to the invoice, or if any form or substitution or alteration occurs after the order is in process. Figure 18-2, in contrast, illustrates a *partial billing procedure*. Note that the invoice is not completed until the shipping charge is determined and added to the invoice in the Billing Section prior to being mailed to the customer.

     There is a clear distinction between the Billing Section and Accounts Receivable Section. Billing relates to invoicing while the Account Receivable Section maintains the record of amounts owed by customers and is responsible for sending periodic statements to customers.

3. *The acknowledgment copy* of the invoice is used only for certain types of businesses. When there is a period of time required for manufacturing or order filling, the acknowledgment to a customer that his order has been received and accepted may be important. When the order is to be filled from stock the acknowledgment copy may not be used as the merchandise could arrive at the customer's business as soon as the acknowledgment copy would arrive.

4. *Invoices should be pre-numbered* so as to provide a control record of all billings and a reference and audit trail for any customer inquiry. Note that a complete numerical control file is maintained. The alphabetical file can often provide important credit history information, and an audit trail to the control file for a specific sale when the number of the invoice is not known.

5. Copies of the invoice provide accurate information to the finished goods warehouse where the order is filled and transmitted to the shipping department. In the shipping department the shipping charges are determined and inserted on the stock request copy which is then transmitted to billing. Billing, having been notified that the order was shipped, can complete the invoice and release the original copy to the customer.

6. The *receivable procedure* must provide for a subsidiary receivable record and for posting the general ledger account receivable control account. It is necessary that a unit ticket type of sales document be provided for the account receivable subsidiary record. If a general purpose accounting machine is used for posting, the accounts receivable copy of the invoice can be sorted into appropriate posting sequence, and can provide the basic input data for the individual customers' account. In a ledgerless bookkeeping system, the copy of the invoice can be filed by customer name and itself become the subsidiary receivable record.

     In many businesses, the account receivable section is provided with several copies of each invoice, and credit follow-up is accomplished by mailing the second copy of the same invoice at the end of 30 days and, when necessary, a third copy at the end of 60 days. Note also that the billing section prepares a prelist of each batch of invoices with the total being transmitted to the general ledger section by journal voucher for appropriate entry. When a general purpose accounting machine is used in the account receivable section, the accumulation in the machine is verified to the general ledger bookkeeper posting as a clerical proof that the control and subsidiary posting agree.

Typical Sales Returns and Allowance Procedure

The sales returns and allowance procedure is of fundamental importance to control in that it is an authorization to remove an asset from the record. Through fraudulent sales returns or allowance authorizations, a shortage in assets can be concealed or a direct embezzlement perpetrated. Sales returns or allowances require careful control.

The major flows of communication media in a typical sales returns and allowance procedure are illustrated in Figure 18-3.

In most situations correspondence is necessary between a customer and the sales order section to determine whether merchandise that is defective or in some way not acceptable to the customer can be returned or if an allowance is to be made with the merchandise being retained by the customer. An authorization must be agreed upon to reduce the amount owed for the merchandise. *Allowances* should be authorized on a special prenumbered form with approval by the selling department and the credit manager, both of whom are independent of the receivable records. When authorized, the billing department would issue a prenumbered credit memorandum as the documentation for relieving the account receivable.

When merchandise is *returned*, there are two important aspects of the control procedure. First, it is necessary that the merchandise get back under accounting control and second, that the asset account be decreased when the merchandise comes into the receiving section. All returned merchandise should be routed through the receiving department where a Sales Return Receiving Slip is prepared. Two copies of this Sales Return Receiving Slip accompany the merchandise to the storeroom where the returned merchandise is picked up in the inventory once again. A copy is stamped to indicate that the item is under accounting control, and routed to the credit manager. When the acknowledgment copy is received by the credit manager, the Sales Return Receiving Slip can be sent to billing where it becomes the documentation for the issuance of a prenumbered credit memorandum.

One copy of the credit memorandum is a unit record that is sent to accounts receivable to reduce the subsidiary account balance, while a control total of all credit memoranda is sent by journal voucher to the general ledger section to reduce the control account.

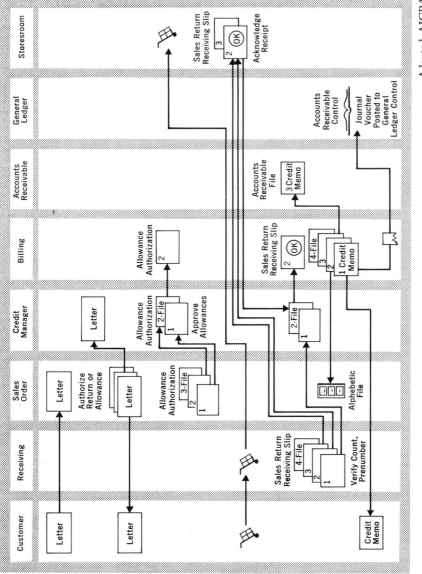

FIGURE 18-3.   Typical Sales Return and Allowance Procedure

Adapted AICPA

Typical Write-off of Accounts Receivable Procedure

Like sales returns and allowance, the write-off of accounts receivable removes an asset from the records, and thus has an important control dimension. Figure 18-4 illustrates a typical write-off of accounts receivable procedure. The account receivable balances owed by customers are analyzed periodically and an aged trial balance prepared. Such an aged trial balance can be the byproduct of establishing new monthly statements for customers, or can be the result of a special analysis. The aged trial balance is transmitted to the credit manager who has responsibility for collection and follow-up. After the appropriate collection activity, including the use of collection agencies and legal assistance, there may be evidence that the account is

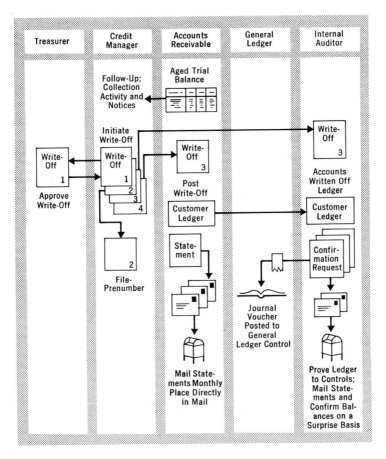

Adapted AICPA

FIGURE 18-4. Typical Write-off of Accounts Receivable Procedure

worthless. In such an instance the credit manager would initiate a write-off which, with an explanation and documentation, would be sent to an officer, probably the treasurer, for approval. On approval, one copy of the write-off authorization is sent to the auditor while a second copy is sent to accounts receivable. When the accounts receivable section is notified of the write-off, it posts the customers' ledger with an appropriate notation that the account was written off, and the account is transmitted to the auditor.

The internal auditor has responsibility for maintaining a ledger of written off accounts. There is no accounting control over this ledger; therefore special care is necessary. When a new written-off account is obtained, the auditor sends a confirmation request to the customer. Such a request could be in the form of a routine billing or a special letter to confirm the amount due. This request should be mailed directly to the customer by the auditor to make certain that no collections have been made on written-off accounts. The auditor would initiate the action to relieve the accounts receivable control account in the general ledger for the balance written off so that the sub-sidiary and control will be in agreement.

Note that the procedure makes it impossible for the credit manager to retain any amounts that had been sent directly to him in connection with this follow-up activity. A confirmation request going directly to the customer from the auditor would result in a customer complaint and disclosure if the amount had actually been paid. There is no way to relieve the account receivable control in the general ledger without a confirmation request having been sent out.

When the accounts receivable department sends out the monthly state-ments to customers, it is important that they be mailed directly by the ac-counts receivable section. In this way another method is available whereby any deletion of either cash-received-on-account, sales returns, or accounts written off would be disclosed by a customer complaint.

One of the characteristics of a procedure in which accounts receivable are written off is that the customer whose account is being written off is not aware of the action that has been taken. Periodic collection efforts should be continued and billing should not be halted. At the time of the annual independent audit, the external auditor can be requested to confirm the written-off ledger in its entirety unless there has been an audit verification of such events as bankruptcy, and the auditor is satisfied that there is no hope for additional collection. The current address for accounts written-off is often difficult to secure.

Internal Control of Sales and Receivables

An internal control questionnaire for sales and receivables is illustrated in Appendix A. Each question suggests good points of effective internal control. Careful study of specific and relevant questions should be helpful in evaluating a given procedure. Its use as a check list would be of great assistance to a systems analyst.

Sales and Receivables Questions, Problems, and Cases

1. The customer billing and collection functions of the Robinson Company, a small paint manufacturer, are attended to by a receptionist, an accounts receivable clerk and a cashier who also serves as a secretary. The company's paint products are sold to wholesalers and retail stores.

   The following describes all of the procedures performed by the employees of the Robinson Company pertaining to customer billings and collections:

   a. The mail is opened by the receptionist who gives the customers' purchase orders to the accounts receivable clerk. Fifteen to twenty orders are received each day. Under instructions to expedite the shipment of orders, the accounts receivable clerk at once prepares a five-copy sales invoice form which is distributed as follows:

   (1) Copy #1 is the customer billing copy and is held by the accounts receivable clerk until notice of shipment is received.
   (2) Copy #2 is the accounts receivable department copy and is held for ultimate posting of the accounts receivable records.
   (3) Copies #3 and #4 are sent to the shipping department.
   (4) Copy #5 is sent to the storeroom as authority for release of the goods to the shipping department.

   b. After the paint ordered has been moved from the storeroom to the shipping department, the shipping department prepares the bills of lading and labels the cartons. Sales invoice copy #4 is inserted in a carton as a packing slip. After the trucker has picked up the shipment the customer's copy of the bill of lading and copy #3, on which are noted any undershipments, are returned to the accounts receivable clerk. The company does not "back order" in the event of undershipments; customers are expected to reorder the merchandise. The Robinson Company's copy of the bill of lading is filed by the shipping department.

   c. When copy #3 and the customer's copy of the bill of lading are received by the accounts receivable clerk, copies #1 and #2 are completed by numbering them and inserting quantities shipped, unit prices, extensions, discounts, and totals. The accounts receivable clerk then mails copy #1 and the copy of the bill of lading to the customer. Copies #2 and #3 are stapled together.

   d. The individual accounts receivable ledger cards are posted by the accounts receivable clerk by a bookkeeping machine procedure whereby the sales register is prepared as a carbon copy of the postings. Postings are made from copy #2 which is then filed, along with staple-attached copy #3, in numerical order. Monthly the general ledger clerk summarizes the sales register for posting to the general ledger accounts.

e. Since the Robinson Company is short of cash, the deposit of receipts is also expedited. The receptionist turns over all mail receipts and related correspondence to the accounts receivable clerk who examines the checks and determines that the accompanying vouchers or correspondence contains enough detail to permit posting of the accounts. The accounts receivable clerk then endorses the checks and gives them to the cashier who prepares the daily deposit. No currency is received in the mail and no paint is sold over the counter at the factory.

f. The accounts receivable clerk uses the vouchers or correspondence that accompanied the checks to post the accounts receivable ledger cards. The bookkeeping machine prepares a cash receipts register as a carbon copy of the postings. Monthly the general ledger clerk summarizes the cash receipts register for posting to the general ledger accounts. The accounts receivable clerk also corresponds with customers about unauthorized deductions for discounts, freight or advertising allowances, returns, etc. and prepares the appropriate credit memos. Disputed items of large amount are turned over to the sales manager for settlement. Each month the accounts receivable clerk prepares a trial balance of the open accounts receivable and compares the resultant total with the general ledger control account for accounts receivable.

Required: Discuss the internal control weaknesses in the Robinson Company's procedures related to customer billings and remittances and the accounting for these transactions. In your discussion, in addition to identifying the weaknesses, explain what could happen as a result of each weakness. (AICPA Examination)

2. You have been employed as a systems analyst to study the portion of the Ace Manufacturing Company system that governs the sales—billing—accounts receivable—cash receipts procedures. After a careful investigation you conclude that most of the difficulties in the existing system are due to violations of the reasonable cost, reliability, organization structure, and human factors principles.

   a. (1) How important is the reasonable cost principle in the design of the system?

       (2) In the application of the reasonable cost principle, what are the "needs of management for information and internal control"?

       (3) What are the "reasonable costs" in the application of the reasonable cost principle?

   b. (1) What are the reliability, organization structure, and human factors principles of systems design?

       (2) How are they related, and what would be the application of each?

   c. Distinguish between the billing function and the accounts receivable function.

3. You audit a small corporation which publishes fiction and other nontechnical books. Sales are made by four salesmen to about 1,000 retail bookstores. Because of his familiarity with the bookstores, the sales manager has been asked to approve each order before shipment is made. In the case of delinquent accounts the sales manager decides whether or not further credit

should be extended and his approval is necessary for any write-off of bad accounts. One bookkeeper and two billing clerks handle the accounting records. The other personnel are three editors and their secretaries and one production man who contracts with printers for the manufacture of the books. Shipments are made from the printers' warehouses directly to the bookstores. In what ways are you, as an auditor, affected by the internal control over credit? Explain. (AICPA Examination)

4. You are in the process of designing an order-billing procedure to replace a procedure in which the order and the bill are prepared in separate operations. What are several of the major problems with the type of procedure you are attempting to design?

5. Describe briefly a punched card billing operation utilizing prepunched, end-printed cards in a tub file plan. For each item in the inventory there is a punched card in the tub file. Identify the cards that would be used to write the invoice. What uses could be made of the product cards and the summary cards after the billing is completed?

6. James Thomas opened a retail shoe store in 1963. The business was incorporated under the name of Thomas Shoe Fair, Inc. Toward the end of 1967, the corporation made purchases far in excess of those previously made. Early in 1968, it filed a petition in bankruptcy showing very little inventory and cash but large accounts payable for purchases. Thomas asserts that the shoes were sold at very low prices to attract new business and that he unwittingly outran his resources. A weekly entry of cash receipts in the check book was his only record of sales, and the creditors suspect fraud. You have been retained by the creditors to investigate.
   a. Outline the procedures you would follow in your investigation.
   b. Indicate the general contents of your report to the creditors. (AICPA Examination)

7. Enumerate five very important items which should be considered by an auditor in the evaluation of the nature and extent of the internal check and control relating to accounts receivable of a merchandising company. (AICPA Examination)

8. Order billing systems may be classified into three distinct types or groups. Identify them.

9. In a customer billing system, the customer often fails to return the billhead with the payment, causing difficulty in matching the payment with the proper account. How might a department store use form design to solve the problem?

10. For several years you have been making the annual audit of a manufacturing company as of December 31st. In order to spread out your work as much as is feasible, you have decided to do as much interim work as can profitably be done on this engagement, starting about two months before the year-end.
   a. You are to prepare an audit program in detail for preliminary work to be done in November on accounts receivable and sales.

b. You are to prepare a program in detail for the year-end examination of accounts receivable and sales, taking into account the work done in the preliminary examination.

Prepare your programs taking into consideration the procedures and controls described below. Your files reveal the following information:

> All sales are charged to accounts receivable, any cash collected before or at the time of sale being credited to the customer's account. For each sale an order is written up (usually by the salesman obtaining the order); a shipping order is prepared in the production planning department; a shipping notice is prepared in the shipping department; and, based on these forms and the order, an invoice is prepared in the billing department. Prenumbered forms are used. The invoices are recapped daily by products and recorded in the sales register. Posting to customers' accounts is from a copy of the invoice. A credit to the perpetual inventory is based on the shipping notice. Sales are all 2/10, n/30 from date of invoice. Credit memoranda for returns, etc., are supported by a receiving report, or are approved by the sales manager if they involve an adjustment or allowance.

> Most collections are checks received by mail. The mail is opened by a clerk who prepares a list of the checks, which list is sent to the accounting department where it is later reconciled to the cashier's report for the day. The checks are turned over to a clerk who records them on a cash report after checking them as to the correctness of the discount, irregularities, etc. The checks are then turned over to the cashier who summarizes and enters them in the cash book, prepares the deposit ticket and deposits them. The cash report goes to the accounts receivable bookkeeping section for use in posting to individual accounts. Checks or currency received from customers not remitting by mail are paid directly to the cashier, who issues a prenumbered receipt to the customer and sends one copy of the receipt to the clerk writing up the cash report.

> Write-off of accounts as uncollectible is recommended by the credit manager and approved by the treasurer. There are about 3,500 accounts in the customers' ledger, which is divided into eight sections each with a control summary.

> Posting is by machine which accumulates the totals posted into each section of the ledger. These totals are posted to the section control. The average sale is $500 with a range of individual sales of from $50 to $10,000. (AICPA Examination)

11. The Green Manufacturing Company, a medium-sized company, maintained a ledgerless Account Receivable file. At the end of each month the Account Receivable bookkeeper prepares an aged trial balance and checks the total of the trial balance to the control account. Prepare a procedural flow chart illustrating a procedure for the write-off of bad accounts. Make any comments on the chart that are necessary to reflect good internal control.

12. The Groves Wholesale Company has established the practice of requiring all sales returns to be processed through the Receiving Room. Prepare a procedural flow chart illustrating a procedure for the return of merchandise.

Make any comments on the chart that are necessary to reflect good internal control.

13. You are auditing the Alaska Branch of Far Distributing Co. This branch has substantial annual sales which are billed and collected locally. As a part of your audit you find that the procedures for handling cash receipts are as follows:

    Cash collections on over-the-counter sales and C.O.D. sales are received from the customer or delivery service by the cashier. Upon receipt of cash the cashier stamps the sales ticket "paid" and files a copy for future reference. The only record of C.O.D. sales is a copy of the sales ticket which is given to the cashier to hold until the cash is received from the delivery service.

    Mail is opened by the secretary to the credit manager and remittances are given to the credit manager for his review. The credit manager then places the remittances in a tray on the cashier's desk. At the daily deposit cut-off time the cashier delivers the checks and cash on hand to the assistant credit manager who prepares remittance lists and makes up the bank deposit which he also takes to the bank. The assistant credit manager also posts remittances to the accounts receivable ledger cards and verifies the cash discount allowable.

    You also ascertain that the credit manager obtains approval from the executive office of Far Distributing Co., located in Chicago, to write off uncollectible accounts, and that he has retained in his custody as of the end of the fiscal year some remittances that were received on various days during the last month.

    Required: a. Describe the irregularities that might occur under the procedures now in effect for handling cash collections and remittances. b. Give procedures that you would recommend to strengthen internal control over cash collections and remittances. (AICPA Examination)

14. Indicate three different methods of accomplishing "posting" to subsidiary accounts receivable records. It is not necessary to assume the usage of any particular machines or devices in your answer. Describe each of the three in 25 words or less.

15. Both cycle billing and ledgerless bookkeeping involve temporary filing of original documents to constitute a ledger. In what respects do they differ?

16. Blank Wholesalers has a limited number of accounts receivable customers, most of whose accounts are fairly active. Posting to their accounts is done on a bookkeeping machine. Media are accumulated for a week and then posted at one time. Commonly about one-half of the accounts in the ledger are affected on a typical posting run. Blank started out using "old and new balance" proof to verify posting and continues to use this proof method even though certain changes in the pattern of customer activity have evolved. Do you recommend continuance of use of this proof method? If not, what alternate plan would you suggest? Give reasons to support your choice.

17. The Reliable Company receives all sales orders through the mail from about 2,000 different customers, most of whom place an order about every two

months. Credit approval is necessary before any order can be written up, but only orders from new customers are routed to the credit department for approval. Orders are normally filled from stock and shipped prepaid to customers within four days, with actual shipping charges being billed to the customer. A ledgerless bookkeeping system is used for accounts receivable. You have been asked to recommend a more complete procedure. Answer the questions that follow *without* changing any of the above facts.

a. Describe the credit authorization procedure you recommend.

b. What type of billing procedure do you recommend? Would a prebilling procedure be more desirable than a partial billing procedure? Explain.

c. Explain ledger bookkeeping. How does it work?

d. What type of billing system would you recommend? Would cycle billing be appropriate?

e. What weaknesses or limitations do you see in the procedure you have described for ledgerless bookkeeping?

f. Prepare a procedural flow chart for the sales procedure you recommend.

18. In studying a given sales procedure, discuss briefly the main points of inquiry.

19. Why is adequate control over credit memorandums issued important in the internal control of accounts receivable? Describe or illustrate using a procedural flow chart a system in which adequate control is provided.

20. Describe briefly the principal elements of a sound credit administration.

21. Name two specific sources of credit information outside the business other than that furnished by the customer.

22. XYZ Company operates an electronics supply business in a small midwestern city. While the company has some customers who live in the immediate area and who come to its place of business for making selections and taking delivery of merchandise, the bulk of its orders (over 95 per cent) are received through the mail. Customers order the company's advertised specials from ads which appear in some electronics magazines with national distribution. Principally, however, they order from a 150-page catalog which anyone can receive the first time by sending in a coupon appearing in the ads. (Thereafter the annual catalog is sent only to customers who ordered $10 or more of goods in the preceding year.)

The company stocks over 25,000 different items. However, many of these are simply different sizes of similar components. For example, customers may select from over 40 different values of ½ watt resistors, another 40 of one watt resistors, etc. The inventory is divided into eight major categories, each of which is in a separate section of the business. The entire operation is in a three-story building which covers about half a city block.

Except for large quantity orders, all customers pay the same unit prices for merchandise. Customers fall principally into two major categories: (a) hobbyists who order parts, hi-fi kits, receivers, antennas, etc., and (b) TV and radio repair shops which order tubes, repair and replacement parts, etc. Type (a) customers send cash for the most part, though on orders totaling $40 or more installment payments can be arranged. Type (b) customers mostly buy on 30-day terms and pay by the invoice, though some send cash with their orders.

Delivery of goods is effected principally by (1) parcel post on shipments up to 20 pounds or (2) freight or express. Parcel post charges are always either remitted by the customer or billed to him. Freight or express charges are invariably paid by the customer upon delivery of goods by the carrier.

a. Design a tear-out order form suitable for inclusion in the company's catalogs. (You may ignore credit application information which appears on the reverse side.)

b. Design an invoice suitable for mailing to credit customers when shipments are made. Fill in the data which might appear if two different items were sold and had been shipped parcel post.

c. If the data on a customer order from the catalog are transferred to a shipping order form and to other related forms immediately upon receipt of the order, what forms might receive some or all of this information?

d. Show typical sales analyses which the company might make. You need not try to describe the merchandise or types of merchandise, but simply refer to these as A, B, C, etc.

e. What would be the more important considerations confronted in the design of procedures for over-the-counter sales to customers who come to XYZ Company and are served by a sales clerk who delivers goods to customers. Emphasize control aspects over sales and goods; minimize those relating to cash.

23. Several basic types of statements can be sent to customers. Describe each briefly. Indicate which type would probably be used in connection with (a) machine-posted records, and (b) ledgerless bookkeeping.

24. Design statement and ledger forms for use on a posting machine. Enter the following transactions reflected in a manual posting situation onto your statement form. Be careful to be both neat and complete in filling in the data.

Jim Farr, 321 Oak St., Bee, Texas

Feb. 29	Balance	$30.00	Mar. 8	SR1	$10.00
Mar. 5	S1	50.00	Mar. 15	CR1	25.00
Mar. 18	S3	70.00			

25. Many firms feel that giving a customer a sales receipt is a waste of time because most customers throw the receipt away unless it is enclosed in the package. Do you agree? Explain. What procedures can be followed to encourage customers to take their sales slips and even to examine them closely?

26. In analyzing the procedures involved in the business transactions, certain definite information must be obtained. Illustrate what is meant by this in the case of sales transactions.

27. What communication media can be prepared from a single copy of an order provided the latter is specially written on a ditto or hectograph master?

28. The illustration on the following page sets out in visual form the flow of a charge sale in a wholesale establishment. Complete the missing elements.

FLOW OF CHARGE SALE ON WHOLESALE LEVEL

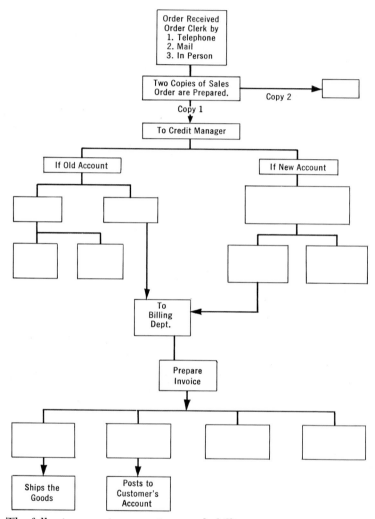

29. The following questions pertain to cycle billing:
    a. What is cycle billing?
    b. Why is it used?
    c. To what kinds of business situations is it generally unsuited?
    d. What problem would cycle billing pose in taking a year-end trial balance?

30. Illustrate or explain the manner in which a "batch," "line proof," and "trial balance proof" can be combined into an account receivable procedure in which a general purpose accounting machine is used.

31. Name and describe briefly methods which can be used to assure that all sales orders received at a processing station are accounted for—that none are lost or handled twice.

32. You have been asked by the editor of a forthcoming *Encyclopedia of Modern Business Practice* to write the section on "Concepts of Receivable Control." The editor knows you can do an authoritative job but has somewhat limited you by specifying that your entry can range only from 250 to 350 words (the work is to be fairly concise and accounting is but one of many subjects in the encyclopedia). The editor states that many contributors are appending a brief bibliography to their entries and that if this is included it does not count in the word limitation as it will be set in small type.

     Prepare a draft of your section in this work. (*Suggestion*: First outline your material, then write in draft.)

33. What special advantages does the punch-card method afford for sales accounting?

34. List as many ways that sales might be classified as you can, giving the reason for each classification and the code which you would use.

35. If a business uses punch card equipment, why would it code its customers?

36. The Utah Manufacturing Company is a large manufacturer of electronic equipment. They issue credit memorandums to customers for both adjustments and returned merchandise through their billing department.
     a. Design a credit memorandum for use by the Utah Manufacturing Company.
     b. Prepare a flow chart for the credit memorandum procedure indicating the necessary internal controls.

37. The following questions pertain to ledgerless bookkeeping:
     a. Of what does the accounts receivable subsidiary ledger consist?
     b. How is control over this ledger maintained as new items enter the ledger?
     c. How are partial payments handled?
     d. In what general type of situation would ledgerless bookkeeping be most effective?
     e. What is a principal advantage of ledgerless bookkeeping?

38. In preparing control reports for shipping and delivery procedures, it is possible to issue cost reports. What other type of report might be used in aiding the management and control of operations of a shipping and delivery department? Give an example as part of your answer.

39. When sales are made on credit and shipped or delivered, three important points of check are available. These are: (a) the sales order, (b) the report of shipment or delivery, and (c) the sales invoice. Explain how each of these could be made to serve to protect the selling concern.

40. Discuss how to achieve internal control over cash sales made over the counter in a retail store.

41. In what factors do the savings in complete pre-billing over separate order system and billing procedures lie? Explain the significance of each factor.

42. From the following chronological history of a customer's account, prepare the different types of statements commonly sent to customers at the end of the

month. You do not need to repeat the common portion after drawing your first statement; merely give the different or variable parts on subsequent exhibits.

March	1	Owed from Feb.	$310	March	21	Purchase Return	$ 45
	5	Purchase	290		25	Payment	290
	7	Payment	310		30	Purchase	115
	12	Purchase	270				

43. It is said that in designing a sales distribution (or any other type of distribution), the entire procedure for recording sales from the moment the original record is produced must be studied. Explain how a step that is preliminary to the actual distribution procedure can affect the method of distribution.

44. Apply the concept of "cost center accumulation" to sales distribution. Assume a firm with headquarters in Chicago and ten sales branches scattered throughout the U.S.

45. The ROL Wholesale Company requires that all merchandise returned by customers be processed through the receiving room, and that a Sales Return Receiving Slip be issued. Recently there has been some concern about whether or not all returned merchandise was being received in the Stores Department. There was also question as to whether both the general and subsidiary customer ledger were being posted properly. Illustrate a procedure to accomplish the above, stating and illustrating specifically all of the controls that are necessary.

46. The Acme Lumber Company receives remittances by mail, but also makes cash sales over the counter. As a part of the control procedure over cash receipts, the company uses a cash sales clearing account. How does the sales clearing account provide control?

47. Outline briefly a system or routine for sales returns which would prevent employees from taking merchandise for their own personal use without proper authorization.

48. The Seashore Company receives sales orders from salesmen on the road, from customers through the mail, by telephone, or directly at the store-warehouse. Many items ordered are not carried in stock and must be back-ordered. What communication media would be basic evidence of the original sale? What provision should be made in the procedure for backorder?

49. In the design of a sales procedure a systems analyst has recommended that the customer be sent an acknowledgment copy of his order. Under what conditions would such a copy be desirable?

50. How is it possible to design a system for control over the write-off of accounts receivable so that there can be little doubt that the accounts being written off have not been collected?

51. In what situation would the use of a "Cash Sales Clearing Account" facilitate control, and how would the control be accomplished?

52. You have been asked to design a system for control of Accounts Receivable. When orders are received from customers, an invoice is prepared in the Sales Order Department in an original plus five copies as follows:

Copy No.	Description	From Sales Order Department To
0	Invoice Copy	Billing
1	Credit Copy	Credit
2	Ledger Copy	Billing
3	Packing Slip Copy	Shipping
4	Stock Request Copy	Finished Goods
5	Acknowledgment	Customer

All cash is received from customers through the mail. At the time cash is received, a single copy of a remittance advise is prepared in the mail room for each receipt and sent to the cash receipt section with the cash. A daily remittance list is also prepared in three copies as follows:

    0 — To Cash Receipts for entry in the Cash Receipts Book

    1 — To Accounts Receivable

    2 — File

Prepare a procedural flow chart for Accounts Receivable illustrating the needed accounting control.

CASH RECEIPTS AND DISBURSEMENTS

There have been a greater number of varied and unique control procedures designed for cash than for any other business asset. Cash must be controlled not only against internal error or embezzlement but also against external pilferage. The liquid and non-traceable nature of cash has much to do with the control problem.

Cash, being difficult to identify specifically and easily transportable, is often the objective of internal manipulation. Procedures or controls that can be devised to minimize cash losses at a reasonable cost are highly desirable. There are instances in which cash is controlled with more enthusiasm than other assets such as tools or merchandise. The possible loss to a business of noncash assets may be as great if not greater than the possible cash loss, yet cash receives the most attention.

Nature and Control of Cash

Cash funds include currency, coins, and negotiable papers such as checks. Procedure relating to control of currency and coins may be different than those relating to checks. In all handling procedures for cash, checks included, an effort must be made to reduce substantially the exposure to loss. Such procedures as immediate deposit, centralization of handling, maintenance of only small balances, and making an immediate record are a part of the major cash control effort.

Checks being received in a business may be drawn to the order of the particular business or, in some instances, they may be drawn to cash. In designing a procedure for handling checks, it is desirable to have them endorsed for deposit at the earliest possible time. In supermarkets, for example, it is customary to use a deposit endorsement at any point where checks are cashed. In this way the checks are endorsed immediately "for deposit only" and are of value only to the depositor. If there should be a holdup or should the checks be misappropriated in any way, they would not be negotiable to the individual that possesses them.

In handling checks received from customers on an account, some provision should be made to distinguish them from checks cashed for customers as an accommodation. There have been instances in which customers have asked that their checks be cashed as an accommodation and at a later date the cancelled check presented as evidence of payment on an account. A special endorsement procedure to identify checks received on account is desirable.

The control of cash requires adequate physical safeguards. For example, a cash register can be utilized as a receptacle for cash received. When cash is removed from the cash register for the preparation of a deposit, it should be kept in the firm's safe if the cash is to be on hand overnight or for some prolonged period of time. When the cash is moved to the bank, it is very likely that an armed messenger service such as Brinks would accompany the cash in its movement as an adequate safeguard. Once the cash has been deposited, the safeguarding is a responsibility of the bank.

Centralization of the cash receiving function reduces the number of individuals handling cash, and thus the exposure to possible loss. In general, the fewer people involved in cash handling, the easier it is to establish effective cash control.

Procedures for Control Prior to the First Record

Many cash shortages occur prior to the establishment of the first record. Once there is an adequate record and cash is controlled physically, such as in a cash register, a misappropriation is much more difficult. In the control of cash the weakest link is prior to the first record. For example, in a retail store a customer may buy ten dollars worth of merchandise. If the clerk should take the money from the customer and put it in his or her pocket, there is no record or proof that would establish the fact or amount of the cash shortage. On the other hand, once it is recorded on a cash register and added into a locked-in total, a record exists that cannot be altered by the person receiving the cash and any shortage could be detected. Business men, however, are not completely helpless against the withholding of cash prior to the initial record. A number of procedures and devices have been developed and used to minimize the probability of such losses.

1. *Customer Audit.* The cash register may be placed in such a way that customers are able to see the amounts that are rung up and flashed in large figures in the windows provided for the purpose. In this way the customer can see the amount that the clerk has registered as the sale and is able to inquire should an amount not be rung up or should a smaller amount be rung up, for example, $.10 instead of $1.10.

Some businesses have gone further in attempting to obtain effective customer audit by the use of cash registers that produce a tape receipt for cash received. Techniques such as posting a sign that will entitle the customer to a dollar if he does not receive his receipt within 30 seconds after he has made his payment, encourage customers to ask for a receipt and thus help in control. Other techniques used in businesses such as short-order restaurants or drive-ins is to post a notice that the customer's food order is free if the receipt from the cash register has a red star or some special mark on it. In such instances every customer will expect a receipt in order to determine whether or not his food is free, again aiding in making certain that all cash has been rung up appropriately on the cash register.

2. *Machine Features.* Most cash registers are constructed so that they will ring at the time the cash drawer is opened. This will signal to anyone in the store that a transaction is being recorded on the cash register, thus affording other people an opportunity to witness amounts flashed by the cash register.

3. *Limits to Cash.* The technique of keeping a limited amount of cash in the cash register can reduce exposure to loss. When a customer comes in with a large bill, it is necessary for the clerk to call one of the managers and obtain the necessary change. In this situation it is difficult for the clerk to fail to ring up the appropriate transaction and less cash is in the cash register, reducing the possibility of a major manipulation. In addition, there is a psychological advantage in that clerks know they are being supervised when they handle cash.

4. *Shopping Services.* Professional shopping services are available to make certain that clerks are following the procedures established for control of cash. At certain intervals shoppers will come into the store and purchase items, noting every detail of the procedure followed by the clerk. Ordinarily purchases will be for large amounts or made in such a way that if employee manipulation is occurring, there would be a temptation on the part of the employee to put the plan into operation. After store hours the shopper returns the merchandise to the store with a report on whether or not proce-

dures were followed. If amounts were not rung up or an irregularity discovered, the clerk would be watched carefully to establish facts more clearly, or he would be called in and the matter corrected.

5. *Internal Audit.* In certain cash operations it is possible to devise internal audit procedures whereby the completeness of initial cash records can be verified. For example, in certain coin-operated machines the cash collected drops into a sealed box. The boxes are brought to a central point under appropriate supervision and opened and an original record recorded. The internal audit procedure would be necessary only when boxes overflow in the machine. The coins would be available to the collector yet there would be no record. Through the internal audit device of counting the overflow coins in certain machines and later verifying the fact that coins were turned in by the collector, the business is assured that all cash received is recorded.

6. *Numerical or Meter Control.* There are many instances in which a reconciliation of sales is possible. For example, when theater tickets are sold they can be pre-numbered and at the end of any given day the number of tickets sold times the amount of admission collected should equal the cash on hand. Numerical control can be extended to many operations in which control would appear to be difficult. In a theater, for example, it is possible for the popcorn concession to account for all cash collected by numbering the bags or boxes in which popcorn is to be sold. Inasmuch as a container is necessary for each sale, there is reasonable certainty that all incoming cash will have been recorded.

7. *Inventory Control.* An effective means of making certain that the business receives cash for all merchandise sold is to charge an individual with the assets that he is attempting to control. Such inventory control systems exist for many route men and also in certain retail stores. In such instances the clerk in the store or the route man is charged with all merchandise at retail price. He must then either have the merchandise in his inventory or turn over the appropriate amount of cash to the cashier. Should any cash be retained a shortage would show up immediately.

This same method can be used in gasoline stations, for example, where meters exist. When gasoline is delivered to a station, it is put in a bulk tank and when it is delivered to a customer, is recorded on a meter. At the end of any given period the attendant should have the amount of cash or customer charges equal to the value of the gasoline metered on the gas pump.

Good control of cash receipts cannot ordinarily be effective enough to remove completely the possibility of some cash shortage. The controls should be effective enough, however, to prevent any sizeable cash defalcation.

An employer has a strong responsibility to his employee for devising a system of control that will remove temptation on the part of the employee. Adequate controls should be provided even though they may cost more than the amount that could be saved. The existence of a good control system may prevent a trusted employee from becoming involved in the unauthorized taking of funds that he would consider as a "temporary loan" but on which he is later unable to make good. It is possible for a good employee to find himself in a situation where "temporary" borrowing from the firm seems to be a solution to a serious problem, such as illness in the family. The employer has a definite obligation to his employees to remove the temptation for unauthorized borrowing and to leave the individual in a position where he cannot possibly be accused of misappropriation. The procedure should eliminate the circumstances in which these misappropriations are possible.

Typical Cash Received on Account Procedure

Cash received on account typically comes into a business through the mail or is paid to a clerk or central cashier. In either instance the customer should have his payment acknowledged. He should receive a receipt or at least a monthly statement with the amount paid shown. A typical cash received on account procedure is as shown in Figure 18-5.

In the design of a procedure to control incoming cash received through the mail, it is important that no one in the mailroom where the correspondence is opened, in the cashier's office where the money is summarized and a deposit prepared, or in the account receivable section where the asset reduction is recorded, have complete control over the transaction. By the separation of duties it is not possible for any individual to withhold cash without the fact being discovered by one of the others. In studying Figure 18-5, it can be noted that when the mail goes to the mailroom the checks or cash are *immediately* withdrawn from the correspondence. A remittance advice is prepared and in many cases authenticated and transmitted to accounts receivable. Note that the remittance advice is a unit ticket and can thus be arranged to match an alphabetic receivable file in such a way as to facilitate posting to reduce the receivable. In many procedures the invoice or statement that is sent to a customer is prepared in such a way that the portion with the name and address of the customer is returned with the payment. This is common with telephone, utility, and department store invoices, and provides good documentation for the payment.

Note that the withdrawal of the checks from the mail is important. Cash, including checks, should not be circulated in an office but should be retained by the cashier for safe keeping. The fallacy that because a check is made out to the company it can be safely circulated has little validity. Whenever there is cash within the business, such as from refunds or cafeteria receipts, from which checks could be cashed, there is little control. Such checks could be included in a valid deposit without even the necessity for forging a signature.

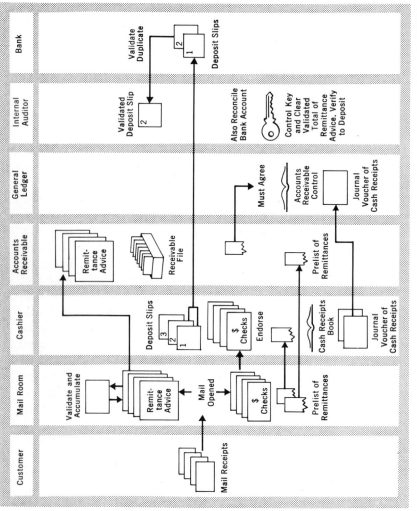

FIGURE 18-5. Typical Cash Received-On-Account Procedure

Adapted AICPA

In the mailroom a prelist of remittance is prepared either as a separate listing or using a validating machine. One copy of the prelist goes to the cashier to notify him of the amount of cash being transmitted, and the second copy goes to accounts receivable with the remittance advice. Note that the source of posting the general ledger is the journal-voucher notification by the cashier of the amount of the deposit of cash receipts. This amount must agree with the accumulated total of the items posted to the subsidiary receivable file. It should also be noted that validated copies of the deposit slip go to a staff accountant such as the internal auditor who will also have responsibility for the reconciliation of the bank account and control the key of the validating and other cash accumulating devices. The accountant has the responsibility for reconciliation and verification of all cash received amounts. Notice that it is not possible for the mailroom clerk, the cashier, the accounts receivable bookkeeper, or the general ledger bookkeeper to withhold funds or manipulate the records without being detected.

Typical Cash Received Over the Counter Procedure

The procedure for handling cash received from customers when there is no asset record, such as a recorded receivable, requires a different control procedure than one in which the accounts receivable are on the books. It can be noted that the internal control duty of supervision is vital when there is no record. For example, when cash is received for promotion items such as flower seeds for 50¢ and a boxtop, supervision is a key control. Another common type of situation in which cash is received and there is no accounts receivable record is a cash sale. A cash register often records the first record of such a transaction. A typical cash received over the counter procedure when there is no account receivable is illustrated in Figure 18-6.

In Figure 18-6 it can be noted that when cash is received from a customer it is rung up on a cash register at the point where the finished goods are delivered. Many cash registers validate the sales ticket and one copy is returned to the customer. In other situations a cash register receipt is delivered to the customer to evidence the amount of cash paid in. In situations in which sales tickets are made for cash sales due to inventory control or other needs, copies are sent to the billing department. A summary that must agree with the cash sale figure accumulated is sent to the general ledger. The cashier, who receives the cash from all cash registers, prepares a deposit slip and reports the amount of cash received. In the general ledger section a cash sales clearing account can be maintained to which the amount of cash received is posted from the separate sources. When the cash sales clearing account *zeroes out,* there has been no error. The amounts reported from independent sources are in agreement.

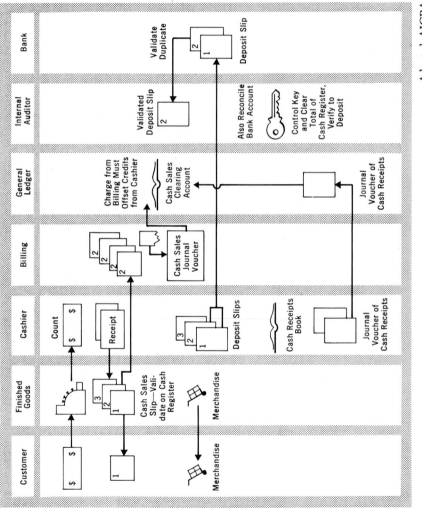

FIGURE 18-6. Typical Cash Received-Over-The-Counter Procedure

Adapted AICPA

Typical Voucher Check Disbursement Procedures

The control over disbursements normally depends upon two procedures —the procedure for controlling check disbursements and the procedure for small "petty cash" payments. The first procedure, covering check disbursement, is very common. Figure 18-7 shows a typical voucher check disbursement procedure.

The voucher check disbursement procedure is centered about a form that combines a check and a remittance advice. The check eventually becomes negotiable and the remittance advice provides the vendor with information about the invoice or invoices being paid by the check or the

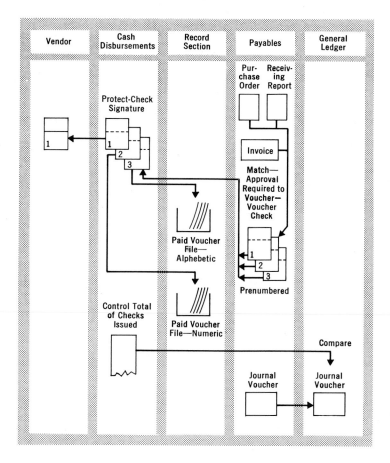

FIGURE 18-7. Typical Voucher Check Procedure

reason for the payment. Copies of the combined form serve various record needs.

In a typical voucher check disbursement procedure, the record of an amount owed is not recorded in the ledger until payment. The procedure is excellent for situations in which adequate working capital is available so that fully processed invoices can be paid immediately or accumulated and paid on a specific date.

When an invoice is received in the payable section from purchases or other sources with the necessary verifications, it is matched with the appropriate purchase order and receiving report. All of the documents are assembled and reviewed for completeness, accuracy, and coding and, if all is well, approval is given for the issuance of a voucher check. If a number of invoices are on hand from the same vendor, they may be accumulated and processed together, with only one check written for the several invoices. Some payable sections accumulate invoices and issue checks only at specific periods, for example on the 10th, 20th, and last day of the month. This procedure may conserve effort to some extent as several invoices can be accumulated and paid by one check. Such procedures are called "build-up voucher" procedures.

In a voucher check disbursement procedure, the data from approved invoices are entered on a remittance advice, and the attached check is drawn for the appropriate amount. One copy of the voucher check (copy 2) is also a voucher jacket in which supporting documents are accumulated and filed in numeric order. Copy 3 is filed in alphabetic order to provide an audit trail.

In some voucher check procedures, documents are not attached to the voucher, but control is obtained by centralization of voucher responsibility and strict numerical document control. Such procedures usually provide an audit trail to supporting documentation. For example, in a voucher check disbursement procedure of a Savings and Loan Association, the check can be traced to signed withdrawal slips, loan papers, etc.

The voucher check set is sent from payable to the cash disbursement section for imprinting the signature and processing through a check protector. The original copy of the signed and protected voucher check is sent directly to the vendor by the cash disbursement section. The voucher check copy filed in numerical sequence also serves the function of a check register and facilitates bank reconciliation. Actual reconciliation is accomplished by a staff accountant rather than someone from the cash disbursement section. The voucher jacket copy and attached documents are mutilated or marked paid to eliminate the possibility of any of the documents being presented for payment a second time, and are then transferred to the Records Section for storage. The third copy is filed in an alphabetic file to enable the location of the control voucher when an inquiry is received in which the name of a vendor is known but not the voucher number.

Periodically, a journal voucher is prepared to transfer the accumulated total of voucher checks issued to the general ledger section. The total of cash disbursements is also reported to the general ledger section. The total amount of disbursements is compared and, if in agreement, posted. Voucher check disbursements may be controlled by batch and by number.

The signature on the check is not the real control over disbursements in most organizations although it serves to make the check negotiable. The signature on a check is often imprinted at the rate of several hundred per minute. The real control over disbursements is the final review of documents that evidence the completion of processing and verification operations, approval of the coding, and authorization to issue the check.

Certain types of disbursement transactions may require special review and approval by officers. For example, the payment of amounts over a specified total or payments for capital acquisitions may require approval of the treasurer.

Where there is an expense control account in the general ledger rather than individual expense accounts, a copy of the voucher check may be sent to the subsidiary purchases and expense section. In this manner the necessary "unit tickets" are provided for an accurate debit distribution. When certain detailed cost data are required, the debit distribution procedure may be expanded.

Typical Imprest Petty Cash Disbursement Procedure

For complete control over cash disbursements a procedure must be implemented for cash pay outs along with the check disbursement procedure. If all cash receipts are deposited intact daily, the complete disbursement procedure can be well controlled.

In the instance of small cash refunds when a cash register is utilized, cash paid outs from receipts are not unusual nor do they necessarily invalidate the control procedure. The small businessman, for example, may personally be in control of all cash handling operations and can see no control advantage of not paying small bills out of the cash register if the necessary documentation is obtained and the "paid outs" are recorded on the cash register. Small refund paid outs are made in the supermarket where bottles are returned as part of the standard operation along with the redemption of coupons and the like. The need for customer service must be balanced with the control advantage of not making small payments from receipts, but establishment of a separate petty cash fund from which to make small payments. Cash registers can be arranged in such a manner that there is a maximum of supervision.

Except for the small business, the advantages of being able to reconcile receipts with deposits and the lessening of exposure that comes by requiring that all cash to be deposited at least daily and intact, may provide a substantial control advantage. In such situations a petty cash disbursements procedure is vital. Figure 18-8 shows a typical imprest petty cash disbursement procedure.

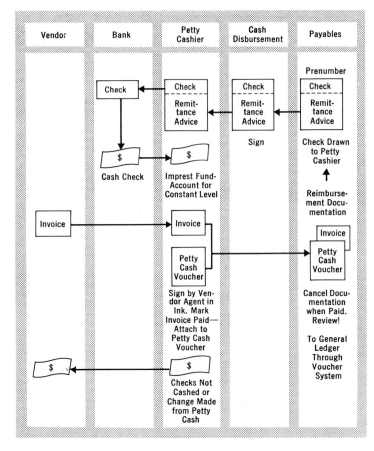

FIGURE 18-8. Typical Imprest Petty Cash Disbursement Procedure

The imprest concept is one that is used for different purposes in systems design. There may be an imprest payroll account, imprest change fund or imprest petty cash funds. Imprint funds are those maintained at a stipulated dollar amount so that control is relatively simple. In studying Figure 18-8 it can be noted that in the imprest petty cash fund a petty cashier is assigned responsibility for the fund. In drawing a check to establish or reimburse the petty cash fund, it should be made out to the petty cashier so that there is evidence that all such payment checks have gone to the appropriate individual. Establishment of the fund at a given level enables the responsible petty cashier to have either cash in the fund or receipts for cash that has been disbursed equal to the fund total.

An imprest petty cash fund should be large enough to cover the necessary disbursements for a specific period of time, such as one or two weeks. The actual cash amount of the fund could be quite large. There is often a policy establishing the maximum size of disbursement that does not require a check, such as $10 or $20. Such policies do not preclude the issuance of checks for small amounts through the check disbursement procedure.

When a vendor or other creditor presents an invoice for payment the petty cashier will have the individual sign a receipt in ink to prevent alteration. The invoice is attached to the petty cash receipt and is retained in the petty cash fund until such time as the fund is reimbursed. Upon reimbursement, the petty cash receipt and attached documentation is sent to the payable section where the disbursements are reviewed and a reimbursement check authorized to maintain the fund at the prescribed level. It should be noted that the petty cash fund should not be used as a change fund or fund out of which checks can be cashed. Proper utilization of the fund minimizes the opportunities of manipulation.

Internal Control of Cash Receipts and Disbursements

Appendix A illustrates an internal control questionnaire. Each question suggests points of good or efficient internal control of cash receipts, cash disbursements and/or petty cash funds. Careful study of individual questions should be helpful in comprehending adequate internal control procedures. Use as a check list against which to measure a procedure is also helpful.

Cash Receipts and Cash Disbursements Questions, Problems, and Cases

1. The Telephone Company has developed a system of control over cash received through pay telephones. The system centralizes the handling of cash, thus in part reducing exposure to possible loss. All cash deposited in pay telephones drops into a locked-in, sealed container. The empty sealed containers are carefully accounted for when issued to the men making collections. The procedure followed is for the collectors to unlock pay telephones, remove the sealed container including cash, and insert a new but empty sealed container back in the telephone. When there is an overflow of cash it is placed in an envelope on which the container number is written and attached to the appropriate sealed container.

    Sealed containers with cash included are checked into the central counting room where the seal of each container is broken, the cash counted and an adequate record made of receipts by telephone. The cash is then sent to the bank for deposit in the company bank account.

    It has been suggested that the Telephone Company system does not provide adequate internal control. You are convinced that there is adequate internal control, but a number of the necessary internal control duties have not been mentioned above.

    (a) Identify seven basic internal control duties, and (b) indicate the ways each can be applied to the system to provide good internal control. When your solution is complete all of the internal control duties for the system should have been identified.

2. Outline measures you would recommend for achieving control over the cash receipts of the types of enterprises named below. If your procedures in the second instance involve repetition, just say "see #4 above" or words to that effect. If you make assumptions about the circumstances affecting amounts of revenue per customer, the physical environment, etc., it would be well to indicate what these are. Such assumptions must be realistic and not intended solely to achieve a simplification of your answers.

     The types of enterprise are (a) a conventional (i.e., not a drive-in) movie theater, and (b) a parking lot wherein customers pay somewhat in proportion to time vehicles are left and which has no "contract (i.e., monthly) customers.

3. The R Company operates a retail store in which all sales are made for cash at the time of the sale and recorded on cash registers by the clerks who make the sales.

     State with reasons what records of cash and sales the R Company should keep in order to enable an auditor to make a satisfactory verification of these items in a detailed audit of the company's records. (AICPA Examination)

4. The manager of a summer resort hotel noticed after a few months' operations that the receipts of the cigar counter had been less than those in corresponding periods of previous seasons. The receipts from other hotel activities had not decreased, and he asked his auditor to investigate.

     It was found that:
a. Four office employees were allowed to serve customers at the counter.
b. All sales are at the established unit selling prices.
c. All cash in excess of a ten-dollar change fund, representing the day's receipts, was to be deposited with the cashier at the close of each day.
d. No stocks had been carried over at the counter from the previous season.
e. Cigars and cigarettes were added to the counter from the general storeroom in full boxes and cartons, as needed.
f. No inventory records were kept at the counter.
g. The cashier's record showed $576.95 received up to date of examination.

     An inventory was taken under supervision of the auditor and he thereupon prepared the following statement:

BOXES OF 50 CIGARS
CARTONS OF 10 PACKAGES CIGARETTES

Unit selling price	Received from stock room	Inventory Boxes and cartons	Inventory Single cigars and packages	Cost per box or carton
Cigars				
25¢	10 boxes	3	25	$9.00
2/25¢	20 boxes	4	10	4.50
10¢	30 boxes	6	40	3.75
Cigarettes				
20¢	25 cartons	4	6	1.50
15¢	300 cartons	77	5	1.20

From the foregoing data prepare:

(a) A summary of cigar-counter transactions, also showing amount of shortage.

(b) Recommendations for maintaining adequate internal check and general-ledger accounting control. (AICPA Examination)

5. It is your client's policy to have invoices and supporting documents accompany all checks presented for signature. The signing officer insists that the invoices and documents be marked "paid" before he will review them and sign the checks. His objective is to preclude resubmission of the same invoices and documents in support of another check. Do you believe this procedure is effective? Explain. (AICPA Examination)

6. Prepare a questionnaire for the evaluation of internal control covering cash receipts for use in your initial annual audit of a large manufacturing company whose sales are made directly to retailers. (AICPA Examination)

7. In what ways can the use of cash registers contribute to the effectiveness of internal control over receipts from cash sales? (AICPA Examination)

8. a. Briefly describe the imprest system for operating a cash fund.
   b. State the principal advantages of the imprest system from the standpoint of internal control.
   c. Prepare a detailed questionnaire to be used by your staff employees in evaluating the internal control over a petty cash fund. (AICPA Examination)

9. a. Outline a division of duties among several employees to secure good internal control over incoming mail receipts on accounts receivable.
   b. Point out the controls over error or fraud on the part of each employee. (AICPA Examination)

10. Describe five methods that may be employed in the abstraction of (and failure to account for) cash receipts in a company that makes both cash and charge sales.

    For each of the above methods, state the internal control procedures you would recommend in order to prevent the fraud and the audit procedures you would employ to discover the fraud. Your internal control recommendations should not be predicated upon the existence of controls other than those which you specifically mention in your answer. (AICPA Examination)

11. Diagram or describe a procedure for control over receipts of cash by mail where some remittances are in settlement of accounts and others accompany orders. Be sure you have provided for proper control without making the system awkward.

12. The United Charities organization in your town has engaged you to examine its statement of receipts and disbursements. United Charities solicits contributions from local donors and then apportions the contributions among local charitable organizations.

    The officers and directors are local bankers, professional men, and other leaders of the community. A cashier and a clerk are the only full-time salaried employees. The only records maintained by the organization are a cashbook and a checkbook. The directors prefer not to have a system of pledges.

Contributions are solicited by a number of volunteer workers. The workers are not restricted as to the area of their solicitation and may work among their friends, neighbors, co-workers, etc., as is convenient for them. To assure blanket coverage of the town new volunteer workers are welcomed.

Contributions are in the form of cash or checks. They are received by United Charities from the solicitors, who personally deliver the contributions they have collected, or directly from the donors by mail or by personal delivery.

The solicitors complete official receipts which they give to the donors when they receive contributions. These official receipts have attached stubs which the solicitors fill in with the names of the donors and the amounts of the contributions. The solicitors turn in the stubs with the contributions to the cashier. No control is maintained over the number of blank receipts given to the solicitors or the number of receipt stubs turned in with the contributions.

Discuss the control procedures you would recommend for greater assurance that all contributions received by the solicitors are turned over to the organization. (Do not discuss the control of the funds in the organization's office.) (AICPA Examination)

13. A teller in a bank prepares a daily proof of his transactions. This proof is prepared by listing on the debit side the opening cash balance as a starting figure. The amounts of the various kinds of transactions handled during the day are then entered as debits or credits as indicated by the transactions. The cash balance at the close of the day is determined by actual count and entered in the proof. The proof should balance at that point unless there is an overage or shortage. Any overage or shortage would then be entered in the proof.

The following list includes all of the transactions handled by the head teller of the X Bank on November 10, 1968. From these transactions, you are to prepare a proof, including the closing cash balance as determined from the proof, assuming there is no overage or shortage.

A.M. cash balance	$1,200
Deposits received	5,500
Checks received on other banks	3,600
Checks received on depositors	4,500
Loans granted	1,000
Interest collected	200
Expenses paid	100
Checks certified for depositors	300
Cashiers checks redeemed	500
Loans collected from borrowers	5,000
Remittance to Federal Reserve for credit to our account	2,000
Certified checks redeemed	400

(AICPA Examination)

14. The Patricia Company had poor internal control over its cash transactions. Facts about its cash position at November 30, 1968, were as follows:

The cash books showed a balance of $18,901.62, which included cash on hand. A credit of $100 on the bank's records did not appear on the books of the company. The balance per the bank statement was $15,550, and outstanding checks were #62 for $116.25, #183 for $150, #284 for $253.25, #8621 for $190.71, #8623 for $206.80, and #8632 for $145.28.

The cashier removed all of the cash on hand in excess of $3,794.41 and then prepared the following reconciliation:

Balance per books, Nov. 30, 1968		$18,901.62
Add—Outstanding checks:		
#8621	$190.71	
#8623	206.80	
#8632	145.28	442.79
		$19,344.41
Add—Cash on hand		3,794.41
Balance per bank, Nov. 30, 1968		$15,550.00
Deduct—Unrecorded credit		100.00
True cash, Nov. 30, 1968		$15,450.00

a. How much did the cashier remove and how did he attempt to conceal his theft?
b. Taking only the information given, name two specific features of internal control which were apparently missing.
c. If the cashier's October 31 reconciliation is known to be in order and you start your audit on December 5, 1968, for the year ended November 30, 1968, what specific auditing procedures would uncover the fraud? (AICPA Examination)

15. Your client, who sells on credit, has several bank accounts. A reconciliation of one of these accounts as of the balance-sheet date appears as follows:

Balance per bank, December 31, 1968	$5,000
Add—Deposit in transit	1,000
Total	$6,000
Less—Outstanding checks	50
Balance per books, December 31, 1968	$5,950

The book balance of $5,950 is shown as cash on the balance-sheet. As to the $1,000 shown as a deposit in transit, you are to:
a. Briefly describe the major possibilities of fraud or error.
b. List the audit procedures that might be followed in a regular annual audit which would help to verify the deposit in transit. Explain fully how these procedures would help to verify the deposit in transit and detect possible fraud or error. (AICPA Examination)

16. Prepare a simple illustration of "lapping" of cash receipts, showing actual transactions and the cash book entries. (AICPA Examination)

17. Lapping has been described as a practice in which the improper abstraction of cash out of current receipts is covered by the omission of an entry or entries or receipts represented by checks. These checks are then deposited in lieu of the cash abstracted. Later entries are made for the items previously omitted and the shortage is either made up by the return of the cash abstracted or continued by the failure to enter other receipt items.

Outline and discuss briefly an audit procedure which would disclose the existence of the practice above described. (AICPA Examination)

18. The owner of the Bitty Bite Grill, open 24 hours each day, seven days per week, is certain that all cash received is not getting into his daily bank deposits. He has asked you as a systems analyst to study his system and to make the appropriate recommendations for improvement. After a study of the system you observe the following:

There are ten employees, four work from 7:00 a.m. to 3:00 p.m., four work from 3:00 p.m. to 11:00 p.m., and two work from 11:00 p.m. to 7:00 a.m. The owner is usually there during busy periods, and devotes full time to the business. One employee each shift is the short order cook and does not wait on customers, while the others serve customers, with each performing all functions necessary for the operation of the grill except cooking. When a customer comes into the grill he places his order and the waitress prepares a guest check. Customers pay as they leave the grill. One of the waitresses takes the money and rings it up on a cash register close to the door, but behind the counter. The guest checks are placed on a spindle next to the cash register after cash is rung up. The cash register has an adequate number of accumulators so that each of the waitresses can ring up her sales on a separate key. About 620 sales tickets are made up each day. They are packaged by date and retained for six months.

Cigarettes, candy, gum, etc., are displayed next to the cash register and are sold for cash. These sales are not recorded on guest checks, but are rung up as miscellaneous sales. Each day at about 8:00 a.m. and again at about 2:00 p.m. the owner clears the cash register, records the register readings including cash paid outs, and prepares a deposit. On Saturday and Sunday the deposits are made through the after-hour depository service of a bank located a block away. The necessary change is acquired by taking an adequate amount of cash (currency) from the cash register, and when the deposit is taken to the bank by the owner, the necessary change is obtained and placed in the cash register.

No controls or procedures exist that have not been specifically set forth above.

1. List the specific weaknesses of the procedure for the control of cash receipts.

2. For each of the weaknesses listed in 1 above, make a recommendation to correct the weakness or at least improve the situation. Recommendations must conform to the reasonable cost and the reliability principles of systems design.

3. The owner has agreed to your recommendations, and has asked you

to install the new procedure. How would the human factors principle of systems design apply to your assignment? Explain.

4. Assuming that your recommendations have been implemented, indicate how each type of internal control duty has contributed to the effectiveness of your system. If all internal control duties are not illustrated in your system, identify and explain each.

19. You have purchased a drive-in at the city limits of Madison that specializes in the sale of root beer, sandwiches, ice cream, etc., to customers who arrive by automobile. The drive-in is open from 9 a.m. through 2:00 a.m. Customers get out of their automobiles and walk up to one of three service windows to place an order. At rush periods five cooks and helpers are employed in addition to the clerks. When they receive the order they pay the clerk and return to the automobile to enjoy their snack. There are two cash registers, one located between service windows 1 and 2 while the other is between 2 and 3.

   You plan to change the system to employ four waiters (fewer during slack periods) who will walk to the car, take the order, return to a service window to have the order filled, and then deliver the order to the customer who is to pay at the time the order is delivered.
   a. In outline form describe the system necessary to control adequately the cash received at the service window through its deposit at the local bank assuming no waiters.
   b. In outline form describe the system necessary to control adequately the cash received by the waiter from the customer through its deposit at the local bank assuming the planned service.
   c. For the proposed system only (requirement b), indicate the seven internal control duties and the role each has in the system. If any internal control duty is not part of the system, explain the duty and indicate why.

20. What internal control would the proprietor of a small retail business (three clerks) need to establish to have good internal control over cash receipts from over the counter *and* from customers through the mail.

21. The cashier of the Easy Company intercepted customer A's check payable to the company in the amount of $500 and deposited it in a bank account which was part of the company petty cash fund, of which he was custodian. He then drew a $500 check on the petty cash fund bank account payable to himself, signed it, and cashed it. At the end of the month while processing the monthly statements to customers, he was able to change the statement to customer A so as to show that A had received credit for the $500 check that had been intercepted. Ten days later he made an entry in the cash received book which purported to record receipt of a remittance of $500 from customer A, thus restoring A's account to its proper balance, but overstating cash in bank. He covered the overstatement by omitting from the list of outstanding checks in the bank reconcilement, two checks, the aggregate amount of which was $500.

   List what you regard as five important deficiencies in the system of internal control in the above situation, and state the proper remedy for each deficiency. (AICPA Examination)

22. The following article appeared in a newspaper:

> Kaiser Aluminum & Chemical Co. is handing out signed blank checks, and saving money.
>
> Formerly, when the company bought something, it sent out a purchase order and then a payment order, as most everyone else does.
>
> Now, Kaiser sends out the order and includes with it a signed check that the vendor fills out with correct amount and cashes as immediate payment. No crisscross correspondence over varying prices. No rush to meet a 10 day discount deadline. The deal is closed immediately.
>
> This is done for all orders of $1,000 or less, a category that embraces 92 per cent of all its orders.
>
> Says Kaiser purchasing director Duncan Gregg, "We have cut clerical and paperwork operations at all 21 purchasing locations. We have eliminated an enormous amount of filing, retrieving, posting, check writing, stuffing, mailing, typing and handwriting."
>
> The idea, he said, is based on the apparently reasonable assumption—there have been no major wrinkles—that Kaiser suppliers are honest, want to keep doing business with Kaiser, and "are just as anxious as we are to cut paperwork."
>
> There's nothing to prevent someone kiting the payment, but this will be spotted when the returned check is matched in a computer with the original order.
>
> "No one would get a chance to do that to us twice," said a Kaiser representative.

    a. From the internal control viewpoint of Kaiser Aluminum, what appear to be the weaknesses of this plan? Be complete and specific, considering internal control of purchases, accounts payable, and cash disbursements.

    b. In view of the weaknesses listed in step a., above, why might Kaiser Aluminum still install the procedure?

    c. From the internal control viewpoint of the supplier, what are the difficulties with this procedure?

    d. As a supplier, would you elect this plan if given the opportunity? Give the reasons why it should be considered.

    e. Would you expect this plan to "catch on" and become a common method of doing business? Explain, using reasons not included under steps a. and c., above.

23. A suburban hospital is planning a drive for contributions to a construction fund. Solicitation will be by mail and by personal appeals made by volunteer workers.

    What controls would you suggest over the receiving of contributions? As to each control, include a brief statement of its specific purpose. (AICPA Examination)

24. Name some desirable internal control features of a check-signing equipment if the volume of checks is so large it is not feasible to sign them manually.

25. The Professional Men's Association of Middleton is made up of men in the various professions, including CPA's. From the start it has been tax exempt from federal income and excise taxes, other than payroll.

    The dues for members are $40 a year, after an initiation fee of $100. The Association has had a consistent policy of operating on a cash basis. It does not deposit initiation fees received with applications and does not consider them as income until the membership committee has acted thereon. Then the successful applicants' fees are deposited and the unsuccessful applicants' checks are returned to them.

    The fiscal year ends August 31. Each year the directors choose from the membership a CPA to make a thorough audit; and no one is allowed to audit two consecutive years. This year you have been selected for the first time, but you are solemnly warned that the directors will not tolerate any suggestion of putting the accounts on an accrual basis. You accept. An adequate fee is provided.

    The secretary furnishes you with the following information:

Membership at September 1, 19A		2,980
Elected during the year		123
Dropped for nonpayment of dues	15	
Died	37	
Expelled	1	53
Net gain		70

    Your examination of records shows the following:

    Notices that "dues are due" are sent out in August. Dues for a full year, not to be prorated, must be paid when elected to membership. Prior to the end of the preceding fiscal year 410 members had paid their dues and in the current fiscal year 457 members had paid their dues for the year beginning September 19B. One of these had died very suddenly on August 30 and is included in the 37 above. No refunds are made for deaths taking place after the fiscal year begins; however, refunds of one-half the dues are made to expelled members. There were 36 applications pending at the end of the fiscal year. During the course of your audit, the committee met and approved of 34. You further find that at the *beginning* of the year there were 47 such applications and that 45 had been acted upon favorably and are included in the 123 above.

    The directors are interested in learning if there is a substantial difference between the income from dues on a cash basis as compared to the accrual basis.

    a. Prepare a schedule of income from membership showing:
        1. Changes in members.
        2. Income from initiation fees.
        3. Income from dues for the year, accrual basis.
        4. Income from dues for the year, cash basis.
        5. Total income from membership.

6. Reconciliation of income from dues cash basis to the accrual basis. (AICPA Examination)

b. Do you agree with the directors on this policy of keeping the accounts on a cash basis? Why?

c. Recommend an "internal control system" for income from membership.

26. The Nelson Wholesale Company receives cash from two sources, through the mail and from salesmen in the field. There are 20 salesmen, each of whom covers a sales territory once each week. All sales are by salesmen, with daily shipments from the warehouse based on written or telephoned orders originating in the field. Some customers prefer to pay salesmen, thus good business consideration demands that salesmen collect when desired by the customer.

Cash received through the mail is recorded in the mail room on a prenumbered duplicate receipt. The original receipt is mailed back to the customer and the duplicate is sent with the cash to the central cashier. The central cashier runs a tape of the duplicate receipts, verifies the cash received, and if the two agree, marks the duplicate receipt with a rubber stamp showing the date and the word "Processed." The duplicate receipt is then sent to the Accounts Receivable Section for posting to the subsidiary ledger, and the tape is sent to the General Ledger Section as the basis for the control account entry.

Each salesman collects on the average of $450 per day. A prenumbered duplicate receipt is prepared when cash is received, and the customer is given the original. Each salesman has two bank accounts, maintained in the name of the company, one in a town serviced on Wednesday, and the other in a town serviced late Friday afternoon. All cash collected is deposited on Wednesday or Friday, and the salesman then sends a check for collections direct to the cashier with the duplicate copies of the receipts. Salesmen remit funds in a special type envelope which is transmitted by the mailroom direct to the cashier without opening. The cashier's procedure thereafter is the same as that for cash received from the mailroom.

Deposits are made by the cashier each afternoon for all receipts processed by 2 p.m. After verifying the deposit, the bank teller stamps the deposit slip and returns it to the cashier as the deposit record. At the same time the deposit is made the necessary change is obtained for the change funds by presenting bills and checks brought to the bank in a special change container.

All employees handling cash are bonded and are required to take regular vacations. There is no internal audit section. The open-item statement plan is used for billing accounts receivable.

Management has been satisfied with the present plan; however, you note a number of suggestions for improvement. You are therefore asked to:

a. Prepare a flow chart of the *procedure described above.*

b. List your suggestions for changing the present system to obtain better internal control, and for each suggestion state the reason *why* the present procedure is not adequate.

27. In a cash receipts procedure in which all receipts are by check, a systems analyst wants to use the checks themselves as posting media for Accounts

Receivable. Explain whether or not this could be done without violating good internal control.

28. What is a remittance advice? Of what value would it be in a cash receiving system?

29. The Model Company has asked that you design a system for the control of cash receipts. You note that cash is received from three sources, namely from customers through the mail, from customers and employees by a central cashier, and by a cashier in the company cafeteria. Large amounts of cash are received at each source, thus any reasonable number of employees or amount of equipment could be justified.

    In *outline form*, follow the cash from *each* source, step by step until it is deposited, indicating the control at each step. Identify specifically (a) machines that should be used, (b) the accounting control that is obtained, and (c) other controls.

30. You have just completed the design of an internal control system for the cash receipts for a large manufacturing company. Indicate whether each of the following is a good internal control and why or why not.
    a. Deposit all receipts intact and daily.
    b. Use a cash sales clearing account.
    c. Obtain a remittance advice for each receipt.
    d. Prepare an initial record (daily remittance list) in the mail room.
    e. Require all incoming checks from customers to be withdrawn from correspondence in the mail room.

31. Explain the basic differences between procedures for receiving cash from customers as between (a) a manufacturing concern offering terms of 2/10, n/30 whose customers, for the most part, avail themselves of the discount and (b) a retail department store selling for cash and on credit whose credit customers, for the most part, pay for purchases of the preceding month within the first ten days of the following month.

32. You have been asked to design a procedure for receiving cash from customers on account. Each customer is to receive a receipt for the amount paid in. A copy of the receipt is to be controlled and used as a basis for posting ledger records. Control is desired over cash.
    a. What two devices (pieces of equipment) could be recommended to implement such a procedure?
    b. What are two features of the procedure that would enable control over the posting copy of receipts?

33. You have been retained by a municipal water district to conduct an audit of the books and records for the year ended June 30, 1968. The Board of Commissioners advise you that they wish a *certified audit* for the year and that the last time the books of the District had been audited by a certified public accountant was as of June 30, 1964.

    During the audit, you discover that the bank account appears to be short in the amount of $3,750. You also note that the shortage appears to represent the difference between the acknowledged receipts and the deposits to the bank for the months of July to February, inclusive. You also note that all funds have been properly recorded and deposited subsequent to February, at which time a new manager was hired for the District. You also learn that at the same time an old and trusted veteran office worker retired from service. During your discussion of general procedures and bookkeeping routine with the manager, another office clerk with six years' service to the District submitted notice of resignation to become effective in two weeks. The manager also advises you that during the month of April 1968, there had been a shortage of $40 in one day's receipts and that he had been unable to determine the cause of this shortage.

   a. Outline the audit steps you would take in connection with this cash shortage.

   b. Could you render an unqualified opinion in your report on this engagement?

   c. Describe briefly the comments you would include in your report regarding the cash shortage. (AICPA Examination)

34. The cashier of a bank is also treasurer of a local charity. He is authorized to purchase $10,000 U.S. bonds for the bank and a similar amount for the charity. He makes both purchases but misappropriates the bonds belonging to the charity. When an audit is made of the charity, the treasurer borrows the bonds from the bank and places them in the charity's safe deposit box.

   What internal controls would you recommend for the charity to prevent the occurrence of this manipulation? (AICPA Examination)

35. The owner of the Carstairs, a transient hotel located in an industrial city of 100,000 population, requests you to devise a system of accounting control over income.

   Your investigation reveals that the hotel had income from the following sources:

   a. Room rentals. Established rates for the 400 transient rooms begin at $9.00 for room with bath.

   b. Commissions on guest's laundry and cleaning service. A 25 per cent commission is earned on gross charges to guests. These charges are billed to the hotel which in turn bills them to guests.

   c. Dining room and coffee shop. Both are serviced by one kitchen. Hotel guests may sign their checks. Both dining room and coffee shop enjoy a good volume of patronage from others than guests of the hotel. This includes bridge parties, wedding receptions, etc.

   d. Cocktail lounge. All sales here are made for cash, except that service to dining room guests is included on the cafe check and the income is included as dining room income.

   e. Telephone. Guests are charged 20¢ for local calls and are charged the exact amount of tolls plus 10¢ for service.

   f. Cigar stand. All sales—cigars, cigarettes, and candy—are made for cash.

   g. Sundry income includes charges to guests for breakage and damage, income of "26" game operated by the clerk at the cigar counter, and commissions from pin ball machines in the cocktail lounge.

You find that income and related costs have not been adequately segregated to permit determination of departmental revenues. In fact, the income from dining room, coffee shop, cocktail lounge, and cigar stand have been combined in one account.

Outline a system of accounting control over cash and income for the Carstairs Hotel. State specifically the Internal Controls applicable. Outline the basic characteristics of the hotel system, with special attention to the method of keeping guest receivable records, in addition to your discussion of items a. through g. above.

36. List the questions that management needs to have answered in order to maintain control over cash receipts. After each question, tell briefly how the answer is ascertained.

37. What specific fraudulent procedures concerning cash can be broken up by rotation of employees? Who should reconcile bank accounts?

38. Some specific ways in which cash receipts are not properly accounted for include:
   a. Theft of cash from sales of both regular merchandise and scrap.
   b. Underfooting the cash receipts book so it agrees with the "short" cash.
   c. Overstating discounts allowed customers.
   d. Debiting an account other than cash when money is received.
   e. Write-off of good accounts as bad debts, then pocketing remittances.
   f. Use of fictitious customer accounts later written off.
   g. Undercharging customers on the books and pocketing remittances.
   h. Lapping.
   i. Failure to account for unclaimed returned checks.
   Indicate procedures leading to prevention and/or detection of the above.

39. Design a combination voucher-check form for use by XYZ Wholesalers, Inc. The company uses an alphameric posting machine to write checks and make postings to other forms simultaneously. What other forms might be involved when different elements of the voucher-check form are being written?

40. Relatively small but repetitive theft or "borrowing" from Petty Cash is said to be a common practice. Describe measures designed to prevent various petty cash irregularities.

41. What are some features of cash registers that aid in the internal control of cash? What advantage is there, if any, in spending $1.00 in clerical expense to save 25¢ in fraud by the petty cash clerk?

42. Name some of the techniques which would encourage customers to check cash register receipts against the amount actually paid.

43. List some essentials, from an internal control standpoint, in the accounting for and handling of petty cash.

44. Certain measures designed to thwart the misappropriation of cash and petty cash are listed below. You are to indicate what type of fraud each measure is designed to prevent.

    a. Cancelling paid vouchers by perforating them at the time of payment.

    b. Simultaneous reconciliation of all bank accounts at an interim date.

    c. Using renumbered checks and carefully accounting for used and unused checks.

    d. Maintaining a record of numbers of all stock certificates and bonds.

    e. Making surprise counts of imprest funds.

    f. Having registers read and cleared by internal auditors rather than cashiers.

    g. Comparing totals of mail receipts with duplicate bank deposit records (daily).

    h. Having credit manager scrutinize detailed list of all accounts written off as uncollectible and comparing total of list with debits to "Reserve for Bad Debts."

    i. Having periodic comparison of personnel department rosters with payroll registers.

    j. Verifying footing of cash disbursements journal.

    k. Requiring receiving report in support of all vouchers for purchases.

    l. Rotation of duties among clerks handling different segments of accounts receivable ledger posting.

    m. Requiring documentary approval of all sales returns and allowances and comparing total authorized with totals posted.

    n. Having checks mailed by persons other than those causing them to be drawn.

    o. Providing multi-drawer cash registers.

    p. Offering bonuses to customers for "red stars" or other special symbols on sales tickets.

    q. Verifying footing of payroll registers.

    r. Having payrolls prepared by persons other than those making the actual payoff.

45. The selling office of the BBS Company (cosmetics) is maintained in New York City, together with the offices of the executive head of the business. The manufacturing, the warehousing, and the shipping departments, together with the accounting offices—where purchases are ordered, sales are billed, and collections are received—are established in a city in an adjoining state.

    The New York City cash receipts—relatively small compared with those arriving at the manufacturing plant—are deposited in a local bank, subject to check only by the chief executive.

    All receipts at the plant—chiefly in settlement for invoices of goods shipped and from cash sales to employees—are opened and accepted by the chief accounting officer and turned over by him, after a control list of such receipts has been made, to the accounts receivable ledger clerks for credit to the proper accounts. The checks, which provide the principal memoranda for entry, are then returned to the accounting officer and deposited by him in a local bank. Against these funds checks may be drawn only by the executive officers in New York City.

The accounting officer mentioned above is also the plant executive and has been selected for his post because of his integrity and loyalty to the president. The business has had a phenomenal growth in the past three or four years and now has sales of approximately $10,000,000 per year. There are one general ledger clerk (all records are kept on a general-purpose accounting machine), one chief clerk in charge of subsidiary ledger records with assistants in charge of accounts receivable and of vouchers payable, seven accounts receivable posting clerks, and four billing clerks who prepare the invoices after orders have been filled; and there are three purchase order or voucher clerks who prepare orders for raw materials and check the receipts of goods and various features of the invoices received.

Checks in payment of approved vouchers are drawn in New York after the vouchers have been forwarded for that purpose by the plant, usually well in advance of the end of the discount period. The payroll is prepared in New York and sent by armored truck to the plant.

a. Answer the following questions pertaining to the cash-handling procedures described above:
   1. Do you think it preferable that all cash should be received and recorded in one office?
   2. If your answer to item 1. is affirmative, where should this recording occur?
   3. Give reasons for your answer to item 1., above.
   4. Do you regard the procedures at the plant involving the control list as satisfactory?
   5. Give reasons for your answer to item 4., above.
   6. What do you see as the main weakness in the cash receiving process?
b. Questions as to other elements of the case:
   1. What do you see as the principal weakness in the voucher-paying procedure?
   2. List any other elements of weakness you detect in the BBS situation.
   3. Aside from any corrections implicit in your answers to preceding questions on this case, what coordinate control steps, if any, would you recommend?

CHAPTER 19

Functional Procedures—2

THERE ARE MANY FUNCTIONAL PROCEDURES THAT ARE COMBINED TO PROVIDE a complete financial information system. In Chapter 18 some of the more common procedures were briefly presented along with related questions, problems, and cases. In Chapter 19, additional procedures are presented, also with relevant questions, problems, and cases. While all procedures cannot be presented in this text, the more common and basic procedures were selected. Others can be developed easily by application of the systems theory provided by the text.

PAYROLL

Payroll Processing

Payroll is the procedure that is relevant in all companies with one or more employees and requires the special attention of the systems analyst. It is an area in which the law imposes not only a fine but a jail sentence for willful negligence in maintaining adequate records. It is a vital procedure for control purposes, since in every step of the procedure an error or fraudulent figure can change a paycheck. At the end of the payroll procedure is a disbursement that must be controlled if assets are to be safeguarded.

Payroll can be one of the more complicated procedures. In general, it can be reduced to four fundamental routines: (1) daily processing, (2) periodic processing, (3) payroll writing, and (4) periodic reporting. In addition there is special processing both at the time of employment and at termination.

All payroll processing is vital to the payroll procedure and, though short of a "total system," the fundamental routines are separate and distinct. In *daily processing* the time records are obtained and assurance is provided that the employee has worked the number of hours recorded on the time record. In general, daily processing relates to keeping attendance and time records, and verification that time worked is correct for each individual. *Periodic processing* is the summarization of the daily time worked in the period, the reconciliation of clock time to job time, and other processing prior to payroll writing. Included as other processing is the change of rates and provision for sickness, vacations, and other similar matters. Both daily and periodic processing are time consuming and involve relatively large amounts of work. In computer systems, for example, it is sometimes difficult to realize that daily and periodic processing must occur to obtain the data used for computer input.

The most glamorous of all phases of payroll processing is *payroll writing*. Payroll writing occurs at the end of a period and may well take a relatively short time as contrasted to the time necessary to collect data on which the payroll is based. In many concerns the payroll writing is a simple and short operation. Like other disbursements, the signature on the paycheck serves primarily as a means of making a check negotiable and has little to do with the adequacy of the procedure.

The payroll procedure must be designed to facilitate the control of labor costs and to enable the periodic reporting required by the Government and others. Employers are required to act as agents and to withhold authorized amounts from employee paychecks. In addition, certain taxes are based on the payroll. In the design of a payroll procedure, it is necessary that the data for all payroll reports be available through the regular procedure and without reprocessing. Included are data used to report, periodically, the amounts of federal income taxes withheld and the FICA tax. The year-end wage and tax statement must be provided to the employee and to the Internal Revenue Service to document the amount of income and FICA taxes withheld. Federal and State unemployment compensation insurance returns must be filed, and select information reported concerning employees who claim benefits. Data for city, county, and state payroll tax reports are required in processing. All situations in which the employer acts as an agent requires reports. The amounts to be reported must be accumulated. The procedure must enable deductions to be stopped when a given level of income is reached each year by the employee. In a properly designed procedure the periodic reporting need not be burdensome.

In *special processing*, the initial records of employment such as payroll deduction authorizations and other personnel records are assembled. The procedures at the time of employment are vital to the implementation of all procedures. Included is the application of the human factor principle of systems design which requires the recognition of the individual abilities and qualifications. Proper determination of ability, follow-up of references, and good selections are effective in assuring competent and qualified employees, and can eliminate difficult problems before they occur. Well developed termination procedures are also important in the planning and control of human resources and in an adequate system of internal control.

Nature and Control of Payroll

In the design of the payroll procedure, the specific routines must be designed to facilitate control. In general there are at least five basic controls to be included in the payroll procedure. They are as follows:

1. Authorizations through personnel.
2. Separation of incompatible duties.
3. Double calculation.
4. Controlled processing.
5. Payment control.

Authorizations Through Personnel. The personnel section provides a key function in the control of payroll. Not only do they control the number of positions that exist within each organization unit of the firm, but they conduct the necessary studies and establish rates and authorize changes to rates. They also are responsible for the approval of all terminations. In determining the amount that each employee is to receive, in general, the calculation is the rate times the number of hours worked. Thus the authorization of starts, rates, rate changes, absences from work, and terminations must be the separate responsibility of the personnel section. This, when combined with the separation of the supervision and certification of work, adds a key dimension to the procedure.

Separation of Incompatible Duties. In the preparation of a payroll, it is important that no one element in the calculation of pay be under the control of any one individual. Thus it would be an incompatible duty for the supervisor to have complete control over the number of hours that an employee works. Rather the time record should be compiled under the supervision of the timekeeping section. Time cards should be approved and signed by the supervisor. To carry the illustration further, the timekeeper who makes a floor check of the employees who are working to verify the hours recorded on the clock cards should not prepare the payroll or be involved in making wage payments.

Double Calculation. The amount of the paycheck for each employee must be calculated accurately. If an error is made in the arithmetic of multiplying hours times rate, the amount of the gross pay will be incorrect. Not only must each of the components in the formula to determine pay be accurate, but the calculations must also be verified. In a payroll system it is important that there be a double calculation or controlled machine calculations to verify amounts.

CONTROLLED PROCESSING. As in other procedures, the payroll data being processed must be under control. The processing is normally accomplished by department or cost center in order that control totals can be established so that the processing is a controlled operation. The payroll processing must establish controlled total of hours, deductions, and net pay so that, during processing, these totals can be verified. Processing normally is by department or cost center for this purpose.

When fixed payroll deductions are authorized, the total of such deductions can be verified in the processing of the payroll for a given department. For example, a deduction for hospital insurance must be specifically authorized by each individual employee. All such deductions of the employee in a given department can be added together to obtain the total that would be verified as a part of the payroll writing process.

PAYMENT CONTROL. Payroll can be paid either by check or cash. In either instance, control of payment is vital. With a check payment, a receipt is automatically obtained by the employer in the form of an endorsement on the back of the check. In a cash payroll system it is vital that the signature of the employee be obtained as an acknowledgement of receiving his pay. Each employee being paid should be identified. There should be an occasional surprise payoff by the internal auditor to make certain that payments are being made only to authorized employees. The payroll procedure does not differ materially if check disbursement is used as compared to cash disbursement. The difference relates primarily to the preparation of a pay envelope instead of a check as a part of the procedure and to the steps that relate to the filling of pay envelopes and their distribution. In either system the complete control over unclaimed payroll checks or envelopes is important. Such amounts should be redeposited as soon as practicable.

Typical Payroll Procedure

Figure 19-1 illustrates a typical payroll procedure. Note the key role that is assumed by the personnel department in the typical payroll procedure. No one can be added to the payroll, paid at any other than a given rate, or be removed from the payroll without authorization from personnel. All payroll deduction authorizations are obtained by the personnel department and sent to the payroll section. In the typical payroll procedure, a job time ticket is maintained in the shop. Each employee punches both on and off a given job. The timekeeping department reconciles the job time tickets to clock cards to make certain that all hours worked are appropriately charged. Note the double calculation of the payroll in that the total of the payroll is also calculated in the cost distribution section. In addition, the gross payroll from

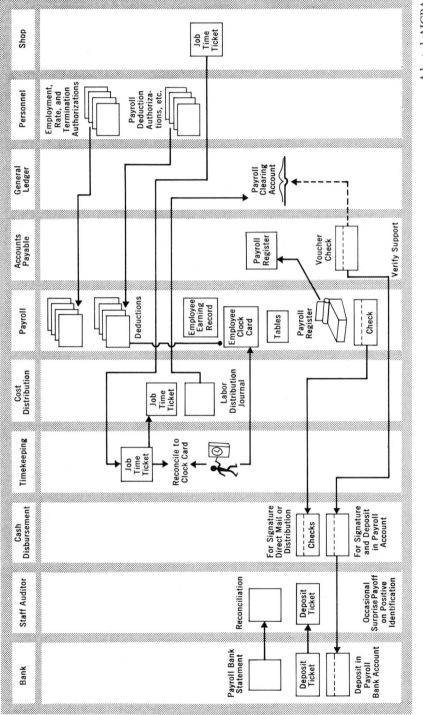

FIGURE 19-1. Typical Payroll Procedure

Adapted AICPA

the payroll register and voucher check is reported to the general ledger book-keeper and must agree with the amount obtained from the labor distribution journal.

The typical payroll procedure is being performed on a general purpose accounting machine. Each employee has an earnings record on which has been accumulated earnings to date, plus all of the key information that is necessary for payroll writing. Included would be such figures as the number of withholding exemptions, any special shift premium, wage rate, and the like. The clock card is also an important record as is the employee check with the employee earning statement attached. The employee earning statement is required by law to inform the employee of the amounts that have been deducted from his pay. If a non-descriptive general purpose machine is used, the checks must have the name and clock number of the individual inserted prior to the time of payroll writing. Tables to provide for the necessary variable deductions, such as income taxes, must also be available. In many payroll procedures, the combined tables for income taxes withheld and FICA taxes are used with the appropriate division for each individual being made only at the end of the year. In payroll writing with the general purpose machine, all of the records must be in sequence, usually by clock number, with processing being done by department or cost center. The payroll register is the backing sheet that is provided as a copy of all the information that is relevant to each paycheck written.

In many medium and large sized firms a special payroll bank account may be maintained. One check is drawn for the take-home pay of all employees, which is deposited, then the individual paychecks are drawn against the payroll bank account.

INTERNAL CONTROL FOR PAYROLL. Appendix A illustrates an internal control questionnaire that includes a series of questions on payroll. The number of questions asked is greater than for many of the other procedures because of the importance of controlling payroll. A careful study of responses to questions on the internal control questionnaire can disclose both the strength and weaknesses of internal control. The use of the internal control questionnaire as a check list against which to test a procedure is often advantageous.

Payroll Questions, Problems, and Cases

1. The Generous Loan Company has 100 branch loan offices. Each office has a manager and four or five subordinates who are employed by the manager. Branch managers prepare the weekly payroll, including their own salaries, and pay employees from cash on hand. The employee signs the payroll sheet signifying receipt of his salary. Hours worked by hourly personnel are inserted in the payroll sheet from time cards prepared by the employees and approved by the manager.

The weekly payroll sheets are sent to the home office along with other accounting statements and reports. The home office compiles employee earnings records and prepares all federal and state salary reports from the weekly payroll sheets.

Salaries are established by home office job evaluation schedules. Salary adjustments, promotions, and transfers of full-time employees are approved by a home office salary committee based upon the recommendations of branch managers and area supervisors. Branch managers advise the salary committee of new full-time employees and terminations. Part-time and temporary employees are hired without referral to the salary committee.

    a. Based upon your review of the payroll system, how might funds for payroll be diverted?

    b. Prepare a payroll audit program to be used in the home office to audit the branch office payrolls of the Generous Loan Company. (AICPA Examination)

2. You are engaged in auditing the financial statements of Henry Brown, a large independent contractor. All employees are paid in cash because Mr. Brown believes this arrangement reduces clerical expenses and is preferred by his employees.

    During the audit you find in the petty cash fund approximately $200 of which $185 is stated to be unclaimed wages. Further investigation reveals that Mr. Brown has installed the procedure of putting any unclaimed wages in the petty cash fund so that the cash can be used for disbursements. When the claimant to the wages appears, he is paid from the petty cash fund. Mr. Brown contends that this procedure reduces the number of checks drawn to replenish the petty cash fund and centers the responsibility for all cash on hand in one person inasmuch as the petty cash custodian distributes the pay envelopes.

    a. Does Mr. Brown's system provide proper internal control of unclaimed wages? Explain fully.

    b. Because Mr. Brown insists on paying salaries in cash, what procedures would you recommend to provide better internal control over unclaimed wages? (AICPA Examination)

3. Describe the highlights of machine posting in a payroll procedure, giving attention to the steps involved, proof techniques, simultaneous preparation of documents, advantages, use of multiple registers, and any other matters you regard as relatively important.

4. The review of the system of internal control by an independent certified public accountant is fundamental in every examination of financial statements, upon which he must express an opinion.

    You have been engaged to examine the financial statements of a manufacturing company which pays all payrolls in currency.

    a. State what questions you would ask in your review of the system of internal control and procedures relative to payrolls. (The answer may be in the form of an appropriate questionnaire.)

b. Give your reasons for asking the above questions, including an explanation of how you would use the questions in deciding on the effectiveness of the control over payrolls. (AICPA Examination)

5. Why might you recommend a writing board for a payroll procedure? Explain.

6. You are the senior on an audit of a manufacturing corporation with about 600 employees. A portion of your firm's internal control questionnaire on payroll shows the following:

a. Who prepares the payroll?   Answer—Payroll clerk
b. Who prepares payroll checks?   Answer—Payroll clerk
c. Who approves the payroll?   Answer—Chief accountant
d. Who signs payroll checks?   Answer—Assistant treasurer
e. Who distributes pay checks?   Answer—Department foremen
f. Who authorizes pay rates?   Answer—Plant superintendent
g. Who reconciles payroll account?   Answer—Chief accountant
h. Who controls unclaimed checks?   Answer—Chief accountant

    What further questions should be included in the questionnaire to permit an appraisal of the effectiveness of the internal control over payroll? Explain why each of the additional questions is needed. (AICPA Examination)

7. All employees of a company are paid in cash once a week. The company has 200 employees, all of whom work at one plant; 50 of these employees are on a night shift. All employees are paid on Friday (or Saturday morning with respect to the night crew) for the week ended on the preceding Tuesday. One employee, the payroll clerk, prepares the payroll from time sheets signed by the respective foremen. He also checks time cards against these payroll sheets, and hands out the pay envelopes.

    Prepare an internal control evaluation of payroll in connection with the regular annual examination of financial statements. (Adopted AICPA Examination)

8. Where payrolls are paid in cash rather than by check, internal control is almost sure to be weaker. State reasons why this may be true.

9. The general ledger of the XY Manufacturing Company contains a payroll clearing account. Debits to the account originate in the payroll section of the factory accounting office. Credits to the account originate in the cost distribution section. The company does not use standard or estimated costs. On the assumption that there is effective internal control over payrolls you are to:

a. State the information needed by the payroll section and indicate the source of this information.
b. State the information needed by the cost distribution section and the source of the information.
c. State the principal controls over the payroll in the system as you have described it. (AICPA Examination)

10. Your client has several accounts in the same bank. One of these accounts is restricted to weekly payroll disbursements and is operated on an imprest basis. The account should always reconcile to a zero balance and for this reason your client has not bothered to reconcile the account at any time during the year under review. The account does not appear in the general ledger.

   In the course of your audit of the payroll account you examine all cancelled checks returned by the bank during the eight weeks following the balance-sheet date. Included among these are checks totaling $2,600 which are dated prior to the balance-sheet. The paymaster also has on hand unclaimed payroll checks for $200 dated prior to the balance-sheet. The bank statement shows a balance of $2,300 at the balance-sheet date.

   Assuming that no fraud is involved and that no errors in footing have been made, give three possible explanations of the situation indicated by the figures. For each explanation, give the procedures you would follow to determine if the explanation were correct. (AICPA Examination)

11. Mention five different methods to which dishonest employees may resort in manipulating payrolls. (Do not give variations of the same method.) (AICPA Examination)

12. XYZ Company operates on a standard one-shift basis, all employees starting at 8 a.m. and finishing at 4:30 p.m. Would you recommend a horizontal or vertical clock card? Why?

13. There is a duality of time reporting in many productive units. Why is this so, and what is the nature of the two reports? Aside from variations in time worked, what are some factors which commonly affect the amount of gross pay earned by (a) factory employees, and (b) non-factory employees?

14. In connection with preparation and payment of a factory payroll by check, indicate six instances of laxity that might exist if the internal control system is weak. Very briefly set out a remedy for each deficiency cited.

15. The following questions relate to payroll time clock cards.
   a. Assuming your plant employs 8,000 persons and a weekly clock card is used, what means would you recommend of printing names on cards?
   b. In addition to names, what other information might well be printed on each employee's time card?
   c. Where on the cards should employee names be printed and why?
   d. What kinds of timing systems do time clocks use?
   e. Assuming horizontal or vertical clocks cost the same, which would you prefer and why?

16. This question concerns payroll distribution.
   a. What is the primary internal control check?
   b. Name some typical objects (not objectives) of payroll distribution in a manufacturing enterprise.
   c. Name some typical functions of payroll distribution in a typical large auto dealership.
   d. What are the principal source media likely to be employed in payroll distribution work?

17. Design an employee earnings record for machine posting and enter specimen data for two pay periods. Assume the employee has allotted $6.25 per pay period to be applied to the purchase of U.S. savings bonds and that he is subject to the usual statutory deductions.

18. Design a payroll register form for hourly employees to be posted by machine. Enter data for two employees, one of whom has worked 40 hours at $2.10 per hour; the other has worked 44 hours (including four hours overtime at time and one-half) and his basic hourly pay rate is $2.60. Assume the first employee pays hospitalization insurance at $5.20 per week by payroll allotment and that the other does not. Both are subject to the usual statutory deductions.

19. The Kowal Manufacturing Company employs about 50 production workers and has the following payroll procedures.

    The factory foreman interviews applicants and on the basis of the interview either hires or rejects the applicants. When the applicant is hired he prepares a W-4 form (Employee's Withholding Exemption Certificate) and gives it to the foreman. The foreman writes the hourly rate of pay for the new employee in the corner of the W-4 form and then gives the form to a payroll clerk as notice that the worker has been employed. The foreman verbally advises the payroll department of rate adjustments.

    A supply of blank time cards is kept in a box near the entrance to the factory. Each worker takes a time card on Monday morning, fills in his name, and notes in pencil on the time card his daily arrival and departure times. At the end of the week the workers drop the time cards in a box near the door to the factory.

    The completed time cards are taken from the box on Monday morning by a payroll clerk. Two payroll clerks divide the cards alphabetically between them, one taking the A to L section of the payroll and the other taking the M to Z section. Each clerk is fully responsible for her section of the payroll. She computes the gross pay, deductions and net pay, posts the details to the employee's earnings records, and prepares and numbers the payroll checks. Employees are automatically removed from the payroll when they fail to turn in a time card.

    The payroll checks are manually signed by the chief accountant and given to the foreman. The foreman distributes the checks to the workers in the factory and arranges for the delivery of the checks to the workers who are absent. The payroll bank account is reconciled by the chief accountant who also prepares the various quarterly and annual payroll tax reports.

    List your suggestions for improving the Kowal Manufacturing Company's system of internal control for the factory hiring practices *and* payroll procedures. (AICPA Examination)

20. Following is a partial write-up of daily timekeeping procedure in a certain company. The steps are given in mixed order, but when placed in their proper sequence they represent a logical functioning of time-keeping. Give each step a priority number in order to organize a proper sequence of the work.

    a. Give absentee report to department foreman.

    b. Time keeper is to work from 8 to 12 and 12:30 to 4:30.

    c. Compute elapsed time on each job ticket.

    d. At 8 a.m. remove attendance cards from clock racks.

    e. Arrange attendance cards in clock number order.

    f. From each job ticket, post employee number, date, quantities produced on Production Record card for item produced.

    g. List absentees on report form used for the purpose.

    h. Arrange job tickets for previous day in clock number order.

21. The Real Wholesale Company has 500 employees working in ten departments, all of whom are salaried. An employment office performs the customary personnel functions and is responsible to the vice-president of labor relations. The union contract requires (a) that employees be paid each Wednesday by check for the prior week's work and (b) for the deduction of union dues. Approximately 20 per cent of the employees have authorized a weekly deduction of $1, $2, or $5 for Series E Savings Bonds. Bonds are purchased and turned over to the employee when a sufficient amount has been accumulated. All payroll checks are to be written using a *non-descriptive*, multiple-purpose accounting machine. An imprest payroll fund is used.

    a. Prepare a procedural flow chart for payroll designed to illustrate good procedures and internal control. Your flow chart should show clearly all *machines* or equipment necessary and the manner in which *accounting control* is accomplished. Illustrate specifically how you propose to control both fixed and variable payroll deductions.

    b. (1) List the necessary payroll records, reports, or returns not specifically illustrated and identified on the flow chart required above, (2) state the source of the information for each, and (3) state how often each would be prepared.

    c. How would the system be modified if employees are paid in cash instead of by check?

22. In the design of a payroll system certain records and reports must be prepared. Identify each of the following and indicate the source of the information from which each would be prepared.

Form 941	Form W-3
Form W-2	Payroll Check
Form 940	Earnings Record
Form W-4	Earnings Statement

23. In connection with payroll preparation and payment:

    a. What internal control matching or reconciliation feature would be essential in a business employing cost accounting?

    b. What advantages attend payment by check rather than in currency?

    c. Where payment is made by check, what is the principal advantage of special bank accounts for payroll?

24. You have been assigned to an engagement that requires the design of an information system for the Melborne Wholesale Company, a large mail order

distributor. Your job is to design a machine payroll procedure to replace the writing board payroll procedure now in use. A standard, multiple-purpose, nondescriptive accounting machine is to be used in the new procedure.

The company is organized into five major divisions, namely women and children's clothing, men's clothing, furniture and appliances, automotive and farm equipment, and general. Each division has its own warehousing facilities. Time clocks are under the supervision of the Timekeeping Section. In addition to the usual payroll deductions required by law, management has authorized deduction of union dues, blue cross health insurance, and united givers contributions. The company has been paying by cash, but now intends to pay by check.

You have designed an optimum payroll procedure for the company, and your supervisor now asks several questions you are requested to answer, as follows:

a. How will your procedure control or eliminate the possibility of:
   1. Paying a man for work not performed?
   2. Paying at rates that are in excess of those authorized?
   3. The inclusion of fictitious employees on the payroll?
   4. Paying a man for periods after he has been terminated?
   5. Errors in calculation?
   6. Shortages in unclaimed wages?
   7. The operator of the machine on which pay checks are written from increasing his own check by $50 without authorization?
   8. A timekeeping employee from increasing the time worked on his own time card?
b. How would fixed deductions be controlled?
c. From what source or sources would information be obtained for the following:

1. Form 941	5. Form W-4
2. Form 940	6. Form 501
3. Form W-2	7. State UC Report
4. Form W-3	

d. You have decided to use the combined withholding and FICA tax tables in payroll processing. Explain.
e. How would the non-descriptive feature of the machine change the basic procedure?
f. Describe the portion of the procedure, including records and forms, that relates to writing the payroll checks.

25. The Royal Ann Company pays all employees in cash. The payroll system is as follows:

Employment Procedures. When an employee is hired, the personnel section obtains and forwards all pay data to the payroll section. This includes all payroll deduction authorizations and the rate.

Time Records. Each employee punches the time clock just inside the factory door when arriving and leaving the plant. The time card is sent to the payroll section where the pay is computed. Time is also recorded in the plant on job order cost tickets which go directly to the cost accounting section.

Payroll Preparation. The payroll is prepared and computed in the payroll section from time cards, deduction authorizations, and pay rates that are on file. The completed payroll is sent to the paymaster.

Payment of the Payroll. The paymaster verifies all payroll computations and corrects any errors. He then has a check drawn for the total amount of the payroll to obtain cash to fill pay envelopes. Pay envelopes are filled and delivered to the paymaster by Brink's service. On payday supervisors draw the pay for their section from the paymaster, and distribute it to the men on the job, thus eliminating long lines waiting for pay and permitting positive identification of the worker by the supervisor.

Unclaimed Wages. Pay envelopes not claimed are returned to the paymaster who retains them for five days before depositing the money. The amount of the deposit is accrued in a special liability account for Unclaimed Wages.

Rate Changes. Supervisors in the factory must authorize any pay rate change. They must fill in an "Authorization for Change of Rate" form, which is sent to the payroll section.

Termination of Employment. Employees whose employment is terminated on a day other than the end of the regular pay period are paid by check. A "Report of Termination of Employment" is prepared by the supervisor, and a copy sent to the payroll section who prepares a voucher for the check, or drops the individual from the payroll.

Vacation and Sick Leave. Supervisors report on a "Vacation and Sick Leave Authorization" form to the payroll section any pay that is to be stopped temporarily due to additional unpaid vacation or excessive sick leave.

Overtime. No employee will be paid overtime unless approved by the supervisor of the section concerned.

Paid Payroll Vouchers. Paid payroll vouchers are the basis for the preparation of a journal voucher that is sent to the accounting department for posting. A detailed report of the payroll is sent to the cost section. The paid payroll is stamped "paid" and retained by the paymaster who prepares Form W-2 statements. Individual wage records are also prepared as a part of a machine operation to enter payroll data on the pay envelope by the paymaster.

a. List specific weaknesses of the present system and state the reason why you would consider the practice a violation of good internal control. Your solution should be in two columns, the first for the weakness of the present system, and the second for why the practice is a violation of good internal control.

b. List in outline form an ideal system of internal control for the Royal Ann Company, assuming that it is desirable to pay in cash, and state the purpose of each control. Do *not* assume any control to be in operation unless it is specifically stated above. Your solution is to be in two columns, the first for the control, and the second for the purpose.

c. Prepare a procedural flow chart revised for your system.

26. Discuss the advantages of payroll payments by check over currency payments.

27. In order to prevent the padding of payrolls with fictitious employees a certain business which uses time clocks had each department head make a regular

daily count of employees in his department, sign for correctness of the name and number of employees, and distribute pay envelopes to them. Do you think any "deadheads" could be paid under such a procedure? If so, how could the procedure be tightened?

28. This question relates to payroll preparation and payment in a factory employing about 1,300 hourly employees. Normally all of them work an eight-hour shift at regular hourly rates of pay. Their time, for the most part, is chargeable to various different job orders rather than to a single account such as Departmental Supervision or Janitorial Expense. Of course occasionally some time of productive employees is chargeable to some kind of idle time expense account because of shortages, down time, etc. Turnover averages about ten new employees per week (with about the same number leaving). In addition, wage reclassifications, transfers, promotions, etc., average about 15 per week.

    All employees clock in at the start of their workday and out at its close, using weekly clock cards. Performance time is accounted for and reported by supervisors. On the average, each employee works on two different job orders per day; sometimes the number runs as high as four or five in a single day.

    With emphasis on the systems aspects of the case, you are to respond to the following:

a. When an employee is hired, leaves, or changes status, what action should be taken by the personnel department? What communication media would be used and what disposition would be made of them? Indicate the probable data added to the communication media used.

b. Describe or illustrate two different methods of computing the income withholding tax for these employees.

c. Beginning around August and continuing through the remainder of the year, clerks preparing payrolls for these employees will need to consult the individual earnings records frequently. Why is this so?

29. Prepare a procedural flow chart for payroll to portray good internal control for the New Wholesale Company. There are 600 employees working in nine different warehouses. All employees are paid by the hour and punch a time clock. A *non-descriptive* general-purpose accounting machine is to be used in check writing. In addition to the usual variable deductions, fixed deductions for union dues and the purchase of savings bonds are authorized. Show *all machines* on the chart that are used in your system, and each of the *forms* they process.

INVENTORY AND PRODUCTION CONTROL

    The responsibility for inventory and production control normally is assigned to the manufacturing function within a company. An efficient operation requires that men, materials, and productive facilities be utilized in an optimum way to accomplish company objectives. Having the right items at the right time, in the right place, and in the right quantity requires effective control and a good information flow.

Production Control

Production control requires the optimum use of facilities and other resources. Men, machines, and materials must be available when needed, and neither in excess nor in short supply. All of the special problems of production scheduling, special priorities, and optimizing are involved. The system design problems of production control can be identified readily, although solutions are not quite so easy.

The focus of this section is on inventory control rather than production control, although the two are so interrelated they cannot be separated clearly. The refinements and special control problems of work-in-process and finished goods inventories are not developed in detail. The application of the general systems theory to detailed problems should provide adequate guidelines.

Inventory Management

The management of inventories, including raw material, work-in-process and finished goods, is usually a responsibility of specialists. It is their obligation to recommend whether a given item should be manufactured or purchased; their function is beyond that of analysis and reporting of items on hand, items received, and items issued. They are responsible that a safety stock is maintained so that there are no stock-outs that could cripple production or cause customer dissatisfaction. Inventory must be maintained in proper balance to assure a reasonable inventory carrying cost. Information for basic inventory decisions, including economic lot size, inventory risk, and the acquisition costs and carrying costs, must be available.

Inventory Controls

The control of inventories is usually a function of its value, size, and composition. Many inventory records are maintained in terms of units rather than in dollars. Certain items are controlled through a continuous or perpetual record. While all items do not have detailed control, the basic control of inventory usually is by unit. Perpetual inventory procedures enable the best control as a record of each inventory item is maintained. Such records can consist of a stock ledger card for all similar items, a unit card for each item in the inventory, or some other record depending on the procedure or control needed.

Control over inventory includes methods of storing and handling. Items need to be classified and properly identified so that they can be located appropriately and so that proper verification and reporting is possible. The housing and handling of the items must be accomplished to provide security against embezzlement, to protect the material against damage or spoilage, to avoid obsolescence, and to provide assurance of proper control.

When appropriate, special sub-procedures are designed to control special inventories such as goods on consignment, in the hands of processors, in outside warehouses, or with customers. Such inventories, whether owned or in custody but belonging to others, should be controlled.

Nature of Inventory Control

The control of inventories is generally accomplished through a series of inventory records and reports that provide such information as inventory usage, inventory balances, and minimum and maximum level. Reorder points and procedures are established.

The inventory record, whether a separate record or stored internally in a computer, provides the best source of inventory information. The units in the beginning inventory, on order, receipts, issues and balance on hand should be included in the record.

Internal control duties are vital for appropriate control of inventories. It is basic that the individual who has responsibility for the asset not have access to the inventory record that controls the asset. No one individual should have complete control over inventory transactions.

Appropriate control over inventories requires that there be a periodic verification of items that are on hand. This can be done on a rotating basis when perpetual inventory records exist, or it can be done with a periodic physical count. The planning of a physical inventory is essential to control. Only through careful planning is it possible to make certain that all items are properly counted and have been reported.

An important part of inventory control is the evaluation of inventory turnover to determine the age, condition, and status of stock. Special control should be established to write down obsolete and slow-moving inventory items, and to compare the balance to an appropriately established inventory level. A stock status report showing detailed use by period is especially helpful in maintaining the inventory at a proper level, and controlling slow-moving items. The financial information system should be designed to facilitate a smooth flow of both inventory and production reports.

Internal Control of Inventory

Appendix A illustrates an internal control questionnaire on inventories. The use of such a questionnaire as a check list against which to test an inventory control procedure will provide an insight into the effectiveness of the internal control and suggest weaknesses in a procedure or strengthening that may be possible.

Inventory and Production Control Questions, Problems, and Cases

1. Aside from prevention of fraud, internal check is also designed to improve the accuracy of the record-keeping system. Name some specific procedures aimed at enhancing the accuracy of inventory records.

2. The Irving Manufacturing Company uses a system of shop orders in its plant. This system includes a series of orders for construction and installation of fixed assets, another series for retirement of assets, and a third series for maintenance work. There are "standing order" numbers for minor repetitive maintenance items and special orders for unusual or major maintenance items.

   In connection with a regular annual audit of the Irving Manufacturing Company, prepare a program for work to be done on the maintenance orders. Assume that there appears to be reasonable internal control in the company. Prepare your program to avoid doing any more work than is necessary to meet acceptable auditing standards and explain the purpose or objective of each of your proposed steps. (AICPA Examination)

3. In what specific ways do you feel that existence of a clerical inventory record such as perpetual, retail, etc., strengthens control over inventory?

4. a. Design an inventory tag and stub for use by a client conducting a moderate-sized wholesale plumbing material and supply business.
   b. Write a memorandum of instructions such as might be necessary to instruct the client's employees in the use of the tag and stub. (AICPA Examination)

5. Suppose you had a stack of materials issue tickets, averaging three items per ticket, and you were to post the issues to perpetual inventory cards. List the steps you would take to do the job, in the order in which you would perform the steps.

6. One important feature of production control in both specific order and repetitive process industries is the maintenance of machine and load files. What should the records show for each major machine?

7. List the principal functions of a production control department.

8. The Martin Johnson Manufacturing Company has had many difficulties in material control, and has recently discovered a serious raw material inventory shortage. In the resulting investigation the following was determined:

Stock ledger cards. Stock ledger cards were maintained in the storeroom, and indicated the reorder point for each item. When the reorder point was reached, or when a special production order was received, the store ledger clerk would call the purchasing agent and instruct him to order the item or items required.

Purchase order. The purchasing agent prepared the purchase order in two copies, sending the original to the vendor and retaining the duplicate as the company record.

Receiving. All incoming materials are delivered directly to the storeroom. A receiving report is prepared and is the basis for posting stock ledger cards.

Invoices. Invoices are received by the purchasing agent who verifies price, terms, extension, etc. He sends them to the stock ledger clerk who verifies the receipt of the item from stock ledger card postings. If the material has been received the invoice is sent to the cash disbursement section for payment.

Inventory Procedure. The stock ledger clerk verified the balances shown by stock ledger cards with materials actually on hand as filler work. There has been little time recently to check ledger cards since two clerks have been sick. No annual inventory is taken.

a. Divide your answer sheet into two parts. In one part list the weaknesses of the present system and opposite, in the other part, your recommendation for improvement. Do not assume any control to exist that has not been specifically stated.

b. Prepare a procedural flow chart for purchases showing the system after installation of the changes recommended above.

9. You are engaged to devise an inventory procedure for a new book store stocking approximately 50,000 volumes under 4,500 different titles. The store has been in operation ten months and it is almost time to take the first inventory under the procedure you are to design. An adequate records system has been maintained, but the store does not keep perpetual inventory records. Your answer should list, in sequence, steps to be taken and will include specimens of forms to be used. You may state such assumptions as you wish, provided, of course, they are not inconsistent with other facts given.

10. Refer to Figure 19-2 which sets out the production schedule of finished product No. 1 from raw materials a and a' and b and b'.

Assume the following quantities are required to turn out 100 units of finished product No. 1.

Raw Material or Subassembly	Unspoiled Units	Spoilage Rate
A	300	10%
B	400	5%
a	600	15%
a'	50	10%
b	700	0%
b'	100	20%

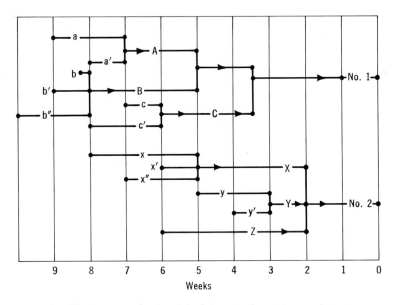

FIGURE 19-2.   Production Schedule—Products No. 1 and No. 2

a. How many units will have to be ordered assuming that inventories of raw materials are to be unchanged after the production? Prepare a specimen *bill of materials* covering the 100 unit lot of product No. 1.

b. How many units will have to be ordered if raw material inventories are to be reduced 50 per cent and prior to start of production are respectively $a = 500$, $a' = 80$, $b = 1,000$, and $b' = 100$?

c. If the finished product is wanted as of the close of business on July 23, what are the latest dates on which orders can be placed for raw materials? (Ignore Sunday, holidays, etc.)

11. Refer to Figure 19-2 which sets out the production schedule of finished product No. 2 from raw materials x and x' and y and y'.

Assume the following quantities are required for 500 units of finished product No. 2.

Raw Material or Subassembly	Unfinished Units	Spoilage Rate
X	200	0%
Y	800	10%
x	1000	10%
x'	500	0%
y	2000	15%
y'	500	20%

a. Prepare a specimen bill of materials covering the 500 units lot of product No. 2. How many units will have to be ordered assuming that inventories of raw materials are to be unchanged after the production?

b. How many units will have to be ordered if inventories are to be increased 40 per cent and prior to start of production are, respectively, $x = 800$, $x' = 800$, $y = 3000$, and $y' = 500$?

c. If the finished product is wanted as of the close of business on July 23, what are the latest dates on which orders can be placed for raw materials? (Ignore Sundays, holidays, etc.)

12. Refer to the data of problem 17. Assume that A is processed by machines, each of which is capable of producing 15 units per day and that spoilage occurs at the end of the production process. How many machines would be required to turn out 100 finished units of product No. 1 in three days?

13. Refer to the data of problem 18. Prepare the *requisition* for commodities y and y'.

14. Visit a local factory and for their simplest final product ascertain the contents of a bill of materials. Draw a replica of their bill of materials form, entering the data for a production batch of the product selected.

15. Refer to a library electronics publication such as *Radio Amateurs' Handbook*, *QST* magazine, or some other electronics magazine which prints circuits and lists parts required to make such things as radios or amplifiers. Prepare a *bill of materials* covering production of ten units for which the circuit and parts are shown.

16. Visit a local factory and obtain a specimen of their *production order* form. Turn in a copy of the form together with the following information:
    a. The title of the employee who prepares it.
    b. By what physical means are data entered on the form?
    c. By what means is routing determined?
    d. By what means is delivery or distribution of the form effected?
    e. How does a typical recipient file the form while the job is in process?
    f. What disposition is made of copies after the job has been completed?

17. In connection with the *production order* form:
    a. What are the essential elements?
    b. What determines its distribution?
    c. What disposition would you recommend after the job covered has been completed?

18. What is the relationship of a *requisition* and a *material credit slip*? Why should they not be on paper of the same color?

19. Describe the contents of an *open order* file.

20. Visit a local factory and ascertain what kinds of visual reporting and control devices such as Gantt charts, production boards, etc., they are using. In connection with your findings write a report detailing the following matters:
    a. Brief description of the devices used.
    b. Frequency with which changes are reflected on the devices used.
    c. Departments making use of the data reflected.

    d. Department responsible for recording data on the devices.

    e. Means, if any, by which visual data are made a matter of permanent record.

    f. Difficulties reported in the use of the devices.

21. a. Briefly describe the Gantt Chart.

    b. Describe how a production control board operates.

22. A Telecontrol system is used in a factory using punch presses, mills, lathes, hobbers, and wedging and winding machines. The factory turns out about 600 different items consisting on the average of 300 parts apiece. The Telecontrol system cost $40,000 to purchase and install and costs $11,000 annually to operate and maintain.

    As a result of the Telecontrol installation the following benefits have been derived:

    a. Saving of six minutes per day per productive worker. (Assume a five-day week, $2 per hour wages for 200 workers).

    b. Transfer of four timekeepers (annual savings $4,000 each) to other duties.

    c. Reduction of downtime by 40 per cent; prior to this system downtime costs were $40,000 per year.

    d. Transfer of three dispatchers (annual savings $5,000 each) to other duties.

    Prepare a report showing how soon the installation should "pay for itself."

23. Discuss the kinds of information cost accounting should furnish to production control.

24. The H Manufacturing Company is engaged in manufacturing items to fill specific orders received from its customers. While at any given time it may have substantial inventories of work in process and finished goods, all such amounts are assignable to firm sales orders which it has received.

    The company's operations, including the administrative and sales functions, are completely departmentalized. Its cost system is on a job order basis. Direct materials and direct labor are identified with jobs by the use of material issue tickets and daily time cards. Overhead costs are accumulated for each factory service, administrative, and selling department. These overhead costs, including administrative and selling expenses, are then allocated to productive departments and an overhead rate computed for each productive department. This rate is used to apply overhead to jobs on the basis of direct labor hours. The result is that all costs and expenses incurred during any month are charged to work-in-process accounts for the jobs.

    a. You are to compare this system, as it affects inventory valuation, with the usual system for manufacturing businesses.

    b. You are to criticize the system as it affects inventory valuation and income determination.

    c. You are to state any justification which you see for the use of the H Company's system. (AICPA Examination)

FIXED PROPERTIES AND INVESTMENTS

Fixed Properties

The heart of control for fixed properties is an adequate subsidiary property ledger. The property ledger provides the necessary detail to support the total amount for all fixed property and the detail of each property. Such records are important to the determination of adequate insurance coverage, or, in the event of loss, the insurance claim. They can also provide the basis for information that is helpful in decisions such as trade *vs.* sell, buy *vs.* lease, make *vs.* buy, and the like.

In the design of a purchase procedure, the necessary provisions should be made so that capital expenditures receive both special authorization and special processing. In most companies capital expenditures over a specific dollar amount are not authorized without special written authority. Such authority normally flows from the approved capital expenditure program.

On acquisition of fixed property, procedures should exist to establish proper accounting control and custodial responsibility. In the processing of the invoice for payment, proper pick-up of the asset in the property record is essential. Periodic reports can be sent to each custodian to verify the physical existence of the asset. Procedures for fixed properties should involve the assigning of an owner's number which is affixed to the asset in a prescribed manner. Any items with manufacturers' serial numbers, such as typewriters or calculators, should have that serial number included as a part of the property record.

In the design of a procedure for fixed property, the problems of physical custody of the asset and the periodic determination that the asset is still on hand and in use are important. Operating records, depreciation history, repairs and such information are often important and summarized on the property record periodically.

One of the important uses of fixed properties records is to control disposition. When a property is replaced or scrapped, it is important that it be removed from the record and the appropriate recognition be given to the transaction. If the asset is sold, the funds from the sale should be traceable into the business and a record should exist of the items that have been disposed. Generally, items that are disposed of or that are not in use should be assembled in the appropriate place, and documentation initiated and approved for items to make them available where they might be useful within the company, or to have them sold, traded, or scrapped.

Investments

Investments, like fixed properties, require special records. The investments themselves normally should be contained in a fireproof safe or safe-deposit box, and the record separated from the custody. The record should include all possible identification such as certificate numbers, par values, dates, etc.

All investments should be held appropriately in the name of the business. It is also desirable that, when investments are in a safe-deposit box, two individuals are required to be present to get into the box. In this manner it is not possible for anyone to withdraw securities from the box without authorization and a witness. No custodian can individually be accused of improper actions.

All investment transactions should be authorized appropriately in corporate minutes. The internal auditor should examine certificates and verify their physical existence periodically to supplement external audit.

Internal Control of Fixed Properties and Investments

Appendix A illustrates an internal control questionnaire with questions relating to fixed properties and investments. Careful study of the questionnaire suggests strengths and weaknesses of given procedures. The use of the questionnaire as a check list against which a given procedure can be measured for appropriate safeguards and internal control can be most helpful in system design.

Fixed Assets and Investments Questions, Problems, and Cases

1. Prepare a questionnaire to be used in the evaluation of internal control relating to property, plant, and equipment. (AICPA Examination)

2. What are some of the principal benefits to be derived from maintenance of a good set of plant and equipment records?

3. Assuming the same degree of adequacy, why might the investments records systems of two businesses of like size quite possibly differ a great deal?

4. Describe the physical safeguards usually employed in connection with securities investments.

5. In a large organization which uses the voucher system and trades in securities regularly, what steps are likely to precede the actual purchase of new securities?

6. Record the following securities transactions in an investment register form:
   a. On January 7, bought 50 shares of ABC Company 5 per cent preferred shares at 25½ plus total brokerage fees of $60. (Par value is $10 per share.)
   b. On March 1 bought ten bonds issued by Bossler Corporation for a total

consideration of $10,300. Since this is an interest date, the price does not include accrued interest.

   c. On May 1 bought ten bonds issued by Pierce and Sloan, Inc., for a total consideration of $10,750. These bonds pay 4 per cent per annum interest each February 1 and August 1.

   d. On July 8 sold the ABC Company 5 per cent preferred shares at 27 and incurred costs of $80 in making the sale.

7. Refer to the data of 6. Suppose you are employed by an organization which deals so actively in securities an individual ledger card is maintained for each stock and bond owned. Enter the data of transactions a. and c. on suitable subsidiary records.

8. Describe the frequency and manner of inventorying securities in a well-run organization. Does the fact that some securities owned are not on hand necessarily indicate something is amiss?

9. Aside from inventorying, indicate the principal internal control measures applicable to securities investments.

10. Mallow Furniture Store began business as a relatively small operation, but due to good values and service, sound management, and growth of the community, has experienced considerable growth.

    Initially the company found it feasible to have a local trucking service make its deliveries. Growth of the business has led management to believe this is no longer economical. The company contemplates acquiring two small vans and two panel delivery trucks to handle customer deliveries.

    Design unit asset records suitable for the new delivery procedure.

11. Refer to the problem above. If management desires a cost comparison of the old and new customer delivery procedure, what data will be needed from the information system after the change in order to supply the comparison without special analysis?

12. Sam Smith opened a newsstand with the following equipment:

   a. Four indoor magazine racks built by a carpenter at a total cost of $360.

   b. Two rotary book racks suitable for display of paperback books which cost $70 each.

   c. One outdoor rack suitable for display of newspapers which cost $30.

   d. Used cash register costing $225.

   e. Miscellaneous second-hand furniture costing $150.

    Assume the business began July 1 and will operate on a calendar year basis. All assets except item d. have an estimated eight year life and salvage value amounting to 20 per cent of cost. The cash register is estimated to have a twelve year life and $45 scrap value.

    Prepare a fixed asset register and reflect depreciation for the first half year and the first full year that follows.

13. Refer to *The Accountants' Index*; look under Fixed Assets. Find an article describing a fixed assets acquisition program. Summarize the article and copy two of the important specimen forms illustrated. Turn in full reference data including author's full name, exact title, page numbers, date, etc.

14. Alternate 13 to be used if *Accountants' Index* is not available but back issues of *N.A.A. Bulletin* (then *N.A.C.A. Bulletins*) are available. Find the article by Kramer in Volume 33, summarize it, and copy three of the filled-out forms he illustrates in describing the acquisition program of Deere and Company.

15. Discuss the type of fixed assets records needed by a motel with 28 room units operating in a single location.

16. Would a railroad probably need to maintain separate records for property tax purposes only? Why would the regular asset records probably not suffice for this special purpose? What would the property tax records contain?

17. Wherein would a bus line connecting 27 cities in three different states have a different fixed assets record problem than a railroad serving the same territory?

18. Design an Authorization for Capital Expenditure form suitable for use on your campus.

19. How would you recommend that a restaurant or cafeteria account for such items as dishes, linens, and silverware? What are some of the unique problems faced?

20. Refer to a book on restaurant, hotel, or hospital accounting. Describe the treatment recommended or set out for accounting for dishes and linens.

21. Suppose all of the adding machines in one of your statistics laboratories are to be transferred to the auditor's or controller's office in the central administration of your school for the summer and the transfer is to be recorded on a form designed for the purpose. Prepare a suitable form and fill in the data to the best of your ability.

22. What are some reasons for maintaining fairly detailed records in connection with leased properties?

23. Indicate the types of retirements of fixed assets that can occur. Describe the procedure that should attend each.

24. Assume that a depreciation method such as straight-line, declining balance, or sum-of-the-digits has been selected. From a systems standpoint, what has to be done in respect to depreciation in a manufacturing business?

25. If a business decides to adopt guidelines depreciation, what implications does this have as to fixed assets records?

26. How and by whom should fixed assets be inventoried? What follow-up action would normally be indicated after such an inventory?

27. Visit some large organization and interview someone in the controller's department about reports to management that are made concerning the entity's fixed assets. Prepare a brief report.

28. If you were to study the system of a large business which had the reputation of having good internal control, what features would you expect to find in respect to accounting for and control over fixed assets?

WORK SIMPLIFICATION AND COST REDUCTION

Administrative costs have risen steadily and markedly, absolutely and relatively. This is a depressing fact of modern business life. Some of the rise is attributable to inflation, i.e., most cost elements—salaries, supplies, depreciation, and others—have been in a continuous ascent since the early 1930's. Inflation might account largely for some elements of cost increases. It does not account for all of them, and it does not begin to explain the *relative* rise in office costs. The systems analyst must (1) take cognizance of the causes of office cost increases, (2) be able to describe some generally effective counter measures, and (3) recommend work simplification and cost reduction actions. At the outset it is important to emphasize that unit costs are equal to costs incurred divided by units of work produced, and that office costs are incurred primarily for facilities (employee time, space, and equipment).

Much of the writing on the subject of office costs in recent years begins by noting that in 1900 the ratio of factory to office employees was about 10 to 1, and that today the ratio is only around 4 to 1. There is evidence that, computers, automation, and other gadgetry notwithstanding, the trend has not been reversed though it may have been arrested. Many causes for this condition can be found. As business units grow larger (through expansion, merger, and diversification), they become harder to manage. Need for information increases as top management gets farther from actual operations and as the span of control increases. Management has grown more sophisticated and demands more information which is often of a type not called for earlier. Demands of government for accounting and other data have multiplied vastly. Three decades ago these commonplace items were almost unknown—payroll withholding taxes, information reports on payments to employees and others, and excise tax reports, to name but a few. Today an atmosphere of disclosure of business data prevails; this contrasts with an earlier tendency to keep most data confidential (assuming it even existed). The web of economic inter-relationships has grown markedly so that it is now common for corporations to file frequent reports with governmental units at all levels, pension trusts, unions, insurance companies, and others.

Clerical Work Measurement

A prerequisite to successfully combat the office cost situation just described is the ability to measure and, thereby, to cost clerical work output. Reduced to its simplest terms, *work measurement* involves counting production and measuring the time required to achieve it.

Diverse groups concerned with rising office costs increasingly have turned attention to clerical work measurement in recent years. Progressive top management, alert office supervisors, staff systems men, industrial engineers, and consultants such as CPA firms have combined efforts and talents to bring about rewarding results in a good number of companies. The surface has barely been scratched, however, as the number of potential users of work simplification dwarfs actual users to date.

Simply stated, work measurement is the counting of production and measuring of time required for it. More broadly, it entails comparison with a standard. Its essential value is that it provides a basis for determining progress by comparing what has been done with what is being done or should be done.

Types of work which have been successfully measured include calculating, posting, filing, billing, typing, tabulating (including key punching, verifying, sorting, and reproducing), sorting and collating, preparing vouchers, duplicating, together with most payroll operations. This list is by no means exhaustive; it is given as a representation of what is feasible. On the other hand, it is not feasible to attempt work measurement for some creative types of activities (e.g., research, planning) or for situations where someone must be employed regardless of the work volume (e.g., a single cashier).

Clerical work measurement programs are warranted in those situations in which existing inefficiency is great enough that the potential savings will more than pay for the programs. This obvious statement is easier to make than to implement. How does one determine that there is serious inefficiency in office operations? By what standard can a given procedure be characterized as inefficient? Even if inefficiency is known to exist, how can one be reasonably sure it is curable or that the benefits of doing so are worth the effort? These questions are not easily answered. It is fairly safe to assume that any operation or procedure is being performed with less than optimum efficiency, but this is not to say it should be altered or even investigated. It is generally agreed that high-volume operations employing relatively large numbers of employees offer potentially more fruitful grounds for possible savings than low-volume ones where few people are engaged. Clues such as employment of a larger number of employees in a given activity than in comparable firms are significant. Independent consultants such as CPA's are in a particularly good position to be of help in advising on whether or where a work measurement program should be initiated because of their wide knowledge of business generally and their background of experience which enables them to compare the client's situation with that of others.

It should be noted that trouble is not always where it may superficially appear to be. A given department may have a very large number of clerks who spend most of their time dealing with complaints resulting from delays or errors occurring in other departments. For example, if the shipping department often packs shipments erroneously, the billing department will probably need additional personnel to handle adjustments, answer complaints, etc.

Delays in one clerical department can cause irregular flow of work to a subsequent department; at first glance the latter may look inefficient in that its employees are idled at times because no work has come down and must work overtime at others to catch up. The overtime costs would appear on expense sheets of the second department which is not at fault at all. Inefficiencies in such departments as production control, inspection, or delivery could involve some clerical department in difficulties which would send the latter's costs soaring.

Clerical Work Standards

Clerical work standards are performance goals related to office work. As in the case of cost accounting standards, there are various kinds of standards, and there are several approaches to the development of clerical work standards. Two methods of clerical work measurement, (1) maintenance of records of output and (2) work sampling, can lead to the development of clerical work standards. Time and motion study may inherently involve them. Maintenance of records of clerical productivity or work sampling can be used to develop standards provided certain sensible precautions are observed. Time and motion studies may involve the application of standard times to what is under observation.

Clerical work standards based on data obtained by maintenance of clerical productivity or on work sampling must take into account whether the procedures under consideration were reasonably efficient at the time and were being done by competent personnel. operating at respectable efficiency. Obviously if the procedure itself is faulty, and the personnel implementing it were not performing efficiently, data based on what was being done at the time would not be a suitable basis for developing performance goals. Standards based on measured performance which is poor could result in employees being excessively compensated for doing an ordinary job.

Achieving Work Simplification

A fruitful source of work simplification suggestions is the employees themselves. If supervisors will begin by looking for easier ways to do things, they will soon develop a habit and consciousness that will be observed and picked up by the employees. Once the employees become convinced there is a genuine interest in work simplification, they will come forth with suggestions. On the plus side it can be said they are experts in the performance of their tasks and should know wherein lie the potential improvements. On the negative side it can be noted that as creatures of habit, many persons simply cannot conceive of doing their tasks differently from the way they were taught to do them. Incentive suggestion programs are fairly widespread. These give cash or other rewards for money-saving suggestions that are adopted. Their implementation requires some special precautions, and discussion of these is beyond the scope of this text. Suffice it to say that many organizations (both business and non-profit) have found ways to make incentive suggestion programs effective and worth-while.

Examples of Work Simplification

Since the concern is with *simplification*, it is logical to expect that many of the specific examples of what is meant by work simplification entail commonplace, common sense practices rather than profound or obscure ones.

Transcribing information from forms prepared by someone else in the organization is a major waste of energy. Relevant parts can be put on specially designed form sets through carbon paper; irrelevant portions can be deleted through use of block outs, narrow carbons, or narrow copy forms. Are data typed which could be handwritten? In many businesses people spend time recopying information from handwritten records which could have been used directly as sources of data. Poor housekeeping results in much wasted human energy. The man hours wasted in some offices cost staggering sums simply because data sought are not in convenient locations or in devices which would increase their accessibility. Information kept in books or binders would be more accessible in a tub file, drawer with a flip end so (one or more) hands are not required to hold back the forms not wanted. Payroll clerks are sometimes found using books of hourly pay rates when a small roll-type desk top file might better serve the purpose. Accounts receivable ought to be near the credit department which probably uses them as much or more in many organizations than the personnel who maintain them.

Traffic through or even in sight of a clerical area causes waste by the interruptions which arise from it. People approaching or passing through work areas cause those employed there to look up. If each such look takes three seconds, and twenty clerks look up when a visitor arrives, the equivalent of a man-minute has been lost. This may not sound like much, but suppose it happens once every ten minutes (a low frequency for most offices); in a month the time lost by all 20 clerks would amount to about three weeks' time for a single clerk!

Cost Reduction

Many economies can be achieved without changing noticeably either the *how* or *what* that employees are processing. Such economies are probably easiest of all to effect, but some of them are so obvious and simple it is quite difficult to detect or conceive them. As an example, consider the matter of filling orders of customers for spare parts. Frequently these have a fairly nominal value; even so, few persons would conceive of giving them away; yet it might be cheaper to do so. It may cost several dollars to bill and collect less than a dollar (the cost of the parts concerned). Manifestly, if this is true, it would be cheaper to send the parts to the customer free of charge; doing so would probably build considerable goodwill as well. It is just as costly to bill a customer for $1 as $1,000. An analysis of the cost of billing could lead to substantial saving. Many firms absorb the costs of shipping orders which exceed a certain minimum amount. Again, this is often worth while because it may cost just as much to fill small orders as large ones.

Cost reduction in mailing, supplies, duplicating, communication media and their preparation, can be worth the expenditure of substantial effort.

Work Simplification and Cost Reduction Questions, Problems, and Cases

1. What factors account for the *relative* rise in office costs?

2. For what reasons has office work measurement lagged behind work measurement in the factory and other operating segments of business enterprises?

3. What advantages can accrue from adoption of a clerical work measurement program?

4. In what lines of activity has adoption of incentive compensation plans for office employees lagged somewhat?

5. Under what circumstances is clerical work measurement feasible? Give specific examples of accounting applications in large businesses which should lend themselves to clerical work measurement.

6. If a given clerical department consistently runs up costs which seem excessive, does this fact indicate it is functioning inefficiently? Why or why not?

7. Under a clerical work sampling program the observation period covered 50 hours, during which time 1,100 observations were made. Element D was noted to occur 78 times. What is the average actual time required to perform this element? If the delay allowance is reduced from 30 per cent to 20 per cent, what time should be required to perform Element D?

8. Design a worksheet suitable for recording time-and-motion observations of an operation involving sorting of charge sales tickets for a department store which arrive in batches of approximately 300. There are 17 departmental classifications; the work is performed by three clerks. All sales tickets are handwritten by sales clerks and are supposed to have been validated by being rung up on cash registers operated by central cashiers, each of whom serves an average of three departments. Fill in some hypothetical data in your worksheet.

9. Analyze the following data incident to machine posting of checks drawn by bank depositors:

Number of checks posted	570
Total elapsed minutes	480
Rest period minutes	20
Interruption and delay minutes	20

Develop a standard time per check. In terms of percentage, what is the rest and delay allowance?

10. Why is it important to adopt qualitative standards at the same time quantitative standards are adopted in an office?

11. Suggest some simplifications of registration procedures followed on your campus at the start of a semester or quarter.

12. Suggest some simplifications of the procedure of checking out library materials on your campus.

13. Interview a local business man. Ask him to name three specific ways in which his organization has cut office costs within the past two years.

14. Consult one of the following Indexes: *Accountants' Index, Business Periodicals Index, Public Affairs Information Service Index*. Prepare a report (two to four typewritten pages) covering three specific instances in which office costs were reduced as a result of some deliberate program seeking such improvements.

OTHER QUESTIONS, PROBLEMS, AND CASES

The "Other" portion of Chapter 19 is designed to provide a format to include special questions, problems, and cases common to more than one procedure, or that relate to the tools and techniques of the systems analyst. Also included are questions, problems, and cases from specific procedures not presented separately. The basic requirements for a systems term report is also included. For reference purposes, the "other questions, problems, and cases" are organized into the following groups:

> Term Report—Systems Analysis
> Organization
> Internal Control
> Simplified Systems
> Machines and Devices
> Miscellaneous

Term Report—Systems Analysis

1. You are given the assignment as a systems analyst to study an actual procedure. You are to utilize fully the tools and techniques of the systems analyst

and to report your findings, including the strong points and weaknesses of the procedure you have selected for study. The project has been assigned early to provide holiday periods to gather data in the event the entity under study is located in the community in which you live rather than where you are going to school.

Physical Requirements. Your report is to be typewritten (double-spaced) unless specific permission is obtained to the contrary, and is to be bound in a report binder. Flow charts should be principally in ink and neatly done, though pencil is allowed for colored portions or other parts which would be unduly difficult to prepare in ink. Specimen forms should be actual forms used by the business, in which case they should be firmly affixed. If specimen forms are not actually available, facsimiles should be faithfully and neatly prepared.

The Entity Suveyed. In selecting an actual business in which to make your study, you should seek an entity which is neither too small nor too large. While no limitations are imposed as to maximum size, you must observe this criterion as to minimum size. The accounting and related activities of the business must require the equivalent of at least one full-time employee. If the business insists its identity must not be disclosed you must, of course, honor this request. It would necessitate your identifying it by a fictitious name and address and deletion of its name from specimen actual forms. If you do use a fictitious name this fact must be stated.

Phase of System Reported Upon. Your report is to deal with some limited phase such as Order and Customer Billing *or* Payroll. In the former case procedures reported on would start with taking the customers' order, include preparation of invoices or sales tickets, posting of accounts receivable, and end with preparation and mailing of statements to customers. If you select Payroll instead, your starting point would be hiring procedures and timekeeping, include payroll calculation and preparation, and end with disbursement to employees. Year-end procedures such as preparation of W-2 forms need not be included.

Elements of Your Report. The elements of the term report should include at least the following:

a. Your report must indicate the nature of the procedure involved. You can use a combination of narrative description, listing of steps, filling in data on specimen forms, even pictures or drawings. An overall flow chart must be prepared, and partial flow charts covering phases of operation are, of course, allowed.

b. The principal forms used must be included. These are to be filled in with *hypothetical* data to such an extent as to convey an accurate impression of how the forms are used. Forms should be mounted in the report where they are discussed, not at the end.

c. Machines used are to be listed and their functions are to be described briefly.

d. Volume statistics such as number of active customer accounts, number of invoices per month, number of employees, usual working hours, etc. are to be included. Money amounts need not be disclosed, though they may be.

    e. Internal control measures are to be listed in a separate portion of the report though they may be referred to in conjunction with preceding material.

    f. Your report is to conclude with a "creative" section in which you evaluate the effectiveness of the procedures, criticize weak points, and make recommendations for improvements if these would be significant.

    Other Points. Obviously a guide such as this cannot cover every point on which questions may arise. When you are in doubt as to what you should do, confer with your teacher.

    You will explain to the company representative with whom you first talk that your job is to make an accurate description of an actual procedure, that no confidential information will be disclosed, and that the organization name will not even be used in the report if this is desired.

    Evaluation. In the evaluation of the project, weight will be given to general appearance, clarity of writing, adequacy of descriptions, use of the tools of the systems analyst, and the quality of analysis of strong points and weaknesses. A letter on company stationery, signed by a responsible individual, saying that your report has been checked for accuracy and completeness, would add to the validity of your report but is not required.

Organization

2. The Nationwide Petroleum Company is one commonly known as an "integrated refiner." It consists of three rather independent divisions. Two of the divisions are refining and marketing operations, one on the East coast of the United States, and the other on the West coast. The third division, located in the South and Southwest, owns large petroleum reserves and produces much of the oil refined and marketed by the other two organizations.

    Historically, each division was once an independent company which subsequently was merged to form the Nationwide Petroleum Company. Even though technically merged, for many years each division has operated autonomously. In fact, one of the company's problems is a lack of uniformity among these units in almost every field or function.

    The president has witnessed an increase in the sales of the company to an annual volume of approximately $400,000,000. However, in comparison with the industry, the rate of return on capital employed and net income, expressed as a per cent of net sales, has declined steadily in the past six years. Under the circumstances, he has called upon the vice-president—finance to discuss the need for re-organizing the financial-accounting function and adopting some modern concepts of responsibility reporting, etc. The president has expressed the opinion that, in view of an inability to control prices of gasoline, an extensive cost reduction program must be adopted in an effort to restore "old margins." Moreover, he feels that an independent reporting organization is necessary to have "absolutely honest and objective measurement of results against goals."

    At the present time, each division has its own financial-accounting organization under the direct supervision of a division controller. The division controller, in turn, reports to the division general manager. A similar pattern exists for the manufacturing, marketing production, purchasing, and research functions in that they report to the division general manager, and have a functional relationship to the applicable home office staff.

The organization of each division controller's staff is as follows:

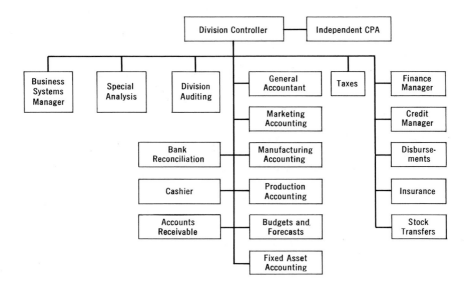

The home office financial group is structured as follows:

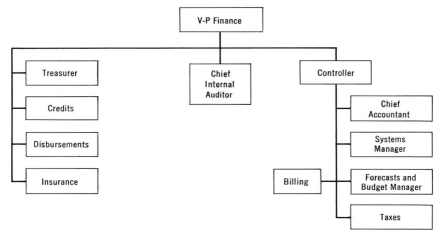

The duties of the home office staff have been a responsibility of the V-P Finance and restricted largely to an advisory role except for the consolidation of over-all operating results, and general corporate financing.

The functions of each group are quite as expected. Divisional auditing has been confined to routine checking of invoices, etc., as contrasted to the broader scope managerial auditing. The business systems manager does all systems work for the division and is presently engaged on a computer installation for the division. The special analysis department does any special project work or analysis required by the division controller.

In studying the organization structure, the division general managers have expressed the opinion that the division controller organization should be retained intact and report to them in order to have proper control information to be held accountable for their operations. Give your views on the subject, including:

a. Any change desired in the structure of the information function. Explain each change.

b. Responsibilities of home office and division groups.

3. Internal auditing is a staff function found in virtually every large corporation. The internal audit function is also performed in many smaller companies as a part-time activity of individuals who may or may not be called internal auditors. The differences between the audits by independent public accountants and the work of internal auditors are more basic than is generally recognized.

a. Briefly discuss the auditing work performed by the independent public accountant and the internal auditor with regard to:

(1) Auditing objectives.

(2) General nature of auditing work.

b. In conducting his audit the independent public accountant must evaluate the work of the internal auditor. Discuss briefly the reason for this evaluation.

c. List the auditing procedures used by an independent public accountant in evaluating the work of the internal auditor (AICPA Examination)

4. The TRK Manufacturing Company is a large single-plant organization. Where within their organization structure should responsibility for the following be assigned and why?

a. Budgeting.

b. Internal audit.

c. Cashier.

d. External auditor.

e. Bank reconciliation.

f. Credit and collections.

g. Organization planning.

5. During a systems study of a single-plant manufacturing company you note that the organization chart reflects the following organization units as a part of the controller's organization.

a. Indicate whether each organization unit should be a part of the controller's organization, and, if not, the reason:

Organization Unit

Accounts receivable	Organization planning
Cashier	Economic studies
Systems and procedures	Taxes
Accounts payable	General ledger
External auditor	Cost accounting
Internal auditor	Payroll
Bank reconciliation	Purchase and expense ledger
Credit and collection	Vouchers payable
Insurance	Purchasing

b. You note that the span of control is too long at both the top and bottom level of the controller's organization. Explain. You also note that similar functions are not grouped. Explain.

6. The Madison Manufacturing Corporation has three specific managerial levels, namely the top management level, the division level, and the plant level. Investigation of the company definitely establishes the following:

a. Profit responsibility has been delegated to the divisional level only, with the exception of Plant A in Division B, to which full profit responsibility has been delegated. Other plants have been delegated only responsibility for cost control and budget performance.

b. There are three divisions, Division A, B, and C. Each division has ten plants. The organization of the three divisions and plants within the division is comparable except for Plant A, Division B, mentioned in item a., above.

c. The top management level organization, and portions of the rest of the organization are as follows:

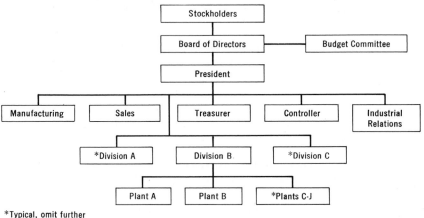

*Typical, omit further detail from solutions

Recopy, changing where desired, the above organization chart. Reflect principles of good organization. Leave sufficient room to add the following:

a. The basic business functions on each level, if appropriate.

    b. The controller or responsible accounting officer at each level, if appropriate.

    c. The following organization units, on the appropriate level or levels, if appropriate:

Accounts receivable	Operations research
Payroll	Bank reconciliation
Timekeeping	General ledger
Billing	Systems and procedure
Internal audit	External auditor
Budgeting	Purchase and expense ledger
Cashier	Amounts payable
Taxes	Cost accounting
Economic forecasts	Insurance
Tabulation	Credit
Mail room	Production control

7. You are employed in the Management Services Department of a national public accounting firm. At a recent professional meeting you were sitting next to the controller of the Paper Bag Manufacturing Company, a large company, who informs you that they are reviewing their system of internal reporting. During the course of the evening, he made the following comments:

> We are extremely pleased with our progress in revising internal reporting procedures. All reports are now channeled through a Report Analysis Section headed by an assistant controller. He investigates unusual items and encloses an analysis of problem areas with reports being sent to line executives. He is also responsible for follow-up on suggestions made in his reports. Duplication of effort is being eliminated by sending copies of detailed reports to all organizational levels, removing the necessity for many summaries that did not reveal the full information. All reports are now designed to compare current data to that of prior years, and are prepared directly by machine. Accuracy has been greatly improved due to the practice of verifying reports to the ledger at the time data are prepared.

> Indicate the strengths and weaknesses of the internal reporting system of the Paper Bag Manufacturing Company as it relates to (a) the Report Analysis Section, (b) elimination of duplication of effort, (c) comparisons, and (d) accuracy.

8. Zee Manufacturing Company, after careful consideration of the project, has decided to create a new subsidiary corporation for the purpose of diversifying its operations and investing some excess funds which otherwise would probably be used for extra dividend payments. The new corporation is to be unrelated operationally to its parent; hence there is no problem of coordinating accounting matters other than choosing the same fiscal period. Key personnel and most top managers are to transfer from Zee, but an outsider is to be hired as controller.

    As a practicing CPA you are called in to advise on design of the system of the new company. Within the framework set out above and assuming the company will initially employ around 1,400 persons (of whom about 35 will be engaged in accounting) and will operate in three locations, you are free to assume whatever you wish in answering the following questions. You must, however, state your assumptions if they materially affect your answers.

   a. If the nature of the business is one on which you have limited background, what sources would you consult to fill in the gaps?

   b. How would you go about determining the new company's accounting requirements?

   c. What principal factors would influence the design of the chart of accounts?

   d. If, instead of as stated above, the new subsidiary is to be operationally related to the parent company, what differences would this make in your approach to the design of the system?

9. Ernest, Hard, Werker and Co., CPA's, have numerous clients in the furniture manufacturing business, an industry which tends to be concentrated in a fairly limited geographical region. One day a furniture manufacturer who has not been one of their clients telephones and says he thinks he needs a complete modernization of his accounting system and replacement of his non-cost system with cost accounting set up. The general nature of this manufacturer's operations is well known to the partners of the CPA firm because he operates principally in the community in which the accounting firm is headquartered. Will it be necessary to make a preliminary survey of this furniture manufacturing enterprise prior to undertaking design of a new system? Support your answer in some detail.

Internal Control

10. An important procedure in the CPA's audit programs is his review of the client's system of internal control.

   a. Distinguish between accounting controls and administrative controls in a properly coordinate system of internal control.

   b. List the essential features of a sound system of accounting control.

   c. Explain why the CPA is concerned about the separation of responsibilities for operating custodianship, financial custodianship, and controllership. (AICPA Examination)

11. Aside from prevention of fraud, internal check and control is also designed to improve the accuracy of the record-keeping system. Name some specific procedures aimed at achievement of this goal.

12. Name two specific acts which should not be performed by the same individual in each of the following procedures:

   a. Bad debt write-off.

   b. Payroll preparation.

    c. Sales returns.

    d. Inventory purchases.

13. The CPA frequently completes an internal control questionnaire designed to aid him in evaluating existing controls and determining the extent of his application of auditing procedures. The questionnaire is frequently so worded that a "no" answer suggests the existence of a weakness of internal control.

    It was possible for the following unrelated incidents to occur or to remain undetected because of internal control weaknesses. The questions below each incident may appear on an internal control questionnaire. In each case there is one question that, if answered "no" by the CPA after his investigation, would have been most likely to disclose the internal control weakness that permitted the incident to occur or to remain undetected.

    Select the *best* answer choice for each of the following items. State the appropriate letter to indicate your answer choice.

1. Unclaimed salary checks are left with the custodian of the petty cash fund until claimed. The custodian cashed an unclaimed salary check (and took the proceeds) by forging the payee's endorsement and depositing the check along with salary checks that he had cashed for employees by the use of petty cash funds.

    a. Are unclaimed wages deposited in a separate bank account and recorded as a liability?

    b. Are paid checks examined for amount, date, payee, authorized signatures, and endorsements as a part of the bank reconciliation process?

    c. Are employee separations reported immediately to the payroll department?

    d. Is the payroll paid through a separate bank account?

2. A manufacturing company received a substantial sales return in the last month of the year, but the credit memorandum for the return was not prepared until after the auditors had completed their field work. The returned merchandise was included in the physical inventory.

    a. Are aging schedules of accounts receivable prepared periodically?

    b. Are credit memoranda prenumbered and all numbers accounted for?

    c. Is a reconciliation of the trial balance of customers' ledgers with the general ledger control prepared periodically?

    d. Are receiving reports prepared for all materials received and such reports numerically controlled?

3. The sales manager credited a salesman, Jack Smith, with sales that were actually "house account" sales. Later Smith divided his excess sales commissions with the sales manager.

    a. Are the summary sales entries checked periodically by persons independent of sales functions?

    b. Are sales orders reviewed and approved by persons independent of the sales department?

    c. Does the internal auditor compare the sales commission statements with the cash disbursements record?

    d. Are sales orders prenumbered and all numbers accounted for?

4. Over a three-month period the person in charge of the mail room took a substantial amount of postage stamps and sold them to a stamp dealer.

    a. Are all petty cash and stamp funds in the custody of one person?

    b. Are all petty cash funds on an imprest basis?

    c. Are periodic expense reports to management compared with reports of prior periods and with budgets?

    d. Are surprise counts of petty cash funds made by responsible officials?

5. A sales invoice for $5,200 was computed correctly but, in error, was posted as $2,500 to the sales journal and to the accounts receivable ledger. The customer remitted only $2,500, the amount on his monthly statement.

    a. Are prelistings and predetermined totals used to control posting routines?

    b. Are sales invoice serial numbers, prices, discounts, extensions and footings independently checked?

    c. Are the customers' monthly statements verified and mailed by a responsible person other than the bookkeeper who prepared them?

    d. Are unauthorized remittance deductions made by customers or other matters in dispute investigated promptly by a person independent of the accounts receivable function?

6. The president of Company A did not disclose to its board of directors that he is a principal stockholder of Company B. The president compelled Company A's purchasing agent to purchase supplies from Company B at prices in excess of typical prices for such supplies.

    a. Are purchase requisitions used to originate purchasing activity?

    b. Are formal written purchase orders required for all significant purchases?

    c. Is the list of stockholders kept up-to-date and reviewed periodically by the board of directors?

    d. Are vendors selected on the basis of competitive bids?

7. The purchasing agent of Company A used a regular written purchase order to order building materials for the company. Later he instructed the building material supply company by telephone to deliver the materials to his home and to charge the account of Company A.

    a. Are purchases made on behalf of employees?

    b. Is a receiving report an essential part of each voucher?

    c. Are purchase orders and changes therein subject to approval, before commitments are made, by a responsible official?

    d. Are purchase orders prenumbered and all numbers accounted for?

8. Long Company purchased some bearer bonds as a temporary investment. The bonds were kept in the company's safe-deposit box at the local bank. The treasurer of Long Company removed the bonds from the safe-deposit box and used them as collateral for a personal loan.

    a. Are registered securities made out in the name of the Company or so endorsed?

    b. Does the accounting department keep a list of all securities in the safe-deposit box?

    c. Are all persons who have access to securities covered by a fidelity bond?

    d. Is the presence of two or more responsible persons required for access to the safe-deposit box?

9. The CPA's count of the petty cash fund at the beginning of the interim audit on November 15 disclosed that it included the cashier's I.O.U. for $100. The I.O.U. was dated September 1.

    a. Is the petty cash fund on an imprest basis?

    b. Is the petty cash box adequately safeguarded?

    c. Are surprise counts of the petty cash fund made by responsible officials?

    d. Are petty cash vouchers cancelled at the time of replenishing the fund to prevent their reuse?

10. Copies of sales invoices show different unit prices for apparently identical items.

    a. Are all sales invoices checked as to all details after their preparation?

    b. Are differences reported by customers satisfactorily investigated?

    c. If statistical sales data are compiled, are they reconciled with recorded sales?

    d. Are all sales invoices compared with the customers' purchase orders?

11. A factory foreman discharged an hourly worker but did not notify the payroll department. The foreman then forged the worker's signature on time cards and work tickets and, when giving out the checks, diverted to his own use the payroll check drawn for the worker.

    a. Are written authorizations required for all employees added to or taken off the payroll?

    b. Is distribution of payroll checks made by a paymaster who has no other payroll responsibility?

    c. Is custody of unclaimed wages vested in someone other than persons who prepare or distribute the payroll?

    d. Are persons distributing the payroll rotated from time to time?

12. A job order cost system was employed, and overhead at the rate of 125 per cent of direct labor was used for estimating and costing purposes. The year-end audit showed that the actual overhead rate was 200 per cent.

    a. Does the cost system provide for obtaining unit or job order costs for work in process?

    b. Are monthly financial statements showing overhead variances prepared and reviewed?

    c. Is an expense budget prepared?

    d. Are job order cost sheets reconciled with the work in process control account?

13. A vendor was paid twice for the same shipment. One payment was made upon receipt of the invoice. The second payment was made upon receipt of the monthly statement which showed the amount of the open invoice but not the remittance. No stop-payment order was issued for either check and the vendor deposited both checks without comment.

    a. Does the person signing the check examine supporting data at the time of signing?

    b. Are vouchers, invoices, and supporting papers cancelled upon payment?

    c. Is a cash disbursement record maintained which lists in numerical sequence each check issued?

    d. Are all payments made on predetermined days?

14. A newly-employed storeroom clerk stole numerous small tools and other supplies by placing them in his lunch box or wrapping them in paper so that the package appeared to be personal property. The shortages were discovered when a physical inventory disclosed discrepancies between the items on hand and the perpetual records.

    a. Are tools and supplies issued from storerooms only on the basis of signed requisitions?

    b. Are detailed stores records kept by persons other than custodians of the actual goods?

    c. Are the plant grounds fenced and guards stationed at the gates?

  d. Are only authorized persons permitted access to storerooms? (AICPA Examination)

14. A company's system of internal control (which consists of accounting and administrative controls) is strengthened by including in the system procedures that have specific functions or purposes. For example, the system of internal control may include a voucher system that provides for all invoices to be checked for accuracy, approved for propriety, and recorded before being paid. The system reduces the likelihood that an invoice will be mislaid or the discount lost, and it provides assurance that improper or unauthorized disbursements are not likely to be made.

    Give the purposes or functions of each of the following procedures or techniques that may be included in a system of internal control, and explain how each purpose or function is helpful in strengthening accounting and administrative internal control.

    a. Fidelity bonding of employees.

    b. Budgeting of capital expenditures.

    c. Listing of mail remittances by the mail department when the mail is opened.

    d. Maintaining a plant ledger for fixed assets. (AICPA Examination)

15. In conducting his examination in accordance with generally accepted auditing standards, the CPA studies and evaluates the existing internal control of his client.

    a. List and discuss the general elements or basic characteristics of a satisfactory system of internal control.

    b. List the purposes for which the CPA reviews his client's system of internal control. (AICPA Examination)

16. Are internal control concepts different for a small business than for a large business? Explain.

17. What must be done by the proprietor of a small business if there is to be adequate internal control? Explain.

18. Internal control questionnaires are frequently so worded that a "no" answer suggests the existence of an internal control weakness. Which of the following questions from an internal control questionnaire, if answered 'no', would be more likely to disclose an internal weakness if a cashier diverted cash

received over the counter from a customer to his own use and wrote off the receivable as a bad debt?

a. Are aging schedules of accounts receivable prepared periodically and reviewed by a responsible official?

b. Are journal entries approved by a responsible official?

c. Are receipts given directly to the cashier by the person who opens the mail?

d. Are remittance advices, letters or envelopes which accompany receipts separated and given directly to the accounting department? (AICPA Examination)

19. The Witt Company is engaged in manufacturing. Certain features of its operating methods are described below.

You are to consider the procedure for each of the activities as described and point out the existing deficiencies, if any, in internal control, including an explanation of the errors or manipulations which might occur in view of the weakness and your recommendations as to changes in procedures which could be made to correct the weakness.

The company has an employee bond subscription plan under which employees subscribe to bonds and pay in installments by deductions from their salaries. The cashier keeps the supply of unissued bonds in a safe together with the records showing each employee's subscription and payments to date. The amounts of unissued bonds in the hands of the cashier and the balances due from employees are controlled on the general ledger, kept in another department. However, the employees may, if they desire, pay any remaining balance to the cashier and receive their bonds.

When an employee makes a prepayment, the cashier notes the amount on his account, delivers the bond, and receives a receipt from the employee for the amount of the bond. The cashier deposits bond cash received in an employee bond bank account and submits a report showing the transaction to the general ledger department; this report is used as a basis for the necessary adjustments of the control accounts. Periodic surprise counts of bonds on hand are made by independent employees, who check the amounts of unissued bonds and employees' unpaid balances with the control accounts.

During the cashier's lunch hour or at other times when he is required to be absent from his position, another employee, with keys to the safe in which unissued bonds and employee bond payment records are kept, comes in and carries out the same procedures as enumerated above. (AICPA Examination)

Simplified Systems

20. The Hardware and Furniture Company (a sole proprietorship) did not have complete records on a double-entry basis. However, from your investigation of their records you have established the information shown below. Using that information you are to prepare a balance-sheet as of December 31, 1969 and an income statement for the year.

a. The assets and liabilities as of December 31, 1968 were:

	Debit	Credit
Cash	$ 5,175	$ 740
Accounts receivable	10,556	
Allowance for loss on accounts		740
Fixtures	3,130	
Accumulated depreciation		1,110
Prepaid insurance	158	
Prepaid supplies	79	
Accounts payable		4,244
Accrued miscellaneous expenses		206
Accrued taxes		202
Merchandise inventory	19,243	
Note payable		5,000
Roberts, capital		26,839

b. A summary of the transactions for 1969 as recorded in the check book shows:

Deposits for the year (including the redeposit of $304 of checks charged back by the bank) ...	$83,187
Checks drawn during the year	84,070
Customers' checks charged back by the bank	304
Bank service charges	22

c. The following information is available as to accounts payable:

Purchases on account during year	$57,789
Returns of merchandise allowed as credits against accounts by vendors	1,418
Payments of accounts by check	55,461

d. Information as to accounts receivable shows the following:

Accounts written off	$ 812
Accounts collected	43,083
Balance of accounts December 31, 1969 (Of this balance $700 is estimated to be uncollectible)..	11,921

e. Checks drawn during the year include checks for the following items:

Salaries	$10,988
Rent	3,600
Heat, light, and telephone	394
Supplies	280
Insurance	341
Taxes and licenses	1,017
Drawings of proprietor	6,140
Miscellaneous expense	769
Merchandise purchases	2,080
Note payable	3,000
	$28,609

f. Merchandise inventory December 31, 1969 was $17,807. Prepaid insurance amounted to $122 and supplies on hand to $105 as of December 31,

1969. Accrued taxes were $216 and miscellaneous accrued expenses were $73 at the year end.

g. Cash sales for the year are assumed to account for all cash received other than that collected on accounts. Fixtures are to be depreciated at the rate of 10 per cent per annum. (AICPA Examination)

21. You have been asked to design a single entry, cash basis system for a local attorney.
  a. In the design of this system, would you recommend a general ledger?
  b. Why might you recommend a single entry system over an accrual system?
  c. Which of the following items would be reflected directly on the cash basis Income Statement?
    1. Cash paid for supplies still on hand.
    2. Billings to clients not yet received.
    3. Collections from clients for last year services.
    4. Reimbursement by insurance company for damage to business automobile in accident.
    5. Purchase for cash of new business automobile.
    6. Payment in cash of attorney's personal life insurance premium.
    7. Cash repaid on a bank loan.
    8. Cash paid for office supplies used last year.
    9. Depreciation on office equipment.
    10. Collection of bad account written off three years ago.
    11. Client account written off—uncollectible.
    12. Collection of current year billings.

22. You have been employed in the Small Business Division of a national firm of Certified Public Accountants. As a part of your training you have been asked to (a) identify (describe); (b) indicate the prime systems contribution or contributions; and (c) give a good illustration of system application for each of the following:
    1. Autographic register.   5. Keysort.
    2. Writing board.   6. Flexowriter.
    3. Summary strip accounting.   7. Analysis and distribution
    4. Cash register.   machine.

23. You have been asked to design a system for a small grocery store. The proprietor has no knowledge of accounting. There is an excellent cash register available. You, as a qualified accountant and systems analyst, are to go in once each month and prepare financial statements, plus prepare all payroll and income tax returns.
  a. Would single or double entry records be most appropriate? Explain.
  b. Should records be on a cash or accrual basis? Explain.
  c. Describe the contributions and controls that can be provided by the cash register.

24. What are the characteristics of the system in which the following would be especially appropriate?
  a. Keysort.
  b. Writing board.

    c. Strip accounting.

    d. Single entry.

25. Accounting writing boards are adaptable to a variety of applications. In each case the aim is to take advantage of carbon and placement of communication media so that one writing simultaneously is entered on several papers. A typical board and communication media set-up is pictured below.

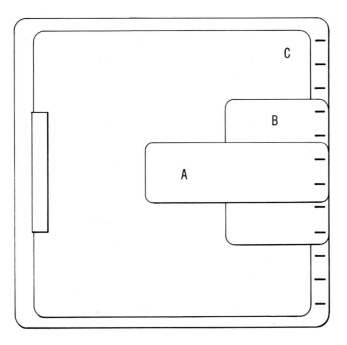

    Identify the probable uses of communication media A, B, and C if the board is being used (a) for payroll work, (b) in connection with receivables, and (c) in connection with payables.

26. a. Assume a needle-sort card has 60 notching positions, 20 each on the top and bottom and ten each on the sides. How many classifications can be accommodated by direct notching? By sequence or number code notching? By alphabetical code notching?

    b. Why are the corners clipped on needle-sort cards?

    c. What are the advantages and limitations of needle-sort cards?

    d. Explain how a group of needle-sort cards can be arranged in numerical order.

27. State the advantages and disadvantages of a single entry system over a double entry system. Cash basis over accrual basis.

28. The manager of a small manufacturing company doesn't believe in accounting. He says he gets all the information he needs from his filing system, which consists of the files named below. Each month an adding machine tape

is run of new documents in each file, and the Income Statement is updated to show the cumulative year-to-date figures.

a. File of all unfilled orders.
b. File of all sales invoices collected.
c. File of all uncollected sales invoices.   (b + c is Sales)
d. File of deposit slips.
e. File of materials purchase orders.   (Cost of sales)
f. File of extended clock cards.   (Direct Labor)
g. File of voucher checks.   (Total cost and expense)
h. File of cancelled checks.

Discuss the shortcomings of this system.

Machines and Devices

29. Listed below are a number of punch card accounting machines which are identified by letter. Using these letters, indicate which machine performs the functions described.

a. Interpreter.
b. Key punch.
c. Electronic coupler.
d. Multiplying punch.
e. Verifying punch.
f. Collator.
g. Sorter.
h. Summary punch.
i. Reproducing punch.
j. Tabulator.

1. Helps determine data punched in cards is accurately punched.
2. Merges like cards from two separate groups.
3. When coupled to another machine, produces a new card each time the other machine encounters a different card (control break).
4. Arranges cards in alphabetical order.
5. Accumulates and prints totals of a group of cards.
6. Automatically computes extensions and punches them into cards.
7. Prints data on a card that is punched in that card.

30. What is a register? Give some specific examples of situations where registers might advantageously be maintained.

31. Suppose you were a salesman for a manufacturer of punch card equipment and called on a prospect who said he was satisfied with his present system which used principally a numeric posting machine which was capable of printing the date and a limited number of symbols. He says he cannot see any advantage to the use of punch cards because by the time a key punch operator punches a card for an item (say an invoice), one of his posting machine operators could have the item journalized and posted (simultaneous operations). Further, after a card is punched, the information in it is not "recorded" until it is run through one or more machines. The prospect also says it is his understanding that each card, in effect, has to be punched twice because of the necessity of verifying it.

    What would you say in answer to his arguments? What advantages might punch card equipment have over his present installation and why?

32. Distinguish between MICR and optical scanning.

33. Common-language communication between machines is a vital link in integrated data processing systems. Describe the roles of punched paper tapes in this context.

34. A new division of a multiple-division company is to be located 900 miles from the home office. About 60 employees will be hired to manufacture, sell, and distribute a new product. As the systems analyst you must recommend a system for the division payroll. You have been asked to make a specific recommendation as to whether a descriptive multiple-purpose accounting machine should be acquired, or whether a writing board is more desirable.
    a. What major advantage or advantages exist in common for both the descriptive multiple-purpose accounting machine and the writing board? Explain.
    b. (1) Assume that the writing board is ruled out as not meeting the systems need. Would you recommend a descriptive multiple-purpose machine? Explain.
       (2) What factors would be important in deciding between machines manufactured by different companies?
    c. In the use of a multiple-purpose machine in the payroll procedure there are at least six kinds of errors possible. Identify the kinds of errors that might be made. Recommend and briefly describe a proof method to prevent each of the errors.
    d. You decide that management of the new division should be decentralized, but accounting should be centralized. Explain what is meant, and the systems consequences.

35. During a conversation concerning the use of a multiple-purpose accounting machine, several comments were made as follows:
    a. Multiple-purpose accounting machines are of great value due to their flexibility. A simple screwdriver adjustment is all that is required to change from one procedure to another.
    b. The "one-writing" feature of a machine procedure is not available in manual systems.
    c. The number of accumulators in a multiple-purpose accounting machine is especially important to facilitate the preparation of pre-list tapes.
    d. The most important factor in the decision to purchase one model accounting machine over another is the cost of the machine.
    e. The posting operation is often slow as feeding the ledger card into a machine in the same manner as paper is put in a typewriter, upside down from the back, makes spacing to a specific line difficult.
       State whether each of the above statements is "true" or "false" *and* explain the reasons.

36. In the left-hand column several kinds of equipment or machines are named. The right-hand column lists the function or usage of these. Select the usage or description which best agrees with each piece of equipment or machine.

a. Hectograph machine.

b. Listing adding machine.

c. Split-platen, listing adding machine.

d. Multiple register machine.

e. Comptometer.

f. Calculator.

g. Printing calculator.

h. Addressograph.

i. Viewer.

j. Autographic register.

k. Multiple drawer register.

1. Multiple addressing machine.

2. Used to review tapes produced on printing calculator.

3. Files tapes.

4. Driven by a rotary motor.

5. Key-driven machine.

6. Provides each clerk with a separate cash storage drawer.

7. Used to maintain internal control in handling sales slips.

8. Used to inspect files recorded on microfilm.

9. Provides the operator with a direct proof.

10. Accumulated posted totals.

11. Used to check and recheck sales.

12. Posts accounts with date and amounts.

13. Provides the operator with a complete tape of all adding, subtracting, division, and multiplication.

Miscellaneous

37. What is meant by the "exception principle" in reporting?

38. "Various methods of estimating inventories are found in practice." Discuss.

39. "Nearly every concern has a 'natural' business year." Discuss.

40. "Tax laws are but one of a number of ways the regulating hand of law is felt by a concern." Explain and illustrate.

41. a. In designing the chart of accounts for a sporting goods store, if the primary basis of expense breakdown is to be by *object*, what would be a typical list of expense accounts?

    b. Suppose instead a *functional* expense classification is to be used; what would be a typical list of accounts?

    c. Give one example of an expense account classification which combines function and object.

42. The following questions pertain to use of codes in systems work:

    a. Name three types of codes (other than sequence or straight numbering) and provide a brief illustration of each adequate to demonstrate that you know each type named.

    b. Give four different advantages of use of codes.

43. There are *at least three steps* in establishing a good communication media control program. To centralize is one of the steps. Explain the detail that would have to be accomplished to "centralize" in a company where communication media control does not exist.

44. Identify three standardized adjusting entries which could be prefabricated for use in monthly closings.

45. Discuss some systems problems peculiar to department store accounting paying attention to such matters as inventory accounting, leased departments, employee compensation, and departmental profits.

46. What effect, if any, would the use of a systems manual have on a systems report? The problem of writing a systems report for installation in a new business, branch, or subsidiary is entirely different from that covering a revision of the system in an existing business unit. Discuss this briefly.

47. Answer the following questions relating to the design of communication media:
    a. Why is the recommendation of suitable communication media and office equipment an essential part of a systems analyst's work?
    b. What preparation by the systems analyst is necessary to enable him to be of greatest service in recommending communication media and equipment?
    c. What are controlling factors in deciding between bound and loose-leaf records?
    d. What factors should be considered in deciding on the size of new communication media?
    e. As to physical characteristics of paper, what kinds of data must be supplied to a printer in having special communication media made?
    f. What are the advantages of standard stock sheets?
    g. Why is selection of proper color combinations important?
    h. What are advantages of non-black or non-blue ink?
    i. Does paper color have much to do with eye fatigue?
    j. Why make copies of a set of identical media in various copies?
    k. What are disadvantages of color communication media sets?
    l. Should back or bottom copies of multi-color media sets be lighter or darker colors?

48. This question relates to features or elements which should be incorporated into business media if they are to be well designed and of maximum effectiveness.
    a. Name an element essential on external communication media but not on internal ones.
    b. Name an element essential on every media whether internal or external.
    c. Name an element required if the media themselves are to be accounted for.
    d. Media involving responsibility for such things as cash, securities, inventory, etc., usually provide spaces for certain things not required on media such as invoices, time tickets, etc. What goes in such spaces?

e. In a multi-color media set what considerations should govern the choice of colors?

49. Complete the following:

a. One of the more important account listings in a systems manual in which one system has superseded another is _____ _____ .

b. If the first two digits of a code always indicate a certain class of information, the next two another class, etc., the _____ _____ coding system is being used.

c. Use of a voucher register eliminates the need for a _____ _____ journal.

d. To facilitate the making of changes, systems manuals are usually in _____ form.

e. When recording of transactions occurs at several places (e.g., home office, branches, etc.), the _____ is a useful form for transmittal of accounting data.

f. Typically _____ distributions have fewer classifications or breakdowns than any other class of distribution.

g. When a voucher register is in use, in addition to the "Cash Credit" column, the check register will have money columns for _____ _____ and, in addition to a date column, will have a numerical column for _____ .

h. In addition to setting out account titles and codes to be debited or credited, standard journal entries usually also set out _____ _____ and _____ .

i. _____ is the usual title of the chief accounting officer in a large business.

j. _____ is a feature common to both cycle billing and the ledgerless system of maintaining the receivables ledger.

k. The instructions which tell a computer what to do are called _____ .

50. A CPA recently said "One of the fundamental means by which accounting control is effected is *comparisons*." What did he have in mind?

APPENDIX A

Internal Control Questionnaire

THE IMPORTANCE OF THE INTERNAL CONTROL QUESTIONNAIRE IS BRIEFLY discussed in Chapter 7. Its use by the systems analyst as a check list in the analysis and synthesis steps of a systems investigation provides clues to systems strengths and weaknesses as well as reasonable assurance that basic internal control duties have been prescribed. The extent of exposure to error or embezzlement can be evaluated and a deliberate decision made to either include or exclude the applicable internal control duties.

Appendix A is an Internal Control Questionnaire designed for use by the staff of a large Certified Public Accounting firm to evaluate internal control in audit engagements. Each question is included to get at a specific internal control relationship. Note that major sections provide the opportunity for an evaluation in narrative form when the staff man is asked to "comment on the adequacy of internal control." Not shown is space provided after *each* section to insert the name of the staff man by whom the questionnaire was originally prepared and the date. Also omitted is the name of the staff man reviewing the questionnaire in subsequent examinations with the date and his comments.

Appendix A will be of great assistance in providing clues to internal control deficiencies in actual systems situations, as well as in the preparation of solutions to the problems and cases in this text. It should be of special assistance in the solution of systems problems and cases in Chapter 18 and 19. The instructions for the use of the questionnaire and the questionnaire itself are on the pages that follow.

INTERNAL CONTROL QUESTIONNAIRE

INSTRUCTIONS FOR USE

1. This questionnaire has been designed to assist members of the staff in the determination of the adequacy or inadequacy of the client's system of internal check and control. It does not purport to be complete as regards all engagements and is not intended to preclude the insertion of additional questions which, in the opinion of the user, may be pertinent in considering the methods of internal control employed by a particular client.

2. The questionnaire is to be used subject to the modifications set forth in the succeeding paragraph. If the related examination covers the accounts of a group of companies, a questionnaire will usually be required for each company in the group. Similarly, if the client maintains branch plants and/or offices, a questionnaire should be developed for the head office, as well as for each branch plant or office, to the extent to which the decentralization of the accounting or other office routine renders such questionnaire applicable. For example, where a branch office has no general books of account but carries and records certain cash transactions and maintains a local payroll, only those sections of the questionnaire dealing with such matters should be used.

3. In the case of clients who employ only a small number of persons, or who are engaged in certain special activities, such as brokerage firms, banks, etc., it may be found that the questionnaire is either entirely inappropriate or usable only in small part. In such instances it is expected that the matter of internal control will, nevertheless, have the full and adequate consideration of the accountant in charge, and separate supplemental pages should be used when the regular questionnaire is not appropriate.

4. The regular pages of the questionnaire have been prepared with spaces to indicate affirmative or negative answers to the majority of the questions. Each question should be answered by a check-mark in the appropriate column, or a reason stated for there being no answer; e.g., "not applicable." This latter may be abbreviated as "N.A." and should be recorded in the "Yes" column.

5. The questions have been so devised that an affirmative answer would indicate a satisfactory degree of internal control. Negative answers should influence the examiner to consider whether, in order to make the questionnaire as informative as possible, such negative answers should be amplified or the related question covered by a supplemental statement. For example, it may be that a negative answer should be coupled with a statement to the effect that some alternative procedure followed by the client has the same degree of adequate control in the circumstances.

6. The answering of the questions does not complete the investigation of the system of internal check and control; the accountant in charge must satisfy himself, by observation and/or test-check, that the procedures indicated by the answers are being carried out in practice.

7. Space is also provided at the end of each section of the questionnaire for notations as to the adequacy or inadequacy of the system as it relates to the particular section. (Use insert pages if necessary.)

8. Major shortcomings in the system as revealed by our survey, before being taken up with the client, should be discussed with the executive in charge, who will decide what action should be taken. Each section of the questionnaire should be signed by the accountant making the survey of that particular phase of the internal control; the questionnaire as a whole should be signed by the accountant in charge and, after review by the executive in charge of the work, should be filed with the working papers in the permanent file.

9. During subsequent examinations, the questionnaire must be reviewed and brought up to date as follows:
   a. The auditor performing each section of the examination shall take the previously completed questionnaire and in conjunction with and as a part of his examination shall determine what changes, if any, have been made by the client in the system of internal control.
   b. The changes, if few in number for a particular section, will be made by crossing out the original answers and indicating the new answers, and the auditor's verifications in red.
   c. The changes, if numerous in a section, will be made by marking the original page superseded in the comment space provided for subsequent examinations, signing and dating the page and transferring it to the inactive file, and by filling out a revised section of the questionnaire as if it were a part of an original questionnaire and filing it in its proper place.
   d. The auditor, when he has completed the review of a section during each examination, shall sign and date each section, and shall note in the comment space the results of his review, i.e., "No change," "Control strengthened, see comments above," "Control weakened, see comments on supplemental page," etc., as may be appropriate.
   e. The in-charge senior and executive shall review the entire questionnaire at each examination date and indicate their review in the appropriate place on the title page.

INTERNAL CONTROL QUESTIONNAIRE

| | ANSWER | | ANSWER BASED ON: | | |
	YES	NO	IN-QUIRY	OBSER-VATION	TEST
I. GENERAL					
1. Does the client have a chart of organization?	___	___	___	___	___
2. Does the client have a chart of accounts?	___	___	___	___	___
3. Is the accounting routine set forth in accounting manuals?	___	___	___	___	___
4. Do we have copies of such charts and manuals in our permanent file for this client?	___	___	___	___	___
5. Does the client have: a. A controller?	___	___	___	___	___

| | ANSWER | | ANSWER BASED ON: | | |
	YES	NO	IN-QUIRY	OBSER-VATION	TEST

I. General (Continued)

    b. An internal auditor or audit staff?

6. If internal auditors are employed:
    a. Do they render written reports on the results of their examinations?
    b. Are they directly responsible to, and do they report to, an executive officer other than the chief accounting officer? Designate:
    c. Have we reviewed their reports?

7. Is the general accounting department completely separated from:
    a. The purchasing department?
    b. The sales department?
    c. Manufacturing and/or cost departments?
    d. Cash receipts and disbursements?

8. Are all employees who handle cash, securities, and other valuables bonded?

9. Are all such employees required to take regular vacations, their regular duties then being assigned to other employees?

10. Does head office accounting control over branch offices appear to be adequate?

11. Are expenses and costs under budgetary control?

12. Is insurance coverage under the supervision of a responsible official or employee?

13. Are journal entries approved by:
    a. The controller?
    b. Other designated employee?

14. Does the client use standard journal entries for the regularly recurring monthly closing entries?

15. Are journal entries adequately explained or supported by vouchers bearing adequate substantiating data?

		ANSWER BASED ON:		
	ANSWER	IN- OBSER-	
YES	NO	QUIRY VATION	TEST

I. GENERAL (*Continued*)

16. Are periodic financial statements prepared for submission to the management? ____ ____ ____ ____ ____

17. If so, are these sufficiently informative to bring to light abnormal fluctuations in costs, revenues, inventories, etc., and other discrepancies? ____ ____ ____ ____ ____

18. a. List names of officials and employees exercising the function noted:
    Treasurer _____
    Secretary _____
    Controller _____
    Internal auditor (chief) _____
    Chief accountant _____
    General ledger bookkeeper _____
    Accounts receivable bookkeeper _____
    Accounts payable bookkeeper _____
    Cashier _____
    Department heads:
    Purchasing _____
    Sales _____
    Credit _____
    Cost _____
    Receiving _____
    Shipping _____
    Pay roll _____
    Personnel _____
    Tax _____
    b. Is any one of the above, to the best of your information, a relative of any other? ____ ____ ____ ____ ____
    c. If so, who? _____

II. CASH RECEIPTS

A. Mail receipts:

1. Is the mail opened by someone other than the cashier or accounts receivable bookkeeper? ____ ____ ____ ____ ____

2. Does the mail routine prohibit the delivery of unopened mail (other than personal mail) to employees having access to the accounting records? ____ ____ ____ ____ ____

| | ANSWER | | ANSWER BASED ON: | | |
| | YES | NO | IN-QUIRY | OBSER-VATION | TEST |

II. Cash Receipts (*Continued*)

3. a. Is a record of the money and checks received prepared by the person opening the mail?

     b. If so, is this record given to someone other than the cashier for independent verification of the amount recorded?

     c. Is this record compared with the cash receipts book regularly?

B. Other receipts:

1. Are the receipts of currency relatively insignificant?

2. Are receipts recorded by cash registers or other mechanical devices?

3. If so, are the machine totals checked independently by the accounting department?

4. Are sales books or receipt books used?

5. If so:

     a. Are the slips or receipts prenumbered?

     b. Are the daily totals and numerical sequence checked independently by the accounting department?

     c. Are unused books safeguarded?

6. If neither of the above methods are in use, is some other adequate system of control in force? If so, explain.

7. Is there an adequate safeguard against misappropriation of cash through the recording of fictitious discounts or allowances by the cashier?

8. Are miscellaneous receipts, such as from sale of scrap, salvage, etc., reported to the accounting department by the recipient as well as to the cashier?

9. Does the accounting department check such reports against the related cash book entries?

		ANSWER BASED ON:		
ANSWER		IN-	OBSER-	
YES	NO	QUIRY	VATION	TEST

II. Cash Receipts (*Continued*)

C. General:

1. Are each day's receipts deposited in the bank intact and without delay?

2. Does someone other than the cashier or accounts receivable bookkeeper take the deposits to the bank?

3. Is a duplicate deposit slip checked and held for the auditors by someone other than the employee making up the deposit?

4. Are bank debit advices (such as for N.S.F. checks) delivered directly to a responsible employee (other than the cashier) for investigation?

5. Are the duties of the cashier entirely separate from the recording of notes and accounts receivable?

6. Is the general ledger posted by an employee who is not from the cashier's department?

7. Is the office routine so arranged that the cashier is denied access to the accounts receivable ledgers and monthly statements?

8. Are all other cash funds (i.e., other than cash receipts) and securities handled by someone other than the cashier?

9. If the cashier handles such funds:
   a. List the items hereunder:
   b. Are such items counted by us during our examination?

10. Where branch offices make collections, are such collections deposited in a bank account subject to withdrawal only by the head office?

11. Are rents, dividends, interest, and similar revenues adequately controlled in such manner that their non-receipt would be noted and investigated?

| | | ANSWER | | ANSWER BASED ON: | | |
		YES	NO	IN-QUIRY	OBSER-VATION	TEST

II. Cash Receipts (Continued)

12. Is the cashier responsible for the cash receipts from the time they are received in his department until they are sent to the bank?

13. Are proper physical safeguards and facilities employed to protect cash and cash transactions?

14. Does any employee having custody of client funds also have custody of non-client funds (e.g., credit union, employee benefit association, etc.)?

Comment on adequacy of internal control:

III. Cash Disbursements

1. Are all disbursements, except from petty cash, made by check?

2. Are all checks prenumbered?

3. Are voided checks properly defaced or mutilated and held available for subsequent inspection?

4. Are checks required to be counter-signed?

5. a. Is the signing of checks in advance prohibited?
   b. Is the countersigning of checks in advance prohibited?

6. Are authorized signatures limited to officers or employees who have no access to accounting records or to cash?

| | | ANSWER | | ANSWER BASED ON: | | |
		YES	NO	IN-QUIRY	OBSER-VATION	TEST

III. CASH DISBURSEMENTS
(*Continued*)

7. Is the practice of drawing checks to "cash" or "bearer" prohibited?

8. If not, are checks so drawn limited to pay rolls and/or petty cash reimbursement?

9. Are monthly bank statements and paid checks received directly by the accounting department?

10. Are the bank accounts independently reconciled by someone other than the employees who keep the cash records?

11. Is the sequence of check numbers accounted for when reconciling the bank accounts?

12. Is the practice of examining paid checks for date, name, cancellation, and endorsement followed by the employee reconciling the bank accounts?

13. Are vouchers or other supporting documents presented together with the checks submitted for signature?

14. Do the signers make adequate investigation before signing checks?

15. If a check-signing machine is in use, are the machine and signature plates kept under effective control?

16. Are checks mailed out without allowing them to return to the employee who drew the checks or to the accounts payable bookkeeper?

17. Are the supporting documents impressed with a "paid" stamp or other mark so as to prevent their use for duplicate payment?

18. Are pay roll checks drawn against a separate pay roll bank account?

19. Is the pay roll bank account on an imprest basis?

20. Are dividend checks drawn against a separate dividend bank account?

	ANSWER		ANSWER BASED ON:		
	YES	NO	IN-QUIRY	OBSER-VATION	TEST

III. Cash Disbursements (*Continued*)

21. Are transfers from one bank to another under effective accounting control?

Comment on adequacy of internal control:

IV. Petty Cash Fund

1. Is imprest fund system in use?
2. Is the responsibility for each fund vested in one person only?
3. Is the custodian independent of the cashier or other employees handling remittances from customers and other cash receipts?
4. Is the amount of the fund restricted so as to require reimbursement at relatively short intervals?
5. a. Has a maximum figure for individual payments from the fund been established?
   b. If so, state maximum figure.
6. Are payees required to sign vouchers for all disbursements?
7. Is adequate approval required for advances to employees and I.O.U.'s?
8. a. Is the cashing of personal checks prohibited?
   b. If not, state whether such checks are recashed at bank or are included as vouchers supporting request for reimbursement.
9. a. Are vouchers and supporting documents checked by a re-

	ANSWER		ANSWER BASED ON:		
	YES	NO	IN-QUIRY	OBSER-VATION	TEST

IV. PETTY CASH FUND (*Continued*)

       sponsible employee at the time of reimbursement?

    b. Does that employee verify the unexpended balance of the fund?

10. Are the amounts of the vouchers spelled out in words as well as written in numerals?

11. Are vouchers marked so as to preclude their re-use?

12. a. Is any part of the fund represented by cash in bank?

    b. Are checks drawn on this account signed by the custodian only?

13. Are checks for reimbursement made out to the order of the custodian?

14. Is the fund checked at reasonable intervals by surprise counts made by an internal auditor or other employee independent of the custodian?

15. Describe the operation of the fund if the same is in part represented by a bank account. (e.g., If an imprest fund, are all reimbursements deposited in the bank and a small working cash balance replenished therefrom, or does the custodian transfer amounts from cash to bank and vice versa in his discretion?)

Comment on adequacy of internal control:

		ANSWER		ANSWER BASED ON:		
				IN-	OBSER-	
		YES	NO	QUIRY	VATION	TEST

V. Security Investments

1. Are securities kept in a safe deposit vault in the name of the client?

2. If so:
   a. Does access thereto require the signatures or presence of two or more designated persons?
   b. Is a record maintained by the client of visits to safe deposit vault?

3. If not:
   a. Are they kept in safekeeping by an independent person?
   b. Are they kept in a safe place under control of an officer?

4. Is a record kept by the accounting or the financial department of each security, including certificate numbers?

5. Are all securities, except "bearer" bonds, in the name of the client?

6. Are securities periodically inspected and agreed with the record by internal auditors or other designated officers or employees?

7. Are purchases and sales of securities authorized by:
   a. The board of directors?
   b. An officer?
   c. The financial department?

8. Are securities held for others, or as collateral, recorded and safeguarded in similar manner to those owned by the client?

9. Are security investments which have been written off or fully reserved against followed up as to possible realization?

10. Are satisfactory records kept to insure the proper and prompt receipt of income on securities owned?

ANSWER BASED ON:

	ANSWER		IN- QUIRY	OBSER- VATION	TEST
	YES	NO			

V. SECURITY INVESTMENTS
(*Continued*)

Comment on adequacy of internal
control:

VI. NOTES AND ACCOUNTS RECEIVABLE

1. a. Are notes authorized by a responsible official?
   b. Are renewals of notes authorized by a responsible official?

2. a. Is the custodian of notes receivable independent of the cashier or bookkeepers?
   b. Is the custodian of negotiable collateral independent of the cashier or bookkeepers?

3. Are the customers' ledgers kept by employees who have no access to cash receipts?

4. Are the customers' ledgers balanced at least monthly and the totals agreed with the general ledger control account?

5. a. Are statements of open items mailed to all customers monthly?
   If not, to what extent are they mailed?
   b. If so, is this done by an employee who has no access to cash and who is independent

| | ANSWER | | ANSWER BASED ON: | | |
| | YES | NO | IN-QUIRY | OBSER-VATION | TEST |

VI. NOTES AND ACCOUNTS
RECEIVABLE (*Continued*)

of the accounts receivable bookkeepers and the billing clerks?

c. Does this employee retain control of the statements until mailed?

d. Are differences reported by customers routed to this same employee for investigation?

6. Are delinquent accounts listed periodically for review by an official other than the credit manager?

7. Are write-offs of bad debts approved by an official other than the credit manager?

8. Are charged-off accounts kept under memo ledger control and followed up? Explain.

9. Are credit memos approved by a responsible official?

10. Are such credit memos under numerical control?

11. Is approval of a responsible official required for discounts allowed after the discount date or in excess of normal credit terms?

12. Are credits for returned goods checked against receiving reports?

13. Are direct confirmations of notes and accounts receivable obtained periodically:
a. By internal auditors?
b. By other designated employees?

14. Is the management of the credit department entirely divorced from the sales department?

15. Is the cashier denied access to the accounts receivable ledgers?

16. a. Is merchandise out on consignment recorded in a memorandum accounts receivable ledger?

		ANSWER		ANSWER BASED ON:		
		YES	NO	IN-QUIRY	OBSER-VATION	TEST

VI. NOTES AND ACCOUNTS
RECEIVABLE (*Continued*)

    b. If consigned merchandise is a material and/or continuing factor, outline the client's procedures in this respect on a separate page, with a cross reference hereto.

17. Are journal entries affecting accounts receivable approved by someone senior to the accounts receivable bookkeeper?

Comment on adequacy of internal control:

VII. INVENTORIES

A. Physical control:

1. Are designated stores keepers held responsible for the control of:
    a. Raw materials?
    b. Purchased parts?
    c. Semi-finished merchandise?
    d. Finished merchandise?
    e. Supplies and repair parts?

2. Do the stores keepers notify the accounting department of all receipts by means of receiving or production reports?

3. Are issues made only against signed requisitions or shipping orders?

		ANSWER		ANSWER BASED ON:		
		YES	NO	IN-QUIRY	OBSER-VATION	TEST

VII. INVENTORIES (*Continued*)

4. Are the quantities on hand counted:
   a. At the end of the fiscal year? ___ ___ ___ ___ ___
   b. Periodically during the year? ___ ___ ___ ___ ___

5. Are such counts made independent of the stores keepers or other employees responsible for the custody of the items being counted? ___ ___ ___ ___ ___

6. Are the following classes of inventories under effective accounting control:
   a. Goods out on consignment? ___ ___ ___ ___ ___
   b. Materials in hands of processors, suppliers, etc.? ___ ___ ___ ___ ___
   c. Materials or merchandise in bonded or other outside warehouses? ___ ___ ___ ___ ___
   d. Returnable containers, pallets, etc. ___ ___ ___ ___ ___

7. Is merchandise on hand which is not the property of the client (consignments-in, etc.,) physically segregated and under effective accounting control? ___ ___ ___ ___ ___

8. With respect to the determination of inventory values:
   a. Are priced inventory sheets double-checked as to:
      i. Cost prices? ___ ___ ___ ___
      ii. Market prices? ___ ___ ___ ___
      iii. Extensions, footings, and summarizations? ___ ___ ___ ___
   b. Is a review made by a responsible official or designated employee as to overstock and as to slow-moving or obsolete items? ___ ___ ___ ___ ___

9. Is a reasonable degree of control maintained over stationery and other supplies which are charged directly against operations? ___ ___ ___ ___ ___

10. Are scrap, salvaged materials, and "no value" inventories under such accounting control as should assure

| | ANSWER | | ANSWER BASED ON: | | |
	YES	NO	IN-QUIRY	OBSER-VATION	TEST

VII. INVENTORIES (*Continued*)

the proper recording of the sale or re-use of such items?

11. Are there adequate safeguards to insure that the costs of partial shipments billed to customers are eliminated from inventories at time of billing?

12. If standard costs are used, is there an established procedure for revising them periodically?

B. Perpetual inventory records:

1. Are perpetual inventory records maintained for:
   a. Raw materials?
   b. Supplies and repair parts?
   c. Work in process?
   d. Finished product?

NOTE: If no perpetual records are maintained, the following six questions (2 to 7 inclusive) are not applicable.

2. Do such perpetual records show:
   a. Quantities only?
   b. Quantities and values?

3. Are such perpetual records kept by employees other than the stores keepers?

4. Are such records controlled by accounts in the general ledger?

5. Are perpetual records checked by physical stocktaking at least once annually?

6. Are the perpetual records regularly adjusted as a result of the physical stocktaking?

7. Do such adjustments require the approval of a responsible official or employee?

C. Planning and scheduling:
Outline briefly the client's practices and their effectiveness in controlling inventories.

	ANSWER		ANSWER BASED ON:		
	YES	NO	IN-QUIRY	OBSER-VATION	TEST

VII. INVENTORIES (*Continued*)

D. Commitments:
Outline briefly the client's practices and their effectiveness in controlling inventories.

Comment on adequacy of internal control:

VIII. PROPERTIES AND PATENTS

1. Are detailed plant ledgers maintained for the various units of property?

2. Are such records balanced at least annually with general ledger control accounts?

3. Does the client:
   a. Take periodic inventory of plant items?
   b. Have periodic appraisals, for insurance or other purpose?

4. Is a satisfactory system in effect for the control of small tools?

5. Is a work order system in use:
   a. For capital expenditures?
   b. For major repair jobs?
   c. For research and development projects?

6. Is prior authorization for capital expenditures required:
   a. From the board of directors?
   b. From officers?

7. When actual exepnditures exceed the amount authorized, is the excess approved as in Question 6 above?

	ANSWER		ANSWER BASED ON:		
	YES	NO	IN-QUIRY	OBSER-VATION	TEST

VIII. PROPERTIES AND PATENTS (*Continued*)

8. Is there a sound policy in force for the differentiation between capital additions and maintenance and repairs?
   Explain:

9. Is the recording and the accounting for capital replacement items so devised as to insure the proper accounting treatment for the removal of items replaced?

10. Is the approval of a designated official required for the retirement or dismantling of plant items?

11. Is there an effective procedure to insure that property physically retired is removed from the records and that the proceeds from salvage and sales are accounted for?

12. Are reserves for depreciation carried by units or groups corresponding with the classifications or grouping of depreciable plant items?

13. Is the client assured that patents arising from its research expenditures are issued in its name and not in the name of some individual?

Comment on adequacy of internal control:

| | ANSWER | | ANSWER BASED ON: | | |
	YES	NO	IN-QUIRY	OBSER-VATION	TEST

IX. Notes and Accounts Payable and Long-Term Debt

A. Notes and accounts payable:

1. Are borrowings on notes payable authorized by the board of directors?

2. Are two or more signatures required on notes payable?

3. Is a notes payable register kept by an employee who is not authorized to sign checks or notes?

4. Are paid notes canceled and retained?

5. Is the voucher register, or accounts payable ledger, regularly reconciled with the general ledger control account?

6. Are statements from vendors regularly compared with the related ledger accounts (or with open items in voucher register)?

7. Are appropriate adjustments made as a result of this comparison?

8. Are adjustments of accounts payable (including the writing off of debit balances) required to be supported by the approval of a designated official?

B. Long-term debt:

1. Are an independent trustee and an independent interest-paying agent employed?

2. Are redeemed notes, bonds, and interest coupons effectively mutilated?

Comment on adequacy of internal control:

	ANSWER		ANSWER BASED ON:		
	YES	NO	IN-QUIRY	OBSER-VATION	TEST

X. CAPITAL STOCKS

1. a. Does the client employ an independent registrar?

   b. Transfer agent?

2. If not:

   a. Are unissued certificates and stock certificate stubs in the custody of an officer?

   b. Are surrendered certificates effectively canceled?

   c. Are documentary stamps under proper control?

3. Does the client employ independent dividend-paying agents?

4. If not, is proper control exercised in preparing and mailing dividends? (i.e., separate bank account, etc.)

5. Are returned or unclaimed dividend checks promptly redeposited and set up in the accounts as liabilities?

Comment as to adequacy of internal control:

XI. SALES AND SHIPPING

1. Are sales orders adequately controlled?

2. Are all orders approved by the credit manager or department before shipment?

3. Is the credit department entirely independent of the sales department?

ANSWER BASED ON:

	ANSWER		IN-	OBSER-	
	YES	NO	QUIRY	VATION	TEST

XI. Sales and Shipping (Continued)

4. Are sales prices and credit terms based on approved standard price lists?

5. If so, are any deviations from standard approved:
   a. By an officer?
   b. By another? Explain.

6. If not, are all sales prices and credit terms approved by the sales manager or in the sales department?

7. Are prenumbered shipping advices prepared for all goods shipped?

8. Are the quantities shown on the shipping advices double-checked in the shipping department?

9. Does the billing clerk or some other designated employee receive the shipping advices directly from the shipping department?
   (If so, identify this employee.)

10. Does this employee check the numerical sequence of shipping advices to assure that all are accounted for?

11. Are sales invoices checked:
    a. As to prices?
    b. As to quantities?
    c. As to credit terms?
    d. As to extensions and footings?
    e. Against customers' orders?
    f. Against shipping advices?
    (Identify the department or individual responsible for the above.)

12. Are sales invoices prenumbered?

13. Is there a check on the arithmetical accuracy of total sales by means of a statistical or product analysis?

14. Are total sales for the respective accounting periods (e.g., monthly) reported directly to the general ledger bookkeeper independently of the work of the accounts receivable bookkeepers?

| | ANSWER | | ANSWER BASED ON: | | |
| | YES | NO | IN-QUIRY | OBSER-VATION | TEST |

XI. SALES AND SHIPPING (*Continued*)

15. Are there adequate safeguards against understatement of sales through the suppression of sales invoices or shipping advices? ___ ___ ___ ___ ___

16. Are returned sales cleared through the receiving department (i.e., the department receiving incoming purchased materials and supplies)? ___ ___ ___ ___ ___

17. Are credit memos for returned sales supported by adequate data from the receiving department as to quantity, description, and condition? ___ ___ ___ ___ ___

18. Are the following classes of sales accounted for in substantially the same manner as regular credit sales of merchandise:
    a. Sales to employees? ___ ___ ___ ___ ___
    b. C.O.D. sales? ___ ___ ___ ___ ___
    c. Sales of property and equipment? ___ ___ ___ ___ ___
    d. Cash sales of merchandise? ___ ___ ___ ___ ___
    e. Scrap and waste? ___ ___ ___ ___ ___
    (If the answers are in any case in the negative, amplify by a concise description of the procedures.)

19. Is there an adequate check on freight allowances:
    a. By reference to terms of sale? ___ ___ ___ ___ ___
    b. By checking against freight bills or established and up-to-date schedule of freight rates? ___ ___ ___ ___ ___
    c. Other? (If any, explain.) ___ ___ ___ ___ ___

Comment on adequacy of internal control:

| | ANSWER | | ANSWER BASED ON: | | |
	YES	NO	IN-QUIRY	OBSER-VATION	TEST

XII. Purchases and Expenses

1. Is there a purchasing department? ___ ___ ___ ___ ___

2. If so, is it entirely independent of:
   a. The accounting department? ___ ___ ___ ___ ___
   b. The receiving and shipping departments? ___ ___ ___ ___ ___

3. Are purchases made only on the basis of purchase requisitions signed by the respective department heads? ___ ___ ___ ___ ___

4. Are all purchases (except small items purchased from petty cash) routed through the purchasing department? ___ ___ ___ ___ ___

5. Are all purchases made by means of the client's purchase orders sent to the vendors? ___ ___ ___ ___ ___

6. Are the purchase order forms prenumbered? ___ ___ ___ ___ ___

7. Are certain items required to be purchased subject to competitive bidding? ___ ___ ___ ___ ___

8. If so, does the procedure followed indicate the result of the review of the bids received? ___ ___ ___ ___ ___

9. Are purchase prices approved:
   a. By responsible official in purchasing department? ___ ___ ___ ___ ___
   b. If not, by any other responsible official? ___ ___ ___ ___ ___

10. Is the quantity and condition of goods received determined at the time of receipt by someone independent of the purchasing department? ___ ___ ___ ___ ___

11. Is the receiving department denied reference to copies of the purchase orders for authority to accept materials, etc.? ___ ___ ___ ___ ___

12. Are receiving reports prepared by receiving department? ___ ___ ___ ___ ___
    a. Are such reports prenumbered? ___ ___ ___ ___ ___

13. Are copies of receiving reports:
    a. Filed permanently in the receiving department? ___ ___ ___ ___ ___

	ANSWER		ANSWER BASED ON:		
			IN-	OBSER-	
	YES	NO	QUIRY	VATION	TEST

XII. PURCHASES AND EXPENSES
(*Continued*)

  b. Furnished to the accounting department?

  c. Furnished to the purchasing department?

14. Is the accounting department notified promptly of purchased goods returned to the vendor?

15. Are unmatched receiving reports reviewed periodically and investigated for proper recording?

16. Are purchases returned to the vendor cleared through the shipping department?

17. Are vendors' invoices registered immediately upon receipt?

18. Are vendors' invoices delivered in the first instance to the purchasing department?

19. If so, are the invoices checked in the purchasing department:
  a. Against purchase orders?
  b. Against receiving reports (as to quantity and condition)?

20. If not, are the invoices checked as above by:
  a. The accounting department?
  b. Others? Explain.

21. Is there an adequate system for the recording and checking of partial deliveries applicable to a purchase order?

22. Are invoices approved for payment by a responsible official?

23. Is there a definite responsibility for the checking of invoices as to:
  a. Prices and credit terms?
  b. Extensions?
  c. Freight charges or allowances?

24. Is a designated employee made responsible for the determination of the distribution of invoices (pursuant to an established accounting policy) to proper general ledger accounts?

	ANSWER		ANSWER BASED ON:		
			IN-	OBSER-	
	YES	NO	QUIRY	VATION	TEST

XII. Purchases and Expenses
(Continued)

25. Is the distribution so determined tested or double-checked periodically?

26. Are invoices not involving materials or supplies (e.g., fees, rentals, power and light bills, taxes, etc.) approved by department heads or executives prior to payment?

27. Is there a satisfactory check to insure that merchandise purchased for direct delivery to customers is billed to the recipients? Explain.

28. Are purchases made for employees cleared in regular manner through the receiving, purchasing, and accounting departments?

29. Are the vouchers, supporting documents, and expense or other distributions reviewed and initialed by an auditor of disbursements or other designated employee before payment is authorized?

30. If the answer to Question 29 is in the negative, is the accounts payable clerk or bookkeeper instructed to accept only those invoices which bear complete approval (i.e., rubber stamp endorsement, or equivalent, fully completed)?

31. Are all purchases (materials, merchandise, services, and expenses) routed through a purchase register or voucher record and not directly through cash disbursements?

32. If any purchases or expenses are booked originally directly in the cash disbursement records, are adequate vouchers filed therefor? Explain.

33. Is the accounts payable ledger or voucher register balanced monthly with the general ledger controlling account?

	ANSWER		ANSWER BASED ON:		
	YES	NO	IN-QUIRY	OBSER-VATION	TEST

XII. PURCHASES AND EXPENSES (*Continued*)

34. Are statements received from vendors regularly checked by the accounting department with the individual creditors' accounts or against open items in the voucher register?

35. Is a postage meter used for outgoing mail?

Comment on adequacy of internal control:

XIII. PAY ROLLS

1. Is a time clock system in use:
   a. For factory workers?
   b. For general office workers?

2. If so, are the time cards:
   a. Prepared and controlled by the pay roll department, independent of foremen?
   b. Punched by the employees in the presence of the foremen or other designated employees?
   c. Signed by the foremen at the close of the pay roll period?

3. Are piece-work production reports (if any) signed by:
   a. The employees?
   b. The foremen?

4. Are time cards and piece-work production reports checked to or compared with:

	ANSWER		ANSWER BASED ON:		
	YES	NO	IN-QUIRY	OBSER-VATION	TEST

XIII. PAY ROLLS (Continued)

    a. Production schedules?

    b. Pay roll distribution?

5. Does preparation of the pay roll require more than one employee?

6. Are the duties of those preparing the pay roll rotated?

7. Are the names of employees hired reported in writing by the personnel office to the pay roll department?

8. Are the names of employees resigned or discharged reported in writing by the personnel office to the pay roll department?

9. Is the pay roll checked at regular intervals against the personnel records?

10. Are all wage rates fixed by union contract, or authorized in writing by a designated official or employee?

11. Are vacation and sick-leave payments similarly fixed or authorized?

12. Is there adequate check against payments for vacation, etc., in excess of amounts authorized?

13. Is the pay roll double-checked as to:

    a. Hours?

    b. Rates?

    c. Deductions?

    d. Extensions?

    e. Footings?

14. Are signed authorizations on file for all deductions being made from employees' wages?

15. Is there a time department independent of the pay roll department?

16. Is the pay roll signed prior to payment by:

    a. The employee preparing the pay roll?

				ANSWER BASED ON:		
		ANSWER		IN-	OBSER-	
		YES	NO	QUIRY	VATION	TEST

XIII. PAY ROLLS (*Continued*)

    b. The employee rechecking the pay roll?

    c. The factory manager?

17. Are salary pay rolls approved by a responsible official prior to payment?

18. Are all employees paid by check?

19. If paid by check, are the checks pre-numbered?

20. Are checks drawn and signed by employees who do not:
    a. Prepare the pay roll?
    b. Have custody of cash funds?
    c. Keep the accounting records?

21. Are checks distributed to employees by someone other than the foreman?

22. Are pay roll disbursements made from a special pay roll bank account?

23. Is the pay roll bank account reconciled by employees who do not prepare the pay rolls, sign checks, or handle the pay-offs?

24. If so, does the reconciliation procedure include the comparison of the paid checks with the pay roll and the scrutiny of endorsements?

25. To the extent that wages are paid in cash:
    a. Is an independent pay agent (such as armored car service) employed?
    b. Is the currency placed in pay envelopes by employees who do not prepare the pay rolls?
    c. Are pay roll receipts obtained from employees?
    d. Are the workers identified by their foremen?
    e. Are different employees assigned to the pay-off from time to time without prior notice?

26. Are unclaimed wages relatively insignificant?

| | ANSWER | | ANSWER BASED ON: | | |
| | YES | NO | IN-QUIRY | OBSER-VATION | TEST |

XIII. Pay Rolls (*Continued*)

27. Is proper control maintained over back pay and unclaimed wages?

28. Are wages which remain unclaimed for a specified period redeposited in a bank account and liability set up therefor?

29. Are pay rolls audited periodically:
    a. By internal auditors?
    b. By other designated employees?

30. If so, do the auditors:
    a. Attend occasional pay-offs?
    b. Cover unclaimed wages?

Comment on adequacy of internal control:

APPENDIX B

Industrial Parts Company Case

The application of principles of systems design, especially the *Reliability, Organization Structure and Human Factors principles* that serve as the primary basis for internal control, and the more detailed *standards of internal control* and *internal control duties*, is difficult and involves interrelationships and implications that are often concealed by the situation. The Industrial Parts Company Case provides a situation for the student to flow-chart, study, and analyze. The facts in the case have been compiled from an actual situation.[1]

The Case

The Industrial Parts Company is located in Chicago, Illinois. The company acts as a jobber in replacement parts for certain types of industrial equipment. The company has been successful in finding manufacturers for practically all of the various parts which are needed for repair and maintenance of the equipment. Sales are made to established distributors all over the country and in some foreign countries. In many instances, these distributors act not only as vendors of the parts, but also operate maintenance bases for the equipment in their regions.

The company occupies a two-story brick building. Part of the building is used for storage of large parts, and for parts which are very slow moving items. The smaller parts and fast moving items are stored on the second floor. (See Figure B-1.) Most of the parts are stored in bins. There are six rows of bins, and four units in each row. Each unit of bins has 30 to 40 bins on each side. There are two rows of general shelf storage, and the outside wall is used for general storage of the bulkier parts.

---

[1] This case was compiled in the field by Professor W. E. Thomas of the University of Illinois who has kindly consented to its inclusion here.

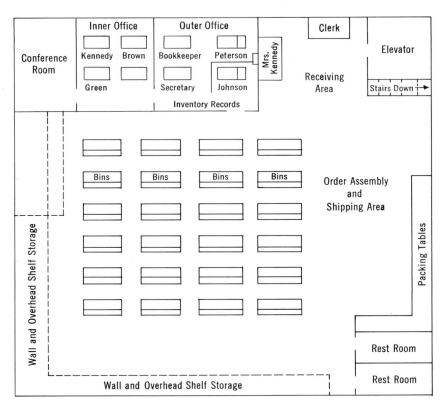

FIGURE B-1.   Second Floor Layout

The offices of the company are also located on the second floor. Approximately six to eight people are employed in the warehouse operation of the company. They do the receiving, place the material in the bins, pick orders, gather material together in the shipping area, and do the packing. The crews are under the general supervision of Mrs. Kennedy, wife of one of the partners. In the outer office are the desks for four of the office employees. One of the employees is Peterson whose duties include typing purchase orders, sales orders, handling export papers, shipping papers, and expediting traffic. Another employee is Johnson, whose duties involve primarily the posting of inventory records. He also assists with some of the clerical duties of others. The bookkeeper performs the usual bookkeeping function. The books are closed and statements prepared at the end of each month by a firm of public accountants. The secretary does general secretarial and clerical work, and employed on a part-time basis. In the inner office are the partners and their assistant. The partners are Mr. Kennedy and Mr. Brown. Their assistant's name is Mr. Green. Mr. Kennedy and Mr. Brown work together closely on all company problems. Both of them purchase parts, each specializing in certain types of parts. Mr. Kennedy is perhaps more active in sales work than is Mr. Brown; he travels widely and, when he is gone, Mr. Brown takes the full responsibility for the operation of the office. Mr. Green works primarily in the field of engineering and in the procurement of parts.

Purchasing and Receiving Procedures. The procurement process may be initiated in any one of three ways: (1) Mrs. Kennedy, in directing her force of workers, may note that certain bins are low in stock and may tell Mr. Kennedy that purchases need to be made. (2) When the pickers are unable to gather items for some of the sales orders and must note that the item has to be back ordered, Mrs. Kennedy keeps a record of items which must be back ordered, and transmits that information to Mr. Kennedy or to Mr. Brown for the placement of orders with manufacturers so that the customers' orders can be filled. (3) The third way in which purchasing may be originated is with the extension of items in the line. Decisions as to what new items should be ordered rests solely with Mr. Kennedy and Mr. Brown. Based upon information from these three sources, Mr. Kennedy or Mr. Brown, depending upon who is responsible for the items involved, places the purchase orders, almost always by telephone. The follow-up by means of a confirming purchase order is always made. The information to be placed on the purchase order is given to Peterson on a memo. Peterson types up this purchase order, making four copies. The original of the copies goes to the vendor; the second copy is placed in a permanent serial file. This permanent serial file is the source for postings to the inventory control record by Johnson, who enters the items as being on order. The third copy of the purchase order is given to the bookkeeper. This is the copy which is used to check against the invoice with respect to the prices and descriptions of items which have been ordered. The fourth copy is sent back to Mr. Kennedy or to Mr. Brown for purposes of reference, in connection with following up of unfilled orders, expediting shipments, and checking back on sources of supply.

When the invoice comes into the office, it is given directly to the book-keeper. The material is received in the receiving area under the general directions of Mrs. Kennedy. The merchandise is checked, counted, and the receiving report is prepared in four copies. One copy of the receiving report is sent to Johnson for entry in the inventory control. After the posting has been made, Johnson files it away for permanent reference. Copies two and three are both sent to the book-keeper for comparison with the invoice, with the purchase order, and as a basis for supporting eventual payment of the invoice. Copy four is retained in the receiving department as a file copy. It should be noted that approximately 10 per cent of the purchases made by this company are received in partial shipments; some of them involving as many as five or six shipments over a period of several months.

Sales Orders and Shipping Procedures. When a sales order is received, Johnson reviews the order and converts any old stock numbers to new numbers using a cross reference file for that purpose. Also, as he reviews the numbers, he places beside each the number of the bin in which the part is kept. This facilitates picking of the order by the warehouseman. The customer's order is then forwarded to the warehouse for picking by the crew under the supervision of Mrs. Kennedy. As the order is picked, it is marked for the items which are available and are being accumulated for the shipment. Any items which cannot be prepared for shipment are noted on the customer's order as being on back order. When the order has been completely picked, insofar as possible considering back orders, it is sent to

Peterson who prepares the customer's invoice. Five copies of the invoice are prepared. Two of them are sent to the customer, one is placed in the sales journal for posting to the accounts receivable control account of the general ledger, one is placed in the packing carton as a packing slip, and one is given to the book-keeper who attaches the original order of the customer and uses the papers as a basis for posting to the accounts receivable ledger.

The sources for posting to the inventory control records is from the sales journal. Johnson goes through the invoices each day, posting to mimeographed

| Part Number | Week Ending 2-26 | | | | | TOTAL |
---	M	T	W	T	F	
I-D-04	5-5 5-10	7-3	3-2	10-3	2	55
I-D-05						
I-D-06						
I-F-436						
I-C-628						
1-C-710						
1-F-840						
1-M-11020						
1-M-11024						
1-M-11030						
1-M-11040						
1-M-11050						
1-M-11054						
1-M-11060						
1-M-11104						
1-M-11150						
1-M-12016						
1-M-12024						
1-M-12034						

FIGURE B-2.   Weekly Summary of Units Sold

sheets. (*See* Figure B-2.) On the line for each part number under each day, he makes a notation of the number of items which have been sold. The line is totaled for the week, and the weekly total sales is entered on the stock ledger card for the particular part involved. (*See* Figure B-3.)

Back Order Procedure. The sales back ordering procedure is controlled through a system of back order slips. When the customer's order has been marked by the warehouseman as not being in stock, Mrs. Kennedy uses that customer's order as a basis for preparing back order slips. One back order slip is prepared for each item not in stock which must be back ordered. Each slip contains the following information: the part number, the quantity, the description, customer purchase order number, customer name, invoice number, and the date of the customer's purchase order. These back order slips are filed in Mrs. Kennedy's desk drawer, clipped together by customer's names. Periodically, she reviews these back order slips, refreshing her memory with respect to the different items which are on back order. As Mrs. Kennedy is also in general charge of the receiving procedure, when she notes that items are being received which are on back order she pulls the back order slip and sends it through the regular procedure as the customer's order. The back order is the authorization for setting aside merchandise and for generating the invoice procedure which involves the preparation of copy number four, the packing slip which is the authorization for final shipment to the customer. Mentioned above in the purchasing and receiving procedure, when back orders are first prepared, Mrs. Kennedy reports verbally to Mr. Kennedy or Mr. Brown so that they may check to ascertain whether the merchandise is in transit or whether purchase orders must be placed in the customer's requirements.

Observations. It is not our purpose here to analyze exhaustively the above case but merely to point out several observations to provide a starting point for

ORDERS				RECEIPTS						PRICE CHANGES	
Date	Order No.	Quan.	Vendor	Date	Quan.	Bal. Due	Date	Quan.	Bal. Due	Date	Price
1/6	276	100	Western	2/12	100				'		
4/5	402	200	Western	4/8	200						

ISSUES			BALANCE	ISSUES			BALANCE	ISSUES			BALANCE
Date	Order No.	Quan.		Date	Order No.	Quan.		Date	Order No.	Quan.	
2/12			100								
2/19	601	20	80								
2/26	703	55	25								
3/5	806	5	20								
3/19	904	10	10								
4/2	945	5	5								
4/8			205								
4/9	997	10	195								

SIZE OR PART NO.			ARTICLE		MAX.	MIN.	SECTION	BIN	UNIT

FIGURE B-3. **Front Stock Ledger Card**

student analysis. Violation of internal control standards 1 and 2 (See Chapter 7) is evident in that no one has been designated to correlate partial shipments with the original purchase order. Since approximately 10% of all shipment from vendors are partial shipments, this lack of specific responsibility for correlating shipments with the purchase order could result in the Industrial Parts Company receiving and paying for more merchandise than was actually ordered; or could result in an unnecessary out of stock situation.

From the facts in the case there is no provision for reconciling the stock ledger cards with a physical count of the inventory items on hand. This is an essential proof measure which is omitted and does not measure up to the second internal control standard.

Another standard which has not been achieved is internal control standard 4. Physical access to the parts stored in bins or on the floor on both levels of the building is not restricted to any employee. Unless peculiar circumstances are present which may cause this standard to be waived by management, the veracity of the perpetual inventory records is impaired because the inventory ledger clerk has full access to the merchandise whose transactions he is recording.

A good example of measuring up to internal control standard 6 is the comparisons which the bookkeeper makes among the purchase order, receiving report, and vendor invoice before vouchering the invoice for payment.

APPENDIX C

A Model Evaluation Report

December 4, 1968

Mr. John Smith, President
XYZ Corporation
Milwaukee, Wisconsin 53202

Dear Mr. Smith:

At the conclusion of our recent meeting, you suggested that I summarize some of the ideas expressed to you about the performance of the financial department so that you might give further consideration to them. It is the purpose of this letter to provide you with such a summary.

We have had the pleasure of being your company's independent public accountants for a number of years. During this time we have had the opportunity to become familiar with your company, its strengths and its problems, and with the characteristics of the industry in which it operates. During the course of our examinations we have worked extensively with members of the finance department and are well acquainted with that department's work. With the growth in size and complexity of your company we have come increasingly to question whether the financial function, as the result of its people, its methods, its philosophy and its performance, makes the kind of significant contribution to the successful management of the business which should be expected of a topflight financial organization. More specifically, we have come to believe that the department does not assist management in planning and controlling the business to the extent which is practical and desirable under the circumstances.

We have discussed the basic ideas expressed in this letter with the chief financial executive for several years. Because we believe that inadequate progress is being made, we concluded that we should also bring this matter to your attention.

The finance department continues to provide excellent routine bookkeeping services in such areas as payroll preparation, billing customers and paying suppliers, and in preparing the required financial statements for stockholders. The department has conceived this to be its major function and has staffed itself at both the supervisory and the clerical levels with individuals who by training, experience and temperament fit in best with this concept.

It has been well established by observing the performance of many of the outstanding companies of today that financial information designed to meet the needs of management can and does contribute to the quality of business decisions and to the effective planning, execution and evaluation of results. Operating executives in your company make very limited use of financial information for these purposes, largely because there are severe deficiencies in the information provided for managerial purposes and because the key individuals in the financial department make a minimum personal impact upon other key executives in the company.

The company has achieved a reasonable measure of success over the years, in part as the result of the capabilities of its top management, in part as the result of the intrinsic value of its product line, and in part because the business was basically straightforward enough so that significant financial and operating data could be readily obtained or "sensed" from the information available. The addition, through acquisition and internal development, of other product lines with different manufacturing and distribution processes has created a substantially new set of managerial problems and responsibilities. It is no longer sufficient to know merely how well the company as a whole is doing; information is equally vital about the component parts which in total make up the company. It is the failure to understand the changing nature of the business and an apparent unwillingness to accept the more responsive role which this change requires, which are the causes of our greatest concern.

It is our opinion that the company would find it to its substantial advantage as soon as practical to (1) develop and install an accounting system which would show the results of operations by divisions and within divisions by product lines, (2) identify revenues and cost or expenses with the individuals who have the responsibility for these items and budget and report results by these responsibility centers, and (3) improve the financial techniques which are employed in evaluating the relative attractiveness of proposed expenditures for fixed asset additions. This program will fall considerably short of providing you with a complete financial service, but it would constitute a much-needed start which would be particularly valuable in terms of the problems which currently face your company. As you suggested during our meeting, it would be well for us to set aside a period of time during which the specifics of the three items mentioned above could be discussed with you and others of your management group whom you might desire to have present.

Companies which have used financial information effectively have found that a great deal of the value came from making the chief financial officer an active participant in the top management group. This has been done (1) because financial terminology and principles are, for obvious reasons, not completely understood by operating executives, (2) because financial statements are often not self-explanatory, and (3) because the financial executive who is present when management problems or decisions are under consideration can often orally supplement the data contained in regular and special financial reports or can make available the financial point of view during the course of discussion. We believe the company would gain distinct and important advantages if its chief financial officer were included as a member of top management in the manner indicated. At present we find that this is not the case and, based upon our discussions with you and other operating officers, we believe that this is not likely to happen so long as the incumbent occupies this position. The present financial officer can continue to make a valuable contribution to the company in those areas in which he is particularly qualified, but someone with a different point of view and type of experience should be obtained in order to enable the finance department to contribute more significantly and directly to the management of the company.

It is likely that a new chief financial executive will find it necessary or desirable to make other personnel changes in his organization, particularly by providing additional strength in the financial analysis and systems and procedures areas. These changes would presumably be the responsibility of the chief financial executive and thus it is the latter position with which top management would be most concerned.

We would like to suggest that we discuss the ideas set forth in this letter again in the relatively near future. I shall therefore call you in a few weeks to set up a mutually agreeable date. In the meantime, if you have questions I hope you will not hesitate to call me.

Sincerely yours,

A. R. Cole Company
Certified Public Accountants

INDEX